DATE DUE

MY 20 '93			
NO 4 '94			
NO 27 '95			
MR 8 '96			
SE 10 '97			
OC 13 '97			
OC 22 '97			
MR 19 '09			
DE 2 '00			
NY 29 '01			
DE 6 '01			
NY 7 '02			
SE 29 05			
FE 3 09			
OC 17 19			

DEMCO 38-296

The Sign and the Seal

'And as concerning the Ark of the Covenant . . . the work thereof is marvellous. It catcheth the eye by force, and it astonisheth the mind and stupefieth it with wonder. It is a spiritual thing and is full of compassion; it is a heavenly thing and is full of light; it is a thing of freedom and a habitation of the Godhead, Whose habitation is in heaven and Whose place of movement is on the earth . . .'

Kebra Nagast, Ethiopia, thirteenth century

ለፍቅርተየ፡የዋህ፡ምልአት፡ጸጋዊ፡መንፈስ፡እንተ፡ቱነግድ፡ምስሌየ፡
ማእምንተ፡አልባብ፡ዐርክ፡ውህብት፡ለሕይወትየ፡
መኑ፡አነቲ፡ተአምሪ፡ጥቀ፡ቅሩበ፡እሙን፡ልብየ።

Also by Graham Hancock

Journey through Pakistan
Ethiopia: the Challenge of Hunger
AIDS: the Deadly Epidemic
Lords of Poverty
African Ark: Peoples of the Horn

The Sign and the Seal

The Quest for the Lost Ark of the Covenant

Graham Hancock

CROWN PUBLISHERS, INC.
NEW YORK

Copyright © 1992 by Graham Hancock

Published by Crown Publishers, Inc., 201 East 50th Street, New York, New York 10022. Member of the Crown Publishing Group.

CROWN is a trademark of Crown Publishers, Inc.

Manufactured in the United States of America

LIBRARY OF CONGRESS CATALOGING-IN-PUBLICATION DATA

Hancock, Graham.
   The sign and the seal : the quest for the lost Ark of the Covenant / Graham Hancock.
     p.   cm.
   1. Ark of the Covenant—Miscellanea.   2. Ethiopia—Description and travel—1981–   3. Hancock, Graham—Journeys—Ethiopia.   I. Title.
BM657.A8H36   1992
916.304′7—dc20   91-39041
                                      CIP

ISBN 0-517-57813-1
10 9 8 7 6 5 4 3

Contents

Acknowledgements

First and foremost I want to thank Carol, my partner of ten years, for the precious gifts she gave me. Our marriage did not survive this book. I hope that our friendship will. Thanks, too, to my children: Sean and Leila, Luke and Gabrielle. You've paid a heavy price for your dad's commitment to his quest. I mean to make it up to you. I'm enormously grateful to Donald and Muriel Hancock, to James Macaulay, and to Harold Elborn, for their constant support and interest, for their many readings of the evolving manuscript, and for the wealth of helpful suggestions and advice that they have offered. I would also like to put on record the appreciation that I feel for the invaluable contributions made by my friends Colin Skinner, Caroline Lasko, and Claire Lasko. As well as reading the manuscript at various stages, and commenting on it, they offered me consolation and solidarity in times of trouble and put up patiently with my often exasperating behaviour. In Ethiopia, Professor Richard Pankhurst was both a friend and a colleague to me. I'm honoured to have worked so closely with him. And in England I benefitted greatly from the input of a series of research assistants: Sadie Maine, Alex MacIntyre, Claire Wise, David Mestecky and Julia Hallawell. In addition, my Anglophone editors on both sides of the Atlantic, Tom Weldon at Heinemann, Jim Wade at Crown, John Pearce at Doubleday Canada, as well as my literary agents Bill Hamilton and Sara Fisher, have all shown an interest in this project and a commitment to it that has been above and beyond the call of duty.

Many other people in many different walks of life have also helped along the way. Some would not want to be mentioned at all and others will, I hope, forgive me for not setting out here a list that would be too long for the available space. I cannot close, however, without expressing my very special thanks and gratitude to one person in particular – Santha, who took most of the photographs in this book and who saved my life.

Graham Hancock, March 1992

Part I: Ethiopia, 1983
Legend

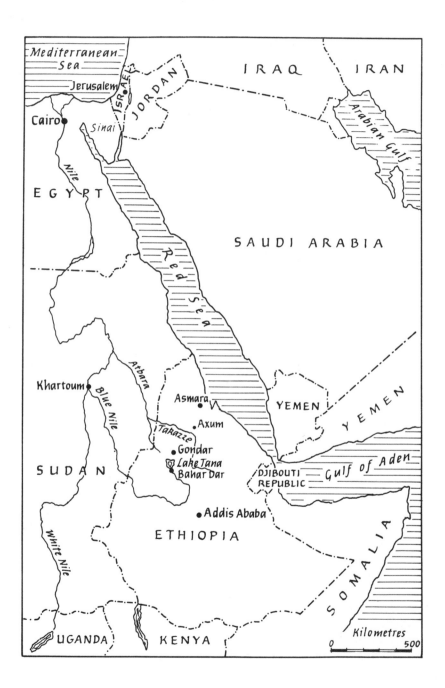

Chapter 1

Initiation: 1983

It was growing dark and the air of the Ethiopian highlands was chill when the monk appeared. Stooped and leaning on a prayer stick he shuffled towards me from the doorway of the sanctuary chapel and listened attentively as I was introduced to him. Speaking in Tigrigna, the local language, he then sought clarification through my interpreter about my character and my motives: from which country had I come, what work did I do there, was I a Christian, what was it that I wanted from him?

I answered each of these questions fully, squinting through the gloom as I talked, trying to make out the details of my inquisitor's face. Milky cataracts veiled his small sunken eyes and deep lines furrowed his black skin. He was bearded and probably toothless – for although his voice was resonant it was also oddly slurred. All I could be sure of, however, was that he was an old man, as old as the century perhaps, that he had his wits about him, and that he did not seem to be seeking information about me out of idle curiosity. Only when he was satisfied with everything that I had said did he condescend to shake hands with me. His grip was dry and delicate as papyrus and from the thick robes that he wore, faint but unmistakable, arose the holy odour of frankincense.

Now that the formalities were over I got straight to the point. Gesturing in the direction of the building that loomed in shadowy outline behind us, I said: 'I have heard of an Ethiopian tradition that the Ark of the Covenant is kept here . . . in this chapel. I have also heard that you are the guardian of the Ark. Are these things true?'

'They are true.'

'But in other countries nobody believes these stories. Few

know about your traditions anyway, but those who do say that they are false.'

'People may believe what they wish. People may say what they wish. Nevertheless we *do* possess the sacred *Tabot*, that is to say the Ark of the Covenant, and I *am* its guardian . . .'

'Let me be clear about this,' I interjected. 'Are you referring to the *original* Ark of the Covenant – the box made of wood and gold in which the Ten Commandments were placed by the prophet Moses?'

'Yes. God Himself inscribed the ten words of the law upon two tablets of stone. Moses then placed these tablets inside the Ark of the Covenant – which afterwards accompanied the Israelites during their wanderings in the wilderness and their conquest of the Promised Land. It brought them victory wherever they went and made them a great people. At last, when its work was done, King Solomon placed it in the Holy of Holies of the Temple that he had built in Jerusalem. And from there, not long afterwards, it was removed and brought to Ethiopia . . .'

'Tell me how this happened,' I asked. 'What I know of your traditions is only that the Queen of Sheba is supposed to have been an Ethiopian monarch. The legends I have read say that when she made her famous journey to Jerusalem she was impregnated by King Solomon and bore him a son – a royal prince – who in later years stole the Ark . . .'

The monk sighed. 'The name of the prince you are speaking of was Menelik – which in our language means "the son of the wise man". Although he was conceived in Jerusalem he was born in Ethiopia where the Queen of Sheba had returned after discovering that she was carrying Solomon's child. When he had reached the age of twenty, Menelik himself travelled from Ethiopia to Israel and arrived at his father's court. There he was instantly recognized and accorded great honour. After a year had passed, however, the elders of the land became jealous of him. They complained that Solomon showed him too much favour and they insisted that he must go back to Ethiopia. This the king accepted on the condition that the first-born sons of all the elders should also be sent to accompany him. Amongst these latter was Azarius, son of Zadok the High Priest of Israel, and it was Azarius, not Menelik, who stole the Ark of the Covenant from its place in the

Holy of Holies in the Temple. Indeed the group of young men did not reveal the theft to Menelik until they were far away from Jerusalem. When at last they told him what they had done he understood that they could not have succeeded in so bold a venture unless God had willed it. Therefore he agreed that the Ark should remain with them. And it was thus that it was brought to Ethiopia, to this sacred city . . . and here it has remained ever since.'

'And are you telling me that this legend is literally true?'

'It is not a legend. It is history.'

'How can you be so sure of that?'

'Because I am the guardian. I know the nature of the object that has been placed in my care.'

We sat in silence for a few moments while I adjusted my mind to the calm and rational way in which the monk had told me these bizarre and impossible things. Then I asked him how and why he had been appointed to his position. He replied that it was a great honour that he should have been chosen, that he had been nominated with the last words of his predecessor, and that when he himself lay on his death-bed his turn would come to nominate his own successor.

'What qualities will you look for in that man?'

'Love of God, purity of heart, cleanliness of mind and body.'

'Other than you,' I asked next, 'is anyone else allowed to see the Ark?'

'No. I alone may see it.'

'So does that mean that it is never brought out of the sanctuary chapel?'

The guardian paused for a long while before answering this question. Then, finally, he told me that in the very distant past the relic had been brought out during all the most important church festivals. More recently its use in religious processions had been limited to just one occasion a year. That occasion was the ceremony known as *Timkat* which took place every January.

'So if I come back next January will I have a chance of seeing the Ark?'

The monk looked at me in a way that I found strangely disconcerting and then said: 'You must know that there is turmoil and civil war in the land . . . Our government is evil, the people oppose it, and the fighting comes closer every day. In such circumstances it is unlikely that the true Ark will be used again in the ceremonies. We cannot risk the possibility that any harm might come to something so precious . . . Besides, even in time of peace you would not be able to see it. It is my responsibility to wrap it entirely in thick cloths before it is carried in the processions . . .'

'Why do you wrap it?'

'To protect the laity from it.'

I remember asking my interpreter to clarify the translation of this last puzzling remark: had the monk really meant 'to protect the laity from it'? Or had he meant 'to protect it from the laity'?

It was some time before I got my answer. 'To protect the laity from it. The Ark is powerful.'

A great mystery of the Bible

In early Old Testament times the Ark of the Covenant was worshipped by the Israelites as the embodiment of God Himself, as the sign and the seal of His presence on earth, as the stronghold of His power, and as the instrument of His ineffable will.[1] Built to contain the tablets of stone upon which the Ten Commandments had been written, it was a wooden chest measuring three feet nine inches long by two feet three inches high and wide.[2] It was lined inside and out with pure gold and was surmounted by two winged figures of cherubim that faced each other across its heavy golden lid.[3]

Biblical and other archaic sources speak of the Ark blazing with fire and light, inflicting cancerous tumours and severe burns, levelling mountains, stopping rivers, blasting whole armies and laying waste cities. The same sources also leave no doubt that it was, for a very long time, the cornerstone of the evolving Jewish faith: indeed when King Solomon built the First Temple in Jerusalem his sole motive was to create 'an house of rest for the Ark of the Covenant of the Lord'.[4] At some unknown date between the tenth and the sixth century BC, however, this uniquely precious and puissant object vanished from its place in the Holy of Holies of that Temple, vanished without song or lamentation in the Scriptures – almost as though it had never existed at all. The evidence suggests that it was already long gone when the armies of Nebuchadnezzar burned Jerusalem in 587 BC. Certainly it was not in the Second Temple which was built over the ruins of the First after the Jews had returned from their exile in Babylon in 538 BC. Neither does it seem to have been taken as booty by the Babylonians.

Writing in 1987, Richard Elliott Friedman, Professor of Hebrew and Comparative Religion at the University of California, expressed a view shared by many scholars when he described the disappearance of the sacred relic as 'one of the great mysteries of the Bible':

> There is no report that the Ark was carried away or destroyed or hidden. There is not even any comment such as 'And then the Ark disappeared and we do not know what happened to it' or 'And no one knows where it is to this day'. The most important object in the world, in the biblical view, simply ceases to be in the story.'[5]

Indeed so. A close reading of the Old Testament reveals more than two hundred separate references to the Ark of the Covenant *up until the time of Solomon* (970–931 BC); after the reign of that wise and splendid king it is almost never mentioned again.[6] And this, surely, is the central problem, the real historical enigma: not, human nature being what it is, that an immensely valuable golden chest should go missing, but – given its supreme religious significance – that it should go missing amidst such a deafening, improbable silence. Like a black hole in space, or a negative photographic image, it is identifiable in the later books of the Old Testament only by what it is not – it is, in short, conspicuous only by its absence.

From this it seems reasonable to suggest that some sort of cover-up may have taken place – a cover-up devised by priests and scribes to ensure that the whereabouts of the sacred relic would remain forever a secret. If so then it is a secret that many have tried to penetrate – a secret that has inspired several treasure-hunting expeditions (all of which have failed) and also one enormously successful Hollywood fantasy, *Raiders of the Lost*

Ark, which was first released in the USA and Europe in 1981 with Harrison Ford in the starring role as Indiana Jones.

I was living in Kenya at the time and had no opportunity to see the film until it finally arrived in Nairobi's cinemas early in 1983. I enjoyed the combination of action, adventure and archaeology and I remember thinking what a sensation it would be if someone were really to find the Ark. Then, only a few months later, I made an extended visit to Ethiopia during which I travelled to the north-west of the war-torn province of Tigray. It was there, in Axum – the so-called 'sacred city of the Ethiopians'[7] – that I had my encounter with the guardian monk reported earlier in this chapter.

1983: a country at war

On 28 May 1991, after years of brutal fighting, the government of Ethiopia was finally toppled by a formidable coalition of rebel forces in which the Tigray People's Liberation Front had played a leading role. When I went to Axum in 1983, however, the TPLF was still a relatively small guerilla force and the sacred city, although besieged, was still in government hands. Other than myself, no foreigners had been there since 1974 when a team of British archaeologists had been driven out by the revolution that had overthrown Emperor Haile Selassie and that had installed one of Africa's bloodiest dictators, Lieutenant-Colonel Mengistu Haile Mariam, as Head of State.

Lamentably the free access that I was granted to Axum did not result from any special enterprise or initiative of my own but from the fact that I was working for Mengistu. As a result of a business deal that I was later bitterly to regret I was engaged in 1983 in the production of a coffee-table book about Ethiopia – a book that Mengistu's government had commissioned in order to proclaim the underlying unity in the country's cultural diversity, and to emphasize the ancient historical integrity of the political boundaries that the rebels were trying so hard to redraw. It had been agreed before I began work that there would be no overt promotion of the government's cause, and it was written into my contract that no particular individuals (Mengistu included) would be praised or vilified. Nevertheless I was under no illusions about how the project was viewed by senior figures in the regime: they would not have footed the bills, or permitted me to visit historic sites forbidden to others, if they did not think that what I was doing would be helpful to them.

Even so it was by no means easy for me to get to Axum. Intense rebel activity along the main roads and around the sacred city itself meant that driving was completely out of the question. The only option, therefore, was to fly in. To this end – together with my wife and researcher Carol and my photographer Duncan Willetts – I travelled first to Asmara (the regional capital of Eritrea) where I hoped that it might be possible for us to hitch a ride over the battle lines on one of the many military aircraft stationed there.

Standing on a high and fertile plateau overlooking the fearsome deserts of the Eritrean coastal strip, Asmara is a most attractive place with a markedly Latin character – not surprising since it was first occupied by Italian forces in 1889 and remained an Italian stronghold until the decolonization of Eritrea (and its annexation by the Ethiopian state) in the 1950s.[8] Everywhere we looked we saw gardens erupting with the colour of bougain-villaea, flamboyants and jacaranda, while the warm, sunny air that surrounded us had an unmistakable Mediterranean bouquet. There was also another element that was hard to miss: the presence of large numbers of Soviet and Cuban combat 'advisers' wearing camouflage fatigues and carrying Kalashnikov assault rifles as they swaggered up and down the fragrant pastel-shaded boulevards.

The advice that these thickset men were giving to the Ethiopian army in its campaign against Eritrean separatists did not, however, appear to us to be very good. Asmara's hospitals were crammed to bursting point with casualties of the war and the government officials we met exuded an air of pessimism and tension.

Our concerns were heightened a few nights later in the bar of Asmara's rather splendid Ambasoira Hotel where we met two Zambian pilots who were on temporary secondment to Ethiopian Airlines. They had thought that they were going to be spending six months expanding their practical experience of commercial flying. What they were actually doing, however, was ferrying injured soldiers from the battle fronts in Tigray and Eritrea to the hospitals in Asmara. They had tried to get the airline to release them from this hazardous duty; on checking the small print of their contracts, however, they had discovered that they were bound to do it.

After several weeks of almost continuous sorties in aged DC3 passenger planes converted to carry wounded troops, the two pilots were shell-shocked, shaky and embittered. They told us that they had both taken to the bottle to drown their sorrows: 'I can't sleep at night unless I'm completely drunk,' one of them confided. 'I keep getting these pictures passing through my mind of the things that I've seen.' He went on to describe the teenage boy who, that morning, had been dragged aboard his aircraft with his left foot blown away by a mine, and another young soldier who had lost half his skull after a mortar bomb had exploded nearby. 'The shrapnel wounds are the worst ... people with huge injuries in their backs, stomachs, faces ... it's horrible ... sometimes the whole cabin is just swilling with blood and guts ... we carry as many as forty casualties at a time – way above the operating limits of a DC3, but we have to take the risk, we can't just leave those people to die.'

They were required to fly three, sometimes four, missions each day, the other pilot now added. In the past week he had been twice to Axum and on both occasions his plane had been hit by machine-gun fire. 'It's a very difficult airport – a gravel runway surrounded by hills. The TPLF just sit up there and take pot-shots at us as we land and take off. They're not fooled by the Ethiopian Airlines livery. They know we're on military business ...'

Overjoyed to have found some sympathetic non-Russian and non-Cuban foreigners to share their woes with, the Zambians had not yet asked us what we were doing in Ethiopia. They did so now, and seemed highly amused when we replied that we were producing a coffee-table book for the government. We then explained that we needed to get to Axum ourselves.

'Why?' they asked, dumbfounded.

'Well, because it's one of the oldest and most important archaeological sites and because it was there that Ethiopian Christianity first got started. It was the capital for hundreds of years. Our book's going to look really sick without it.'

'We might be able to take you,' one of the pilots now suggested.

'What – you mean when you next go to pick up wounded?'

'No. You definitely wouldn't be allowed on those flights. But a delegation of military top brass are supposed to be going there the day after tomorrow to inspect the garrison. Maybe you could hitch a ride then. It would depend on what sort of strings you're able to pull back in Addis. Why don't you check it out?'

Into Axum

We spent most of the next day on the telephone to Addis Ababa talking to the minister directly responsible for our project. It was touch and go, but his influence finally did get us seats on the flight that our Zambian friends had told us about. In the event, however, they were not to be our pilots; a fully Ethiopian crew was on board the DC3 for the short hop to Axum.

During the one-hour delay before our morning take-off from Asmara airport, and during the turbulent thirty-five-minute journey itself, I completed my background reading – reassuring myself in the process that the visit really was worthwhile.

The early historical references painted a picture of an important and cosmopolitan urban centre. In AD 64, for example, the anonymous author of a Greek trading manual known as the *Periplus of the Erythrean Sea* had referred to the Axumite ruler as being 'a prince superior to most and educated with a knowledge of Greek'.[9] Some hundreds of years later a certain Julian, ambassador of the Roman Emperor Justinian, described Axum in glowing terms as 'the greatest city of all Ethiopia'. The king, he added, was almost naked, wearing only a garment of linen embroidered with gold from his waist to his loins and straps set with pearls over his back and stomach. He wore golden bracelets on his arms, a golden collar around his neck, and on his head a linen turban – also embroidered with gold – from which hung four fillets on either side. When receiving the ambassador's credentials, this monarch apparently stood on a four-wheeled chariot drawn by four elephants; the body of the chariot was high and covered with gold plates.[10]

In the sixth century AD, a much-travelled Christian monk, Cosmas Indicopleustes, added further colour to the impression conveyed by Julian. After his visit to the city he reported that the 'four-towered palace of the King of Ethiopia' was adorned with 'four brazen figures' of a unicorn, as well as the skin of a rhinoceros 'stuffed with chaff'. He also saw several giraffes which had been caught 'by command of the King when young and tamed to make a show for his amusement'.[11]

These images of barbaric splendour well befitted the capital of what had by that time become the most important power between the Roman Empire and Persia – a power that sent its merchant navies as far afield as Egypt, India, Ceylon and China and that had adopted Christianity as its state religion as early as the fourth century AD.

The story of the conversion of Ethiopia is preserved in the writings of the fourth-century Byzantine theologian Rufinius – an authority highly regarded by modern historians. Apparently a certain Meropius, a Christian merchant described by Rufinius as a 'philosopher of Tyre', once made a voyage to India, taking with him two Syrian boys whom he was educating in 'humane studies'. The elder was called Frumentius and the younger Aedesius. On their return journey through the Red Sea the ship was seized off the Ethiopian coast in an act of reprisal against the Eastern Roman Empire which had broken a treaty with the people of the area.

Meropius was killed in the fighting. The boys, however, survived and were taken to the Axumite King, Ella Amida, who promptly made Aedesius his cup-bearer and Frumentius – the more sagacious and prudent of the two – his treasurer and secretary. The boys were held in great honour and affection by the king who, however, died shortly afterwards leaving his widow and an infant son – Ezana – as his heir. Before his death, Ella Amida had given the two Syrians their freedom but now the widowed queen begged them, with tears in her eyes, to stay with her until her son came of age. She asked in particular for the help of Frumentius – for Aedesius, though loyal and honest at heart, was simple.

During the years that followed, the influence of Frumentius in the Axumite kingdom grew. He sought out such foreign traders who were Christians and urged them 'to establish conventicles in various places to which they might resort for prayer.' He also provided them with 'whatever was needed, supplying sites for buildings and in every way promoting the growth of the seed of Christianity in the country.'

At around the time that Ezana finally ascended the throne, Aedesius returned to Tyre. Frumentius for his part journeyed to Alexandria, in Egypt – then a great centre of Christianity – where he informed Patriarch Athanasius of the work so far accomplished for the faith in Ethiopia. The young man begged the ecclesiastical leader 'to look for some worthy man to send as bishop over the many Christians already congregated.' Athanasius, having carefully weighed and considered the words of Frumentius, declared in a council of priests: 'What other man shall we find in whom the spirit of God is as in thee who can accomplish these things?' He therefore 'consecrated him and bade him return in the Grace of God whence he came.'[12]

Frumentius accordingly went back to Axum as Ethiopia's first Christian bishop and there he continued his missionary endeavours – which were rewarded, in the year AD 331, by the conversion of the king himself. The surviving coins of Ezana's reign record the transition: the earlier ones bear crescent and disk images of the new and full moon; later examples are stamped uncompromisingly with the cross – amongst the earliest coins of any country to carry this Christian symbol.[13]

Important as the seed-bed of Ethiopian Christianity – and as the capital of the Ethiopian empire from the first until approximately the tenth century AD – Axum's interest in terms of our project was nevertheless much broader than this. Here, I read, we would come across many imposing pre-Christian ruins of great archaeological merit (including the remains of several immense palaces), and also – still well preserved – the monuments for which the city was best known: its ancient obelisks, some more than two thousand years old, attesting to a high level of advancement in art and architecture at a date far earlier than that of any other civilization in sub-Saharan Africa. Nor were such physical artefacts the only witnesses to Axum's unique stature. To my astonishment, the reference works I had with me reported that according to Ethiopian legends the Ark of the Covenant was kept here in a small chapel adjacent to an especially sacred church. The legends were connected to Ethiopia's claim to have been the realm of the biblical

Queen of Sheba but were generally dismissed by historians as preposterous fictions.

Having only recently seen the first Indiana Jones movie, *Raiders of the Lost Ark*, I was naturally intrigued by the possibility – however remote – that the most precious and mystical relic of Old Testament times, a relic believed to have been lost for almost three thousand years, might actually rest in the city I was about to visit. I therefore decided that I would not leave without learning more about this strange tradition and I looked down with renewed interest when the captain announced that Axum was directly beneath us.

The DC3's descent to the narrow runway far below was unorthodox in the extreme – and quite alarming. Instead of the usual long, low and slow approach, the pilot brought the plane down very fast from a considerable altitude in a tight corkscrew pattern that kept us at all times directly above the town. This, one of the military men riding with us explained, was so as to minimize the time that we would be a target for snipers in the surrounding hills. I remembered what the Zambians had said about regularly getting hit by machine-gun fire when landing at Axum and prayed silently that this would not happen to us. It was an unpleasant feeling to be strapped into a flimsy seat in a narrow tube of metal hundreds of feet above the ground and to wonder whether, at any moment, bullets were going to start plunking through the cabin floor and walls.

Fortunately nothing so bad happened that morning and we touched down safely. I remember the red gravel of the strip, the dust that flew up as the wheels made contact, and the sight of large numbers of Ethiopian soldiers – all armed to the teeth and dressed in combat fatigues – staring at us intently as we taxied to a halt. I noticed other things as well: trenches had been dug on both sides of the runway and there were numerous pits, covered with camouflage netting, out of which protruded the barrels of heavy artillery pieces. I recall several armoured personnel carriers lined up near the tower and perhaps half-a-dozen Soviet tanks. Parked off to one side, on the apron, there were also two Mi-24 helicopter gunships with rocket pods visible beneath their stubby stabilizing fins.

From the beginning to the end of our visit, Axum never for a second shed the jittery and watchful atmosphere of a city under siege. We were permitted to stay only one night but we felt as though our time there was drawn-out, protracted, almost infinite.

Palaces, catacombs and obelisks

Our work began the moment that we arrived. Waiting to greet us as we stepped down from the plane was an elderly Abyssinian gentleman wearing a slightly threadbare three-piece suit and a most splendid patriarchal beard. In quaint but excellent English, he introduced himself as Berhane Meskel Zelelew and explained that he had been contacted by radio from Addis Ababa and ordered to guide us and act as our interpreter. He was employed, he said, by the Ministry of Culture 'to keep an eye on the antiquities of Axum'. In this capacity he had helped the archaeologists from the British Institute in Eastern Africa whose excavations of some of the city's most interesting ruins had been interrupted by the revolution of 1974.[14] 'It's *so* nice to see other British people here after such a long time,' he exclaimed as we introduced ourselves.

We climbed into a vintage Land Rover with a lime-green paint job and two neat bullet holes in the front windscreen. 'Fortunately no one was killed,' Zelelew reassured us when we asked him about these. Laughing nervously as we drove away from the airfield, I then explained what we had come to do, listed the historic sites that we wanted to visit, and told him that I was particularly intrigued by Axum's claim to be the last resting place of the Ark of the Covenant.

'Do you believe that the Ark is here?' I asked.

'Yes. Certainly.'

'And where is it exactly?'

'It is deposited in a chapel near the centre of the city.'

'Is this chapel very old?'

'No. Its construction was ordered by our late Emperor . . . in 1965 I think. Before that the relic had rested for many hundreds of years within the Holy of Holies of the nearby church of Saint Mary of Zion . . .' Zelelew paused, then added: 'Haile Selassie had a special interest in this matter, by the way . . . He was the two hundred and twenty-fifth direct-line descendant of Menelik, son of the Queen of Sheba and King Solomon. It was Menelik who brought the Ark of the Covenant to our country . . .'

I was all for visiting the chapel at once, but Zelelew persuaded me that there was little point in hurrying: 'you will not be allowed anywhere near the Ark. Where it rests is holy ground. The monks and the citizens of Axum protect it and they would not hesitate to kill anyone who tried to break in. Just one man is allowed to enter and he is the monk responsible for guarding the Ark. We will try to meet him later today, but first let us go and see the Queen of Sheba's palace.'

After we had assented to this attractive proposition we turned on to a bumpy, potholed road that – had we been able to follow it all the way – would eventually have led us hundreds of miles south-west, through the gigantic peaks and valleys of the Simien mountains, to the city of Gondar near Lake Tana. In open country barely a mile from the centre of Axum, however, we stopped within sight of an extensively fortified military post which, Zelelew explained, marked the limit of the government-controlled sector. He waved expressively at the nearby hills: 'Everything else TPLF, so we cannot go. It's a pity. There are so many interesting things to see . . . There, just around that corner in the road, are the granite quarries where all the stelae were cut. One still remains partially unexcavated from the rock. And there is a beautiful carving of a lioness. It is very ancient. It was put there before the coming of Christianity. But unfortunately we cannot reach it.'

'How far is it exactly?' I asked, tantalized.

'Very close, less than three kilometres. But the military will not let us past the checkpoint and if they did we would certainly be taken by the guerillas. Even here we should not stand around for too long. Your foreign faces will be noticed by the TPLF snipers. They might think you are Russians and decide to shoot at you . . .' He laughed: 'That would be highly undesirable, would it not? Come, follow me.'

He led the way into fields to the north of the road and we quickly began to stumble across the remains of what must, once, have been an imposing building. 'This was the Queen of Sheba's palace,' Zelelew announced proudly. 'According to our traditions her name was Makeda and Axum was her capital. I know that foreigners do not accept that she was an Ethiopian at all. Nevertheless no other country has a stronger claim than ours.'

I asked whether any archaeology had ever been done on the site to test the legends.

'Yes, in the late 1960s the Ethiopian Institute of Archaeology conducted some excavations here . . . I helped on the dig.'

'And what was discovered?'

Zelelew made a mournful face. 'The opinion was that the palace was not sufficiently old to have been the residence of the Queen of Sheba.'

What the archaeologists had unearthed, and what we now spent some time exploring, were the ruins of a great and well built edifice with finely mortared stone walls, deep foundations and an impressive drainage system. We saw a still-intact flagstone floor – which Zelelew claimed was a large throne room – and a number of stair-wells which hinted at the existence of at least one upper storey. There were also private bathing areas of sophisticated design and a well-preserved kitchen dominated by two brick ovens.

Across the road, in a field facing the palace, we then inspected a number of rough-hewn granite stelae, some standing more than fifteen feet high, some fallen and broken. Most were undecorated but one, the largest, was carved with four horizontal bands, each band topped by a row of circles in relief – like protruding beam ends in a building made of wood and stone. This crude obelisk, Zelelew told us, was thought by the townspeople to mark the grave of the Queen of Sheba. No excavation work had been carried out beneath it, however, and the field was now entirely given over to farmers who grew crops for the Axum garrison. Even as we talked we saw two peasant boys approach with an ox, which they harnessed to a wooden plough. Oblivious to the history that lay all around them, and apparently indifferent to our presence as well, they began to till the soil.

After we had finished taking pictures and notes we drove back into the centre of the city and then out again to the north-east to another palace complex, this one on a hill-top with commanding views of the whole area. Square in plan, the structure measured about two hundred feet on each side. The walls, which had long since crumbled, showed signs of having originally been projected at the corners to form four towers – possibly the very towers which, in the sixth century, the monk Cosmas had described as being adorned with brass unicorns.

Beneath the fortress Zelelew then led us down steep stone stairways into a number of underground galleries and chambers which were roofed and walled with massive dressed granite blocks that fitted precisely against one another without any mortar in the joints. Local tradition, he said, identified this cool dark warren as the treasury used by Emperor Kaleb (AD 514– 542) and also by his son Gebre-Maskal. With the aid of a flashlight we saw the empty stone coffers which lay within – coffers believed to have once contained great riches in gold and pearls.[15] Further rooms, as yet unexcavated, extended into the hillside from there, blocked off behind thick granite walls.

Eventually we left the hill-top fortress and made our way down into the centre of Axum on a gravel road. Near the bottom of the gradient, to our left, we paused to photograph a large, open deep-water reservoir dug down into the red granite of the hillside and approached by means of rough-hewn stairways. Known as the Mai Shum, it seemed to us very old – an impression that Zelelew confirmed when he remarked that it was originally the Queen of Sheba's pleasure bath: 'At least so our people believe. Since the beginning of Christian times it has been used for baptismal ceremonies to celebrate the Holy Epiphany, which we call *Timkat*. And of course the peasants still come here every day to draw their water.' As though to confirm this last observation he pointed to a group of women carefully descending the time-worn steps bearing gourds on their heads.

By now, without any of us really noticing how the time had passed, it was already well past the middle of the afternoon. Zelelew urged us to hurry, pointing out that we were scheduled to fly back to Asmara at first light the next day and that we still had much to see.

Our next destination was close by, the so-called 'Park of the Stelae' – certainly the focal point of Axum's archaeological interest. Here we examined and photographed a remarkable series of giant obelisks carved from slabs of solid granite. The most massive of these, a tumbled fractured ruin, was believed to have fallen to the ground more than a thousand years previously. In its heyday, though, it had stood one hundred and ten feet tall and must have dominated the entire area. I remembered from the reading I had done on the flight that its weight was estimated to exceed five hundred tons. It was thought to be the largest single piece of stone ever successfully quarried and erected in the ancient world.

This fallen stele was painstakingly hewn to mimic a high, slender building of thirteen storeys – each storey complete with elaborate representations of windows and other details, and demarcated from the next by a row of symbolic beam-ends. At the base could be discerned a false door complete with a knocker and lock, all perfectly carved in stone.

Another fallen – but much smaller and unbroken – obelisk, Zelelew told us, had been stolen during the Italian occupation of 1935–41, transported with enormous difficulty to Rome by Mussolini, and re-erected near the Arch of Constantine. Since it, too, was elaborately carved – and therefore of great artistic value – the Ethiopian government was campaigning for its return. In the meantime, however, it was fortunate that a third decorated monolith still remained *in situ* in the stelae park.

With a flourish our guide now pointed to this towering stone needle, more than seventy feet high and topped with a curved headpiece shaped like a half moon. We strolled over to examine it properly and found that, like its huge neighbour, it had been carved to resemble a conventional built-up structure – in this case a nine-storey building in the fashion of a tower-house. Once again, the main decoration on the front elevation was provided by the semblance of windows and of beams of timber supposedly inserted horizontally into the walls. The intervals between each of the floors were defined by rows of symbolic log-ends, and the house-like appearance was further enhanced by the presence of a false door.

Several other stelae of varying sizes were ranged around this refined monument – all of them clearly the products of an advanced, well organized and prosperous culture. Nowhere else in sub-Saharan Africa had anything even remotely similar been built and, for this reason, Axum was a mystery – its antecedents unknown, the sources of its inspiration unremembered.

The sanctuary chapel

Across the road, directly opposite the park of the stelae, stood a spacious walled compound containing two churches – one old and the other obviously much more recent. These, Zelelew told us, were both dedicated to Saint Mary of Zion. The new one, which had a domed roof and a lofty bell-tower in the shape of an obelisk, had been built by Haile Selassie in the 1960s. The other dated back to the mid-seventeenth century and was the work of Emperor Fasilidas – who, like so many Ethiopian monarchs before and since, had been crowned in Axum and had venerated the sacred city despite making his capital elsewhere.

We found Haile Selassie's pretentious modern 'cathedral' as unpleasant as it was uninteresting. We were attracted, however, to the Fasilidas construction which, with its turrets and crenel-lated battlements, seemed to us 'half church of God, half castle' – and thus to belong to a truly ancient Ethiopian tradition in which the distinctions between the military and the clergy were often blurred.

In the dimly lit interior I was able to study several striking murals including one depicting the story of the life of Mary, another that of the Crucifixion and Resurrection of Christ, and a third the legend of Saint Yared – the supposed inventor of Ethiopia's eerie church music. Faded with age, this latter work showed Yared performing before King Gebre-Maskal. The saint's foot had been pierced by a spear dropped from the monarch's hand but both men were so entranced by the music of sistrum and drum that they had not noticed.

Not far from the old church were the ruins of a building that must once have been very extensive but was now reduced to little more than its deeply entrenched foundations. These, Zelelew explained, were the remains of the *original* Saint Mary of Zion – which had been built in the fourth century AD at the time of the conversion of the Axumite kingdom to Christianity. Some twelve hundred years later, in 1535, it had been razed to the ground by a fanatical Muslim invader, Ahmed Gragn ('the left-handed'), whose forces swept across the Horn of Africa from Harar in the east and, at one time, threatened the complete extinction of Ethiopian Christendom.

Shortly before its destruction, this 'first Saint Mary's' – as Zelelew called it – was visited by an itinerant Portuguese friar named Francisco Alvarez. I later looked up his description of it – the only one that survives:

> It is very large and has five naves of a good width and of a great length, vaulted above, and all the vaults are covered up, and the ceiling and sides are all painted; it also has a choir after our fashion . . . This noble church has a very large circuit, paved with flagstones, like gravestones, and it has a large enclosure, and is surrounded by another large enclosure like the wall of a large town or city.[16]

Zelelew rightly dated the start of construction works on the first Saint Mary's at AD 372[17] – which meant that this was quite possibly the earliest Christian church in sub-Saharan Africa. A great five-aisled basilica, it was regarded from its inauguration as the most sacred place in all Ethiopia. This was so because it was built to house the Ark of the Covenant – which, if there was any truth to the legends, must have arrived in the country long before the birth of Jesus and must then have been co-opted by the Christian hierarchy at some point after the new religion had been officially adopted by the Axumite state.

When Alvarez visited Saint Mary's in the 1520s – becoming, in the process, the first European to document the Ethiopian version of the legend of the Queen of Sheba and the birth of her only son Menelik[18] – the Ark was still in the Holy of Holies of the ancient church. It did not stay there for very much longer, however. In the early 1530s, with the invading armies of Ahmed Gragn drawing ever closer, the sacred relic was removed 'to some other place of safekeeping' (Zelelew did not know where). It thus escaped the destruction and looting that the Muslims unleashed upon Axum in 1535.

A hundred years later, with peace restored throughout the empire, the Ark was brought back in triumph and installed in the second Saint Mary's – built by Fasilidas beside the razed remains of the first. And there apparently it stayed until 1965 when Haile Selassie had it moved to the new and more secure chapel put up at the same time as his own grandiose cathedral but annexed to the seventeenth-century church.

It was in the grounds of Haile Selassie's chapel that the guardian monk told me his astonishing story about the Ark and warned me that it was 'powerful'.

'How powerful?' I asked. 'What do you mean?'

The guardian's posture stiffened and he seemed suddenly to grow more alert. There was a pause. Then he chuckled and put a question to me: 'Have you seen the stelae?'

'Yes', I replied, 'I have seen them.'

'How do you think they were raised up?'

I confessed that I did not know.

'The Ark was used,' whispered the monk darkly, 'the Ark and the celestial fire. Men alone could never have done such a thing.'

On my return to the Ethiopian capital Addis Ababa, I took the opportunity to conduct some research into the historical merits of the legend that the guardian had related to me. I wanted to find out whether there was any possibility at all that the Queen of Sheba could have been an Ethiopian monarch. And if there was, then could she really have journeyed to Israel in the time of Solomon – around three thousand years ago? Could she have been impregnated by the Jewish king? Could she have borne him a son named Menelik? Most importantly, could that son have made his way to Jerusalem as a young man, spent a year there at his father's court, and then returned to Axum with the Ark of the Covenant?

Chapter 2

Disenchantment

Questions of the kind that I needed to ask in order to evaluate Axum's claim to be the last resting place of the Ark of the Covenant were not entirely welcome in Addis Ababa in 1983. There was still a certain amount of revolutionary jingoism in the air less than nine years after Haile Selassie had been overthrown (and less than eight after he had been smothered with a pillow by the man who had engineered his downfall – Lieutenant-Colonel Mengistu Haile Mariam). Mistrust, hatred and rank fear could also be detected everywhere: people remembered bitterly the period in the late 1970s when Mengistu's forces had unleashed the 'Red Terror' against those seeking to restore the monarchy. State-sponsored death squads had roamed the streets rooting out suspects from their homes and executing them on the spot. The families of the victims of these purges had then had to reimburse the cost of the bullets used to kill their relatives before they were allowed to claim back the bodies for burial.

It was in the emotional climate fostered by such atrocities that I was obliged to conduct my preliminary research into a subject that had explicit connections with Ethiopia's last emperor and with the Solomonic dynasty to which he had belonged. Just how close these connections in fact were was made clear to me when a friend passed me a *samizdat* copy of a document prepared at the peak of Haile Selassie's power and popularity – the 1955 Revised Constitution. Implemented with the intent of encouraging 'the modern Ethiopian to accustom himself to take part in the direction of all departments of State' and 'to share in the mighty task which Ethiopian Sovereigns have had to accomplish alone in the past', this remarkable piece of legislation nevertheless contained the following unequivocal confirmation of the age-old monarchy's Divine Right to rule:

> The Imperial dignity shall remain perpetually attached to the line of Haile Selassie I, whose line descends without interruption from the dynasty of Menelik I, son of the Queen of Ethiopia, the Queen of Sheba, and King Solomon of Jerusalem . . . By virtue of His Imperial Blood, as well as by the anointing which He has received, the person of the Emperor is sacred, His Dignity inviolable and His Power indisputable.[1]

I quickly established that Zelelew, our guide in Axum, had been correct about at least one of the things that he had told us: the Emperor *had* claimed to be the two hundred and twenty-fifth direct-line descendant of Menelik. Furthermore, very few of the Ethiopians to whom I talked in Addis Ababa – even the most revolutionary amongst them – seriously doubted the sacral pedigree of the Solomonic dynasty. Indeed, it was whispered that President Mengistu himself had plucked the ring of Solomon from Haile Selassie's dead hand and now wore it on his own middle finger – as though, by this device, he could appropriate some of the charisma and supposed magical powers of his predecessor.

Such whispers and rumours were interesting enough. They did not, however, satisfy my desire for hard information about the Ark of the Covenant and about its mystical associations with the deposed 'line of Haile Selassie I'. The problem was that most of my Ethiopian contacts were too terrified to tell me what they knew and shut up like clams whenever I mentioned the Ark, the former emperor, or indeed anything to do with the pre-revolutionary period that might possibly be interpreted as seditious. I therefore only managed to make progress when a knowledgeable colleague arrived in Addis Ababa from England – Professor Richard Pankhurst, whom I had invited to join me as co-author in the book that I was preparing for the government.

Grandson of the famous English suffragette Emmeline Pankhurst, and the son of Sylvia Pankhurst – who had fought heroically alongside the Abyssinian resistance during the Italian occupation in the 1930s – Richard was, and remains, the leading historian of Ethiopia. In the time of Emperor Haile Selassie he had founded the scholarly and well respected Institute of Ethiopian Studies at Addis Ababa University. Shortly after the revolution in 1974 he had left the country with his family, but was now anxious to get reinvolved; our book project, therefore, suited his own requirements well and he had taken a few days off from his work at the Royal Asiatic Society in London in order to discuss our collaboration on the text.

A tall but rather stooped man in his late fifties, he had a diffident, almost apologetic manner which – as I had discovered some time previously – disguised great self-confidence and a wicked sense of humour. His knowledge of Ethiopian history was comprehensive and one of the first matters I discussed with him was the Ark of the Covenant and the seemingly far-fetched claim that it might now rest in Axum. Did he think there could be any factual basis at all to this tradition?

He replied that the story of Solomon and Sheba that I had heard in the sacred city had an ancient pedigree in Ethiopia. There were many versions of it, both oral and written. Amongst the latter the oldest still surviving was contained in a thirteenth-century manuscript known as the *Kebra Nagast* – which was greatly revered and which most Ethiopians believed to tell 'the truth, the whole truth and nothing but the truth'. As a historian, however, he could not accept this – particularly since the homeland of the Queen of Sheba had almost certainly been located in Arabia and not in Ethiopia at all. Nevertheless he could not entirely dismiss the possibility that the legend might contain 'some scintilla of veracity'. There *had* been well documented contacts between Ethiopia and Jerusalem in antiquity (though not as far back as the time of Solomon) and there could be no doubt that Ethiopian culture did contain a strong 'flavour' of Judaism. This was best illustrated by the presence in the country of a group of indigenous Jews – known as the Falashas – who lived in the Simien mountains to the south of Axum and around the shores of Lake Tana. There were also certain widespread customs (many of which Abyssinian Christians shared with their Falasha neighbours) which provided at least circumstantial evidence of early ties with Judaic civilization. These customs included circumcision, the following of food proscriptions very close to those outlined in the book of Leviticus, and the practice (still adhered to in isolated rural communities) of celebrating the Sabbath on Saturdays rather than on Sundays.

I was already aware of the existence of the Falashas and had requested (but not yet been granted) official permission to visit and photograph at least one of their villages on our next field trip – which would take us to Lake Tana and thence northwards to the city of Gondar and hopefully also to the Simien mountains. I knew next to nothing about the so-called 'Black Jews of Ethiopia', however, and asked Richard to tell me more about them.

He replied that in physical appearance and in dress they were quite indistinguishable from other Abyssinian highlanders. Their mother tongue, too, was indigenous, being a dialect of the Agaw language which – although now rapidly being replaced by Amharic, the national *lingua franca* – had once been spoken extensively in the northern provinces. In short, the only really unique quality that the Falashas possessed was their religion – which was undoubtedly Jewish, though of a very archaic and idiosyncratic kind. Their adherence to ancient customs, long abandoned elsewhere, had led a number of romantic and excitable visitors to proclaim them as 'the lost tribe of Israel'. And in the last decade this notion had received the official blessing of the Ashkenazi and Sephardi Chief Rabbis in Jerusalem who had defined the Falashas unequivocally as Jews – a status that rendered them eligible for Israeli citizenship under the terms of the Law of Return.

But, I asked, where had the Falashas come from in the first place? And how exactly had they been marooned in the middle of Ethiopia nearly two thousand miles from Israel?

Richard admitted that there were no easy answers to these questions. The view accepted by most scholars was that a number of Jews had migrated to the Abyssinian mainland from south-western Arabia in the first and second centuries AD and had subsequently converted some sections of the local population to their faith; the Falashas were therefore seen as the descendants of these converts. It was true, he added, that an important Jewish community *had* established itself in the Yemen following persecution by the Roman occupiers of Palestine in the first century AD – so it was theoretically possible that missionaries and traders had crossed the narrow Red Sea straits of Bab-el-Mandeb and entered Ethiopia. Nevertheless he knew of no historical evidence which confirmed that this was really what had happened.

And what did the Falashas themselves say?

Richard smiled: 'That they are descended from King Solomon of course . . . Their legend is basically the same as the Christian one but a bit more elaborate. If I remember correctly, they claim that Solomon not only made the Queen of Sheba pregnant but also her maidservant – thus fathering not only Menelik but also a half-brother who founded a dynasty of Falasha

kings. All the rest of the Jews in Ethiopia today are supposed to be the descendants of the bodyguard made up of the first-born sons of the elders of Israel who accompanied Menelik with the Ark of the Covenant.'

'And do you think there's any possibility that what they say might be true – I mean that the Ark could really have been stolen from Solomon's Temple in Jerusalem and brought to Axum?'

Richard made a wry face: 'Frankly no. No possibility at all. As a matter of fact Axum didn't even *exist* in the period when this is supposed to have happened. It simply wasn't there . . . Look, Solomon died – I don't know exactly when but it must have been around the 940s or 930s BC. If Menelik was his son then it would have had to have been around those dates – maybe even ten or fifteen years earlier – that he brought the Ark to Axum. But there's absolutely no way that he could have done that. You see, Axum wasn't founded until at least the third century BC, perhaps not even until the second century BC – in other words about seven or eight hundred years *after* the supposed theft of the Ark.'

'Well,' I said, 'that rather puts paid to the whole story doesn't it?'

'Yes – although I expect it's just feasible that the Ark could have been brought to some other place in Ethiopia which later got mixed up with Axum in the traditions that have been handed down. There are, however, many other fallacies, anachronisms and inaccuracies in the legend – which is why no historian or archaeologist worth his salt has ever been prepared to spend time investigating it ... Nevertheless not all the things that the Falashas say about themselves are complete fantasies and some aspects of their origins would merit further research.'

'What, for example?'

'The claim I mentioned that there was once a dynasty of Jewish kings in Ethiopia ... If we go back to say the fifteenth and sixteenth centuries AD we find quite a lot of evidence to support that view – and it's probable that they had a monarchic system long before then as well. In fact, by all accounts, the Jews were once a force to be reckoned with in this country: sometimes they even fought successful wars with the Christian rulers in order to preserve their independence. But over the years they gradually weakened and began to disappear. We know that their numbers were greatly reduced between the fifteenth and eighteenth centuries. And unfortunately they've continued to be in steady decline ever since. There are probably no more than twenty thousand of them left now – and most of them are trying to get to Israel.'

Richard and I worked together in Addis for the next three days – during which time I benefited enormously from the detailed briefings that he gave me about Ethiopian culture and history. Then he returned to London and Carol, Duncan and I embarked on the field trip that would take us to Lake Tana, Gondar and the Simiens.

Tabots: replicas of the Ark

Driving out of Addis Ababa in the battered Toyota Landcruiser that the government had provided to facilitate our work we climbed the immense eucalyptus-covered shoulder of Mount Entoto and then travelled in a north-westerly direction for many miles across high, bleak moorlands.

At Debra Libanos (the name means 'Mount Lebanon'), we paused to photograph a sixteenth-century church where thousands of pilgrims had congregated to celebrate the life and miracles of Tekla Haimanot, a famous Ethiopian saint. We saw normally shy and conservative men and women casting off all their clothes to bathe naked in a spring of holy water. Possessed by the demanding spirit of their own religious fervour, they seemed enraptured, entranced, lost to the world.

Further north still we crossed the spectacular Blue Nile gorge before finally arriving at Bahar Dar, a small town at the southern tip of Lake Tana, Ethiopia's mighty inland sea. Here we spent several days puttering about on the reed-fringed waters in a large diesel-engined launch provided to us by the Maritime Authority. We visited some of the twenty monasteries on the lake's numerous islands and photographed their wonderful collections of old illuminated manuscripts, religious paintings and murals.

Because of their literal 'isolation', we learned, these monasteries had frequently been used during times of trouble as places of safety for art treasures and for sacred relics from all parts of the country. Their main purpose, however, was to provide their inmates with peace and solitude. One monk told me that he had not left his tiny, wooded island for twenty-five years and had no intention of ever doing so. 'By cutting myself off like this,' he said, 'I get real happiness. All my days I have been loyal to God and will remain so until I die. I have separated myself from the life of the world. I am free from its distractions.'

Every monastic community had its own church – and these buildings, usually circular in plan rather than rectangular, were often very old. Typically they would have an outer walkway, open at the sides but covered by the projecting thatch of the roof, then an inner circuit (the *k'ane mahlet*) richly decorated with paintings, then a second circuit (the *keddest*, used for communion) which in turn surrounded a walled central enclosure (the *mak'das*) containing the Holy of Holies.

I had been in many Ethiopian churches before, but those on Lake Tana were the first in which I began to get some idea of the significance of the Holy of Holies. I discovered that each of these inner sanctums – which only the most senior priests could enter – contained an object regarded as being immensely sacred. Speaking through our government interpreter at the fourteenth-century monastery of Kebran Gabriel, I asked what this sacred object was.

'It is the *tabot*,' replied my informant, ninety-year-old Abba Haile Mariam.

The word sounded familiar and, after a moment's reflection, I remembered that I had heard it in Axum when I had sat in the grounds of the sanctuary chapel talking to the guardian monk: it was the Ethiopian name for the Ark of the Covenant.

'What does he mean by *tabot*?' I asked our interpreter. 'Does he mean the Ark of the Covenant? We were just in Axum a couple of weeks ago and we were told that the Ark was there . . .' I paused, genuinely puzzled, then concluded rather lamely: 'I don't see how it can be here as well.'

A lengthy discussion followed, into which several of the other monks were drawn. For a while I despaired of ever learning anything of substance from these people who – quiet and withdrawn until a moment before – were now garrulous, animated and argumentative. Eventually, however, with further probing from me and much clarification by the interpreter, a clear picture began to emerge.

Every Orthodox church in Ethiopia, it seemed, had its own Holy of Holies, and in every Holy of Holies was a *tabot*. No claim was made that any of these objects were actually *the* Ark of the Covenant. There was only one true Ark and that, properly known as *Tabota Zion*, had indeed been brought by Menelik to Ethiopia in the time of Solomon and now stood in the sanctuary chapel in Axum. All the others throughout the length and breadth of the land were merely replicas of that sacred and inviolable original.

These replicas, however, were important. Indeed they were supremely important. Symbolic on several levels, it appeared from what I was told that they fully embodied the intangible notion of sanctity. As Abba Haile Mariam painstakingly explained to me during our interview at Kebran Gabriel: 'It is the *tabots*, rather than the churches that they stand in, that are consecrated; without a *tabot* at its heart, in its Holy of Holies, a church is just an empty husk – a dead building of no greater or lesser significance than any other.'

The black Jews of Ethiopia

When our work at the island monasteries was complete we returned to Bahar Dar and then drove north, around the curving eastern shore of Lake Tana, to the city of Gondar – founded in the seventeenth century by Fasilidas, the same emperor who had rebuilt the church of Saint Mary of Zion at Axum. During the journey I had time to give further consideration to the *tabot* tradition that I had just learned about.

At the very least, I remember thinking, it was intriguing and odd that the Ethiopian Christians should ascribe so much importance to the Ark of the Covenant that they felt the need to place replicas of it in every single one of their churches. The Ark, after all, was a *pre-Christian* relic and had absolutely nothing to do with the teachings of Jesus. So what on earth was going on here?

Inevitably I began to wonder again about the validity of the Axumite claims concerning the Queen of Sheba, King Solomon and their son Menelik. Perhaps, after all, there was some substance to the legends. The presence of indigenous black Jews in the country, whose origin seemed to be shrouded in mystery, was also intriguing – and could, it seemed to me, quite possibly be connected. I therefore found myself looking forward with interest to visiting the Falasha settlements which I knew that we would encounter with increasing frequency on the next stage of our field trip.

Before leaving Gondar, however, we were warned by a senior official that we should on no account try to interview or photograph any Ethiopian Jews. Under the circumstances I was extremely frustrated by this, and even more frustrated – and annoyed – when our interpreter and official guide explained the reason for the ban. With an absolutely straight face he told me: 'This year the position of our government is that the Falashas don't exist. And if they don't exist then obviously you can't talk to any of them or take their pictures . . . It would be a contradiction.'

Less than ten minutes' drive beyond the city limits, however, I spotted a Star of David positioned on top of a hut in a small village by the side of the road. 'Come on, Balcha,' I said to the interpreter, 'that's a Falasha house isn't it?'

Balcha was an intelligent, sensitive and highly educated man who had spent several years in the United States. He was vastly over-qualified for the government job he was now doing. He was also quite obviously impatient with the more lunatic edicts of the bureaucrats in Addis Ababa and, indeed, with official secrecy in general. Although we had already left the Falasha village behind I

therefore made a determined effort to persuade him to let us turn
back.

He cast me a discomfited glance out of the corner of his eye:
'Really it is very difficult. We never know from one day to the next
what line our bosses are going to take . . . Late last year I brought a
Canadian film crew to that very village . . . they were interested in
the Jews and they had all the official permissions and everything.
Anyway, they poked around and asked a lot of leading questions
about religious freedom, political persecution and so on – all of
which I had to translate. Afterwards I was arrested by the security
police and locked up for a few weeks accused of facilitating anti-
state propaganda. Do you really want that to happen to me again?'

'No, of course not. But I'm certain there won't be any
problems. I mean we're actually here working *for* the government
and trying to produce a worthwhile book about the peoples and
cultures of this country. Surely that makes a big difference?'

'Not necessarily. Last year, when I came with the film crew,
the Falashas officially existed – the government wasn't denying
them – but I still ended up in jail. This year there are supposed to
be no Jews in Ethiopia, so I think if I take you to one of their
villages I will be in serious trouble.'

I had to admit that Balcha's logic was faultless. As we drove on
through increasingly mountainous terrain, I asked him to explain
the official position – if he could.

Part of the problem, he replied, was that most of 'the bosses' in
Addis Ababa belonged to the dominant Amhara ethnic group.
The Falashas lived mainly in the provinces of Gondar and
Gojjam – which were both Amhara strongholds – and, as a result,
there was tension between the two peoples. In the past there had
been occasional massacres as well as sustained economic
persecution, and the Jews were still looked down upon and
despised by their Amhara neighbours today. Since the revolution
some efforts had been made to improve the situation, but
members of the ruling elite continued to suffer from a kind of
collective guilty conscience about the whole matter and did not
want any foreigners 'sticking their noses in'. Moreover, since the
beginning of the 1980s, official paranoia had been greatly
heightened by the strong anti-government line taken by visiting
American and British Jews, who had openly and vociferously

expressed concern about Falasha welfare. 'This has been seen as meddling in our internal affairs,' Balcha explained.

As we talked I learned that there were other more complex considerations too. Instinctively lowering his voice – though our driver spoke no English – Balcha pointed out that Addis Ababa was the Headquarters of the Organization of African Unity and that Ethiopia had joined other African states in ending its diplomatic relationship with Israel after the last Arab–Israeli war. The fact was, however, that clandestine links did still continue between the two countries: indeed the Israelis were providing a certain amount of military assistance to the regime. In return for this help, some hundreds of Falashas had quietly been permitted to emigrate every year to Israel. The problem was, however, that thousands more had fled illegally by trekking across the border into refugee camps in the Sudan – from whence, they hoped, they might eventually be airlifted to Tel Aviv.

As a result of all this, the entire issue had now become very sensitive. On the one hand the government feared that its covert guns-for-people deal with the Israelis might at any moment be exposed, thus causing maximum embarrassment within the OAU. On the other hand there was real resentment at the fact that large numbers of Ethiopian citizens were being lured into refugee camps in a neighbouring and not entirely friendly country. This, Balcha said, made 'the big-shots in Addis' look as though they were no longer fully in control – which was true but not something that they wanted to publicize.

During the next three days I had little time to give further consideration to the Falasha question. Our journey had brought us into the heart of the Simien mountains – an Afro-Alpine wilderness, all of which lay at more than six thousand feet above sea level, much at nine thousand feet or more, and a not insignificant portion at thirteen thousand feet plus. The giant of the range, the snow-capped peak of Mount Ras Dashen, soared up to fourteen thousand nine hundred and ten feet – making it the highest point in Ethiopia and the fourth highest in the whole continent of Africa.

At an altitude of ten thousand feet, the camp that we had established as the base for our photography and research was freezing cold at night – so cold that we had to keep a huge fire stoked and burning. In the mornings, however, as the dawn mists evaporated beneath the rising sun, warmth filled the air and astonishing views unfolded in all directions over a surreal landscape which ancient seismic activity, followed by millions of years of erosion, had left folded and fissured, cut through with steep valleys, and dominated by isolated, jutting crags.

Our treks frequently took us up above twelve thousand feet on to remote, unpopulated heaths. At lower altitudes, however, we saw frequent signs of human habitation: grassy meadows that provided grazing for sheep, goats and cattle, and terraced hillsides divided into allotments and planted with cereals. Viewing these tidy smallholdings, I had the sense of a very old, long-established pattern of agricultural life and of a peasant culture that probably had experienced no significant change in the past century – nor even in the past millennium.

There were a few Falasha communities – which, at Balcha's insistence, we rigorously avoided. The majority of the population, however, were Amharas who lived not in villages but in small hamlets – usually of six houses or less – that tended to be inhabited by single extended families. Typically their homes were circular structures with walls made of wattle-and-daub or sometimes of stone, and with conical thatched roofs supported by wooden poles rising through the centre.

The peasant whom we met and talked to were poor, in some cases very poor indeed, and their lives were clearly ruled by the iron rods of soil and season. Nevertheless they were also dignified and proud and this, Balcha told us, was because they felt – with good reason – that they belonged to a 'master race'. Over an astonishing period of more than seven hundred years, from AD 1270 until the overthrow of Emperor Haile Selassie in 1974, all but one of the rulers of Ethiopia had been Amharas. It was their mother-tongue, furthermore – Amharic – that had been adopted as the country's official language.

Inevitably, therefore, Amhara culture – expressed through an almost universal dedication to the Christian faith – had had an enormous impact. In the past few centuries, whole tribes and peoples had become 'Amharized', and this process was still continuing in many different parts of Ethiopia. In such a context, Balcha concluded, it was little short of a miracle that subject groups like the Falashas had managed to survive at all, let alone maintain their own distinct identity.

A maverick at heart, Balcha (who some years later defected to the United States) surprised us on our journey back to Gondar by ordering our driver to stop at the same Falasha village that we had seen on our way out. 'Go on,' he said, 'I'll give you ten minutes.' He then folded his arms and pretended to fall asleep.

From the moment we climbed down from the Landcruiser we were besieged by women and children all shouting '*Shalom, Shalom*' – which, it quickly transpired, was just about the only word of Hebrew that they knew. With Balcha steadfastly refusing to interpret for us, we at first had some difficulty in communicating; soon, however, we found a young man who spoke some English and, in exchange for a small sum of money, he agreed to show us around.

There was not much to see. Sprawled up a slope at the side of the road, the village – it was called Weleka – was dirty and seething with flies. Many of the people who pressed around us seemed to think that we ourselves must be Jewish and that we had come to take them away to Israel. Others ran towards us with armloads of souvenirs – for the most part baked clay representations of the Star of David and of the supposed bed-time scene between Solomon and Sheba. The plaintive earnestness with which these items were touted touched me and I asked our guide how long it had been since there had been any foreigners here to buy their goods. 'Not since year before,' he replied.

In the short time we had at our disposal we photographed what we could. Here a loom stood positioned for a weaver above a hole in the ground; there pieces of iron lay scattered around a fire, in the flickering flames of which a blacksmith was forging an axe-head; in one hut clay was being baked; in another we found a woman at work fashioning pottery. The Amharas, Balcha told us later, despised such lowly trades – indeed, in their language, the word for 'manual worker' (*tabib*) had the same meaning as 'one with the evil eye'.

By the time we left Weleka I felt thoroughly jaded. Partly prompted by what Richard Pankhurst had told me about the medieval history of the Falashas, and partly because I was intrigued by the possible connection of this people to the Ark of the Covenant story that I had heard in Axum, I had built up some rather unrealistic and extravagant expectations. A romantic at heart, I had nurtured dreams of encountering a noble and ancient Judaic civilization. The reality, however, seemed to be a degraded and impoverished peasant culture overanxious to pander to the enthusiasms of foreigners. Even the place of worship, which the Falashas called a *mesgid*, turned out to be filled with chintzy gifts from Israel: boxes of *matsos* were stacked in one corner and nobody could read the Torah – which had been printed in Tel Aviv – because it was written in Hebrew.

Just before we drove away I bought one of the miniature sculptures of Solomon and Sheba in bed together. I have it still. At the time I remember thinking that its cheap workmanship and sentimental imagery appropriately symbolized the deficiencies of the legend itself. Disappointed and disenchanted I glowered out of the window of the Landcruiser as we motored back into Gondar.

Coup de grâce

By the end of 1983 I had entirely lost interest in the Axumite claim to the Ark of the Covenant. The *coup de grâce*, however, was not delivered by the tawdry Falasha village but by what I saw when I followed up the one issue still outstanding after the completion of our field work – the question of the *tabots*, the replicas of the Ark, which were lodged in every Ethiopian Christian church. This custom had struck me as being of possible relevance and I wanted to find out more about it.

I raised the matter in the late autumn of 1983 on a visit that I made to Richard Pankhurst's home in London's elegant Hampstead district. Over tea and biscuits the historian confirmed that *tabots* were indeed supposed to be replicas of the Ark and added: 'It's a most curious tradition. As far as I'm aware there's no precedent for it in any other brand of Christianity.'

I asked if he knew how long *tabots* had been in use in Ethiopia. He replied that he honestly had no idea. 'The first historical mention was probably made by Father Francisco Alvarez who visited the north of the country in the sixteenth century. But it's clear that he was witnessing a tradition that was already very old at that time.'

Richard then pulled down from his bookshelf a slim volume, printed in 1970, entitled *The Ethiopian Orthodox Church*. 'This is an official church publication,' he said, 'let's have a look and see if it offers any enlightenment on the subject.'

There was no index, but we checked first in a chapter entitled 'The Consecration of a Church'. Here I read:

> The consecration of a church is a solemn and impressive ceremony with rites symbolic of the sacred uses to which the edifice is dedicated. The various parts of the service are of very ancient date . . . The *Tabot*, or Ark, previously consecrated by the Patriarch, is installed with grandeur and is the chief feature of the ceremony.[2]

In another chapter, 'Church Buildings', I came across this passage: 'It is the *Tabot* which gives sanctity to the church in which it is placed.'[3] Finally, in the glossary, I found the word *tabot* defined simply as 'Ark of the Covenant'.[4]

I next asked Richard if he had any idea what *tabots* looked like. 'The Bible says that the original Ark of the Covenant was a wood and gold box about the size of a tea-chest. Do the *tabots* fit that description?'

'Well, no, I'm afraid they don't. Of course lay people aren't supposed to see them at all. Even when they're brought out in procession they're always covered in cloth wrappings. But they're certainly much smaller than the biblical description. We needn't speculate on this though. You can go and see some *tabots* for yourself at the British Museum. They were looted from Ethiopia during the Napier Expedition to Magdala in the nineteenth century and brought back to England. I don't think they're on public display any more, but you'll find them in the Ethnographic Store in Hackney.'

The next morning, after I had made a few phone calls, I drove over to Orsman Road, London N1, where the Ethnographic Store was located. It was a modern and fundamentally unattractive building with quite a high level of security: 'People sometimes try to break in here and nick our stuff,' explained the caretaker as I signed in.

He took me in a lift to one of the upper floors and then into an enormous warehouse of a room completely filled with rows of metal filing racks. These extended from floor to ceiling and were separated only by narrow walkways badly lit by overhead fluorescent tubes. The caretaker now consulted a voluminous index, muttering incomprehensibly to himself as he did so. 'I think it's this way,' he said finally. 'Follow me.'

As we walked I was reminded irresistibly of the closing scene in *Raiders of the Lost Ark* – the scene in which the sacred relic is sealed in a wooden crate and dumped in a federal depository amidst thousands of other anonymous containers. This parallel continued when, after quite a few false turns in the maze of shelves, we finally arrived at the right spot. Here, with a certain amount of ceremony, the caretaker pulled out . . . a large box.

I felt a thrill of excitement as he opened it up. Inside, however, there was nothing that bore even the remotest resemblance to my image of the Ark of the Covenant. Separated by sheets of crêpe paper there were, instead, nine wooden slabs, some square, some rectangular, none exceeding eighteen inches in length and width, and none more than three inches thick. The majority were very plain but all bore writing which I recognized as *Ge'ez*, the ancient liturgical language of Ethiopia. A few were additionally engraved with crosses and other devices.

I asked the caretaker to check his index. Could he possibly have made a mistake? Could we be looking at the wrong things?

He squinted at the list in his hands, then replied: 'No. No mistake. These are your *tabots* all right. From the Holmes collection. Brought back by the British Expedition to Abyssinia in 1867/8. That's what it says here.'

I thanked him for his trouble and left, satisfied that I had finally laid the whole matter to rest. These pathetic lumps of wood were supposed to be replicas of the sacred relic in the sanctuary chapel at Axum. Whatever that relic might be, therefore, one thing was now absolutely clear: it was *not* the Ark of the Covenant.

'So that's the end of that,' I remember thinking as I stepped out on to Orsman Road and ran to my car through a dismal shower of rain.

I could not have been more wrong.

Part II: Europe, 1989
Holy Ark
and Holy Grail

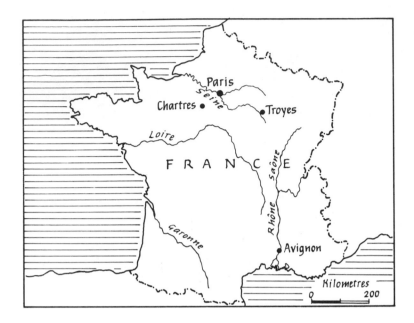

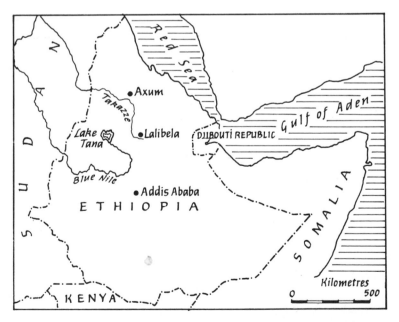

Chapter 3

The Grail Cipher

It was in 1983 that I visited Axum and learned at first hand about Ethiopia's audacious claim to be the last resting place of the Ark of the Covenant. I had been living in Africa at the time. In 1984 I moved to England with my family. Nevertheless in the years that followed I continued to travel regularly to Addis Ababa, producing a number of publications for the government and generally strengthening my contacts with those in power – including President Mengistu Haile Mariam himself. The dictator had a bad reputation for abusing human rights but I cultivated him assiduously and won a number of useful privileges as a result – notably access to many areas that were normally closed to foreigners. If I had wanted to look further into the Ark mystery there is no doubt that I would have been strongly placed to do so. I was just not interested, however. I therefore did not feel even a twinge of regret when, at the end of 1988, the forces of the Tigray People's Liberation Front launched a massive offensive against Axum and captured it in a single day of bloody hand-to-hand fighting – during which more than two thousand of the governments troops were killed or captured. At that stage my involvement with the Mengistu regime had become so close that the rebels' success meant the doors of the sacred city were now effectively closed to me. But I had no particular reason to want to go back there anyway. Or at least so I thought.

The Queen of Sheba at Chartres

I spent most of the second half of 1988 and the first quarter of 1989 writing the accompanying commentary for an illustrated book focussing on the historic northern regions of Ethiopia and on the religious ceremonies and customs of the peoples living there. This project was not commissioned by the government but was the work of two internationally renowned photographers, Angela Fisher and Carol Beckwith[1] – both of whom were close friends of mine.

Because of the nature of the subject, I had to do some quite detailed background research into several different ethnic groups – amongst them the Falashas, the indigenous black Jews of the Ethiopian highlands whom I had first encountered in 1983. At the same time, because of its formative role in Abyssinian religious culture, I found it necessary to read an ancient text to which Professor Richard Pankhurst had long before drawn my attention. Called the *Kebra Nagast* ('Glory of Kings') this text dated from the thirteenth century AD and had originally been written in *Ge'ez*. It contained the earliest-surviving version of the story told to me in Axum about the Queen of Sheba and King Solomon, the birth of their son Menelik, and the eventual abduction of the Ark of the Covenant from the First Temple in Jerusalem. An English translation had been made in the 1920s by Sir E. A. Wallis Budge, formerly Keeper of Egyptian and Assyrian Antiquities at the British Museum. It was out of print, but I managed to obtain a photocopy which I studied closely and drew on at various stages in the book I was writing.

My manuscript was not finalized until the end of March 1989. In April, wanting a complete break, I went on holiday to France with my family. We hired a car in Paris and then, with no particular itinerary in mind, headed south. Our first stop was Versailles where we spent a couple of days looking at the palace and at the châteaux. Then we went on to Chartres, a lovely old town in the *département* of Eure-et-Loire that is famous for its Gothic cathedral – a cathedral dedicated, like the great church at Axum, to Saint Mary the Mother of Christ.

Chartres has been an important Christian site since at least the sixth century AD and a focal point for the cult of the Madonna since the ninth century when Charles the Bald, grandson of the famous Charlemagne, presented the town with its most precious religious relic – a veil said to have been worn by Mary when she gave birth to Jesus. In the eleventh century the church built by Charles the Bald was burnt down and a new, much enlarged, cathedral was erected on its foundations. Following classical, 'Romanesque' design principles that emphasized horizontal solidity, this cathedral, too, was badly damaged by fire. Subsequently, during the twelfth and thirteenth centuries, its surviving shell was extensively modified and enlarged in the new, soaring, upward-striving style that came to be known as 'Gothic'. Indeed the high north tower of Chartres cathedral, completed in the year 1134, is thought to be the world's earliest example of Gothic architecture.[2] The south tower was added over the next two decades, as were further features such as the west-facing Royal Portal. Then, in a concentrated burst of building between 1194 and 1225 most of the rest of the superb Gothic exterior was put in place – remaining intact and virtually unaltered ever since.[3]

When I visited Chartres with my family in April 1989 I was initially much less interested in the history of the cathedral than in its spectacular and glorious beauty. It was such a vast construction, with so much complex sculpture around its walls, that I realized it might take a lifetime to get to know it properly. We had other things to do and see, however, and decided to stay in the town for just three days before moving on towards the south.

I spent the greater part of those three days walking slowly around the cathedral, gradually imbibing its powerful and numinous atmosphere – the remarkable stained glass windows telling biblical stories and illuminating the inner gloom with strange patterns of light, the enigmatic labyrinth mapped out with paving stones in the centre of the nave, the flying buttresses supporting the soaring walls, the pointed arches, and the overwhelming sensation of harmony and proportion conveyed by the grace and agility of the architecture.

Guidebooks that I had purchased stressed that nothing was accidental here. The entire edifice had been carefully and explicitly designed as a key to the deeper religious mysteries. Thus, for example, the architects and masons had made use of *gematria* (an ancient Hebrew cipher that substitutes numbers for the letters of the alphabet) to 'spell out' obscure liturgical phrases in many of the key dimensions of the great building.[4] Similarly the sculptors and glaziers – working usually to the instructions of the higher clergy – had carefully concealed complex messages about human nature, about the past, and about the prophetic meaning of the Scriptures in the thousands of different devices and designs that they had created. The statues and windows were in themselves works of art and beauty that were capable, at the most superficial level of understanding, of providing satisfaction, moral guidance and even entertainment to the viewer. The challenge, however, was to delve deeper and to decode the information concealed beneath the more obvious surface interpretations of this or that set of sculptures, this or that arrangement of stained glass.[5]

I was initially rather unconvinced by arguments like these and found it hard to accept that there could be anything more to the building than its outward appearance. Gradually, however, as I explored further and joined several specialist tours, I began to see that the vast structure was indeed a kind of 'book in stone' – an intricate and provocative opus that could be approached and understood at several different levels.

Soon enough, therefore, I too started to play the game – and several times entertained myself by trying to work out the deeper significance of various pieces of statuary that caught my eye. When I thought I had found the correct answer to a particular arrangement or tableau I would then check in the guidebooks to see whether I was right or not.

Then something unexpected happened. Opposite the cathedral's south porch I stopped for a snack in a café called *La Reine de Saba*. My recent reading of the *Kebra Nagast* containing the Ethiopian legend of the Queen of Sheba was still fresh in my mind and I asked one of the waiters why this name had been chosen.

'Because there is a sculpture of the Queen of Sheba in the porch over there,' he explained.

My curiosity aroused, I crossed the road and climbed the seventeen steps to the ornate porch – which consisted of a wide central archway sandwiched between two slightly narrower bays. Here, on almost every available square inch of masonry, were hundreds and hundreds of statuettes and many full-size statues. I could find none, however, that seemed obviously to represent the

Queen of Sheba. I therefore checked in the guidebooks I had
with me, the most detailed of which, *Chartres: Guide of the
Cathedral*, told me where to look:

> The inner archivolt of the outer arch has twenty-eight
> statuettes of kings and queens of the Old Testament: we
> recognise David with his harp, Solomon with a sceptre,
> and the Queen of Sheba holding a flower in her left hand.
> At the top, the four major prophets, bearded, talk with
> four minor prophets who are clean shaven.[6]

The book also informed me that the whole of the south porch had
been built in the first quarter of the thirteenth century – the same
century in which the *Kebra Nagast* had been compiled in Ethiopia
to tell the story of the Queen of Sheba, Menelik and the theft of
the Ark.

This struck me as an amusing coincidence and I therefore
examined the statuette of the Queen of Sheba with some
considerable interest. I could see absolutely nothing about it,
however, that made it special in any way – other than the fact that it
seemed to be a little out of place in the august company of a large
number of Jewish monarchs and prophets. I knew that according to
the *Kebra Nagast* the queen had been converted to Judaism,[7] but I
also knew that the relatively short biblical account of her visit to
Jerusalem made no mention of this. In Chapter 10 of the book of
Kings and in Chapter 9 of the book of Chronicles – the only places
where she was specifically named in the Scriptures – she arrived at
Solomon's court a heathen and apparently left there a heathen still.[8]
It was her paganism, therefore, that made her the odd one out –
unless, of course, the builders of Chartres cathedral had been
familiar with the Ethiopian story of her conversion. This, however,
seemed most unlikely – indeed the Old Testament did not even hint
that she might have come from Ethiopia at all and the majority of
scholars believed her to have been a South Arabian monarch who
had hailed quite specifically from Saba or Sabaea in what is now the
Yemen.[9]

I might very well have left the matter there, as a minor
anomaly amongst the sculptures in the south porch of Chartres
cathedral, if I had not discovered, by reading further in my

guidebook, that there was a second statue of the Queen of Sheba in the north porch. That porch, too, had been built between the years 1200 and 1225, and was devoted to an extensive portrayal of Old Testament themes.[10]

The Ark and the inscriptions

I suppose, on that first visit, that I spent two hours in the north porch trying to puzzle out the convoluted stories told by the sculptures.

The left bay contained several representations of the Virgin Mary and of the infant Christ together with Old Testament prophets like Isaiah and Daniel. There were also moral tales – notably one which portrayed the triumph of the Virtues over the Vices, and another which depicted the beatitudes of the body and soul as described by the great twelfth-century cleric Saint Bernard of Clairvaux.

The central bay was dominated by a group of Old Testament patriarchs and prophets, notably the figure of Melchizedek – the mysterious priest-king of Salem described in Chapter 14 of the book of Genesis and in Psalm 110.[11] Abraham, Moses, Samuel and David were there also, as were Elisha and Saint Peter. Other scenes included the Garden of Eden, with its four rivers, and the Virgin Mary crowned and seated on the heavenly throne beside Jesus.

It was in the right bay that I found the Queen of Sheba. This time she was not an obscure statuette on the arch, as had been the case in the south porch, but rather a full-size statue. She was placed next to a figure of Solomon, which made sense given the biblical context. What immediately caught my eye, however, was that beneath her feet crouched an African – described in one of my guidebooks as 'her negroid servant',[12] and in another as 'her Ethiopian slave'.[13]

No further details were given. Nevertheless I had seen enough to be satisfied that the sculptors who had worked in the north porch of Chartres in the thirteenth century had wanted to place the queen unmistakably in an African context. This meant that I could no longer so easily dismiss the possibility that those sculptors might have been familiar with the Ethiopian traditions about her which, in the thirteenth century, had been set down in the *Kebra Nagast*. That, at least, would explain why an apparently pagan monarch had been given so much importance in the iconography of a Christian cathedral: as noted above, it had only been in the *Kebra Nagast*, and not in the Bible, that she had been described as a convert to the true faith of the patriarchs. At the same time, however, it raised another difficult question: how and by what means could the Ethiopian story have filtered into northern France at so early a date?

It was with such thoughts passing through my mind that, on a column between the central and right-hand bays, I came across a piece of sculpture that was to have an even more powerful impact on me. Miniaturized – no more than a few inches high and wide – it depicted a box or chest of some sort being transported on an ox-cart. Beneath it, in capital letters, were carved these two words:

ARCHA CEDERIS

Moving on around the column in an anti-clockwise direction I then found a separate scene, badly damaged and eroded, which seemed to show a man stooping over the same box or chest. There was an inscription here, too, a little difficult to make out:

HIC AMICITUR ARCHA CEDERIS (or possibly HIC
AMITTITUR ARCHA CEDERIS, or HIC
AMITITUR ARCHA CEDERIS, or even HIC
AMIGITUR ARCHA CEDERIS).

The style of the lettering was archaic, jumbled up and obscure. I realized that it must be Latin, or a form of Latin. However, having been obliged by my schoolmasters to abandon that subject at the age of thirteen (on account of my own linguistic incompetence), I made no attempt at a full translation. It seemed to me, however, that the word ARCHA must mean 'Ark' – as in Ark of the Covenant. I could also see that the box or chest depicted in the sculptures was about the right size (scaled against the other figures) to have been the Ark described in the book of Exodus.[14]

If I was correct in this assumption, I reasoned, then the positioning of an image of the Ark within a very few feet of an image of the Queen of Sheba strengthened the hypothesis that the builders of Chartres might, in some as yet unexplained way, have been influenced by the Ethiopian traditions set down in the *Kebra Nagast*. Indeed the fact the sculptors had placed the queen so unambiguously in an African context made this hypothesis look much more plausible than it had seemed when it had first occurred to me in the south porch. I therefore felt that it would be worth my while to establish whether the miniaturized devices on the columns were really images of the Ark and to work out the meaning of the Latin inscriptions.

I sat down on the paving of the north porch and pored through my guidebooks. Only two of them made any mention at all of the decorations on the columns I was interested in. One offered no translation of the inscriptions but confirmed that the scenes depicted did indeed relate to the Ark of the Covenant.[15] The other provided the following translation – which I found interesting, but also rather suspect:

ARCHA CEDERIS: 'You are to work through the Ark.'

HIC AMITITUR ARCHA CEDERIS: 'Here things take their course; you are to work through the Ark.'[16]

Even my schoolboy Latin was sufficient to suggest that these interpretations were probably incorrect. I therefore decided that I would have to refer the matter to an expert for clarification and it occurred to me that in just a few days I would be passing quite close to the home of a man well qualified to help – Professor Peter Lasko, an art historian and a former director of the University of London's Courtauld Institute, who now spent six months of every year living in southern France. The father of a close friend of mine, Lasko had made a lifetime study of the sacred art and architecture of the medieval period and could probably give me an authoritative opinion – or at any rate point me in the right direction.

Accordingly I carefully copied out the inscriptions and then stood up to try to produce a sketch of the whole north porch. As I was doing so I noticed something else that was possibly significant: the Ark tableau, though standing to the front of the porch on the supporting columns, was positioned exactly mid-way between Melchizedek, the Old Testament priest-king whose statue dominated the central bay, and the statue of the Queen of Sheba, which dominated the right-hand bay. Indeed I found that I could draw a neat triangle connecting up all three pieces of sculpture – with Melchizedek and the Queen of Sheba at either end of the long base and the Ark of the Covenant at the apex of the two shorter sides.

Nor was this all. As I studied the layout of images in the two bays I realized that the Ark on its little cart had been depicted as moving *away* from Melchizedek and directly *towards* the Queen of Sheba – along the side of the triangle I had drawn. Given the cryptic nature of much of the sculpture at Chartres, and the way in which different figures were often deliberately juxtaposed in order to tell stories and convey information, it seemed to me that this particular arrangement was unlikely to have been accidental. On the contrary it looked very much like another piece of evidence to support my evolving hypothesis that the builders of Chartres must, somehow, have been exposed to the Ethiopian legend of the Queen of Sheba as related in the *Kebra Nagast*. Though there was far too little to go on here to justify any firm conclusions, it was at least possible that the curious iconography of the north porch did contain echoes of the tradition that the Ark of the Covenant had been taken *away* from ancient Israel (represented by the priest-king Melchizedek) and *to* Ethiopia (represented by the Queen of Sheba).

I therefore paid special attention to the statue of Melchizedek before leaving the north porch. He had caught my eye when I had first arrived, but now, as I sketched him, I began to notice more details. Dangling beneath his right hand, for example, was a censer very similar to those that I had often seen in use in Ethiopian church services – where copious quantities of incense were routinely burned. Meanwhile he held in his left hand a long-stemmed chalice or cup containing not liquid but rather some sort of solid cylindrical object.

I searched through my guidebooks again, but could find no reference to the censer and only conflicting explanations of the cup. One source said that Melchizedek was intended here to be viewed as a precursor of Christ and that the chalice and the object within it were thus meant to represent 'the bread and the wine, the symbols of the Eucharist'.[17] Another captioned its photograph of the statue with these words: 'Melchizedek bearing the Grail cup out of which comes the Stone', and then added (somewhat puzzlingly):

> With this we may connect the poem of Wolfram von Eschenbach, who is said to have been a Templar – though there is no proof of this – for whom the Grail is a Stone.[18]

None the wiser, I eventually left the north porch and joined my wife and children in the gardens behind the great cathedral. The next day we drove south from Chartres in the direction of Bordeaux and Biarritz. And some time after that, now heading east towards the Côte d'Azur, we arrived in the *département* of Tarn-et-Garonne near the city of Toulouse. There, with the aid of a good map, I eventually found the home of the art historian Professor Peter Lasko whom I had telephoned from Chartres and who had expressed a willingness to talk to me about the sculptures in the north porch – though, he had modestly added, he could not claim to be an expert on them.

An Ethiopian connection?

I spent an afternoon with Peter Lasko at his house in the village of Montaigu de Quercy. A distinguished, grey-haired man in his sixties, I had met him several times before and he knew that, as a writer, I specialized in Ethiopia and the Horn of Africa. He therefore began by asking me why I had suddenly taken an interest in medieval French cathedrals.

I replied by outlining my theory that the sculptures I had seen in the north porch of Chartres might in some way have been influenced by the *Kebra Nagast*: 'Melchizedek with his cup could represent Old Testament Israel,' I concluded. 'He was priest-king of Salem, after all, which a number of scholars have identified with Jerusalem.[19] Then the Queen of Sheba with her African servant could represent Ethiopia. And then we have the

Ark between the two, going in the direction of Ethiopia. So the message would be that the Ark had gone from Jerusalem to Ethiopia – which is exactly what the *Kebra Nagast* says. How does that sound to you?'

'To be perfectly honest, Graham, it sounds preposterous.'

'Why?'

'Well . . . I suppose it's just possible that Ethiopian traditions could have filtered into Europe as early as the thirteenth century – in fact, come to think of it, there has been at least one scholarly paper which does suggest that this could have happened. I rather doubt that view myself. Nevertheless, even if the *Kebra Nagast* story was known in Chartres at the right time I just don't see why anyone would have felt motivated to translate it into the iconography of the cathedral. That would have been a most peculiar thing to do – particularly in the north porch which is mainly about the Old Testament forerunners of Christ. Melchizedek is there for that very reason, by the way. He's specifically identified with Christ in the book of Hebrews.'[20]

'He's shown holding a cup in the sculpture and there's also some kind of cylindrical object in the cup.'

'Probably meant to represent bread – the bread and the wine of the Eucharist.'

'That's what one of my guidebooks says. But there's another one which identifies the cup with the Holy Grail and which argues that the cylindrical object is a stone.'

Peter Lasko raised a quizzical eyebrow. 'I've never heard such a thing before. It sounds even more far-fetched than your theory of an Ethiopian connection . . .' He paused reflectively, then added: 'There is one thing though. That scholarly paper which I mentioned – the one that talks about Ethiopian ideas finding their way into medieval Europe . . .'

'Yes.'

'Well oddly enough it's about the Holy Grail. If I remember rightly it argues that Wolfram von Eschenbach's Grail – which was a stone, not a cup – was influenced by some sort of Christian Ethiopian tradition.'

I sat forward in my chair: 'That's interesting . . . Wolfram von Eschenbach was also mentioned in my guidebook. Who was he?'

'One of the earliest of the medieval poets to concern himself with the Holy Grail. He wrote a book-length work on the subject called *Parzival*.'

'Isn't that the name of an opera?'

'Yes, by Wagner. He was inspired by Wolfram.'

'And this Wolfram . . . when did he write?'

'Late twelfth or early thirteenth century.'

'In other words at the same time that the north porch of Chartres cathedral was built?'

'Yes.'

We both remained silent for a while, then I said: 'The paper that you told me about which argues that Wolfram's work was influenced by Ethiopian traditions – I don't suppose you happen to remember the title of it do you?'

'. . . Ah. No. I'm afraid not. It must have been at least twenty years ago when I read it. It was by someone or other Adolf, I think. That name sticks in my mind, anyway. Wolfram was a German so you really need to talk to a specialist in Middle High German literature to find out more details.'

Silently resolving that I would do just that, I then asked Peter if he could help me with a translation of the inscriptions that had so intrigued me at Chartres. My guidebook, I told him, had rendered ARCHA CEDERIS as 'You are to work through the Ark' and HIC AMITITUR ARCHA CEDERIS as 'Here things take their course; you are to work through the Ark.' These interpretations, however, were in his view completely wrong. ARCHA certainly meant Ark and CEDERIS was most probably a corruption of FOEDERIS – meaning Covenant. On this reading, therefore, ARCHA CEDERIS would translate very simply and logically as 'Ark of the Covenant'. Another alternative, however, was that the word CEDERIS was intended as a form of the verb *cedere* – meaning to yield or to give up or to go away. The tense was unorthodox, but the best translation of ARCHA CEDERIS if this was the case would be 'the Ark that you will yield' (or 'give up' or 'send away').

As to the longer inscription, the problem was the obscurity of the fourth letter of the second word. My guidebook had presumed it to be a single 'T'. It was much more likely to be an abbreviation representing a double 'T', however (because there was no Latin word spelt AMITITUR with a single 'T'). If a double

'T' had indeed been intended then the phrase would read HIC AMITTITUR ARCHA CEDERIS, meaning something like 'Here it is let go, the Ark that you will yield', or perhaps 'Here it is let go, Oh Ark, you are yielded', or alternatively – if CEDERIS was a corruption of FOEDERIS – 'Here it is let go, the Ark of the Covenant'.

It was also possible, however, that the fourth letter of the second word was a 'C' of some kind (which was actually what it looked like). If so then the relevant phrase became HIC AMICITUR ARCHA CEDERIS – which would translate either
as 'Here is hidden the Ark of the Covenant', or 'Here is hidden the Ark that you will yield' (or 'give up' or 'send away').

'Even the word "hidden" isn't definite,' concluded Peter as he closed his Latin dictionary. '*Amicitur* in this context could equally well mean "covered up" – although that does convey the same sort of idea doesn't it? I don't know. The whole thing's a bit of a puzzle really.'

I agreed wholeheartedly with him on this point. The whole thing was indeed a puzzle. It was, moreover, a puzzle that I felt challenged, intrigued and tantalized by and that I very much wanted to solve.

During the remainder of my holiday in France my thoughts kept wandering back to the north porch of Chartres where I had seen the little sculptures. What I could not forget was the way in which the relic on its ox-cart had appeared to be moving towards the Queen of Sheba; nor could I dismiss from my mind the possibility that this suggested movement or a journey towards Ethiopia.

I knew that I was indulging in wild speculation for which there was no academic justification whatsoever and I fully accepted Peter Lasko's argument that the sculptors of Chartres would not have allowed themselves to be influenced by an Ethiopian legend in their choice of subject matter. This, however, left me with a much more exciting possibility to contemplate: perhaps those responsible for the north porch of the cathedral (which had also been called 'the door of the initiates'[21]) had been drawing a cryptic map for future generations to follow – a map that hinted at the location of the most sacred and precious treasure that the world had ever known. Perhaps they had discovered that the Ark of the Covenant really had been let go, or yielded (or sent away?) from Israel in Old Testament times and that it had subsequently been hidden (or covered up?) in Ethiopia. Perhaps this was the true meaning of the little sculptures with their puzzling inscriptions. If so then the implications were truly breathtaking and the Axumite traditions that I had so readily dismissed in 1983 would, at the very least, merit a close second look.

Mary, the Grail and the Ark

When I returned from France at the end of April 1989 I set my research assistant to work on the problem of the scholarly paper that Peter Lasko had mentioned to me. I knew that it might have been written by someone named Adolf and I knew that the subject matter had to do with a possible Ethiopian influence on Wolfram von Eschenbach's story of the Holy Grail. I did not know where, or when, the paper had been published, or even in what language, but I advised my researcher to contact the universities to see if there were any specialists on medieval German literature who might be able to help.

While waiting for an answer on this I went out and bought a number of different versions of the Grail 'romance'. These included Chrétien de Troyes's *Conte du Graal*, left unfinished by the author in AD 1182,[22] Sir Thomas Malory's *Le Morte D'Arthur*, a much later epic dated to the mid-fifteenth century,[23] and last but not least *Parzival*, which Wolfram von Eschenbach was thought to have written between the years 1195 and 1210[24] – dates that coincided almost exactly with the main phase of construction work on the north porch of Chartres cathedral.

I began to read these books and initially found Malory's the most accessible – since it had been the inspiration for a number of stories and films dealing with the quest for the Holy Grail that I had enjoyed as a child.

I quickly discovered, however, that Malory had presented an idealized, sanitized and above all *Christianized* account of 'the only true quest'. Wolfram's story, by contrast, was more earthy, provided a more accurate portrayal of the realities of human behaviour, and – most important of all – was completely devoid of New Testament symbolism where the Grail itself was concerned.

In Malory the sacred relic was described as a 'vessel of gold' carried by a 'perfect clean maiden' and containing 'part of the blood of Our Lord Jesus Christ'.[25] This, as I was well aware, was precisely the image that had long been enshrined in popular culture, where the Grail was always portrayed as a cup or a bowl (usually that in which Joseph of Arimathea caught a few drops of Christ's blood when the Saviour hung suffering on the cross).

I myself had been so influenced by this conception that I found it difficult to think of the Grail as anything other than a cup. When I turned to Wolfram's *Parzival*, however, I found confirmation of what I had learned in France, namely that the relic – although carried by a maiden just as in Malory – was depicted as a *stone*:

> However ill a mortal man may be, from the day on which
> he sees the Stone he cannot die for that week, nor does
> he lose his colour. For if anyone, maid or man, were to
> look at the Gral for two hundred years, you would have to
> admit that his colour was as fresh as in his early prime . . .
> Such powers does the Stone confer on mortal men that
> their flesh and bones are soon made young again. This
> Stone is called 'The Gral'.[26]

I was struck by this odd and compelling imagery, and it raised a nagging question in my mind: why should the *Morte D'Arthur* have depicted the Grail as 'a vessel' when the far earlier *Parzival* had unambiguously described it as 'a Stone'? What was going on here?

I investigated further and learnt from one authority on quest literature that Malory was 'merely embroidering a theme, the meaning of which [he] did not understand' when he wrote the *Morte D'Arthur*.[27] That theme had been most definitively spelled out in Wolfram's *Parzival* and in Chrétien de Troyes's *Conte du Graal*,[28] both of which were more than two hundred years older than the *Morte*.

Encouraged by this advice I turned to my copy of Chrétien's unfinished story and there read the following description of the Grail – the first in literature (and, for that matter, in history). As in both Wolfram and Malory, the precious object was carried by a damsel:

Once she had entered with this grail that she held, so
great a radiance appeared that the candles lost their
brilliance just as the stars do at the rising of the sun and
the moon . . . The grail . . . was of pure refined gold [and]
was set with many kinds of precious stones, the richest
and most costly in sea or earth.[29]

At no point, I discovered, did Chrétien's manuscript explicitly
state that the Grail was a cup or bowl. It was clear from the
context, however, that this was precisely what he saw it as. In
several places he referred to a central character – 'the Fisher
King' – being 'served from the grail',[30] and later added: 'he's
served with a single consecrated wafer brought to him in that
grail – that supports his life in full vigour, so holy a thing is the
grail'.[31] On checking further I learned that the very word 'grail'
was itself derived from the Old French *gradale* (Latin *gradalis*)
meaning 'a wide and somewhat hollowed-out vessel in which
delicious food is served'. In the colloquial parlance of Chrétien's
day *gradale* was often pronounced *greal*. And even in more recent
times *grazal*, *grazau*, and *grial* continued to be used in parts of the
south of France to denote receptacles of various kinds.[32]

Here, therefore, was the origin of Malory's conception of the
sacred object as a vessel. Other than the mention of 'a
consecrated wafer', however, Chrétien's treatment offered no
unequivocal connections with Christianity (not even in the
notion of the Grail being a 'holy thing' – which could as easily
have been inspired by the Old Testament as by the New[33]). Like
Wolfram, the French poet did not mention Christ's blood at all
and certainly did not suggest that the relic was a container for it.

It followed that the 'sacred blood' imagery associated with the
Grail in popular culture was a gloss added by later authors – a
gloss that broadened, but also to some extent obscured, the
original theme. With a little more work on the subject I was able
to satisfy myself that this process of 'Christianization' had been
sponsored by the Cistercian monastic order.[34] And the
Cistercians in their turn had been profoundly influenced and
shaped by one man – Saint Bernard of Clairvaux, who had joined
the Order in the year 1112 and who was regarded by many
scholars as the most significant religious figure of his era.[35]

This same Saint Bernard, I then discovered, had also played a formative role in the evolution and dissemination of the Gothic architectural formula in its early days (he had been at the height of his powers in 1134 when the soaring north tower of Chartres cathedral had been built, and he had constantly stressed the principles of sacred geometry that had been put into practice in that tower and throughout the whole wonderful building).[36] Moreover, long after his death in 1153, his sermons and ideas had continued to serve as prime sources of inspiration for the further evolution of Gothic architecture and also for statuary and sculptures like those I had seen in the north porch at Chartres.[37]

The principal bridge between the earlier non-Christian versions of the story of the Holy Grail and the stylized New Testament tract that it had become by Malory's time had been formed by the so-called *Queste del Saint Graal* – compiled by Cistercian monks in the thirteenth century.[38] Moreover, although he was already dead when this great anthology was begun, it seemed to me that the strong hand of Saint Bernard could also be seen at work here – reaching out from beyond the grave as it were. I arrived at this conclusion because, in his extensive writings, this immensely influential cleric had propounded a mystical view of Christ's blood, a view that was incorporated by the compilers of the *Queste* into their new concept of the Grail itself.[39] From now on Wolfram's Stone was completely forgotten and Chrétien's 'vessel', although preserved, was filled up with the blood of Christ.

What I found interesting about this notion was the way in which it had immediately begun to be interpreted by the church. In hymns, sermons and epistles, I learned, subsequent generations of Christians all over Europe had gone to great lengths to equate the Grail symbolically with the Blessed Virgin Mary – to whom, I remembered, Chartres cathedral had been dedicated. The reasoning underlying this pious allegory was as follows: the Grail (according to the *Queste* and other later recensions of the legend) contained the holy blood of Christ; before she gave birth to him, Mary had contained Christ himself within her womb; therefore, QED, the Grail was – and always had been – a symbol for Mary.[40]

According to this logic, *Mary Theotokos*, the 'God Bearer', was the sacred vessel who had contained the Spirit made flesh. Thus, in the sixteenth-century Litany of Loretto,[41] she was the *vas spirituale* (spiritual vessel), the *vas honorabile* (vessel of honour), and the *vas insigne devotionis* (singular vessel of devotion).[42]

Why did this symbolism attract my attention? Quite simply because the Litany of Loretto had also referred to the Blessed Virgin as *arca foederis*[43] – which, as I already knew, was Latin for 'the Ark of the Covenant'. I researched this coincidence further and discovered that the Litany was not the only place in which it cropped up. In the twelfth century, the redoubtable Saint Bernard of Clairvaux had also explicitly compared Mary to the Ark of the Covenant – indeed he had done so in a number of his writings.[44] And as early as the fourth century Saint Ambrose, the Bishop of Milan, had preached a sermon in which he had argued that the Ark had been a prophetic allegory for Mary: just as it had contained the Old Law in the form of the Ten Commandments, so she had contained the New Law in the form of the body of Christ.[45]

I was subsequently to discover that concepts like these had persisted into the twentieth century and had been woven into the fabric of modern Christian worship. On a trip to Israel, for example, I came across a small and beautiful Dominican church built in 1924 and dedicated *A la Vièrge Marie Arche d'Alliance* – in other words 'To the Virgin Mary Ark of the Covenant'. The church stood at Kiriath-Jearim, overlooking the road between Tel Aviv and Jerusalem, and its seven-metre steeple was topped off with a full-sized representation of the Ark. There were also several paintings of the sacred relic arranged around the interior walls of the building itself. During my visit I was given the following (very 'Ambrosian') explanation of the dedication – and of the symbolism – by a senior church official, Sister Raphael Mikhail:

'We compare Mary to a living Ark. Mary was the mother of Jesus, who was the master of the Law and of the Covenant. The tablets of stone with the Ten Commandments of the Law were placed inside the Ark by Moses; so also God placed Jesus in the womb of Mary. So she is the living Ark.'

It seemed to me highly significant that both the Ark and the Grail, apparently so different, should nevertheless have been compared repeatedly to the *same* biblical personality, and in exactly the same way. If Mary was both a 'living Ark' and a 'living Grail', I speculated, then surely this suggested that the two sacred objects might not in fact have been so very different – that they might, indeed, have been *one and the same thing*.

This struck me as a truly electrifying possibility. And, far-fetched though it at first appeared, it did shed interesting light on the choice and juxtaposition of statuary in the north porch of Chartres cathedral. If I was correct then Melchizedek's 'Grail' cup with the 'Stone' inside it would at one level have represented Mary but could, at another, have been intended to serve as an esoteric symbol for the Ark of the Covenant and for the stone tablets that it had contained.

Such an interpretation, I felt, added considerable weight to the hypothesis that the other iconography of the north porch signalled the removal of the sacred relic to Ethiopia. But I also realized that I had no really firm grounds on which to base a conclusion of this magnitude – only coincidence, guesswork and a strong intuition that I might be on to something important.

I have always been inclined to follow my intuitions to see where they lead. However, it seemed to me that if I was going to involve myself in a proper, thorough, expensive and time-consuming investigation then I needed something rather more solid to go on than a few happy accidents and presentiments.

I did not have to wait long. In June 1989 my researcher finally managed to locate the academic paper that, according to Peter Lasko, had suggested a possible Ethiopian influence on the portrayal of the Holy Grail in Wolfram von Eschenbach's *Parzival*. The encouragement given to me by that paper launched me on the quest that was to dominate my life for the next two years.

Literary influence – or something more?

The paper, entitled 'New Light on Oriental Sources for Wolfram's *Parzival*', had appeared in 1947 in the academic journal *PMLA* (*Publications of the Modern Languages Association of*

America).[46] The author was Helen Adolf, a highly regarded medievalist who had taken a special interest in the literary pedigree of the Holy Grail. The thesis that she put forward (for which she admitted that she was indebted to two earlier authorities[47]) was that Wolfram – although largely influenced by Chrétien de Troyes – must also 'have known, besides Chrétien, a Grail story in Oriental setting'.[48]

When I began to read Helen Adolf's paper I was already aware,

from the background research that I had done, that Chrétien de Troyes had effectively 'invented' the Grail in 1182. Prior to that date it had existed neither in history, nor in myth. Most authorities on the subject agreed that there were earlier legends – dealing, for example, with magic cauldrons, heroic quests, and deeds of chivalry done by King Arthur and his Knights – which the courtly poets and raconteurs had drawn upon to add texture to their Grail stories.[49] These older lays, however, which had been handed down by word of mouth from generation to generation, had been too well known, too 'tried and tested', in short too familiar to all and sundry, to have provided the creative impulse for the distinct cycle of romances that Chrétien initiated in the late twelfth century.

The great French poet had never finished his famous *Conte du Graal*. Within a very few years, however, Wolfram von Eschenbach capitalized on the good start that had been made, extending and completing his predecessor's story – while at the same time rather churlishly accusing Chrétien of 'doing wrong' by it and adding that his own German text was the 'authentic tale'.[50]

What made such protestations seem odd was the fact that Wolfram had obviously lifted many details directly from the *Conte du Graal* and, by and large, had remained faithful to its plot and characters.[51] Indeed there was only one glaringly obvious difference – the bizarre innovation of making the Grail a Stone. The motive for this innovation did, therefore, look like a genuine mystery to some scholars. It could not have been a simple mistake on Wolfram's part – he was much too clever and precise a raconteur to have made an error of such significance. The only reasonable conclusion, therefore, was that he had described the relic in the way he did for some special reason of his own.

It was to precisely this question that Helen Adolf addressed herself in her short paper. And she offered an answer to it that I found most intriguing. Somehow or other, she argued, Wolfram must have gained access to the *Kebra Nagast*, enjoyed the story about the Ark of the Covenant being removed from Jerusalem to Axum, and decided to work elements of it into his own *Parzival*. The influence was only 'indirect', she thought; nevertheless the most likely explanation for the curious character of Wolfram's Grail could be traced to the use, 'in every Abyssinian church', of what she described as 'a so-called *Tabot*, a slab of wood or stone'.[52]

Adolf explained that this practice had its origins in the religious traditions set down in the *Kebra Nagast* – an observation that I knew to be correct. In 1983 I had learned that *Tabot* was the local name for the sacred relic – believed to be the Ark of the Covenant – that Menelik had supposedly brought from Jerusalem and that was now kept in the sanctuary chapel at Axum. Moreover, as the reader will recall, I had subsequently discovered, as Adolf also affirmed, that each and every Ethiopian Orthodox church possessed its own *tabot*. These objects, which were often spoken of as *replicas* of the original in Axum, were not boxes or chests but took the form of flat slabs. The ones I had seen had all been made of wood. Researching the matter further, however, I discovered that many were indeed made of stone.[53]

On the basis of several comparisons Adolf asserted that Wolfram, too, had known this and had derived his Grail-Stone from the Ethiopian *tabot*. She also pointed out that not all the characters in *Parzival* had been borrowed from Chrétien de Troyes; there were a few additional figures whose origins were mysterious and who might well have been inspired by the *Kebra Nagast*. She could offer no solid explanation as to how the German raconteur could have become familiar with the *Kebra Nagast* but suggested rather tentatively that wandering Jews might have brought it to Europe. In the medieval period, she pointed out, 'the Jews were not only the mediators between Arabs and Christians in general. They had a special stake in Ethiopia, where they formed, and still form, an important part of the population.'[54]

I found Adolf's arguments persuasive but extremely limited in scope. She had confined herself to the specialized field of literary criticism, and accordingly her concerns had been of an entirely literary nature. Having set out to prove the possibility of a connection between the *Kebra Nagast* and *Parzival* (with the former 'indirectly influencing' the latter) she had been quite happy to stop when she felt she had achieved this goal. I was enormously grateful to her, however, because she had opened my eyes to something far more exciting – something of infinitely greater significance.

On the basis of the comparisons cited earlier between the Ark of the Covenant, the Holy Grail, and Mary the Mother of Christ, I had already begun to wonder whether the identities of the Ark and the Grail were really as distinct and separate as they seemed at first sight. Now it occurred to me that if Wolfram's Grail looked as if it had been influenced by Ethiopian traditions concerning the Ark then there was just a chance that there could be more to this – perhaps much more – than Helen Adolf had ever guessed. To cut a long story short, I began to wonder whether the German poet might not have deliberately constructed his fictional Grail as a kind of 'code' for the real and historical Ark. If so then the quest that formed the central theme of *Parzival* could also be a code that might, like some cryptic treasure map, point the way to the last resting place of the Ark itself.

I had already become intrigued by the possibility that a similar code in the north porch of Chartres cathedral – though carved in stone rather than written in a book – might hint that the relic had been taken to Ethiopia. It was therefore with real enthusiasm and excitement that I set out to try to 'decode' *Parzival*.

Celestial writing, laws and oracles

It seemed to me that my initial task should be to determine whether Wolfram's Grail could indeed have been designed as a sort of cryptogram for the Ark of the Covenant. To this end I decided that I would temporarily postpone further examination of the Ethiopian connection suggested by Adolf. Instead I would look for direct parallels between the characteristics of the Grail and the characteristics of the Ark as described in the Old Testament and other ancient Jewish sources. Only if those parallels proved persuasive would there be any point in going further.

The first thing that attracted my attention was the way in which Wolfram had transformed Chrétien's Grail cup – or vessel – into a stone. It occurred to me that the French poet's description of the Grail had been sufficiently vague and mystical to allow Wolfram to *impose* an identity on it, to mould his predecessor's rather imprecise concept of a sacred receptacle into a shape that suited his own purposes – in short to *define* that receptacle by speaking not directly of it but of its *contents*.

The Ark of the Covenant was, after all, a receptacle too, and it did indeed contain a stone – or rather two stone tablets upon which the Ten Commandments had been inscribed by the finger of God. I therefore found it intriguing that Wolfram's Grail, like the Tablets of the Law, bore – from time to time – the imprint of a celestial script which set out certain rules.[55]

There were other such coincidences – for example, the oracular function that the Grail played for the community that depended on it:

> We fell on our knees before the Gral, where suddenly we
> saw it written that a knight would come to us and were he
> heard to ask a Question there, our sorrows would be at an
> end; but that if any child, maiden or man were to
> forewarn him of the Question it would fail in its effect,
> and the injury would be as it was and give rise to deeper
> pain. 'Have you understood?' asked the Writing. 'If you
> alert him it could prove harmful. If he omits the question
> on the first evening, its power will pass away. But if he
> asks his Question in season he shall have the
> Kingdom.'[56]

The Ark, too, frequently served as an oracle, dispensing advice that was crucial to the survival of the Israelites. In the book of Judges, for example, where the identity of God Himself was often completely fused with that of the Ark, I found this passage:

> And the children of Israel enquired of the Lord, (for the
> Ark of the Covenant of God was there in those days, and

Phinehas, the son of Eleazar, the son of Aaron, stood before it in those days), saying Shall I yet again go out to battle against the children of Benjamin my brother, or shall I cease?' And the Lord said, Go up: for tomorrow I will deliver them into thine hand.[57]

I also came across a much later biblical passage which stated that it had become rare for the Ark actually to speak and that 'visions' were now 'uncommon'. Nevertheless, as the prophet Samuel lay down 'in the house of the Lord, where the Ark of God was', a voice issued forth from the sacred relic warning: 'Behold, I will do a thing in Israel at which both the ears of everyone that heareth it shall tingle.'[58]

Neither were utterances and visions the only ways in which the Ark communicated its oracular messages. Like the Grail, it also used the written word from time to time – notably to impart to King David the blueprint for the Temple that his son Solomon was to build.[59]

The weight of sin, the golden calf, and stones from heaven

As my research progressed I discovered many other shared characteristics linking the Grail to the Ark – and particularly to the Tablets of Stone. One example concerned the way in which the weight of the relic seemed to be spiritually controlled. According to Wolfram: 'the Gral [while it may be carried by the pure of heart] is so heavy that sinful mortals could not lift it from its place.'[60]

In this, I thought there might well be a connection to an ancient Jewish legend which described the moment when the prophet Moses descended from Mount Sinai carrying the Tablets of Stone, then freshly inscribed with the divine words of the Ten Commandments. As he came into camp the prophet caught the children of Israel in the act of worshipping the golden calf, a sin so unspeakable that:

All at once he saw the writing vanish from the tablets, and at the same time became aware of their enormous weight;

for while the celestial writing was upon them they carried
their own weight and did not burden Moses, but with the
disappearance of the writing all this changed.[61]

In Wolfram's cryptic prose the golden calf, too, made an
appearance. It did so, moreover, in a context so crucial that I felt
certain that the author was using it quite deliberately to convey a
message – a message further identifying the Grail with the Ark:

> There was a heathen named Flegetanis [I read in Chapter
> 9 of *Parzival*] who was highly renowned for his
> acquirements. This same physicus was descended from
> Solomon, begotten of Israelitish kin all the way down
> from ancient times . . . He wrote of the marvels of the
> Gral. Flegetanis, *who worshipped a calf as though it were his
> god*, was a heathen by his father . . . [and] was able to
> define for us the recession of each planet and its return,
> and how long each revolves in its orbit before it stands at
> its mark again. All human kind are affected by the
> revolutions of the planets. With his own eyes the heathen
> Flegetanis saw – and he spoke of it reverentially – hidden
> secrets in the constellations. He declared there was a
> thing called the Gral, whose name he read in the stars
> without more ado. 'A troop [of Angels] left it on earth and
> then rose high above the stars, as if their innocence drew
> them back again.'[62]

To my mind what was really important about this passage was the
way in which it used Flegetanis (with his intriguingly Solomonic
and Jewish/pagan background) to signal an *astral* origin for the
Grail.

Why important? Simply because some of the most serious
biblical scholarship that I studied argued that the Tablets of
Stone contained within the Ark of the Covenant had, in reality,
been two pieces of a *meteorite*.[63] Neither was this merely some
latter-day interpretation that could not have been shared by
Moses and by the Levitical priests who attended the Ark. On the
contrary, since ancient times, Semitic tribes such as the children

of Israel had been known to venerate stones that 'fell from heaven'.[64]

The best illustration of this custom, since it had continued into modern times, was the special reverence accorded by Muslims to the sacred Black Stone built into a corner of the wall of the *Ka'aba* in Mecca. Kissed by every pilgrim making the *Haj* to the holy site, this stone was declared by the Prophet Muhammad to have *fallen from heaven* to earth where it was first given to Adam to absorb his sins after his expulsion from the Garden of Eden; later it was presented by the angel Gabriel to Abraham, the Hebrew Patriarch; finally it became the cornerstone of the *Ka'aba* – the 'beating heart' of the Islamic world.[65]

Geologists, I learned, unhesitatingly attributed a meteoric origin to the Black Stone.[66] Likewise the *pairs* of sacred stones, known as *betyls*, that some pre-Islamic Arab tribes carried on their desert wanderings were believed to have been aerolites – and it was recognized that a direct line of cultural transmission linked these *betyls* (which were often placed in portable shrines) with the Black Stone of the *Ka'aba* and with the stone Tablets of the Law contained within the Ark.[67]

I then discovered that *betyls* had been known in medieval Europe as *lapis betilis* – a name:

> stemming from Semitic origins and taken over at a late
> date by the Greeks and Romans for sacred stones that
> were assumed to possess a divine life, stones with a soul
> [that were used] for divers superstitions, for magic and
> for fortunetelling. They were meteoric stones fallen from
> the sky.[68]

In such a context, I found it hard to believe that Wolfram had merely been indulging in flights of fancy when he had specified a meteoric origin for his Grail-Stone. Not only did he use his character Flegetanis to this end but also, a few pages further on, he provided a strange alternative name for the Grail – '*Lapsit exillis*'.[69] Although I came across a variety of interpretations for the real meaning of this pseudo-Latin epithet,[70] the most plausible by far was that it had been derived from *lapis ex caelis* ('stone from heaven'), *lapsit ex caelis* ('it fell from heaven'), or even *lapis, lapsus ex caelis*, 'stone fallen from heaven'.[71] At the same time it seemed to me that the bastardized words *Lapsit exillis* were quite close enough to *lapis betilis* to raise the suspicion that the German poet had intended a deliberate – and characteristically cryptic – pun.

Benedictions, supernatural light, and the power of choice

Another and quite different area of comparison lay in Wolfram's repeated descriptions of the Grail as a source of blessing and fertility for those pure-hearted people who came into contact with it. To cite one example amongst many,[72] I found this passage in Chapter 5 of *Parzival*:

> Whatever one stretched out one's hand for in the
> presence of the Gral, it was waiting, one found it all ready
> and to hand – dishes warm, dishes cold, new-fangled
> dishes and old favourites . . . for the Gral was the very
> fruit of bliss, a cornucopia of the sweets of this world.[73]

It seemed to me quite probable that this description echoed an ancient Talmudic commentary which had it that:

> When Solomon brought the Ark into the Temple, all the
> golden trees that were in the Temple were filled with
> moisture and produced abundant fruit, to the great profit
> and enjoyment of the priestly guild.[74]

I found an even closer correspondence between the Ark and the Grail in the otherworldly *luminescence* said to have been given off by both objects. The Holy of Holies in Solomon's Temple (where the Ark was installed before it mysteriously vanished) was a place of 'thick darkness' according to the Bible.[75] Talmudic sources recorded, however, that: 'The High Priest of Israel entered and left *by the light that the Holy Ark issued forth*' – a convenient state of affairs that changed after the relic disappeared. From then on the Priest 'groped his way in the dark'.[76]

The Ark, therefore, was a source of paranormal lambency: a

dazzling radiance was emitted by it – as numerous biblical passages confirmed.[77] In similar fashion Chrétien's Grail, which I thought that Wolfram had been happy to accept (because it provided the receptacle part of the Ark cipher that he then completed with his Stone), sent out a radiance 'so great . . . that . . . candles lost their brilliance just as the stars do at the rising of the sun or moon.'[78]

Chrétien's Grail was likewise made of 'pure gold'[79] while the Ark was 'overlaid with pure gold, within and without'[80] and was covered with a lid (known as the 'mercy seat') which was also 'of pure gold'.[81] But it was not from this precious metal that Ark and Grail derived their light-generating quality; rather this was the product of their shared impregnation with a fiery celestial energy. And it was this same energy (cast forth by the Tablets of Stone after the Ten Commandments had been inscribed upon them by the finger of God) that caused Moses' face to shine with an eerie, supernatural brilliance when he descended from Mount Sinai:

> As he came down from the mountain, Moses had the two Tablets of the Testimony in his hands. He did not know that the skin on his face was radiant . . . And when Aaron and all the sons of Israel saw Moses, the skin on his face shone so much that they would not venture near him.[82]

I therefore thought it not entirely coincidental that Wolfram's Grail-Stone, on its very first appearance in *Parzival*, was carried in procession in the hands of a certain Repanse de Schoye whose face 'shed such refulgence that all imagined it was sunrise.'[83]

The heaven-destined hero

Repanse de Schoye was a 'Princess'[84] and was also 'of perfect chastity'.[85] Her most important characteristic, however, was that the Grail had *chosen* her: 'She whom the Gral suffered to carry itself', Wolfram explained, 'had the name Repanse de Schoye . . . By her alone, no other I am told, did the Gral let itself be carried.'[86]

Such phrases seemed to imply that the relic possessed a kind of sentience. And linked to this was another quality: 'No man can win the Gral,' Wolfram stated in Chapter 9 of *Parzival*, 'other than one who is acknowledged in Heaven as destined for it.'[87] The same point was then forcefully reiterated in Chapter 15: 'No man could ever win the Gral by force, except the one who is summoned there by God.'[88]

These two notions – of the Grail exercising powers of choice and of it being a prize to be won only by those who were 'Heaven-destined' – were of great importance in Wolfram's overall scheme of things. I concluded, moreover, that precedents were provided for both of them in biblical descriptions of the Ark of the Covenant. In Numbers 10:33, for instance, it *chose* the route that the children of Israel were to take through the desert, and it also determined where they should camp. Meanwhile in the book of Chronicles there was this example of certain individuals being 'Heaven-destined' for the Ark:

> None ought to carry the Ark of God but the Levites; for them hath the Lord chosen to carry the Ark of God and to minister unto it.[89]

It was not in the Bible, however, that I found the closest correspondences between the Ark of the Covenant and Wolfram's sentient, Heaven-destined Grail. These came rather in the *Kebra Nagast*, which told the story of the Ark's abduction to Ethiopia. In Sir E. A. Wallis Budge's authoritative English translation[90] I came across this passage in which the sacred relic was referred to almost as though it were a feminine person (who, like all ladies, could change her mind):

> And as for what thou sayest concerning the going of the Ark of the Covenant to their city, to the country of Ethiopia, if God willed it and she herself willed it, there is no one who could prevent her; for of her own will she went and of her own will she will return if God pleaseth.[91]

Next I noted the following strange references which seemed to imply that the relic possessed intelligence and also that the honour of keeping it was granted as a result of heavenly predestination:

> The Ark goeth of its own free will whithersoever it wisheth, and it cannot be removed from its seat if it does not desire it.[92]

> Without the Will of God the Ark of God will not dwell in any place.[93]

> But the chosen ones of the Lord are the people of Ethiopia. For there is the habitation of God, the heavenly ZION,[94] the Ark of His Covenant.[95]

Last but not least, in Chapter 60 of the *Kebra Nagast*, I found a lengthy lamentation supposedly uttered by Solomon when he learned that the Ark had been abducted by his son Menelik from the Holy of Holies of the Temple in Jerusalem. At the moment of his bitterest grief an angel appeared to him and asked:

> 'Why art thou thus sorrowful? For this hath happened by the Will of God. The Ark hath . . . been given . . . to thy first-born son . . .' And the King was comforted by this word, and he said, 'The will of God be done and not the will of man.'[96]

Could this not be, I wondered, exactly what had been in Wolfram's mind when he had written that 'no man could ever win the Gral by force except the one who is summoned there by God'? In other words, if the Grail was indeed a cryptogram for the Ark then might not the prototype for the German poet's 'Heaven-destined' hero have been none other than Menelik himself?

To answer this question I read *Parzival* again. I was not looking, however, for literary influences from the *Kebra Nagast* – as Helen Adolf had done – but rather for the presence of explicit clues embedded within the text which pointed in the direction of Ethiopia. I wanted to know whether there was there anything at all to suggest that Ethiopia might in fact *be* Wolfram's mysterious

Terre Salvaesche[97] – the land of the Grail and, therefore, by implication, the land of the Ark.

Chapter 4

A Map to Hidden Treasure

My readings of *Parzival* during the spring and summer of 1989 had brought a startling possibility to my attention: the fictional object known as the Holy Grail could have been devised to serve as a complex symbol for the Ark of the Covenant. This in turn had led me to formulate another hypothesis – namely that behind Wolfram von Eschenbach's Heaven-destined Grail hero, there might lie another figure who, once recognized, would point the way to the heart of the mystery of the whereabouts of the Ark – a figure whose real identity the poet had therefore disguised beneath layers of arcane and sometimes deliberately misleading details. This figure, I suspected, might be none other than Menelik I – the son of the Queen of Sheba and King Solomon who, according to Abyssinian legends, had brought the Ark of the Covenant to Ethiopia. If there was anything at all to this speculation, I reasoned, then I might hope to find further clues embedded in *Parzival* – cryptic clues that might be obscured by frequent false trails, that might be scattered here and there amongst widely separated chapters, that might be calculatedly vague and ambiguous, but that would, nevertheless, serve to reinforce the Ethiopian connection if only they could be gathered together and made sense of.

Ebony and ivory

I found the first of these clues early in the text of *Parzival* in a chapter which spoke of a far-off land called 'Zazamanc' where the people 'were all as dark as night'.[1] To this land came a wandering European aristocrat, 'Gahmuret of Anjou',[2] and there he fell in love with no lesser personage than the queen – 'sweet and constant Belacane'.[3]

In 'Belacane' I could not help but hear an echo of 'Makeda', the Ethiopian name for the Queen of Sheba that I had first become acquainted with when I had visited Axum in 1983. I was also aware that this same monarch had been known in Muslim tradition as Bilquis.[4] Since I was by this time quite familiar with Wolfram's love of neologisms, and with his tendency to make up new and fanciful names by running old ones together, it seemed to me rash totally to reject the possibility that 'Belacane' might be a kind of composite of 'Bilquis' and 'Makeda' – and doubly rash since the poet described her as a 'dusky queen'.[5]

When I looked more closely at the love affair between Belacane and Gahmuret, recounted at length in the first chapter of *Parzival*, I found further echoes of the King Solomon and Queen of Sheba story told in the *Kebra Nagast* and also, with minor variations, in a range of other Ethiopian legends. In this connection I felt it was not accidental that Wolfram had gone to considerable lengths to make it clear that Gahmuret – like Solomon – was white, while Belacane, like Makeda, was black.

For example, after the arrival of the 'fair complexioned' Angevin knight[6] in Zazamanc, Belacane observed to her hand-maidens: 'His skin is a different colour from ours. I only hope this is no sore point with him?'[7] Certainly it was not, because her romance with Gahmuret blossomed in the following weeks, one thing led to another, and eventually the couple retired to her bedroom in the palace:

> The Queen disarmed him with her own dark hands.
> There was a magnificent bed with a sable coverlet, where
> a new though private honour awaited him. They were
> now alone: the young ladies-in-waiting had left the room
> and closed the doors behind them. The Queen yielded to
> sweet and noble love with Gahmuret, her heart's own
> darling, little though their skins matched in colour.[8]

The lovers married. Because Belacane was an unbaptized heathen, however, and Gahmuret a Christian with many deeds of chivalry still to do, he fled Zazamanc when she was 'twelve weeks gone with child'[9] and left her only this letter:

'Like a thief I have sailed away. I *had* to steal away to spare our tears. Madam, I cannot conceal it that did you but live within my rite I would long for you to all eternity. Even now my passion gives me endless torment! If our child has the aspect of a man, I swear he will be brave.'[10]

Long after his departure Gahmuret continued to suffer agonies of remorse since 'the dusky lady was dearer to him than life'.[11] Later he proclaimed:

'Now many an ignorant fellow may think that it was her black skin I ran away from, but in my eyes she was as bright as the sun! The thought of her womanly excellence afflicts me, for if noblesse were a shield she would be its centre-piece.'[12]

So much then for Belacane and Gahmuret. But what of their child?

When her time came the lady was delivered of a son. His skin was pied. It had pleased God to make a marvel of him, for he was both black and white. The Queen fell to kissing his white spots, time and time again. The name she gave her little boy was Feirefiz the Angevin. When he grew up he cleared whole forests – so many lances did he shatter, punching holes in shields. His hair and all his skin were particoloured like a magpie.[13]

Wolfram could hardly have found a more graphic way to emphasize that Feirefiz was a half-caste – the product of a union between a black woman and a white man. This half-caste Feirefiz, furthermore, was to go on to play a crucial role in the story of *Parzival*. His father, the amorous Gahmuret, returned to Europe after deserting Belacane and there married another queen, a certain Herzeloyde, whom he immediately set about making pregnant. He then abandoned her also, went off to have several more adventures, earned great honour in a series of battles, and eventually managed to get himself killed. 'A fortnight later,' Wolfram related, Herzeloyde 'was delivered of a babe, a son so big in the bone that she scarce survived.'[14] That son was Parzival himself, the eponymous hero of Wolfram's tale and – through Gahmuret – the half-brother of Feirefiz.[15]

In the *Kebra Nagast* and other relevant Ethiopian legends there were, I discovered, numerous parallels to the complex of relationships involving Gahmuret, Belacane, Feirefiz, Parzival *et al*. These parallels were often of an indirect kind; nevertheless I had come to expect such tantalizing hints from Wolfram and I became increasingly confident that he was laying down a trail of clues that – through snares and mazes – would lead me to Ethiopia in the end.

The constant references to the contrasting blackness and whiteness of Belacane and Gahmuret had been unmissable features of the opening sections of *Parzival*. In the *Kebra Nagast* the lovers were King Solomon and the Queen of Sheba. Like Gahmuret and Belacane they had retired to bed together.[16] Like Gahmuret and Belacane, one of them (in this case Makeda) had deserted the other and gone on a long journey.[17] Like Gahmuret and Belacane the fruit of their union had been a half-caste son, in this case Menelik.[18] And again like Gahmuret and Belacane, the difference in their colour was repeatedly emphasized in the relevant text, in this case the *Kebra Nagast*. In a typical scene the Jewish monarch was upbraided for Menelik's abduction of the Ark in the following unambiguous terms:

> Thy son hath carried away the Ark of the Covenant,[19] thy son whom thou hast begotten, who springeth from an alien people into which God hath not commanded you to marry, that is to say from an Ethiopian woman, who is not of thy colour, and is not akin to thy country, and who is, moreover, black.[20]

There were, in addition, certain parallels between Menelik and Feirefiz which went beyond their shared identity as half-castes. Amongst these, for example, was the curiosity of the very name 'Feirefiz'. What language did it belong to, and what – if anything – did it mean? I checked and discovered that literary critics had quite firm ideas on this subject. Most interpreted the strange-sounding epithet as a characteristic Wolfram neologism based on the French words 'vair fils' meaning, literally, 'piebald son'.[21] Another school of thought, however, derived it equally plausibly from 'vrai fils' – 'true son'.[22]

In the *Kebra Nagast* itself I could find no comparison directly reflecting either etymology (although, in Chapter 36, Solomon declared, on first being introduced to Menelik: 'Look ye, this is my son'[23]). In a somewhat different but equally ancient Ethiopic recension of the same legend, however (translated into English in 1904 by Professor Erno Littman of Princeton University), the moment of the meeting between Solomon and Menelik was also described, and contained this passage:

> At once Menelik went to him and took his hand to greet him. Then said Solomon: 'Thou art my true son'.[24]

'Vrai fils', in other words!

Devious mechanisms

Coincidences like these made it increasingly difficult for me to resist the notion that Wolfram had indeed linked his Feirefiz with Menelik. Why should he have done that? Not, I speculated, because he had been *influenced* by the *Kebra Nagast* (as the scholar Helen Adolf had suggested in the 1940s[25]) but rather because he had *known* the final resting place of the Ark of the Covenant to be in Ethiopia, and because he had set out to encode this knowledge within the story of *Parzival* – which was thus a kind of literary 'treasure map' that used the Grail as a cryptogram for the Ark itself.

Wolfram had been addicted to ingenious tricks – to a species of verbal legerdemain that was as baffling as it was entertaining. I felt, however, that I was beginning to see through most of his illusions and also to recognize the decoys that he so frequently set up in order to lure his readers away from the secret that lay hidden at the heart of his story. I was therefore undisturbed by the fact that it was not Feirefiz himself who was depicted as being on a quest for the Grail – nor Feirefiz who was eventually accorded the honour of finding the precious relic. Such an outcome would have provided much too *direct* and obvious a pointer. And, besides, Wolfram could not have afforded to allow the heathen half-caste son of a black queen to become the hero of a romance written for the amusement of medieval European Christians.

For these reasons, it seemed to me that the clever German poet had been quite content to let all-white, all-good Parzival win through to the non-existent Grail – which was the only thing that most of his audience would be interested in. Meanwhile, for the discerning few, it would be Feirefiz – the *true son* – who would point the way to the Ark.

I realized, however, that I needed something more solid to support this hypothesis than just a series of coincidences – no matter how suggestive and intriguing these coincidences might seem. I therefore set about the brain-bending task of combing through *Parzival* yet again.

Eventually I found what I was looking for. I remembered from my previous readings that Feirefiz had ended up marrying Repanse de Schoye[26] – the pure and perfect Grail-bearer who, surrounded by an aura of sanctity and power, had appeared and disappeared constantly throughout the story. Now I came across a small but highly significant detail contained in a single line that I had missed before: according to Wolfram's 'happily-ever-after' conclusion, the son of Feirefiz and Repanse de Schoye had been named 'Prester John'.[27]

It was obvious to me at once that this could be a momentous clue. I knew that the first Europeans to arrive in Ethiopia had addressed the monarchs of that country as 'Prester John'.[28] I also knew that the legendary founder of the self-styled 'Solomonic' dynasty to which those monarchs had belonged had been Menelik I – the supposed son of Solomon and the Queen of Sheba. I therefore could not help but be excited to read that Repanse de Schoye had given Feirefiz 'a son named "John" ' and, moreover, that 'They called him "Prester John", and, ever since, they call their kings by no other name.'[29]

It would have been very nice if I had been able, there and then, to demonstrate that the land of the Grail – *Terre Salvaesche* – was in fact the same as the land ruled by 'Prester John'. Such a direct linkage would, at the very least, have enormously strengthened what I was coming to think of as my 'treasure map' theory of

Wolfram's work. Unfortunately, however, there was not a single shred of evidence in *Parzival* to support this view: the location of *Terre Salvaesche* was never spelled out in anything other than the most dreamlike and indefinite terms and at no point was it suggested that its king was 'Prester John'.

I was about to conclude that I had marched optimistically into an extremely depressing *cul de sac* when I discovered that there was another medieval German epic in which Prester John did become the guardian of the Grail. Called *Der Jüngerer Titurel* ('The Younger Titurel'), it was written in a style so close to that of *Parzival* that scholars had long attributed it to Wolfram himself (this attribution dated back to the thirteenth century).[30] Relatively recently, however, the hand of a slightly later author had been detected. Thought to have been a certain Albrecht von Scharfenberg, this author was believed to have compiled 'The Younger Titurel' between 1270 and 1275 (about fifty years after Wolfram's death) and *to have based it on previously uncirculated fragments of Wolfram's own work.*[31] Indeed Albrecht's identification with 'his master'[32] had been so complete that he had actually claimed to *be* Wolfram, 'adopting not just his name and subject matter but also his mannerisms as a narrator and even the details of his personal history.'[33]

I knew that there was a well established tradition in medieval literature of later writers extending and completing the work of their predecessors. Wolfram's *Parzival* had itself grown out of Chrétien de Troyes's original story of the Holy Grail. Now it seemed that it had been left to a third poet, Albrecht, to provide an ending to that story – an ending in which the Grail found its last resting place.

This last resting place, as 'The Younger Titurel' stated clearly, was the land of Prester John.[34] I thought it highly significant that such a statement existed in the literature of the Grail and, moreover, that it had been made by a Wolfram acolyte who appeared to have had privileged access to the notes and jottings of Wolfram himself. This, in my opinion, was just the sort of devious mechanism that 'the master' might have set up in order not to have to spell out his Ethiopian secret too bluntly in *Parzival* – while at the same time ensuring that that secret would be transmitted to future generations.

Perhaps this conclusion was warranted; perhaps it was not. Its significance, however, lay less in its academic merits than in the fact that it encouraged me to take Wolfram's own brief mention of 'Prester John' seriously – and thus to persevere with what turned out to be an exhausting but ultimately fruitful investigation.

The purpose of that investigation was to find the answer to a single question: when Wolfram talked of 'Prester John' could he have had an *Ethiopian* monarch in mind?

The first indications were that he had not; indeed he stated plainly that 'Prester John's' birth had taken place in 'India'[35] – a country of which Feirefiz was apparently the king and to which he and Repanse de Schoye had returned after the adventures described in *Parzival* were over.

To complicate the picture further the same paragraph then went on to advise that 'India' was also known as 'Tribalibot' ('Here we call it "India": there it is "Tribalibot"'[36]). Checking back I found earlier passages in which Feirefiz had been spoken of as the 'Lord of Tribalibot'[37] – which was consistent enough since I now knew that his son 'Prester John' had ultimately succeeded him as the ruler of Tribalibot/India. However, I could hardly forget that Feirefiz was himself the son of Belacane the Queen of 'Zazamanc'. I was therefore not surprised to learn that Wolfram had also referred to Feirefiz as the 'King of Zazamanc'.[38]

The only reasonable conclusion to be drawn from this confetti of exotic titles and appellations was that 'Zazamanc', 'Tribalibot' and 'India' were all, in fact, the same place. But could this place possibly be Ethiopia? Wasn't it much more reasonable to assume – since he had actually named it – that Wolfram had had the subcontinent of India in mind all along?

I decided to research the real, historical pedigree of 'Prester John' to see if this would shed any more light on the problem.

A real king

The name 'Prester John', I discovered, had been completely unknown before the twelfth century – a century during which European Crusaders had occupied the Holy City of Jerusalem for a continuous period of more than eighty years (they were finally expelled by the Saracens in 1187). Historians agreed that the very first mention of Prester John had been made roughly half-way through this period – in 1145 in the *Chronicle* of Bishop Otto of Freisingen. Claiming that his informant was a Syrian churchman, the bishop had written of a certain 'John, king and priest [*rex et sacerdos*]', a Christian who lived in 'the uttermost East' where he commanded enormous armies which, apparently, he wished to put at the disposal of the defenders of Jerusalem. This 'Prester John – for so he was wont to be styled' was said to be so rich that he used a sceptre of solid emerald.[39]

Subsequently, in 1165, a letter purporting to have been written by Prester John himself and addressed to 'various Christian kings, especially to the Emperor Manuel of Constantinople and the Roman Emperor Frederick',[40] was circulated widely in Europe. Filled with the most preposterous, legendary and supernatural claims, this lengthy epistle stated, *inter alia*, that the Prester's realm was divided into four parts 'for there are so many Indias'.[41]

The next development came in 1177 when Pope Alexander III (writing from Venice) addressed a letter to his *'dearest son in Christ, John, illustrious and magnificent King of the Indians'*.[42] Although the Pope certainly believed that he was replying to the author of the 1165 letter he made it clear that he had also had information about 'the Prester' from another source. He spoke, for example, of his personal physician, 'the leech Philip', who had apparently been approached in Jerusalem by the Prester's emissaries. Significantly these emissaries, who were referred to as 'honourable persons of the monarch's kingdom', had expressed their ruler's desire to be granted something that had not even been mentioned in the 1165 letter – a sanctuary in the Church of the Holy Sepulchre in Jerusalem.[43] Responding to this request, the Pope commented:

> The more nobly and magnanimously thou conductest thyself, and the less thou vauntest of thy wealth and power, the more readily shall we regard thy wish as to the concession of [an altar] in the Church of the Lord's Sepulchre at Jerusalem.[44]

There was much that was puzzling in these twelfth-century documents. But the one thing that was clear from all of them was that Prester John, in his earliest incarnations, had been explicitly associated with 'India'. As I looked more deeply into the whole issue I was able to confirm that this was indeed the case: again and again 'the Prester's' realms were referred to as India or, more loosely, 'the Indies'.

It was quite obvious, however, that none of the medieval authorities concerned had had any firm idea in their own minds as to where exactly India and/or the Indies were. And it was equally obvious, when they talked about 'India', that they were only rarely speaking of the subcontinent itself. The majority of the references were quite clearly to some other place, perhaps in Africa, perhaps elsewhere – although nobody really seemed to know.

As I researched the subject further I began to understand what the source of all this uncertainty might have been: for more than a thousand years *before* the earliest mention of Prester John a profound terminological muddle had existed in which 'India' had frequently been confused with 'Ethiopia'. Indeed from the first century BC (when Virgil had written of the Nile rising in 'India'), until at least the time of Marco Polo – when all the countries that bordered on the Indian Ocean were still referred to as 'the Indies'[45] – the terms 'Ethiopia' and 'India' appeared to have been used as though they were completely interchangeable.

The classic example of this lay in the works of Rufinius, the fourth-century Byzantine theologian who had compiled the definitive account of Ethiopia's conversion to Christianity that I had studied in 1983.[46] The details of this important treatise (which included place names such as Axum and historically recognized figures such as Frumentius and King Ezana) confirmed beyond all doubt that the country Rufinius had talked about had indeed been Ethiopia; nevertheless he had referred to it throughout as 'India'.[47]

This had happened, as one historian explained, because 'the early geographers had always regarded Ethiopia as the western part of the great empire of India'.[48] Moreover, it seemed that this same geographical mistake, coupled with the curious letters that had circulated in the twelfth century, had helped to create the impression that Prester John was an Asiatic, indeed an Indian, king.

This impression, though erroneous, had proved so tenacious that it was still in evidence long after 'the Prester' had ceased to be a mythical figure – and long after his realms had been firmly located in the Horn of Africa. In the late thirteenth century, for example, Marco Polo provided some insight into the conventional wisdom of his era when he wrote that 'Abyssinia is a large province and is called middle or second India. The ruler of this country is a Christian.'[49] Similarly, in the fourteenth century, the Florentine traveller Simone Sigoli was still speaking of 'Presto Giovanni' as a monarch dwelling in India; this 'India', however, was a land which bordered on the dominions of the Sultan of Egypt and its king was described as being the 'master of the Nile', the flow of which into Egypt he was believed to be able to control.[50] Rather later, when the first official Portuguese embassy was sent to Ethiopia in the sixteenth century, its members believed that they were going to meet 'the Prester John of the Indies'. The authorised account of this mission was subsequently written by Father Francisco Alvarez, who disembarked at the Red Sea port of Massawa in April 1520 and then spent the next six years travelling overland around Ethiopia. Despite this arduous physical tour of what was unmistakably part of the *African* mainland, the title of his work continued to reflect the old terminological confusion: '*Verdadera Informacam das terras do Preste Joam das Indias*' ('Truthful information about the countries of the Prester John of the Indies').[51]

Throughout his scholarly and informative book, Alvarez always referred to the Emperor of Ethiopia as 'the Prester' or as 'Prester John'.[52] I was also able to establish that much earlier than this – in 1352 – the Franciscan Giovanni de Marignolli, apostolic legate in Asia, had spoken (in his *Chronica*) of 'Ethiopia where the negroes are and which is called the land of Prester John'.[53] Similarly in 1328 a certain Friar Jordanus 'Catalani' had referred to the Emperor of the Ethiopians '*quem vos vocatis Prestre Johan*'.[54] And, later, in 1459, Fra Mauro's well regarded map of the then known world indicated a great city within the boundaries of present-day Ethiopia with the rubric: '*Qui il Preste Janni fa residentia principal.*'[55]

Surveying all the conflicting references before me I felt literally dazed: sometimes, it seemed, Prester John had been

unambiguously located in Ethiopia; on other occasions he had
been located in Ethiopia but spoken of as the ruler of the 'Indies';
and sometimes he had been located in India itself – or elsewhere
in the far east. Behind all this confusion, however, there seemed
to be no doubt that the real Prester John, the source of all the
myth-making, must all along have been the ruler of Ethiopia –
the only non-European Christian kingdom that had existed
anywhere in the world in medieval times, and therefore the only
model that Wolfram could possibly have drawn on when he had
talked of an 'India' being ruled by 'Prester John', the Christian
son of Fierfiz and Rapanse de Schoye.

For a final and hopefully definitive word I turned to the
Encyclopaedia Britannica, which observed:

> It is not improbable that from a very early date the title
> 'Prester John' was assigned to the Abyssinian king,
> though for a time this identification was overshadowed by
> the prevalence of the Asiatic legend. At the bottom of the
> double allocation there was, no doubt, that confusion of
> Ethiopia with India which is as old as Virgil or perhaps
> older.[56]

Significantly for my purposes, the *Encyclopaedia* concluded its
entry with a reference to the exchange of letters between the
Pope and Prester John that, as noted earlier, had taken place in
the second half of the twelfth century:

> However vague may have been the ideas of Pope
> Alexander III respecting the geographical position of the
> potentate whom he addressed from Venice in 1177, the
> only real person to whom the letter can have been sent
> was the king of Abyssinia. Let it be observed that the
> 'honourable persons of the monarch's kingdom' whom
> the leech Philip had met with in the East must have been
> the representatives of some real power, and not of a
> phantom. It must have been a real king who professed to
> desire . . . the assignation of . . . an altar at Jerusalem.
> *Moreover we know that the Ethiopic Church did long possess a
> chapel and altar in the Church of the Holy Sepulchre.*[57]

Indeed so. In fact, as I was soon able to ascertain, the chapel and the altar had first been granted to Ethiopia in the year 1189 – and not by the Pope (who by then was no longer in a position to distribute such favours) but by the Muslim general Saladin who had wrested Jerusalem from the hands of the Crusaders in 1187. Most important of all, these special privileges in the Holy Sepulchre had been obtained for the Ethiopian Orthodox Church as a result of a direct appeal to Saladin by no lesser person than the King of Ethiopia himself.[58]

These events had taken place just a decade before unknown stonemasons in northern France had left enigmatic representations of the Holy Grail, of the Ark of the Covenant, and of an Ethiopian Queen of Sheba in the north porch of Chartres cathedral – and also just a decade before Wolfram von Eschenbach had begun to write his *Parzival*. It seemed to me, moreover, that such coincidences were unlikely to be *just* coincidences. On the contrary, I now felt that the circumstantial evidence very strongly supported my hypothesis that the Chartres sculptures and Wolfram's remarkable narrative poem had been explicitly created to serve as esoteric treasure maps. And, though not actually marked with an 'X', there seemed to be little doubt that the spot identified by these maps as the hiding place of the treasure could only be Ethiopia – the land of Prester John, the land that had provided the last resting place of the fictional Holy Grail, and thus (if my theory was correct) the land in which the Ark of the Covenant, the real object that the Grail symbolized, would be found.

Now, however, other questions presented themselves:

- How, in the late twelfth century, could information that the Ark might rest in Ethiopia possibly have reached a German poet and a group of French iconographers?
- What connected the former to the latter? – for they *must* have been connected in some way if they had both produced works of art encoding the same message.
- Finally, why should anyone have chosen to express the secret of the Ark's location in a story and in sculptures? I had already concluded that this might have been done

to ensure transmission of the secret to future generations. At the same time, however, the code used – particularly by Wolfram – had been exceptionally difficult to crack. I myself, with all the research resources of the twentieth century at my disposal, had only got as far as I had because I had *been* to Axum and had thus been predisposed to accept that the Ark might be in Ethiopia. In the twelfth and thirteenth centuries, however, that advantage should not have been available to anyone. From this it followed that the hidden message of *Parzival* could not have been decoded in the medieval period at all – unless there had been people with access to some very special and privileged knowledge. Since there would have been no point in creating a code that no one could crack, it seemed to me logical to assume that such people must have existed. But who could they have been?

I did find one group of Europeans who fitted the bill perfectly. As part of the Crusading army of occupation they had maintained a massive presence in Jerusalem in the twelfth century: they had been there in 1145 when the Prester John legends had first begun to circulate, and they had still been there in 1177 when envoys of the King of Ethiopia had visited the Holy City seeking an altar in the Church of the Holy Sepulchre. Direct contact between Ethiopians and members of this European group would therefore have been perfectly possible.

The group in question was, moreover, highly secretive and made regular use of codes and ciphers in its far-flung international communications. It was, in addition, a group that had been involved with the evolution and dissemination of Gothic architecture in Europe (and quite specifically with the architecture and iconography of Chartres cathedral). Finally, and most importantly, it was a group that Wolfram von Eschenbach had several times *mentioned by name* – a name that I had also come across in connection with the curious Grail cup that the sculptors of the north porch of Chartres cathedral had placed in the left hand of their imposing statue of the priest-king Melchizedek[59] (which, incidentally, was almost the *only* depiction of Melchizedek in the whole of medieval Europe[60]).

What then was the name of this strangely influential, powerful and widely travelled group?

Its full and formal title was the 'Poor Knights of Christ and of the Temple of Solomon'[61] – but its members were better known simply as 'Templars', or as Knights Templar. It was, fundamentally, a religious order, an order of warrior monks, and throughout much of the twelfth century it had its headquarters in Jerusalem on the site of Solomon's Temple – the same site from which the Ark of the Covenant had inexplicably vanished in Old Testament times.

1 Ethiopian church painting showing King Solomon
and the Queen of Sheba. According to Ethiopian tradition
their son stole the Ark of the Covenant from the Temple
in Jerusalem and brought it to Ethiopia.

2 This painting, from Israel, depicts the veneration
of the Ark of the Covenant in Old Testament times.
Regarded as the sign and the seal of God's presence
on earth, the Ark was the most sacred relic of the
ancient Judaic faith.

3 Main group of stelae at Axum.

4 Section of the fallen stele. At 500 tonnes in weight
and more than 100 feet tall, it was the largest
single piece of stone ever quarried in the ancient world.

5 According to Axumite traditions the powers of the Ark
of the Covenant were used to raise up this towering
stele. It stands 70 feet tall and weighs 300 tonnes.

6 *Top left*: An Ethiopian painting
  depicting the late Emperor Haile
  Selassie, deposed in 1974.

7 *Above*: A rebel wall poster showing
  the brutality of the Emperor's
  successor, President Mengistu.

8 *Bottom right*: Falasha artefacts
  portraying the supposed bedroom
  scene between Solomon and
  Sheba. Haile Selassie claimed to
  be the 225th direct-line descendant
  of this union.

9 *Bottom left*: Falasha market woman.

10 In one of the island churches on Lake Tana
a Christian priest stands guard at the doorway
to the Holy of Holies.

11 Chartres Cathedral, France. One of the earliest and finest examples of the Gothic style of architecture that blossomed suddenly and mysteriously in the twelfth century AD.

12 Sculpture of Melchizedek, priest-king of ancient Israel, in the north porch of Chartres Cathedral. According to some authorities the cup in his hand is the Holy Grail and the object contained within it is a stone.

13 The Queen of Sheba (central of the three figures),
    her Ethiopian slave at her feet,
    in the north porch of Chartres Cathedral.

14 Tableau in the north porch of Chartres Cathedral
depicting the removal, to some unstated destination,
of the Ark of the Covenant – which is shown
placed upon an ox-cart.

15 A section of the strange inscription
beneath the Ark tableau.

Chapter 5

White Knights, Dark Continent

According to Emma Jung, analyst, lecturer and wife of the eminent psychiatrist Carl Gustav Jung, the way in which the literary genre of the Holy Grail appeared at the end of the twelfth century was both sudden and surprising. In an authoritative study of the Grail legend (which she undertook on behalf of the Jung Foundation) she argued that something of great significance must have lain behind this abrupt and dramatic materialization. Indeed she went so far as to suggest that in Chrétien de Troyes's *Conte du Graal* and Wolfram's *Parzival* – the first two exemplars of the genre – it was almost 'as if a subterranean watercourse had been tapped'.[1] What might that 'subterranean watercourse' have been?

The answer, I thought, lay in the period of history in which the Grail romances began to circulate. This, after all, was the era of the Crusades – an era that had brought Europeans into close contact with Arab and Judaic culture for the first time and that saw the occupation of Jerusalem by Christian armies for eighty-eight years (from AD 1099 until the recapture of the Holy City by Saladin in 1187). It was in 1182 – the eighty-third year of the occupation – that Chrétien produced his version of the Grail story. And shortly after the fall of Jerusalem Wolfram von Eschenbach started work on his own *Parzival*.

I therefore found it difficult to resist the conclusion that these early recensions of the Grail romance must have been based on something that had happened – or on material that had come to light – during the period that Jerusalem had been under the full control of European forces. I looked very carefully at the text of *Parzival* to see whether there was any evidence to support this conjecture and discovered that Wolfram had on several occasions made mention of a mysterious source named 'Kyot' – a man, he said, whom he had relied upon heavily for his information and who fortunately had been:

> a baptized Christian – otherwise this tale would still be unknown. No infidel art would avail us to reveal the nature of the Gral and how one came to know its secrets.[2]

This was by no means the only place in *Parzival* where the German poet had hinted that there might have been more to his Grail than at first met the eye. I was already satisfied that this 'something more' could well have been the Ark of the Covenant – the real object that lay behind the beautiful fictional symbol. Now as I studied the widely scattered references to 'Kyot' it occurred to me that this shadowy figure, whose identity was never clarified, could have been the source who had introduced Wolfram to the secret of the Ark's hiding place in Ethiopia. Referred to at one point as 'Kyot, who sent us the authentic tale',[3] he was clearly very important. But who was he?

There were few obvious clues in *Parzival* itself. Here Kyot was spoken of as a 'Master'[4] and there it was suggested that his mother tongue had been French.[5] But beyond such hints there was very little to go on. I therefore turned to the literary scholars and found that several of them had identified Kyot quite specifically with a twelfth-century French poet, Guyot de Provins, who had made a pilgrimage to Jerusalem shortly before the recapture of the Holy City by the Saracens[6] – and who had also been attached for a while to the court of the Holy Roman Emperor Frederick Barbarossa.[7]

This latter fact caught my eye because I knew that Frederick – like Wolfram – had been a German by birth (before his election as Emperor in 1152 he had been Duke of Swabia[8]). And I also knew (see previous chapter) that this same Frederick had been one of the two monarchs specifically named amongst the various Christian kings to whom the 'letter of Prester John' had been addressed in the year 1165.

Investigating further I then learned something else –

something that turned out to be of major importance: Guyot/Kyot had been closely associated with the Knights Templar[9] who, according to Emma Jung's study, 'were considered to be the guardians of Solomon's Temple'.[10] I also knew that it was from Solomon's Temple that the Ark of the Covenant had mysteriously disappeared in Old Testament times. I was therefore excited to discover that, in *Parzival*, Wolfram had described *the guardians of the Grail* as 'Templars'[11] and had referred to them, flatteringly, as:

> a noble Brotherhood . . . who, by force of arms, have
> warded off men from every land, with the result that the
> Gral has been revealed only to those who have been
> summoned to Munsalvaesche to join the Gral
> Company.[12]

Were Wolfram's 'Templars' the same as the famous military order of that name?

I found that the word translated into English as 'Templars' had, in the Middle High German of *Parzival*, been *Templeis*.[13] Amongst the scholars there was some debate about what exactly had been meant by this. The consensus, however, was that the term was 'an obvious variant of the regular forms *templarius*, *templier*, Eng. *Templar*'[14] and that Wolfram's 'Order of Knighthood dedicated to the service of the Gral' could therefore be 'identified with the order of the Knights Templar'.[15]

I then remembered that one of the guidebooks I had used on my visit to Chartres cathedral had spoken of 'Wolfram von Eschenbach, who is said to have been a Templar – though there is no proof of this'.[16] On further investigation I was able to establish that there had indeed been persistent rumours to this effect.[17] I also learned that several well respected scholars had suggested that the German poet might himself have paid a visit to the Holy Land whilst writing *Parzival*.[18]

Digging for hidden treasure?

I had been intrigued by Emma Jung's assertion that the Templars in Wolfram's time 'were considered to be the guardians of Solomon's Temple'. I had not understood why this should have been so. However, when I began to research the order, I discovered that it had derived its official title ('The Poor Knights of Christ and of the Temple of Solomon') from the fact that its Jerusalem headquarters had been located on the summit of Mount Moriah – where Solomon's Temple had stood until its destruction by the Babylonians in 587 BC. That Temple had been built in the tenth century BC and its explicit – indeed its *only* – purpose had been to serve, as the Bible put it, as 'an house of rest for the Ark of the Covenant of the Lord'.[19]

By identifying themselves with Solomon's Temple, therefore, it seemed to me that there was a very real sense in which the knights had also identified themselves with the Ark of the Covenant. And my feeling that this was so strengthened as I began to investigate the curious history of the order.

The Templars, I learned, had been founded by nine French noblemen who had made their way to the Holy Land in AD 1119 – twenty years after Jerusalem had been captured and occupied by the European powers. The twelfth-century historian, Archbishop William of Tyre, noted that 'foremost and most distinguished' amongst these nine men 'were the venerable Hugh de Payens and Godfrey de St Omer.'[20]

On checking further I discovered something interesting. Hugh de Payens, who was in fact the first Grand Master of the Order,[21] had been born in the village of Payens, eight miles north of the city of Troyes in the old French county of Champagne.[22] Moreover it seemed that the nine founders were all from the same region.[23] In this there were several coincidences:

1 Chartres, with its great cathedral, had – in both the twelfth and thirteenth centuries – been a dominion of the Counts of Champagne.[24]

2 One of the original nine knights, André de Montbard (who later became the fifth Grand Master), was an uncle of Saint Bernard of Clairvaux[25] – who was himself a native of Champagne. This enormously influential cleric had taken a special interest both in Gothic architecture and in the Grail romances.[26]

3 The city of Troyes, so close to the birthplace of Hugh de Payens, the first Templar Grand Master, was also

the home of Chrétien de Troyes, the 'inventor' of the Holy Grail.

4 Hugh de Payens was a cousin of the Count of Champagne,[27] and, in the year 1125, the Count of Champagne joined the Templars.[28]

5 When Chrétien de Troyes rose to prominence rather later in the twelfth century his principal patron was the Countess of Champagne.[29]

Noting this string of coincidences with some interest, I went on to learn more about the early history of the Templars.

There was much that was strange. Perhaps strangest of all, however, was the way in which the nine original knights were received by King Baldwin I of Jerusalem in 1119. As soon as they had arrived in the Holy City they told him that they wanted to establish their headquarters on the Temple Mount[30] – where the monarch had recently converted the Al-Aqsa Mosque to serve as his own royal palace. Rather astonishingly he complied at once with their request, giving them, for their exclusive use, a large part of the former mosque and its outbuildings immediately adjacent to the famous 'Dome of the Rock', which marked the site where Solomon's Temple had once stood.[31]

Thereafter, like latter-day archaeologists with an important dig to complete, the knights lived, ate, slept and worked on this uniquely precious site: indeed for almost seven years after their arrival they rarely left it and adamantly refused admission to any outside party. In public pronouncements they had declared that their mission in the Holy Land was to 'to keep the road from the coast to Jerusalem free from bandits'.[32] I could find no evidence, however, to suggest that they took any steps to fulfil this mission during those first seven years of their existence; on the contrary, as one authority put it, 'the new Order apparently did very little' in this period.[33] Besides, simple logic suggested that nine men could hardly have protected anybody on a highway almost fifty miles long – and their number stayed at nine until they were joined by the Count of Champagne in 1125. Moreover, the members of an older and far larger military order – the Knights of Saint John – were already doing the job of protecting pilgrims when the Templars arrived.[34]

I could only conclude, therefore, that Hugh de Payens and his colleagues must have had some other, undeclared, purpose. As noted above, they largely confined themselves to the precincts of the Temple Mount during the first seven years of their sojourn in Jerusalem – and this suggested very strongly that their real motive must have had to do with that very special site.

From the beginning their behaviour was secretive and I found, as a result, that there was no really hard evidence about what they had been up to there. It seemed at least possible, however, that they might have been looking for something, and this suspicion deepened when I learned that they had indeed used their occupancy of the Temple Mount to conduct quite extensive excavations.

Because the Temple Mount today contains the third and fourth most sacred sites of Islam – the Dome of the Rock and the Al-Aqsa Mosque – modern archaeologists have never been permitted to work there. In recent years, however, Israeli teams have operated freely immediately to the south of the Mount, and there they found the exit-point of a tunnel which they identified as having being dug by the Templars in the twelfth century.[35] In their official report the archaeologists stated:

> The tunnel leads inward for a distance of about thirty metres from the southern wall before being blocked by pieces of stone and debris. We know that it continues further, but we had made it a hard-and-fast rule not to excavate within the bounds of the Temple Mount, which is currently under Moslem jurisdiction, without first acquiring the permission of the appropriate Moslem authorities. In this case they permitted us only to measure and photograph the exposed section of the tunnel, not to conduct an excavation of any kind. Upon concluding this work . . . we sealed up the tunnel's exit with stones.[36]

And that was all that was known, or could be said, about the Templar tunnel. The archaeologists had only been able to confirm that it continued further than they themselves had been allowed to go. Extending inwards from the southern wall, however, I realized that it might well have penetrated into the very heart of the sacred precincts, quite possibly passing directly beneath the Dome of the Rock a hundred or so metres to the north of the Al-Aqsa Mosque.

The Dome of the Rock, I discovered, was so named because within it lay a huge stone, known to the Jews as the *Shetiyyah* (literally the 'Foundation'). When the Temple of Solomon had been erected on this exact spot in the mid-900s BC, the Ark of the Covenant had been placed on the *Shetiyyah*, which had formed the floor of the Holy of Holies.[37] Then, in 587 BC, the Temple had been destroyed by the Babylonians and most of the population of Jerusalem had been carried off into exile. There was no evidence, however, to suggest that the conquerors had also carried off the Ark; on the contrary, it appeared to have vanished into thin air.[38]

Subsequently a legend began to circulate which provided a possible explanation for what had happened – an explanation that was accepted by most Jews. According to this legend, only moments before the Babylonian looters had burst into the Holy of Holies, the sacred relic had been hidden away in a sealed and secret cavern directly beneath the *Shetiyyah*.[39]

Expressed as it was in a variety of Talmudic and Midrashic scrolls, and in the popular apocalypse known as the 'Vision of Baruch'[40] – all of which were still very much in circulation in Jerusalem in the twelfth century AD – it occurred to me that the Templars might easily have learned the details of this intriguing legend. Moreover, with a little further research, I was able to establish that they could well have done so some years *before* 1119 – the date of their official arrival in Jerusalem. Hugh de Payens, the founder of the order, had made a pilgrimage to the Holy Land in 1104 in the company of the Count of Champagne.[41] The two men had then returned to France and were known to have been together there in 1113.[42] Three years later Hugh went back to the Holy Land alone[43] and then returned once more – this time to gather together the eight knights who travelled with him in 1119 and who formed the nucleus of the Templar order.

The more I thought about this sequence of events the more likely it seemed to me that Hugh and the Count of Champagne could, on their 1104 pilgrimage, have heard of the startling possibility that the Ark of the Covenant might lie concealed somewhere within the Temple Mount. If so, I speculated, then was it not also probable that they could have formulated a plan to try to recover the sacred relic? And did this not explain the determined manner in which the nine knights had taken control of the Temple Mount in 1119 – and also the many other curiosities of their behaviour in the early years of the order's existence?

I found tangential support for this conjecture in Emma Jung's authoritative study of the Grail legend. There, in an excursus, the psychoanalyst argued that the European occupation of Jerusalem in the twelfth century had been inspired, at least in part, by a belief that some puissant, sacred and incalculably precious relic lay concealed in that city. As she commented:

> This deeply-rooted concept of hidden treasure
> contributed to the fact that the summons to liberate the
> Holy Sepulchre awakened a resounding echo [and]
> imparted [an] inflammatory motive power to the Crusades
> – if it did not actually cause them.[44]

There could have been no treasure more precious or more sacred than the lost Ark of the Covenant – which, in a century that was unusually obsessed with the recovery of religious relics,[45] could well have looked like the ultimate prize. It therefore seemed to me not just possible, but actually highly probable, that Hugh de Payens and his backer the Count of Champagne could indeed have been motivated by a desire to find the Ark – and that they could have established the Templars, and taken control of the Temple Mount, in order to achieve this goal.

If so, however, then they failed in their objective. In the twelfth century, as one expert put it, 'the asset value of a famous relic was prodigious'.[46] Possession of a relic as uniquely significant as the Ark of the Covenant would, in addition, have brought enormous power and prestige to its owners. From this it followed, that if the Templars had found the Ark, they would certainly have brought it back to Europe in triumph. Since that had not happened it seemed to me quite safe to conclude that they had *not* found it.

Yet rumours persisted that they had found *something* in their seven years of intensive digging on the Temple Mount. None of these rumours had any academic authority whatsoever – but some were intriguing. According to one mystical work, which attempted to address what the Templars had really been up to in Jerusalem between 1119 and 1126:

> The real task of the nine knights was to carry out research in the area in order to obtain certain relics and manuscripts which contained the essence of the secret traditions of Judaism and ancient Egypt, some of which probably went back to the days of Moses . . . There is no doubt that [they] fulfilled this particular mission and that the knowledge obtained from their finds was taught in the oral tradition of the Order's . . . secret circles.[47]

No documentary proof was offered to back up this attractive assertion. In the same source, however, I was interested to note a name that I had come across several times before in my research – Saint Bernard of Clairvaux, who here was said (again without any supporting evidence) to have *sent* the nine knights to Jerusalem.[48]

I already knew that Bernard had been the nephew of one of the nine founder knights. I was also aware that he had joined the Cistercian order in 1112, that he had become an abbot by 1115[49] and that he had risen to a position of considerable prominence in French religious circles by 1119 when the first Templars had arrived in Jerusalem. I therefore thought that it would be most unwise to dismiss out of hand the possibility that he might have played some role in the formulation of their mission. This suspicion intensified considerably when I began to look into what had happened to the Templars after their first curious seven years.

A trade-off?

Late in 1126 Hugh de Payens suddenly left Jerusalem and returned to Europe accompanied by none other than André de Montbard,[50] the uncle of Saint Bernard. The knights arrived in

France in 1127 and, in January 1128, participated in what was to be the most significant event in the early history of the Templars. That event was the Synod of Troyes, which had been convened with the explicit objective of procuring the Church's official backing for the Templar order.[51]

Three things particularly interested me about this important meeting. First, it took place in the home town of the poet who, some years later, was to invent the Holy Grail; second, it was presided over by Saint Bernard, in his capacity as its secretary;[52] and third, during the course of the Synod, it was Bernard himself who drew up the formal Rule of the Knights Templar that, henceforth, was to guide the evolution and development of the order.[53]

If my suspicions were justified, therefore, it seemed that the original nine knights had initially been preoccupied with their excavations on the Temple Mount in Jerusalem. Whatever else they might have unearthed there, however, it had become clear to them by 1126 that they were not going to find the prime object of their search, the Ark of the Covenant. This realization had made it necessary for them to consider their future: specifically, having lost their *raison d'être*, should they simply cease to exist as an order, or should they try to forge ahead?

History showed that they had indeed suffered a crisis of identity in 1126, that they had resolved it and decided to forge ahead, and that they had enlisted the powerful support of Saint Bernard in this enterprise. At the Synod of Troyes he drew up their Rule and obtained the full backing of the Church for their expansion. And thereafter, in a series of sermons and glowing panegyrics such as *De laude novae militae*,[54] he vigorously promoted the young order – thus using his own prestige and influence to guarantee its success.

The results were spectacular. New recruits flocked in from all over France and later from many other parts of Europe as well. Donations of land and money were received from wealthy patrons, and political power quickly followed. By the late twelfth century the order had become phenomenally rich, was operating a sophisticated international banking system,[55] and owned properties throughout the known world.

And all this, in a sense, it owed to the intervention of Saint

Bernard in 1128 – and to his continued solidarity and support in the years that followed. Had he played this role on behalf of the Templars purely out of a sense of altruism? Or had they perhaps given him something in return?

Remembering that the 1130s were the decade in which Gothic architecture had suddenly and mysteriously burst upon the scene in France, remembering that Bernard had been a prime mover in the dissemination of the Gothic formula, and remembering too the persistent rumours that the Templars had gained access in Jerusalem to some deep and ancient source of knowledge, I could not help but wonder if this had been the trade-off. To be sure, the knights had failed to find the Ark of the Covenant. But what if, in their excavations on the Temple Mount, they had unearthed scrolls, manuscripts, theorems or blueprints relating to Solomon's Temple itself? What if these discoveries had included the lost architectural secrets of geometry, proportion, balance and harmony that had been known to the builders of the pyramids and other great monuments of antiquity? And what if the Templars had shared these secrets with Saint Bernard in return for his enthusiastic backing for their order?

These speculations were not entirely without foundation. On the contrary, one of the oddities of the Templars was the fact that they had been great architects. In 1139, Pope Innocent II (whose candidacy, incidentally, had also been enthusiastically backed by Saint Bernard[56]), granted the order a unique privilege – the right to build their own churches.[57] This was a privilege that they subsequently exercised to the full: beautiful places of worship, often circular in plan like the Temple Church in London, became a hallmark of Templar activities.

The knights also excelled in military architecture and their castles in Palestine were exceptionally well designed and virtually impregnable. Foremost amongst these imposing fortresses was Atlit (Château Pélérin or Castle Pilgrim) which, I discovered, had been built in the year 1218 by the fourteenth Grand Master of the Templars, William of Chartres[58] – in whose name was revealed yet another connection to the great Gothic cathedral.

Standing to the south of Haifa on a spur of land surrounded on three sides by the sea, Atlit in its heyday was well supplied with orchards, fresh water, and vegetable gardens and even possessed its own harbour and ship-yard together with a jetty two hundred feet long. Often besieged by the Saracens but never captured, it had been capable of sheltering as many as four thousand people. Its massive walls, resting on unusually deep foundations, were more than ninety feet high and sixteen feet thick[59] – and were so well made that large sections of them still survive intact. The site was thoroughly excavated by the archaeologist C. N. Johns in 1932. He concluded that the skills of the Templar architects and masons had been astonishingly advanced by comparison with the norm in the Middle Ages and had, indeed, been 'exceptional' even by modern standards.[60]

The Templars also built extensively in Jerusalem where they continued to maintain their headquarters on the Temple Mount until the Holy City was recaptured by the Muslim general Saladin in 1187. I learned that a German monk named Theoderic had made a pilgrimage to Jerusalem in 1174 – at which time he reported that all the buildings within the precincts of the Dome of the Rock were still 'in the possession of the Templar soldiers'.[61] He added:

> They are garrisoned in these and other buildings
> belonging to them . . . Below them they have stables once
> erected by King Solomon . . . with vaults, arches, and
> roofs of many varieties . . . According to our estimation
> they will hold ten thousand horses with grooms.[62]

In fact the 'stables' had not been erected by King Solomon, but dated back to the reign of Herod the Great (around the time of Christ). The vaults, arches and roofs, however, had been the work of the Templars themselves, who greatly extended these subterranean halls and who were the first and only people to use them to accommodate horses.[63]

Theoderic's eyewitness account of the Temple Mount in 1174 continued with these words:

> On the other side of the palace [i.e. the Al-Aqsa Mosque]
> the Templars have built a new house, whose height,
> length and breadth, and all its cellars and refectories,

staircase and roof, are far beyond the custom of this land. Indeed its roof is so high that, if I were to mention how high it is, those who listen would hardly believe me.[64]

The 'new house' that Theoderic had referred to in 1174 was, unfortunately, knocked down in the 1950s during some renovations undertaken on the Temple Mount by the Muslim authorities. The German monk's testimony was, however, valuable in itself – and what I found most valuable about it was its breathless tone. Clearly he had regarded the Templars' architectural skills as almost supernaturally advanced and had been particularly impressed by the soaring roofs and arches that they had built. Reviewing his statements I thought it far from accidental that soaring roofs and arches had also been the distinguishing features of the Gothic architectural formula as expressed at Chartres and other French cathedrals in the twelfth century – cathedrals that I knew were regarded by some observers as 'scientifically . . . far beyond what can be allowed for in the knowledge of the epoch'.[65]

And this brought me back again to Saint Bernard of Clairvaux. Looking more thoroughly into what was known about his life and ideas, I was able to confirm my earlier impression that his influence on the iconography of the Gothic cathedrals had been massive, but indirect, taking the form mainly of groups of sculptures and of stained-glass windows that had been inspired by his sermons and writings, often after his death.[66] Indeed, in his lifetime, Bernard had frequently *opposed* the unnecessary proliferation of images and had stated: 'There must be no decoration, only proportion.'[67]

This emphasis on proportion, harmony and balance in architecture was, I knew, the key to the strange magic of Gothic architecture and, as I became more familiar with Saint Bernard's thinking, I realized that it was in this area that his influence on the design of Chartres and other cathedrals had been most profound. In those great edifices, the introduction of a number of remarkable technical innovations like ribbed vaulting, ogive arches and flying buttresses had enabled the builders to use geometrical perfection to give expression to complex religious ideas. Indeed, in a very real sense, it seemed that architecture and faith had merged in twelfth-century Gothic to form a new synthesis. This synthesis had been summed up by Saint Bernard himself when he had asked 'What is God?' – and had then replied to his own rhetorical question with these surprising words: 'He is length, width, height and depth.'[68]

Gothic architecture, as I already knew, had been born at Chartres cathedral with the start of construction work on the north tower in 1134. This, I now learned, was no accident. In the years immediately prior to 1134 Bernard had cultivated a particularly close friendship with Geoffrey the Bishop of Chartres,[69] inspiring him with an 'uncommon enthusiasm' for the Gothic formula[70] and holding 'almost daily negotiations with the builders themselves'.[71]

Interesting though it was in itself, the great significance of this piece of information for my purposes lay in the fact that 'the years immediately prior to 1134' were also the years immediately *after* the Synod of Troyes, at which Saint Bernard had obtained official Church recognition for the Order of the Poor Knights of Christ and of the Temple of Solomon. Historians had never been able to account adequately for the sudden way in which Gothic architecture had emerged in France in the 1130s. But my earlier speculation that the Templars might have had a hand in it now looked increasingly plausible. Reviewing all the evidence I had gathered I felt satisfied that they could indeed have unearthed on the Temple Mount some repository of ancient knowledge concerning the science of building, and that they could have passed on what they had learned to Saint Bernard in return for his support.

Moreover Templar interest in the Ark of the Covenant, and the Templar connections with Wolfram and with Chartres, also rather neatly tied together the two cryptic 'maps' that I believed I had identified (one carved in stone in the north porch of the cathedral, the other encoded in the plot of *Parzival*). Those 'maps' had appeared to suggest that Ethiopia was the last resting place of the Ark. The question I now needed to address, therefore, was this: how could the Templars have come to the conclusion that the sacred relic (which they had failed to find after seven years of digging in Jerusalem) had in fact been removed to Ethiopia? What could have led them to think this way?

A possible answer, I discovered, lay in Jerusalem itself – where an exiled Ethiopian prince had sojourned for a quarter of a century before returning to his homeland to claim his kingdom in 1185.[72] Not much more than a decade later Wolfram began to write his *Parzival* and work started on the north porch of Chartres cathedral.

An Ethiopian prince in Jerusalem

The name of the prince who had spent so long in exile in Jerusalem was Lalibela. I became interested in him because of the 'letter of Prester John' referred to in the last chapter. That letter had been written in 1165 and I knew that in 1177 Pope Alexander III had written a letter of his own to 'Prester John' in response to a request from 'the Prester's' emissaries for the concession of an altar and a chapel in the Church of the Holy Sepulchre in Jerusalem. According to the *Encyclopaedia Britannica*, 'the only real person' to whom the Pope's letter could have been sent was the King of Ethiopia.[73] I had therefore naturally wondered *which* king had sat on the Ethiopian throne in 1177. On researching the matter I had discovered that it had been a man named Harbay and that the concession requested had not been granted to him but rather to his successor, Lalibela.

Neither Harbay nor Lalibela had stemmed from the line of monarchs supposedly descended from King Solomon and the Queen of Sheba through Menelik I. Instead they had both belonged to a usurper dynasty known as the Zagwe which had ruled in Ethiopia from roughly AD 1030 until 1270 when the Solomonids were finally restored to the throne.[74]

This was a period of Ethiopian history about which very little was known. I was able to confirm, however, that the Solomonic line had been interrupted around AD 980 and that this *coup d'état* had been the work of a tribal chieftainess named Gudit, who adhered to the Jewish faith and who seemed to have been motivated above all else by a desire to obliterate the Christian religion. At any rate she attacked Axum, razed much of the ancient city to the ground, and succeeded in killing its Solomonic emperor. Two of the royal princes were also murdered but a third escaped with his life and fled to the province of Shoa, far to the south, where he married and produced children, thus ensuring the survival of the old dynasty, although in much reduced circumstances.[75]

Gudit was the head of a large tribal confederation known as the Agaw – to which the Falashas, the indigenous black Jews of Ethiopia, also belonged.[76] Although it was by no means certain that she had left any direct successor, historians accepted that within fifty years of her death most of northern Ethiopia had been united under the Zagwe monarchs who, like her, were all of Agaw extraction.

In its early days this dynasty could – again like Gudit – have been Jewish.[77] If so, however (and the case was not proved), it had certainly converted to Christianity well before the birth of Prince Lalibela – which took place in the ancient mountain town of Roha, in what is now the province of Wollo, around the year 1140.

The younger half-brother of King Harbay, Lalibela appeared to have been destined for greatness from the moment when his mother saw a dense swarm of bees surrounding him as he lay in his crib. Recalling an old belief that the animal world could foretell the future of important personages, the legends said that she had been seized by the spirit of prophecy and had cried out 'Lalibela' – meaning, literally, 'the bees recognize his sovereignty'.[78]

Thus the prince received his name. The prophecy that it expressed caused Harbay to fear for the safety of his throne to such an extent that he tried to have Lalibela murdered while he was still a babe in arms. This first attempt failed, but persecutions of one kind or another continued for several years, culminating in the administration of a deadly poison that plunged the young prince into a cataleptic sleep. Ethiopian legends said that the stupor lasted for three days, during which time Lalibela was transported by angels to the first, second and third Heavens. There he was addressed directly by the Almighty who told him to have no anxiety as to his life or future sovereignty. A Purpose had been mapped out for him, for which reason he had been anointed. After awaking from his trance he was to flee Ethiopia and seek refuge in Jerusalem. He could rest secure, however, that when the time was right he would return as king to Roha, his birthplace. Moreover it was his destiny that he would build a number of wonderful churches there, the like of which the world had never seen before. God then gave Lalibela detailed instructions as to the method of construction that was to be used, the form that each of the churches was to take, their locations and even their interior and exterior decorations.[79]

Legend and history coincided at this point in a single well documented fact: Lalibela did indeed suffer a long period of exile in Jerusalem while his half-brother Harbay continued to occupy the throne of Ethiopia.[80] This exile, I learned, began around the year 1160 – when Lalibela would have been about twenty years old – and ended in 1185 when he returned in triumph to his own country, deposed Harbay and proclaimed himself king.[81]

From that date onwards there were reliable chronicles of his rule, which lasted until AD 1211.[82] He made his capital at Roha, where he had been born and which was now renamed 'Lalibela' in his honour.[83] There, perhaps in fulfilment of his legendary vision, he almost immediately set about building eleven spectacular monolithic churches – churches that were literally carved out of solid volcanic rock (I myself had visited those churches in 1983 some weeks after my trip to Axum, and had found that they were still places of living worship).

Neither did Lalibela forget his twenty-five-year sojourn in the Holy Land – many of the features of which he attempted to reproduce in Roha-Lalibela. For example, the river running through the town was renamed 'Jordan'; one of the eleven churches – *Beta Golgotha* – was specifically designed to symbolize the Church of the Holy Sepulchre in Jerusalem; and a nearby hill was called *Debra Zeit* ('Mount of Olives') so that it might represent the place where Christ was captured.[84]

Not content with making his capital a kind of 'New Jerusalem', the Ethiopian king also sought, throughout his reign, to maintain close links with Jerusalem itself. There was, I discovered, nothing particularly new about this. Since the late fourth century AD clergy from the Ethiopian Orthodox Church had been permanently stationed in the Holy City.[85] It had been a desire to increase and consolidate this presence that had led to Harbay's request to Pope Alexander III to grant the concession of an altar and a chapel in the Church of the Holy Sepulchre. Nothing had come of that – other than the Pope's rather tentative letter sent in 1177 in reply to Harbay's initial approach. A decade later, however, there had been two important developments: in 1185 Lalibela had seized the Ethiopian throne, and in 1187 Saladin had driven the Crusaders out of the Holy City and had forced Jerusalem's Ethiopian community, together with other Eastern Christians, to flee to Cyprus.[86]

The royal chronicles showed that Lalibela had been deeply disturbed by this turn of events and, in 1189, his envoys had managed to persuade Saladin to allow the Ethiopians to return and also to grant them, for the first time, a key site of their own – the Chapel of the Invention of the Cross, in the Church of the Holy Sepulchre.[87] Subsequently, in relatively modern times, these privileges had again been lost; in consequence, I learned, Abyssinian pilgrims were now obliged to make their devotions on the roof of the chapel – where they had established a monastery.[88] They also still possessed two other churches in Jerusalem as well as a substantial Patriarchate situated in the heart of the Old City within a few minutes' walk of the Church of the Holy Sepulchre.

Both in terms of foreign and domestic policy, and also in terms of architectural expression and spiritual development, Lalibela's reign had represented the zenith of the Zagwe dynasty's powers and achievements. After his death a steep decline set in. Finally, in AD 1270, his grandson Naakuto Laab was persuaded to abdicate in favour of Yekuno Amlak – a monarch claiming Solomonic descent.[89] Thereafter, until Haile Selassie was deposed during the communist revolution of 1974, all but one of Ethiopia's emperors had belonged to the royal line that traced its heritage back, through Menelik I, to King Solomon of Jerusalem.

A pattern of coincidences

Reviewing what I had learned about Lalibela's illustrious reign, I realized that it fitted perfectly into the beguiling pattern of coincidences that I had already identified as being associated with the Crusades, with the Templars, and with the twelfth century:

- At the very beginning of the twelfth century (or more properly in 1099, the last year of the eleventh century) Jerusalem was seized by the Crusaders.
- In 1119 the nine founding knights of the Templar order – all French noblemen – arrived in Jerusalem and took up residence on the site of the original Temple of Solomon.
- In 1128 Saint Bernard of Clairvaux won official church recognition for the Templars at the Synod of Troyes.
- In 1134 work started on the north tower of Chartres cathedral, the first-ever example of Gothic architecture.
- In 1145 the name 'Prester John' was first heard in Europe.
- In 1160 Prince Lalibela, the future monarch of Ethiopia, arrived in Jerusalem as a political exile fleeing the persecutions of his half-brother Harbay (who then occupied the throne).
- In 1165 a letter purporting to have been written by 'Prester John' and making a series of awe-inspiring claims about the size of his armies, his wealth and his power, had been circulated in Europe addressed to 'various Christian kings'.
- In 1177 Pope Alexander III issued a response to the above document but, significantly, made reference in it to another communication that he had received somewhat later – a request from 'Prester John' to be granted an altar in the Church of the Holy Sepulchre in Jerusalem. It seemed that this request had been lodged by 'the Prester's' emissaries who had spoken to the Pope's personal physician Philip during a visit that the latter had made to Palestine. (The 'Prester John' who had asked for this concession could only have been Lalibela's half-brother Harbay who, in 1177, was still on the throne of Ethiopia.)
- In 1182 the Holy Grail made its first-ever appearance in literature (and, for that matter, in history) in an uncompleted narrative poem by Chrétien de Troyes.

- In 1185 Prince Lalibela left Jerusalem and returned to Ethiopia where he successfully deposed Harbay and seized the throne. Almost immediately thereafter he began building a group of spectacular rock-hewn churches in his capital Roha – later renamed 'Lalibela' in his honour.
- In 1187 Jerusalem fell to the Muslim forces of Sultan Saladin and the Crusaders were driven out, along with members of the Ethiopian community in the Holy City – who sought temporary refuge in Cyprus. (Some Templars also went to Cyprus – indeed, after the fall of Jerusalem, the knights bought the island which became, for a while, their headquarters.⁹⁰)
- In 1189 emissaries sent to Saladin by King Lalibela managed to persuade the Muslim general to allow the Ethiopians to return to Jerusalem and also to grant them a privilege that they had never enjoyed before, the same privilege that Harbay had sought from the Pope in 1177 – namely a chapel and altar in the Church of the Holy Sepulchre.
- Between the years 1195 and 1200 Wolfram von Eschenbach began to write *Parzival*, which continued the earlier work done by Chrétien de Troyes and which, in the process, transformed the Grail into a Stone, incorporated many Ethiopic elements into the story, and specifically mentioned not only 'Prester John' but also the Templars.
- At exactly the same time work started on the north porch of Chartres cathedral with its Ethiopic Queen of Sheba, its Grail (containing a Stone), and its representation of the Ark of the Covenant.

The Templars, Gothic architecture, the Holy Grail and the notion that somewhere in the world there existed a powerful non-European Christian king called 'Prester John' had therefore all been the products of the twelfth century. And in that same century, just before *Parzival* was written and the north porch of Chartres cathedral built, a future Christian king of Ethiopia – Lalibela – had returned to his homeland to claim his throne after spending twenty-five years in Jerusalem.

It seemed to me, from everything I had learned, that all these matters must have been intricately connected by some common factor that had remained hidden from history, perhaps because it had been deliberately concealed. Proof positive of a Templar quest for the lost Ark of the Covenant, first in Jerusalem and then later in Ethiopia, would provide that hidden but common factor – the missing link in the complex chain of inter-related events, ideas and personalities that I had identified. I knew, at least for the moment, that I had gone as far as I could with the part of my investigation that related to Jerusalem. But what about Ethiopia? Was there really any evidence at all that the Templars might have gone there to look for the Ark – and that they might subsequently have arranged for the results of their quest to be encoded by Wolfram in the arcane symbolism of his 'Stone called the Gral'?

'Those treacherous Templars . . .'

The first breakthrough came when I received an English translation of the full text of the letter supposedly written by Prester John himself to various Christian kings in the year 1165. Unlike Pope Alexander III's letter to Prester John, written in 1177 (which was a genuine document intended, as I now knew, for Lalibela's half-brother Harbay) the 1165 letter was regarded with great suspicion by scholars. Its date was authentic, but it was thought most unlikely that it could have been written by anyone with a real claim to the title 'Prester John' – and it was therefore regarded as an elaborate hoax.[91]

As I read it I could understand why. If the writer was to be believed his 'realms' contained, amongst other things: 'wild hares as big as sheep'; 'birds called griffins who can easily carry an ox or a horse into their nest'; 'horned men who have but one eye in front and three or four in the back'; 'other men who have hoofed legs like horses'; 'bowmen who from the waist up are men, but whose lower part is that of a horse'; the fountain of youth; a 'sandy sea' from which 'every piece of debris . . . turns into precious stones'; 'the tree of life'; 'seven-headed dragons' – and so on and so forth.[92] Just about every mythical beast and object ever dreamed of, it seemed, was to be found in the land of Prester John. Where exactly this land was located, however, was nowhere specified in the letter – except in the loose reference to the 'many Indias' quoted in the previous chapter (a reference, as I now knew, that was more likely to have applied to Ethiopia than to the subcontinent). Moreover, scattered here and there amongst the fabulous creatures were other animals that did seem to belong to the real world: 'elephants' and 'dromedaries', for example, and also 'unicorns' with 'a single horn in front' which sounded very much like rhinoceroses – all the more so since, apparently, they were sometimes known to 'kill lions'.[93]

Such details made me wonder whether the writer of the letter might have been something more than a hoaxer – might, in fact, have had direct knowledge of Ethiopia (where, of course, camels, elephants, lions and rhinos were all to be found). My suspicion that this might have been so deepened when I noticed that mention was also made of 'King Alexander of Macedonia' in a context that linked him to 'Gog and Magog'.[94] This caught my eye because I remembered that Alexander, Gog and Magog had been connected in an almost identical manner in a very ancient Ethiopic manuscript known as the *Lefafa Sedek*, the 'Bandlet of Righteousness',[95] which was supposedly unknown outside Abyssinia until the nineteenth century.

Another point of interest was that 'Prester John' claimed in the letter that his Christian kingdom contained large numbers of Jews – who seemed to be semi-autonomous and with whom wars were often fought. Again this had a certain flavour of genuine Ethiopian conditions: following the tenth-century Jewish uprising by Gudit (which had temporarily overthrown the Solomonic dynasty) there had in fact been several hundred years of conflict between Ethiopia's Jews and Christians.[96]

All in all, therefore, despite the many fantastic and obviously apocryphal aspects of the letter, I was not disposed to believe that it was entirely an imposture. It seemed to me, furthermore, that its prime objective might have been to impress and scare the European powers to whom it was addressed. In this regard I noted in particular the frequent references that it made to the size of 'the Prester's' armed forces – for example:

We have . . . forty-two castles, which are the strongest
and most beautiful in the world, and many men to defend

them, to wit ten thousand knights, six thousand crossbowmen, fifteen thousand archers, and forty thousand troopers . . . Whenever we go to war . . . know that in front of us there march forty thousand clerics and an equal number of knights. Then come two hundred thousand men on foot, not counting the wagons with provisions, and the elephants and camels which carry arms and ammunition.[97]

This was unmistakably fighting talk, but what was most notable about it was that it was closely tied to something else – specific, and hostile, mention of the Templars. In a section apparently intended for the 'King of France' the letter suggested:

There are Frenchmen among you, of your lineage and from your retinue, who hold with the Saracens. You confide in them and trust in them that they should and will help you, but they are false and treacherous . . . may you be brave and of great courage and, pray, do not forget to put to death those treacherous Templars.[98]

Reviewing this ominous suggestion in the context of the rest of the bizarre letter I asked myself a question: in the year 1165, which candidate for the role of 'Prester John' could possibly have had a motive (a) to try to frighten off the European powers in general by boasting of his own overwhelming military strength, and (b) to attempt to smear the Knights Templar in particular and to request that they should be 'put to death'?

The answer I came up with was Harbay, who, in 1165, had been the reigning Zagwe monarch of Ethiopia, and who, as I have already observed, had certainly been the intended recipient of the letter written to Prester John by Pope Alexander III in 1177.

One of my reasons for pinpointing Harbay as the real author of the supposedly hoax letter of 1165 was terminological. I had discovered, as my research had progressed, that all the Zagwe monarchs had favoured the use of the Ethiopic term *Jan* in their string of titles.[99] Derived from *Jano*, a reddish-purple toga worn only by royalty, the word meant 'King' or 'Majesty' and might easily have been confused with 'John'; indeed it could have been precisely because of this (coupled with the fact that several of the

Zagwe rulers were also priests) that the phrase 'Prester John' had first been coined.

But there was a stronger reason to suspect Harbay. He, after all, had been a man with a burgeoning political problem in the year 1165. By then his disaffected half-brother Lalibela (who was eventually to depose him) had already been in exile in Jerusalem for five years – long enough, I speculated, for him to have got to know the Templars and to have made friends amongst them. Perhaps he had even asked the knights to help him to overthrow Harbay and perhaps Harbay had got wind of this plot.

Such a scenario, I thought, was not entirely implausible. The slightly later request to the Pope for a concession in the Church of the Holy Sepulchre (a request presented in Palestine by 'honourable persons' of 'Prester John's' kingdom) suggested that Harbay regularly sent emissaries to Jerusalem; such emissaries, therefore, could easily have picked up intelligence of a conspiracy brewing between Lalibela and the Templars in 1165. If this had been what had happened then it would undoubtedly go a long way to explain the strangely menacing suggestion to the King of France that it might be a good idea if he were to have the 'treacherous Templars' (still mainly Frenchmen at that time) executed forthwith. The 'letter of Prester John' – at least according to this hypothesis – would therefore have been concocted by Harbay's agents in Jerusalem as a deliberate strategy to deter collusion between the Templars and Prince Lalibela.

This was obviously an attractive line of reasoning. It was also dangerously speculative, however, and I would have been reluctant to follow it any further if I had not found certain passages in *Parzival* which seemed to confirm that the Templars might indeed have entered into precisely the sort of alliance with Lalibela that Harbay would have feared.

'Deep into Africa . . .'

Written some years *after* Lalibela had forcefully deposed Harbay from the throne of Ethiopia, *Parzival* contained a number of direct references to the Templars – who, as I have already noted, were depicted as being members of 'the Grail Company'.[100]

What I found intriguing was the specific suggestion, which Wolfram repeated several times, that these Templars were occasionally sent on missions overseas – missions that were highly secretive and that were to do with winning political power. For example:

> Writing was seen on the Gral to the effect that any
> Templar whom God should bestow on a distant people
> . . . must forbid them to ask his name or lineage, but must
> help them gain their rights. When such a question is put
> to him the people there cannot keep him any longer.[101]

Or similarly:

> If a land should lose its lord, and its people see the hand
> of God in it and ask for a new lord from the Gral
> Company, their prayer is granted . . . God sends the men
> out in secret.[102]

This was all very interesting, but the passage that really caught my attention came one page later in a lengthy monologue by a member of the Grail Company who spoke, amongst other things, of riding '*deep into Africa . . . past the Rohas*'.[103]

Scholars, I discovered, had tentatively identified 'the Rohas' with the Rohitscher Berg in Saangau Styria.[104] But this derivation looked completely spurious to me: it was not at all suggested by a context that had just mentioned Africa and I was quite unconvinced by the reasons given for it.[105] I knew something, however, that the Wolfram specialists in universities in Germany and England could not have been expected to know: *Roha* was the old name for a town in the remotest highlands of Ethiopia – a town now called Lalibela in honour of the great king who was born there and who made it his capital when he returned to it in triumph in the year of our Lord 1185. Neither was there any reason for the experts in medieval German literature to have been aware that this same Lalibela had spent the previous quarter of a century in Jerusalem rubbing shoulders with the knights of a military-religious order whose headquarters stood on the site of the Temple of Solomon – knights who would have had a special interest in any contender to the throne of a country which claimed to possess the lost Ark that the Temple had originally been built to house. The question that I now needed to address, therefore, was this: was there any evidence at all to suggest that Lalibela might have been accompanied by a contingent of Templars when he returned to Ethiopia in 1185 and deposed Harbay?

I did not think that the answer to this question would be easy to find. Luckily, however, I had been to the town of Lalibela in 1983 while working on my book for the Ethiopian government, and I had kept field notes. I therefore studied these notes with great care. To my surprise, I almost immediately came across something of interest.

On the ceiling of the rock-hewn church of Beta Mariam (yet another place of worship dedicated to Saint Mary the Mother of Christ) I had noticed 'faded red-painted crosses of the Crusader type'. I had then remarked: 'These don't look at all like any of the normal Ethiopian crosses – check out origins when back in Addis.' I had even made a rough sketch of one of these 'Crusader crosses' (which had triangular arms widening outwards). And, although I could not remember doing so, I had obviously followed the matter up to some extent: beneath the sketch and in a different pen I had later added the technical term *croix pattée*.

What I had not known in 1983 was that the Templars' emblem – adopted after the Synod of Troyes had given official recognition to the order in 1128 – had been a red *croix pattée*.[106] I did know this in 1989, however. Moreover I also knew that the Templars had been associated throughout their history with the construction of wonderful churches.

Almost inevitably, further questions began to form in my mind. By a considerable margin, the eleven rock-hewn churches of Lalibela were the most architecturally advanced buildings that Ethiopia had ever known (indeed, in the considered opinion of UNESCO, they deserved to be ranked amongst the wonders of the world).[107] Moreover, a certain air of mystery clung to them: there were other rock-hewn churches in the country, to be sure, but none were even of a remotely comparable standard. Indeed, in terms of overall conception, of workmanship, and of aesthetic expression, the Lalibela monoliths were unique. No expert had been able to suggest exactly how they had been built, and there had been persistent rumours of foreign involvement in their construction. Several academics had speculated that Indians, or Egyptian Copts, had been hired as masons by King Lalibela.[108] Ethiopian legends, by contrast, attributed the work to angels! I now had to ask myself, however, whether the true artificers of the Lalibela churches might not have been the Templars.

Certainly, my 1983 field notes painted a picture of a fantastic architectural complex:

Towering edifices [I had written], the churches remain places of living worship eight hundred years after they were built. It is important to stress, however, that they were not *built* at all in the conventional sense, but instead were excavated and hewn directly out of the solid red volcanic tuff on which they stand. In consequence, they seem superhuman – not only in scale, but also in workmanship and in conception.

Close examination is required before the full extent of the achievement that thcy rcpresent can be appreciated. This is because, like medieval Mysteries, considerable efforts have been made to cloak their real natures: some lie almost completely concealed within deep trenches, while others hide in the open mouths of huge quarried caves. Connecting them all is a complex and bewildering labyrinth of tunnels and narrow passageways with offset crypts, grottoes and galleries – a cool, lichen-enshrouded, subterranean world, shaded and damp, silent but for the faint echoes of distant footfalls as priests and deacons go about their timeless business.

Four of the churches are completely free-standing, being attached to the surrounding rock only by their bases. Although their individual dimensions and configurations are very different, they all take the form of great hills of stone, precisely sculptured to resemble normal buildings. They are wholly isolated within the deep courtyards excavated around them and the most striking of them is *Beta Giorghis* (the Church of Saint

George). It rests in majestic isolation at a considerable distance from all the others. Standing more than forty feet high in the centre of a deep, almost well-like pit, it has been hewn both externally and internally to resemble a cross. Inside there is a faultless dome over the sanctuary and, throughout, the craftsmanship is superb.

I concluded my 1983 notes – from which I have copied only the brief extract above – with the following question:

Setting aside the assistance supposedly provided by angels, how exactly were Lalibela's wonders created? Today, if truth be told, no one really knows: the techniques that made possible the excavation and chiselling of stone on so dramatic a scale, and with such perfection, have long been lost in the mists of history.

In the summer of 1989, looking back at what I had written six years previously, I was uncomfortably aware of how little those mists had cleared – and of how much there remained for me to find out. Intuitively I had a strong feeling that the Templars could have been involved in the creation of the Lalibela complex. The fact was, however, that there was really nothing to support this view other than the red 'Crusader crosses' that I had observed painted on the ceiling of Saint Mary's (one of the four completely free-standing churches).

Nevertheless there *was* a genuine mystery surrounding the origin of the churches. This mystery was reflected in the inability of scholars to explain how they had been excavated or who their architects could have been. It also found an echo in the quaint insistence of some of the inhabitants of Lalibela that angels had been involved in the work. Now, as I studied my 1983 field notes I discovered that there were other dimensions to the enigma.

Inside Saint Mary's, I had recorded, a priest had taken me close to the veiled entrance of the Holy of Holies and there had pointed out a tall pillar. I had described this pillar in the following terms:

About as thick as a good-sized tree-trunk, it soars
upwards out of the rock floor and disappears into the
gloom above. It is completely wrapped, spiral-fashion, in
a very old, discoloured shroud of cloth that bears faint
traces of washed-out dyes. The priest says that the pillar
is sacred and that engraved upon it are certain writings by
King Lalibela himself. Apparently these writings tell the
secrets of how the rock-hewn churches were made. I
asked if the cloth could be drawn back so that I could
read these secrets, but the poor priest was horrified.
'That would be sacrilege,' he told me, 'the covering is
never removed.'

Gallingly, my notes had nothing else to add on this point. I had
gone on to scribble my little entry on the 'Crusader crosses' and
then had left Saint Mary's for the next church in the complex.

Closing the battered foolscap jotter that had travelled everywhere with me in 1983, I felt what I can only describe as a sense
of retrospective fury at my earlier lack of curiosity. There had
been so *much* in Lalibela that I had failed to investigate. There
had been so many questions that I should have asked and had
failed to ask. Golden opportunities had thrown themselves
wantonly at me from every direction and I had ignored them.

Rather wearily I turned my attention to the hefty stack of
primary and secondary reference materials that I had accumulated on Ethiopia. The bulk of what I had consisted of
photocopies of worthy but irrelevant academic papers. There
was, however, one book which looked rather promising. Entitled
The Prester John of the Indies, it was an English translation of the
narrative of the Portuguese embassy to Ethiopia in 1520–6.
Written by Father Francisco Alvarez, this narrative – running to
more than five hundred pages – had first been printed in Lisbon
in 1540 and had been rendered into English in 1881 by the ninth
Baron Stanley of Alderley.

It was Lord Stanley's translation that I had before me – in a
relatively new edition issued by the Hakluyt Society in 1961. The
editors, Professors C. F. Beckingham and G. W. B. Huntingford
of the University of London, described Alvarez as 'rarely silly or

incredible . . . a kind, tactful, sensible man . . . free from the dishonesty of the traveller who tries to exaggerate his own knowledge.' As a result his book was universally regarded by scholars as being 'of great interest . . . incomparably detailed [and] a very important source for Ethiopian history.'[109]

With this glowing testimonial fresh in my mind I turned to page 205 of Volume I, where Alvarez began his account of his own visit to Lalibela. A lengthy church-by-church description followed which I could only admire for its exhaustive detail and for its plain, no-nonsense language. What I found most striking of all was how little things seemed to have changed in the four and a half centuries that had elapsed between Alvarez's visit and my own. Even the covering on the pillar in Saint Mary's had been there! After giving an account of other aspects of that church the Portuguese traveller had added: 'It had besides a high column in the cross of the transept over which is fixed a canopy, the tracery of which looks as if it had been stamped in wax.'[110]

Referring to the fact that all the churches were 'entirely excavated in the living rock, very well hewn' Alvarez exclaimed at one point:

I weary of writing more about these buildings, because it seems to me that I shall not be believed if I write more, and because regarding what I have already written they may blame me for untruth. Therefore I swear by God, in whose power I am, that all I have written is the truth, to which nothing has been added, and there is much more than what I have written, and I have left it that they may not tax me with its being falsehood, so great was my desire to make known this splendour to the world.[111]

Like the good reporter he undoubtedly was, Alvarez talked to some of the senior priests at the end of his visit – a visit, it is worth remembering, that was made only three and a half centuries after the churches were built. Amazed by everything he had seen, the Portuguese cleric asked his informants if they knew how long the carving and excavation of the monoliths had taken and who had carried out the work. The reply he was given, unencumbered by later superstitions, caused my pulse to race:

They told me that all the work on these churches was
done in twenty-four years, and that this is written, and
that they were made by white men . . . They say that King
Lalibela ordered this to be done.[112]

Coming at the end of everything else I had learned, I felt that I
could not disregard this pure and early piece of testimony. To be
sure, the history books on my shelves made no mention of any
'white men' going to Ethiopia before the time of Alvarez himself.
That, however, did not rule out the possibility that white men *had*
gone – white men who had belonged to a military-religious order
that was renowned for its international outreach and for its
secretiveness; white men who, in the words of Wolfram von
Eschenbach, were 'forever averse to questioning';[113] white men
who were sometimes sent to 'distant people . . . to . . . help them
gain their rights';[114] white men whose headquarters in the
twelfth century had stood over the foundations of the Temple of
Solomon in Jerusalem.

The priests' strange statement about the 'white men' who had
come to Lalibela therefore struck me as being a matter of the
utmost importance. Above all else, it strengthened my conviction
that Wolfram had been indulging in something more than mere
whimsy when, in *Parsival*, he had linked the Templars so closely
to his Grail cryptogram and to Ethiopia. He had never, anyway,
been a whimsical writer; on the contrary he had been pragmatic,
clever and highly focussed. I thus now felt increasingly confident
that my suspicions about him were justified and that he had
indeed been admitted to the inner circles of a great and terrible
mystery – the secret of the last resting place of the Ark of the
Covenant. Perhaps through the good offices of his 'source', the
Templar acolyte Guyot de Provins, or perhaps by means of a
more direct contact, he had been commissioned by the order to
encrypt that secret in a compelling story that would go on being
told and retold for centuries.

Why should the Templars have wanted Wolfram to do such a
thing? I could think of at least one possible answer. Written down
and placed in some form of container (a chest buried in the
ground for example), the secret of the Ark's whereabouts might
easily have been lost or forgotten within a century or so, and

would then only have come to light if somebody physically dug it up again. Cleverly encoded in a popular vehicle such as *Parzival*, however (which, I discovered, had been translated into almost all modern languages and reprinted in English five times in the 1980s in the Penguin Classics edition alone), the same secret would have stood an excellent chance of being preserved indefinitely in world culture. In this way, through all the passing centuries, it would have continued to be available to those with the capacity to decipher Wolfram's code. It would, in short, have been hidden in full view, enjoyed by all as a 'cracking good yarn', but accessible only to a few – initiates, insiders, determined seekers – as the treasure map that it really was.

This photograph of the ceiling of the rock-hewn church of Saint Mary's was provided to me by my Canadian publisher John Pearce in November 1991 – shortly before this book went to press. Pearce took it on a visit that he made to Lalibela in 1982. On the arch can be seen a stylised *croix pattée* contained within a Star of David – a most unusual symbol in a Christian place of worship, but one to which it is known that the Knights Templar were particularly attached. Behind the arch can be seen a section of the cloth-wrapped column said by the priests to have been engraved by King Lalibela himself with the secrets of how the rock-hewn churches were made.

16 In medieval times the Virgin Mary was repeatedly compared to both the Ark of the Covenant and the Holy Grail. This church steeple reflects these ideas by depicting Mary standing above the Ark.

17 and 18 Amongst many other shared characteristics, the Holy Grail (illustrated above right) and the Ark of the Convenant (on the horizon below) were both said to have given off a bright supernatural radiance.

19 In this illustration from a rare 14th century manuscript, the German poet Wolfram von Eschenbach is depicted second from the left amongst a group of other minstrels. In his *Parsival*, Wolfram described the Holy Grail not as a cup or container but as a stone.

20 Saint Bernard of Clairvaux, the force behind the formation of the Knights Templar in the twelfth century, is shown here urging the Second Crusade.

21 A Knight Templar showing the *croix-pattée*
that characterised the Order.

22 The great Muslim mosque known as the Dome of the Rock was built in the seventh century AD and stands at the site originally occupied by Solomon's Temple on Jerusalem's Temple Mount.

23 Interior of the Dome of the Rock showing the *Shetiyya*, the 'foundation stone of the world', which formed the floor of the Holy of Holies of Solomon's Temple. It was here that Solomon placed the Ark 3,000 years ago and it was from here, at some unknown date, that the sacred relic vanished.

24 and 25. *Above*: Porch of the Al Aqsa Mosque on Jerusalem's Temple Mount 100 metres to the south of the Dome of the Rock. The porch, in Gothic style with three central bays, was built by the Knights Templar in the twelfth century when they used the Al Aqsa Mosque as their palace. *Below*: for comparison, the Gothic north porch of Chartres Cathedral.

26 Interior of the circular Temple Church in London, with effigies of
knights on the floor in the foreground. An early example of Gothic
architecture, the church was built by the Templars in the 12th century.

27 Frontispiece of Alvarez' text, written in the 1520's, describing the first
official Portuguese mission to the court of Prester John in Ethiopia.

28 The rock-hewn monolithic church of Saint Mary in the ancient
Ethiopian settlement of Lalibela. Dating to the late 12th century, the
church was 'built by white men' according to a local tradition recorded
by Alvarez on his visit in the 1520's. Could these white men have been
Templars?

29 Twelfth century rock-hewn church of Saint George at Lalibela. The
double-cross device on its roof is a variant of the Templar cross and
was later adopted by their successors – the Portuguese Knights of
Christ.

30 Grand Master of the Templars being burnt at the stake in the early 14th
century. The suppression of the Templars began in 1307 and was
instigated by Pope Clement V and King Philip IV of France. Less than
a year earlier the first-ever Ethiopian mission to Europe had held an
audience – in France – with Pope Clement V.

31 *Top left*: Pope Clement V. 32 *Top centre*: Robert the Bruce, who gave shelter to fugitive Templars in Scotland. 33 *Top right*: Prince Henry the Navigator (1394–1460), Grand Master of the Knights of Christ, who inherited Templar traditions and who showed an exceptional interest in Ethiopia.

34   Vasco da Gama, a member of the Knights of Christ, whose son Don Christopher da Gama was killed in Ethiopia in 1542.

35 James Bruce of Kinnaird, who claimed to be descended from Robert the Bruce and whose epic journey to Ethiopia in the late eighteenth century shows evidence of a hidden agenda concerning the Ark of the Covenant. Though he kept it secret during his lifetime, Bruce was a Freemason and an inheritor of Templar traditions in Scotland.

Chapter 6

Resolving Doubts

My visit to Chartres cathedral and my readings of Wolfram's *Parzival* during the spring and summer of 1989 had opened my eyes to many things that I had missed before – notably to the revolutionary possibility that the Knights Templar could have made an expedition to Ethiopia in the twelfth century in search of the lost Ark. As explained in Chapter 5, I did not find it difficult to see how and why they might have been motivated to do that. But what I now needed to establish was this: other than the Templar 'quest' that I thought I had identified, was there really any convincing evidence to suggest that the last resting place of the Ark of the Covenant might actually be in the sanctuary chapel at Axum?

After all, there were literally hundreds of cities and churches around the world which boasted of possessing holy relics of one kind or another – fragments of the True Cross, Christ's shroud, the finger-bone of Saint Sebastian, the lance of Longinus, and so on and so forth. In almost every case where a proper investigation had been conducted such boasts had turned out to be hollow. Why, therefore, should Axum be any different? The fact that its citizens obviously *believed* their own legends certainly didn't prove anything – except, perhaps, that they were a susceptible and superstitious lot.

And, on the face of things, there seemed to be several good reasons for concluding that the Ethiopians did not possess the Ark of the Covenant.

Trouble with *tabots*

First and foremost, in the mid-nineteenth century, a legate of the Armenian Patriarch had visited Axum determined to prove that the tradition of the Ark's presence there, 'which the whole of Abyssinia believed to be the truth', was in fact 'an appalling lie'.[1] After putting some pressure on the Axumite priests, the legate – whose name was Dimotheos – had been shown a slab of 'reddish-coloured marble, twenty-four centimetres long, twenty-two centimetres wide and only three centimetres thick'[2] which the priests had said was one of the two tablets of stone contained within the Ark. They had not shown him the object believed by Ethiopians to be the Ark itself and had clearly hoped that he would be satisfied with a glimpse of the tablet – which they had referred to as 'the *Tabot* of Moses'.[3]

Dimotheos had indeed been satisfied. He reported with the obvious pleasure of a man who has just debunked a great myth:

> The stone was virtually intact, and showed no sign of age. At the most it dated from the thirteenth or fourteenth century of the present era . . . Stupid people like the Abyssinians who blindly accept this stone as the original are basking in a useless glory by possessing it, [for it is] not the true original at all. Those that know the Holy Scriptures do not require any further proof of this: the fact is that the tablets on which the divine laws were inscribed were placed inside the Ark of the Covenant and lost forever.[4]

What was I to make of this? If the slab of stone shown to the Armenian legate had really come from the relic claimed by the Axumites to be the Ark of the Covenant then he was right to suggest that they were basking in useless glory, because it went without saying that something made in 'the thirteenth or fourteenth century of the present era' could not possibly have been one of the two 'tablets of the law' on which the Ten Commandments had supposedly been inscribed more than twelve hundred years before the birth of Christ. In other words, if the contents were bogus then it followed that the container must be bogus too, which meant that the entire Axumite tradition was indeed 'an appalling lie'.

But that was a conclusion, I felt, that it would be premature to accept before attempting to find the answer to an important question: had Dimotheos been shown the object believed to be the genuine *Tabot* of Moses, or had he in fact been shown something else?

This question was particularly pertinent because the Armenian legate had so obviously been affronted and outraged by the possibility that a people as 'stupid' as the Ethiopians might possess a relic as precious as the Ark of the Covenant – and had therefore very much wanted to prove that they did not. Moreover, as I read and re-read his account, it became apparent to me that his desire to vindicate his own prejudices had over-ridden any proper investigative spirit on his part – and that he had also absolutely failed to recognize the subtle and devious nature of the Ethiopian character.

When he had visited Axum in the 1860s the specially dedicated sanctuary chapel had not yet been built[5] and the Ark – or the object believed to be the Ark – was still kept in the Holy of Holies of the church of Saint Mary of Zion (where, in the seventeenth century, it had been installed by Emperor Fasilidas after the reconstruction of that great edifice[6]). Dimotheos, however, had *not* been permitted to enter the Holy of Holies. Instead he had been taken to a rickety wooden outbuilding 'situated with some other rooms outside the church on the left'.[7] It had been in this outbuilding that the 'reddish-coloured marble stone' had been revealed to him.[8]

Because of this it seemed to me that there was a very high degree of probability that the Armenian legate had been duped by the priests. The Ark, I knew, was regarded as uniquely sacred by the Ethiopian Orthodox Church. It was therefore inconceivable that it, or any part of its contents, would have been removed even temporarily from the Holy of Holies of Saint Mary of Zion unless there had been some extremely compelling reason. The voyeuristic whim of a vulgar foreigner would certainly not have qualified as such a reason. At the same time, however, this foreigner had been an emissary of the Armenian Patriarch in Jerusalem and it would therefore have been thought wise to treat him with a certain amount of respect. What to do? The answer, I suspected, was that the priests had decided to show him one of the many *tabots* kept at Axum. And because he had so forcefully expressed his wish to see something connected to the Ark, if not the Ark itself, it would only have been kindly and polite to massage his ears with words that he obviously very much wanted to hear, namely that what he was being shown was the 'original *Tabot* of Moses'.

Needing to be sure that I was right about this I made a long-distance telephone call to Addis Ababa, where Professor Richard Pankhurst – my co-author on the government book in 1983 – was now living (he had moved back to the city in 1987 to take up his old post at the Institute of Ethiopian Studies). After telling him a little about my re-awakened interest in the Axumite tradition concerning the Ark of the Covenant, I asked him about the Dimotheos incident. Did he think that the *Tabot* that the Armenian legate had been shown could actually have been one of the objects believed by Ethiopians to have been placed in the Ark by Moses?

'Most unlikely,' Richard replied. 'They wouldn't show such a sacred thing to any outsider. Besides, I've read Dimotheos's book and it's full of mistakes and misapprehensions. He was a pompous man, pretty unscrupulous in his dealings with the Ethiopian Orthodox Church, and not entirely honest. I imagine the Axum clergy would have seen through him very quickly and fobbed him off with some other *tabot* that wasn't of any great importance to them.'

We talked for some time longer and Richard supplied me with the names and telephone numbers of two Ethiopian scholars who he thought might be able to help me with my research – Dr Belai Gedai (who had spent several years making an exhaustive study of his country's ancient history, drawing heavily on rare Amharic and *Ge'ez* documents) and Dr Sergew Hable-Selassie of the Institute of Ethiopian Studies, the author of a highly respected work entitled *Ancient and Medieval Ethiopian History to 1270*[9] with which I was already familiar.

The question of what Dimotheos had or had not seen in Axum was still very much at the forefront of my mind and I decided that I would put the problem to Hable-Selassie. I therefore called him, introduced myself, and asked for his opinion on the matter.

He laughed: 'Well certainly that fellow did not see the original *Tabot* of Moses. To satisfy his wish the priests showed him a substitute – not the real one . . . Here in Ethiopia it is normal for each church to have more than one *tabot*. In fact some have as many as ten or twelve, which they use for different ceremonial purposes. So he would have been shown one of these. There's no doubt about that at all.'

The confident nature of the historian's response laid to rest any remaining uncertainty that I may have felt about the merits of the Armenian legate's testimony. The 'reddish-coloured marble stone' that he had seen had no value as evidence either for or against Ethiopia's claim to possess the Ark of the Covenant. Nevertheless his account of his visit to Axum had raised another complicated reservation in my mind – a reservation to do with the whole issue of *tabots* as a category of sacred objects. As far as I was aware these objects were supposed to be *replicas* of the Ark of the Covenant – which, as I knew very well, had been a box about the size of a tea-chest. Yet the small marble slab that Dimotheos had been shown had been called a *tabot* and it had been described as one of the *tablets of stone* contained inside the Ark.

This was something that I really needed to clarify. Every Ethiopian church had its own *tabot* (and, as I now knew, they sometimes had several). But were these *tabots* really supposed to be replicas of the sacred object, thought to be the Ark, that was kept in the sanctuary chapel in Axum? If that were the case, and if all *tabots* were flat slabs, then the implication was that that sacred object, too, must be a flat slab – which meant that it could not be the Ark (although it might possibly be one of the tablets of the law on which the Ten Commandments had been inscribed).

Certainly the *tabots* that I had seen over my many years of acquaintance with Ethiopia had all been slabs rather than boxes – slabs that had been made sometimes of wood, and sometimes of stone. And certainly, also, it had been this very characteristic that had led the scholar Helen Adolf to conclude that Wolfram von Eschenbach must have had some knowledge of *tabots* when he had devised his Grail Stone.[10]

That was all very well – if *tabots* were meant to represent the stone tablets that the Ark had contained. On the other hand, if these objects were thought of as replicas of the Ark itself then the Axumite claim to that relic would be severely damaged. I could hardly forget that it had been precisely this problem – brought starkly to my attention after my visit to the British Museum Ethnographic Store in 1983 – that had caused me to abandon my initial research into the great mystery that was now clamouring for my attention once again. Before going any further, therefore, I felt that it was imperative to establish once and for all exactly what *tabots* were supposed to be. To this end I telephoned Dr Belai Gedai, the other Ethiopian scholar whom Richard Pankhurst had recommended to me. After introducing myself I got straight to the point: 'Do you believe,' I asked, 'that the Ark of the Covenant is in Ethiopia?'

'Yes,' he replied emphatically. 'Not only me but all Ethiopians believe that the Ark of the Covenant is in Ethiopia, kept in the church of Saint Mary of Zion in Axum. It was brought here after the visit of Emperor Menelik I to his father Solomon in Jerusalem.'

'And what about the Ethiopian word *tabot*? Does that mean "Ark"? Are *tabots* supposed to be replicas of the Ark in Axum?'

'In our language the correct plural of *tabot* is *tabotat*. And, yes, they are replicas. Because there is only one original Ark and because the ordinary people need something tangible to which they may attach their faith, all the other churches make use of these replicas. There are now more than twenty thousand churches and monasteries in Ethiopia and every one of them has at least one *tabot*.'

'That's what I thought. But I'm puzzled.'

'Why?'

'Mainly because none of the *tabotat* I've seen looked anything like the biblical description of the Ark. They were all slabs, sometimes made of wood, sometimes made of stone, and none of them were much more than a foot long and wide or more than two or three inches thick. If objects like these are supposed to be replicas of the relic kept in the church of Saint Mary of Zion in Axum then the logical deduction is that that relic can't be the Ark of the Covenant after all . . .'

'Why?'

'Because of the biblical description. Exodus clearly depicts the Ark as a fair-sized rectangular chest. Hang on, I'll look up the details . . .'

I took down my copy of the Jerusalem Bible from the bookshelf above my desk, turned to Chapter 37 of Exodus, found the relevant passage, and read out how the artificer Bezaleel had built the Ark according to the divine plan given to him by Moses:

Bezaleel made the Ark of acacia wood, two and a half cubits long, one and a half cubits wide, one and a half cubits high. He plated it, inside and out, with pure gold.[11]

'How long exactly is a cubit?' Gedai asked.

'Approximately the length of a forearm from the elbow to the tip of the middle finger – in other words about eighteen inches. So that means the Ark would have been about three feet nine inches in length and two feet three inches in width and depth. *Tabotat* simply don't fit those dimensions. They're much too small.'

'You are right,' Gedai mused. 'Nevertheless we do have the original Ark of the Covenant. This is certain. In fact there is even an eyewitness description.'

'You mean the one given by the Armenian legate Dimotheos?'

'No, no. Certainly not. He saw nothing. I am referring to someone who came much earlier, a geographer named Abu Salih – who was also an Armenian, by the way. He lived in the very early thirteenth century and he made a survey of Christian churches and monasteries. These churches and monasteries were mainly in Egypt. In addition, however, he visited some neighbouring countries, including Ethiopia, and his book contains material on these countries as well. That is where the description of the Ark is given. If I remember correctly it does accord quite well with what you have just read me from Exodus.'

'This book of Abu Salih's? Has it ever been translated into English?'

'Oh yes. A very good translation was made in the nineteenth century. You should be able to find a copy. The editor was a certain Mr Evetts . . .'

Two days later I emerged triumphantly from the stacks of the library of the School of Oriental and African Studies in London. In my hand was B. T. Evetts's translation of Abu Salih's monumental *Churches and Monasteries of Egypt and some Neighbouring Countries.*[12] On page 284, in small print, I found the subheading 'Abyssinia' followed by eight pages of observations and comments. Amongst them was this reference:

> The Abyssinians possess the Ark of the Covenant, in which are the two tables of stone inscribed by the finger of God with the commandments which he ordained for the Children of Israel. The Ark of the Covenant is placed upon the altar, but is not so wide as the altar; it is as high as the knee of a man and is overlaid with gold.[13]

I borrowed a ruler from the librarian and measured my own leg from the sole of my foot to my knee: twenty-three inches. This, I felt, was close enough to the twenty-seven inches given in Exodus to be significant – particularly if the statement 'as high as the knee of a man' had referred to a man wearing shoes or boots. I knew that such a rough measure could never be conclusive as a piece of evidence; on the other hand it by no means excluded the possibility that the Armenian geographer *had* seen the original Ark of the Covenant when he had made his visit to Ethiopia in the thirteenth century. And anyway, from my point of view, the real importance of the account that he had given was this: it indisputably described a substantial box or chest covered with gold rather than a slab of wood or stone a few inches thick like the *tabotat* that I had seen – or, for that matter, like the *tabot* that had been shown to Dimotheos in the nineteenth century.

Equally significantly, Abu Salih had given some details about how the object that he had seen had been used by the Christians of Axum:

> The liturgy is celebrated upon the Ark four times in the year, within the palace of the king; and a canopy is spread over it when it is taken out from its own church to the church which is in the palace of the king: namely on the feast of the great Nativity, on the feast of the glorious

Baptism, on the feast of the Holy Resurrection, and on the feast of the illuminating cross.[14]

There could, it seemed to me, be no question but that this early and quite matter-of-fact eyewitness account provided considerable support for Ethiopia's claim to be the last resting place of the genuine Ark of the Covenant. The dimensions and appearance were roughly right and even Abu Salih's description of the way in which the relic that he had seen had been covered with a 'canopy' when transported was in accord with the regulations laid down in the Bible:

And when the camp setteth forward . . . they shall take down the covering veil and cover the Ark with it. And they shall . . . spread over it a cloth.[15]

So far so good. But though the Armenian geographer was helpful, he still did not provide me with any answer to the knotty problem posed by the shape of that category of objects known as *tabotat*. Nor was this problem one that I could afford to ignore. I therefore decided to check out the etymology of the Ethiopic word. In its pure and original form, I wondered, did *tabot* actually mean 'Ark'? Or did it mean 'stone tablet'? Or did it mean something else altogether?

My investigation into this matter took me into intellectual territory that I had never charted before (and that I would prefer never to have to chart again), namely linguistics. Ploughing through reams of obscure and boring documents I established that the ancient Ethiopian language known as *Ge'ez*, together with its modern and widely spoken descendant Amharic, are both members of the Semitic family of languages, to which Hebrew also belongs.[16]

I then learned that the word most frequently used in biblical Hebrew to refer to the Ark of the Covenant was *'aron*,[17] which obviously bore no similarity whatsoever to *tabot*. There was another Hebrew word, however – *tebah* – from which scholars agreed that the Ethiopic *tabot* had undoubtedly been derived.[18]

I next sought to confirm whether this word *tebah* had featured in the Hebrew Old Testament, and, after further research, I discovered that it had – though only twice. Significantly, in both cases, it had been used to refer to a ship-like *container*: first the ark of Noah which contained the survivors of the human race after the flood,[19] and secondly the ark of bulrushes which contained the infant Moses after his mother had set him adrift on the Nile to save him from the wrath of Pharaoh.[20]

Turning to the *Kebra Nagast* I then found one passage in which the Ark of the Covenant was specifically described as 'the belly of a ship . . . Two cubits and half a cubit shall be the length thereof, and a cubit and half a cubit the breadth thereof, and thou shalt cover it with pure gold, both the outside thereof and the inside thereof.'[21] Within this 'belly of a ship', furthermore, were to be placed 'the Two Tables which were written by the finger of God'.[22]

Such language left no room for doubt. Both in terms of its etymology and its early usage the Ethiopic word *tabot* unambiguously connoted the biblical Ark of the Covenant in its original form as a gold-covered container – a form for which the 'belly of a ship' could serve as a clever metaphor capable not only of summoning up an image of the object but also of linking it conceptually to earlier 'ships': the ark of Noah and the ark of bulrushes, which of course had both also contained sacred and precious things.

By the same token, however, *tabot* definitely did not mean or in any way connote flat solid slabs of wood or stone. So there was still a genuine mystery here. That mystery, however, was finally resolved for me by Professor Edward Ullendorff, Fellow of the British Academy and the first incumbent of the Chair of Ethiopian Studies at the University of London. Now retired and living in Oxford, this renowned scholar insisted that he could see no difficulty in explaining how slabs of wood or stone had come to be referred to as 'Arks' by the Ethiopians:

The genuine Ark is supposed to rest at Axum; all other churches can only possess replicas. In most cases they are not, however, replicas of the whole Ark, but merely of its supposed contents, i.e. the tablets of the Law . . . In other words: the description of these stone or wooden tablets as *tabotat* is simply by way of a *pars pro toto* referring to the

most important part of the Ark, the tables of the
Covenant.[23]

Flies in amber

By eliminating an apparent contradiction, Ullendorff's solution
to the *tabot* problem lifted one of the clouds of doubt that hovered
over Ethiopia's claim to possess the lost Ark. Other clouds
remained, however. Amongst them, one of the darkest was
brought to my attention by Ullendorff himself. In a paper entitled
'The Queen of Sheba in Ethiopian Tradition' he had indicated
very strongly that the *Kebra Nagast* was not to be taken seriously
as a work of history; rather its purpose had been to glorify
Ethiopia and it was to this end that the Ark had been introduced
into it.[24]

Nor was Ullendorff alone in the view that the *Kebra Nagast* was
largely apocryphal. In the Introduction to his translation of that
great epic, for example, Sir E. A. Wallis Budge pointed out that it
was most unlikely that the Queen of Sheba could have been an
Ethiopian at all: 'It is far more probable', he wrote (rehearsing an
argument with which I was already somewhat familiar), 'that her
home was Sebha, or Saba, in the south-west of Arabia.'[25]

Several authorities made much of the fact that in Solomon's
time – a thousand years before Christ – Ethiopia had not
possessed any real civilization of its own and certainly had not
boasted an advanced urban society capable of producing so
illustrious a monarch as the Queen of Sheba. Indeed, the
consensus was that enlightenment had not even begun to dawn in
the Abyssinian highlands until about the sixth century BC and
had not reached any level of sophistication until some four
hundred years after that. Neither could this period of progress be
regarded as an Ethiopian achievement: instead the catalyst had
been an influx of Arab tribesmen whose 'superior qualities' had
revolutionized the sluggish culture of the native inhabitants.
Coming mainly from the Yemen, these Semitic immigrants had

> settled in the north of Ethiopia and in the process of
> assimilation with the local population brought about a
> cultural transformation. They brought with them gifts

beyond price: religion, a more highly-developed social organization, architecture and art, and a system of writing.[26]

In short, Ethiopian civilization was not only much more recent than the Axumite legends implied but also had been borrowed from elsewhere. In their heart of hearts, furthermore, most Ethiopians knew this to be true and felt deeply insecure about their heritage. Indeed one standard work of history went so far as to suggest that the *Kebra Nagast* was popular because it filled a deep psychological need on the part of the Abyssinians 'to prove their ancient origins ... Parvenu peoples, like parvenu individuals, hanker after ancestors, and peoples have as little scruple in forging family trees as have individuals.'[27]

In my view the importance of all these arguments lay less in the notion that the *Kebra Nagast* was mainly a work of fiction (since that did not preclude the possibility that what it had to say about the abduction of the Ark could have been based on some real event), but rather in the consensus that Ethiopian civilization was relatively young and that it had been derived from South Arabia.

This consensus had a real bearing on my attempts to establish the legitimacy of the Ethiopian claim to the Ark because it applied not only to the general civilization of the highlands but also – and quite specifically – to the Falashas. The *Kebra Nagast* stated quite plainly that the Jewish faith had been introduced into Ethiopia in the 950s BC when Menelik and his companions had arrived with the Ark (indeed it even said that the Queen of Sheba herself had been converted to Judaism).[28] On the face of things, therefore, the existence of indigenous black Jews in Ethiopia looked like significant corroborative evidence for the Ark's presence. On closer examination, however, this turned out not to be the case – or at least not according to the scholars. As Richard Pankhurst had told me in 1983,[29] the academic establishment was overwhelmingly of the opinion that the Jewish faith was unlikely to have reached Ethiopia before the second century AD, and that it had been brought across the Red Sea from the Yemen where a large Jewish community had indeed been established after AD 70 by emigrants fleeing Roman persecutions in Palestine.[30]

One of the strongest proponents of this view was Professor

Ullendorff, who presented a long argument on the subject in his influential *Ethiopia and the Bible* and who concluded quite emphatically that the ancestors of the Falashas must have been converted by Jews who had 'entered Ethiopia via South Arabia' over a lengthy period from AD 70 through until about AD 550.[31]

I decided that I would have to investigate this issue very thoroughly. If the Judaism of the Falashas was indeed less than two thousand years old – and had come from Arabia – then a great swathe of apparently convincing 'cultural corroboration' for direct contacts between Ethiopia and Jerusalem in Old Testament times would be obliterated at a stroke and Axum's lcandidacy as the last resting place of the Ark would lose much if not all of its credibility.

Soon after I began this new phase of my research, however, it became apparent to me that the scholarly consensus in favour of 'the Yemeni theory' had largely come about because there was an absence of evidence for any alternative theory. There was nothing whatever which proved that the Jewish faith could *not* have arrived by some other route; on the other hand there was no proof that it had. The tendency therefore had been to focus on South Arabia as the likely source because it was known that there had been other migratory movements from that region into Ethiopia.[32]

This struck me as a deplorable failure of logic in which absence of evidence, which was one thing, was in fact being treated as evidence of absence – which was quite another. To reiterate, the problem was a lack of proof that Judaism might have arrived in Ethiopia much earlier and by a different route than the scholars believed; but there was no proof at all that this could *not* have been the case.

I therefore felt that the field was open and that what I needed to do in order to satisfy myself one way or the other was to study the traditions, beliefs and behaviour of the Falashas themselves and to draw my own conclusions about their origins from these. I thought it likely, however, that their religious observances would have been adulterated during the twentieth century by extensive exposure to western and Israeli visitors. I therefore turned to older accounts that depicted their way of life before it had been contaminated by modern cultural change.

Ironically, several of these accounts were written by foreigners who came to Ethiopia with the express intention of engineering cultural change, notably nineteenth-century Christian missionaries who had heard rumours of the existence of a sizeable population of Abyssinian Jews and who had rushed to convert them.

One such evangelist was Martin Flad, a young German who arrived in Ethiopia in 1855 to proselytize on behalf of the London Society for Promoting Christianity amongst the Jews.[33] His book, *The Falashas of Abyssinia*, was published in 1869. I found a worn and much-handled copy of it in the British Library and soon became intrigued by several passages in which the author insisted that there must have been Jews in Ethiopia at least since the time of the prophet Jeremiah (around 627 BC[34]), and possibly since the reign of Solomon. Flad based this assertion in part on the fact that:

> The Falashas know nothing of either the Babylonian or
> the Jerusalem Talmud, which were composed during and
> after the time of the captivity. They also do not observe
> the Feasts of Purim and of the Dedication of the Temple,
> which . . . are still solemnly kept by the Jews of our
> time.[35]

On further investigation, I discovered that the Feast of the Dedication of the Temple was properly known as Hanukkah (meaning, literally, 'Dedication'). From my point of view the most significant fact about it was that it was instituted in 164 BC[36] and therefore would certainly have been observed by the Jewish community that established itself in the Yemen after AD 70. The academic orthodoxy which had previously persuaded me to see the Falashas as the descendants of Ethiopians converted by these Yemeni Jews thus suddenly began to look very suspect. To put matters as plainly as possible, non-observance of Hanukkah suggested only one rational conclusion: the Falashas must have acquired their Judaism *before* 164 BC and thus not from the Yemen but from some other source.

I next researched the Feast of Purim of which Flad had also found Ethiopia's Jews to be ignorant. This festival, too, I learned, had been observed since at least the second century BC. Indeed it was quite possibly of even earlier provenance than that: the events that it commemorated took place in the mid-fifth century BC and several of the authorities whom I consulted suggested that its observance had become widely popular by 425 BC.[37] This raised the interesting possibility – of which Flad himself had obviously been convinced – that the Falashas had become isolated from the evolving body of world Judaism well before that date, perhaps during the sixth century BC.

I now had a growing sense that the gap between Abyssinian legend and historical fact was closing fast: five hundred years before Christ, after all, was only four hundred years after Solomon. It was beginning to look more and more probable that the Judaism of the Falashas *had* arrived in Ethiopia in early Old Testament times – just as the *Kebra Nagast* and the Falashas themselves had always claimed. If this were so, then the implications were clear: at the very least the story of the abduction of the Ark to Ethiopia by Menelik deserved to be taken much more seriously than the academics had hitherto allowed.

I found further evidence for this point of view in the account of another nineteenth-century missionary, Henry Aaron Stern, who was himself a German-Jewish convert to Christianity. He had worked and travelled with Flad in Ethiopia and had published his own *Wanderings among the Falashas in Abyssinia* in 1862.

As I read this 300-page volume I developed an intense dislike for its author, who came across as an arrogant, brutal and unscrupulous proselytizer with no respect whatsoever for the culture or traditions of the people amongst whom he was working. In general, too, I felt that his descriptions of Falasha religion and lifestyle were thin and poorly observed. As a result, by the time I was halfway through the book I had become thoroughly impatient with it.

Then, on page 188, I came across something interesting. Here, after a lengthy treatise on the absolute interdiction amongst the Falashas of 'intermarriages with those of another tribe or creed', Stern described the Ethiopian Jews as being faithful to the law of Moses 'which . . . is the formula after which they have moulded their worship.' He then added:

> It sounds strange to hear in central Africa of a Jewish
> altar and atoning sacrifices . . . [Yet], in the rear of every
> place of worship is a small enclosure with a huge stone in
> the centre; and on this crude altar the victim is
> slaughtered, and all other sacrificial rites performed.[38]

Though at this stage my general knowledge about Judaism was
limited to say the least, I was well aware that animal sacrifice was
no longer practised anywhere in the world by modern Jews. I had
no idea whether this ancient institution still existed amongst the
Falashas in the late twentieth century; Stern's account, however,
made it quite clear that it had flourished a hundred and thirty
years earlier.

Continuing his description of the sacrificial enclosure, the
German missionary next remarked:

> This sanctum is sacredly guarded from unlawful intrusion
> . . . and woe betide the stranger who, ignorant of Falasha
> customs, ventures too close to the forbidden precincts . . .
> I was one day on the very verge of committing this
> unpardonable offence. It was a very sultry and close noon
> when, after several hours' fatiguing march, we reached a
> Falasha village. Eager to obtain a short rest, I went in
> quest of a cool and quiet shelter, when accidentally I
> espied in the midst of a secluded grassy spot a smooth
> block that looked as if it had been charitably placed there
> to invite the weary to solitude and repose. The thorny
> stockade easily yielded to the iron of my lance, and I was
> just about to ensconce myself behind the flattened stone
> when a chorus of angry voices . . . reminded me of my
> mistake, and urged me to beat a hasty retreat.[39]

I found myself wishing that Stern had received the punishment
he deserved for vandalizing a holy place.[40] At the same time,
however, I could not help but be grateful to him for drawing my
attention to the practice of sacrifice amongst the Falashas. This
was a lead well worth following up since it might provide another
clue to the date at which Ethiopia's Jews became separated from
the main body of their co-religionists.

I devoted considerable effort to researching the obscure subject of Judaic sacrifice in Old Testament times. The picture that eventually emerged from the fog of scholarly references was of a constantly evolving institution that started out as a simple offering to God which anyone, priest or layman, could make and in virtually any place where a local shrine had been established. This state of relative unregulation, however, began to change after the Exodus from Egypt around 1250 BC.[41] During the Hebrews' wanderings in the wilderness of Sinai the Ark of the Covenant was built and housed in a portable tent or 'tabernacle'. Thenceforward all sacrifices were to be made at the door of this tabernacle and anyone disobeying the new law was to be punished by banishment:

> Whatsoever man there be of the House of Israel . . . that offereth a burnt offering or sacrifice and bringeth it not to the door of the tabernacle of the congregation, to offer it unto the Lord; even that man shall be cut off from among his people.[42]

I learned, however, that this prohibition was rather less absolute than it sounded. The main point of the code was not to abolish sacrifice at local shrines in all circumstances but rather to ensure that sacrifices were carried out exclusively at a centralized national place of worship *when and if such a place existed*. In the wilderness the tabernacle housing the Ark was such a central point. Later, from roughly 1200 to 1000 BC, a national sanctuary was established in Israel at Shiloh, which thus became the new sacrificial centre. Significantly, however, there were periods of political upheaval when Shiloh was abandoned and during these periods the Hebrews were permitted to sacrifice once again at local shrines.[43]

By the 950s BC Solomon's Temple in Jerusalem had superseded Shiloh as the national religious centre. There is evidence, however, that local sacrifices did take place elsewhere from time to time, particularly amongst those Jews living far from the capital. Indeed it was not until the reign of King Josiah (640-609 BC) that a blanket ban on all forms of sacrifice other than at the Temple began to be strictly enforced.[44]

So seriously was this prohibition taken that the Jews appear not to have attempted sacrifice of any kind in the decades immediately following the Temple's destruction by Nebuchadnezzar in 587 BC. The early tradition of reverting to local shrines in the absence of a centralized national place of worship seems to have been irrevocably abandoned. Quite simply, while there was no Temple there could be no sacrifice.[45]

After the return from the Babylonian Exile, the Second Temple was built in Jerusalem and the institution of sacrifice was re-established exclusively within its precincts; meanwhile the absolute prohibition on local offerings was reinforced and appears to have been strictly obeyed. This system of centralized sacrifice remained firmly in place from 520 BC, when the Second Temple was dedicated, until 70 AD when it was razed to the ground by the Roman Emperor Titus.[46]

No Third Temple had ever been contemplated, other than by millennial groups who linked the fulfilment of that dream with the coming of the still-awaited Messiah.[47] In consequence, since AD 70, sacrifice had everywhere been abandoned by the Jews. *The Falashas were the sole exception to this rule.*[48] Moreover Stern's account suggested that they had offered sacrifices at all their places of worship when he had worked amongst them in the nineteenth century. With a little further research I was able to confirm that this tradition was so strong that sacrifices continued to be made by the majority of Falasha communities today despite their increased exposure to modern Jewish practices.[49]

As I considered this fact, I realized that there might be a number of possible explanations for it. The most obvious and attractive of these explanations, however, was also the simplest – and therefore the most likely to be correct. I wrote in my notebook:

> The ancestors of today's Falashas must have been
> converted to Judaism at a time when it was still acceptable
> for those far away from the centralized national sanctuary
> to practise local sacrifice. That would suggest that the
> conversion took place before King Josiah's ban – i.e. no
> later than the seventh century BC and possibly even
> earlier than that.

HYPOTHESIS: At some stage after the building of Solomon's Temple (mid-900s BC) but before Josiah (mid-600s BC) a group of Jews migrated from Israel and settled in Ethiopia. They established local shrines at which they conducted sacrifices to their God and they began to convert the natives of the country to their faith. Perhaps they initially maintained contact with their homeland. The distance was great, however, and it is reasonable to suppose that they would eventually have became completely isolated. They would thus have been untouched by the great revolutions in theological thought that took place in the Judaic world in subsequent centuries.

This explains why the Falashas are the only Jews still practising sacrifice. Frozen like flies in amber, trapped in a time-warp, they are the last surviving practitioners of genuine First Temple Judaism.

So far so good. But QUESTION: *why* would a group of Jews have migrated from Israel to somewhere as far away as Ethiopia? We are talking the tenth to seventh centuries BC here, not exactly the jet age. The émigrés must therefore have had a very strong motive. What could that have been?

ANSWER: The *Kebra Nagast* is in no doubt about what the motive was. It says that the migrants were the first-born sons of the elders of Israel, and that they came to Ethiopia in the entourage of Menelik to attend the Holy Ark of the Covenant which they had abducted from the Temple.

Decline and fall

If the *Kebra Nagast*'s account of the arrival of Judaism in Ethiopia were true, I reasoned, then I might expect to find evidence somewhere in the historical annals to prove that the Jewish faith had formerly enjoyed a much greater prominence in that country than it did today. That certainly would make sense if it had originally been associated with so exalted a figure as Menelik I. I remembered, moreover, that my old friend Richard Pankhurst had mentioned something to me that was relevant to this line of inquiry. When we had worked together in 1983 he had told me that the Falashas had once been a prosperous and powerful people with kings of their own.

I therefore placed another telephone call to Richard in Addis Ababa to see if he could recommend any sources that might shed light on the decline and fall of the Falashas.

He directed me to a book with which I was already slightly familiar: *Travels to Discover the Source of the Nile in the Years 1768–1773* written by the Scottish adventurer James Bruce of Kinnaird. Pankhurst also suggested that I should look into the 'Royal Chronicles' compiled during the reigns of a number of Ethiopian emperors since medieval times. These, he said, documented a series of wars that had been fought between the Christians and the Jews and could be of interest. 'Other than that,' he added, 'I'm not sure where you can get the kind of information you want. The problem is that almost nothing in depth was ever written about the Falashas before Bruce.'

James Bruce of Kinnaird, as I was to discover, was something of an enigma. Hailing from a staunchly Presbyterian Stirlingshire family, he had belonged to the minor aristocracy and had inherited sufficient wealth to indulge a lifelong passion for overseas travel. Initially it seemed to me that it was only this wanderlust that had lured him into the heart of the Ethiopian highlands. When I began to look at his work on the Falashas, however, it gradually dawned on me that his interest in these people had been too intense and too sustained to be explained away merely as the normal curiosity of an intelligent traveller. Over a period of several years he had carried out meticulous research into the faith, customs and historical origins of Abyssinia's black Jews. In the process, interviewing elders and religious figures, he had recorded many ancient traditions that would otherwise most certainly have been lost to history.

Amongst these traditions was one which stated that King Ezana of Axum had been reading the Psalms of David when he was first introduced to Frumentius, the young Syrian who later converted him to Christianity.[50] Bruce, furthermore, made it quite clear that the monarch's acquaintance with this book of Old Testament verse resulted *from the widespread prevalence of Judaism in Ethiopia at that time*[51] – i.e. the early part of the fourth century AD.

In the context of what I now knew about Falasha customs, I was happy to give credence to this assertion. Indeed I took it as additional support for my own rapidly evolving hypothesis – namely that a form of the Jewish faith incorporating archaic traditions of blood sacrifice had been in Ethiopia for at least a thousand years before Frumentius turned up to preach the gospel of Christ.

I was soon to find further confirmation of this in an old and rare Ethiopic manuscript that had once rested in the Tigrayan fortress of Magdala (stormed and looted by British forces under General Napier in the nineteenth century). Entitled *A History and Genealogy of the Ancient Kings* it contained the following passage:

Christianity was introduced into Abyssinia 331 years after the birth of Christ by Abuna Salama, whose former name was Frumentos or Frumentius. At that time the Ethiopian kings reigned over Axum. *Before the Christian religion was known in Ethiopia half the inhabitants were Jews, who observed the Law;* the other half were worshippers of Sando, the dragon.[52]

The reference to worshippers of 'the dragon' – presumably a rubric for all sorts of primitive animistic gods – was interesting. It suggested that Judaism had at no point become the exclusive state religion of Ethiopia and that, in the pre-Christian era, the Falashas – like Jews everywhere – had accepted the coexistence of many pagan creeds. I reasoned, however, that they would undoubtedly have been put on their guard, and been tempted to abandon their traditional tolerance, by the arrival of a militantly evangelistic monotheistic sect like the Christians, whom they would have had good reason to see as a real threat to their pre-eminence and to their beliefs. The conversion of the Axumite king would have looked particularly ominous in such a context and thereafter Jews and Christians might well have found themselves locked in bitter struggle.

There was considerable support for this analysis amongst the traditions recorded by Bruce. The Scottish adventurer asserted, for example, that the Falashas

were very powerful at the time of the conversion to
Christianity or, as they term it, 'the Apostasy'. At this
time they declared a prince of the tribe of Judah, and of
the race of Solomon and Menelik, to be their sovereign
... This prince ... refused to abandon the religion of his
forefathers.[53]

Such a state of affairs, Bruce added, was bound to lead to conflict
since the Christians, too, claimed to be ruled by a king descended
from the line of Solomon. The conflict, when it came, was thus
precipitated by concerns that were entirely secular:

Although there was no bloodshed upon difference of
religion, yet, each having a distinct king with the same
pretensions, many battles were fought from motives of
ambition and rivalship of sovereign power.[54]

Bruce provided no details of these 'many battles' and the history
books, too, were silent concerning them – other than noting that
in the sixth century AD Kaleb, a Christian king of Axum,
assembled a vast army and took it across the Red Sea to do battle
with a Jewish monarch in the Yemen.[55] Was it not quite
probable, I now speculated, that this Arabian campaign had been
an escalation of fighting between Jews and Christians in Ethiopia
itself?

Evidence that this might indeed have been the case was
contained in the *Kebra Nagast*. Towards the end of the great epic
I found specific mention of King Kaleb in a chapter that seethed
with anti-Judaic sentiments: here, for no apparent reason, the
Ethiopian Jews were suddenly described as the 'enemies of God';
furthermore, the text advocated that they should be 'cut to pieces'
and that their lands should be laid waste.[56]

All this was said in a context that ascribed two sons to Kaleb.
One of these sons was named 'Israel' while the other was referred
to as 'Gebra Maskal' (an Ethiopic term meaning 'Slave of the
Cross'). The symbolism of a Jewish–Christian rift was hard to
miss (with the Christian faction, of course, being represented by
Gebra Maskal and the Jewish faction by Israel). And this analysis
began to look even more credible when I remembered that the

Falashas never referred to themselves as 'Falashas' but always as 'Beta Israel', i.e. 'House of Israel'.[57]

The basic message, therefore, seemed clear enough; nevertheless, the whole passage was complicated by dense and obscure imagery. Several times, for example, the words 'Chariot' and 'Zion' cropped up. I could make little or no sense of the former. I already knew very well, however, that the latter – 'Zion' – was one of a number of different epithets for the Ark of the Covenant used frequently in the *Kebra Nagast*.[58]

Everything became clear when I read that Israel and Gebra Maskal were destined to fight each other. After this battle, the text continued:

God will say to *Gebra Maskal*, 'Choose thou between the Chariot and Zion', and He will cause him to take Zion, and he shall reign openly upon the throne of his father. And God will make *Israel* to choose the chariot, and he shall reign secretly and he shall not be visible.[59]

In this fashion, the *Kebra Nagast* concluded:

The kingdom of the Jews shall be made an end of and the Kingdom of Christ shall be constituted . . . Thus hath God made for the King of Ethiopia more glory and grace and majesty than for all the other kings of the earth because of the greatness of Zion, the Ark of the Law of God.[60]

It seemed to me beyond any reasonable doubt that what was being described here, albeit in arcane and symbolic language, was a conflict between the Jews and Christians of Ethiopia – a battle for supremacy in which the followers of the new religion triumphed while the followers of the older faith were vanquished, thereafter to live invisibly in secret places. It was also clear that the Ark of the Covenant – 'Zion' – had stood at the heart of this struggle for power and that the Christians had in some way managed to wrest it from the Jews who thenceforward had had to content themselves with the 'Chariot', in other words with second best.

As my researches continued, however, it became obvious that the Falashas had *not* tamely accepted the invisibility and second-class status that the Christians had sought to impose on them. On the contrary, I found a considerable body of evidence to suggest that they had fought back – and, furthermore, that they had done so with great determination and over a rather lengthy period.

The first tantalizing hint of sustained warfare between Abyssinia's Jews and Christians came in an account written by a ninth-century traveller named Eldad Hadani – better known as Eldad 'the Danite' because he claimed descent from the lost Israeli tribe of Dan. Exactly who he was, or where he came from, was by no means clear. In a widely circulated letter written in AD 833, however, he had claimed that the Danites – and three other 'lost' Jewish clans – lived in Ethiopia where they were locked in permanent antagonism with the Christian rulers of that country: 'And they slew the men of Ethiopia and unto this very day they fight with the children of the kingdoms of Ethiopia.'[61]

On investigating further I discovered that several authorities regarded Eldad as a charlatan and his letter as an improbable piece of fiction. Others, however, felt that much of what he said was firmly grounded in fact.[62] I had no hesitation in aligning myself with the latter camp – simply because Eldad's references to the Abyssinian Jews were too close to the truth about the Falashas to have been pure fabrications. He insisted, for example, that they had emigrated from the Holy Land to Ethiopia in First Temple times, shortly after the separation of the kingdoms of Judah and Israel (i.e. around 931 BC[63]). In consequence, he said, they did not celebrate festivals instituted after that date such as Purim and Hanukkah. Neither did they have rabbis 'for these were of the Second Temple and they did not reach them.'[64]

I was already well aware of the non-observance of the later festivals by the Falashas, and of the implications of this. On checking I now discovered that they did not have rabbis either: indeed their religious officials were called *kahen*, a word derived from the Hebrew *kohen* (more familiar as the common name Cohen) meaning 'priest' and dating back to the era of the First Temple.[65]

All in all, therefore, it did sound very much as though Eldad had been in Ethiopia as he had claimed, and had given a faithful enough description of the state of Judaism there in the mid-ninth century AD. His report of sustained fighting between the Abyssinian Jews and their neighbours during this period thus also looked quite plausible:

And their banner is white and written thereon in black is 'Hear O *Israel*, the Lord our God is one God' . . . They are numerous as the sands of the sea, and have no employment but war and, whensoever they fight, they say it is not good for mighty men to flee, let them die young, but let them not flee, let them strengthen their heart unto God, and several times they say and cry all of them together, 'Hear O *Israel*, our God is one God', and then they all take heed.[66]

Eldad concluded that the Jewish tribes in Ethiopia had been successful in their warlike endeavours and had 'placed their hands on the necks of their enemies'.[67] This, it seemed to me, was nothing more nor less than a fairly accurate description of the true balance of power between Christians and Jews in the ninth and early tenth centuries AD. It was, after all, at precisely this time that the Christian Solomonic dynasty of Axum had been overthrown. And I already knew from my previous research that this *coup d'état* had been the work of a Jewish monarch – a great queen named Gudit (or Judit, or possibly Yehudit).

As outlined in Chapter 5, Gudit's brief and bloody reign was followed, perhaps half a century later, by the establishment of the Zagwe dynasty, to which King Lalibela had belonged. Although they were almost certainly Jews at the outset, the Zagwes themselves later converted to Christianity and subsequently (about fifty years after Lalibela's death) abdicated the throne in favour of a monarch claiming Solomonic descent.

Whatever else it achieved, however, it quickly became apparent to me that the Zagwe interregnum had not halted the chronic state of conflict between the Abyssinian Jews and Christians. As my researches continued I learned that Benjamin of Tudela, a widely travelled Spanish merchant who lived in the twelfth century, had reported the existence of Jews in Ethiopia who were 'not under the yoke of the Gentiles', and who had 'cities and castles on the summits of mountains'. He spoke of wars with the Christians in which the Falashas were normally successful, taking 'spoil and booty' at will because no man could 'prevail against them'.[68]

Then, in the fifteenth century, the Jewish traveller Elijah of Ferrara related that he had met a young Falasha in Jerusalem and was told how his co-religionists 'preserved their independence in a mountainous region from which they launched continual wars against the Christian emperors of Ethiopia.'[69]

A hundred years later the Jesuit Bishop of Oviedo asserted that the Falashas hid away in 'great inaccessible mountains; and they had dispossessed the Christians of many lands which they were masters of, and the kings of Ethiopia could not subdue them, because they have but small forces, and it is very difficult to penetrate into the fastnesses of their rocks.'[70]

The bishop was wrong, however. His statement was made in 1557 – by which date, far from 'dispossessing' anyone, the Falashas were actually under sustained attack from Christian forces bent, apparently, on genocide. Sarsa Dengel, the Solomonic emperor who ruled from 1563 to 1594, waged a seventeen-year campaign against them – a campaign described by one respected scholar as 'a veritable crusade, inspired by religious fanaticism.'[71]

During the fighting, which saw brutal onslaughts against Falasha strongholds in the Simien mountains west and south of the Takazze river, the defenders acquitted themselves with great dignity. Even Sarsa Dengel's sycophantic chronicler could not avoid expressing admiration for the courage of one group of Jewish women who, rather than be captured and used by the emperor's men, hurled themselves off a cliff with the cry *Adonai* [God] help me'.[72]

Later the Falasha king, Radai, was taken prisoner. Offered his life if only he would beg the Virgin Mary for mercy – and death if he would not – he is reported to have said: 'Is not the mention of the name of Mary forbidden? Make haste! It is better for me that I should depart from a world of lies to a world of justice, from the darkness to the light; kill me, swiftly.' The emperor's general,

Yonael, answered: 'If you prefer death, die bravely and bow your head.' Radai then bowed and Yonael struck him with a great sword: the single blow instantly decapitated the Falasha monarch and passed through his knees also, the blade finally burying itself in the ground. Those who witnessed this horrible scene were said to have admired 'the courage of the Jew in death who declared the things of the earth are bad and the things of heaven are good.'[73]

Towards the end of the same campaign the last two Falasha fortresses in the high Simiens were attacked and overwhelmed despite the bravery of the defenders. In both cases the leaders and their picked men chose suicide rather than captivity.

This did not bring an end to the persecutions, however. On the contrary, even worse atrocities were committed after 1607 when Emperor Susneyos ascended the throne. He launched a pogrom against all Falashas still living in the vast highland expanses between Lake Tana and the Simien mountains. During the next twenty years of 'unwarrantable butchery' thousands were killed in fierce fighting and their children were sold as slaves. The few survivors, according to the detailed account given by the Scottish traveller James Bruce:

> were ordered upon pain of death to renounce their
> religion, and be baptised. To this they consented, seeing
> there was no remedy . . . Many of them were baptised
> accordingly, and they were all ordered to plough and
> harrow on the Sabbath day.[74]

The upshot of such sustained and vindictive oppression was that it forever deprived Ethiopia's Jews of the autonomous statehood that they had obviously once enjoyed – and thus hastened their slide into obscurity. Looking back through the admittedly sketchy historical documents at my disposal, I found that it was even possible to chart this gradual submergence and disappearance in numerical terms.

In the early 1600s, for example, the Falashas were said to have numbered some '100,000 effective men'.[75] Assuming one 'effective man' per family of five, this would give a total population for that period of around 500,000. Nearly three hundred years later – in the late nineteenth century – the Jewish scholar Joseph Halévy put total Falasha numbers at around 150,000.[76] By the end of the first quarter of the twentieth century this figure had plummeted to just 50,000 – according to the undoubtedly well-informed estimate of another Jewish investigator, Jacques Faitlovich.[77] Sixty years on, in the famine year of 1984, the Falasha population of Ethiopia was reliably estimated at 28,000.[78]

My reading left me in no doubt that the watershed had come at the beginning of the seventeenth century with the Susneyos campaigns, which had clearly broken the back of Falasha resistance. Before that they had been a populous and powerful folk with kings and a kingdom of their own; afterwards, disenfranchised and beaten, their numbers remorselessly declined.

The historical record, therefore, more than adequately resolved the contradiction that had been bothering me, namely how to explain the latter-day victimization and impoverishment of the Falashas if it were true that Judaism had been brought to Ethiopia by so exalted a figure as Menelik I – who had also brought the Holy Ark of the Covenant, the most precious and prestigious relic of the ancient world. I now realized that there was no contradiction at all. Indeed a scenario in which the Jewish religion had once enjoyed great influence suggested the only possible motive for the merciless pogroms, killings and mass enslavements that Susneyos and other Christian emperors had inflicted upon their Falasha compatriots. Simply stated, such bizarre and apparently psychopathic behaviour made a twisted kind of sense if the Christians had actively *feared* the possibility of a resurgence of Judaism – and if their fear had stemmed from the fact that this rival monotheistic faith had earlier represented an extremely strong and enduring theme in Ethiopian life.

'Consummation of heart's desire . . .'

All this, I reasoned, strongly supported the view that Judaism had arrived in Ethiopia long before Christianity. By the same token it also added some social corroboration to the legendary account of Menelik's abduction of the Ark. To summarize, I now knew that:

- The Falashas' archaic traditions of blood sacrifice – as well as some of their other religious practices – cast grave doubt on the academic orthodoxy which favoured a late (and South Arabian) origin for Ethiopian Judaism. On the contrary the evidence suggested quite compellingly that the Jewish faith must have come to Ethiopia in First Temple times and must then have been isolated there. Furthermore, the best possible account of how and why Judaism had taken root in the heart of Africa at so early a date was provided by the *Kebra Nagast*. Since the story of the abduction of the Ark was central to that account it followed that Ethiopia's claim to possess the sacred relic deserved to be taken seriously.
- There was clear evidence to suggest that the Jewish faith had been an important force in Ethiopia long before the arrival of Christianity in the fourth century AD. This evidence also suggested that Jews and Christians had subsequently engaged in a protracted struggle to the death. The winners of this struggle had been the Christians – who had, in the process, captured the Ark of the Covenant. Thereafter they had gradually incorporated it into their own non-Jewish religious ceremonies. This was the only satisfactory explanation for what was otherwise an incomprehensible anomaly – namely the crucial role, unique in the Christian world, played in all Ethiopian church services by replicas of an Old Testament relic.
- These replicas depicted the contents of the Ark – i.e. the tablets of stone – rather than the Ark itself. This had originally confused me; I now understood, however, that it was merely an example of a culture being 'economical with its symbols'. In the Holy of Holies of every one of the more than twenty thousand Orthodox churches in Ethiopia was a *tabot*. Behind these *tabotat* – and directly responsible for the superstitious dread which they inspired in the general population – lay a mysterious and puissant object. There now seemed to me to be every possibility that

that object might indeed be the Holy Ark of the
Covenant.

Of course there were still several loose ends. These included
the important issue of the ethnic identity of the Queen of Sheba
(could she really have been an Ethiopian?). Linked to this, and of
at least equal weight, was another legitimate doubt that the
scholars had raised: in the era of Solomon was it really possible
that Ethiopia could have possessed a sufficiently 'high' civilization to have engaged in direct cultural contact with ancient Israel?
Finally there was the problem of Axum – to which Richard
Pankhurst had drawn my attention in 1983.[79] The sacred city
had not even existed in Solomon's time and therefore the Ark
could not have been brought to it. This did not preclude the
possibility that the relic might have been deposited at some other
place in Ethiopia and then moved to Axum at a later date. If so,
where was that 'other place' and why had I encountered no
traditions concerning it?

These, I realized, were questions for which I would eventually
have to seek answers. There were others, too. Indeed it was
perhaps intrinsic to the occult and recondite nature of the Ark of
the Covenant that it would *always* generate questions, con-
fusions, ambiguities and misgivings. An object so rare and
precious, imbued with such power, venerated with such fervour
over so many centuries – and charged with the numinous energy
of God – could hardly be expected to yield up its secrets easily or
to any casual inquirer.

I felt, however, that the evidence I had already unearthed in
support of Ethiopia's claim to be the last resting place of the relic
was sufficiently thought-provoking to merit further research.
Moreover, when I combined this evidence with the results of the
decoding exercise that I had just carried out on Wolfram's
Parzival, I found it difficult to resist the conclusion that two plus
two did indeed equal four.

In short, knowing what I knew now, it seemed to me hardly
surprising that the clandestine tradition of quest that I had
identified should have focussed on the Abyssinian highlands.
After all, for a group of knights whose very identity was bound up
with the mysteries of Solomon's Temple, no real historical relic

other than the Ark could possibly have served as a more fitting object of chivalric endeavour. By the same token, there was only one country in which such an endeavour might have been undertaken with any genuine hope of success – a country which had a living institution of Ark-worship, a Solomonic heritage, and a credible claim to possess the Ark itself.

I therefore believed I was right in my hypothesis that the Templars had launched a quest in Ethiopia in the late twelfth century and I believed that they had found the precious relic which Wolfram had described as 'the consummation of heart's desire'.[80] As I shall recount in the next chapter, however, I also believed that they had lost it again – that it had been wrested from them and that they had been obliged to quit Ethiopia without it.

Why? Because a very few intrepid men continued to travel to Ethiopia in search of the Ark long after the utter destruction of the Knights of the Temple of Solomon in the fourteenth century. Furthermore, though they travelled at different periods, and were born in different lands, all these later adventurers were directly linked to the Templars and had inherited their traditions.

Chapter 7

A Secret and
Never-Ending Quest

From the first to the sixth century AD the empire centred on the city of Axum in northern Ethiopia could rightly claim to rank amongst the most powerful and prosperous in the known world. It dealt on equal terms with Rome and Persia and sent its navies sailing to ports as far afield as Egypt, India, Ceylon and China. Its architectural and artistic achievements were impressive and it became the first bastion of Christianity in sub-Saharan Africa, adopting the new faith as its official religion in the early fourth century AD (coincidentally at much the same time as the miraculous conversion of Constantine the Great).[1]

By the seventh century, however, Axum's light had begun to dim; the embassies that it sent abroad were now few and far between and its once formidable military power was clearly in decline. This marked change, which eventually led to total isolation, had much to do with the advance of the belligerent forces of Islam and the encirclement of Abyssinian Christianity during and after the lifetime of the Prophet Muhammad (AD 570–632). 'Encompassed by the enemies of their religion,' wrote Edward Gibbon in his *Decline and Fall of the Roman Empire*, 'the Ethiopians slept for near a thousand years, forgetful of the world by whom they were forgotten.'[2]

The millennium to which the great English historian referred lasted from roughly the seventh to the sixteenth centuries, during which time it would be fair to say that Ethiopia all but disappeared from world consciousness. Formerly well known to outsiders, and relatively well travelled, this Christian country in the remote highlands of Africa was gradually transformed into a mysterious realm of myth and magic in which dragons and other monsters were believed to dwell – a *terra incognita* where no one dared (or wanted) to venture.

It would have been tempting to assume that the Abyssinians had reverted to barbarism or stagnated during the long, dark hole in their history. My researches had shown me, however, that the opposite was true: as the extraordinary rock-hewn churches of Lalibela proved, a rich and idiosyncratic culture had been preserved throughout. Moreover, although this culture was introverted and suspicious of the motives of foreign powers, it *had* stayed in contact with the outside world. Prince Lalibela himself had spent twenty-five years as an exile in Jerusalem in the second half of the twelfth century. And it had been from Jerusalem that he had returned to Ethiopia to claim his kingdom and to build the monolithic churches that now bear his name.

As outlined in Chapter 5, my findings had convinced me of the possibility that Lalibela might have been accompanied by a contingent of Templars when he left the Holy Land in 1185 to win back his throne. These knights, I believed, would have been motivated first and foremost by a desire to seek out the Ark of the Covenant in Ethiopia. In furtherance of this end it seemed logical to suppose that they would have been more than willing to assist the prince to achieve his own political objectives – since by so doing they might reasonably have expected to gain great influence.

The reader will recall that I then learned of an Ethiopian tradition which told of the involvement of mysterious 'white men' in the construction of the Lalibela churches. This tradition was an ancient one. Indeed, it had already been very old when it had first been recorded in the early sixteenth century by a Portuguese visitor, Father Francisco Alvarez. I knew that the Templars had been great builders and architects,[3] and it was therefore difficult to resist the conclusion that they might have been the 'white men' who had had a hand in the creation of the rock-hewn monoliths. Furthermore, since the churches were twenty-four years in the making, the implication was that the knights had – at the very least – had a sustained presence in Ethiopia and perhaps had entertained plans for an even longer-term involvement in the affairs of that country.

The suspicion that this might indeed have been the case

deepened as my research continued. In order to explain why, it is first of all necessary to acquaint the reader with what happened to the Templars during and immediately after the brutal suppression of the order in the early fourteenth century. It is also necessary to cross-reference this information with certain events that took place in Ethiopia at around the same time.

A period involved in darkness

Founded in the year 1119, and given official recognition by the church in 1128 at the Synod of Troyes, the Templars quickly rose to a position of great international power, wealth and prestige – a position from which they were nevertheless doomed to fall within two centuries. The history of the order's catastrophic collapse has been too frequently and thoroughly recounted elsewhere to require extensive repetition here.[4] Suffice it to say that quite suddenly, on Friday 13 October 1307, all Templars residing in France were arrested. This was a well co-ordinated operation that saw simultaneous dawn swoops on hundreds of Templar properties by the bailiffs and seneschals of the French king, Philip IV. By nightfall 15,000 men were in chains and Friday the 13th had won a unique place for itself in the popular imagination as the most unlucky and inauspicious date in the calendar.

The charges levelled against the Templars to justify their dramatic and humiliating arrests were as lurid as they were imaginative. They were accused, for example, of denying Christ and spitting on His image, and of giving each other indecent kisses 'in shame of human dignity, according to the profane rite of the order' (these kisses were said to be placed on the anus, navel and mouth of each initiate at the time of his induction). It was also alleged that they engaged in a wide range of other homosexual practices (which were 'required without the possibility of refusal'), and – last but not least – that they made offerings to idols.[5]

At this time (and until 1377) the official residence of the Papacy was the city of Avignon in Provence. The reasons for the abandonment of the Vatican need not be gone into here.[6] Obviously, however, the removal of the Holy See to a point so close to French territory gave King Philip great influence over the Pope (Clement V who had been crowned at Lyons in Philip's presence in 1305[7]). This influence was exercised to the detriment of the Templars, whose destruction Philip was determined to ensure not only in France but also in every other country in which they were established. To this end the French monarch put pressure on Clement V who in due course issued a bull (*Pastoralis praeeminentiae*, dated 22 November 1307) which ordered the arrest of the Templars throughout the Christian world.[8]

Proceedings followed as far afield as England, Spain, Germany, Italy and Cyprus and, in 1312, another bull from the puppet Pope officially suppressed the order. Meanwhile thousands of Templars had been subjected to the most horrific tortures and inquisitions. Many were subsequently burned at the stake – including Grand Master Jacques de Molay and the Preceptor of Normandy, Geoffroi de Charnay.[9]

It is not my intention here to go in any depth into the persecution, trial and destruction of the Templars. I only became interested in these matters because of the evidence I had unearthed which suggested a possible Templar quest for the Ark in Ethiopia in the late twelfth century. Having established that a group of knights could have accompanied Lalibela from Jerusalem in the year 1185 I naturally wondered what might have happened next – and this curiosity led me to look for clues in the subsequent history of the Templar Order.

That history, of course, was rather short: less than 130 years after Lalibela's accession to the throne of Ethiopia the Templars had been rounded up, tortured, and burnt at the stake. Their properties and money had been shared out amongst the ruling houses of Europe; their order had ceased to exist; and their good name had been tainted by charges of sodomy, blasphemy and idolatry.

Nor, in the records of the last century of their existence, could I find a single shred of evidence to support the view of a sustained Templar quest in Ethiopia. After the early 1200s the trail simply went cold; from then until the arrests in 1307 the order seemed to have been concerned solely with its campaigns in the Near East and with the build-up of its own considerable power and wealth.

Where else, I wondered, might I find the information I was looking for? Few attempts had been made to chronicle developments in Ethiopia in the period that now concerned me. I knew, however, that James Bruce had done his utmost to gather and record ancient traditions during his lengthy visit in the eighteenth century. I therefore turned to his *Travels* – which I now kept constantly on my desk.

Towards the end of Volume I, as I had hoped, I came across several pages devoted to the reign of King Lalibela. Unfortunately much of what the Scottish adventurer had written was irrelevant to my own investigation. There was, however, one particular detail that attracted my attention. Drawing on 'the histories and traditions ... thought the most authentic' in Ethiopia,[10] Bruce reported that Lalibela had promoted a scheme to reduce the downstream flow of water into the Nile river system in order 'to famish Egypt'.[11] After 'an exact survey and calculation', it seemed this illustrious monarch of the Zagwe dynasty had ascertained:

> that there ran on the summit, or highest part [of
> Ethiopia], several rivers which could be intercepted by
> mines, and their stream directed into the low country
> southward, instead of joining the Nile, augmenting it and
> running northward. By this he found he should be able so
> to disappoint its increase, that it never would rise to a
> height proper to fit Egypt for cultivation.[12]

Such a project, I could not help but think, would certainly have suited Templar ambitions which, by the end of Lalibela's reign (AD 1211), had begun to focus on the conquest of Egypt. Several extensive battles were fought at this time on the banks of the Nile, and the Templars spent more than a year besieging the Arab fortress at Damietta in the delta.[13] There could be no doubt, therefore, that a 'famished' and weakened Egypt would have been very much to their liking.

In the event, however, the diversion of the rivers was never completed: 'Death, the ordinary enemy of all these stupendous undertakings, interposed here and put a stop to this enterprise of

Lalibela.'[14] Bruce then added a comment on the last two monarchs of the Zagwe dynasty:

> To Lalibela succeeded Imrahana Christos, remarkable for nothing but being son of such a father as Lalibela, and father to such a son as Naakuto Laab; both of them distinguished for works very extraordinary, though very different in their kind. The first, that is those of the father, we have already hinted at, consisting in great mechanical undertakings. The other was an operation of the mind, of still more difficult nature, a victory over ambition, the voluntary abdication of a crown.[15]

I was already familiar with the historical details that followed. In 1270, Naakuto Laab – the last of the Zagwes – was persuaded to abdicate his throne in favour of a certain Yekuno Amlak, a monarch claiming Solomonic descent. This king, as the reader may recall, had been biding his time in the distant province of Shoa where the Solomonic line had been preserved by the descendants of the single royal prince who had escaped the uprising of the Jewish queen Gudit in the tenth century.[16]

Bruce had little or nothing to say about Yekuno Amlak himself, or about his immediate successors, Yagba Zion (1285–94) and Wedem Ara'ad (who ruled until the year 1314). Indeed, it seemed that the normally fastidious research methods favoured by the Scottish traveller had failed to yield any solid information at all for the century that followed Lalibela's death in AD 1211: 'All this period is involved in darkness,' Bruce complained. 'We might guess, but since we are not able to do more, it answers no good purpose to do so much.'[17]

Similar darkness, as I already knew, also enshrouded the period *before* Lalibela's accession to the throne. I was therefore left with a host of unanswered questions. Of these by far the most important concerned the Ark of the Covenant: I needed to know what had happened to it during the roughly 300 years (from the tenth to the thirteenth century) in which the rule of the Solomonic dynasty had been interrupted. And I needed to know whether the Templars might have gained direct access to the sacred relic if, as I supposed, they had established themselves in Ethiopia during Lalibela's reign.

Once again I telephoned the historian Belai Gedai in Addis Ababa to see if he could enlighten me with his knowledge of local traditions.

'In the tenth century', he told me, 'we Ethiopians say that the Ark was removed from Axum by the priests and the people in order to keep it safe from the ravages of Queen Gudit, and we say that it was brought to an island on Lake Zwai . . .'

'You mean in the Rift Valley – south of Addis Ababa?'

'Yes.'

'That was a hell of a long way for it to be moved.'

'Yes, but no lesser distance would have been safe. Gudit was Jewish, you know. She wanted to establish the Falasha religion all over the country and she wanted to destroy Christianity. She came to burn and rob the churches at Axum. So the priests carried off the Ark to prevent it from falling into her hands, and they brought it very far – all the way to Zwai! – where they were sure that it would be out of her reach.'

'Do you know how long it remained on the island?'

'Our traditions say that it was there for seventy years and that after that it was taken back to Axum.'

I thanked Gedai for his help and rang off. What he had told me fitted – more or less – with the picture of Ethiopian medieval history that I had thus far managed to piece together. I knew that the throne of Ethiopia had been held by Gudit for some years after she had deposed the Solomonids. I also knew that she had eventually been succeeded by the first monarch of the Zagwe dynasty, himself probably a Jew.

Later, however (and certainly well before Lalibela's time), the Zagwes had converted to Christianity. It therefore seemed quite possible that they might have permitted the safe return of the Ark to its customary resting place in Axum – where, presumably, it would still have been when Lalibela came to power.

Of obvious relevance to this argument was the eyewitness account of the Ark in Ethiopia given by the Armenian geographer Abu Salih in his *Churches and Monasteries of Egypt and some Neighbouring Countries*. From internal textual evidence (the translator and editor of this important work explained in his

Introduction), it was clear that it had been written 'in the first years of the thirteenth century'[18] – in other words during the reign of Lalibela himself. And although Abu Salih at no point stated in *which* Ethiopian city he had seen the sacred relic, there was no good reason to suppose that this city had not been Axum. Moreover, as I re-read the relevant passage, I was struck by a few words that I had overlooked before. Describing the transportation of the Ark on certain ceremonial occasions, the geographer had noted that it was 'attended and carried' by bearers who were *'white and red in complexion, with red hair'.*[19]

With a shock of genuine excitement I realized that I was looking at a second piece of pure and early testimony suggesting the presence of mysterious white men in Ethiopia at the time of King Lalibela (particularly so since another authoritative translation of the same passage rendered 'red hair' as 'blond hair'[20]). Alvarez had already alerted me to the old tradition that white men had built the wonderful rock-hewn churches – a tradition that fitted well with what I knew about the advanced architectural skills possessed by the Templars. Now, as though to bear out my own evolving theory, here was Abu Salih addressing me across seven centuries with the electrifying news that men who were white and red in complexion, men with red or even blond hair – men, in other words, who sounded very much like northern Europeans – had been associated closely and directly with the Ark of the Covenant itself.

The possibility that these men might have been Templars was a very seductive one, but it still left my investigation stranded in the early thirteenth century and it still left the key questions unanswered. If the northern Europeans seen by Abu Salih had indeed been Templars then had they just contented themselves with carrying the relic from time to time or had they perhaps tried to remove it from Ethiopia and take it back to Europe? Most important of all – if they had tried, had they succeeded?

On all these points, I had to admit, I was effectively blocked by the absolute lack of historical information. Obsessively secretive as the Templars had undoubtedly been,[21] it did not really surprise me that their own documents and records yielded so little. Nor was there any comfort to be gained from Ethiopian annals: after examining a wide range of different sources, I was forced to accept that the century after the death of King Lalibela had indeed been a period 'involved in darkness', just as James Bruce had observed. Almost nothing was known about what had gone on in these years.

I was by now feeling extremely pessimistic about the prospects of ever breaking the research deadlock. Nevertheless I telephoned Richard Pankhurst in Addis Ababa and asked him if there were *any* records which might suggest that there had been contacts of any kind between Ethiopians and Europeans during the period in question.

'None that I know of before 1300,' he replied.

'And how about after 1300? I suppose the first documented European contact was with the Portuguese embassy that arrived in Ethiopia in 1520?'

'Not quite. A small number of missions travelled in the other direction before that – I mean from Ethiopia to Europe. As it happens, the very first of these *was* sent within a century of Lalibela's death – so that does put it into the period you're interested in.'

I sat forward in my chair: 'Do you happen to know the exact date?'

'Yes, I do,' Richard replied. 'It was 1306, and it was quite a large mission. It was sent by the Emperor Wedem Ara'ad and it had, I believe, about thirty members.'

'Do you remember what the purpose of this mission was?'

'I'm not absolutely certain. You would have to check the source. But I do know that its destination was Avignon in the south of France.'

A final solution?

Richard did not realize it, but he had just dropped a small bombshell. Avignon had been the seat of Pope Clement V – who had been crowned at Lyons in 1305 in the presence of King Philip of France. Moreover, as I was already well aware, it had been Clement V who had ordered the arrest of the Templars throughout Christendom in 1307. Now I had learned that a high-level Ethiopian delegation (the first ever to be sent to Europe) had visited Avignon in 1306 – just a year before the arrests. Were these dates and events clustered together by coincidence? Or was there, perhaps, some underlying pattern of cause and effect? To get answers to these questions I would have to try to establish whether the Abyssinian envoys had in fact met with the Pope during their visit and, if they had, I would also have to try to learn what had passed between them.

The original source of information on the 1306 mission had been a Genoese cartographer, Giovanni da Carignano, who had been active in map-making during the years 1291–1329.[22] I was intrigued to discover that this same Carignano had been responsible for a major shift in European ideas about Ethiopia: after centuries of confusion (see discussion in Chapter 4) he had been the first authority to affirm unambiguously that 'Prester John' ruled in Africa rather than in 'India'.[23]

Carignano had met with the members of the Ethiopian embassy when they had passed through Genoa in 1306 on their way back from Avignon to their homeland. Because of adverse winds they had spent 'many days' in the Italian port and there the cartographer had questioned them about 'their rites, customs and regions'. [24]

Regrettably, however, Carignano's treatise containing all the information that the Ethiopians had given him had subsequently been lost. All that remained of it today was a brief abstract preserved in a Bergamese chronicle of the late fifteenth century written by a certain Jacopo Filippo Foresti.[25]

I finally managed to get my hands on an English translation of the abstract in question. It consisted of only a single paragraph in which Foresti praised and then summarized Carignano's treatise:

> Amongst many things written in it about the state of [the Ethiopians] . . . it is said that their emperor is most Christian, to whom seventy-four kings and almost innumerable princes pay allegiance . . . It is known that this emperor in the . . . year of our salvation 1306 sent thirty envoys [who] . . . presented themselves reverentially before Pope Clement V at Avignon.[26]

And that – apart from a few frills and the 'Prester John' reference already mentioned – was all that was known about the first-ever Ethiopian mission to Europe. Skimpy though the data was, however, it did confirm my suspicion that the envoys had met with Pope Clement V[27] – and that they had done so just a year before he authorized the mass arrests of the Knights Templar.

No information was given concerning the substance of the meeting; nor was there the slightest hint as to *why* the Emperor of Ethiopia should have been so anxious to make contact with Pope Clement V in the year 1306. It seemed to me improbable, however, that Wedem Ara'ad would have sent so large an embassy on such a long and unprecedented mission if he had not had a very strong motive indeed. I now felt at liberty to speculate about what that motive might have been.

Opening my notebook I jotted down the following series of propositions, conjectures and hypotheses:

Assume for the moment that the Templars did go from Jerusalem to Ethiopia with Prince Lalibela in 1185 – and that they did help to install him on his throne. Assume that the 'white men' said to have built the Lalibela churches were in fact Templars. Assume also that the 'white men' seen acting as bearers for the Ark of the Covenant in Ethiopia in the early 1200s were these same Templars.

The implication is that the order had succeeded in winning a position of power, trust and influence with Lalibela, and with the Zagwe dynasty to which he belonged. If so then it would be reasonable to assume that the last two Zagwe monarchs (Imrahana Christos and Naakuto Laab) would also have had a good relationship with the Templars – whom they might have continued to grant privileged access to the Ark.

Assume that this was what happened and that during the six decades after Lalibela's death in 1211 the Templars were allowed to approach the sacred relic but not, of course, to take it out of Ethiopia. Perhaps they *planned* to take it but were simply biding their time until a favourable opportunity presented itself. Meanwhile, as the knights who had originally come to Ethiopia grew old the order would have sent out others from the Holy Land to replace them. There would have been no particular sense of urgency; indeed they might have been quite content for the Ark to stay in Ethiopia.

This state of affairs would have changed dramatically in 1270, however, when (for whatever reasons) Naakuto Laab was persuaded to abdicate his throne and was replaced by Yekuno Amlak – a monarch claiming Solomonic descent. Unlike the Zagwes, the very identity of the Solomonids was irrevocably bound up with the Ark of the Covenant and with the notion that Menelik I – the founder of their dynasty – had brought it from Jerusalem during the reign of King Solomon himself. In this context it is worth remembering that the first *written* version of the *Kebra Nagast* was prepared on the orders of Yekuno Amlak.[28] In other words, although the legend was by then already very old in oral form,[29] Yekuno Amlak wanted it formalized. Why? Because it served to legitimize and glorify his title to the throne.

From this it follows that Yekuno Amlak would have been horrified by the presence in his country of a body of armed, militant (and technologically advanced) foreigners like the Templars: foreigners who could call on reinforcements from amongst the thousands of other members of their order in the Near East; foreigners who clearly had a special interest in the Ark and who were possibly plotting to steal away with it.

Assume, however, that Yekuno Amlak (new to the throne and still insecure) initially tried to placate these powerful and dangerous white men, perhaps by giving them the false impression that he was willing to co-operate with them in much the same way as the Zagwes had done. That would have been a logical strategy – particularly since it is known that his army was very small[30] – and would explain why nothing spectacular happened during his reign. It would therefore have been up to his successors to seek a final solution to the problem of how to get rid of the Templars and retain the Ark.

Yekuno Amlak's son (Yagba Zion, 1285–94) was, if anything, even weaker than his father in military terms.

Yagba Zion, however, was succeeded by a much stronger character, Wedem Ara'ad, who reigned until 1314. Significantly it was Wedem Ara'ad who sent a large embassy to Pope Clement V at Avignon in 1306.

Is it not possible that the purpose of that embassy was to stir up trouble for the Templars – and perhaps to give the Pope and the French king (Philip IV) an urgent motive to destroy the order? Such a motive could have been provided by the suggestion that the knights were planning to bring the Ark of the Covenant to France. After all, this was a period when deep superstitions ruled the popular imagination. With so sacred and so powerful a relic in their hands the Templars would have been in a unique position to challenge both the secular and religious authorities of the land – and those authorities would certainly have taken any steps they could to prevent such an eventuality.

This theory begins to look particularly attractive when set against the backdrop of the arrests of the Templars in France and elsewhere. All these arrests took place in 1307 – i.e. about a year after the departure of the Ethiopian mission from Avignon. This fits perfectly with what is known about the behaviour of King Philip IV: there is evidence that he began to plan his operation against the Templars about a year in advance of its implementation[31] (i.e. in 1306) and there is also evidence that on several occasions during that year he discussed his plans with Pope Clement.[32]

It would of course be folly to imagine that the destruction of the Templars was occasioned *only* by the lobbying of the Ethiopian envoys. Malice and greed on the part of Philip IV also played a role (the former because the king had several times been snubbed by the order; the latter because he undoubtedly had his eyes on the huge sums of money resting in Templar treasuries throughout his realm).

By the same token, however, it would be folly to imagine that the Ethiopian mission to Avignon in 1306 had *nothing* to do with the events of 1307. On the contrary it is more than probable that there was a link – and that link, I am convinced, was the Ark of the Covenant.

Portuguese and Scottish connections

The Templars were a rich and powerful international brother-hood of religious warriors. As such, despite the best efforts of King Philip IV and Pope Clement V, they did not prove easy to destroy. The suppression was most effectively and completely implemented in France; even there, however, some brothers managed to evade capture[33] (as did the entire Templar fleet which slipped out of the Atlantic port of La Rochelle on the morning of the arrests and was never seen again[34]).

In other countries the trials and inquisitions were pursued with much less vigour than in France; nevertheless, tortures, imprisonments, executions, confiscation of property and the final dissolution of the order were the end result in England (after some considerable delay), in Spain, in Italy, in Germany, in Cyprus and elsewhere.[35]

In Portugal and Scotland, however, the Templars appear to have escaped persecution almost completely. Indeed, circum-stances were so favourable in these countries that, under different disguises, the order managed to live on in both of them.

At the time when Pope Clement V issued his bull ordering the arrests of the Templars throughout Christendom – November 1307 – Scotland was locked in a fierce struggle to preserve its national independence against the colonial aspirations of England. Leading this struggle was the most famous of all Scots monarchs – King Robert the Bruce who, at the battle of Bannockburn in 1314, was to inflict such a crushing defeat upon the English that his country's freedom was guaranteed for centuries afterwards. With all his energies focussed on the war, Bruce had no interest whatsoever in pursuing the papal vendetta against the Templars. He therefore only went through the motions of suppressing them: just two knights were arrested[36] and the most that appears to have been required of the remainder was that they should keep a low profile.

There was method in the Scottish king's behaviour: all the evidence suggests that he granted safe haven not only to local Templars but also to members of the order fleeing persecution in other lands.[37] Not naturally altruistic, it seems that he adopted this generous policy in order to encourage fugitive knights to join his army.[38] It has, furthermore, been cogently argued that a Templar contingent *did* fight on Bruce's side at Bannockburn[39] – a suggestion that looks worthy of further research when it is remembered that the victorious Scots marched behind a tiny Ark-shaped reliquary at that famous battle.[40]

The favour that Bruce showed towards the Templars in Scotland, and the fact that many knights escaped arrest in England (because of a delay in implementing the papal bull there), made it possible for the order to go underground in the British Isles – in other words to survive in a secret and hidden form rather than to be completely destroyed. For hundreds of years it has been rumoured that this secret survival took the form of Freemasonry[41] – a view supported by a specific Masonic tradition that the oldest Scottish lodge (Kilwinning) was founded by King Robert the Bruce after the battle of Bannockburn 'for the reception of those Knights Templar who had fled from France'.[42] In the eighteenth century Andrew Ramsay, a prominent Scots Mason and historian, added credibility to this tradition with a considerable body of work on the connections between Freemasonry and the Templars.[43] And at around the same time Baron Carl von Hund, a leading German Mason, declared that 'Freemasonry originated in Knight Templary, and that, in consequence, every Mason is a Templar.'[44]

That such forthright statements should have been made in the eighteenth century (rather than in any earlier century) is not surprising: this was the period in which Freemasons finally 'came out of the closet' and began to talk about themselves and about their history.[45] Subsequently, as the new spirit of openness encouraged further research, it became clear that 'Knight Templarism' was and always had been an important force within the Masonic system.[46] This research, together with much other material not previously uncovered, has recently been incorporated into a detailed and authoritative study which itemizes the many ways in which Freemasonry was shaped and influenced by fugitive Templars.[47]

It is not my intention here to participate at all in what is undoubtedly a heated, convoluted and highly specialized debate. The point I wish to make is simply that the Masonic system did inherit many of the most central traditions of the Order of the

Temple of Solomon, and that this inheritance was first passed on in the British Isles in the years 1307–14 by Templars who had survived papal persecution because of the specially favourable conditions then prevailing in Scotland.

Nor, as I have already noted, was Scotland the only country in which the Templars were left unscathed. In Portugal they were tried but found to be free of guilt, and thus neither tortured nor imprisoned.[48] Of course, as a good Catholic, the Portuguese monarch (Dennis I) could not afford to ignore papal instructions completely: accordingly lip service was paid to these instructions and the Templars were officially dissolved in 1312. Just six years later, however, they were reborn under a new name: the Militia of Jesus Christ (also known as the Knights of Christ or, more simply, as the Order of Christ).[49]

This transformation of one order into another enabled the Portuguese Templars not only to survive the fires of the Inquisition during the years 1307 to 1314 but also to emerge phoenix-like from the ashes in 1318 – after which date they seem to have carried on with business very much as usual. All Templar properties and funds in Portugal were transferred intact to the Order of Christ, as were all personnel.[50] Moreover, on 14 March 1319, the newly formed entity received the approval and confirmation of Pope John XXII (Clement meanwhile having died).[51]

In summary, therefore, despite the harshness of the suppression in France and elsewhere, the Portuguese Order of Christ, and British (and especially Scottish) Freemasonry, were the means by which Templar traditions were preserved and carried forward into the distant future – perhaps right up to modern times.

As my research continued I was to become increasingly sure that one of the traditions thus perpetuated was the quest for the Ark of the Covenant.

'After battle like wolves and after slaughter like lions . . .'

Even if my theory about the Templars in Ethiopia was correct, I knew that there was no way that I could establish what might have happened to them in that country after the persecutions began in

Europe in 1307. Historical records from the reign of Wedem Ara'ad were virtually non-existent. After sending his mission to Avignon, however, my guess was that he would have stayed in touch with developments and would have been informed of the order's destruction. Secure in the knowledge that no further knights could now be sent to vex him, the Emperor would then have moved against those Templars who remained in Ethiopia and either expelled them or wiped them out – most probably the latter.

That, at any rate, was my working hypothesis, and probably I would have thought no more about this aspect of my investigation if I had not learnt about the 'Portuguese connection' represented by the Order of Christ. You see, with just two unimportant exceptions,[52] *all* the known early visitors to Ethiopia were Portuguese. Moreover, this Portuguese interest in the realm of 'Prester John' was already pronounced within a century of the destruction of the Templars and was, from the beginning, spearheaded by members of the Order of Christ.

In this endeavour, the first and most active figure on whom any solid information is available was Prince Henry the Navigator, Grand Master of the Order of Christ and a man described by his biographer as possessing 'strength of heart and keenness of mind to a very excellent degree . . . [who] was, beyond comparison, ambitious of achieving great and lofty deeds.'[53]

Born in 1394, and actively involved in seafaring by 1415,[54] Henry's greatest ambition – as he himself declared – was that he would 'have knowledge of the land of Prester John'.[55] Chroniclers who were his contemporaries, as well as modern historians, are in full agreement that he devoted the greater part of his illustrious career to the pursuit of precisely this goal.[56] Yet an atmosphere of mystery and intrigue surrounds all his efforts. As Edgar Prestage, the late Camoens Professor of Portuguese Language, Literature and History at the University of London, observed:

> Our knowledge of the Henrican voyages is inadequate, and this is largely due to the adoption of a policy of secrecy which included the suppression of facts . . . historical works . . . nautical guides, maps, instructions to navigators and their reports.[57]

Indeed, so great was the commitment to secrecy in Henry's time that the release of information on the results of the various exploratory voyages that were undertaken was punishable by death.[58] Despite this, however, it is known that the prince was obsessed with the notion of making direct contact with Ethiopia – and that he sought to achieve this end by circumnavigating Africa (since the shorter route through the Mediterranean and then into the Red Sea via Egypt was blocked by hostile Muslim forces[59]). Moreover, even before the Cape of Good Hope was rounded, the masters of Portuguese vessels venturing down the West African coast were instructed to enquire after 'Prester John' to see whether it might not be quicker to approach his kingdom overland.[60]

One can only speculate as to the true objective of the Portuguese prince. The common view is that he intended – as a 'good crusader'[61] – to forge an anti-Islamic alliance with the Christian Ethiopian emperor. Perhaps he did. Since all serious plans to win the Holy Land for Christendom had been abandoned more than a century before Henry was born, however, I found it difficult to resist the notion that he must have had some other motive – some hidden agenda, perhaps, that would have accounted both for his secrecy and for his fascination with Prester John.

As I studied the life of the great navigator further I became more and more certain that this motive was rooted and grounded in his identity as Grand Master of the Order of Christ, in which capacity he would have inherited all the mystical traditions of the Order of the Temple of Solomon. It is notable that he immersed himself in the study of mathematics and cosmography, 'the course of the heavens and astrology',[62] and that he was constantly surrounded by Jewish doctors and astronomers[63] –men in every way reminiscent of Wolfram's character Flegetanis who 'saw hidden secrets in the constellations [and] declared there was a thing called the Gral whose name he read in the stars without more ado.'[64]

Another factor which suggested to me that the Portuguese prince was profoundly influenced by Templar traditions was his celibacy. The Knights of Christ were not bound by such strict rules as their predecessors in the Order of the Temple.

Nevertheless, like the Templar Grand Masters before him, Henry 'would never marry, but preserved great chastity [and] remained a virgin till his death.'[65] Likewise, I could not help but wonder whether it was entirely a matter of coincidence that the illustrious navigator chose to make his last will and testament on 13 October 1460[66] – the 153rd anniversary of the arrests of the Templars in France (which took place on 13 October 1307).

Henry died in 1460, shortly after making his will, and it was not until the early years of the twentieth century that certain secret archives pertaining to the last decade of his life came to light. Amongst these archives (details of which were published by Dr Jaime Cortezao in 1924 in the review *Lusitania*[67]) a brief note was found to the effect that 'an ambassador of Prester John visited Lisbon eight years before Henry's death'.[68] It is not known what the purpose of this mission was, or what the prince and the Ethiopian envoy discussed. Nevertheless, two years after their meeting it can hardly have been accidental that King Alfonso V of Portugal granted spiritual jurisdiction over Ethiopia to the Order of Christ.[69] 'We are', admits Professor Prestage, 'still ignorant of the motives that led to this concession.'[70]

In the year that Henry the Navigator died – 1460 – a fitting successor was born at Sines, a seaport in the south of Portugal. That successor, also a Knight of the Order of Christ,[71] was Vasco da Gama, who was to open up the Cape route to India in 1497.

It is notable that when he set off on this famous voyage da Gama was carrying two things: a white silk banner with the double red cross of the Order of Christ embroidered upon it; and letters of credence for delivery to Prester John.[72] Moreover, although his ultimate destination was indeed India, the Portuguese admiral devoted a considerable part of the expedition to African exploration and is reported to have wept for joy when, at anchor off Mozambique, he was rightly told that Prester John lived in the interior far to the north.[73] It was also claimed by the same informants that the Ethiopian emperor 'held many cities along the coast'.[74] This claim was incorrect, but da Gama's subsequent stop-overs at Malindi, Mombasa, Brava (where he built a lighthouse that still stands) and Mogadishu were in part motivated by his continuing desire to make contact with Prester John.[75]

Meanwhile, in 1487 – a decade before da Gama set off – the Order of Christ had sponsored a different initiative also aimed at reaching Ethiopia. In that year King John II of Portugal, then Grand Master of the Order, had sent his trusted aide Pero de Covilhan on a perilous journey to the court of Prester John via the Mediterranean, Egypt and the Red Sea. Disguised as a merchant, Covilhan passed through Alexandria and Cairo to Suakin and there, in 1488, he took ship in a small Arab barque for the Yemeni port of Aden. He then became caught up in various adventures which delayed him considerably. As a result it was not until 1493 that he finally succeeded in entering Abyssinia.[76] Once there, however, he made his way immediately to the emperor's court where he was first welcomed but later placed under comfortable house arrest. One can only speculate as to why this happened, but since it is known that Covilhan's greatest skill was as a spy (he had previously worked as a secret agent in Spain[77]) it is difficult to resist the notion that the Order of Christ may have commissioned him to gather intelligence on the whereabouts of the Ark of the Covenant. Perhaps he aroused suspicion by making enquiries about the sacred relic; perhaps not. At any rate he was detained in Ethiopia for the rest of his life.[78]

Covilhan was still alive when the first official Portuguese embassy to the court of Prester John landed at the port of Massawa in 1520 and made its way inland to meet with Lebna Dengel, the Solomonic emperor who had been on the throne since 1508. One of the members of this embassy was Father Francisco Alvarez – and the reader will recall that it was Alvarez who had been told by priests of the ancient tradition that the rock-hewn churches of Lalibela had been 'made by white men'.[79]

I now turned back to the English translation of the lengthy narrative that Alvarez had written after leaving Ethiopia in 1526. Re-reading his chapter on Lalibela I was struck by the description he gave of the church of Saint George. Carved into the roof of this great edifice, he said, was 'a double cross, that is, one within the other, like the crosses of the Order of Christ.'[80]

Of course, as I already knew, the Lalibela churches had been hewn in the time of the Templars, long before the Order of

Christ was created to follow in their footsteps. It seemed logical to suppose, however, that the cross of the Order of Christ was derived from a design that would have been significant to the Templars. It was therefore intriguing to learn that this design had been used on Saint George's – undoubtedly the finest church in the Lalibela complex. Casting my mind back to my own visit there in 1983, I could not recall the double cross motif. I was sufficiently interested, however, to look out the photographs that had been taken on that trip; these confirmed that the description that Alvarez had given of Saint George's was absolutely correct: the double cross was there.

In the mid-1520s, while the Portuguese embassy was still at the court of Lebna Dengel, it became clear that Ethiopia would soon come under attack from Muslim forces massing in the emirate of Harar in the eastern part of the Horn of Africa. These forces were led by a redoubtable and charismatic warlord, Ahmed Ibn Ibrahim el Ghazi, whose nickname was 'Gragn' (meaning 'the left-handed').

After some years of careful preparations, Gragn eventually declared his holy war in 1528 and led hordes of wild Somali troops (supported by Arab mercenaries and Turkish matchlock-men) on a rampage into the Christian highlands.[81] This turned out to be no brief campaign but rather continued, year in year out, without any remit. Across the length and breadth of Ethiopia towns and villages were burnt, churches were destroyed, price-less treasures were looted, and thousands of people were put to the sword.[82]

Lebna Dengel had been somewhat cool towards the Portuguese. During the six years that their embassy had been in his country (1520–6) he had constantly stressed his own self-sufficiency, saying, in spite of the Muslim threat (which was very apparent by 1526), that he saw no point in hastening into an alliance with any foreign power.[83] This strangely aloof attitude, I believe, could have been occasioned by concerns as to the true motives of the European visitors – particularly as regards the Ark of the Covenant.

Whatever fears the emperor may have entertained, however, it gradually became apparent to him that Gragn posed a far greater threat than the white men ever would – and not only to the sacred relic but also to the very existence of Ethiopian Christendom. In 1535 the Muslims attacked Axum and razed to the ground the ancient and most holy church of Saint Mary of Zion[84] (from which, as I shall recount later in this chapter, the priests had already taken the Ark to another place for safekeeping). In 1535, too –and not by coincidence – Lebna Dengel at last overcame his antipathy towards foreign alliances and sent an envoy to the king of Portugal with an urgent request for military assistance.[85]

Meanwhile communications between Ethiopia and Europe had become much more difficult (because the Turks had won control of much of the coast of the Horn of Africa as well as many of the Red Sea ports). It took a long while for the emperor's SOS to reach its destination and, in consequence, it was not until 1541 that a contingent of 450 Portuguese musketeers landed at Massawa to lend their support to the Abyssinian army – which appeared at that point to be utterly beaten and demoralized (Lebna Dengel, after years on the run, had died of exhaustion and had been succeeded by his son Claudius, then barely out of his teens).[86]

Since they were armed with matchlocks, hand-guns, and several pieces of heavy artillery, much hope was pinned upon the intervention of the Portuguese troops. The Ethiopian royal chronicle for 1541 speaks of the confident manner in which they marched up into the highlands from the coast, praising them as 'bold and courageous men who thirsted after battle like wolves and after slaughter like lions'.[87] Nor did this description overstate their qualities: though small in numbers they fought with inspiring valour and won a series of decisive victories. The British historian Edward Gibbon was later to summarize their achievements in just nine words: 'Ethiopia was saved by four hundred and fifty Portuguese.'[88]

Significantly in my opinion, the commander of the relief force was none other than Don Christopher da Gama, son of the famous Vasco and, like his father, a Knight of the Order of Christ.[89] James Bruce was inordinately interested in the character of this young adventurer and described him in the following terms:

He was brave to a fault; rash and vehement; jealous of

what he thought military honour; and obstinate in his
resolutions . . . [However], in a long catalogue of virtues
which he possessed to a very eminent degree, [he] had
not the smallest claim to that of patience, so very
necessary to those that command armies.[90]

I believe that, as a Knight of the Order of Christ, Don
Christopher may well have had an ulterior motive for his
operations in Ethiopia: first he would defeat the Muslims; later
he would seek out the Ark of the Covenant. His rashness and lack
of patience, however, were to cost him his life before either
objective could be achieved.

Despite overwhelming odds, he repeatedly engaged Ahmed
Gragn's forces in battle (on one occasion, deserted by the
Abyssinians, the Portuguese faced 10,000 spearmen – and beat
them). Such feats of derring-do, however, were loaded with risks
and, in 1542, Don Christopher was taken prisoner (an eyewitness described how, shortly before his capture, he 'had been
shot in the right knee and was fighting with his sword in his left
hand, for his right arm had been broken by another shot'[91]).

The Portuguese commander was first horribly tortured and
then, according to Bruce's account of his last hours, was

brought into the presence of the Moorish general Gragn,
who loaded him with reproaches; to which he replied with
such a share of invectives that the Moor, in the violence
of his passion, drew his sword and cut off his head with
his own hand.[92]

Barely a year later, however, the Muslim leader too was killed.
In a battle fought on the shores of Lake Tana on 10 February
1543 he was shot dead by a certain Peter Leon,

a man of low stature, but very active and valiant, who had
been *valet de chambre* to Don Christopher . . . The
Moorish army no sooner missed the presence of their
general than, concluding all lost, they fell into confusion
and were pursued by the Portuguese and Abyssinians
with a great slaughter till the evening.[93]

Thus, after fifteen years of unparalleled destruction and violence, ended the Muslim attempt to subdue the Christian empire of Ethiopia. The costs to the Portuguese relief force were considerable: as well as the redoubtable Don Christopher, more than half of the original contingent of 450 musketeers were killed in the fighting. Abyssinian casualties, of course, were far greater (running into tens of thousands) and the cultural damage – in terms of burnt manuscripts, icons and paintings, razed churches and looted treasures – was to cast a shadow over the civilization of the highlands for centuries to come.

The greatest treasure of all, however, was saved: moved out of Axum by the priests only days before that city was burnt in 1535, the Ark had been taken to one of the many island-monasteries on Lake Tana. There it was kept in safety until long after Gragn's death. Then, in the mid 1600s, Emperor Fasilidas (described by Bruce as 'the greatest king that ever sat upon the Abyssinian throne'[94]) built a new cathedral of Saint Mary of Zion over the gutted ruins of the old – and there, with due ceremony, the sacred relic was at last re-installed in all its former glory.[95]

Fasilidas did one other thing also. Despite the debt of gratitude that his country owed to the Portuguese (whose numbers had been allowed to increase steadily after the success-ful conclusion of the war with Gragn) he made it his business to throw all the settlers out. Indeed, he seemed so wary of their intentions that he entered into a business arrangement with the Turks at Massawa: any Portuguese travellers arriving there and seeking entry into Ethiopia were to be apprehended and decapitated – with a substantial sum in gold payable for each head thus obtained.[96]

The source of a mystery

After the death of Don Christopher da Gama the intense and focussed interest that the Order of Christ had shown in Ethiopia seemed to come to an end. And after the reign of Fasilidas there was no longer any way in which that interest could have been pursued by *any* Portuguese.

However, as noted earlier, the Order of Christ was not the only vehicle in which Templar traditions were perpetuated. Scottish

Freemasonry, too, inherited some portions of the mystical legacy of the Temple of Solomon – in which the Ark of the Covenant played such a central role. Because of this Scottish connection, and because he had claimed to be a distant descendant of the king who had welcomed the fugitive Templars in the fourteenth century,[97] I felt that a closer investigation was warranted into the activities of one of the most audacious and determined foreigners ever to visit Ethiopia: James Bruce of Kinnaird.

Standing rather more than six feet four inches tall, and with a girth to match, Bruce was a giant of a man ('the tallest man you ever saw *gratis*', as one contemporary described him). He was also wealthy and well educated. Born in 1730 in the lowlands of Scotland on the family estate at Kinnaird, he was sent at the age of twelve to Harrow school, where his work in the classical languages was considered excellent by his teachers. He later completed his studies at Edinburgh University.

A period of illness followed and when he recovered he went to London intending to take up a job offer with the East India Company. Once there, however, he fell passionately in love with a beautiful woman named Adriane Allan, whom he married in 1753. Soon afterwards he joined his father-in-law's wine-trading business as a partner.

Tragedy followed. On a trip to France in 1754 Adriane died suddenly and, though he remarried much later and fathered several children, Bruce seems to have taken a long time to recover from the loss of his first wife.

Restless and depressed, he began to travel almost continuously, learning new languages with great facility wherever he went. His peregrinations took him first to Europe, where he fought a duel in Belgium, sailed down the Rhine, inspected Roman ruins in Italy, and studied Arabic manuscripts in Spain and Portugal. Subsequently – after his linguistic ability had been recognized by his government – he was given a diplomatic posting as British consul in Algiers. From there he later travelled extensively along the North African coast, visiting the ruins of Carthage, before journeying onwards to the Holy Land where he explored several other ancient sites. He also found the time to return occasionally to Scotland to attend to the family estates of which he was now the laird, his father having died in 1758.

During this period the young Scotsman became something of an astronomer, acquiring two state-of-the art telescopes that subsequently went everywhere with him. He also picked up surveying and navigational skills that would be invaluable to him on his travels in Abyssinia.

It is not clear exactly when he conceived of this last adventure, but there is evidence that he had been planning it for a considerable while (it is known, for example, that he had begun to learn *Ge'ez*, the classical language of Ethiopia, as early as 1759[98]). Because of such preparations, which included detailed readings of the works of all previous travellers, he had accumulated a great deal of background knowledge about the country by the time that he arrived in Cairo in 1768 to begin his epic journey.

What was it that inspired Bruce to go to Ethiopia? His own account of his motives is unambiguous: he went, he said, risking 'numberless dangers and sufferings, the least of which would have overwhelmed me but for the continual goodness and protection of Providence', in order to discover the source of the Nile.[99] Lest anyone should be in any doubt that this was indeed his ambition he enshrined it conspicuously in the full title of the immense book that he later wrote: *Travels to Discover the Source of the Nile in the Years 1768, 1769, 1770, 1771, 1772 and 1773.*

There is a mystery here, however, which has attracted the attention of more than one historian (though no solution has ever been proposed to it).[100] The mystery is this: long before he set out for Ethiopia, James Bruce *knew* that the Blue Nile's source had already been visited and thoroughly explored by two other Europeans: Pedro Paez and Jeronimo Lobo (both of whom were Portuguese priests who had lived in Ethiopia in the 1600s before the Fasilidas ban was put into effect).

As my research into the Ark of the Covenant progressed during 1989, the mystery of Bruce's objectives came to engage my attention more and more. The five hefty volumes of his *Travels* had become essential reference works for me because they provided a unique picture of Ethiopian culture at a time when that culture was still not too far separated from its own archaic origins. Moreover, I knew the Scottish adventurer to have been a considerable scholar, and I was impressed from the outset by the solid accuracy of his observations and by the general worth of his judgments and opinions on matters of history. I also regarded him as an honest man, not overly prone to hyperbole, exaggeration or misrepresentation. How then, I had to ask myself – since it was clear from many of his own comments that he had carefully read the works of both Paez and Lobo[101] – could I account for the fact that he had failed to give them credit for their achievements?[102] Since I fully agreed with the subsequent judgment of history (namely that 'Bruce, far from being a romancer, was a most reliable guide'[103]) I found myself increasingly puzzled by his obvious dishonesty over this crucially important issue – a dishonesty which he compounded with the bald assertion that 'none of the Portuguese . . . ever saw, or indeed pretended to have seen, the source of the Nile'.[104]

I was soon to discover that this was not the only matter about which Bruce had lied. On the subject of the Ark of the Covenant he was even more evasive and deceitful. Describing his own visit to the sacred city of Axum, he commented on the destruction by Ahmed Gragn of the first church of Saint Mary of Zion and added – correctly – that another had now been built in its place:

> In it [is] supposed to be preserved the Ark of the
> Covenant . . . which Menelik . . . is said, in their fabulous
> legends, to have stolen from his father Solomon on his
> return to Ethiopia . . . Some ancient copy of the Old
> Testament, I do believe, was deposited here . . . but
> whatever this might be, it was destroyed . . . by Gragn,
> though pretended falsely to subsist there still. This I had
> from the King himself.[105]

In summary, what Bruce appeared to be saying was that the Ark had never been brought to Axum (since the story of Menelik and Solomon was just a 'fabulous legend'), that the relic once stored in the church could therefore only have been 'some ancient copy of the Old Testament', and that even this relic no longer existed since it had been 'destroyed by Gragn'. These statements were then backed up with the assertion that they had been corroborated by 'the King himself'.

Had it not been for that last remark I might have been content to believe that Bruce had simply never learned of how the Ark had been saved during the war with the Muslims, and of how it had later been returned to Axum after the rebuilding of Saint Mary of Zion. The claim that 'the King himself' had attested to the destruction of the relic was patently false, however: in 1690 – long after the Gragn campaigns and just eighty years before Bruce's own visit – an Ethiopian monarch had entered the Holy of Holies of the new Saint Mary's where he had actually *seen* the Ark (thus confirming its continued existence). The monarch in question (Iyasu the Great) had been a priest as well as a king, and because of this he had been allowed not only to view the sacred relic but also to open it and gaze inside it.[106] Since it is inconceivable that the king in Bruce's day would not have known of this famous and unprecedented incident, I had to conclude that the Scottish traveller was once again being 'economical with the truth'.[107]

My conviction that this was so deepened further when I realized – contrary to his own statement quoted above – that Bruce had *not* in fact regarded the Ethiopian tradition of Menelik, Solomon and the Queen of Sheba as a 'fabulous legend'. On the contrary, he had treated it with the utmost respect. In Volume I of his *Travels* – some thousand pages before his account of his visit to Axum – he had written at great length about the close cultural and commercial connections between Ethiopia and the Holy Land in early Old Testament times.[108] Here, amongst other things, he had unequivocally stated his own view that the Queen of Sheba had been a real historical person (rather than a mythical figure),[109] that she had indeed made her voyage to the court of King Solomon in Jerusalem ('there can be no doubt of this expedition'[110]) and – most important of all – that she had come from Ethiopia rather than from any other country: '[Others] have thought this Queen was an Arab,' he concluded, '[but] many reasons . . . convince me that she was an Ethiopian.'[111]

He next went on to describe as 'by no means improbable'[112] the account given in the *Kebra Nagast* of the queen's love affair with Solomon and the subsequent birth of Menelik. In the same vein he then retold the story of Menelik's own visit to Jerusalem and ultimate return to Ethiopia bringing with him 'a colony of

Jews, among whom were many doctors of the law of Moses'.[113] These events, Bruce concluded, had led to 'the foundation of an Ethiopian monarchy, and the continuation of the sceptre in the tribe of Judah down to this day . . . first when Jews, then . . . after they had embraced Christianity.'[114]

All this was nothing more nor less than a straightforward précis of the *Kebra Nagast* in a context that granted it a great deal of weight and historical authenticity. Strangely, however, while covering every other major detail, Bruce at this point made absolutely no mention of the Ark of the Covenant – an omission that could only have been deliberate given the central and all-pervasive role played by the sacred relic in the Ethiopian national epic.

Once again, therefore, I was forced to conclude that the Scottish traveller had knowingly misled his readers about the Ark. But why should he have wanted to do that? What possible motive could he have had? My curiosity aroused, I carefully re-read his description of Axum and came across an important detail that I had completely overlooked before: his own visit there had taken place on 18 and 19 of January 1770.[115]

This timing, I suddenly realized, could have been no accident, for on precisely those two days he would have witnessed the celebration of *Timkat*, the most important festival of the Ethiopian Orthodox Church. During this festival, and at no other time – as I had established when I talked to the guardian-priest in 1983 – the Ark of the Covenant was traditionally wrapped in rich brocades ('to protect the laity from it'[116]) and carried out in procession.[117] Bruce had therefore chosen to be in Axum on the single occasion in the year when, as a layman, he might have had a reasonable opportunity to get close to the sacred relic.

I was by now seriously beginning to wonder whether it had not been the Ark all along that had lured the Scottish traveller to Ethiopia: his claim to have gone there to find the source of the Nile did not stand up to close scrutiny and bore all the hallmarks of a 'cover story' intended to veil the real object of his quest. Moreover his evasiveness on the subject of the Ark itself was most peculiar and really only made sense if he had indeed had a special interest in it – an interest that he had wanted to keep secret.

Soon I learned other things that deepened my suspicions. I discovered, for example, that Bruce had been fluent in ancient Hebrew, Aramaic and Syriac[118] – dead languages that he could have had no reason to learn unless he had wished to make an intimate study of early biblical texts. Moreover, there could be no doubt that he *had* made such a study: his knowledge of the Old Testament, which shone out from nearly every page of the *Travels*, was described by one scriptural expert as 'outstanding'.[119]

Nor was this the only example of Bruce's 'more than common erudition'.[120] As I already knew, he had also carried out meticulous and original research into the culture and traditions of the black Jews of Ethiopia. 'I did not', as he himself had put it, 'spare my utmost pains in inquiring into the history of this curious people, and lived in friendship with several esteemed the most knowing and learned among them.'[121] Because of such efforts he had managed to make a lasting contribution to the study of Falasha society – a contribution that, like so much else, did not jibe at all with his professed enthusiasm for geographical exploration but that was entirely consistent with a quest for the lost Ark.

I telephoned the historian Belai Gedai in Addis Ababa and asked him whether he had any views on Bruce's motives. His reply shook me: 'As a matter of fact what we Ethiopians say is that Mr James Bruce did not come to our country to discover the source of the Nile. We say that he was just pretending that. We say that he had another reason.'

'Tell me more,' I requested. 'What do you think his objective could have been if it wasn't the Nile?'

'The real reason he came was to steal our treasures,' Gedai said resentfully, 'our cultural treasures. He took many precious manuscripts back to Europe. The book of Enoch, for example. Also from the imperial repository at Gondar he carried off an ancient copy of the *Kebra Nagast*.'

This was news to me – but exciting news if true. I investigated further and in due course confirmed that Gedai was absolutely correct. On leaving Ethiopia Bruce had indeed carried the *Kebra Nagast* with him – and not just the single splendid copy taken from the imperial repository but also a *copy* of that copy that he had made himself (his knowledge of *Ge'ez*, the classical Ethiopic language, being near-perfect[122]). Much later he gave both manuscripts to the Bodleian Library at Oxford, where they remain to this day (as 'Bruce 93' and 'Bruce 97').[123]

Nor was this all. Prior to the eighteenth century, scholars had believed the book of Enoch to be irretrievably lost: composed long before the birth of Christ,[124] and considered to be one of the most important pieces of Jewish mystical literature, it was only known from fragments and from references to it in other texts. James Bruce changed all this by procuring several copies of the missing work during his stay in Ethiopia. *These were the first complete editions of the book of Enoch ever to be seen in Europe.*[125]

I was of course interested to discover that Bruce had brought back the *Kebra Nagast* to Europe – and that he had also gone to the trouble of copying out the entire massive volume by hand. This made the omission of the Ark of the Covenant in his summary of that work look even more suspicious than I had originally thought. Suspicions are not certainties, however. It was therefore only when I got the full story of the Book of Enoch, and of the service that the Scottish adventurer had performed for scholarship in this regard, that I finally felt sure that I was on the right track.

I learned that the Book of Enoch has always been of great significance to Freemasons, and that certain rituals dating back to long before Bruce's time identified Enoch himself with Thoth, the Egyptian god of wisdom.[126] I then found a lengthy entry in the *Royal Masonic Cyclopaedia* which recorded other relevant traditions of the order – for example that Enoch was the inventor of writing, 'that he taught men the art of building', and that, before the flood, he 'feared that the real secrets would be lost – to prevent which he concealed the Grand Secret, engraven on a white oriental porphyry stone, in the bowels of the earth.' The entry in the *Cyclcopaedia* concluded with these words: 'The Book of Enoch was known to exist from very ancient times, and is continually alluded to by the fathers of the Church. Bruce brought home three copies from Abyssinia.'[127]

This brief and familiar mention of Bruce, coupled with the fact that he had gone to such great lengths to obtain not one but three copies of the Book of Enoch, raised the possibility that he might himself have been a Freemason. If so, then a solution to all the puzzles about his evasiveness and dishonesty suggested itself. I was already convinced that he had a special interest in the Ark of the Covenant – an interest that he had been determined to conceal. Now I could see exactly how he might have acquired that interest (and why he might have wanted to keep it secret). As a Freemason – and a Scottish Freemason to boot – he could have been exposed to the Templar traditions concerning the Ark's presence in Ethiopia.

But was Bruce a Mason? Finding the answer to this question was by no means easy. In the more than 3,000 pages of his *Travels* there was not a single clue that would have enabled me even to arrive at an informed opinion on the matter. Nor was any enlightenment shed by the two detailed and extensive biographies that had been written about him (the first in 1836[128] and the second in 1968[129]).

It was not until August 1990 that I was at last able to travel to Scotland to visit Bruce's family estate, where I hoped I might be able to obtain some definitive information. I found Kinnaird House on the outskirts of the Falkirk suburb of Larbert. Situated well back from the main road in extensive and secluded grounds, it was an imposing edifice of grey stone. After some understandable hesitation, its present owner – Mr John Findlay Russell – invited me in and showed me around. It was quite obvious from many architectural details, however, that the building did not date back to Bruce's time.

'That's quite right,' Findlay Russell agreed. 'Kinnaird House passed out of the possession of the Bruce family in 1895 and was knocked down by its new owner, a Dr Robert Orr. He built the present mansion in 1897.'

We were standing in an immense panelled hallway directly in front of a broad stone staircase. Findlay Russell now pointed to these stairs and added proudly: 'They're just about the only original feature to have been preserved. Dr Orr left them in place and built his house around them. They're of some historic significance you know.'

'Oh, really? Why?'

'Because James Bruce died on them. It was in 1794. He'd been giving a dinner in one of the upstairs rooms and he was escorting a guest down the stairs when he tripped and pitched over on his head. That was the end of him. A great tragedy.'

Before leaving I asked Findlay Russell if he had any idea whether Bruce might have been a Freemason or not.

'No,' he said. 'No idea at all. Of course I take a great interest in him, but I wouldn't claim to be an expert.'

I nodded, disappointed. As I was walking out of the door, however, another question occurred to me: 'Do you happen to know where he's buried?'

'Larbert Old Church. You'll have a job finding the tomb though. There used to be a great iron obelisk raised up over it, but that was pulled down some years ago because it was rusting away. It was considered a danger to the public.'

The drive to the church took only ten minutes. Locating the last resting place of one of Scotland's greatest explorers took much longer, however.

It was a miserable, rainy afternoon and I grew more and more depressed as I hunted up and down the rows of gravestones. As a personality, there was no doubt that Bruce had had many failings. Nevertheless, I felt strongly that this brave and enigmatic man deserved some lasting monument: it seemed shameful that he should have been left to lie in a completely unmarked patch of ground.

After I had thoroughly searched the main cemetery and found nothing, I noticed a thickly overgrown area surrounded by a low stone wall set into which was a small gate. I opened this gate and then walked down a flight of three steps which led . . . to a rubbish tip. Piles of old clothing, discarded shoes, tin cans and bits of broken furniture lay scattered around amidst dense patches of stinging nettles and brambles. Several massive trees locked branches overhead and their intertwined leaves formed a dripping green canopy that allowed very little light to penetrate.

Cursing the swarms of midges and wasps that rose up to greet me, I proceeded to stamp down as much of the vegetation as I could. I had looked everywhere else, I reasoned, so I might as well look here too. I had almost given up hope, however, when finally, in the centre of the enclosure, I stumbled upon several solid stone slabs laid flat on the ground and completely covered with moss, lichen and vile nettles. With a sense of reverence – but also of anger – I cleared the slabs as best I could and gazed down at them. There was nothing to say that they covered Bruce's remains but, somehow, I felt sure that they did. Involuntarily a lump rose in my throat. Here lay a man – a great man – who had preceded me to Ethiopia. Moreover, if my guess about his Masonic connections was correct, then there could be little doubt that he had gone to that far country in quest of the lost Ark. Now, however, it seemed that I might never be able to prove those connections. The only thing that was certain was that Bruce was lost himself – lost and forgotten in the land of his birth.

I stayed there for a while, thinking my gloomy thoughts. Then I left the little enclosure, not by the gate through which I had entered it but rather by clambering over the surrounding wall into a courtyard beyond. There, almost immediately, I saw something interesting: lying on its side quite close to where I stood was an enormous metal obelisk. I approached and found that James Bruce's name was engraved upon it, together with the following epitaph:

His life was spent performing useful and splendid actions.
He explored many distant regions.
He discovered the fountains of the Nile.
He was an affectionate husband, an indulgent parent,
An ardent lover of his country.
By the unanimous voice of mankind his name is
Enrolled with those who were conspicuous
For genius, for valour, and for virtue.

What I found most exciting of all about the obelisk was that it was intact – not rusting and crumbling – and that it was covered with fresh red primer paint. Someone, clearly, was still taking an interest in the explorer – enough of an interest to have had his monument restored, though not yet set up over his grave again.

Later that afternoon I made enquiries with the church authorities and discovered the identity of the mysterious bene-factor. It seemed that the obelisk had been taken away for repairs some years previously and had only been returned to Larbert the day before my own arrival. The restoration work had been organized and paid for by no lesser person than the titular head of the Bruce family in Scotland – the Earl of Elgin and Kincardine, himself a Master Mason.[130]

This was a promising lead and I followed it all the way to Broomhall, the beautiful estate just north of the Firth of Forth where Lord Elgin lived. I telephoned first – the Broomhall number was not ex-directory – and made an appointment for Saturday morning, 4 August.

'I can't give you more than about fifteen minutes,' the earl warned.

'Fifteen minutes will be enough,' I replied.

Elgin turned out to be a short, stocky, elderly man with a pronounced limp (apparently the result of injuries received while a prisoner of the Japanese during the Second World War). Without much ceremony he ushered me into a splendid drawing room dominated by family portraits and suggested that I get straight to the point.

So far his manner had been a little abrupt. As we talked about Bruce, however, he softened – and it gradually became clear to me from his detailed and extensive knowledge that he had made a close study of the life of the Scottish explorer. At one stage he took me into another room and showed me several shelves filled with old and esoteric books in many different languages. 'These were from Bruce's personal library,' he explained. 'He was a man of very wide interests . . . I also have his telescope, his quadrant and his compass . . . I can look them out for you if you like.'

While all this was going on, the quarter of an hour I had been promised had turned into an hour and a half. Spellbound by Elgin's enthusiasm, I had somehow still not managed to ask him the question that had brought me here. Now, quite suddenly, he glanced at his watch and said: 'Gosh, look at the time. I'm afraid you'll have to go. Things to do . . . I'm off to the Highlands this afternoon. Perhaps you can come back on some other occasion?'

'Er . . . yes. I'd like that very much.'

At this, beaming graciously, the earl stood up. I stood too and we shook hands. I felt distinctly foolish but I was determined not to leave without satisfying my curiosity.

'If you don't mind,' I said, 'there's one other thing I particularly wanted to ask you. It's to do with a theory I've been developing about the motives that led Bruce to make his expedition to Ethiopia. Do you happen to know . . . er . . . um . . . I mean is there any chance, any possibility at all, that he might have been a Freemason?'

Elgin looked slightly amazed. 'My dear boy,' he replied. 'Of *course* he was a Mason. It was a very, *very* important part of his life.'

Part III: Ethiopia, 1989–90
Labyrinth

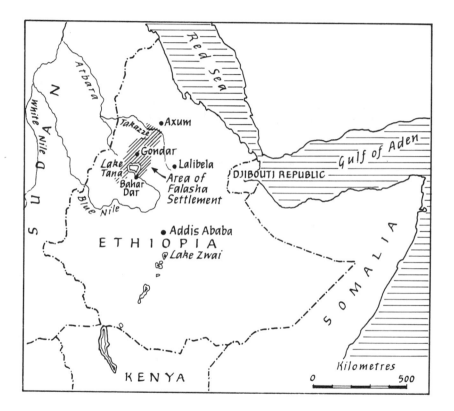

Chapter 8

Into Ethiopia

On my visit to his estate in Scotland, the Earl of Elgin confirmed that my suspicions about James Bruce were correct: the explorer had indeed been a Freemason (a member of Canongate Kilwinning Lodge No. 2 in the city of Edinburgh).

Elgin also told me that Bruce had been very much involved in the 'speculative' side of Freemasonry – as distinct from the more pragmatic and mundane 'craft' Masonry. This meant that he would have cultivated an interest in the esoteric and occult traditions of the brotherhood – traditions, including 'Knight Templarism', that most modern Masons neither knew nor cared anything about.

I should add, at this point, that I had never felt that all Masons would have had access to the Templar legacy; on the contrary, it was reasonable to suppose that such access would at all times have been restricted to a very few people.

Bruce, however, looked like an ideal candidate for membership of that privileged group. With his extensive knowledge of the Scriptures, his scholarly attraction to mystical works such as the Book of Enoch, and his 'speculative' leanings within the Masonic system, he was precisely the kind of man who would have investigated Templar traditions concerning the last resting place of the Ark of the Covenant.

After my meeting with Lord Elgin, therefore, I felt more confident than ever that it had been the Ark all along, rather than the Nile, that had lured the Scottish adventurer to Ethiopia in 1768. His paradoxical dishonesty on certain key issues (paradoxical because he was normally so truthful) now made sense to me; his evasiveness and secrecy were now explained. I might never know what mysteries he had uncovered in the Abyssinian highlands all those many years ago; now, however, I could at least be reasonably sure about his motives.

It had been in the summer of 1989 when I had first begun to wonder whether Bruce might have been a Mason, but it was not until August 1990 that I had my discussion with Lord Elgin. Meanwhile, as recounted in the last chapter, I had followed up the 'Portuguese connection' represented by members of the Order of Christ who had travelled to Ethiopia in the fifteenth and sixteenth centuries.

All the evidence that I had unearthed seemed to point in the direction of a continuing quest for the Ark – a covert venture that had drawn travellers hailing from quite different historical periods and from different lands towards the same lofty and enduring goal. Moreover, if this had been the case in centuries past then might it not still be the case today? Might not others be seeking the Ark in Ethiopia just as I was? As my research progressed I kept an open mind on this question while continually adding to my files on people like James Bruce and Christopher da Gama. Even without the stimulus of competition, however, my findings during the spring and summer of 1989 had convinced me that it was high time for me to return to Ethiopia to add some detailed field work to what had hitherto been primarily an intellectual exercise.

Difficult times

I took this decision as early as June 1989, but several months were to elapse before I was finally able to implement it. Why? Because on 19 May of that year a violent *coup* had been attempted in Addis Ababa throwing the whole of Ethiopia into turmoil.

The government of President Mengistu Haile-Mariam survived, but only at great cost. After the dust had settled one hundred and seventy-six rebellious officers were rounded up and arrested, including no less than twenty-four generals, amongst them the Commander of Ground Forces and the Chief of Operations. Rather than be captured and face trial, the Armed Forces Chief of Staff and the Commander of the Air Force committed suicide. Eleven other generals were killed in the fighting and the Minister of Defence was shot dead by the *coup* plotters.

The consequences of this ugly bloodbath were to haunt Mengistu and his regime for a very long while to come: with the officer corps effectively gutted, the military's decision-making capacity was reduced virtually to zero, a state of affairs that quickly translated itself into reverses on the battlefield. Indeed, in the months immediately following the *coup*, the Ethiopian army suffered a series of crushing defeats that ended in its total expulsion from the province of Tigray (which the TPLF declared a 'liberated zone') and from most of Eritrea as well (where the EPLF was already laying in place the structures for an independent state). The fighting also spread with alarming rapidity into other areas – including north-east Wollo, where the ancient city of Lalibela was overrun in September 1989, and Gondar, where the regional capital was besieged.

The worst setback of all, at least from my own selfish perspective, was that the government was no longer in control of Axum. Indeed, as noted in Chapter 3, the sacred city had been seized by the TPLF at the end of 1988, some months before the attempted *coup*. I had at first hoped that this would be a temporary state of affairs. As the dismal events of the second half of 1989 began to unfold, however, I had to face up to the possibility that the guerillas might be able to hold on to Axum indefinitely.

This, of course, left me with the option of approaching the TPLF in London and trying to win their co-operation in getting into the areas that they now administered. I was, however, not ready to pursue this option immediately. My own long-standing connections with the Ethiopian government meant that the Liberation Front would regard any overtures from me with intense suspicion. One possible outcome, unless I played my cards very cleverly indeed, was that they would point-blank refuse my request to go to Axum. But frankly I was more concerned about the safety of my skin if they did agree to take me in: as a known friend of the hated Mengistu regime wasn't there a chance, on the long and dangerous road into Tigray, that some local guerilla commander might decide I was a spy and have me shot – even if the London office had cleared me for the visit?

In the post-*coup* atmosphere nothing could be certain in

Ethiopia; no plans could be made with any degree of confidence; and there was no way of predicting what might happen from one week to the next. Any number of dramatic developments looked theoretically possible – not least the fall of Mengistu and a complete victory for the combined forces of the EPLF and the TPLF. I decided, therefore, that I would focus my efforts on other aspects of my research until a clearer picture had emerged. It was thus not until November 1989 that I finally returned to Ethiopia.

A secret hiding place?

The information that precipitated my return was provided to me by the Very Reverend Liqa Berhanat Solomon Gabre Selassie. I first encountered the man who owned this extremely long name in London on 12 June 1989, at which time I discovered that he also had an extremely long and full grey beard, nut-brown skin, twinkling eyes, splendid ceremonial robes, and – suspended around his neck – an elaborate wooden crucifix. Archpriest of the Saint Mary of Zion Ethiopian Orthodox Church in the United Kingdom, he was, in fact, a missionary. He had been sent to Britain some years previously by the Patriarchate in Addis Ababa in order to spread the Orthodox message. Moreover he had succeeded in winning a number of converts, mainly young Londoners of West Indian origin, some of whom he brought with him to our meeting – which I had arranged in order to pump him for information about the Ark.

Archpriest Solomon was, for me, the very image of an Old Testament patriarch. The venerable beard, the sagacious and yet slightly roguish manner, the charismatic personality leavened with genuine humility, and the absolute conviction of a deeply held faith all added irresistibly to this impression.

It quickly became clear to me as we talked that he possessed an unshakable belief that the sacred relic was indeed in Ethiopia. An intelligent and obviously highly educated man who spouted out biblical references with an assurance born of a lifetime of study, he expressed this view firmly and calmly and refused to accept that there was any possibility at all that he might be mistaken.

On a sheet of paper in front of me I took careful notes as he forcefully reiterated this point: the original Ark of the Covenant which had been constructed at the foot of Mount Sinai to contain the tablets of stone bearing the Ten Commandments – that very same pure and authentic object now rested in Axum. Furthermore, he insisted, it still had 'its powers, thanks to the Grace of God' and was, in addition, 'protected by the entire population of Tigray'. 'It remains today', he concluded, 'in the safe hands of the church and Christian people who are constantly seen around the church's compound.'

Before the archpriest left, I wrote down a list of fifteen questions that I wanted him to answer in detail. When his considered replies arrived at my home by post in mid-July, however, I was far away in Egypt. On my return some weeks later I barely glanced at the ten pages of mixed handwriting and typescript that he had sent me. Indeed I was so busy analysing and working through the Egyptian material I had gathered that I didn't even bother to send him a note of thanks.

In an idle moment in early November I finally turned my attention to the document which I had placed in the 'pending' tray on my desk more than three months previously. I found that it contained point-by-point responses to all my fifteen questions. Some of the answers, furthermore, were both intriguing and provocative.

For example, I had asked whether the alleged 'supernatural' powers of the Ark had ever been harnessed by the rulers of Ethiopia to bring victory in war. The Bible made it clear that this had been done on several occasions in ancient Israel.[1] If the Ark was really in Ethiopia, therefore, wasn't it logical to suppose that this tradition would have been maintained?

'In the teaching of our Church', Solomon had replied, 'God is the only power in the universe. He is the creator of all existing life, visible and invisible. He himself is the uncreated eternal light, which gives us light and power and grace. There is, however, a tangible dimension in which we can understand the relation between God and the Ark, for since the Ark contains the ten sacred words of the Law, written by God, the gift of His holiness cannot be diminished within it. Up to this day, therefore, His grace still rests upon the Ark, so by the name of God it is holy and of great spiritual significance.'

The former rulers of Ethiopia, the archpriest's answer continued, had known this. Since their prime function was to protect and defend the Orthodox Christian faith they had, during the many wars fought over the passing centuries, made use of the Ark from time to time 'as a source of spiritual strength against the aggressors . . . The King would rally the people for battle and the priests would stand as on the day when Joshua carried the Ark around the city of Jericho. Likewise our priests carried the Ark, chanting and going into battle in the glory of God.'

This use of the sacred relic as a war palladium – and as an effective one at that – was not, according to Archpriest Solomon, just something that had happened in Ethiopia's distant past. On the contrary: 'As recently as 1896 when the King of Kings Menelik the Second fought against the Italian aggressors at the battle of Adowa in Tigray region, the priests carried the Ark of the Covenant into the field to confront the invaders. As a result of this, Menelik was very victorious and returned to Addis Ababa in great honour.'

I re-read this part of the reply with considerable interest because I knew that Menelik II had indeed been 'very victorious' in 1896. In that year, under the command of General Baratieri, 17,700 Italian troops equipped with heavy artillery and the latest weapons had marched up into the Abyssinian highlands from the Eritrean coastal strip intent on colonizing the whole country. Menelik's forces, though ill prepared and less well armed, had met them at Adowa on the morning of 1 March, winning in less than six hours what one historian had subsequently described as 'the most notable victory of an African over a European army since the time of Hannibal'.[2] In a similar tone, the London *Spectator* of 7 March 1896 commented: 'The Italians have suffered a great disaster . . . greater than has ever occurred to white men in Africa.'

The tantalizing hint that the Ark had been used at Adowa raised in my mind the half-serious possibility that it might still be being used today – perhaps by the TPLF, who now had control of Axum and who, like Menelik II, had certainly been very victorious in recent months. Solomon, however, did not specu- late about this in his written answers. Instead (in his reply to a question that I had asked concerning the security of the Ark in the sanctuary chapel during the current all-out war being fought between government and rebel forces) he went on to suggest a completely different scenario.

When I had talked to him in June he had seemed confident that the sacred relic was still in its usual place, 'protected by the entire population of Tigray'. Now he did not seem so sure. 'There have been very infrequent occasions', he explained, 'during periods of great violence and tribulation, when the guardian monk, who watches the Ark day and night until he dies, has been obliged to cover it up and bring it out of Axum to safety. We know, for instance, that this happened in the sixteenth century when Tigray was invaded by the Muslim armies of Ahmed Gragn and most of Axum was destroyed. Then the guardian took the Ark to the monastery of Daga Stephanos, which stands on an island in Lake Tana. There it was hidden in a secret place.'

It was the archpriest's conclusion that really caused me to sit up and pay attention. Under the present circumstances of war and chaos in Tigray, he said, it was quite possible that the guardian could have taken the Ark out of Axum again.

Two lakes, two islands

I flew back to Addis Ababa on Tuesday 14 November 1989, arriving on the morning of Wednesday 15 November. Despite the continuing fighting in almost all parts of northern Ethiopia, I was quite clear in my own mind about the objectives of this trip. If Archpriest Solomon's analysis was correct, I reasoned, might not the sacred relic believed to be the Ark of the Covenant be resting even now on the monastic island of Daga Stephanos – in that same 'secret place' to which it had been taken in the sixteenth century?

This, furthermore, was not the only location in which it might have been concealed. I also remembered very well that Dr Belai Gedai had told me in one of our several long-distance telephone conversations of another, earlier tradition concerning the saving of the Ark during the uprising of Queen Gudit in the tenth century. At the time, the Ethiopian historian had explained, it had been brought to one of the islands on Lake Zwai.

I had therefore come to Ethiopia to check out both Lake Tana and Lake Zwai: the former lying in the war-torn north, though still in an area controlled by the government; the latter in safer territory about two hours' drive to the south of Addis Ababa.

I felt a tremendous sense of urgency during my first few days in the Ethiopian capital. I had left England less than a week after reading Archpriest Solomon's answers to my questions, and the reason why I was in such a hurry was quite simple: though Lake Zwai was secure enough, for the present at least, there was absolutely no guarantee that Lake Tana was going to remain in government hands for very much longer. Rebel forces, I knew, had surrounded the fortress city of Gondar, which stood some thirty miles to the north of the vast lake. Meanwhile, sporadic artillery and hit-and-run attacks had also been directed against the port of Bahar Dar on the southern shore. Since the only way for me to reach Daga Stephanos was through Bahar Dar I felt that I had no time to lose.

There could be no question of going through the normal bureaucratic channels to arrange the internal travel permit. Accompanied by my old friend Richard Pankhurst, who had taken a few days off from the Institute of Ethiopian Studies in order to help me out, I therefore went along to a meeting with one of my highest-ranking contacts – Shimelis Mazengia, Head of Ideology and a senior member of the ruling Politburo of the Workers' Party of Ethiopia.

A tall slim man in his forties who spoke fluent English, Shimelis was a committed Marxist but also one of the most intelligent and cultured of the Politburo members. His power within the regime was considerable and I knew him to have a genuine enthusiasm for the ancient history of his country. I therefore hoped that he might be persuaded to use his influence to back the research that I wanted to do – and in this I was not disappointed. After I had outlined my project to him he agreed readily to my proposed field trips to Lake Tana and to Lake Zwai. The only condition was that my stay in the Tana area should be kept as short as possible. 'Do you have a schedule in mind?' he asked.

I pulled out my diary and, after a moment's thought, proposed Monday the 20th for my departure to Lake Tana: 'I'll fly to Bahar Dar, hire a launch from the Maritime Authority, visit Daga

Stephanos and then come back to Addis on – say – Wednesday the 22nd. That should give me enough time . . . If it's OK with you I'd then like to drive down to Zwai on Thursday the 23rd.'

Shimelis turned to Richard: 'And will you be going as well, Professor Pankhurst?'

'Well, if it is acceptable . . . of course I would like very much to go.'

'Certainly it is acceptable.'

Shimelis then telephoned the Headquarters of the National Security Police in Addis Ababa and spoke rapidly in Amharic to someone in authority. After he had hung up he told us that our permits would be ready for collection that afternoon.

'Come back and see me next Friday,' he said, 'after you have finished at Lake Tana and Lake Zwai. You can make an appointment with my secretary.'

We left the Party building in high spirits. 'I never thought it would be so easy,' I said to Richard.

Chapter 9

Sacred Lake

The morning flight from Addis Ababa to Bahar Dar on the southern shore of Lake Tana took about an hour and a half. Despite the fighting reported in the area, no special procedures were observed during the landing, and the plane made a low, slow, scenic approach over the Blue Nile Falls before touching down on the bumpy gravel strip. From there, after hiring a taxi, Richard Pankhurst and I motored the few remaining kilometres into town along roads lined with jacaranda and flame trees.

We checked into two of the hundred empty rooms at the Tana Hotel on the lake's edge and then drove to the Maritime Authority pier where the motor launch that we hoped to use was moored. After protracted negotiations with the officials concerned it was eventually agreed that we could charter the boat – but not until the next day, Tuesday 21 November, and then only if we were prepared to pay the piratical hire of 50 US dollars an hour. Since I had no other choice I grudgingly accepted this extortionate figure and asked that the vessel should be made ready for a 5 a.m. departure.

With time to kill that afternoon we drove out of Bahar Dar to the nearby village of Tissisat and then hiked through tawny countryside overlaid with a patchwork of fields until we came to a massive stone bridge thrown across a steep gorge. Built by the Portuguese in the early seventeenth century, this crumbling edifice looked highly dangerous; Richard assured me, however, that it was still serviceable. We crossed it, and climbed a hillside – at the top of which two militiamen suddenly appeared out of a clump of shrubbery. They searched us, looked at our passports (classically, mine was examined upside down) and then waved us on.

Fifteen minutes later, after negotiating a narrow goat-track lined with thick tropical shrubbery and yellow daisies, we began to sense a low, thundering vibration underfoot. We walked on, aware of an increasing dampness in the air, and in a short while caught a first glimpse of what we had come to see – the spectacular basalt cliff over which, with tremendous power, the Blue Nile hurls itself before embarking on its epic journey out of the Abyssinian highlands.

The local name for the Blue Nile Falls, and for the village through which one must approach them, is Tissisat, meaning 'water that smokes'. As I stood enraptured, gazing at the rainbows playing amongst the fine spumes of spray thrown high into the air by the boiling cataract, I could well understand why.

I was also reminded – and struck by the accuracy – of the description given by the Scottish explorer James Bruce after his visit here in 1770:

> The river . . . fell in one sheet of water, without any interval, above half an English mile in breadth, with a force and a noise that was truly terrible, and which stunned and made me, for a time, perfectly dizzy. A thick fume, or haze, covered the fall all around, and hung over the course of the stream both above and below, marking its track, though the water was not seen . . . It was a most magnificent sight, that ages, added to the greatest length of human life, would not deface or eradicate from my memory; it struck me with a kind of stupor, and a total oblivion of where I was, and of every other sublunary concern.[1]

Ethiopia, I reflected, was a country in which time really could stand still: there was nothing at all, in the scene now laid out before me, which suggested that more than two centuries had elapsed since Bruce had been here. Not for the last time I felt a deep sense of empathy with the Scottish traveller whose family name I happened by coincidence to share (through the maternal line – my grandmother was born a Bruce, and Bruce, too, is my own middle name).

Later, surrounded by crowds of local children who had

materialized from nowhere in order to demand money, pens and sweets, Richard and I set off on the walk back towards Tissisat village. Thus far there had been something almost idyllically peaceful and rustic about the afternoon; even the militiamen who had searched us earlier had done so lethargically and with good humour. Now, however, as we re-crossed the Portuguese bridge with the first chill of evening setting in, we were confronted by an incongruous and jarring spectacle: at least three hundred heavily armed soldiers dressed in green battle fatigues advancing towards us from the other direction.

It was impossible to be sure whether we were looking at government or rebel troops. They wore no regimental insignia, nor any other identifying paraphernalia. Neither did they appear to be disciplined or even under the command of an officer: rather than being organized into a discernible marching order they slouched oafishly along with angry and resentful glares. I also noticed that a number of the men were carrying their weapons very sloppily: one used his rifle as a walking stick; another held an AK-47 barrel-forwards across his shoulder; a third was loosely waving a loaded rocket launcher which, if fired accidentally, could have demolished a fair-sized building – or, for that matter, the bridge we were all standing on.

Richard, whose Amharic is better than mine, greeted several individual members of this surly rabble in a familiar manner, shook hands heartily with perhaps a dozen more, and made eccentric gestures of friendship towards most of the rest. 'They think all foreigners are slightly mad,' he explained to me in a stage whisper. 'I'm just living up to the stereotype. Believe me, it's the best thing to do.'

The Jewel of Ethiopia

The next morning we arrived at the Maritime Authority pier at 5 a.m. There was no sign of activity and Richard, who was wrapped in a blanket against the cold, muttered something about the '*maambfak* syndrome'.

'What's that?' I asked.

'Many appointments are made but few are kept,' the historian grumbled.

Within half an hour, however, the captain of the MV *Dahlak* had arrived. So too had a clean-shaven young man in a well cut suit who introduced himself as Wondemu and informed us, with great humility, that he was the Second Deputy-Assistant Regional Administrator: 'Yesterday afternoon my boss received a phone call from Comrade Shimelis Mazengia in Addis telling him that we should look after you. I immediately reported to your hotel but you were not present. Then from Reception I learned about this research you are conducting today. So,' he concluded with a broad smile, 'here I am.'

By 5.45, shivering in the dawn chill, we were on the water and making good headway towards Daga Stephanos some twenty miles to the north. Above the mountains ringing the eastern shore of the huge lake the sun was already rising. A fresh breeze carried the sounds of birdsong and of barking dogs.

Before too long Richard and Wondemu disappeared into the cabin to chat and drink tea. Entranced by the view, by the invigorating Alpine quality of the air, and by the romance of travel, I remained on deck gazing out at the ever-shifting lacustrine panorama and fretting subliminally about exactly how much this little pleasure cruise was going to cost me. To reach Daga, the captain had said, would take about two and a half hours. Since we would need to be on the island for at least that long and would then require a further two and a half hours to get back, it looked like I was going to end up shelling out almost 400 dollars.

I was interrupted in this slightly depressing piece of mental arithmetic by the striking spectacle of two native long boats with high, curved prows pulling out towards us from the distant shore. Silhouetted in the pink light of the early sun I could discern five or six men crouched down inside each vessel wielding paddles which, in unison, they raised and dipped into the water, raised and dipped, raised and dipped.

Known as *tankwas*, I remembered from my previous visit in 1983 that local craft such as these were a common sight on Lake Tana. The two now running briefly parallel to us, but heading in the opposite direction, were much larger than any that I had seen before. Nevertheless they were clearly of the same basic design, being made of bundles of papyrus reeds bound together.

Having spent a considerable fraction of the previous few months studying archaeological sites in Egypt I was now able to confirm with my own eyes something which I knew that several historians had already observed – namely that the Ethiopian *tankwas* bore an uncanny resemblance to the reed boats used by the Pharaohs for transportation, hunting and fishing on the Nile.[2] I had seen representations of high-prowed vessels just like these in frescoes decorating the tombs in the Valley of the Kings and also in reliefs carved into the temple walls at Karnak and Luxor.

Not for the first time I found myself wondering whether the ancient Egyptians had ever visited the Tana area. It was not just the similarity in boat design, suggestive as it was of a strong cultural influence, that led me to this speculation, but also the lake's importance as the principal reservoir of the Blue Nile.

Tana is not itself officially regarded as the source of that great river, identified as twin springs, in the mountains to the south, that were visited by Bruce and by other travellers before him.[3] At these springs rises a river known as the 'Little Abai' which flows across the southern edge of the lake (there is a discernible current) and then out again as the 'Big Abai', the local name for the Blue Nile.

To all intents and purposes, however, as geographers and engineers now accept,[4] the Blue Nile's real source *is* Lake Tana, which is fed not only by the 'Little Abai' but also by many other rivers, thus draining a huge expanse of the Abyssinian highlands. Indeed, with a surface area of 3,673 square kilometres, this vast inland sea provides an estimated six-sevenths of the total volume of water in the combined streams of the Blue and the White Niles.[5] Most important of all, it is Ethiopia's long rainy season – which causes a veritable flood to race out of Lake Tana and along the Blue Nile – that has been responsible since time immemorial for the annual inundation that brings silt and fertility to Egypt's Delta. By comparison the longer White Nile – which loses more than half of its volume in the swamplands of southern Sudan – contributes almost nothing.[6]

As I sat watching the papyrus-reed *tankwas*, therefore, it seemed to me inconceivable that the priests of Karnak and Luxor – who worshipped the Nile as a life-giving force and also, symbolically, as a blessed god – would not at some stage in their long history have made their way to Ethiopia. There were no records to prove this, just another hunch; but nevertheless, in the numinous dawn glow of that November morning, I felt confident that the ancient Egyptians must at some point have visited Tana – and venerated it.

Certainly the Greek geographer Strabo, who lived around the time of Christ and who was deeply versed in Egyptian learning, was aware (as later scholars were not) that the Blue Nile rose in a giant lake in Ethiopia, a lake which he called 'Pseboe'.[7] In the second century AD the Egyptian geographer Claudius Ptolemy expressed a similar opinion, although the name that he gave to Tana was 'Coloe'.[8] I also thought that the Athenian dramatist Aeschylus might have been inspired by more than just poetic fancy when he wrote hauntingly in the fifth century BC of 'a copper-tinted lake . . . that is the jewel of Ethiopia, where the all-pervading sun returns again and again to plunge his immortal form, and finds a solace for his weary round in gentle ripples that are but a warm caress.'[9]

These, I knew, were not the only references linking the mysterious waters of Lake Tana to the ancient cultures of Greece, Egypt and the Middle East. As I sat on the deck of the MV *Dahlak en route* to Daga Stephanos I also remembered that the Abyssinians themselves firmly believed the Blue Nile to be nothing less than the Gihon of Genesis 2:13 – 'the second river' that 'compasseth the whole land of Ethiopia'. This, furthermore, was a very old tradition,[10] almost certainly pre-Christian, and thus added considerable weight to the notion that the lake, together with its rivers and islands, might indeed have some genuine connection with the Ark of the Covenant.

It was therefore with a certain flush of optimism that I looked ahead, across the intervening miles, to the green slopes of Daga island rising above the shining waters like the peak of some submerged mountain.

Daga Stephanos

It was around 8.30 when we finally moored at Daga. The sun was now high in the sky and, despite the altitude (Tana stands more than 6,000 feet above sea level), the morning was hot, humid and breathless.

We were met on the wooden jetty by a delegation of monks dressed in astonishingly dirty robes. They had obviously been monitoring our approach for some time but did not appear to be in the least bit pleased to see us. Wondemu had a word with them and eventually, with obvious reluctance, they led us through a small banana plantation and then up a steep, winding path towards the summit of the island.

As we walked I stripped off the pullover I had been wearing, stretched my arms and took a few deep breaths. The track that we were following passed through the midst of a dense forest of tall gnarled trees, the leaves of which formed a canopy above us. The air was laden with the loamy scent of freshly turned earth and with the fragrance of tropical flowers. Bees and other large insects buzzed industriously about and, in the distance, I could hear the monotonous ringing of a traditional stone bell.

Eventually, some 300 feet above the surface of the lake, we began to come across low round buildings with thatched roofs – the dwellings of the monks. Next we passed under an arch set into a high stone wall and finally entered a grassy clearing at the centre of which stood the church of Saint Stephanos. This was a long rectangular structure, curved at the ends, with a covered walkway extending all around it.

'Doesn't look all that old,' I said to Richard.

'It isn't,' he replied. 'The original building was burnt down in a grass fire about a hundred years ago.'

'I suppose that would have been the one that they brought the Ark to in the sixteenth century?'

'Yes. In fact there's probably been some sort of church on this site for at least a thousand years. Maybe even for longer than that. Daga is reckoned to be one of the holiest places on Lake Tana. Because of that the mummified bodies of five former emperors are kept here.'

Wondemu, in his self-appointed role as our guide and interlocutor, had been talking quietly to some of the monks. Now he detached one member of the group – whose vestments were slightly cleaner than those of his fellows – and led him by the hand towards us. 'This,' he announced proudly, 'is

Archpriest Kifle-Mariam Mengist. He will answer all your questions.'

The archpriest, however, seemed to have ideas of his own on this subject. His wrinkled, prune-like features registered a curious mixture of hostility, resentment and greed. In silence he sized Richard and me up, then turned to Wondemu and whispered something in Amharic.

'Ah . . . ,' sighed our guide, 'I am afraid he wants money. It is to purchase candles, incense and . . . er . . . other necessary church items.'

'How much?' I asked.

'Whatever you feel is appropriate.'

I proposed 10 Ethiopian birr – about 5 US dollars – but Kifle-Mariam indicated that this sum was not sufficient. Indeed, he declared, the proffered note was so lacking in the quality of sufficiency that he could not even bring himself to detach it from my fingers.

'I think you should pay more,' Wondemu hissed politely in my ear.

'I'll be happy to do that, of course,' I said. 'But I'd like to know what I'll be getting in return.'

'In return he will talk to you. Otherwise he says he has much to do.'

We settled, after further debate, on 30 birr. The money was quickly folded and conjured away in some noisome fold or pouch in the priestly robes. Then we strolled over to the arcade surrounding the church and sat down in the shade beneath the overhanging eaves of the thatched roof. Several of the other monks followed us and lurked about looking self-consciously contemplative and pretending not to listen to our conversation.

Kifle-Mariam Mengist began by telling us that he had been on the island for eighteen years and had become an expert on all matters concerning the monastery. As though to prove this point he then launched into a kind of potted history – which went on, and on, and on.

'Right,' I interrupted after Wondemu had given me the drift of this boring speech. 'I *do* want to get a general picture. But first I'd like to ask the archpriest a specific question – which is this: I've heard it said that the Ark of the Covenant was brought here in the sixteenth century when Axum was attacked by the armies of Ahmed Gragn. Does he know this story? And is it true?'

Fifteen or twenty minutes of incomprehensible argument followed, at the end of which Wondemu announced that the priest definitely did not know the story. Moreover, since he did not know it, he was not able to tell us whether it was true or not.

I tried a different tack. 'Do they have a *tabot* of their own? Here. Inside this church?' Through the open doorway behind us I pointed expressively towards the entrance of the Holy of Holies, which was just visible in the gloom within.

After another Amharic question-and-answer session Wondemu announced: 'Yes. Of course they have their *tabot*.'

'Good. Well I'm glad we've established that at any rate. Now, ask him this: does he accept that their *tabot* is a copy – a replica – of the original *tabot* in Axum?'

'Perhaps,' came the enigmatic reply.

'I see. OK. Well in that case I'd like you to ask him whether he knows anything at all about the Ark of the Covenant. How it came to Axum. Who brought it. Things like that. Get him to tell us the story in his own words.'

An immediate and perfunctory response was given to this question. 'He says he does not know the story,' Wondemu translated rather mournfully. 'He says he is not an authority on such matters.'

'Is there anyone else who is?' I asked in exasperation

'No. Kifle-Mariam Mengist is the senior priest on the island. If he does not know then it is impossible that anyone else will know.'

I looked at Richard: 'What's going on here? I've never, never *ever*, met an Ethiopian priest who didn't know the *Kebra Nagast* story about the Ark.'

The historian shrugged: 'Nor have I. It's very peculiar. Perhaps you should offer him . . . a further inducement.'

I groaned. It always came down to money in the end, didn't it? If a few more birr was what it would take to get this tight-lipped old bastard talking, however, then it would be best to pay up quickly. After all, I'd come all the way from London to check Daga Stephanos out – and even now the MV *Dahlak* was moored at the jetty with its meter running at the rate of approximately a dollar a minute. With grim resignation I passed over another small handful of crumpled notes.

This latest act of generosity, however, did me absolutely no good at all. The priest had nothing further to say on any subject of interest. When this had finally sunk in – and it took some time – I leaned back against one of the pillars that supported the roof, inspected my fingernails, and tried to decide what to do next.

There were, I realized, two possible explanations for the apparent ignorance of Kifle-Mariam Mengist. One, the least likely, was that the man was genuinely stupid. The other, more probable by far, was that he was lying.

But why should he lie? Well, I reasoned, there were two possible explanations for that as well. The first – and the least likely – was that he had something important to hide. The second – more probable by far – was that he wanted to extract further notes from my rapidly diminishing wad of Ethiopian currency.

I stood up and said to Wondemu: 'Ask him again. Ask him if the Ark of the Covenant was brought here from Axum in the sixteenth century . . . and ask him whether it's here now. Tell him I'll make it worth his while if he'll show it to me.'

Our guide raised a quizzical eyebrow. What I had just proposed was not in good taste. 'Go on,' I urged. 'Just ask him.'

More Amharic, then this from Wondemu: 'He says the same as before. He does not know about the Ark of the Covenant. But he also says that nothing has been brought to Daga Stephanos from outside for a very long time.'

The group of monks who had been standing in a semi-circle eavesdropping on my conversation with Kifle-Mariam Mengist dispersed at this point. One of them, however – barefoot, toothless and dressed in such poor rags that he would have passed for a beggar on any street in Addis Ababa – accompanied us as we walked back down the steep track to the jetty. Before we climbed on board the launch he pulled Wondemu aside and whispered something in his ear.

'What was that?' I asked sharply, expecting a further demand for payment of some kind.

Money, however, turned out not to be the issue this time. Wondemu frowned: 'He says that we should go to Tana Kirkos.

Apparently we will learn something about the Ark there . . .
something important.'

'What's Tana Kirkos?'

'It is another island . . . east of here. Quite far.'

'Ask him to tell us more. What does he mean by something
important?'

Wondemu put the question again and translated the answer.
'He says that the Ark of the Covenant is on Tana Kirkos. That is
all he knows.'

My first reaction to this astonishing piece of news was to roll
my eyes heavenwards, tug distractedly at my hair, and kick the
side of the launch. Meanwhile the monk, whom I wanted more
information from, had hobbled back along the jetty and vanished
into the banana grove.

I looked at my watch. It was now almost noon. We had been out
of Bahar Dar for six hours, or 300 dollars.

'Is Tana Kirkos on our way back?' I asked Wondemu.

'No,' he replied, 'I have never been there. No one ever goes
there. But I know it is more or less due east. Bahar Dar is south.'

'I see. Any idea how long it will take us?'

'No. I shall ask the captain.'

Wondemu did that. It would take us about an hour and a half.

'And after that, how long back to Bahar Dar?'

'About three more hours.'

I did some rapid calculations in my head. Say two hours on
Tana Kirkos, plus an hour and a half to get there, plus three
hours to Bahar Dar . . . that's six and a half hours. Call it seven,
plus the six we've already had. That's, let's see, thirteen hours.
Thirteen bloody hours! At fifty bucks an hour. Six hundred and
fifty dollars minimum. Christ!

I fulminated inwardly for some time longer. Eventually,
however – with a heart as heavy as my wallet was light – I made up
my mind to go.

Of course the Ark wouldn't actually *be* on Tana Kirkos. I knew
that. In fact the most likely scenario was that I would be given the
run-around again, just as on Daga Stephanos. Money would be
extracted from me in dribs and drabs until the point was reached
where I was obviously not prepared to hand over any more. Then
another tantalizing little hint would be dropped naming yet

another island – and off I would go, banknotes at the ready, to enrich yet another community of needy anchorites.

James Bruce, I remembered, had been to Tana in the eighteenth century. 'There are forty-five inhabited islands in the lake,' he had written, 'if you believe the Abyssinians, who, in everything, are very great liars . . .'[11]

Tana Kirkos

I was not in a receptive frame of mind when we arrived at Tana Kirkos. Nevertheless, as I stood in the bows of the MV *Dahlak* scowling at the island ahead, I had to admit that it was a beautiful and unusual place. Completely covered in dense green shrubbery, flowering trees and tall cactus plants, it rose steeply from the water to a high peak on which I could just make out the thatched roof of a circular dwelling. Hummingbirds, kingfishers and bright blue starlings darted through the air. On the shore of a small sandy bay, on a makeshift jetty, stood a group of monks. Smiling.

We dropped anchor and clambered out of the boat. Wondemu did the usual round of introductions and explanations. Hands were shaken. Lengthy greetings were exchanged. Finally we were led up a narrow, overgrown path cut out of the side of a grey cliff, through an archway at the top – again hewn out of the bare stone – and finally into a clearing containing three or four dilapidated buildings and a dozen ragged monks.

Set back behind natural rock walls, the grassy space in which we stood was enclosed, silent and dark. The light that did penetrate, filtered as it was through the overarching trees and bushes, seemed muted and green. Against my better judgment, I began to suspect that there might be something worth seeing here after all. I could not have explained why, but Tana Kirkos felt 'right' in a way that Daga Stephanos had not.

The senior priest now arrived and introduced himself, through Wondemu, as Memhir Fisseha. He was lean and smelled of incense. He did not ask for money, but he did ask whether or not we had security clearance.

I was nonplussed by such a question, coming as it did from a traditional figure in clerical robes.

'As a matter of fact,' I said, 'yes we do.' I pulled from my pocket the permit we had obtained from the security police in Addis and gave this to Wondemu, who in turn passed it to Memhir Fisseha. The old man – were all priests in Ethiopia so old? – studied the document with an abstracted air and then handed it back to me. He seemed to be satisfied.

Wondemu now explained that I wanted to ask some questions about Tana Kirkos and about the Ark of the Covenant. Would that be OK?

'Yes,' the priest replied, rather sadly I thought. He directed us to the doorway of what, from the blackened pots and pans lying inside, appeared to be a kitchen. Here, on a small stool, he sat down, indicating that we should join him.

'Do you believe,' I began, 'that the Ark of the Covenant was brought from Jerusalem to Ethiopia by Emperor Menelik I?'

'Yes,' Wondemu translated.

I heaved a sigh of relief. This was already *much* better than Daga Stephanos.

'I have heard a story', I continued, 'that the Ark is now here – on the island of Tana Kirkos. Is that story true?'

An anguished expression crossed Memhir Fisseha's leathery face as he answered: 'It was true.'

Was true? What on earth did that signify? 'Get him to elaborate,' I barked at Wondemu in some agitation. 'What does he mean by *was* true?'

The priest's response excited and distressed me in roughly equal measure: 'It was true. But the Ark of the Covenant is not here any longer. It has been taken to Axum.'

'Taken back to Axum!' I exclaimed. 'When? When did they take it?'

An intense discussion followed in Amharic, with the main point obviously being clarified several times. Finally Wondemu translated: 'The Ark was taken to Axum one thousand six hundred years ago, in the time of King Ezana. It was not taken *back*. It was simply taken there, and it has stayed there ever since.'

I felt perplexed and frustrated. 'Let me get this clear,' I said after a moment's thought. 'He's not telling us that the Ark was here recently and has now gone back to Axum, is he? He's telling us that it went there a very long time ago.'

'Exactly. One thousand six hundred years ago. That is what he says.'

'OK, then ask him this. How did the Ark get here in the first place? Did it come here from Axum, and then go back there? Or was it here *before* it was ever taken to Axum? That seems to be what he means, but I want to be absolutely sure.'

Slowly and painfully the story emerged. Extracting it was like extracting the stump of a rotten tooth from an inflamed gum. Several times consultation was required with the other monks and once a huge, leather-bound book written in ancient *Ge'ez* was referred to and a passage read out.

In summary, what Memhir Fisseha told us was that the Ark had been stolen from the Temple of Solomon in Jerusalem by Menelik I and his companions. They had brought it out of Israel, he explained, and into Egypt. Then they had followed the Nile – first the Nile and afterwards its tributary the Takazze – until they had reached Ethiopia.

This, of course, was the tradition of the theft of the Ark reported in the *Kebra Nagast*. What came next, however, was completely new.

Looking for somewhere safe and appropriate where they might install the precious relic, the old priest continued, the travellers had come to Tana. At that time, he said, the entire lake was sacred. It was dear to God. A holy place. So they had come to Tana, to its eastern shore, and they had chosen this island, now called Kirkos, as the resting place for the Ark.

'How long did it stay here?' I asked.

'For eight hundred years,' came the reply. 'It blessed us with its presence for eight hundred years.'

'Was there a building? Was it put into some sort of temple?'

'There was no building. The Holy Ark was placed inside a tent. And it stayed within that tent, here on Tana Kirkos, for eight hundred years. We were Jews then. Afterwards, when we became Christians, King Ezana took the Ark to Axum and placed it in the great church in that city.'

'And you say the Ark was taken to Axum one thousand six hundred years ago?'

'Yes.'

'So if it was on Tana Kirkos for eight hundred years before

that, then – let's see – it must have arrived here something like two thousand four hundred years ago. Is that right? Are you telling me it came here about four hundred years before the birth of Christ?'

'Yes.'

'You do know that 400 BC was a long time *after* Solomon – who was supposed to be Menelik's father? In fact Solomon would have been dead for about five centuries by then. What do you say to that?'

'I say nothing. I have told you our tradition as it is recorded in our sacred books and in our memory.'

A remark that the priest had made a few moments earlier had interested me enormously, and I now picked him up on this: 'You told me that you were Jews then? What did that mean? What kind of religion did you have?'

'We were Jews. We performed sacrifice . . . the sacrificial lamb. And we continued with this practice until the Ark was taken from us to Axum. Then Abba Salama came and he taught us the Christian faith, and we built a church here.'

Abba Salama, I knew, was the Ethiopic name for Frumentius, the Syrian bishop who had converted King Ezana and the entire Axumite kingdom to Christianity in the 330s AD. This meant that the periods of time that Memhir Fisseha had given me made sense – or at least were internally consistent. The only contradiction was the huge gap between the known dates for Solomon – mid 900s BC – and the date that the Ark had supposedly been brought to Tana Kirkos (which, if I subtracted eight hundred years from 330 AD, would have been 470 BC).

I pressed on: 'Before Abba Salama came and taught you Christianity you had no church here?'

'No church. I told you. We were Jews. We performed sacrifice.' He paused, then added: 'The blood from the lamb was collected in a bowl . . . a *gomer*. Then it was scattered over some stones, some small stones. They are here still, up to this day.'

'Sorry. Come again. What are here to this day?'

'The stones that we used for sacrifice when we were Jews. Those stones are here. On the island. They are here now.'

'Can we see them?' I asked. I felt a tiny thrill of excitement. If what Memhir Fisseha had just said was true, then he was talking about physical evidence – real physical evidence to support the strange but curiously convincing story that he had told.

'You can see them,' he replied. He got to his feet. 'Follow me. I will show you.'

Scattering the blood

The priest led us to a high point on the cliff edge near the summit of the island, overlooking Lake Tana. Here, on a raised plinth made of natural unhewn rock, he showed us three short stone pillars grouped closely together. The tallest of the three – perhaps a metre and a half high – was square in section, with a cup-shaped declivity hollowed out in its top. The remaining two were each about a metre high, circular in section, and as thick as a man's thigh. At the top they also had been hollowed out to a depth of approximately 10 centimetres.

Though copious quantities of green lichen grew on them I was able to establish that the three pillars were all monoliths, that they were freestanding, and that they had been carved from the same type of grey granite. They looked old, and I asked Richard for his opinion on this.

'Of course,' he replied, 'I'm not an archaeologist. But I would say from the way they are cut, the style – particularly the square one . . . I would say they are at least from the Axumite period, if not earlier.'

I asked Memhir Fisseha what the cup-shaped declivities were for.

'To contain blood,' was his answer. 'After the sacrifice, some was scattered over the stones and some on to the tent that contained the Ark. The remainder was poured into these hollows.'

'Can you show me how it was done?'

The old priest beckoned one of the other monks and gave him an instruction in a low voice. He strode off and returned a few minutes later carrying a wide but shallow bowl so corroded and tarnished with age that I could not even guess of what metal it was made. This, we were told, was the *gomer* in which the sacrificial blood was first collected.

'What exactly does *gomer* mean?' I asked Wondemu.

He shrugged: 'I don't know. It is not an Amharic word, nor Tigrigna. It does not sound like it belongs to any Ethiopian language.'

I looked to Richard for enlightenment but he confessed that he was not familiar with the word either.

Memhir Fisseha said simply that it was called a *gomer* and had always been called a *gomer* and that was all he knew. He then positioned himself next to the stones with the bowl in his left hand, dipped into it with his right forefinger, swept his right hand above the level of his head and commenced an up-and-down motion. 'The blood was scattered in this way,' he said, 'over the stones and over the tent of the Ark. Afterwards, as I told you, what was left was poured thus.' He then tipped the bowl sideways above the cup-shaped hollows in the tops of the pillars.

I asked the priest if he knew where exactly on the island the Ark had been kept in its tent. All he would say, however, was 'near here . . . somewhere near here'.

I then sought clarification of our earlier discussion: 'You told me that it was taken from Tana Kirkos to Axum one thousand six hundred years ago. Is that correct?'

Wondemu translated the question. Memhir Fisseha nodded affirmatively.

'OK,' I continued. 'Now what I want to know is this: has it ever been brought back here? At any time, for any reason, has the Ark ever come back to this island?'

'No. It was taken to Axum and it stayed in Axum.'

'And as far as you are aware it is still there to this day?'

'Yes.'

No further information seemed likely to be forthcoming, but I was more than satisfied with what I had got – particularly since the information given had at no point been bartered for money. Grateful for this I handed over a 100 birr note as a voluntary contribution to the monastery's expenses. Then, with Memhir Fisseha's permission, I set about photographing the sacrificial pillars from a variety of different angles.

We were back in Bahar Dar shortly before eight that evening. We had been out and about on Lake Tana for more than fourteen hours and the final bill for the hire of the MV *Dahlak* came to 750 US dollars.

36 The Blue Nile Falls near Lake Tana, Ethiopia.

37 Papyrus-reed boat on Lake Tana.

38 Hollowed stones on the island of Tana Kirkos, said to have been used
to contain blood during sacrifices in the presence of the Ark of the
Covenant. The monks claim that the Ark remained on their island for
eight hundred years before being taken to Axum.

39 Qemant High Priest, centre, in dark cloak.
The Qemant, a pagan tribe whose religion nevertheless contains strong
elements of Judaism, say that they came to Ethiopia 'from the land of
Canaan.'

40 Falasha priest at the village of Anbober, near Gondar, photographed in
1990. A year later almost all of Ethiopia's Falasha population had been
airlifted to Israel.

41 Falasha priest displaying a copy of the Torah
witten in *Ge'ēz*, the ancient liturgical language
of Ethiopia. The illumination shows the prophet
Moses holding the Ten Commandments.

42 and 43
Christian priests at Gondar
carrying *Tabots* on their heads
during the *Timkat* ceremony.

44 Christian priests performing
the dance of David before the Ark
during the *Timkat* ceremony at Gondar.

45 *Timkat* reveller in
traditional warrior's head-dress.

46 Ethiopian priests with sistra. Musical instruments
exactly like these were used in religious ceremonies in
Israel in Old Testament times.

47 The medieval castle and baptismal pool
that provide the focus for the climax
of the *Timkat* ceremony in Gondar.

It had been, by any standards, a costly day. I no longer begrudged the expense, however. Indeed, the doubts that had beset me so forcefully on Daga Stephanos had been completely banished by Tana Kirkos and I felt that I could now continue the quest with a renewed sense of commitment and optimism.

This positive mood received a further boost back in Addis Ababa. There, before I set out for the planned trip to Lake Zwai on Thursday 23 November, I had the opportunity to visit the University Library and examine a number of references concerning the use of sacrificial stones in Old Testament Judaism.

What I discovered was that pillars similar to those that I had seen on Tana Kirkos had been associated with the very earliest phases of the religion – both in Sinai and in Palestine. Known as *masseboth*, they were set up as altars on high places and were used for cultic and sacrificial purposes.[12]

I then looked in the Bible to see if I could find any specific details concerning the proper performance of sacrifices in Old Testament times. I did find such details and, as I read and re-read the relevant passages, I realized that what Memhir Fisseha had described to me on the island had been an authentic and very ancient ceremony. No doubt much had become muddled and confused in the memories of the tradition that had been handed down from generation to generation. When he had talked about the scattering of blood, however, he had been astonishingly close to the mark.

In Chapter 4 of the book of Leviticus, for example, I came across this verse: 'And the priest shall dip his finger in the blood, and sprinkle of the blood seven times before the Lord, before the veil of the sanctuary.'[13] Likewise in Chapter 5 I read: 'And he shall sprinkle of the blood of the sin offering upon the side of the altar; and the rest of the blood shall be wrung out at the bottom of the altar.'[14]

It was not until I turned to the Mishnah, however, the compilation in written form of early oral Jewish law, that I realized just how authentic Memhir Fisseha's account in fact had been. In the tractate known as *Yoma*, in the second division of the Mishnah, I found detailed descriptions of the sacrificial rituals carried out by the High Priest within Solomon's Temple in front of the curtain that shielded the Ark of the Covenant from the gaze of the laity.

I read that the blood of the victim – whether lamb, goat, or bullock – was collected in a basin and given 'to one that should stir it up . . . so that it should not congeal'. Then the priest, having emerged from the sanctuary, 'took the blood from him that was stirring it and entered again into the place where he had entered and stood again on the place whereon he had stood, and sprinkled the blood once upwards and seven times downwards.'[15]

And where, exactly, did the priest sprinkle this blood? According to the Mishnah he sprinkled it 'on the curtain outside, opposite the Ark, once upwards and seven times downwards, not as though he intended to sprinkle upwards or downwards, but as though he were wielding a whip . . . He then sprinkled the cleansed surface of the altar seven times and poured out the residue of the blood.'[16]

It seemed to me highly improbable that Memhir Fisseha had ever read the Mishnah. As a Christian he would have no reason to do so; nor would he have had access to such a book on his remote island; nor could he have understood any of the languages into which it had been translated. Yet his hand movements, when he had shown me how the scattering of the blood was done, had been precisely those of a man wielding a whip. And he had spoken confidently of the blood being poured not only upon the altar stones but also 'on the tent of the Ark'.

The correspondences were too close to be ignored and I felt sure that at some time in the distant past an object of great religious significance had been brought by Jews to the island of Tana Kirkos. Despite the chronological inconsistency in the supposed date of its arrival, there was also every reason to suppose – as Memhir Fisseha himself had so obviously believed – that that object might indeed have been the Holy Ark of the Covenant.

Chapter 10
Ghost in a Maze

During the discussions on Tana Kirkos a comment that the priest had made to me just before he had got to his main point had aroused my curiosity. That comment – the implications of which I now wanted to investigate further in the library at the Institute of Ethiopian Studies – had been to do with the *route* that the Ark had followed on its journey to Ethiopia. After being stolen from the Temple of Solomon in Jerusalem, the priest had said, it had first been carried into Egypt and from there had been brought to Lake Tana by way of the Nile and the Takazze rivers. Despite all the research that I had done during the previous few months, I realized that I had never given serious consideration to the question of Menelik's itinerary. I therefore wanted to see what the *Kebra Nagast* had to say on the matter. I also wanted to know if there was anything in it that specifically contradicted the priest's assertion that the Ark had spent eight hundred years at Tana Kirkos before being taken to Axum.

The only relevant information that I could find in the great epic was contained in Chapter 84. There it was reported that Menelik and his travelling companions had brought the sacred relic to a place called *Debra Makeda* after their arrival in Ethiopia.[1] To my surprise there was no mention of Axum whatsoever. 'Debra Makeda', wherever it might have been, was clearly and unambiguously highlighted as the Ark's first home in Ethiopia. At a stroke this cleared up one of the more serious factual inconsistencies that had bothered me since 1983 – namely that the city of Axum had not been founded until about eight hundred years after the date of Menelik's supposed journey.[2] Several of my original informants had told me that

Axum had been the final destination of that journey and that the Ark had been lodged there from the outset[3] – which, of course, would have been historically impossible. Now, however, I could see that the *Kebra Nagast* made no such claim and said only that Menelik and his companions had brought the relic from Jerusalem to 'Debra Makeda'. I knew that the word 'debra' meant 'mountain' and that 'Makeda' was the name given in Ethiopian tradition to the Queen of Sheba. 'Debra Makeda' therefore meant 'Mount Makeda' – the Queen of Sheba's mountain.

In the *Kebra Nagast*'s brief description I saw nothing to suggest that this 'Queen of Sheba's Mountain' might actually have been Tana Kirkos. By the same token, however, I could find nothing that ruled that possibility out. Seeking further clues I then referred to an authoritative geographical survey of Lake Tana carried out in the 1930s and learned that 'Kirkos' was a name that had been given to the island in relatively recent times (in honour of a Christian saint). 'Before the conversion of Ethiopia to Christianity,' the survey added, 'Tana Kirkos was called *Debra Sehel*.'[4] The obvious question immediately formed itself in my mind: what, exactly, did *Sehel* mean?

To find out I consulted several of the scholars who were then studying in the library. They told me that it was a *Ge'ez* word rooted in the verb 'to forgive'.

'Would I be right', I asked, 'in assuming that a correct translation of the full name *Debra Sehel* would be something like "Mount of Forgiveness"?'

'Yes,' they replied. 'That is correct.'

Now this was interesting. In Wolfram von Eschenbach's *Parzival*, as I remembered very well, the location of the Grail castle – and of the Grail Temple – was given as *Munsalvaesche*.[5] There had been some debate over the exact interpretation of this word *Munsalvaesche*; more than one Wolfram expert, however, had suggested that behind it lay 'the biblical *Mons Salvationis*, Mount of Salvation'.[6]

There could be no doubt that the notions of 'forgiveness' and 'salvation' were linked – since in order to be 'saved', in the religious sense, one must first be 'forgiven'. Moreover, as Psalm 130 puts it: 'If thou, Lord, shouldest mark iniquities . . . who shall stand? But there is *forgiveness* with thee . . . Let Israel hope in the Lord: for with the Lord there is mercy, and with him is plenteous *redemption*.'[7]

'Redemption' is, of course, a close synonym for 'salvation'.[8] I therefore could not help but wonder whether Wolfram's 'Mount of Salvation' might not in some way have been associated with Ethiopia's 'Mount of Forgiveness' – now known as Tana Kirkos.

I was fully aware that speculation of this kind could only ever be tenuous and that it was a long jump indeed from *Debra Sehel* to *Munsalvaesche*. Nevertheless, after my many readings of *Parzival*, I could hardly forget that the mystical Grail Temple ('smooth and rounded as though from a lathe'[9]) had stood on a lake – and quite possibly on an island on that lake.[10] Nor did it seem entirely irrelevant that Ethiopian Orthodox churches and Falasha places of worship were traditionally circular in shape[11] – as were the majority of Templar churches (including several still standing to this day such as the twelfth-century Temple Church off London's Fleet Street). I therefore felt that there were certain correspondences in all of this which it might be unwise for me to ignore entirely (though it would be equally unwise to read too much into them).

Meanwhile there was another and rather less tentative link to consider – that between *Debra Sehel* and *Debra Makeda*. As the former name of Tana Kirkos made clear, Ethiopian islands could acquire the prefix *Debra* (meaning 'Mount'). And, indeed – rising steeply to a high peak that towered above the surface of the lake –Tana Kirkos had looked to me very much like a mountain when I had first set eyes on it. This certainly did not prove that the *Kebra Nagast* had been referring to *Debra Sehel* when it had spoken of the Ark being taken to the Queen of Sheba's mountain. I reasoned, however, that it did at least elevate the island to the status of a candidate for that distinction.

With this established, I moved on to consider the question of the route that Menelik and his companions had followed on their journey. Previously I had always assumed that the travellers had gone by ship – from Solomon's port of Eziongeber (modern Elat on the Gulf of Aqaba),[12] and thence down the Red Sea to the Ethiopian coast. Now, as I pored over the copy of the *Kebra Nagast* provided to me by the librarian, I discovered that my earlier assumption had been quite wrong. Menelik's long journey from Jerusalem had involved a substantial caravan and had been overland throughout.[13]

But *what* overland route had been followed? The description of the trek given in the *Kebra Nagast* had the dreamlike, miraculous and surreal quality of imaginative storytelling, in which recognizable place names and geographical features were not easy to find. Nevertheless there were some details that were both specific and important. After leaving Jerusalem the travellers had first made their way to Gaza (on Israel's Mediterranean coast, where a city of that name still exists). From there, presumably following the well established trade route across the northern edge of the Sinai peninsula,[14] they had crossed into Egypt where, not long afterwards, they had arrived at a great river: 'Let us let down the wagons,' they said at this point, 'for we have come to the water of Ethiopia. This is the Takazze which floweth down from Ethiopia and watereth the valley of Egypt.'[15] It was clear from the context that Menelik and his companions were *still* in 'the valley of Egypt' when they uttered these words – and probably not far south of the site of modern Cairo. The river beside which they had let down their wagons could therefore only have been the Nile. What was striking, however, was that they had immediately identified it with the Takazze – the same great Ethiopian tributary that the priest had mentioned to me on Tana Kirkos.

From the librarian I obtained an atlas and traced the Takazze's course with my fingertip. I found that it rose in Abyssinia's central highlands not far from the ancient town of Lalibela, took a winding path in a north-westerly direction through the Simien mountains, merged with the Atbara in the Sudan, and finally joined the Nile proper some hundreds of miles to the north of the modern city of Khartoum (which stands at the confluence of the Blue and White Niles).

Looking at the map I could immediately see two other things: first that the Nile – from an Ethiopian perspective – might easily have come to be regarded as an extension of the Takazze;[16] secondly that it would have been entirely sensible for the caravan carrying the Ark of the Covenant to have followed the Nile and then the Takazze in order to reach Ethiopia. The alternative would have been to proceed much further southwards through the hostile deserts of the Sudan as far as the confluence of the two Niles and then to follow the Blue Nile into the highlands. However – since the latter river makes a wide curving detour to the south before turning north again towards Lake Tana – this would have required an unnecessarily lengthy expedition; the Takazze route, by contrast, was the best part of a thousand miles shorter.

The map made something else clear as well: a group of travellers following the Takazze to its headwaters would, near the end of their journey, have reached a point less than seventy miles from the eastern shore of Lake Tana. And Tana Kirkos lay not far off that same eastern shore. There was thus no mystery surrounding the tradition that the little island had been the first resting place of the Ark in Ethiopia: indeed, casting around for somewhere safe and close to install the sacred relic, Menelik and his companions could hardly have made a better choice.

Three men in a boat

The next morning when Richard Pankhurst and I travelled to Lake Zwai we were accompanied by an old friend of mine, Yohannes Berhanu, the General Manager of the state-owned National Tour Operation. The three of us met up just before 6 a.m. at the NTO offices, where Yohannes had thoughtfully provided a chauffeur-driven Toyota Landcruiser. Twenty minutes later we had left the slums and skyscrapers of Addis Ababa behind and were rumbling along the broad highway that led south through the town of Debra Zeit into the heart of the Great Rift Valley.

Discounting the Koka reservoir, which is man-made, Lake Zwai is the northernmost of Ethiopia's string of Rift Valley lakes. It has a surface area of some two hundred square miles and a maximum depth of about fifty feet. Oval in shape, it is studded with islands and has marshy shores overgrown with reeds that provide an ideal habitat for storks, pelicans, wild ducks, geese and fish eagles – as well as for great numbers of hippopotami.

Our destination, after the two-hour drive from Addis Ababa, was a jetty on the southern side of the lake. Here we had been told that the Ministry of Fisheries owned and operated a number of boats, one of which would surely be provided for us at minimal cost. Predictably, however, all the larger vessels had gone fishing. Only a single small motorboat was available – and there was no fuel for its outboard engine.

A lengthy palaver followed with the Ministry staff who explained that the motorboat wasn't really big enough to take Richard, Yohannes and me as well as a pilot. Debra Zion, the island to which I had been told that the Ark had been brought for safekeeping in the tenth century, was distant: at least a three-hour journey in this humble craft. Furthermore, with no deck to shelter under, we would be grievously afflicted by the sun. Perhaps, therefore, we would care to come back tomorrow when more suitable transport could be arranged?

Yohannes vehemently declined this suggestion. Professor Pankhurst and Mr Hancock, he said, had important appointments in Addis Ababa tomorrow – appointments which could not under any circumstances be altered. We must, therefore, reach Debra Zion today.

More discussions followed and eventually we trooped along the jetty and sat experimentally in the tiny motorboat. Arranged around its sides we did more or less fit into it, although our combined weight forced it rather low in the water.

What to do? The Fisheries officials seemed dubious but at last agreed to let us have our way. The vessel was ours. They would provide a pilot. And there would be no charge. We, however, would have to arrange for the fuel ourselves. Perhaps we could send our driver into the nearest town with a jerrycan?

We did this. A vast and completely inexplicable delay then ensued. One hour passed. Then another. Growing impatient I stood at the end of the jetty and made the acquaintance of several marabou storks: huge, lugubrious, long-beaked, bald-headed birds obviously descended from pterodactyls. Finally our driver returned with the necessary fuel and – just after 11 a.m. – we started up the outboard motor and set off.

We puttered, very slowly, through the rippling waters, passing one densely wooded island, then another. The reed-fringed shoreline receded and then disappeared behind us, there was no sign of Debra Zion, the sun was now directly overhead, and the boat was leaking in a small but noticeable way.

At this point Yohannes Berhanu rather pointedly reminded us

that the lake was full of hippopotami (which he described as 'very aggressive and untrustworthy animals'). He was, I observed, wearing a life-jacket that he must somehow have acquired before our departure from the jetty. Meanwhile, Richard Pankhurst's nose was turning an interesting shade of lobster pink. And I . . . well I was gritting my teeth and trying to ignore the implications of an increasingly full bladder. Where was that bloody island? And when exactly were we going to get there? I looked impatiently at my watch and was suddenly overtaken by a faint but definite sense of the ridiculous. I mean, *Raiders of the Lost Ark* was one thing but this, to be honest, was more like *Three Men in a Boat*.

The journey to Debra Zion did not take as long as we had been told it would; nevertheless it took quite long enough and I was the first on to dry land when we finally arrived. I dashed past the delegation of monks waiting to greet us, disappeared behind the nearest bush and emerged again some minutes later feeling very much better.

When I rejoined the others, who were deep in conversation with the welcoming committee, I noticed a number of papyrus-reed boats lined up along the shore. They seemed identical in every respect to those I had seen on Lake Tana. I was on the point of asking about this when Yohannes interrupted my chain of thought by announcing excitedly: 'Graham. There is something strange here. It seems that the mother-tongue of these people is Tigrigna.'

This was strange indeed. We were now in the southern part of the province of Shoa, an Amharic-speaking area. Tigrigna, on the other hand, was the language of the sacred city of Axum and of the province of Tigray – hundreds of miles to the north. I knew from direct experience that Ethiopia was a country in which regional distinctions, particularly linguistic distinctions, had very profound implications (profound enough, anyway, to lead to civil war). It was therefore most surprising to find that Amharic was not the first language of the monks of Debra Zion.

Nor, as it turned out, did this peculiarity apply only to the monks. We quickly established that every inhabitant of the island, including the farmers and the fishermen, routinely conversed in a dialect of Tigrigna and only used Amharic (which many of them did not speak at all well) on the rare occasions when they were visited by government officials.

As we hiked up the winding path to the top of the hill where Debra Zion's main church was sited I asked: 'How come you all speak Tigrigna?'

'Because our forefathers came from Tigray,' the monks replied through the medium of Yohannes.

'When did they come?'

'It was around one thousand and thirty years ago.'

I did some quick mental arithmetic. One thousand and thirty years from 1989 gave a date of AD 959. The tenth century, I thought. The century in which Queen Gudit had overthrown the Solomonic dynasty and in which the Ark of the Covenant had supposedly been taken out of Axum and brought to Debra Zion for safekeeping. Without really having begun to interview anybody it was already beginning to look very much as though the tradition reported to me by Belai Gedai had some substance to it.

'Why did they come?' I asked next. 'Get them to tell us the story of how and why they came here.'

Yohannes put this to the monks and then translated their answer: 'You see, their forefathers came here with the *tabot*. It was in the time of Gudit. She attacked the Christians in Tigray. There was much fighting. They were escaping from her. And they came here with the *tabot*.'

'Which *tabot*?'

'They say it was the *tabot* from the Church of Saint Mary of Zion in Axum.'

'By that do they mean the original *tabot* that was brought by Menelik from Jerusalem to Ethiopia? The Ark of the Covenant in other words. Or do they have some other *tabot* in mind? I want to be absolutely clear on this point.'

Yohannes manfully plunged into this minefield of interpretation while we carried on walking up the steep hill. Much argument and debate followed before he finally commented: 'I do not think they are very clear themselves. But they say that it is written . . . that it is all written in a book, kept here in the church, and that we should discuss the whole matter with their senior priest.'

Stolen history

Five minutes later we arrived at the church which, I was not
entirely surprised to discover, was dedicated to Saint Mary of
Zion. It was a plain and unpretentious wattle-and-daub building,
whitewashed on the outside and surmounted by a simple cross.
The view that it commanded from its position on the hilltop was,
however, superb, giving us some idea of the extent of this large
island. Behind us, from the direction we had come, the path
wound back through fields dotted with the poor huts of peasant
farmers. Ahead of us the land sloped steeply away to the lake's
edge through a forest of acacia trees and cactus.

The senior priest, Abba Gebra Christos, now presented
himself. A small wiry man, probably in his late sixties, he wore a
thin grey beard and a threadbare two-piece suit, around the
shoulders of which he had draped a length of white cotton cloth
in traditional highland fashion. His manner was welcoming and
genial enough but there was also a foxy and calculating look about
him that seemed to forebode imminent financial transactions.

I nervously fingered the greasy wad of birr that I had stuffed
into my pocket before leaving Addis and resolved to pay only for
high-quality information. Then, making as little song and dance
as possible, I switched on my tape-recorder and asked my first
question: did he know the story of how Menelik had abducted the
Ark of the Covenant from the Temple of Solomon in Jerusalem?

Yes, Yohannes translated, of course he did.

And did he know what had happened next?

Menelik, the priest replied, had brought the Ark to Ethiopia
where it remained to this day.

'Is he sure', I asked 'that this was the original Ark of the
Covenant, containing the Ten Commandments inscribed on the
Tablets of Stone by the finger of God?'

Yohannes put the question and Abba Gebra Christos replied
gravely: 'Yes. I am sure.'

'OK. Good. Now tell me . . . was this same original Ark ever
brought here to Lake Zwai – to Debra Zion?'

'Yes,' said the priest, 'at the time of Gudit the Ark was brought
here from Axum.'

'But *why* was it brought here?' I asked. 'I mean, why here? Why such a long way? Surely there must have been hundreds of secret places where it could have been hidden in Tigray?'

'Listen . . . This Gudit . . . she was a devil. She burned many churches in Tigray. And in other regions of Ethiopia. It was a time of great fighting, great danger. Our forefathers were very much afraid that she would capture the Ark. So they brought it out of Axum and they carried it to Zwai where they knew that it would be safe. They travelled only by night, hiding by day in forests and in caves. They were very much afraid, I tell you! But in this way they evaded her soldiers and they brought the Ark to Zwai and to this island.'

'Do you know how long it remained here?'

With no hesitation at all Abba Gebra Christos replied: 'After seventy-two years it was returned back to Axum.'

Now, I thought, was the right time to pop the sixty-four thousand dollar question: 'Has there been any other occasion', I asked tentatively, 'when the Ark has been brought here again for safekeeping? Perhaps recently?'

Again there was no hesitation: 'Never.'

'So as far as you know it is still in Axum?'

'Yes.'

'Even now – with all the fighting going on in Tigray?'

He shrugged: 'I believe so. But that is only my opinion. To find out truly you must ask those in Axum.'

Another thought now occurred to me: 'When we were walking up here,' I said, 'some of the monks told us that you have an ancient book in which is written the history of how the Ark came to Debra Zion in Gudit's time. Is that correct? Do you have such a book?'

As Yohannes translated this question, the wizened features of Abba Gebra Christos formed themselves into the expression of one who has just tasted something unexpectedly sour. He responded readily enough, however: 'Yes, there is a book.'

'Can we see it?'

A momentary hesitation, then: 'Yes . . . But the part concerning the Ark is no longer there.'

'I'm sorry. I don't follow. What do you mean exactly?'

'About twenty years ago a certain man came and cut some pages from the book and took those pages away with him. They were the pages in which the story of the Ark was told.'

'This man. Was he a foreigner? Or was he an Ethiopian?'

'Well, he was an Ethiopian. But since that time we have not been able to track him down.'

As I considered the implications of this last answer I could not help but reflect on the bizarre and convoluted nature of the enterprise that I was now involved in. Was the matter of the unknown man who had cut an unknown number of pages from an unknown book something that should concern me? Or was it an irrelevance? Was I picking up the traces of someone else's quest for the Ark of the Covenant? Or was I dealing simply with a local manuscript hunter who twenty years ago had made a fast buck on the antiquities market with the sale of a few illuminated folios?

I suspected that I might never know. Pursuing the Ark through Ethiopia was turning out to be far more daunting and difficult than I had ever imagined. Indeed it was something like pursuing a ghost through a maze. Avenues that seemed promising and open from one perspective turned out, on closer examination, to be impassable dead ends; by contrast apparent dead ends had more than once transformed themselves into paths to understanding.

I sighed, refocussed my mind on the immediate issue, and told Abba Gebra Christos that even if the most important pages were missing, I would still very much like to see the book that he had mentioned. Perhaps he would allow us to photograph it?

This suggestion produced a flurry of nervous objections. No, the old priest said, he could not possibly let us do that. Photographs were out of the question unless specific written permission were given by the Patriarch of the Ethiopian Orthodox Church in Addis Ababa. Did we by any chance have such permission?

No, we did not.

Then, regretfully, we could not photograph the book. We could, however, *see* it if that was what we wanted.

I indicated that we would be grateful even for that small mercy. Abba Gebra Christos nodded sagely, led us inside his church and walked over to a cupboard near the back of the humble building. A tremendous pantomime ensued as he searched in all his pockets for the necessary key – which, after some moments, he confessed that he could not find.

A young deacon was then summoned and sent off somewhere. Ten minutes later, panting and out of breath, the boy returned clutching a bundle of at least twenty keys. One after another these were tried in the lock and eventually – to my considerable surprise – the door was opened. The cupboard, however, was almost bare and the one book that it contained proved to be an early twentieth-century work donated to the church by Princess Zauditu, the daughter of Emperor Menelik II.

At this point Abba Gebra Christos suddenly remembered an important fact: the manuscript we wanted to see was not in the church after all. A few weeks ago he himself had taken it to the repository, which was in a separate building some distance away. If we would like to accompany him he would show it to us there.

I looked at my watch, decided there was just enough time before we had to leave the island, and gave my assent to this plan. A lengthy hike followed and we eventually arrived at a rather decrepit stone-built two-storey house. The priest ushered us grandly into a dank and musty rear room, around the walls of which were arranged dozens of wooden chests and garishly painted tin trunks. After a moment of indecision he advanced towards one of these trunks and threw back its lid revealing a pile of books within. He lifted out the topmost of these – a weighty tome with pages made of cured sheepskin – and passed it over to me.

Richard Pankhurst and Yohannes crowded round as I opened the volume. They immediately confirmed that it was written in *Ge'ez*. Moreover it was undoubtedly very old: 'From the style of the illuminations, and from the binding, I would guess thirteenth century,' volunteered Richard. 'It's certainly not later than the fourteenth century. There's no doubt that it's an early work. Probably very valuable.'

Eagerly we began to turn the pages. At no point, however, was there any indication that anything had been removed. As far as we could tell the manuscript was intact. We pointed this out to Abba Gebra Christos, who had been standing silently watching us, and asked him whether he was absolutely certain that this was the book he had talked to us about.

As it turned out, it was not. Apologetically the old priest then rummaged in a number of other boxes around the room, passing us a series of ancient manuscripts.

'It's quite amazing,' Richard commented at one point. 'So many old books. A real treasure trove. And they're just lying here in complete disarray. They could get damp. They could get stolen. Anything could happen to them. I wish we could move the whole lot of them to the Institute.'

The last volume we looked at was a wood-bound and beautifully illuminated copy of the Ethiopian Book of Saints. It too was intact. When we had finished going through it Richard nudged me in the ribs: 'I think,' he said, 'that we're not getting anywhere here.'

I nodded: 'I think you're right. And it's really late. We'd better go or we'll end up having to cross the whole lake in the dark.'

Before leaving, however, I asked Yohannes to make a final attempt to get some sense out of the priest. Was the book that told the story of the Ark really here or not?

Certainly it was here, Abba Gebra Christos insisted. Of course it was here. The only problem was that he was no longer certain in which box he had placed it. If we would care to wait – just a little longer – he was sure that he could locate it . . .

This was an offer that I felt safe in declining. It seemed to me that the old man was being deliberately evasive – and if that were the case then presumably it meant that he was hiding something. But what? Not, I thought, the Ark itself. Perhaps not even the notorious book. But something, definitely.

Puzzled and a little piqued I led the way back to the motorboat. We said our farewells. Then, with at least an hour of sunlight still left in the sky, we headed out onto the still waters of Lake Zwai.

I wrote in my notebook:

I don't believe there is any purpose in spending further time investigating Debra Zion. After interviewing the monks and the senior priest I feel quite certain that the importance of the island lies solely in the strength of its *ancient* traditions concerning the Ark of the Covenant. Broadly speaking these traditions seem to confirm what Belai Gedai told me in one of our telephone conversations – namely that the Ark was brought to

Debra Zion in the tenth century to keep it safe from Gudit, that it stayed here for about seventy years, and that it was then returned to Axum.

The fact that the mother-tongue of all the islanders is Tigrigna rather than Amharic is strong 'social' evidence in support of the oral history I was given – because the only logical explanation for such an ethnographic peculiarity is that there was indeed a movement of population from the Axum area to Debra Zion in the distant past. Something as momentous as the need to bring the Ark to safety could certainly account for a migration of this sort. Moreover, if the relic did stay here for as long a period as seventy years before being taken back to Axum, then it's quite easy to see why some of the descendants of the original migrants would have wanted to stay on the island, which would have been the only home they knew. It's also to be expected that they would have maintained a folk memory of the glorious events in which their forefathers were involved.

That folk memory is what I've spent most of the afternoon listening to. In the process some intriguing local mysteries surfaced. At no point, however, did I get any sense at all that the Ark might actually be here now. On the contrary, I feel confident in saying that it isn't here – and, furthermore, that it hasn't been here for the best part of a thousand years.

Since the same goes for the islands of Lake Tana as well it's becoming transparently obvious that Axum is still the most probable place for the relic to be. In other words, like it or not, I'm going to have to go to Axum. The best time to do that would be in January during *Timkat*, which is the one occasion when I might be able to get close to the Ark without having to gain access to the sanctuary chapel. And *Timkat* 1770 was when Bruce was there – presumably for the same reason.

I closed my notebook and looked up at Richard and Yohannes. 'Do you think there's any possibility,' I asked, 'that the government will have captured Axum by January? I'd really like to get there in time to attend the next *Timkat*.'

Yohannes said nothing. Richard made a face: 'A nice idea. But you might as well plan to fly to the moon.'

'Well,' I said, 'it was just a thought.'

It was after dark when we finally moored the motorboat at the Ministry of Fisheries jetty, and almost 10 p.m. by the time we reached the sprawling outskirts of Addis Ababa. We instructed our driver to head for Yohannes's office in the centre of town where we had parked our cars that morning (there were still two hours left before curfew and our plan was to grab a quick dinner at a nearby restaurant). As we climbed down out of the Landcruiser, however, we heard a prolonged burst of automatic rifle fire which seemed to come from an apartment block just across the road. Seconds later there were two short answering bursts from a different weapon. Then a profound silence fell.

'What on earth was that all about?' I asked.

'Probably nothing serious,' Richard offered. 'There have been a few isolated incidents since the attempted *coup* . . . shootings here and there. But nothing major.'

'Nevertheless,' said Yohannes gravely, 'I think that it would be wise for us to abandon dinner. Let us all go to our homes.'

An ethnographic fingerprint

Back at the Hilton I slept soundly and awoke before seven the next morning – Friday 24 November. I then took a turn in the pool, had breakfast and telephoned the office of Shimelis Mazengia. The Politburo member had asked Richard and me to report back to him after completing our trips to Lake Tana and Lake Zwai. His secretary now told me that she had been expecting my call and gave us an appointment for three o'clock that same afternoon.

Satisfied with this arrangement, and determined to bring up the question of *Timkat* and Axum despite Richard's pessimism, I left the hotel and drove round to the Institute of Ethiopian Studies.

My research on Wednesday the 22nd had established the plausibility of the Nile/Takazze route mentioned in the *Kebra Nagast* and also by the priest on Tana Kirkos.[17] What I wanted to do now was to test out a hypothesis that had subsequently taken rough shape in my mind. It seemed to me that if Menelik and the first-born sons of the elders of Israel had indeed brought the Ark to Tana Kirkos by following the Takazze river, then this would have had implications for the distribution of the Jewish faith in Ethiopia. If there was some truth to the legend, I reasoned, then the traditional epicentre of the Falasha population should lie between the Takazze and Lake Tana – since it would have been in precisely this area that Menelik would first have begun to convert the local population to Judaism. If the legends were false, however, then I might expect to find that the bulk of the Falashas lived elsewhere – most likely much further north and close to the Red Sea (since academic orthodoxy had it that their forefathers had been converted by Jewish immigrants from the Yemen).

I turned first to James Bruce, whose early work on the Falashas had already impressed me so much. In Volume III of his *Travels* I knew that the Scottish author had devoted a chapter to what might loosely be termed the 'social geography' of eighteenth-century Ethiopia. Though I did not remember the contents of this chapter very clearly I hoped that it would have something to say about the location of the principal Falasha settlements at that time.

I was not disappointed. Bruce's survey began in the north of Ethiopia – at the Red Sea port of Massawa – and worked inland from there. Several ethnic groups were covered but no mention was made of the Falashas in either Eritrea or Tigray. 'After passing the Takazze', however, the country stretching to the south and west as far as Lake Tana was described as being:

> in great part possessed by Jews, and there [the] king and queen of that nation and, as they say, of the house of Judah, maintain still their ancient sovereignty and religion from very early times.[18]

Writing in the nineteenth century (about eighty years after Bruce) the German missionary Martin Flad had recorded a similar distribution of population, noting that the Falashas lived in a total of fourteen provinces – all of which lay 'west of the Takazze'.[19]

The modern sources that I next reviewed painted the same

picture. The vast majority of Ethiopia's Jews inhabited the territory to the west and south of the Takazze river: this was their traditional homeland and their occupation of it was ancient beyond memory.[20] One particularly detailed and authoritative study included a map in which the entire area of Falasha settlement was shaded – a long but relatively narrow strip extending south-west from the Takazze through the Simien mountains and the city of Gondar and then going on, without any interruption, to encompass the whole of Lake Tana.[21]

It would have been difficult to find more telling support for my hypothesis that this – with the unique impetus provided by the presence of the Ark on Tana Kirkos – had been precisely the area in which the conversion of native Abyssinians to Old Testament Judaism had been concentrated. On the basis of my own research (see Chapter 6) I had anyway begun to doubt the merits of the academic theory which held that the Jewish faith had first been imported into the far north of Ethiopia from the Yemen at some point after AD 70. Hitherto my dissatisfaction with such notions had stemmed mainly from their failure to explain the extremely archaic nature of Falasha beliefs and rituals (again, see Chapter 6). Now the ethnographic evidence made the case against the 'Yemeni connection' look even stronger: on the map, the area in which the Falashas lived stood out like a tell-tale fingerprint confirming that the religion of Solomon could only have entered Ethiopia from the west – through Egypt and the Sudan along the ancient and well-travelled trade routes provided by the Nile and Takazze rivers.[22]

The virtue of patience

At three sharp, Richard and I kept our appointment with Shimelis Mazengia. The Politburo member first of all wanted to hear how our trips to Lake Tana and to Lake Zwai had gone. Had we been successful? Had we found anything out?

I replied that our discoveries on Tana Kirkos island – and the strange, archaic traditions that had been reported to us there – had had a profound effect on my thinking. I was now almost certain that this was the region to which the Ark of the Covenant had first been brought before being taken to Axum.

'So you really believe that we have the Ark?' Shimelis asked with a smile.

'I'm increasingly confident of that. The evidence is building up . . .' I hesitated, then turned his question back on him: 'What do you think?'

'I think there is something very special in the sanctuary at Axum. Not necessarily the Ark, mind you, but something very special. It is an ancient tradition. It cannot completely be ignored.'

I asked whether his government had ever made a determined effort to find out whether the sacred – and immensely valuable – relic was really there or not. The Workers' Party of Ethiopia were Marxists, after all, and so presumably were not hampered by reactionary superstitions. It was only quite recently that they'd lost Axum to the TPLF. Prior to that, hadn't they ever thought of taking a look?

'We never for a moment considered it,' Shimelis replied. 'Never for a single moment . . . If we had tried to do something like that I think we would have had' – he smiled ironically – 'a revolution on our hands. Our people are very traditional, as you know, and there would have been an explosion if any government official had ever involved himself in such a matter.'

'Do you think the TPLF have the same attitude?' I asked. 'Now that they control Axum, I mean.'

The Politburo member shrugged: 'That is not for me to say. But they are not renowned for their religious sensitivities . . .'

I was a little hesitant about putting my next question, but did so anyway: 'I'm sorry if this sounds impertinent,' I said, 'but I've got to ask. Is there any chance at all that your side is going to win the city back in the immediate future?'

'Why do you ask?'

'Because I've come to the conclusion that I'm going to have to go there myself. In fact I'd like to get there for the next *Timkat* celebrations.'

'You mean this coming January?'

I nodded my head.

'Impossible,' said Shimelis flatly. 'Besides, why be in such a hurry? If you are right, then the Ark has already been in our country for three millennia. In another year, two at the most, we will recapture Axum and when we do I think I can promise that you will be the first foreigner into the city. So be patient. You will get your chance.'

I had to admit that this was sound advice. In a country like Ethiopia patience was almost always a virtue. I was not prepared to wait two years, however. I therefore silently resolved to aim for Axum not in January 1990, but in January 1991. The confidence that Shimelis had shown had impressed me and I hoped very much that the sacred city would be back in government hands by then. Meanwhile, however – just as a precaution – I thought that I might also try to open up some dialogue with the TPLF. I had hitherto avoided the rebels but it now seemed to me that it might be in my interests to make some preliminary overtures in their direction.

I looked across the table at Shimelis. 'You're right of course,' I said. 'But would you mind if I asked you another favour?'

With an eloquent hand gesture, the Politburo member indicated that I should go ahead.

'I'd still like to attend a *Timkat* ceremony,' I continued, 'and since Axum is obviously out of the question I was wondering whether I might be able to go to Gondar this January instead.'

Beside me Richard coughed politely. The city that I had just named was reportedly besieged by rebel forces and there had been rumours that it might fall any day.

'Why Gondar?' Shimelis asked.

'Because it's in the Lake Tana area – which, as I said, I've identified as being closely associated with the early history of the Ark in this country. And because I understand that many Falashas still live in and around Gondar. I remember passing through Jewish villages just north of the city way back in 1983, but I didn't have a chance to carry out any proper interviews at that time. So what I'd like to do, if it's OK with you, is kill two birds with one stone. I'd like to attend *Timkat* in Gondar. And while I'm there I'd like to carry out some research amongst the Falashas.'

'It may be possible,' replied Shimelis. 'It depends on the military situation, but it may be possible. I shall look into it and let you know.'

Chapter 11

And David danced
before the Ark . . .

On 18 and 19 January 1770 the Scottish adventurer James
Bruce had quietly attended the *Timkat* ceremonials in Axum
and, as outlined in Chapter 7, I believed that he had done so in
order to get as close as possible to the Ark of the Covenant.

Exactly two hundred and twenty years later – on 18 and 19
January 1990 – I attended *Timkat* in the city of Gondar to the
north of Lake Tana. Moreover, although I had not shared my
true feelings with either Richard Pankhurst or with Shimelis
Mazengia, I saw this trip as being of pivotal significance to my
quest.

Immersed as I was in the great historical mystery that
connected the Ark to Ethiopia, it had become clear to me that
sooner or later, somehow or other, I was going to have to go back
to Axum. I had resolved to try to make that hazardous visit in
January 1991 – and to make it under the auspices of the rebels if
necessary. I therefore saw Gondar as a crucial 'dry run': the
closest point to Axum still in government hands, it was also, like
Axum, a former capital of Ethiopia, an important historic site and
a centre of religious learning. In such a setting, I reasoned, I
might hope to prepare myself spiritually and psychologically for
the real ordeal that lay ahead, to familiarize myself with aspects of
the same arcane rituals that Bruce must have witnessed in 1770,
to gather such intelligence as I could, and to quicken my
commitment to the quest.

This, however, was not the only voice within me. Other, less
steadfast thoughts also passed through my mind and I could see
the possibility of a different outcome. If, for example, I were to
discover anything at Gondar which cast serious doubt on the

legitimacy of Ethiopia's claim to be the last resting place of the Ark then might I not – with honour – abandon my plan to go to Axum in 1991?

This was a disturbing but oddly seductive notion to which I found myself increasingly attracted as the date of the Gondar trip approached. That trip itself was for a while in doubt – indeed it was not until 8 January 1990 that I finally received a telex from Shimelis confirming that the necessary permission had been obtained from the military authorities.

Riddles to solve

I knew that I could expect a central feature of the *Timkat* ceremonies to be the carrying in procession of the *tabotat* – the symbols or replicas of the Ark of the Covenant normally kept in the Holy of Holies of every Ethiopian church. Of course in Gondar I would not see the object which the Ethiopians claimed to be the Ark itself (since there was no suggestion that it had ever been lodged there). What I would see, however, was an event otherwise identical in character that was regarded as the supreme festival of the Ethiopian Orthodox calendar.

I had been aware for some time that *Timkat* meant 'Epiphany' – a holy day associated by the western church with the manifestation of Christ to the Gentiles.[1] Epiphany, however, had an entirely different significance amongst eastern Christians, for whom it commemorated the Baptism of Christ.[2] I had established that the Ethiopians were in complete agreement with the rest of the eastern church on this latter point, but that they diverged radically from the norm when it came to the specific rituals employed.[3] In particular, their use of the *tabot* was unique to them, unparalleled in any other culture and unrecognized even by the Coptic Patriarchate in Alexandria[4] (which had supplied Ethiopia with all its archbishops from the date of the conversion of the Axumite kingdom in AD 331 until autocephaly was achieved in 1959[5]).

Against this background I felt that close observation of the *Timkat* rituals and of the role of the *tabotat* within them might help me to fathom what I had long since come to regard as the central paradox of Ethiopian Christianity – namely its infiltration, indeed domination, by a pre-Christian relic: the Ark of the Covenant.

This, however, was not my sole purpose in making the trip to Gondar. While there I also intended to talk to Falashas living in the environs of the city.

I had already mentioned this to Shimelis and he had not objected – for the simple reason that much had changed since my previous visit to the area in 1983. Then, driving north from Gondar into the Simien mountains, official policy had made it almost impossible to do any serious work amongst the black Jews: their villages had been effectively out of bounds and there had been no opportunity to observe their customs or to carry out proper interviews.

This repressive state of affairs had been swept away in November 1989 when, after a sixteen-year break, Addis Ababa and Jerusalem had restored diplomatic relations. At the heart of this agreement was a commitment on Ethiopia's part to allow the Falashas – *all* the Falashas – to emigrate to Israel. By then, anyway, there were few enough left – probably no more than 15,000.[6] All the others had died during the famines of the mid-1980s or had already fled clandestinely to Israel via refugee camps in the Sudan (from which, during 1984/5 alone, the airlift known as 'Operation Moses' had taken more than 12,000 to safety[7]).

The net effect of all this, by January 1990, was that the number of Ethiopian Jews was dwindling fast. In the three months since the restoration of diplomatic relations some 3,000 of them had left the country. Many more had deserted their villages and flocked to Addis Ababa hoping for an early place on the planes out. Inexorable and unstoppable, this latter-day Exodus was gathering pace, and I could see that very soon not a single Falasha would be left in Ethiopia. Thereafter, of course, it would still be possible to interview them and research their folklore and traditions in the Promised Land. This, however, would almost certainly be the last year in which it would be possible to get any impression at all of their traditional life in its traditional surroundings.

I was determined not to miss this chance: the riddle of how there had ever come to be Jews – indigenous, black Jews – in the heart of Ethiopia was intimately connected to the enigma of the Holy Ark; solve one, I felt, and I would solve the other.

Neither were the Falashas the only ethnic group of interest to me in the Gondar area. In the week of research that I had done just prior to my departure from England I had turned up an intriguing reference to another people – a people known as the Qemant who were described as 'Hebraeo-Pagans' in the single anthropological paper written about them.[8] Published in 1969 by an American scholar named Frederick Gamst, this obscure monograph observed that:

> The Hebraism found among the Qemant is an ancient form unaffected by Hebraic religious change of the past two millennia. This Hebraism is dominant in the religion of the Falasha, neighbours of the Qemant . . . sometimes called 'the black Jews of Ethiopia'.[9]

I had hitherto been completely unaware of the Qemant and was therefore intrigued by Gamst's suggestion that their religion contained ancient 'Hebraic' elements. This, I felt, was a matter that obviously merited further investigation since it might help to shed light on the antiquity of Judaic influence in Ethiopia – and also on the pervasiveness of that influence.

The One God and the fetish tree

In his study of the Qemant Gamst had mentioned that he had been befriended by a religious leader who had helped him enormously with his field work in the 1960s. The name of this dignitary, I knew, was Muluna Marsha and his title was *Wambar* (a word meaning 'High Priest' in the Qemant language). In the short time available, it seemed to me that my best strategy would be to try to locate this man (whom Gamst had described as a mine of information) and to interview him about the religious beliefs of his people. I could not be sure, however, whether he would still be alive after so many years – or even whether I would be able to find any Qemant still adhering to the traditional Hebraeo-Pagan faith (since there had been less than five hundred of them in Gamst's time[10]).

After my arrival in Gondar on Wednesday 17 January I discussed this worry with the officials who came to meet me at the airport and was told that there were a very few Qemant – now mostly elderly – who continued to adhere to the old religion. Feelers were then put out, radio messages were sent to Party cadres in remote areas, and, on Thursday the 18th, I got the good news that the Wambar was still alive. His home village, apparently, was inaccessible by road but it was thought possible that he might be persuaded to come to an intermediate point – Aykel, about two hours' drive due west of Gondar. The journey, furthermore, would almost certainly be safe: in recent fighting the rebels had been pushed back and the western region into which we would be going was considered to be secure during daylight hours.

Timkat, which I shall describe later in this chapter, took up all of my attention for the rest of Thursday and all of Friday. Early in the afternoon of Saturday 20 January, however, I was finally able to set off for Aykel in the Toyota Landcruiser that the Party had put at my disposal. In addition to the driver, I was accompanied by Legesse Desta – the young and enthusiastic official who was acting as my interpreter – and by two dour soldiers armed with Kalashnikov assault rifles.

As we bumped along the rough, graded track through glowing fields and golden-brown hills I studied the Michelin map of the Horn of Africa that I now took everywhere with me. I was interested to note that our destination lay not far from the headwaters of the Atbara river which rose about fifty miles to the north-west of Lake Tana and flowed from there into the Sudan, where it was eventually joined by the Takazze before merging with the Nile just above the Fifth Cataract.

Because it passed so close to Tana Kirkos, and because it was specifically mentioned in the *Kebra Nagast*, the Takazze itself still looked to me like the strongest contender for the route of the Ark. Nevertheless it was clear from the map that travellers following the Atbara would also have arrived in this same general area. I considered the implications of this and then remarked in my journal:

The rivers are roads through the desert. In the case of

Ethiopia all these 'roads' – whether the Takazze, the
Atbara, or the Blue Nile – seem to lead to Lake Tana.
The Falashas (and their relatives the 'Hebraeo-Pagan'
Qemant) have always lived in precisely this area and are
indigenous Ethiopians – natives of this country. Since
their Judaism (or 'Hebraism' as Gamst prefers to call it) is
a foreign element in their culture, it is logical to deduce
that it *must* have been imported along the rivers.

As we drove into Aykel we were met by a group of local Party
officials who told us that Wambar Muluna Marsha had arrived
some time ago and was waiting for us. We were then taken to a
large, circular hut with a high beehive-shaped roof and ushered
into the cool semi-darkness within. Thin shafts of sunlight fell
through gaps in the wattle-and-daub, highlighting motes of dust
that hung suspended in the air. From the newly brushed earth
floor there arose a loamy fragrance complicated by a faint note of
sandalwood.

The Wambar, as I had expected, was an elderly man. He had
evidently dressed up for this occasion since he was wearing a
white turban, white ceremonial robes and a fine black cape.
Seated on one of the several chairs that had been arranged inside
the hut, he stood graciously as we came in and, after the
necessary introductions had been made, shook my hand warmly.

Speaking through the interpreter he immediately asked: 'Do
you work with Mr Gamst?'

I had to admit that I did not. 'But,' I added, 'I've read the book
that he wrote about your people. That's why I'm here. I'm very
interested in learning about your religion.'

The Wambar smiled rather mournfully. As he did so I noticed
that one tooth, disconcertingly long, grew down from the left side
of his upper jaw and protruded tusk-like over his lower lip. 'Our
religion', he said, 'has become a thing of the past. Almost nobody
practises it today. The Qemant are now Christians.'

'But you yourself are not a Christian . . . ?'

'No. I am the Wambar. I still follow the old ways.'

'And are there others like you?'

'A few remain.' That smile again. Then, slyly and somewhat
paradoxically: 'Even those who say they are Christians have not

entirely abandoned their former beliefs. The sacred groves are still tended ... The sacrifices are still made.' A pause for thought, a shake of the old, grizzled head, a sigh: 'But things are changing ... Always there is change ...'

'You said "sacred groves". What did you mean by that?'

'Our worship, if it is conducted as it should be, takes place in the open air. And we prefer to make our devotions amongst trees. For this purpose we have set aside special groves called *degegna*.'

I put several more questions on this subject and established that there were in fact two kinds of groves. Some – the *degegna* themselves – were used for annual ceremonies. They had first been planted in the distant past when the founder of the Qemant religion was shown the correct locations in his dreams. In addition there were other much smaller sacred sites – called *qole* – which often consisted of only a single tree where a particularly powerful spirit was believed to reside. These *qole* were normally situated in high places. As it happened there was one on the outskirts of Aykel which I could see if I liked.

I then asked the Wambar if he knew whether the Falashas also venerated sacred groves.

'No,' he replied, 'they do not.'

'Would you say that their religion is in *any* way similar to yours?'

A sage nod: 'Yes. In many ways. We have much in common.' Unprompted he then added: 'The founder of the Qemant religion was called Anayer. He came here to Ethiopia so long ago. He came, after seven years of famine, from his own country, which was far away. As he travelled on the journey with his wife and children he met the founder of the Falasha religion, also travelling on the same journey with his wife and children. A marriage alliance was discussed between the two groups, but it did not succeed.'

'Did Anayer and the founder of the Falasha religion come originally from the same country?'

'Yes. But they were separate. They made no marriage alliance.'

'Nevertheless, the country of their birth was the same?'

'Yes.'

'Do you know where it was?'

'It was far . . . It was in the Middle East.'

'Do you know the name of this country?'

'It was the land of Canaan. Anayer was the grandson of Canaan who was the son of Ham, who was the son of Noah.'

I was intrigued by this genealogy and by the faded memory of an ancestral migration from the Middle East – a memory that also suggested a common locus for the origin of the Falasha and the Qemant religions. I could not get the Wambar to confirm whether the 'Canaan' that he had referred to was the Promised Land of the Bible. Indeed, despite his familiarity with names like Ham and Noah, he claimed never to have read the Bible. I believed him on this point but, at the same time, was in no doubt that there was a scriptural background to what he had just told me. Contained in his account, for example, were echoes of the great trek made by the patriarch Abraham and his wife Sarah who had fled Canaan and 'journeyed, going on still toward the south' because 'there was famine in the land'.[11] At the same time, like Egypt in the book of Genesis, the country that Anayer had come from had been afflicted by seven years of famine.[12]

'Tell me more about your religion,' I now asked the Wambar. 'You mentioned spirits earlier – spirits living in trees. But what about God? Do you believe in *one* God, or many gods?'

'We believe in one God. Only one God. But he is supported by angels.'

The Wambar then went on to list these angels: Jakaranti, Kiberwa, Aderaiki, Kiddisti, Mezgani, Shemani, Anzatatera. Each, apparently, had his own distinctive place in the countryside. 'When our religion was strong, all the Qement used to go to these places to pray to the angels to mediate with God on their behalf. Jakaranti was the most respected, then Mezgani and Anzatatera.'

'And God?' I asked. 'The God of the Qemant. Does he have a name?'

'Of course. His name is Yeadara.'

'Where does he reside?'

'He is everywhere.'

A single God then, and an omnipresent one. I was beginning, already, to see why Gamst had characterized these people as *Hebraeo*-Pagans. This   impression,   furthermore,   was strengthened by almost everything else that the Wambar told me during our long discussion in the village of Aykel. I kept detailed notes of that discussion and, after my return to Addis Ababa, made a careful study of his answers – comparing them point by point with the Scriptures. Only when I had completed this exercise was I able to appreciate just how strong and how *old* the Judaic dimension of Qemant religion really was.

The Wambar had told me, for example, that the Qemant were forbidden to eat any animal that was not cloven-hoofed and that did not chew the cud. In addition, he had said, camels and pigs were regarded as unclean and were strictly forbidden. These restrictions accorded perfectly with those placed upon the Jews in the eleventh chapter of the Old Testament book of Leviticus.[13]

The Wambar had also said that amongst the Qemant even 'clean' animals could not be eaten if they had not been slaughtered properly. 'Their throats must be cut until all the blood is gone,' he had explained – adding that, for the same reason, it was forbidden to eat any animal that had died of natural causes. Both proscriptions, I discovered, were perfectly in line with Judaic law.[14]

Still on the subject of food, the Wambar had told me that the consumption of meat and dairy products at the same table was permitted by Qemant religion. He had added, however, that it was regarded as an abomination to eat the flesh of an animal that had been cooked in milk. I knew that orthodox Jews were forbidden to mix meat and dairy foods in the same meal. When I researched the background to this particular Kosher restriction, however, I learnt that it derived its authority from the books of Exodus and Deuteronomy, both of which stated: 'Thou shalt not seethe a kid in his mother's milk.'[15] This, more or less exactly, was the rule obeyed by the Qemant.

Another area of convergence concerned the Sabbath – which, like the Jews, the Qemant observed on Saturday. 'It is forbidden to work on that day,' the Wambar had told me. 'It is forbidden to light fires on Saturday. And if a field should catch fire accidentally on the Sabbath then that is a field that we must no longer use.'[16]

These restrictions and others like them – all very much in

accord with biblical law – made me more and more confident that a deep and truly ancient Judaic substratum did indeed underlie the religion of the Qemant. What finally convinced me that this was so, however, was the one practice that the Wambar had described to me which had not sounded Judaic at all – namely the veneration of 'sacred groves'.

He had told me during our interview that there was a *qole* site on the outskirts of Aykel where I might see a tree believed to be the residence of a powerful spirit. I did go to look at this tree, which turned out to be a huge, spreading acacia. It stood to the west of the village on a spur of high ground, beyond which, across a hundred descending miles, the land sloped steeply away towards the Sudanese border. A soft afternoon breeze, laden with the fragrance of distant deserts, blew through the tawny canyons beneath me, circulated amongst the ravines and foot-hills, and soared on eagles' wings across the first battlements of the escarpment.

Gnarled and massive, the acacia was so ancient that it would have been easy to believe that it had stood here for hundreds and perhaps even for thousands of years. Inside the walled enclosure that surrounded it, laid out upon the ground, were various offerings – a jar of oil, a heap of millet, small piles of roasted coffee beans, and a trussed chicken awaiting sacrifice. In their own way all these oblations contributed to the peculiar character of the place: numinous and eerie, by no means menacing but none the less distinctly strange.

What multiplied this other-worldly effect, however – and what made this Qemant *qole* site so different from any other place of worship I had ever come across in my travels – was the fact that every branch of the tree to a height of about six feet off the ground had been festooned with woven strips of vari-coloured cloth. Rustling in the wind, these waving pennants and ribbons seemed to whisper and murmur – almost as though they were seeking to impart a message. And I remember thinking that if I could only understand that message then many hidden things might be revealed. Superstitiously I touched the living wood, sensed its age, and returned to my companions who were awaiting me at the bottom of the hill.

Later, back in Addis – after I had looked into the other

comparisons between Qemant religion and Old Testament Judaism – I ran a routine check in the Scriptures and in works of biblical archaeology to see if I could find any references to sacred trees. I did not expect that I would. Much to my surprise, however, I discovered that certain specially planted forest groves *had* been accorded a sacred character in the very earliest phases of the evolution of the Jewish faith. I was also able to confirm that these groves *had* been used as places of active worship. In the twenty-first chapter of the book of Genesis, for example, it was stated that: 'Abraham planted a grove in Beersheba, and called there on the name of the Lord, the everlasting God.'[17]

Reading more widely around the subject I established the following points with certainty: first, that the Hebrews had 'borrowed' the use of sacred groves from the Canaanites (who were the indigenous inhabitants of the Promised Land); second, that the groves were normally situated in high places (known as *bamoth*); and third, that they often contained sacrificial stone pillars of the kind that I had seen on Tana Kirkos and that – as I already knew – were called *masseboth*.[18]

Very little was understood about how the groves had been used, what they had looked like, what sort of ceremonies had gone on within them, or what kind of offerings had been made there. The reason for this ignorance was that the priestly elite of later biblical times had turned savagely against all such practices, cutting down and burning the sacred trees and overthrowing the *masseboth*.[19]

Since it was these same priests who had also been responsible for the compilation and editing of the Scriptures, it was hardly surprising that they had left us with no clear picture of the function and appearance of the groves. Moreover the single reference that did evoke some kind of image was regarded as a mystery by biblical scholars. This reference, in the second book of Kings, spoke of a place 'where the women wove hangings for the grove.'[20] As I read these words, the memory was still fresh in my mind of the strips of woven cloth that hung from every branch of the fetish tree on the outskirts of the village of Aykel. And it seemed to me then (as it seems to me now) that there was no mystery at all about the words in the book of Kings – but much that still cried out for explanation about the Qemant who, in the heart of Africa, had managed to acquire a Judaeo-Canaanite tradition as hoary with age as this one.

The whole issue, I felt sure, was intimately connected to the larger problem of the Falashas, the Qemant's better-known neighbours.

Aswan and Meroe

Despite the strong Judaic flavour of their religion, no one has ever claimed that the Qemant are in fact Jews: there is too much that is pagan and animist about them to have allowed that to happen. The position, however, is quite different for the Falashas. They have been widely regarded as true Jews since the early nineteenth century – though they were not formally recognized as such by the Sephardi Chief Rabbi of Jerusalem until 1973. Two years later the Ashkenazi Chief Rabbi followed suit, opening the way for the Israeli Ministry of the Interior to declare that the Falashas were entitled to automatic citizenship of Israel under the terms of the Law of Return.[21]

Ironically the main reason that rabbinical recognition was so long delayed was the pronouncedly Old Testament character of Falasha religion which did not in any way incorporate or refer to the Talmud (the authoritative body of Jewish law and lore accumulated between 200 BC and AD 500[22]). This made the Falashas seem quite alien to many Israeli and other Jews; it was later accepted, however, that ignorance of Talmudic precepts was simply a function of the fact that the Ethiopian arm of the faith must have been cut off from the evolving body of world Judaism at some extremely early date. This same isolation also explained the Falashas' continuing adherence to practices that had long been forbidden by the rabbis, notably animal sacrifice (see Chapter 6).

The important point – which weighed heavily when official recognition was finally granted in the 1970s – was that the social and religious behaviour of the Falashas did clearly and un-ambiguously conform to the teachings of the Torah (Old Testament). Moreover, *within the Torah*, as one would expect of pre-Talmudic Jews whose religious beliefs were genuinely ancient, they showed the greatest respect for the Pentateuch (i.e.

the five books believed by the orthodox to have been written by Moses himself, namely Genesis, Exodus, Leviticus, Numbers and Deuteronomy).[23]

This 'fundamentalism' within Falasha religion was typified by their strict observance of the food restrictions enumerated in the books of Leviticus and Deuteronomy and by their refusal to eat any animal – 'clean' or not – that had been slaughtered by a Gentile. It was also recognized that they paid meticulous attention to the Mosaic laws of cleanliness and purity. Special huts, for example, were set aside for those members of the community considered to be temporarily in states of ritual impurity – such as menstruating women, who were segregated for seven days in line with a Levitical edict.[24]

Falasha circumcision ceremonies (*gezrat*) were equally traditional, taking place on the eighth day after the birth of a male child, exactly as stipulated in the Pentateuch.[25] Likewise their Sabbath procedures were rigorously orthodox with all fires being extinguished before sunset on Friday, and on the Sabbath itself no work of any kind being done, no water being drawn, no fire being lit, no coffee being boiled, and only the consumption of cold food and drink being permissible.

I was aware of all this when, during my stay in Gondar in January 1990, I visited several Falasha settlements. My objective was to make contact with religious leaders, to whom I wanted to put certain specific questions. Because of the mass migration of Ethiopia's Jews to Israel this was no easy task: many homesteads were completely deserted, stripped of their goods and chattels, their doors left unbarred, and their inhabitants gone. Nevertheless, in the countryside some twenty miles from Gondar I did find one village that still seemed to be functioning. Called Anbober, it straggled across a steep slope in rolling mountainous terrain and was populated almost entirely by women and children, the majority of the menfolk having already left for Israel.

Falashas have neither synagogues nor rabbis; instead their places of worship are called *mesgid* and their religious officials *kahenat* (singular *kahen*, meaning 'priest'). With my interpreter Legesse Desta, I now walked up through the village followed by a rapidly growing crowd of mischievous children. We were making for the *mesgid* – identifiable by the Star of David on its roof –

where I hoped very much that I might find the *kahen* in residence.

On this occasion I was not disappointed: inside the humble building, at a roughly made wooden table, a lean, elderly man sat studying a copy of the Torah (which was beautifully written in *Ge'ez* on cured sheepskin leaves). Legesse began by explaining why we had come and then asked the priest if he would mind answering some questions from me. After a lengthy debate he gave his assent to this and introduced himself as Solomon Alemu. He was, he said, seventy-eight years old. He had been the *kahen* of Anbober for almost thirty years.

We spent the next couple of hours going through numerous aspects of Falasha belief and ritual. All Solomon's answers confirmed the pure Old Testament character of the religion and were very much in line with what I had already learned from my research. In this context I pressed him particularly hard on the issue of blood sacrifice, trying to establish why his people continued with this practice when Jews everywhere else had abandoned it two thousand years previously. 'We believe', he replied with great conviction, 'that God in his throne observes these ceremonies and is pleased.'

Perhaps Solomon knew, perhaps he did not, how close this simple statement was to a verse in the book of Leviticus which described offerings made by fire as being 'of a sweet savour to the Lord'.[26] Certainly, he seemed a wise and well read man. When I complimented him on his scholarship, however, his response – with no trace of false modesty – was to insist that he understood far less about the Judaic traditions of the Falashas than his father had done. And he added that his father, in his turn, had understood less than his grandfather – who had also been *kahen* of Anbober. 'We are forgetting our own past,' he said sadly. 'Day by day we forget our history.'

Taking my cue from this I asked Solomon if he knew for how many centuries there had been Jewish people in Ethiopia.

'We came here', he replied, 'long ago . . . long before the Christians. The Christians are recent compared with us.'

He then proceeded to tell me the familiar story of the Queen of Sheba, Menelik and the bringing of the Ark. In this way, he said, the Jewish faith had arrived in Ethiopia.

I asked casually: 'Do you have any idea what route Menelik and his companions used when they made their journey?'

Though it might have surprised me once I now accepted his answer to this last question with perfect complacency: 'According to our traditions they travelled from Jerusalem through Egypt and Sudan.'

Almost bored, I prompted: 'Presumably they would have followed the river Nile for much of the journey?'

The *kahen* nodded: 'Yes. That is what our traditions say.' He then added two details that were completely new to me: 'On the way,' he said, 'they rested at Aswan and Meroe.'

Aswan, I knew, was in Upper Egypt (near the site of the modern high dam of the same name), and in Pharaonic times had been important as a source of the granite used in the construction of the Pyramids. Meroe, the ancient capital of Nubia, had been located much further to the south, in what is now the Republic of the Sudan.

Intrigued, I pushed Solomon for more details of the Falasha traditions concerning these places. He insisted, however, that the little that he had already said was the sum of his knowledge about them. 'I heard their names', he sighed, 'in stories told to me by my grandfather. He was a wise man . . . but he is gone . . . Soon we will all be gone.'

Ceremony of the Ark

Everything that I learned during my stay in Gondar reinforced my view that it had been to precisely this region of Ethiopia that the Jewish faith had first been brought in antiquity. The Falashas were Jewish through and through, and this was their homeland. Their near neighbours the Qemant also showed convincing signs of an archaic and deeply ingrained Judaic influence.

Nor was this influence limited to the Falashas and the Qemant. On the contrary, in Gondar and throughout Ethiopia, supposedly 'Orthodox' Christians displayed many customs and beliefs that were unmistakably Jewish in origin. Just like the Falashas, as I already knew, they circumcised their sons on the eighth day after birth, a date commanded by the book of Leviticus – a date that, amongst all the peoples of the world, was now observed only by Jews and by Ethiopians.[27] Likewise (in a remarkable instance of the phenomenon known as religious syncretism) the Jewish Sabbath was still being respected in the twentieth century by millions of Abyssinian Christians – not *instead of* the Sunday Sabbath adhered to by their co-religionists elsewhere but *in addition* to it.[28]

There were other holidays which, although superficially Christian, were also clearly Judaic in origin. I had learned, for example, that the Ethiopian New Year feast (*Enkutatsh*) corresponded closely to the Jewish New Year (*Rosh Ha-shanah*). Both were held in September and both were followed a few weeks later by a second festival (known as *Maskal* in Ethiopia and *Yom Kippur* in Israel). In both cultures, furthermore, this second festival was connected to the New Year by a period of expiation and atonement.[29]

Ethiopian Christians also strictly obeyed many of the Pentateuchal laws of cleanliness and purity. No man, for example, would consider going to church after having had sexual intercourse with his wife, nor would he have intercourse prior to having contact with any consecrated thing, nor would he have intercourse during days of fasting, nor would he have intercourse with any menstruating woman.[30] None of these restrictions were called for by Christian lore; all of them, however, were demanded in the Pentateuch (notably in the books of Exodus and Leviticus[31]).

In a similar fashion Ethiopian Christians also observed the Old Testament food laws, scrupulously avoiding the flesh of 'unclean' birds and mammals (pork being particularly abhorred) and even attending to the minutiae such as the 'sinew which shrank' referred to in Chapter 32 of the book of Genesis.[32] This same sinew, I was able to establish, was shunned by all Abyssinian Christians and was known in *Ge'ez* as 'the forbidden muscle'.[33]

Another intriguing link that I had turned up while researching this subject was that Ethiopian clerical vestments seemed to be modelled upon the special garments worn by the priests of ancient Israel[34] – the *k'enat* (belt) corresponding to the High Priest's girdle;[35] the *k'oba* (skull-cap) corresponding to the mitre;[36] and the *askema* (scapular), with its twelve crosses in four rows of three, corresponding to the priestly breast-plate (which, as Chapter 28 of the book of Exodus makes clear, was adorned with twelve precious stones also arranged in four rows of three.[37]

All in all, therefore, I found it difficult to disagree with Archbishop David Matthew who, in 1947, had described 'the whole cast of religious expression in Ethiopia as antique and ceremonial and imbued with an undercurrent of Judaic practice.'[38] It was not until I participated in the Christian *Timkat* celebrations on 18 and 19 January 1990, however, that the real pervasiveness and power of this undercurrent was finally brought home to me.

The preparations for *Timkat* were already well advanced when, in the mid-afternoon of Thursday 18 January, I slipped through a wildly excited crowd, up a flight of steps and on to the exterior walkway of the church of Medhane Alem (literally 'Saviour of the World'). Situated in the oldest part of Gondar, this was a large, circular building laid out in the traditional fashion – somewhat like an archery target if viewed from above – with a series of concentric ambulatories surrounding the Holy of Holies (*mak'das*).

This distinctively Ethiopian pattern, as I already knew, was repeated in a slightly different manner in rectangular and octagonal as well as in round churches, and had been recognized by scholars as being based 'on the threefold division of the Hebrew Temple'.[39] According to Edward Ullendorff, the first Professor of Ethiopian Studies at the University of London:

> The outside ambulatory of the three concentric parts of the Abyssinian church is called *k'ene mahlet*, i.e. the place where hymns are sung, [and] corresponds to the *ulam* of Solomon's Temple. The next chamber is the *k'eddest*, where communion is administered to the people; and the innermost part is the *mak'das* where the *tabot* rests and to which only priests have access ... This division into three chambers applies to all Abyssinian churches, even to the smallest of them. It is thus clear that the form of the Hebrew sanctuary was preferred by Abyssinians to the basilica type which was accepted by early Christians elsewhere.[40]

Professor Ullendorff declined to speculate as to precisely *why* the Abyssinians should have favoured a pre-Christian model for their Christian churches. As I stepped into the first ambulatory of Medhane Alem, however, it seemed to me that the answer was obvious: the Syrian evangelist Frumentius, who was responsible for the conversion of the Axumite kingdom and who was appointed as Ethiopia's first archbishop by the Coptic Patriarch of Alexandria in AD 331, must deliberately have adapted the institutions of the new faith to the pre-existing Judaic traditions of the country.[41] Furthermore, as Ullendorff did admit:

It is clear that these and other traditions, in particular that of the Ark of the Covenant at Axum, must have been an integral part of the Abyssinian national heritage *long before* the introduction of Christianity in the fourth century; for it would be inconceivable that a people recently converted from paganism to Christianity (not by a Christian Jew but by the Syrian missionary Frumentius) should thereafter have begun to boast of Jewish descent and to insist on Israelite connections, customs and institutions.[42]

Walking in stockinged feet – since it is considered sacrilege to wear shoes inside any Ethiopian church – I made a circuit of the *k'ene mahlet* studying the faded paintings of saints and holy men that adorned its walls: here was Saint George, mounted on his white charger, slaying the dragon; there was God Almighty, 'the Ancient of Days', surrounded by the 'living creatures' described by the Prophet Ezekiel; here was John baptizing Christ in the Jordan; there the Kings and Shepherds at the Manger; and over there Moses receiving the Tables of the Law from the hand of God on Mount Sinai.

Standing lost in contemplation before a portrayal of the Queen of Sheba's journey to Jerusalem, I became aware of the slow, deep throb of a *kebero* – the large oval drum, made of cowskin stretched over a wooden frame, that features in so much of the music of the Ethiopian Orthodox Church. To this barbaric sound was now added a chorus of voices chanting a *Ge'ez* hymn, and then the mystic jingle of sistra.

My curiosity aroused, I proceeded round the ambulatory and,

at last, near the doorway that led inwards to the *k'eddest*, I came across a group of priests and deacons gathered about the drummer, who was seated cross-legged on the floor hunched over his *kebero*.

This was a strange and archaic scene: nothing about it belonged to the modern world and, as I watched, I felt myself transported backwards through time, riding the eerie waveforms of the music – which seemed to me to belong neither to Africa nor to Christianity but to some other place and to some infinitely older faith. Dressed in their traditional white robes and black shoulder-capes, leaning on tall prayer sticks, the deacons swayed and chanted, swayed and chanted, absorbed in the primal cadence of the dance. Each held in his hand a silver sistrum which, in the silent interstices between the drum-beats, he raised and then let fall, producing a clear and melodious tintinnabulation.

The chanting was antiphonal in form, with phrases uttered by one group of singers being given their response by others, a dialogue in which verses and choruses were passed back and forth amongst the participants allowing the hymn to build to its ponderous crescendo. This same system, I knew, had been an established part of the Jewish liturgy in Old Testament times.[43]

As I was reflecting on this coincidence a fragrant cloud of incense billowed from the open door of the *k'eddest*. Edging forward I looked inside and saw a swirling figure wrapped in robes of green embroidered with golden threads, a figure out of a dream, half sorcerer, half priest, who whirled and turned with drooping eyes.

Gathered round him were other men, similarly attired, each holding a smoking censer suspended in a fine net of silver chain. I strained my eyes to look beyond these figures through the fumes and darkness and could just make out, at the very centre of the *k'eddest*, the curtained entrance to the Holy of Holies. I knew that beyond that heavy veil, venerated and mysterious, guarded by superstition, concealed and secret within its sanctuary, lay the *tabot* – the symbol of the Ark of the Covenant. And I was reminded that in ancient Israel the High Priest could not approach the Ark unless he had first burnt sufficient quantities of incense to cover it completely with smoke.[44] The thick fumes were thought necessary to protect his life – necessary to ensure, as the book of Leviticus rather chillingly put it, 'that he die not'.[45]

I stepped across the threshold into the *k'eddest* to get a closer look at what was going on there but was almost immediately waved back into the outer ambulatory. At the same time the song of the deacons ceased, the drum-beats stilled and, for a moment, absolute silence fell.

I could sense an intangible atmosphere of imminence, as though a huge charge of lightning were building up within a thundercloud. A general stirring and movement then ensued, with people scurrying in all directions. At the same time a smiling priest took my arm lightly but firmly, and guided me out of the *k'eddest*, through the *k'ene mahlet*, to the main door of the church where I stood blinking in the brilliant afternoon sunlight, amazed at the rapid change of mood that seemed to have overtaken the proceedings.

The crowd, big enough when I had arrived, had now swelled into a huge multitude that completely filled the extensive compound in which Medhane Alem was situated and that also spilled out on to the road as far as I could see. Men and women, small children, the very elderly, lame people, obviously sick and dying people, laughing, happy, healthy people – half of Ethiopia seemed to be here. Many clutched musical instruments of one kind or another: cymbals and trumpets, flutes and fiddles, lyres and biblical harps.

Moments after my own exit from the church, a group of richly robed priests appeared. These were the same men whom I had last seen amidst the incense cloud before the drawn veil of the Holy of Holies, but now one of them – slender and bearded with fine, delicate features and smouldering eyes – bore on his head the *tabot* wrapped in costly brocades of red and gold.

At once the crowd erupted into a frenzy of shouts and stamping feet and, from the women, shrill ululations – a rousing, tremulous vibration that, I knew, had been connected by more than one scholar to 'certain musical utterances in ancient Hebrew worship (Hebrew *hallel*, Ethiopic *ellel*) . . . the mode of exultation is to repeat the sound *ellel* many times, saying *ellellellellellell*, etc. . . . . The proper meaning of "Halleluyah" will probably be "sing *hallel* or *ellel* unto Jehovah." '[46]

After standing at the doorway of the church for some minutes while the agitation of the crowd grew, the priests now wheeled and turned, making a complete circuit of the exterior walkway before descending the flight of steps to ground level. The instant that their feet touched the earth, the multitude parted before them – creating a pathway through which they might pass – and the shouts and ululations, the blowing of trumpets, the whistle of flutes, the strumming of lyres, and the jingle of the tambourines built up to a pitch that deafened the ear and filled the mind with wonder.

I followed as closely as I dared behind the group of priests, drawn along in their turbulent wake. And though the people were gathered in their hundreds on either side of me, though many were intoxicated either by millet beer or by the tumult, though I was repeatedly jostled, and though more than once I was almost knocked off my feet, I did not for a second feel threatened or alarmed.

Sometimes funnelled through narrow alleyways, sometimes spreading out across patches of open land, sometimes stopping inexplicably, sometimes fast, sometimes slow, always bursting with music and song, we progressed through the ancient city. And all the time I struggled to keep my eyes fixed on the red and gold wrappings of the *tabot*, which was now far ahead of me. For a while, as a new horde of revellers joined us from a side street, I completely lost sight of the sacred object. Then standing on tiptoe, craning my neck, I found it and hurried forward. Determined not to be separated from it again I scrambled up a grassy bank, put on a burst of speed, overtook a massed block of two or three hundred people, skidded past the priests, and lumbered back down on to the road perhaps twenty yards in front of them.

Here I found the reason for the curious stop-start, halting, lurching motion of the multitude. In the space ahead of the *tabot* several impromptu troupes of dancers had formed themselves – some of mixed sex, some all male, some all female, some dressed in everyday working clothes, some in church vestments. At the centre of each of these groups was a drummer, his *kebero* slung around his neck, beating out an ancient and savage rhythm, whirling, jumping, turning and shouting while those around him exploded with energy, leaping and gyrating, clapping their hands, beating tambourines and cymbals, pouring with sweat as they capered and reeled.

Now, urged on by trumpet blasts and by shouts, by the thrum of a ten-stringed *begegna*[47] and the haunting tones of a shepherd's flute, a young man dressed in traditional robes of white cotton performed a wild solo dance while the priests stood in their place stopping the eager crowd behind them and bearing the sacred *tabot* aloft. Beautiful in his lithe vigour, splendid in his ferocious energy, the youth seemed entranced. With all eyes upon him he circled the pulsing *kebero*, pirouetting and swaying, shoulders jerking, head bobbing, lost in his own inner rhythms, praising God with every limb, with every ounce of his strength, with every particle of his being. And I thought . . . this was what it must have been like, three thousand years ago at the gates of Jerusalem when

> David and all the house of Israel brought up the Ark of
> the Lord with shouting, and with the sound of the
> trumpet [and] played before the Lord on all manner of
> instruments made of fir wood, even on harps, and on
> psalteries, and on timbrels, and on cornets, and on
> cymbals . . . and David danced before the Lord with all
> his might . . . leaping and dancing before the Lord.[48]

In mid-stride, without any warning, the youth collapsed and sank to the ground in a dead faint. He was picked up by several of the spectators, carried to the roadside and made comfortable. Then the crowd surged forward again much as before, with new dancers constantly taking the place of those who were exhausted.

Soon afterwards a transition occurred. After tumbling and charging down a last narrow street the crowd debouched into a huge open square. And into this same square, from three other directions, I could see three other processions also approaching – each of which was similar in size to our own, each of which was centred upon a *tabot* borne up by a group of priests, and each of which seemed inspired by the same transcendent spirit.

Like four rivers meeting, the separate processions now converged and mixed. The priest carrying the *tabot* from the church of Medhane Alem – whom I had followed faithfully thus far – stood in line with other priests carrying the *tabotat* from three of the other principal churches of Gondar. Behind this first sacred rank were more priests and deacons. And behind them again were the assembled congregations, forming an army that could not have been less than ten thousand strong.

Almost as soon as the processions had joined we were on the move again, welling forth out of the square and down a steep, broad highway with the *tabotat* ahead of us. Now and then children would be pushed close to me and would shyly take my hands, walk with me for a while and then release me . . . An old woman approached and addressed me at length in Amharic, smiling toothlessly . . . Two teenage girls, giggling and nervous, touched my blond hair with fascinated curiosity and then rushed off . . . And in this fashion, entirely caught up in the gaiety and power of the occasion, I allowed myself to be swept along, oblivious to the passing hours of the afternoon.

Then, quite suddenly, an imposing walled compound set amidst grassy woods appeared around a bend in the track like an image out of a legend. At some distance behind the surrounding ramparts, I thought that I could just make out the turrets of a great castle – turrets high and 'marvellously embattled'. Not for the first time in my travels in Ethiopia I was hauntingly reminded of the wondrous Grail sanctuary described by Wolfram von Eschenbach – of the 'impregnable stronghold' with its 'clusters of towers and numerous palaces' that had stood at the edge of a mysterious lake in the realm of Munsalvaesche.[49]

At the centre of the enclosure wall was a narrow arched gateway through which those ahead of me in the procession now began to stream – and towards which I felt myself irresistibly drawn. Indeed there was a tremendous force and compulsion in this human flow, as though we were being sucked helter-skelter into a vortex.

As I was impelled beneath the arch, jostled and crushed by the scrum of eager bodies, I was shoved momentarily against rough stone and my wristwatch was knocked off; almost immediately, however, some unknown person behind me managed to retrieve it from the ground and pressed it back into my hand. Before I could thank or even identify my benefactor I burst through the bottleneck and arrived, slightly dazed, on the wide and open lawns within the compound. In the same second the enormous constriction and compression was relieved and I experienced a delicious sense of freedom . . .

The compound was rectangular in shape and covered an area as large as four city blocks. Set in the midst of this great grassy space was a second walled enclosure about one-third of the size of the first – which in turn contained the tall, turreted castle that I had glimpsed earlier and, to the rear and sides of this structure, a man-made lake half filled with water. The castle itself had been built by Emperor Fasilidas in the seventeenth century and appeared to be accessible only by way of a narrow stone bridge that passed over a deep moat and that led directly to a massive wooden doorway set into the front of the building.

The crowd, I noticed, was still pouring through the narrow archway that I had negotiated a few moments before, and people milled about apparently aimlessly, greeting one another with boisterous and high-spirited bonhomie. Off to my right, directly in front of the castle, a large group of priests and deacons had gathered and I could see that they now carried a total of seven *tabotat*. I therefore surmised that processions from three other Gondarene churches must at some point *en route* have joined with the original four that had converged in the city's main square earlier in the afternoon.

The priests bearing the wrapped *tabotat* on their heads stood in line, shoulder-to-shoulder. Directly behind them were many more priests who held up brightly coloured ceremonial umbrellas that were fringed at the edges and decorated with crosses, stars, suns, crescent moons and other curious devices. Five metres to the left were two further rows of priests, facing each other, carrying long prayer sticks and silver sistra. And between these latter two rows sat a drummer hunched over his *kebero*.

As I edged closer to get a better view, the facing rows of priests began a slow swaying dance before the *tabotat* – a dance acted out to the same mesmerizing rhythm and to the same antiphonal chanting that I had heard earlier in the church of Medhane Alem. A few moments later the dance broke up as suddenly as it had begun, the dancers dispersed and the priests bearing the seven *tabotat* proceeded majestically on to the stone bridge that led over the moat and into the castle. They paused there for a moment, caught in a warm ray of light from the descending sun, and the women in the crowd gave vent to more wild ululations. Then, on oiled hinges, the heavy wooden door of the fortress swung silently open – affording me a transient glimpse of the shadowy interior – and the *tabotat* were carried inside.

Gradually, almost gently, the assembled thousands began to settle down around the gardens. Some had brought blankets, others cotton *shemmas* (shawls) and thicker woollen *gebbis* (cloaks). All, however, had the look of people who were going to be here for the duration of the *Timkat* holiday, and all seemed at peace with themselves – calm now after the effort and exultation of the processions and prepared for the vigil ahead.

By 9 p.m. numerous camp fires had been lit. Around the flickering flames people wrapped in *shemmas* and blankets huddled and murmured secretively – their words, in the old Semitic language of Ethiopia, turning to chill mist as they spoke.

Braced and exhilarated by the cold Afro-Alpine air, I sat down on the grass, reclined, pillowed my head on my hands and gazed upwards, delighting in the clouds of stars that had ascended the sky. My thoughts drifted for a while, then focussed on the sound of water gushing steadily into the lake somewhere quite close to where I sat. At almost the same moment, from within the old castle, a soft cadenced chanting and drumming rose up – an eldritch, heart-stopping resonance that was at first so faint and so muted that I could barely make it out.

I stood and moved closer to the bridge over the moat. It was not my intention to cross it (I did not think that I would be permitted to do so); rather I hoped merely to find a vantage point from which I might hear the archaic music more clearly. Inexplicably, however, I felt many hands pushing me forward – pushing me firmly but gently – and soon I found myself on the bridge. There a child led me to the towering door, opened it and indicated with a smile that I should proceed within.

Rather timidly I crossed the threshold into a large, square, high-ceilinged, incense-fragrant room illuminated by dozens of candles mounted in niches in the rough stone walls. A wintry current insinuated itself under the door that I had now closed behind me and on all sides cold draughts pushed through chinks and gaps in the masonry, causing the little flames to gutter and dim.

In this ghostly half-light I could make out the robed and hooded figures of perhaps fifty people standing in ranks two-deep and forming an almost complete circle that was broken only by the doorway in which I stood. Though it was difficult to be certain it seemed to me that all these folk were men and that most of them were either priests or deacons, for they held prayer sticks and sistra and were chanting a *Ge'ez* psalm so poignant and so evocative that it caused the hairs at the nape of my neck to prickle and stand erect. Directly in front of me, on flagstones strewn with freshly cut grass, sat a drummer wrapped in a white *shemma*, striking the stretched skin of a *kebero* with a quiet but insistent beat.

Now, without any break in tempo, several members of the choir beckoned to me and I felt myself pulled into their circle, warmed in, made a part of it all. A sistrum was pushed into my right hand, a prayer stick into my left and the chant continued, with the singers swaying very gently and very slowly from side to side.

Involuntarily I felt my own body beginning to acquaint itself with the rhythm. Watching the others, shedding all self-consciousness, I raised and let fall my sistrum between the drum beats, and as I did so the little metal disks in the ancient instrument produced a tuneless, rattling jingle. This oddly compelling sound, I knew, was older by far than the Temple of Solomon, was older even than the Pyramids – for sistra just like these had first been used in pre-dynastic Egypt[50] and had passed from there, by way of the priestly guilds of Pharaonic times, into the liturgy of Israel.

How strange this solemn ceremony was, and stranger still that I should have been allowed to participate in it, here in the heart of the Ethiopian highlands at the edge of a sacred lake. With a shiver of excitement I realized that there was nothing in the scene unfolding around me – absolutely nothing at all – that belonged to the twentieth century AD. I might just as easily have been a witness to the arcane rituals of the tenth century BC when the Ark of God was placed by Solomon in the 'thick darkness' of the Holy of Holies and when the priests,

> Being arrayed in white linen, having cymbals and psalteries and harps, stood at the east end of the altar [making] one sound to be heard in praising and thanking the Lord; and when they lifted up their voice with the trumpets and cymbals and instruments of musick, and praised the Lord, saying, For he is good; for his mercy endureth for ever.[51]

Was it not in just this fashion that the priests of Ethiopia – in whose midst I stood – now also praised the Lord? And was it not with just such fervour and conviction that they thanked Him for His mercy and blessed His ineffable name, singing:

> Rise Yahweh God, come to your resting place,
> You and the Ark of your power.
> Your priests, Yahweh God, are vested in salvation,
> Your faithful rejoice in prosperity.[52]

The night passed with a dreamlike sense of real and impossible things randomly mixed up together. There were moments when I hallucinated that the Ark itself was concealed somewhere within the old castle. In my heart, however, I also knew that I had not yet come to the end of my journey, that the Ark was not here in Gondar, and that I still had miles and months to go before I could even hope to approach it. For the present I would have to content myself with the *tabotat* that reposed somewhere within the castle – with the seven cloth-wrapped bundles that the alchemy of blind faith had effortlessly transformed in the past twenty-four hours into objects of immense symbolic weight.

Before dawn the priests ushered me out of the castle and back over the narrow bridge. As light gradually began to infuse the sky I then spent an hour or so exploring the great compound. If there had been ten thousand people there the evening before there were hardly fewer now. Some walked and talked in twos and threes, others stood around in large huddled groups, others still warmed themselves by the pale flames of the fading fires. And I thought that I could detect again the same mood of expectancy, the same sense of eager and restless anticipation, that had preceded the bringing out of the *tabot* at the church of Medhane Alem the previous afternoon.

I made a complete circuit of the inner compound that surrounded the castle and the lake. Reaching the far side of the complex I then climbed the enclosure wall and looked down at a scene both beautiful and bizarre. Below me an earthen embankment perhaps five feet wide ran all the way around the still and shining waters, and on this embankment – on every square inch of it – people stood watchfully, waiting for something to happen, their shimmering reflections picked out by the risen sun.

A balcony projected at the rear of the castle and now, on to this balcony, out of a cloud of incense, stepped a group of priests dressed in splendid robes of green and red. Loud ululations arose from the crowd and a short ceremony ensued which (I learned later) served to bless and consecrate the waters. Then, with amazing suddenness – and apparently oblivious to the morning chill – people began to hurl themselves into the lake. Some leapt in fully clothed, some completely undressed. Here a young woman with ripe breasts thrust her naked baby beneath the surface and brought him up again, coughing and spluttering, in a shower of droplets. There, with movements that were brittle and precise, an old man, lean and wizened, crooked and infirm, waded in up to his chest. Here a group of teenage boys swam and sported. There a middle-aged matron, stripped to the waist, lashed her back and shoulders with a dampened branch . . . Meanwhile, from the main compound in front of the castle, a roar of excitement could be heard as others in their thousands came to join the throng, to splash and dive, to plunge and frolic.

I climbed down from my vantage point on the wall and rushed round to the front of the compound. Amidst all this distraction what I wanted to do was to get back inside the castle. The *tabotat* had not been in the place where I had spent most of the night singing and chanting, dancing and swaying – so where were they? And what would happen next?

Unnoticed by the near-hysterical crowd, I crossed the bridge over the moat, pushed open the door and stepped inside; as I did so I observed that the floor of the great room was still strewn with grass and that its walls were blackened with candle smoke. It was now perhaps 7 a.m. and bright sunlight streamed in, startling a group of deacons who had gathered there. Opposite me there was a curtain drawn across an arch which I had not seen during the night, and now through this curtain a priest appeared. He regarded me quizzically, then smiled and seemed to offer a welcome.

I walked up to him and signalled that I would like to pass through beyond the veil. At this, however, he shook his head vehemently. 'No,' he whispered in English. 'No. Impossible. *Tabot* inside.' Then he withdrew again behind the curtain, beyond which I thought that I could just make out faint stirrings and footfalls.

I called out, hoping to attract the attention of someone in authority, but got no response. Then – crassly – I put my hand on the curtain and made to open it. At this three of the deacons standing in the room behind me leapt on me, grabbed me by the arms and wrestled me to the floor where I received several severe bruises.

I cursed and struggled, not thinking clearly, aware only that I was dazed and shocked: just a few hours earlier I had been made to feel so much at home here; now I was being beaten up. With some difficulty I shook my assailants off and pulled myself to my feet. This action, however, was misinterpreted as the prelude to another attempt on the curtain and I was pummelled and buffeted while several more deacons blocked my way. 'Cannot go in there,' one of them warned, indicating the room beyond the veil. 'Only priests to go inside.' He wagged his finger at me and added: 'You are very bad man.'

I was then unceremoniously bundled out of the castle door and deposited roughly on the narrow bridge in front of several thousand frowning people – and I thought: if I get into this much trouble just for trying to enter a room where some *tabotat* are kept, then what on earth is going to happen to me in Axum when I try to see the Ark itself?

I crossed the bridge, picked my way through the crowd and stood on a patch of clear ground, shaking slightly because of the adrenalin that was pumping through my bloodstream. Taking stock I could see that many people were still in the lake, and I could hear splashes and shouts. The majority, however, were now out of the water and assembled on the broad lawns in front of the castle, leaning forward avidly, craning their necks, excited and yet oddly silent.

Then seven fully robed priests appeared at the castle door with wrapped *tabotat* balanced on their heads. Slowly and deliberately they stepped out on to the bridge and made their way across, followed by yet more priests holding up ceremonial umbrellas. At the same moment the crowd gave vent to a huge collective sigh, an ardent gasp of awe and devotion that was soon enhanced by the familiar high-pitched ululations of the women and by an urgent, distracted jostling as people scrambled backwards and sideways to clear a path for the advancing *tabotat*.

As the morning wore on and as the sun rose towards its zenith I followed the procession back through the streets of Gondar as far as the main square of the old city. There the dance of David before the Ark was again enacted amidst shouting and the sounds of tambourines and cymbals, amidst the blowing of trumpets and the music of sistra and stringed instruments.

Then finally the priests carrying the seven *tabotat* wheeled and separated. As they did so the multitude too divided itself into seven different parts – seven different processions that now streamed out of the square in seven different directions.

Running to keep up, panting and sweating, I followed close behind the *tabot* of Medhane Alem, followed it all the way back to the old round church and there, amidst a thousand exuberant songs and dances, watched as the priest who bore it circled the building once, circled it twice, and then at last, to a tremendous roar of joy and approbation, vanished from my sight into the darkness within – into the Holy of Holies, into the mystery of mysteries.

A year's reprieve . . .

I left Gondar in January 1990, quite certain that I was right to seek the Ark in Ethiopia. Despite a thin and superficial Christian veneer, the central role of the *tabotat* in the ceremonies that I had witnessed, the strange dances of the priests, the frenzied adulation of the laity, the archaic music of sistra and of tambourines, of trumpets, drums and cymbals, were all phenomena lifted straight out of the most distant and recondite past. And it seemed to me then, as it seems to me now, that these intricate rituals, these complex institutions – all of them focussed upon the Old Testament worship of the Ark of the Covenant – would not have been adhered to with such fervour and fidelity over so many weary centuries if all that lay behind them were mere *replicas*.

No. The Ethiopians had the Ark itself. Perhaps in the way described in the *Kebra Nagast*, or perhaps by some other more historically probable means that I might in due course be able to identify, it had come into their possession in the first millennium BC. And now, so near the end of the second millennium AD, they had it still, hidden away, concealed from prying eyes.

But where?'

In answering this last question I felt that I could not ignore the implications of my own research: the sacred relic was not on an island in Lake Zwai; it was not on an island in Lake Tana; instead all the evidence suggested that it lay still in its traditional resting place – safe in the Holy of Holies of the sanctuary chapel at Axum. There could be no absolute certainty, of course, but I felt sure in my own mind that I was right. And twelve months hence, when *Timkat* came around again in January 1991, I would have to go to Axum to seek it – and to see it if I could.

I felt a sense of inevitability about this, as though a challenge had been laid down – laid down as clearly and as compellingly as the Green Knight's taunt to Sir Gawain:

I am known to many, so if to find me thou endeavour,
thou'lt fail not to do so. Therefore come! Or to be called
a craven thou deservest. . . . Yet a respite I'll allow, till a
year and a day go by.[53]

And what would I do in my period of reprieve, in my year of grace? I would, I determined, learn everything I could about the baleful object that beckoned to me – about its origins, and about its powers. I would study the Ark of God and I would attempt to discover whether there might not be a rational explanation for the terrors and the miracles that it was believed to have worked in Old Testament times.

Part IV: Egypt, 1989–90
A Monstrous Instrument

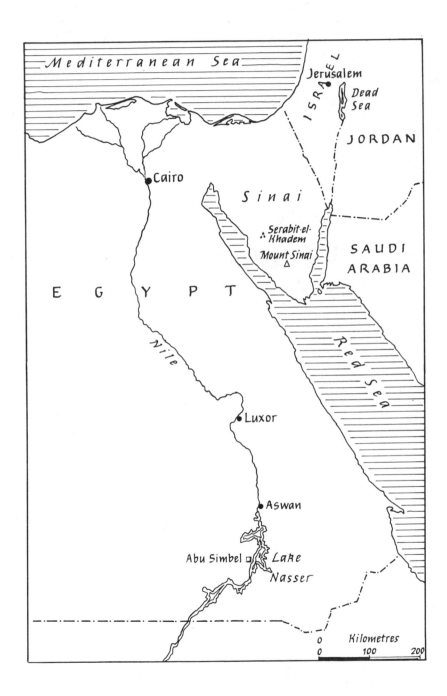

Mediterranean Sea

Jerusalem

Dead
Sea

ISRAEL

JORDAN

Cairo

Sinai

Serabit-el-
Khadem

SAUDI
ARABIA

Mount Sinai

EGYPT

Nile

Red Sea

Luxor

Aswan

Abu Simbel   Lake
Nasser

Kilometres

0   100   200

Chapter 12

Magic . . . or Method?

During 1989 and 1990, as I immersed myself ever more deeply in the mysteries of the lost Ark of the Covenant, I became interested not only in *where* it was but also in *what* it was. Naturally I turned first to the Bible, where the earliest mention of the Ark occurs during the period of the 'wilderness wanderings' immediately after the prophet Moses had led the children of Israel out of their captivity in Egypt (around 1250 BC[1]). In Chapter 25 of the book of Exodus we read that the precise dimensions of the sacred relic and the materials to be used in its construction were revealed to Moses on Mount Sinai by God Himself:

> You are to make me an Ark of acacia wood two and a half cubits long, one and a half cubits wide, and one and a half cubits high [i.e. a rectangular chest measuring three feet nine inches by two feet three inches by two feet three inches[2]]. You are to plate it, inside and out, with pure gold, and decorate it all around with a gold moulding. You will cast four gold rings for the Ark and fix them to its four supports [or corners[3]]: two rings on one side and two rings on the other. You will also make shafts of acacia wood plated with gold and pass the shafts through the rings on the sides of the Ark, to carry the Ark by these. The shafts must remain in the rings of the Ark and not be withdrawn . . . Further you are to make a throne of mercy, of pure gold, two and a half cubits long, and one and a half cubits wide. For the two ends of this throne of mercy you are to make two golden cherubim; you are to

> make them of beaten gold. Make the first cherub for one
> end and the second for the other, and fasten them to the two
> ends of the throne of mercy so that they may make one piece
> with it. The cherubim are to have their wings spread
> upwards so that they overshadow the throne of mercy. They
> must face one another, their faces towards the throne of
> mercy. You must place the throne of mercy on top of the Ark
> . . . There I shall come to meet you: there from above the
> throne of mercy, from between the two cherubim that are on
> the Ark.[4]

This 'divine blueprint' is, surely, one of the very strangest passages in the Bible. After receiving it, Moses passed it on verbatim to an artificer named Bezaleel, a man 'filled with the spirit of God, in wisdom, and in understanding, and in knowledge, and in all manner of workmanship, to devise cunning works.'[5] Bezaleel made the Ark exactly as specified.[6] Then, when it was ready, Moses placed inside it the two tablets of stone, also given to him on Mount Sinai, on which God had inscribed the Ten Commandments.[7] The sacred object, now pregnant with its precious contents, was then installed behind a 'veil' in the Holy of Holies of the Tabernacle[8] – the portable tent-like structure that the Israelites used as their place of worship during their wanderings in the wilderness.

The terrors and the miracles

Soon terrible things began to happen. The first concerned Nadab and Abihu, two of the four sons of Aaron the High Priest, who was Moses's own brother. As members of the priestly family they enjoyed access to the Holy of Holies, into which they one day advanced carrying metal incense burners in their hands.[9] There, according to the book of Leviticus they 'offered strange fire before the Lord, which He commanded them not'.[10] The devastating consequence was that a flame leapt out from the Ark 'and devoured them and they died.'[11]

> And the Lord spake unto Moses after the death of the
> two sons of Aaron, when they offered before the Lord

and died; And the Lord said unto Moses, Speak unto Aaron
thy brother, that he come not at all times into the holy place
within the veil before the throne of mercy, which is upon the
Ark; that he die not: for I will appear in the cloud upon the
throne of mercy.[12]

The throne of mercy – 'mercy seat' in some translations – was
the slab of pure gold that served as the Ark's cover. The reader
will recall that mounted on either end of it – and facing each other
– were two golden figures of cherubim. 'The cloud upon the
throne of mercy' which threatened death to Aaron must
therefore have been visible *between* the cherubim. It was not
always present, but on those occasions when it did materialize the
Israelites believed 'that the demons held sway'[13] – and then even
Moses would not dare to approach.[14]

Other supposedly supernatural phenomena also manifested
themselves 'between the cherubim' that faced each other across
the Ark's golden lid. For example, just a few days[15] after the
unfortunate demise of Aaron's two sons, Moses went into the
Holy of Holies of the Tabernacle, which was then still pitched in
the shadow of Mount Sinai. After he had entered, the prophet
'heard the voice of one speaking unto him from off the mercy seat
that was upon the Ark . . . from between the two cherubim.'[16]
Certain very ancient Jewish legends state that this voice came
from heaven 'in the form of a tube of fire'.[17] And fire – in one
guise or another, with and without the deadly cloud – seems often
to have been associated with the cherubim. According to an
enduring folk memory, for example, 'two sparks [elsewhere
described as "fiery jets"] issued from the cherubim which
shaded the Ark' – sparks which occasionally burned and
destroyed nearby objects.[18]

Eventually the time came for the Israelites to abandon their
camp at the foot of Mount Sinai – also called the 'Mountain of
Yahweh' (after the name of God):

They set out from the mountain of Yahweh and
journeyed for three days. The Ark of the Covenant of
Yahweh went at their head for this journey of three days,
searching out a camping place for them . . . And as the

> Ark set out, Moses would say, 'Arise Yahweh, may your
> enemies be scattered and those who hate you run for their
> lives before you!' And as it came to rest, he would say,
> 'Come back, Yahweh, to the thronging hosts of Israel.'[19]

Travelling at the head of the Israelite column, the sacred relic
was borne on the shoulders of 'the Kohathites' (or 'sons of
Kohath'), a sub-clan of the tribe of Levi to which both Moses and
Aaron also belonged. According to several legends, and to
rabbinical commentaries on the Old Testament, these bearers
were occasionally killed by the 'sparks' which the Ark emitted[20]
and, in addition, were lifted bodily off the ground from time to
time because 'the Ark [was] able to carry its carriers as well as
itself.'[21] Nor is this the only Jewish tradition to suggest that the
Ark might have been able to exert a mysterious force that in some
way was able to counteract gravity. Several other pieces of
learned Midrashic exegesis also testify that it sometimes lifted its
bearers off the ground (thus temporarily relieving them of what
would otherwise have been a considerable burden).[22] In a similar
vein a particularly striking Jewish legend reports an incident
during which the priests attempting to carry the Ark were 'tossed
by an invisible agency into the air and flung to the ground again
and again.'[23] Another tradition describes an occasion when 'the
Ark leaped of itself into the air'.[24]

Imbued as it was with such strange energies it is little wonder,
throughout their wanderings in the wilderness, that the Israelites
were able to use the Ark as a weapon – a weapon with powers so
terrible that it could bring victory even when the odds seemed
overwhelming.[25] An account of one such battle describes the Ark
as first uttering 'a moaning sound', then rising up off the ground
and rushing towards the enemy[26] – who not surprisingly were
plunged into disarray and slaughtered on the spot. On another
occasion, however – and as though to prove the rule – the
Israelites were themselves defeated. This happened, according
to the Bible, because they did *not* have the Ark with them at the
time – Moses had withheld it from them after advising them
against mounting an assault in that particular area:

They set out presumptuously towards the heights of the

highlands. Neither the Ark of the Covenant of Yahweh
nor Moses left the camp. Then the Amalekites came
down . . . which dwelt in that hill country, and smote
them and discomfited them.[27]

According to the Bible, forty years were spent in the
wilderness,[28] years during which the Israelites learned that it was
in their interests to follow Moses's advice to the letter. Thereafter, under his leadership and with the help of the Ark, they
successfully subdued the fierce tribes of the Sinai peninsula,
conquered Transjordania, spoiled the Midianites,[29] and
generally laid waste to all those who opposed them. Finally,
towards the end of their four decades of wandering, they 'pitched
their camp in the plains of Moab . . . opposite Jericho.'[30]

Just across the Jordan river, the Promised Land was now in
sight. By this time Moses's brother Aaron had already died[31] and
had been replaced in the office of High Priest by Eleazar.[32]
Meanwhile Moses himself had been forewarned by Yahweh that
it was not his destiny to enter Canaan and, accordingly, had
invested 'Joshua, the son of Nun' as his successor.[33]

Soon afterwards Moses died,[34] but not before he had initiated
Joshua into the mysteries of the Ark of the Covenant.[35] The new
leader therefore had a formidable weapon at his disposal to
deploy against the fierce resistance that he was about to
encounter in the heavily fortified city of Jericho.

Joshua seemed to know that the Ark was a two-edged sword –
that, if not properly handled, it could harm the Israelites as well
as their enemies. Early in the campaign, while he was planning
the advance across the Jordan river towards Jericho, he sent his
officers throughout the camp to tell the people this:

> When ye see the Ark of the Covenant of the Lord your
> God, and the priests the Levites bearing it, then ye shall
> remove from your place and go after it. *Yet there shall be a*
> *space between you and it, about two thousand cubits by*
> *measure: come not near unto it . . .*[36]

Then, when all was prepared:

> Joshua spake unto the priests, saying, Take up the Ark of the Covenant, and pass over before the people . . . And it came to pass . . . as they that bare the Ark were come unto Jordan . . . [that] the waters which came from above stood and rose up upon an heap . . . and those that came down were cut off . . . and the priests that bare the Ark of the Covenant of the Lord stood firm on dry ground in the midst of Jordan . . . And . . . when the priests . . . were come up out of the midst of Jordan and the soles of the priests' feet were lifted up onto the dry land . . . the waters of Jordan returned unto their place . . . And [Joshua] spake . . . saying . . . the Lord your God dried up the waters of Jordan from before you, until ye were passed over.[37]

Anyone reared in the Judaeo-Christian tradition will be familiar with the details of the assault on Jericho that followed the triumphal crossing of the Jordan. While the main mass of the people stood back at the obligatory distance of two thousand cubits (more than half a mile), a hand-picked group of priests blowing trumpets marched around the walls of the city bearing the Ark. This procedure was repeated every day for six days. Then:

> On the seventh day . . . they rose early about the dawning of the day, and compassed the city after the same manner . . . only on that day they compassed the city seven times. And . . . at the seventh time, when the priests blew with the trumpets, Joshua said unto the people, Shout; for the Lord hath given you the city . . . So the people shouted when the priests blew with the trumpets: and it came to pass, when the people heard the sound of the trumpet, and the people shouted with a great shout, that the wall fell down flat, so that the people went up into the city . . . and they took the city . . . and they utterly destroyed all that was in the city.[38]

In the wilderness, when it was new, the Ark was nigh-on invincible, and during Joshua's campaigns in the Promised Land the biblical testimony suggests that it continued to play a significant military role long after the fall of Jericho.[39] Within about a hundred and fifty years of Joshua's death, however, a change took place: a close examination of the relevant books of the Old Testament shows that, by this time, the relic was no longer routinely being carried into battle; instead it had been installed (in its Tabernacle) at an important shrine-sanctuary known as Shiloh, where it rested permanently.[40]

The reason for this change was the increasing power and confidence of the Israelites themselves who, by the eleventh century BC, had managed to capture, settle and control most of the Promised Land and who evidently felt that it was no longer necessary in such circumstances for them to bring out their secret weapon.[41]

This self-assurance, however, proved misplaced on one significant occasion – the battle of Ebenezer, at which the Israelites were defeated by the Philistines and four thousand of their men were killed.[42] After this *débâcle*:

> The troops returned to the camp and the elders of Israel said . . . 'Let us fetch the Ark of our God from Shiloh so that it may come among us and rescue us from the power of our enemies.'[43]

This suggestion was immediately accepted:

> So the people sent to Shiloh, that they might bring from thence the Ark of the Covenant of the Lord of Hosts, which dwelleth between the cherubim . . . and when the Ark of the Covenant of the Lord came into the camp, all Israel shouted with a great shout so that the earth rang.[44]

Hearing this noise, the Philistines exclaimed:

> 'What can this great shouting in the Hebrew camp mean?' And they realized that the Ark of Yahweh had come into the camp. At this the Philistines were afraid; and they said, 'God has come to the camp'. 'Alas!' they cried. 'This has never happened before. Alas! Who

will save us from the power of this mighty God?. . . But take courage and be men, Philistines, or you will become slaves to the Hebrews . . . Be men and fight.'[45]

Battle was joined again and, to the utter astonishment of all concerned:

> Israel was smitten, and they fled every man into his tent:
> and there was a very great slaughter; for there fell of
> Israel thirty thousand footmen. And the Ark of God was
> taken.[46]

This was truly a catastrophe. Never before had the Israelites suffered defeat when they had carried the Ark into battle and never before had the Ark itself been captured. Such an eventuality had been unthinkable, unimaginable – and yet it had happened.

As the Philistines bore the relic triumphantly away, a runner was sent to carry the bad news to Eli, the High Priest, who had remained behind at Shiloh:

> And . . . lo, Eli sat upon a seat by the wayside watching
> . . . Now Eli was ninety and eight years old and his eyes
> were dim that he could not see. And the man said unto
> Eli, I am he that came out of the army, and I fled today
> out of the army. And he said, What is there done, my
> son? And the messenger answered and said, Israel is fled
> before the Philistines, and there hath been also a great
> slaughter among the people . . . and the Ark of God is
> taken.
>
> When he mentioned the Ark of God, Eli fell backward
> off his seat . . . His neck was broken and he died, for he
> was old and heavy.
>
> [And] his daughter-in-law . . . was with child and near
> her time. When she heard the news that the Ark of God
> had been captured . . . she crouched down and gave birth,
> for her labour pains came on.[47]

The child thus born was called Ichabod meaning 'where is the glory?'[48] This curious name was chosen, the Bible explained, because the mother had given vent to a great cry of grief when she had received the information about the loss of the Ark: 'And she said, The glory is departed from Israel: for the Ark of God is taken.'[49]

Even stranger and more alarming events were to follow:

When the Philistines had captured the Ark of God they brought it from Ebenezer to Ashdod. Taking the Ark of God, the Philistines put it in the temple of [their deity] Dagon, setting it down beside [the statue of] Dagon. Next morning the people of Ashdod went to the temple of Dagon and there lay Dagon face down on the ground before the Ark of Yahweh. They picked Dagon up and put him back in his place. But early next morning there lay Dagon face down again upon the ground before the Ark of Yahweh, and Dagon's head and two hands were lying severed on the threshold; only the trunk of Dagon was left in its place. This is why the priests of Dagon and indeed all who enter Dagon's temple do not step on the threshold of Dagon in Ashdod to the present day.

The hand of Yahweh weighed heavily on the people of Ashdod and struck terror into them, afflicting them with tumours, in Ashdod and its territory. When the men of Ashdod saw what was happening they said, 'The Ark of the God of Israel must not stay here with us, for his hand lies heavy on us and on Dagon our god.' So they summoned all the Philistine chiefs to them, and said, 'What shall we do with the Ark of the God of Israel?' They decided, 'The Ark of the God of Israel must go to Gath.' So they took the Ark of the God of Israel to Gath. But after they had taken it there, the hand of Yahweh lay heavy on that town and a great panic broke out; the people of the town, from youngest to oldest, were struck with tumours that he brought out on them. They then sent the Ark of God to Ekron, but when it came to Ekron the Ekronites shouted, 'They have brought us the Ark of the God of Israel to bring death to us and our people.' They summoned all the Philistine chiefs and said, 'Send the Ark of the God of Israel away; let it not bring death to us and our people' – for there was mortal panic throughout the town; the hand of God was very heavy there. The people who did not die were struck with tumours and the wailing from the town went up to heaven.[50]

Shattered by the horrible afflictions that they had suffered because of the relic, the Philistines eventually decided – after seven months[51] – to 'send it back to where it belongs'.[52] To this end they loaded it onto a 'new cart' hauled by 'two milch kine'[53] and set it rumbling on its way towards Bethshemesh, the nearest point inside Israelite territory.[54]

Another disaster soon followed, and this time the Philistines were not the victims:

> They of Bethshemesh were reaping their wheat harvest in the valley: and they lifted up their eyes, and saw the Ark, and rejoiced to see it. And the cart came unto the field of Joshua, a Bethshemite, and stood there, where there was a great stone: and the men of Bethshemesh offered burnt offerings and sacrificed sacrifices the same day unto the Lord . . . [But] he smote the men of Bethshemesh because they had looked into the Ark of the Lord, even he smote of the people fifty thousand and threescore and ten men; and the people lamented because the Lord had smitten many of the people with great slaughter.[55]

The text quoted above is from the King James Authorized Version of the Bible, produced in the early seventeenth century. Other more recent translations agree that certain men of Bethshemesh were smitten or 'struck down' by the Ark but put the number slain at *seventy* rather than fifty thousand and seventy – and it is the consensus of modern scholarship that this figure is the correct one.[56]

Seventy men, therefore, looked into the Ark of the Covenant after it arrived in the field of Joshua the Bethshemite, and these seventy men died as a result.[57] Nowhere is it stated exactly *how* they died; but there can be no doubt that they were killed by the

Ark – and in a manner sufficiently dramatic and horrible to lead the survivors to conclude: 'No one is safe in the presence of the Lord, this holy God. To whom can we send it to be rid of him?'[58] At this point, suddenly and rather mysteriously, a group of Levitical priests appeared, 'took down the Ark of the Lord,'[59] and carried it off – not to its former home at Shiloh but instead to a place called 'Kiriath-Jearim' where it was installed in 'the house of Abinadab on the hill'.[60]

And on that hill it remained, isolated and guarded,[61] for the next half century or so.[62] Indeed it was not brought down again until David had become King of Israel. A powerful and headstrong man, he had recently captured the city of Jerusalem. Now it was his intention to consolidate his authority by bringing up to his new capital the most sacred relic of his people.

The date would have been somewhere between 1000 and 990 BC.[63] This is what happened:

> They placed the Ark of God on a new cart and brought it
> from Abinadab's house which is on the hill. Uzzah and
> Ahio . . . were leading the cart. Uzzah walked alongside
> the Ark of God and Ahio went in front . . . When they
> came to the threshing floor of Nacon, Uzzah stretched his
> hand out to the Ark of God and steadied it, as the oxen
> were making it tilt. Then the anger of Yahweh blazed out
> against Uzzah, and for this crime God struck him down
> on the spot, and he died there beside the Ark of God.[64]

Quite naturally:

> David was afraid of the Lord that day and said, 'How can
> I harbour the Ark of the Lord after this?' He felt he could
> not take the Ark of the Lord with him to the City of
> David.[65]

Instead he 'turned aside and carried it to the house of Obed-edom the Gittite.'[66] At that house, while the Jewish monarch waited to see if it would kill anyone else, the Ark of the Covenant remained for three months. No further disasters occurred, however. On the contrary: 'Yahweh blessed Obed-edom and his whole family.'[67] The Scriptures are not explicit about the nature of this benediction. According to ancient folk traditions, however, 'it consisted in Obed-edom being blessed with many children ... The women in his house gave birth after a pregnancy of two months only and bore six children at one time.'[68]

The Bible takes up the story again as follows:

> It was told King David, saying, the Lord hath blessed the house of Obed-edom and all that pertaineth unto him, because of the Ark of God. So David went and brought the Ark of God from the house of Obed-edom into the City of David with gladness.[69]

On this journey:

> the children of the Levites bare the Ark of God upon their shoulders with the staves thereon, as Moses had commanded according to the word of God.[70]

Then, finally, David led the joyous procession into Jerusalem 'with shouting and with the sound of the trumpet',[71] and with music played 'on all manner of instruments made of fir wood, even on harps, and on psalteries, and on timbrels, and on coronets, and on cymbals.'[72]

It had been David's hope that he would be able to build a temple in Jerusalem in which the Ark could be housed. In the event, however, he was not to fulfil this ambition and instead had to content himself with placing the relic in a simple tent of the type that had been used during the desert wanderings.[73]

The honour (or the conceit?) of erecting the Temple was therefore left to another man. As David himself put it before he died:

> As for me, I had it in mine heart to build an house of rest for the Ark of the Covenant of the Lord ... and had made ready for the building ... But God said unto me, Thou shalt not build an house for my name ... Solomon thy son, he shall build my house.[74]

This prophecy was duly fulfilled. At Solomon's command, work was started on the Temple around the year 966 BC[75] and was completed rather more than a decade later, probably in 955 BC.[76] Then, when all was done, the Holy of Holies – a place which the Lord had ordered should be utterly dark – was made ready to receive the precious object that it had been built to contain:

> Solomon assembled the elders of Israel, and all the heads of the tribes . . . that they might bring up the Ark of the Covenant of the Lord . . . And all the elders of Israel came, and the priests took up the Ark. And they brought up the Ark of the Lord . . . And King Solomon, and all the congregation of Israel that were assembled unto him, were with him before the Ark, sacrificing sheep and oxen that could not be told nor numbered for multitude. And the priests brought in the Ark of the Covenant of the Lord to its place in the Temple . . . in the Holy of Holies.[77]

And there the sacred relic remained, enveloped in 'thick darkness', until it mysteriously vanished at some unknown date between the tenth and sixth centuries BC.[78] As I have already indicated in Chapter 1, absolutely no explanation exists for its disappearance, which scholars regard as one of the great unsolved riddles of the Bible.[79] Almost equally puzzling, however, are the awesome powers that it seems to have possessed in its heyday – powers portrayed in the Old Testament as stemming directly from God.

Deus ex machina

In trying to understand the Ark, I found myself returning again and again to the perplexing issue of these powers. What could have accounted for them? It seemed to me that there were three possible answers:

  1 The Old Testament was right. The Ark was indeed a
    repository of divine energies and these energies were
    the source of all the 'miracles' that it performed.

2 The Old Testament was wrong. The Ark was just an
ornate casket and the children of Israel were the victims
of a collective mass hallucination that lasted for several
hundred years.

3 The Old Testament was both right and wrong at the same
time. The Ark possessed genuine powers, but those
powers were neither 'supernatural' nor divine. On the
contrary, they were man-made.

I looked into all three options and concluded that I certainly
could not accept the first unless I was also prepared to accept that
Yahweh, the God of the Israelites, was a psychopathic killer – or a
kind of malign genie who lived in a box. Nor could I accept the
second – primarily because the Old Testament, which is a
compilation of books codified in widely different periods, was
remarkably *consistent* where the Ark was concerned. Throughout
the Scriptures it was the *only* artefact explicitly and unambiguously portrayed as being imbued with supernatural
energies. All other man-made objects were treated quite matter-
of-factly. Indeed even exceptionally holy items such as the
seven-branched golden candlestick known as the *menorah*, the
so-called 'table of the showbread', and the altar upon which
sacrifices were performed, were clearly understood to be nothing
more than important pieces of ritual furniture.

The Ark was therefore quite unique, unrivalled in the special
reverence accorded to it by the scribes, and matchless in the
awesome deeds attributed to it throughout the lengthy period in
which it completely dominated the biblical story. Moreover its
alleged powers showed few signs of having fallen victim to
imaginative literary embellishment. On the contrary, from the
time of its construction at the foot of Mount Sinai until its sudden
and unexplained disappearance hundreds of years later, it
continued to exhibit the *same* spectacular but limited repertoire.
Thus it continued to lift itself, its bearers, and other objects
around it off the ground; it continued to emit light; it continued to
be associated with a strange 'cloud' that materialized 'between
the cherubim'; it continued to afflict people with ailments like
'leprosy'[80] and 'tumours'; and it continued to kill those who
accidentally touched or opened it. Significantly, however, it

exhibited none of the other marvellous characteristics that one might have expected if a mass hallucination had been involved or if a great deal of fiction had been allowed to adulterate the record: for example, it did not make rain; it did not turn water into wine; it did not resurrect the dead; it did not drive out devils; and it did not always win the battles into which it was taken (although it usually did).

In other words, throughout its history, it consistently behaved like a powerful machine that had been designed to carry out certain very specific tasks and that only performed effectively within its design parameters – although even then, like all machines, it was fallible because of defects in its construction and because it was subject both to human error and to wear and tear.

I therefore formulated the following hypothesis, in line with the third alternative set out above: the Old Testament had indeed been both right and wrong at the same time. The Ark *had* possessed genuine powers, but those powers had been neither supernatural nor divine; on the contrary, they must have been the products of *human* skill and ingenuity.

This, of course, was only a theory – a speculation intended to guide my further research – and it was confronted by a great many legitimate doubts. Most important of all, how could men possibly have manufactured so potent a device more than three thousand years ago, when technology and civilization had supposedly been at a very rudimentary stage?

This question, I felt, lay at the heart of the mystery. In seeking to answer it I found that I had to consider first and foremost the cultural context of the sacred relic – a context that was almost entirely Egyptian. After all, the Ark was built in the wilderness of Sinai within a very few months after Moses had led his people out of their captivity in Egypt – a captivity that had lasted for more than four hundred years.[81] It therefore followed that Egypt was the most likely place in which to find clues to the Ark's true nature.

Tutankhamen's legacy

I became convinced that I was right about this after I had paid a visit to the Cairo Museum. Located in the heart of Egypt's capital city, close to the east bank of the Nile, this imposing building is an unequalled repository of Pharaonic artefacts dating back as far as the fourth millennium BC. One of the upper floors is given over to a permanent exhibition of objects recovered from the tomb of Tutankhamen, the youthful monarch who ruled Egypt from 1352 to 1343 BC – i.e. about a century before the time of Moses.[82] I was entranced by this exhibition and spent several hours wandering amongst the display cases amazed at the beauty, variety and sheer quantity of the relics on view. It did not surprise me to learn that the renowned British archaeologist Howard Carter had taken six full years to empty the great sepulchre that he had found in the Valley of the Kings in 1922.[83] However, what interested me most of all about the treasures that he had unearthed was that they included dozens of Ark-like chests or boxes, some with carrying poles, some without, but all of them conceptually similar to the Ark of the Covenant.

By far the most striking of these objects were the four shrines that had been built to contain the sarcophagus of Tutankhamen. These shrines, which I studied closely, took the form of large rectangular caskets that had originally been positioned one inside the other but that were now installed in separate display cases. Since each casket was made of wood, and since each, moreover, was plated 'inside and out with pure gold',[84] it was difficult to resist the conclusion that the mind that had conceived the Ark of the Covenant must have been familiar with objects like these.

Further support for this inference was provided by the presence on the doors and rear walls of each of the shrines of two mythical figures: tall and terrible winged women, fierce and imperious in stature and visage – like stern angels of vengeance. These powerful and commanding creatures, placed so as to provide ritual protection for the precious contents of the tomb, were thought to be representations of the goddesses Isis and Nephthys.[85] While that identification in itself held no special significance for me, I could not help but note that the deities had their 'wings spread upwards' just like the cherubim referred to in the biblical description of the Ark. They also faced each other just as the biblical cherubim had done. And although they were shaped in high relief on the flat planes of the doors (rather than being distinct pieces of statuary) they were nevertheless fashioned 'of beaten gold' – again very much like the cherubim described in the Bible.[86]

No scholar, I knew, had ever been able to establish exactly what those cherubim had looked like. There was only consensus that they could in no way have resembled the chubby angelic 'cherubs' of much later western art, which were, at best, sanitized and Christianized interpretations of a truly ancient and pagan concept.[87] Lost in thought in the Cairo Museum, however, it seemed to me that the formidable winged guardians of Tutankhamen's inter-nested shrines were the closest models that I was ever likely to find for the two cherubim of the Ark, which indeed had been conceived as standing sentinel over it and which had also frequently served as channels for its immense and deadly power.

The *tabotat* of Apet

I was subsequently to discover that the Ark's Egyptian background was wider and deeper even than this. Tutankhamen had also left another legacy which helped me to understand the full significance of that background. During a visit to the great temple at Luxor in Upper Egypt in April 1990, while passing through the elegant colonnade that extends eastwards from the court of Rameses II, I came across a story carved in stone – a permanent and richly illustrated account of the important 'Festival of Apet' which had been inscribed here in the fourteenth century BC on Tutankhamen's direct orders.[88]

Although now badly eroded by the passage of the millennia, the faded reliefs on the west and east walls of the colonnade were still sufficiently visible for me to grasp the rudiments of the festival, which in Tutankhamen's time had marked the peak of the annual Nile flood upon which almost all of Egypt's agriculture depended.[89] I already knew that this perennial inundation (today held back by the Aswan High Dam with profoundly unfortunate ecological consequences) had been almost exclusively the product of the long rainy season in the Ethiopian highlands – a deluge that every year roared down out of Lake Tana and along the Blue Nile bestowing hundreds of thousands of tons of rich silt on the farmlands of the Delta and contributing an estimated six-sevenths of the total volume of water in the Nile river system.[90] This opened up the possibility that the Apet ceremonials might in some way prove relevant to my quest: after all, they had celebrated a clear link between the life of ancient Egypt and events in far-off Ethiopia. Most probably this link had been no more than a coincidental one to do with climate and geography; nevertheless I regarded it as being of at least *prima facie* interest.

It turned out to be far more than that.

Studying first the western wall of the colonnade on which the Tutankhamen reliefs were displayed, my eye was caught by what appeared to be an Ark, lifted shoulder high on its carrying poles by a group of priests. Stepping closer I quickly confirmed that this was indeed the case: with the sole proviso that the object being transported took the form of a miniature boat rather than a casket, the scene before me looked like quite a faithful illustration of the passage in the first book of Chronicles which states that the Levitical priests of ancient Israel 'carried the Ark of God with the shafts on their shoulders as Moses had ordered'.[91]

Standing back to get perspective I established that the entire western wall of the colonnade was covered with images very similar to the one that had initially attracted my attention. In what seemed to be a massive and joyous procession I was able to make out the shapes of several different Ark-like boats being carried on the shoulders of several different groups of priests, before whom musicians played on sistra and a variety of other instruments, acrobats performed, and people danced and sang, clapping their hands in excitement.

With my pulse quickening I sat down in a patch of shade around the broken base of a column and reflected on the implications of the huge sense of *déjà vu* that had just overtaken me. It was barely three months since I had attended *Timkat* in the Ethiopian city of Gondar on 18 and 19 January 1990. The details of the ceremonials that I had witnessed during those two days of religious frenzy were therefore still fresh in my mind – so fresh in fact that I could hardly fail to note the similarities between them and the ecstatic procession portrayed on the time-worn stones of this Egyptian temple. Both events, I realized, focussed around a kind of 'Ark worship', with the Arks being borne aloft by groups of priests and adored by hysterical crowds. Nor was this all: *Timkat* had been characterized by the performance of wild dances and the playing of musical instruments before the Arks. This sort of behaviour, it was now clear, had also been an intrinsic part of the Apet festival, right down to the types of musical instruments used, which in many cases were identical to those that I had seen in Gondar. Of course the flat slabs of the *tabotat* carried on the heads of the Ethiopian priests were rather different in appearance from the Ark-like boats carried on the shoulders of their long-dead Egyptian counterparts. From my earlier research, however (detailed at some length in Chapter 6), I could hardly forget that according to established etymologies the original meaning of *tabot* had been 'ship-like container'. Indeed, as I knew very well, the archaic Hebrew word *tebah* (from which the Ethiopic term had been derived[92]) had been used in the Bible to refer specifically to ship-like arks, namely the ark of Noah and the ark of bulrushes in which the infant Moses had been cast adrift on the Nile. Nor, I now realized, could it possibly be irrelevant that the *Kebra Nagast* had at one point described the Ark of the Covenant as 'the belly of a ship'[93] containing 'the Two Tables which were written by the finger of God.'[94]

After catching my breath, I stood up and stepped out from my patch of shade into the fierce mid-day sunlight that bathed the whole of the colonnade area. I then continued my examination of the faded reliefs of the Apet festival which, on the western wall, concerned the bringing of the arks from Karnak to the Temple at Luxor (a distance of about three miles) and, on the eastern wall, showed the procession's eventual return from Luxor back along the Nile to Karnak again where, with all due ceremony, the sacred vessels were reinstalled in their original resting places. Every detail of these complex and beautifully carved scenes reminded me irresistibly of *Timkat* in Gondar – which had also involved an outgoing procession (bringing the *tabotat* from the churches to the 'baptismal' lake beside the old castle) and a returning procession (bringing the *tabotat* back to their home churches again). Moreover, I could now see clearly that the bizarre ceremonies I had witnessed in the early morning of 19 January at the lake itself had also been prefigured in the Apet festival which, at every stage, appeared to have involved a special reverence for water (indeed, the reliefs of the early part of the procession showed that the arks had been carried directly from the temple to the banks of the Nile, where a number of elaborate rituals had then been performed).

Scholarly corroboration

After completing my trip to Egypt in April 1990 I took the opportunity to carry out some further research into the evidence that I had stumbled upon there. I discovered that the experts had no quarrel with my various conjectures. At one meeting, for example, Kenneth Kitchen, Professor of Egyptology at Liverpool University, confirmed that the caskets from Tutankhamen's tomb that I had seen in the Cairo Museum could indeed have been prototypes for the Ark of the Covenant: 'At the very least,' he said in his broad and rather emphatic Yorkshire accent, 'they prove that wooden boxes lined with gold were standard artefacts of the religious furniture of the period and that Moses would therefore have had the technology and skills at his disposal to manufacture the Ark. The methods of construction that he would have employed, and the use of such prefabricated structures for religious purposes, are abundantly attested by actual remains, pictures and texts in Egypt over a long period of time.'[95]

I also found scholarly corroboration for the link that I believed had existed between the festival of Apet and the early Judaic ceremonies surrounding the Ark of the Covenant. Working through piles of reference materials in the British Library I came across a book published in London in 1884 by the Religious Tract Society and entitled *Fresh Light from the Ancient Monuments*. I might have ignored this slim and unprepossessing volume entirely had I not noticed that its author was a certain A. H. Sayce (who at the time had been Deputy Professor of Philology at Oxford University). Remembering that E. A. Wallis Budge, one of the great authorities on Egyptian religion, had held Sayce in the highest regard (describing him as a 'distinguished scholar'[96]) I opened the book at a chapter entitled 'The Exodus out of Egypt' and read that, in Sayce's opinion, 'the law and ritual of the Israelites' had been derived from many sources. Amongst these were 'various festivals and fasts' in which

> The gods were carried in procession in 'ships', which, as
> we learn from the sculptures, resembled in form the
> Hebrew Ark, and were borne on men's shoulders by
> means of staves.[97]

Encouraged by the support for my speculations that the distinguished nineteenth-century professor had given me, I looked further through the reference works at my disposal and was able to confirm that the ship-like arks carried during the Apet ceremonials had indeed contained gods, or rather small statues of various deities in the Egyptian pantheon.[98] These statues had been made of stone and thus, it seemed to me, were not far removed in concept from the stone 'Tablets of the Testimony' that had supposedly been lodged inside the Ark of the Covenant and that the Israelites had regarded as embodying their God. As one Hebrew scholar had put it in a seminal paper published in the 1920s:

> The tradition of the two sacred stone tablets within the
> Ark would point strongly to the conclusion that the
> original contents of the Ark must have been a sacred
> stone . . . [which] was either conceived of as the deity
> himself, or as the object in which the deity was thought to
> reside permanently.[99]

Nor was this the only connection that I was able to establish between the Ark of the Covenant and the ship-like arks that had been carried in the Apet ceremonies. Those ceremonies, it will be remembered, had taken place in the Upper Egyptian town now known as 'Luxor', a relatively recent name derived from the Arabic *L'Ouqsor* (meaning 'the palaces'). Much earlier, during the period of Greek influence in Egypt (from about the fifth century BC) the whole area including the nearby temple at Karnak had been known as *Thebai*. Modern Europeans had subsequently corrupted this name to the more familiar 'Thebes'.[100] In the process, however, they had obscured an intriguing etymology: the word *Thebai* had in fact been derived from *Tapet*, the name by which the Luxor/Karnak religious complex had been known in the era of Tutankhamen and Moses.[101] And *Tapet* in its turn was merely the feminine form of *Apet* – in other words, Luxor and Karnak had originally been named after the great festival for which they had been famous,[102] a festival that had centred upon a procession in which arks had been carried between the two temples. What intrigued me about this, of course, was the phonetic similarity of the words *Tapet* and *Tabot*, a similarity that looked all the less coincidental after I had discovered from one learned source that the shape of the *Tapet* arks had evolved over the passing centuries, gradually ceasing to resemble ships so closely and becoming instead 'more and more like a chest'.[103]

As noted above, I had long since established that the Ethiopic term *Tabot* had been derived from the Hebrew *tebah*, meaning 'ship-like container'. Now I began to wonder whether it was not entirely possible that the word *tebah* had itself originally been derived from the ancient Egyptian *Tapet* – and whether this derivation might not have come about because the ceremonies devised for the Ark of the Covenant had been modelled upon those of the Apet festival.[104]

Such links and coincidences, though by no means attaining the stature of hard evidence, did deepen my conviction that the Ark of the Covenant could only properly be understood in the context of its Egyptian background. Amongst other things, as Professor Kitchen had pointed out, that background demonstrated that Moses would have had the technology and skills at his disposal to fulfil God's command to build an 'Ark of acacia wood' and 'to plate it inside and out with pure gold'.

At the same time, however, the sacred relic had been much more than *just* a wooden box lined with gold. I therefore wondered whether an explanation of its baleful and destructive powers might also be found in Egypt.

Seeking such an explanation I travelled to that country several times and talked to theologians, biblical scholars and archaeologists. I also surrounded myself with rare books, religious texts, folklore, myths and legends and tried to discern whether threads of fact might not lie entangled amongst the wilder fancies.

As my research progressed I became increasingly intrigued by the personality of Moses, the Hebrew prophet and law-giver who challenged Pharaoh, who led the children of Israel to the Promised Land, and who also ordered the construction of the Ark of the Covenant after he had supposedly received the 'blueprint' for its design from God Himself. The more closely I looked at this towering, heroic figure, the more convinced I became that information of fundamental importance to my understanding of the Ark would be found within the records of his life.

'A magician of the highest order . . .'

It is probably the case that every Christian, Muslim and Jew alive in the world today has a shadowy image of the prophet Moses tucked away in some corner of his or her mind. Certainly I was no exception to this rule when I began to think seriously about him and about his role in the mystery of the Ark. My problem, however, was that I needed to flesh out the caricature that I had acquired in Sunday school and, in the process, to gain some real insight into the man who scholars agree was 'the outstanding figure in the emergence and formulation of the Jewish religion'.[105]

Of considerable help to me in completing this task were the extensive and highly regarded historical writings of Flavius Josephus, a Pharisee who lived in Roman-occupied Jerusalem in the first century AD. In his *Antiquities of the Jews*, compiled from traditions and reference materials unavailable today, this diligent scholar chronicled the four hundred years of Hebrew enslavement in Egypt, which lasted roughly from 1650 until 1250 BC, the probable date of the Exodus.[106] The birth of Moses was the key event of this period and was, Josephus said, the subject of a prophecy by an Egyptian 'sacred scribe', a person 'with considerable skill of accurately predicting the future', who informed Pharaoh that there would arise amongst the Israelites

one who would abase the sovereignty of the Egyptians were he reared to manhood, and would surpass all men in virtue and win everlasting renown. Alarmed thereat, the

king, on the sage's advice, ordered that every male child
born to the Israelites should be destroyed by being cast into
the river.[107]

On hearing this edict a certain Amram (Moses's father-to-be)
was plunged into 'grievous perplexity' because 'his wife was then
with child'. God, however, appeared to him in a dream and
comforted him with the news that:

> This child, whose birth has filled the Egyptians with such
> dread that they have condemned to destruction all the
> offspring of the Israelites, shall escape those who are
> watching to destroy him, and, reared in marvellous wise,
> he shall deliver the Hebrew race from their bondage in
> Egypt, and be remembered so long as the universe shall
> endure, not by Hebrews alone but even by alien
> nations.[108]

These two passages were helpful to me because they considerably expanded the biblical narrative on the birth of Moses given
in the opening chapters of the book of Exodus. I noted with
interest that the great legislator of the Jews had indeed been
remembered 'even by alien nations'. More intriguing by far,
however, was the special emphasis put on the prophecy of the
'sacred scribe' who, with his ability to foretell the future, could
only have been an astrologer at the court of the Pharaoh. In
making this point, Josephus seemed to be hinting that – from the
outset – there had been something almost magical about Moses.
In the time-honoured tradition of setting a thief to catch a thief,
what we had here was a magician predicting the coming of a
magician.

The bare bones of the events that occurred after the child was
born are too familiar to require lengthy repetition: aged only
three months he was placed by his parents in a papyrus basket
coated with bitumen and pitch and cast adrift on the Nile;
downriver Pharaoh's daughter was bathing; she saw the floating
crib, heard cries, and sent her handmaiden to rescue the mewling
infant.

Subsequently Moses was brought up in the royal household

where, according to the Bible, he was instructed 'in all the wisdom of the Egyptians'.[109] Josephus had little to add at this point, but another classical authority – Philo, the respected Jewish philosopher who lived around the time of Christ – gave a fairly detailed account of exactly *what* Moses was taught: 'Arithmetic, geometry, the lore of metre, rhythm and harmony were imparted to him by learned Egyptians. These further instructed him in the philosophy conveyed in symbols as displayed in the so-called holy inscriptions.' Meanwhile 'inhabitants of neighbouring countries' were assigned to teach him 'Assyrian letters and the Chaldean science of the heavenly bodies. This he also acquired from the Egyptians, who gave special attention to astrology.'[110]

Reared as an adopted son of the royal family, Moses was seen for a considerable period as a successor to the throne.[111] The implication of this special status, I learned, was that in his youth he would have been given a thorough initiation into all the most arcane priestly secrets and into the mysteries of Egyptian magic[112] – a course of study that would have included not only star-knowledge, as indicated by Philo, but also necromancy, divining and other aspects of occult lore.[113]

A clue that this may indeed have been so was given in the Bible, where Moses was described as being 'mighty in words and deeds'.[114] In the cogent and dependable judgment of that great scholar and linguist Sir E. A. Wallis Budge, this phrase – also and perhaps not coincidentally applied to Jesus Christ[115] – contained the coded suggestion that the Hebrew prophet was 'strong of tongue', like the Egyptian goddess Isis. What this meant, though Moses was self-confessedly lacking in oratorical eloquence,[116] was that he must have been capable of uttering words of power 'which he knew with correct pronunciation, and halted not in his speech, and was perfect both in giving the command and in saying the word.'[117] As such, again like Isis – who was famous for her proficiency in all kinds of witchcraft – he would have been equipped to cast the most potent spells. Others around him would therefore have treated him with a high degree of respect since they would unquestioningly have believed him capable of bending reality and overriding the laws of physics by altering the normal order of things.

I was able to turn up a considerable body of evidence from the Old Testament to support the contention that Moses had been seen in exactly this way. There was, nevertheless, one important proviso: his magic was depicted throughout as being wrought solely at the command of Yahweh, the God of the Hebrews.

According to the book of Exodus, Moses's first encounter with Yahweh took place in a wilderness near the land of Midian (to which he had fled to escape retribution after his anger at the persecution of Hebrew labourers had led him to kill an Egyptian overseer). From the geographical clues that were given, it was clear that this wilderness must have been located in the southern part of the Sinai peninsula, most probably within sight of the peak of Mount Sinai itself[118] (where Moses was later to receive the Ten Commandments and the 'blueprint' for the Ark). The Bible, at any rate, spoke of 'the mountain of God' and placed Moses at its foot when the Lord appeared to him 'in a flame of fire out of the midst of a bush: and he looked, and, behold, the bush burned with fire, and the bush was not consumed.'[119] God instructed Moses that he should return to Egypt in order to lead his people out of their bondage there.[120] Before agreeing, however, the prophet *asked the name* of the strange and powerful being who had addressed him.[121]

This daring question in itself contained evidence of Moses's identity as a sorcerer for, as the great anthropologist Sir James Frazer observed in his seminal work *The Golden Bough*:

> Every Egyptian magician . . . believed that he who possessed the true name possessed the very being of god or man, and could force even a deity to obey him as a slave obeys his master. Thus the art of the magician consisted in obtaining from the gods a revelation of their sacred names, and he left no stone unturned to accomplish his end.[122]

The Lord, however, did not respond directly to the prophet's question. Instead he replied briefly and enigmatically with these words: 'I AM WHO I AM.' By way of further clarification he then added: 'I am the God of thy father, the God of Abraham, the God of Isaac and the God of Jacob.'[123]

The phrase 'I am who I am' (or 'I am what I am', 'I am that I am', depending on the translation) was, I discovered, the root meaning of the name Yahweh used in the Old Testament – and subsequently bastardized in the Authorized King James Version of the Bible as 'Jehovah'. This name, however, was no name; rather it was an evasive formula based loosely on the Hebrew verb 'to be' and written as four consonants which transliterated into the Latin alphabet as 'YHWH'. Known to theologians as the tetragrammaton, these letters revealed nothing beyond the active *existence* of God and thus continued to conceal the divine identity from modern researchers every bit as effectively as they had once done from Moses. Indeed so potent was their mystery that no one today could even claim to know exactly how they should be pronounced; rendering the tetragrammaton as 'Yahweh' by the insertion of the vowels 'a' and 'e' was, however, the accepted convention.[124]

The importance of all this from the biblical perspective was that the deity knew, and pronounced, the name of Moses; Moses, by contrast, only managed to obtain from Him the ritual incantation 'I am who I am'. Henceforward, therefore, the prophet was bound to answer to God and to do his bidding; likewise all his sorcery in the future would derive from the power of God, and from the power of God alone.

It was understandable that the later redactors of the Scriptures should have wanted to present the relationship between omnipotent God and fallible man in precisely this way. What they could not do, however, was erase the evidence that that man had indeed been a sorcerer; neither could they cover up the most convincing demonstrations of his sorcery – the plagues and pestilences that he was soon to inflict upon the Egyptians in order to force Pharaoh to release the children of Israel from captivity.

In working these terrible miracles Moses was assisted by his older half-brother Aaron, who frequently served as his agent and spokesman. Both Moses and Aaron were also equipped with rods – effectively magicians' wands – which they used to work their spells. That of Moses was sometimes referred to as 'the rod of God'[125] and first appeared when the prophet complained to Yahweh that neither Pharaoh, nor the children of Israel, would believe that he had been divinely commissioned, unless he was able to provide some kind of proof. 'What is that in thine hand?' God asked. 'A rod,' Moses replied.[126] God then told him to throw it on the ground 'that they may believe that the Lord God hath appeared unto thee':

> And he cast it on the ground and it became a serpent; and Moses fled from before it. And the Lord said unto Moses, Put forth thine hand and take it by the tail. And he put forth his hand and caught it, and it became a rod in his hand.[127]

Once again the emphasis put by the scriptural text on the primacy of God's role in all of this was understandable. Once again also, however, the connections with Egyptian occult practice were quite unmissable. The turning of an inanimate stick into a snake, and then back again into a stick, was a feat frequently carried out by the magicians of that country; likewise the power to control the movements of venomous reptiles was claimed by Egyptian priests from the very earliest times; last but not least, all Egyptian magicians – amongst them the sage Abaaner and the sorceror-king Nectanebus – possessed marvellous rods made of ebony.[128]

Looked at in this light, I did not find it surprising that the first contests between Moses and Aaron on one side, and the priests at Pharaoh's court on the other, were fairly evenly drawn. To impress the Egyptian tyrant, Aaron threw down his rod – which, of course, became a serpent as soon as it hit the ground. Undaunted Pharaoh called for his own sages and sorcerers, 'and with their witchcraft the magicians of Egypt did the same. Each threw his staff down and these turned into serpents.' Then, however, Aaron's rod – imbued with the superior power of Yahweh – swallowed up the rods of the magicians.[129]

In the next encounter Moses and Aaron turned the waters of the Nile to blood. Remarkable though this trick was, Pharaoh remained unimpressed because 'the magicians of Egypt used their witchcraft to do the same.'[130]

The plague of frogs, which followed, was likewise matched by Pharaoh's sorcerers.[131] But the plague of mosquitoes (gnats in some translations, lice in others) was too much for them: 'The magicians with their witchcraft tried to produce mosquitoes and failed. The mosquitoes attacked men and beasts. So the magicians said to Pharaoh, "This is the finger of God." '[132]

Still the hard-hearted king refused to let the Hebrews go. He was punished for this with a plague of flies[133] and soon afterwards with a pestilence that killed livestock.[134] Moses next caused a plague of boils to break out (he did this by throwing a handful of soot into the air[135]) and then, by using his rod, he procured thunder and hail, a plague of locusts and three days of 'thick darkness'.[136] Finally, the Hebrew prophet arranged for the death of 'all the first-born of the land of Egypt: the first-born of Pharaoh, the first-born of the prisoner in his dungeon, and the first-born of all the cattle.'[137] After this: 'The Egyptians urged the people to hurry up and leave the land because, they said, "Otherwise we shall all be dead".'[138]

So the Exodus began, and with it a prolonged period of danger and enchantment during which, at the foot of Mount Sinai, the Ark of the Covenant was built. Before reaching Sinai, however, the Red Sea had to be crossed. Here Moses gave another dramatic demonstration of his prowess in the occult arts:

And Moses stretched out his hand over the sea; and the Lord caused the sea to go back by a strong east wind all that night, and made the sea dry land, and the waters were divided. And the children of Israel went into the midst of the sea upon the dry ground: and the waters were a wall unto them on their right hand and on their left.[139]

As everyone who has ever attended Sunday school will remember, the pursuing Egyptian forces followed the Israelites into 'the midst of the sea, even all Pharaoh's horses, his chariots and his horsemen.'[140] Then:

Moses stretched forth his hand over the sea – and the waters returned, and covered the chariots, and the horsemen, and all the host of Pharaoh that came into the sea after them; there remained not so much as one of them. But the children of Israel walked upon dry land in the midst of the sea; and the waters were a wall unto them on their right hand, and on their left.[141]

Again, and predictably, the Bible put emphasis on the power of God: Moses may have stretched out his hand a couple of times but it was the Lord who 'caused the waters to go back' – and to 'return'. I found it slightly harder to accept the scriptural party-line on this, however, after I had learned that the ability to command the waters of seas and lakes had also frequently been claimed by Egyptian priests and magicians. For example, one of the ancient documents that I studied (the Westcar Papyrus) related a story from the early Fourth Dynasty – some 1,500 years *before* the time of Moses – which focussed on the doings of a certain Tchatcha-em-ankh, a *Kher Heb* or High Priest attached to the court of Pharaoh Seneferu. Apparently the Pharaoh was out boating one day in the pleasant company of 'twenty young virgins having beautiful heads of hair and lovely forms and shapely limbs.' One of these ladies dropped a much- favoured ornament of hers into the lake and was broken-hearted to have lost it. The Pharaoh, however, summoned Tchatcha-em- ankh who

> spake certain words of power (*hekau*) and having thus caused one section of the water of the lake to go upon the other, he found the ornament lying upon a pot-sherd, and he took it and gave it to the maiden. Now the water was twelve cubits deep, but when Tchatcha-em-ankh had lifted up one section of the water onto the other, that portion became four and twenty cubits deep. The magician again uttered certain words of power, and the water of the lake became as it had been before he had caused one portion of it to go up onto the other.[142]

While of course to do with a much more trivial incident, the story in the Westcar Papyrus nevertheless contained many points that I could only regard as startlingly similar to the parting of the waters of the Red Sea. This, in my view, left no room for doubt that Moses's virtuoso performance in bringing about the great miracle established him firmly in an ancient, and very *Egyptian*, occult tradition. Sir E. A. Wallis Budge, who I had first encountered through his translation of the *Kebra Nagast*, but who had also been keeper of Egyptian and Assyrian Antiquities at the British Museum, had this to say on the subject:

> Moses was a skilled performer of magical rituals and was deeply learned in the knowledge of the accompanying spells, incantations, and magical formulas of every description . . . [Moreover] the miracles which he wrought . . . suggest that he was not only a priest, but a magician of the highest order and perhaps even a *Kher Heb*.[143]

Secret science?

As a *Kher Heb* (High Priest) of the Egyptian temple Moses would undoubtedly have had access to a substantial corpus of esoteric wisdom and of magico-religious 'science' that the priestly guilds kept secret from the laity. I knew that modern Egyptologists accepted that such a body of knowledge had existed.[144] I also knew that they had very little idea as to what it might actually have consisted of: obscure references to it appeared in inscriptions in the tombs of senior temple officials but almost nothing of any substance had survived in written form. A great deal was probably passed on in an exclusively oral tradition confined to initiates.[145] Scholarly opinion had it, however, that most of the rest had been destroyed, either deliberately or accidentally. Who could possibly guess what treasures of learning were lost when fire ravaged the great library at Alexandria – a library that was reputed, by the second century BC, to have contained more than 200,000 scrolls?[146]

There was, however, one matter on which there was no need to speculate: as Herodotus put it in the fifth century BC, 'Egypt has more wonders in it than any country in the world and more works that are beyond description than anywhere else.' Amongst other achievements, this widely travelled Greek historian – whose books are still in print – rightly credited the Egyptians with being 'the first of mankind to invent the year and to make twelve divisions of the seasons for it'. Herodotus also claimed to have penetrated some of the mysteries of the Egyptian priesthood, but then, rather tantalizingly, added that he could not – or would not – reveal what he had learned.[147]

Herodotus was not the first or the last visitor to Egypt to come away with the distinct impression that there were hidden secrets there – and that there might be more to these secrets than mere religious mumbo-jumbo. Indeed the notion that this ancient culture originally promoted itself to greatness through the application of some kind of advanced, but now lost, scientific knowledge was, I discovered, one of the most durable and pervasive in human history: it had proved equally attractive to furious cranks and sober scholars and had been the subject of immense amounts of controversy, acrimony, wild speculation and serious research.

It was a notion, furthermore, that impinged directly upon my quest because it raised an intriguing possibility: as a magician skilled in Egyptian 'sacred science', might not Moses have had at his disposal far more in the way of knowledge and technology than had hitherto been recognized by the archaeologists? And might he not have applied this knowledge and technology to the construction of the Ark of the Covenant?

Such a hypothesis seemed worthy of further investigation. I quickly discovered, however, that what was known about the technological achievements of the ancient Egyptians raised at least as many questions as it answered.

It was clear, for example, that these people were clever metalworkers: their gold jewellery, in particular, was quite exquisite, showing a degree of craftsmanship rarely equalled since. It was also notable, from the very earliest times, that the edges of their copper tools were brought to a remarkable degree of hardness – so hard, in fact, that they could cut through schist and the toughest limestone. No modern blacksmith, I learned, would have been able to achieve such results with copper; it was thought likely, however, that any 'lost art' lay less in the manufacture of the tools than in the manner in which they were manipulated on site by the stonemasons.[148]

A study of many surviving hieroglyphs and papyri left me in no doubt that the ancient Egyptians were – at the very least – moderate mathematicians in the modern sense. They employed unit fractions and appeared to have developed a special form of infinitesimal calculus which enabled them to compute the volume of complex objects.[149] It also seemed highly probable, more than 2,000 years before the Greeks, that they had understood how to use the transcendental number *pi* to derive the circumference of any circle from its diameter.[150]

Egyptian observational astronomy was another area in which great progress appeared to have been made at a very early date. According to Livio Stecchini, an American professor of the history of science and an expert on ancient measurement, astronomical techniques in use as early as 2200 BC had enabled Egyptian priests to calculate the length of a degree of latitude and longitude to within a few hundred feet – an achievement that was not to be equalled by other civilizations for almost 4,000 years.[151]

The Egyptians also excelled in medicine: their surgeons were skilled in a variety of difficult procedures,[152] their understanding of the human nervous system was refined, and their pharmacopoeia included several well known drugs in their first-recorded applications.[153]

I came across many further pieces of evidence which illustrated the relatively advanced state of Egyptian knowledge at a time when the European peoples were still plunged in barbarism. In my view, however, none of the data suggested the existence of any science that we would regard as truly breathtaking today, nor of any branch of technical achievement sufficiently sophisticated to account for the potent energies that the Ark of the Covenant had been able to unleash. Nevertheless, as I have already noted, the belief that the Egyptians were the guardians of some 'great and secret wisdom' was widespread and almost immune to counter-argument.

I knew very well that such ardent conviction often stemmed more from a subconscious desire to glorify the past of the human species than from any rational weighing up of empirical facts. This, certainly, was the dominant opinion of members of the archaeological establishment, most of whom regarded the 'great and secret wisdom' theory as balderdash and claimed to have found nothing extraordinary in Egypt in more than a century of painstaking digging and sifting. I myself am sceptical and pragmatic by nature. Nevertheless I must confess that the physical evidence which I saw everywhere around me during the series of research trips that I made to this beautiful and time-worn land convinced me that the academics did not have all the answers, that much remained to be explained, and that there were a number of aspects of the Egyptian experience which had been lamentably under-researched simply because they were beyond the scope of conventional archaeology – and probably of all other accepted forms of scholarly investigation as well.

Three sites had a particularly profound impact on me: the temple complex at Karnak; the Zoser 'step' pyramid at Saqqara; and the Great Pyramid at Giza on the outskirts of Cairo. It seemed to me that the special composite quality of raw power, delicate grace, imposing grandeur, mystery and immortality that these edifices possessed stemmed from the working out within them of a refined and highly developed understanding of harmony and proportion – an understanding that could reasonably be said to have amounted to a science. Combining engineering, architecture and design, that science had been remarkable by any standards. It had never since been surpassed in its ability to stimulate religious awe, and it had been equalled in Europe only in the great Gothic cathedrals of the Middle Ages such as Chartres.

Was this an accident? Was the essentially similar effect on the senses of the Egyptian monuments and the Gothic cathedrals a matter of pure chance – or was there perhaps a connection?

I had long suspected that there had indeed been a connection and that the Knights Templar, through their discoveries during the Crusades, might have formed the missing link in the chain of transmission of secret architectural knowledge.[154] At Karnak, as I walked slowly past the looming pylons, into the Great Court, and through the forest of giant columns of the Hypostyle Hall, I could not help but remember that Saint Bernard of Clairvaux, the Templars' patron, had defined God – astonishingly for a Christian – as 'length, width, height and depth'.[155] Nor could I forget that the Templars themselves had been great builders and great architects, or that the Cistercian monastic order to which Saint Bernard had belonged had also excelled in this particular field of human endeavour.[156]

Centuries and civilizations before them, however, it had been the ancient Egyptians who had been the first masters of the science of building – the first and still the greatest architect-masons that the world had ever known. Moreover, the monuments that they left behind beggared description and challenged time itself. Typical in this respect were two tall obelisks that dominated the Karnak complex and that I found myself particularly drawn to on my own visits there. One, I discovered, had been erected by Pharaoh Tuthmosis I (1504–1492 BC) and the other by Queen Hatshepsut (1473–1458 BC).[157] Both were perfect monoliths, hewn from single slabs of solid pink granite, the former standing 70 feet in height and weighing an estimated 143 tons, the latter standing 97 feet in height and weighing an estimated 320 tons.[158] A few minutes' walk to the south, overlooking a sacred lake that was used by the temple priests for elaborate purification ceremonies, I found a third, but tumbled and broken, obelisk, the top 30 feet of which – surmounted by a finely pointed pyramidion – were nevertheless quite undamaged. On one occasion, following the advice of a guidebook I had with me,[159] I stepped over the rope perimeter surrounding this fallen giant and placed my ear to the angle of the pyramidion. I then struck the granite firmly with the palm of my hand and listened, entranced, as the entire monolith reverberated with a deep, low-pitched tone like some strange and prodigious musical instrument.

It seemed to me that this phenomenon could not possibly have been accidental. On the contrary, the enormous care and skill required to produce such a monolith (when the same splendid *visual* effect might have been achieved simply by cementing block on block) only really made sense if the ancient Egyptians had wanted to realize some special property inherent in a single piece of stone.

Something, at any rate, other than mere aesthetic considerations must have lain behind the erection of these elegant and flawless stelae. I learned that they had not been hewn locally but rather had been transported by river from granite quarries more than 200 kilometres to the south.

The Nile was a highway broad and deep. It was therefore reasonable to suppose, once the obelisks had been loaded upon barges, that it would not have been so difficult a matter to float them downstream. What I found much harder to understand, however, was the method that the ancient Egyptians had employed to get these massive needles of stone on to the barges in the first place – and then off them again once they had arrived at their destination. One monolith had been left *in situ* at the quarries, only partially separated from the bedrock, because it cracked before it was completely excavated. Had this accident not befallen it, however, it would have made an obelisk 137 feet high and almost 14 feet thick at its base. Obviously, when the work was started, it had been confidently intended that this monstrous object – weighing a staggering 1,168 tons[160] – would be moved and erected somewhere. Yet it was extremely difficult to explain exactly how that would have been done by a people who (according to the archaeologists) lacked even simple winches and pulley systems.[161] Indeed I knew that the task of moving so large a piece of solid stone over a distance of several hundred feet – never mind several hundred kilometres! – would have taxed to the limit the ingenuity of a modern team of construction engineers supported by the most sophisticated and powerful machinery.

Equally puzzling, once the monoliths reached Karnak, was the manner in which they had been set upright on their pedestals with such faultless accuracy. In one of the temples a relief depicted Pharaoh raising an obelisk with no assistance of any kind and making use of just a single piece of rope.[162] It was quite normal for the ruler to be portrayed in heroic poses and perhaps all that was intended here was a symbolic representation of a real process in which hundreds of labourers were trained to pull together on multiple ropes. However, I could not rid myself of the suspicion that there must have been more to it than this. According to John Anthony West, an experienced Egyptologist, the Pharaohs and priests were preoccupied with a principle known as *Ma'at* – often translated as 'equilibrium' or 'balance'. It was possible, he suggested, that this principle might have been carried over into practical spheres and 'that the Egyptians understood and used techniques of mechanical balance unknown to us'. Such techniques would have enabled them to 'manipulate these immense stones with ease and finesse ... What would be magic to us was method to them.'[163]

If the obelisks, at times, seemed like the products of almost
superhuman skill, I had to admit that the Pyramids in all ways
surpassed them. As Jean François Champollion, the founder of
modern Egyptology, once remarked, 'the Egyptians of old
thought like men a hundred feet tall. We in Europe are but
Lilliputians.'[164]

Certainly, when I first entered the Great Pyramid at Giza, I felt
like a Lilliputian – dwarfed and slightly intimidated, not only by
the sheer mass and size of this mountain of stone but also by an
almost tangible sense of the accumulated weight of the ages.

On previous visits I had only seen the exterior of the pyramid,
since I had felt no desire to join the swarms of tourists pouring
inside. Early in the morning of 27 April 1990, however, I
managed by means of a small bribe to get into the great structure
completely on my own. In the dim light provided by a series of low-
wattage bulbs, and bent over almost double to avoid hitting my
head on the rock face above, I climbed the 129 feet of the
ascending passage, and then the 157 feet of the more spacious
Grand Gallery, until I reached the so-called 'King's Chamber'
– a 2:1 rectangle, the floor of which measured 34 feet 4 inches
by 17 feet 2 inches. Just over 19 feet high, the ceiling of this room
– which occupied the very heart of the pyramid – consisted of
nine monolithic blocks of granite each weighing approximately
50 tons.[165]

I do not remember how long I remained in the chamber. The
atmosphere was musty, and the air warm – like the exhalation of
some giant beast. The silence that surrounded me seemed
absolute, all-enveloping, and dense. At some point, for a reason
that I cannot explain, I moved to the middle of the floor and gave
voice to a sustained low-pitched tone like the song of the fallen
obelisk at Karnak. The walls and the ceiling seemed to collect
this sound, to gather and amplify it – and then to project it back at
me so that I could sense the returning vibrations through my feet
and scalp and skin. I felt electrified and energized, excited and at
the same time calm, as though I stood on the brink of some
tremendous and absolutely inevitable revelation.

After my April 1990 visit I was so impressed by the Great
Pyramid that I spent several weeks researching its history. I
discovered that it had been built around 2550 BC for Kufu (or

Cheops), the second Pharaoh of the Fourth Dynasty, and that it was also the single largest edifice ever constructed by man.[166] The conventional belief amongst archaeologists was that it had been designed purely and simply as a tomb. This conjecture, however, struck me as being utterly incomprehensible: no mummy of any Pharaoh had ever been found there, only a poor and undecorated sarcophagus in the so-called King's Chamber (a sarcophagus, by the way, that was lidless and completely empty when it was first brought to light by Caliph Al-Mamun, an Arab ruler of Egypt who broke in with a party of diggers in the ninth century AD.[167])

As I researched the subject further it became clear to me that the real purpose of the Great Pyramid was, in fact, a matter of considerable debate. On one side stood the most orthodox and prosaic scholars insisting that it was nothing more than a mausoleum. On the other side stood the pyramidologists – an apocalyptic tribe who pretended to find all manner of prophecies and signs in virtually every dimension of the immense structure.

The lunacies of this latter group were perhaps best summarized by one US critic who pointed out that it is possible to marshal numbers to prove almost anything: 'If a suitable unit of measurement is used, an exact equivalent to the distance to Timbuktu is certain to be found in the number of street lamps in Bond Street, or the specific gravity of mud, or the mean weight of adult goldfish.'[168]

This, of course, was quite true. Nevertheless, I could see that there were certain surprising features to which the pyramidologists persistently drew attention which did seem unlikely to be accidental. For example, it was a fact that the latitude and longitude lines that intersected at the Great Pyramid (30 degrees north and 31 degrees east) crossed more dry land than any others. This put the edifice at the very centre of the habitable world.[169] Likewise, it was a fact that when a north-facing quadrant (a cake-slice-shaped quarter circle) was drawn on a map with its axis at the pyramid then this quadrant exactly encapsulated the entire Nile Delta.[170] Finally, it was a fact that all the pyramids at Giza were precisely aligned to the cardinal points – north, south, east and west.[171] It was, I thought, extremely difficult to explain how this particular feat of surveying could have been achieved so long before the supposed date of the invention of the compass.

What intrigued me most of all about the Great Pyramid, however, was simply its sheer size and scope. Occupying a ground area of 13.1 acres, I ascertained that the core masonry of the structure was composed of no less than 2.3 million blocks of limestone each weighing approximately 2.5 tonnes.[172] Herodotus, whose informant was an Egyptian priest, claimed that gangs of 100,000 labourers built the edifice in 20 years (working only during the three-month agricultural lay-off season), and that the construction technique involved 'levers made of short timbers' which were used to lift the massive blocks from ground level.[173] No researcher subsequently had been able to guess at exactly what these 'levers' might have been or how they could have been used. However, after taking account of the time required for all the site-clearing, quarrying, levelling and other works that would have had to be done, civil engineer P. Garde-Hanson of the Danish Engineering Institute calculated that 4,000 blocks would have had to be installed each day, at the rate of 6.67 blocks per minute, if the job were indeed to have been completed within 20 years. 'Generally speaking,' he concluded, 'I believe it would demand the combined genius of a Cyrus, an Alexander the Great, and a Julius Caesar, with a Napoleon and Wellington thrown in for good measure, to organize the armies required for carrying out the work as assumed.'[174]

I then learned that a team of Japanese engineers had recently tried to build a 35-feet-high replica of the Great Pyramid (rather smaller than the original, which was 481 feet 5 inches in height). The team started off by limiting itself strictly to techniques proved by archaeology to have been in use during the Fourth Dynasty. However, construction of the replica under these limitations turned out to be impossible and, in due course, modern earth-moving, quarrying and lifting machines were brought to the site. Still no worthwhile progress was made. Ultimately, with some embarrassment, the project had to be abandoned.[175]

All in all, therefore, the Great Pyramid – with its many riddles and mysteries – suggested to me that the ancient Egyptians must have been much more than 'technically accomplished primitives' (as they had often been described), and that there must have existed amongst them a special kind of scientific knowledge. If so then it was entirely possible that the baleful powers of the Ark of the Covenant could have been the products of that science – in which Moses would most certainly have been a leading practitioner.

48 The construction of the Ark of the Covenant
at the foot of Mount Sinai.

49 Glowing with fire and light the Ark is transported
through the wilderness wrapped in thick cloths
to protect its bearers from its unearthly powers.

Uzziah smitten with leprosie II Chron: 26 v. 19

50 The Ark at the destruction of Jericho.

51 King Uzziah smitten with leprosy after approaching the Ark
(see Chapter Fifteen, 'Hidden History', page 413).

52 Nadab and Abihu, two of the sons of Aaron,
are struck dead as they approach the Ark.

The face of Moses shining after receiving the Tables of the Testimony.

53 After receiving the tablets of stone,
   which he later placed inside the Ark,
   Moses' face was burnt and shone so terribly
   that ever afterwards he had to wear a veil.

54 The Temple complex at Karnak, Egypt.

55 Archaeologists at work on the site
of the Jewish Temple on the island
of Elphantine, upper Egypt.

56 and 57. *Above*: this Ark-like chest, transported on two carrying poles, was recovered from the tomb of Tutankhamen. *Below*: the author examining a mysterious engraving on a fallen stele in Axum. The engraving bears an extraordinary resemblance to the Ark from Tutankhamen's tomb and may be the earliest Axumite representation of the Ark of the Covenant. Tutankhamen reigned in Egypt approximately 100 years before Moses led the Exodus. It is therefore probable that the Hebrew prophet devised the Ark according to an Egyptian prototype of precisely the kind found in Tutankhamen's tomb.

58 Priests and deacons
at prayer, *Timkat*, Axum.

59 *Timkat* procession, Axum.

60 The sanctuary of the Ark of the Covenant at Axum.

61 Gebra Mikail,
the Guardian of the Ark.

Chapter 13

Treasures of Darkness

My research had convinced me of the possibility that the ancient Egyptians might have possessed some advanced but secret scientific knowledge which Moses could have applied to the design of the Ark of the Covenant.

But where could such a body of knowledge have come from? Ancient Egypt itself, as I was very well aware, provided a simple – though supernatural – answer to this question. Every relevant surviving record that I had studied claimed unambiguously that it had been given to mankind by the moon-god Thoth, the lord and multiplier of time, the celestial scribe and invigilator of individual destinies, the inventor of writing and of all wisdom, and the patron of magic.[1]

Frequently represented on temple and tomb walls as an ibis, or as an ibis-headed man, and more rarely as a baboon, Thoth was venerated throughout Egypt as a true lunar deity who in some manifestations was identical with the moon itself and in others was the guardian of the moon, charged with ensuring that it kept to its course across the night skies, waxing and waning, vanishing and reappearing, precisely as and when it should. It was in this capacity – as the divine regulative force responsible for all heavenly calculations and annotations – that Thoth measured time, dividing it into months (to the first of which he gave his own name).[2]

His powers, however, were believed to have extended far beyond the mere calibration of the seasons. According to the pervasive and influential teachings of the priestly guild established at the sacred city of Hermopolis in Upper Egypt, Thoth was the universal demiurge who created the world through the sound of his voice alone, bringing it into being with the utterance of a single word of power.[3]

Regarded by the Egyptians as a deity who understood the mysteries of 'all that is hidden under the heavenly vault', Thoth was also believed to have had the ability to bestow wisdom on certain specially selected individuals. It was said that he had inscribed the rudiments of his secret knowledge on 36,535 scrolls and then hidden these scrolls about the earth intending that they should be sought for by future generations but found 'only by the worthy' – who were to use their discoveries for the benefit of mankind.[4]

Later identified by the Greeks with their own god Hermes, Thoth in fact stood at the very centre of an enormous body of Egyptian traditions stretching back into the most distant and impenetrable past. No scholar, I learned, could honestly say how old this moon-god really was, or even make a guess at where and when his cult began. At the dawn of civilization in Egypt, Thoth was there. Furthermore, throughout the entire 3,000 or more years of the dynastic period, he was continuously revered for certain very specific qualities that he was said to possess and for his supposed contributions to human welfare. He was, for example, credited with being the inventor of drawing, of hieroglyphic writing and of all the sciences – specifically architecture, arithmetic, surveying, geometry, astronomy, medicine and surgery. He was also seen as the most powerful of sorcerers, endowed with nothing less than complete knowledge and wisdom. He was exalted as the author of the great and terrible book of magic that was regarded by the priests at Hermopolis as the source of their understanding of the occult. Moreover whole chapters of the famous *Book of the Dead* were attributed to him, as well as almost the entire corpus of closely guarded sacred literature. He was believed, in short, to possess a virtual monopoly on esoteric learning and was therefore called 'the mysterious' and 'the unknown'.[5]

The ancient Egyptians were quite convinced that their first rulers were gods. Not surprisingly, Thoth was one of these divine kings: his reign on earth – during which he passed on to mankind his greatest and most beneficial inventions – was said to have lasted 3,226 years.[6] Before him the Egyptians believed that they had been ruled by another deity – Osiris, who was also closely associated with the moon (and with the numbers seven, fourteen and twenty-eight which relate to physical lunar cycles[7]). Although Osiris and Thoth looked quite different from one another in some of their manifestations, I was able to establish that they were similar or related in others (in certain archaic texts they were described as brothers[8]). A number of papyri and inscriptions went even further and portrayed them as being effectively the *same* entity, or at least as performing the same functions.

They were most commonly associated in the celestial Judgment Hall where the souls of the dead came to be weighed in the Great Scales. Here Osiris – as judge and final arbiter – often seemed to be the superior of the two gods, while Thoth was a mere scribe who recorded the verdict. Many of the tableaux from the *Book of the Dead*, however, reversed this relationship, as did a large vignette of the Judgment Scene found amongst the Theban funerary papyri of the New Kingdom. This latter document portrayed Osiris sitting passively to one side while Thoth determined the verdict, and then recorded and pronounced it.[9] In other words, not only were Thoth and Osiris both gods of the moon, gods of the dead (and perhaps brothers); both were also judges and law-makers.

As my research continued I noted such similarities with interest, but failed, at first, to see their relevance to my own quest for the Ark of the Covenant. Then it occurred to me that there was one invariable link between the two deities which also tied them conceptually to Moses and to all his works: like him they were above all else civilizing heroes who bestowed the benefits of religion, law, social order and prosperity upon their followers.

Thoth, it will be remembered, invented writing and science and brought these and many other wonders of enlightenment into the world in order to improve the lot of the Egyptian people. Likewise, Osiris was universally believed to have played a crucial role in the evolution and development of Egyptian society. When he began his rule on earth as divine monarch the country was barbaric, rude and uncultured and the Egyptians themselves were cannibals. When he ascended to Heaven, however, he left behind an advanced and sophisticated nation. His many contributions included teaching his people to cultivate the soil, to plant grain and barley, to grow vines, to worship the gods, and to abandon their previously savage customs. He also provided them with a code of laws.[10]

Such stories, of course, could have been fabrications. In a speculative frame of mind, however, I found myself wondering whether there might not after all have been something more than pure fancy and legend behind the tradition that Egypt became a great nation because of the gifts of Thoth and Osiris. Was it not just possible, I conjectured, that the all-wise, all-knowing moon-god could have been a mythical version of the truth – a metaphor for some real individual or group of individuals who, in remotest antiquity, brought the benefits of civilization and science to a primitive land?

The civilizers

I might have dismissed this notion out of hand had I not learned shortly afterwards of the existence of a great mystery – a mystery to which no definitive solution had ever been proposed. Rather than developing slowly and painfully, as might have been expected, it seemed that the civilization of Egypt had emerged all at once and fully formed. Indeed, by all accounts, the period of transition from primitive to advanced society had been so short that it really made no kind of historical sense. Technological skills that should have taken hundreds or even thousands of years to evolve had appeared almost literally overnight, and apparently with no antecedents whatsoever.

For example, remains from the pre-dynastic period dated to around 3600 BC showed no trace of writing. Then, quite suddenly and inexplicably, the hieroglyphs familiar from so many of the ruins of ancient Egypt began to appear and to do so, furthermore, in a complete and perfect state. Far from being mere pictures of objects or actions, this written language was complex and structured, with signs that represented sounds only and with a detailed system of numerical symbols. Even the very earliest hieroglyphs were already stylized and conventionalized; it was also clear that an advanced cursive script had come into common usage by the dawn of the First Dynasty.[11]

What struck me as remarkable about all this was that there were absolutely no traces of evolution from simple to more sophisticated styles. The same was true of mathematics, medicine, astronomy and architecture, and also of Egypt's amazingly rich and convoluted religio-mythological system (even such refined works as the *Book of the Dead* existed right at the start of the dynastic period.[12])

Unfortunately, there is not space here to present all or even a tiny part of the data which confirms the sheer suddenness with which Egyptian civilization emerged. By way of summary, however, I will quote the authoritative opinion of Professor Walter Emery, late Edwards Professor of Egyptology at the University of London:

> At a period approximately 3,400 years before Christ, a great change took place in Egypt, and the country passed rapidly from a state of neolithic culture with a complex tribal character to [one of] well-organized monarchy . . .
> At the same time the art of writing appears, monumental architecture and the arts and crafts develop to an astonishing degree, and all the evidence points to the existence of a luxurious civilization. All this was achieved within a comparatively short period of time, *for there appears to be little or no background to these fundamental developments in writing and architecture.*[13]

One explanation, I realized, could simply have been that Egypt had received its sudden and tremendous cultural boost from some other known civilization of the ancient world – Sumer, on the Lower Euphrates in Mesopotamia, being the most likely contender. Moreover, despite many basic differences, I was able to establish that a variety of shared building and architectural styles[14] did suggest a link between the two regions. None of these similarities, however, turned out be strong enough to allow me to infer that the connection had been in any way causal, with one society directly influencing the other. On the contrary, as Professor Emery put it:

> The impression we get is of an *indirect* connection, and

perhaps the existence of a third party, whose influence
spread to both the Euphrates and the Nile . . . Modern
scholars have tended to ignore the possibility of immigration
to both regions from some hypothetical and as yet
undiscovered area. [However], a third party whose cultural
achievements were passed on independently to Egypt and
Mesopotamia would best explain the common features and
fundamental differences between the two civilizations.[15]

This theory, I felt, shed revealing light on the otherwise
mysterious fact that the Egyptians and the Sumerian people of
Mesopotamia worshipped virtually identical lunar deities who
were amongst the very oldest in their respective pantheons.[16]
Exactly like Thoth, the Sumerian moon-god Sin was charged
with measuring the passage of time ('At the month's beginning to
shine on earth, thou shalt show two horns to mark six days. On
the seventh day divide the crown in two. On the fourteenth day,
turn thy full face.'[17]) Like Thoth, too, Sin was regarded as being
all-knowing and all-wise. At the end of every month the other
gods of the Sumerian pantheon came to consult him and he made
decisions for them.[18] Neither was I alone in my intuition that
something more than mere chance might have underpinned
these links between Sin and Thoth. According to the eminent
Egyptologist Sir E. A. Wallis Budge:

The similarity between the two . . . gods is too close to be
accidental . . . It would be wrong to say that the Egyptians
borrowed from the Sumerians or the Sumerians from the
Egyptians, but it may be submitted that the literati of
both peoples borrowed their theological systems from
some common but exceedingly ancient source.[19]

The question, therefore, was this: what was that 'common but
exceedingly ancient source', that 'hypothetical and as yet undiscovered area', that advanced 'third party' to which both Budge
and Emery referred? Having stuck their necks out a long way
already, I was frustrated to find that neither authority was
prepared to speculate much further. Emery, however, did hint at
where he thought the cradle of Egyptian civilization might have

been located: 'Vast tracts of the Middle East and the Red Sea and East African coasts', he rather coyly observed in this context, 'remain unexplored by the archaeologist.'[20]

I was sure that if Egypt had indeed received the gifts of civilization and science from elsewhere then some record of this momentous transaction would have been preserved. The deification of two great civilizers –Thoth and Osiris – was evidence of a kind: although presented as theology, the legends of these gods sounded to my ears much more like the echoes of long-forgotten events which had actually taken place.[21] But I felt I needed something more substantial – something which clearly and indisputably attested to beneficial contacts with an advanced donor society and which also explained how that society had managed to disappear without a trace.

I did find such an account. It was the familiar story of the lost continent of Atlantis – a story that, in recent years, had been so thoroughly degraded by outlandish speculations that it had become a form of professional suicide for any scholar even to appear to take it seriously (let alone to research it properly). After peeling away all the New Age nonsense, however, I was struck by a single significant fact: the earliest-surviving report of Atlantis had come from the Greek philosopher Plato – one of the founders of rational western thought – who had insisted that what he had said on the matter was 'not fiction but true history'.[22] Furthermore, writing around the beginning of the fourth century BC, Plato had added that the original source of his story had been an Egyptian priest – a priest who had spoken of the recurrent destruction of civilizations by floods and who had said of the Greeks:

> You are all young in mind . . . you have no knowledge
> hoary with age. [But] our traditions here are the oldest
> . . . In our temples we have preserved from earliest times
> a written record of any great or splendid achievement or
> notable event which has come to our ears whether it
> occurred in your part of the world, or here, or anywhere
> else; whereas with you, and others, writing and the other
> necessities of civilization have only just been developed
> *when the periodic scourge of the deluge descends*, and spares

none but the unlettered and uncultured, so that you have to begin again like children, in complete ignorance of what has happened in our part of the world or in yours in early times.

Thousands of years before, the priest continued,

There was an island opposite the strait which you call the Pillars of Hercules, an island larger than Libya and Asia combined; from it travellers could in those days reach the other islands, and from them the whole opposite continent which surrounds what can truly be called the ocean. On this island of Atlantis had arisen a powerful and remarkable dynasty of kings . . . Their wealth was greater than that possessed by any previous dynasty, or likely to be accumulated by any later, and they were provided with everything they could require. Because of the extent of their power they received many imports, but for most of their needs the island itself provided. It had mineral resources from which were mined both solid materials and metals, including one metal which survives today only in name, but was then mined in quantities in a number of localities in the island, *orichalc*, in those days the most valuable metal except gold. There was a plentiful supply of timber for structural purposes and every kind of animal domesticated and wild, among them numerous elephants. For there was plenty of grazing for this largest and most voracious of beasts, as well as for all creatures whose habitat is marsh, swamp and river, mountain or plain. Besides all this, the earth bore freely of all the aromatic substances it bears today . . . There were cultivated crops . . . There were the fruits of trees . . . All these were produced by that sacred island, then still beneath the sun, in wonderful quality and profusion.[23]

This paradise was not to remain 'beneath the sun' for much longer, however, because soon – to punish its inhabitants for wrongdoing and an overabundance of materialistic pride – there came 'earthquakes and floods of extraordinary violence, and in a single dreadful day and night the island of Atlantis was swallowed up by the sea and vanished.'[24]

My interest in this story did not stem from what it had to say about Atlantis itself, nor was I convinced by the suggestion as to the island's location 'opposite the pillars of Hercules'. My own view – well supported by geophysical evidence[25] – was that there could never have been such a landmass in the Atlantic Ocean and that those who persisted in looking for it there were fishing for the reddest of red herrings.

It did seem to me, however – and the authorities reluctantly concurred on this point[26] – that Plato's account must have had *some* basis in fact. No doubt he introduced many distortions and exaggerations of his own but he was, nevertheless, recording something that had actually happened, somewhere in the world, and a very long time ago. Furthermore – and of the greatest significance to me – he made it absolutely clear that a memory of this event had been retained by Egyptian priests and set down in the 'priestly writings'.[27]

I reasoned that if a similar memory had been preserved in Mesopotamia then the chance of this being pure coincidence was slight. A far more likely explanation would be that the same cataclysm – wherever it took place – had inspired the traditions of both regions. Accordingly I took a second look at the legends in which I had first noted the similarity between Thoth and the Sumerian moon-god Sin. What I learned did not surprise me: like their Egyptian contemporaries, the Sumerians had not only worshipped a wise lunar deity but had also preserved a record of a flood in ancient times that had destroyed a great, prosperous and powerful society.[28]

As my research progressed, therefore, 'Atlantis' did come to symbolize for me that 'hypothetical and as yet undiscovered area' from whence the wonderful civilizations of Egypt and of Sumer both came. As already noted, I did not believe that the area in question could possibly have been in or even near the Atlantic. Instead, I found myself wholeheartedly agreeing with Professor Emery that it was likely to have stood at a point roughly equidistant from both the Nile Delta and the Lower Euphrates – perhaps in some vanished archipelago similar to the modern Maldives (which scientists believe will be completely inundated within fifty years as a result of rising sea levels linked to global warming[29]), or along the vast unexcavated coasts of the Horn of Africa, or in a flood-prone region of the Indian subcontinent like modern Bangladesh. Such tropical zones looked all the more credible when I remembered that Plato had mentioned the existence of elephants in his 'Atlantis' – creatures that, for many thousands of years, have lived only in Africa, India and South-East Asia.[30]

The more thought I gave to notions like these the more it seemed to me that they possessed genuine merit and were worthy of further investigation. In order to orientate myself in this task I therefore wrote down the following conjectures and hypotheses in my notebook:

Suppose that somewhere around the basin of the Indian Ocean, in the early or middle part of the fourth millennium BC, a technologically advanced society was destroyed by flood. Suppose it was a maritime society. Suppose that there were survivors. And suppose that some of them sailed in their ships to Egypt and Mesopotamia, made landfall there and set about the task of civilizing the primitive inhabitants they encountered.

Most important of all, suppose that in Egypt the priestly traditions of sacred science – to which Moses was exposed from his childhood – were the means by which the skills and know-how of the settlers were deliberately preserved so that they could be passed down to subsequent generations. In Egypt these traditions were associated from the outset with the worship of the moon-god Thoth (and, in Mesopotamia, with the worship of Sin). Perhaps this was because the settlers themselves revered the moon – or perhaps they wittingly and rather cold-bloodedly encouraged the deification of a prominent and familiar but yet frightening and ghostly sidereal object. Their aim, after all, would have been to shape and direct the simple and savage minds of the peoples they had found themselves amongst and to create a durable cult – capable of surviving for millennia – as a vehicle for all their otherwise fragile and easily forgotten knowledge.

In such circumstances, it is really not difficult to see why they might have chosen to focus on a glowing and uncanny lunar god rather than on some more abstract, more sophisticated but less visible and less corporeal divinity.

At any rate, once the cult of Thoth had been established in early Egypt, and once its priests had learned and institutionalized the scientific and technological 'tricks of the trade' brought by the settlers, then it is logical to suppose that a self-perpetuating process would have begun: the new-found and valuable knowledge would have been fenced about with mysteries, protected from outsiders by all kinds of ritual sanctions and then passed from initiate to initiate, from generation to generation, in an exclusive and secret tradition. This knowledge, of course, would have given its possessors unprecedented mastery over the physical world – at least by the rudimentary standards of the native culture prevailing in Egypt before the coming of the settlers – and would have been expressed in ways that would have seemed astounding to laymen (not least in the erection of stupendous and awe-inspiring buildings). It is therefore easy to understand how the belief that the moon-god had 'invented' both science and magic might have taken hold in the population at large, and why it was that the priests of this god were regarded as masters of sorcery.

Saved from water

As my research progressed I turned up several pieces of evidence which seemed to provide strong support for the central hypotheses listed above, namely that a secret tradition of knowledge and enlightenment had been 'carried' and preserved within the cult of Thoth – a tradition that had been started in the most distant past by sophisticated immigrants who had survived a flood. Highly significant, in this respect, was a very strong theme – traces of which I found running through almost all the sacred literature – which repeatedly associated wisdom, and other qualities of the civilizing hero, with individuals who had been 'saved from water'.

The first thing I discovered was that Thoth, who had been

seen by the Egyptians as the source of all their knowledge and science, had been credited with having caused a flood to punish humankind for wickedness.[31] In this episode, related in Chapter CLXXV of the *Book of the Dead*, he had acted jointly with his counterpart Osiris.[32] Both deities had subsequently ruled on earth after the human race had begun to flourish again. I was therefore excited, when I looked more closely at the story of Osiris, to learn that he had been 'saved from water'.

The fullest account of the original Egyptian legend was given by Plutarch[33] and stated that, after improving the condition of his own subjects, teaching them all manner of useful skills and providing them with their first legal code, Osiris left Egypt and travelled about the world in order to bring the benefits of civilization to other nations as well. He never forced the barbarians he encountered to accept his laws, preferring instead to argue with them and to appeal to their reason. It was also recorded that he passed on his teaching to them by means of hymns and songs accompanied by musical instruments.

While he was away, however, he was plotted against by seventy-two members of his court led by his brother-in-law Set. On his return the conspirators invited him to a banquet where a splendid coffer of wood and gold was offered as a prize to any guest who could fit into it exactly. What Osiris did not know was that the coffer had been constructed precisely to his own body measurements. As a result, when the assembled guests tried one by one to get into it they failed. The god-king then took his turn and lay down comfortably inside. Before he had time to get out the conspirators rushed forward, nailed the lid tightly closed and sealed even the cracks with molten lead so that there would be no air to breathe. The coffer was then cast adrift on the Nile where it floated for some time, eventually coming to rest in the papyrus swamps of the eastern Delta.[34]

At this point Isis, the wife of Osiris, intervened. Using all her great magic – and assisted by the moon-god Thoth – she went to look for the coffer, found it, and concealed it in a secret place. Her evil brother Set, however, out hunting in the marshes, discovered the location of the coffer, opened it, and in a mad fury cut the royal corpse into fourteen pieces which he then scattered throughout the land.

Once more Isis set off to 'save' her husband. She made a small boat of papyrus reeds, coated with bitumen and pitch, and embarked on the Nile in search of the remains. When she had found them she called again on the aid of Thoth who helped her to work certain powerful spells which reunited the dismembered parts of the body so that it resumed its old form. Thereafter, in an intact and perfect state, Osiris went through a process of resurrection to become god of the dead and king of the underworld – from which place, the legend had it, he occasionally returned to earth in the guise of a mortal man.[35]

There were three details of this story that I regarded as being of the greatest interest: first the fact that, during his rule on earth, Osiris was a civilizer and a legislator; secondly that he was placed in a wooden coffer and thrown into the Nile; and thirdly that Isis came to rescue his body in a papyrus boat coated with bitumen and pitch. The parallels with the life of Moses could not have been more obvious – he, too, became a great civilizer and lawgiver, he too was cast adrift upon the waters of the Nile, he too floated in a vessel of papyrus coated with bitumen and pitch, and he too was saved by an Egyptian princess. Indeed, as the historian Josephus recorded, the very name 'Moses' meant 'saved from water': 'for the Egyptians call water *mou* and those who are saved *eses*; so they conferred upon him this name compounded of both words.'[36] Philo, the other great classical commentator, concurred with this etymology: 'Since he had been taken up from water, the princess gave him a name derived from this, and called him Moses, for *Mou* is the Egyptian word for water.'[37]

I asked myself whether there might not have been other instances – in Egypt and perhaps in Mesopotamia as well – of civilizing heroes who had been saved from water. A search in ancient annals and legends revealed that there had been many. For example Horus, the son of Isis and Osiris, was murdered by Titans and thrown into the Nile. Isis rescued him and revived him with her sorcery. He then learned from her 'the arts of physic and divination and used them for the benefit of mankind'.[38] Likewise, in Mesopotamia, Sargon the Great – whose rule brought unrivalled wealth, splendour and stability to Sumer and neighbouring territories at the end of the third millennium BC[39] – had claimed quite specifically to have been saved from water:

My mother was a priestess. I did not know my father.
The priestess, my mother, conceived me and gave birth to
me in hiding. She placed me in a basket made of reeds
and closed the lid with pitch. She put the basket in the
river which was not high. The river carried me away and
brought me to Akki who was a man responsible for
libations. Akki looked upon me with kindness and drew
me from the river.[40]

I found that the theme of salvation from water also ran very
strongly through the pages of the Old Testament. The prophet
Jonah, for instance, was thrown into the sea during a raging
tempest, swallowed alive by a giant fish and three days later
'vomited out upon dry land' so that he could preach the word of
God to the citizens of Nineveh and divert them from their evil
ways.[41]

Even more familiar was the much more ancient story of Noah,
who – together with all his family and with 'two of every sort of
living thing'[42] – rode out the primeval deluge in a remarkable
survival ship which we know as the ark ('make it with reeds and
line it with pitch inside and out'[43]). After the flood waters had
receded, Noah's three sons, Shem, Ham and Japheth, heard
God's command to 'be fruitful and multiply' and went out to
repopulate the world.[44]

By far the most famous and influential biblical figure to be
'saved from water', however, was Jesus Christ himself – the only
individual, other than Moses, to be described in the Scriptures as
'mighty in deed and word'[45] (a phrase which, as I already knew,
implied proficiency in the utterance of magical words of power).
Rather than being an actual rescue, the incident in question was
wholly symbolic and took the form of the mysterious rite of
baptism in the waters of the river Jordan. This, Jesus explained,
was absolutely necessary for *salvation*: 'Except a man be born of
water . . . he cannot enter into the kingdom of God.'[46]

And it came to pass in those days, that Jesus came from
Nazareth of Galilee, and was baptized of John in Jordan.
And straightway coming up out of the water, he saw the
heavens opened, and the Spirit like a dove descending

upon him. And there came a voice from heaven saying,
Thou art my beloved Son, in whom I am well pleased.[47]

Though I knew that the vast majority of practising Christians
took this passage from the Gospel of Saint Mark entirely at face
value I could not help but wonder whether a deeper layer of
meaning might not have been encoded in the stirring and
beautiful words. It seemed to me at least possible that what was
really being described here was the initiation of Jesus into the
enlightened knowledge of a secret cult whose founders were
literally 'saved from water' thousands of years earlier. Furthermore, I thought it not accidental that it was only *after* this
initiation that Christ began to work his miracles – most of which
(including healing the sick, restoring the dead to life, multiplying
loaves and fishes, and controlling the elements) would have been
instantly recognizable to the High Priests and sorcerers of
ancient Egypt as 'magic tricks' of the type that they, too, had been
trained to perform.[48]

After considering all the data that I had compiled I made the
following entry in my notebook:

The theme of the civilizer, or founding father, or great
prophet, or legislator, or Messiah who has in one way or
another been 'saved from water' occurs in the Scriptures,
and in Egyptian and Middle Eastern mythology, so
frequently and with such consistency that it cannot be a
matter of pure chance. I am not proposing that all the
individuals concerned were *actual* survivors of that
'hypothetical and as yet undiscovered area', that supposed
technologically advanced society which may have been the
cradle for the civilizations of both Mesopotamia and
Egypt. The fact is that only Noah, Osiris – and perhaps
Horus – belong to a period of pre-history sufficiently
remote to qualify them for that distinction. Sargon,
Moses, Jonah, and Jesus, however (together with many
other important figures in different places and at different
periods), were all also saved from water – either literally
or symbolically. It therefore seems to me that what is
really implied by this recurrent image is initiation of the

individuals concerned into a tradition of secret wisdom started a very long time ago by the survivors of a flood in an effort to preserve vital knowledge and skills that might otherwise have quickly been forgotten.

Going beyond what could be deduced from myths and legends, I also found some rather more tangible evidence in Egypt to support the 'saved from water theory'. I knew that this evidence – the concealment of complete ocean-going boats beside almost all the most important tombs of pharaohs and notables, and also near all the pyramids – had thus far been treated by archaeologists according to the hoary old dictum that 'if you can't understand a particular custom then the safest thing to do is to put it down to religion'. It gradually dawned on me, however, that the practice of boat burial could well have been motivated by something other than a simple desire to install near the grave a 'physical representation of the symbolic craft that would take the soul or spirit of the dead king to its ultimate destination in the sky.'[49]

A prime case in point was the cedarwood ship discovered buried and dismantled in a pit beside the southern edge of the Great Pyramid at Giza and now reassembled in a special museum on site. Still in perfect condition 4,500 years after it was built, I learnt that this giant vessel was more than 142 feet long and had a displacement of around 40 tons. Its design was particularly interesting, incorporating (in the informed opinion of Thor Heyerdahl) 'all the sea-going ship's characteristic properties, with prow and stern soaring upward, higher than in a Viking ship, to ride out the breakers and high seas, not to contend with the little ripples of the Nile.'[50] Another expert felt that the careful and clever construction of this strange pyramid boat would have made it 'a far more seaworthy craft than anything available to Columbus'; indeed, it would probably have had no difficulty in sailing round the world![51]

Since the ancient Egyptians were highly skilled at making scale models and representations of all manner of things for symbolic purposes[52] it seemed to me implausible that they would have gone to such trouble to manufacture and then bury a boat as sophisticated as this one if their only purpose had been to betoken the spiritual vessel that would carry off the soul of the king to heaven. That could have been achieved just as effectively with a much smaller craft. Besides, I learnt that recent research at Giza had revealed the existence of *another* huge boat, also on the south side of the pyramid, still sealed in its pit – and there were also known to be three (now empty) rock-hewn pits on the eastern side. As one otherwise orthodox Egyptologist rather daringly admitted, 'it is difficult to see why so many boat pits should have been thought necessary.' Predictably he then fell back on the great standby of all puzzled scholars and declared: 'it is clear that their presence was required for some religious purpose relating to the afterlife of the king.'[53]

It was precisely this point, however, which was not clear to me at all – particularly since, as noted in the previous chapter, there was absolutely no indication that any pharaoh was ever interred within the Great Pyramid. Furthermore, the earliest funerary boats to be discovered in Egypt dated back to that mysterious period, just before the inception of the First Dynasty, when civilization and technology in the Nile Valley underwent a sudden and inexplicable transformation.[54] I therefore found it difficult to resist the conclusion that the curious practice of boat burial was more likely to be linked to the well established tradition of 'salvation from water' than to any purely religious symbolism. Sturdy ocean-going vessels, I reasoned, would have been of immense importance to a group of foreigners who had survived a flood and who had settled in Egypt after sailing away from the site of the cataclysm. Perhaps they, or those who came after them, had believed that the buried boats might one day be needed – not to enable reincarnated souls to navigate the heavens like celestial pleasure trippers but, instead, to allow living individuals to escape once again from the scourge of some terrible deluge.

Hidden riches of secret places

The really great achievements of ancient Egypt all took place early. The peak period spanned the Third to the Fifth Dynasties – roughly from 2900 BC to 2300 BC. Thereafter, albeit gradually and with some notable resurgences, the general trend was steadily downhill.[55] This scenario – accepted by all scholars – was, I felt, completely consistent with the theory that civilization was brought into the Nile Valley during the fourth millennium BC from some technologically advanced but as yet unidentified area. After all, one would not have expected an imported culture to produce its most perfect forms of expression from the very moment that the settlers arrived; there would undoubtedly have been a great leap forward at that time but the full potential would not have been realized until the native inhabitants had picked up and learned the new techniques.

And this was precisely what seemed to have happened in Egypt. Just before the beginning of the First Dynasty (say around 3400 BC), writing, arithmetic, medicine, astronomy and a complex religion all appeared very suddenly – without, as already noted, any local evidence of prior evolution in any of these spheres. At the same time highly sophisticated monuments and tombs were being built that incorporated advanced architectural concepts – again with no trace of evolution. The First and Second Dynasties (say from 3300 BC onwards) saw the construction of ever more elaborate monuments which embodied with increasing confidence and vigour the new-found skills and knowledge that had arrived in Egypt.[56] And this trend towards greater and greater beauty and excellence received what many modern scholars regarded as its ultimate expression in the remarkable stone edifices of the funerary complex of King Zoser, the first Pharaoh of the Third Dynasty.

The complex, which I visited several times in 1989 and 1990, is dominated by a towering six-tiered pyramid 197 feet high and is located to the south of the city of Cairo at Saqqara. The complete site takes the form of a rectangle nearly 2,000 feet long and 1,000 feet wide and was originally enclosed by a single massive stone wall, large sections of which are still standing. Other features include an extensive colonnade with forty tall columns, an elegant courtyard, and numerous shrines, temples and outbuildings – all on a colossal scale but with clean and delicate lines.

I was able to establish that in Egyptian tradition the conception and design of the entire Zoser complex had been regarded as the work of a single creative genius – Imhotep the Builder, whose other titles were Sage, Sorcerer, Architect, High Priest, Astronomer and Doctor.[57] I became interested in this legendary figure because of the great emphasis put by subsequent generations on his scientific and magical abilities; indeed, like Osiris, his achievements in these fields were so highly regarded that he was eventually deified. With uniquely impressive engineering feats such as the Zoser pyramid to his credit, Imhotep looked to me like an obvious candidate for membership of the cult of Thoth: the monuments at Saqqara seemed eloquently to confirm that he had assimilated and then put brilliantly into practice the technological dexterity peculiar to that cult.

I was therefore excited to discover that Imhotep was often characterized in inscriptions as 'the image and likeness of Thoth'[58] – and also as the 'successor to Thoth' after the deity had ascended to heaven.[59] I then learnt something of even greater significance: in antiquity, Moses too was frequently compared to Thoth (indeed, in the second century BC an entire work was filled with such comparisons by the Judaeo-Greek philosopher Artapanus, who credited the prophet with a range of remarkable and clearly 'scientific' inventions[60]).

The fact that individuals as far apart in history as Moses and Imhotep should have been explicitly linked through the cult of the moon-god struck me as strong circumstantial evidence not only for the existence of a secret wisdom tradition but also for the durability of that tradition. Accordingly I began to wonder whether there had been other magicians and sages like Imhotep to whom the design of particularly sophisticated and advanced buildings had been attributed.

Unfortunately, no record survived of the architect who built the Great Pyramid at Giza. This remarkable edifice was certainly the crowning achievement of the splendid Fourth Dynasty – during which Egyptian civilization reached its zenith. As one authority put it:

The Pharaohs would never again build to such scale and perfection. And this level of expertise carried over into almost every other form of art or craft. Under the Fourth Dynasty the furniture was the most elegant, the linen the finest, the statuary at once the most powerful and the most perfect . . . Certain skills, such as the making of inlaid eyes, reached levels that border on the supernatural. Later dynasties could produce but mediocre versions and ultimately the knowledge disappeared entirely.[61]

I could only agree with most of the above remarks. It seemed to me, however, that the very special technological skills required for the erection of splendid and imposing monuments had been preserved for a considerable period before 'disappearing entirely'. Though not given any practical expression, for example, there was no doubt that these skills had somehow survived the many centuries of cultural stagnation that set in after the Fourth Dynasty and had then reasserted themselves in the remarkable resurgence that occurred during the Eighteenth and Nineteenth Dynasties (1580–1200 BC).

The crowning achievement of this latter era, which filled me with awe every time I set eyes on it, was the beautiful obelisk of Queen Hatshepsut at Karnak. Nearby, on the western side of the Nile, the same monarch had also commissioned a massive mortuary temple that had later come to be regarded as one of the great architectural masterpieces of the world.[62]

I learnt that the name of the long-dead architect responsible for both of these monuments had been Senmut. Intriguingly, an inscription that he himself had composed – and that could still be read on his tomb wall – left little doubt that his special knowledge and abilities had been acquired after he had been admitted to the mysteries of an ancient and secret wisdom tradition. 'Having penetrated all the writings of the Divine Prophets,' he boasted, 'I was ignorant of nothing that has happened since the beginning of time.'[63]

Suppose [I wrote in my notebook] that Moses (who lived barely 200 years after Senmut) was also an initiate in this same secret tradition – a tradition that stretched back beyond the horizon of history through Imhotep to the god-kings Thoth and Osiris, and that extended forward as well to include other great scientists and civilizers like Jesus Christ. If there is anything at all to this hypothesis then is it not possible that some of the truly extraordinary thinkers of more recent years may also have been heirs to the 'occult' knowledge that inspired the builders of the pyramids and obelisks, and that made it possible for Moses to perform his miracles?

In seeking to answer this question, I was drawn back first and foremost to the Knights Templar – who had occupied the original site of the Temple of Solomon in Jerusalem in AD 1119 and who, I believed, had learned something in the Holy City that had subsequently caused them to seek the Ark of the Covenant in Ethiopia. As reported in Chapter 5, the research that I had carried out into the beliefs and behaviour of this strange group of warrior monks had convinced me that they had tapped into some exceedingly ancient wisdom tradition – and that the knowledge they had thus acquired had been put to use in the construction of churches and castles that were architecturally far in advance of other buildings of the twelfth and thirteenth centuries.

Was it not possible, I now asked myself, that the wisdom tradition into which the Templars had been initiated had been the very one to which Moses, Senmut and Imhotep had belonged? And if so then was it not also possible that the knights' quest for the Ark had been connected to this tradition? I knew that it would probably prove impossible to substantiate such esoteric guesswork. Nevertheless, I was excited to discover a number of ancient Jewish traditions which asserted that the Ark had contained 'the root of all knowledge'.[64] In addition, as the reader will recall, the golden lid of the sacred relic had been surmounted by two figures of cherubim. Could it therefore have been pure coincidence that, in Judaic lore, 'the distinctive gift of the cherubim was *knowledge*'?[65]

These were by no means the only tantalizing hints which suggested to me that the quest for the Ark might also have been a quest for wisdom. Equally significant was the fact that when the Templars were persecuted, tortured and put on trial in the early fourteenth century many of them confessed to worshipping a mysterious bearded head, the name of which was given as Baphomet.[66] Several authorities, pointing to the close connections that the knights had cultivated with Islamic mystics, had

identified Baphomet with Muhammad[67] – thus blithely ignoring
the fact that Islam could hardly have inspired such behaviour
(since Muslims, as I was very well aware, regarded their prophet
as human not divine and had an absolute abhorrence of any kind
of idol worship). A far more convincing explanation, however,
was given by Dr Hugh Schonfield, an expert on early
Christianity, who had deciphered a secret code used in a number
of the famous 'Dead Sea Scrolls' – a code that the Templars
might easily have learned during their long residence in the Holy
Land. Dr Schonfield showed that if the name Baphomet were
written in this code and then transliterated the result would be
the Greek word Sophia.[68] And the Greek word Sophia, in its
turn, meant nothing more nor less than 'Wisdom'.[69]

By this analysis, therefore, when the Templars worshipped
Baphomet what they were really doing was worshipping the
principle of Wisdom. And that, of course, was exactly what the
ancient Egyptians had done when they had worshipped Thoth as
'the personification of the mind of God',[70] as 'the author of every
work on every branch of knowledge, both human and divine',[71]
and as 'the inventor of astronomy and astrology, the science of
numbers and mathematics, geometry and land surveying,
medicine and botany'.[72] I was encouraged to look further.

One fact which quite quickly came to light was that the
Freemasons had also held Thoth in special regard. Indeed,
according to a very old Masonic tradition, Thoth 'had played a
major part in preserving knowledge of the mason craft and
transmitting it to mankind after the flood'.[73] And the author of a
well researched academic study on the origins of Freemasonry went
so far as to say that, in their early days, the Masons had regarded
Thoth as their patron.[74] I was already aware (see Chapter 7) that
close links had existed between the Templars and the Freemasons,
with the latter almost certainly being descended from the former.
Now I could see that what I was coming to think of as the 'Thoth
connection' set those links in the ancient and enduring context of a
wisdom tradition stretching back to Pharaonic times. I therefore
asked myself this: in addition to the Templars and the Masons had
there been any other groups or individuals whose works and ideas
had appeared unusually advanced – and who might possibly have
been initiates in the same wisdom tradition?

I found that there had been many. For example, Copernicus, the Renaissance astronomer whose theory of a heliocentric universe had overturned the earth-centred complacency of the Middle Ages, had said quite openly that he had arrived at his revolutionary insights by studying the secret writings of the ancient Egyptians, including the hidden works of Thoth himself.[75] Likewise the seventeenth-century mathematician Kepler (who, amongst other things, compiled an imaginary account of a trip to the moon) admitted that in formulating his laws of the planetary orbits he was merely 'stealing the golden vessels of the Egyptians'.[76]

In a similar vein, Sir Isaac Newton had stated his view that 'the Egyptians concealed mysteries that were above the capacity of the common herd under the veil of religious rites and hieroglyphic symbols.'[77] Amongst these mysteries, he believed, was the knowledge that the earth orbited the sun and not vice-versa: 'It was the most ancient opinion that the planets revolved about the sun, that the earth, as one of the planets, described an annual course about the sun, while by a diurnal motion it turned on its axis, and that the sun remained at rest.'[78]

Newton's profound intellect and scholarship had enabled him to lay the foundations of physics as a modern discipline. His specific achievements had included epoch-making discoveries in mechanics, optics, astronomy and mathematics (the binomial theorem and the differential and integral calculus), huge steps forward in the understanding of the nature of light, and – above all else – the formulation of the universal law of gravitation which had altered forever mankind's vision of the cosmos.

What was much less well known about the great English scientist, however, was the fact that he had spent a significant part of his adult life deeply immersed in hermetic and alchemical literature (more than a tenth of his personal library had been taken up with alchemical treatises[79]). Furthermore he had been obsessed – literally obsessed – with the notion that a secret wisdom lay concealed within the pages of the Scriptures: Daniel of the Old Testament and John of the New particularly attracted him because 'the language of the prophetic writings was symbolic and hieroglyphical and their comprehension required a radically different method of interpretation.'[80]

It seemed to me, as I researched Newton further, that pursuit of this method perhaps explained why he had involved himself in an exacting study of some twenty different versions of the book of Revelation. He had learned Hebrew in order to do the job properly[81] and had then carried out a similarly meticulous exercise on the book of Ezekiel.[82] I was also able to establish that he had drawn on the information contained in this latter work to produce a painstaking reconstruction of the floorplan of the Temple of Solomon. Why? Because he had been convinced that the great edifice built to house the Ark of the Covenant had been a kind of cryptogram of the universe; if he could decipher this cryptogram, he had believed, then he would know the mind of God.[83]

Newton's Temple floorplan had been preserved in the Babson College Library.[84] Meanwhile the seventeenth-century scientist had expressed his other 'theological' findings and observations in private writings that had totalled well over a million words.[85] In the mid-twentieth century these rather surprising manuscripts came to light and were purchased at auction by John Maynard Keynes. 'Newton was *not* the first of the age of reason,' the obviously shaken economist later told the Royal Society, 'he was the last of the magicians, the last of the Babylonians and Sumerians, the last great mind which looked out on the world with the same eyes as those who began to build our intellectual inheritance rather less than ten thousand years ago.' Keynes made an extremely careful study of the manuscripts and concluded – significantly in my view – that Newton saw

> the whole universe and all that is in it *as a riddle*, as a secret which could be read by applying pure thought to certain evidence, certain mystic clues which God had hid about the world to allow a sort of philosopher's treasure hunt to the esoteric brotherhood. He believed that these clues were to be found partly in the evidence of the heavens and in the constitution of elements, but also partly in certain papers and traditions handed down by the brethren in an unbroken chain back to the original cryptic revelation.[86]

Indeed so! And although I knew that I might never be able to prove that the 'brethren' in question had been directly linked to the occult traditions of the moon-god Thoth – and to those scientists and civilizers who had been 'saved from water' – I felt that there was at least sufficient evidence to confirm one intriguing fact. In making his greatest discoveries, Newton had indicated several times that he had drawn not only upon his own genius but also upon some very old and secret repository of wisdom. He had once stated quite explicitly, for instance, that the law of gravitation expounded in his *Principia* was not new but rather had been known and fully understood in ancient times; he had arrived at it by decoding the sacred literature of past ages.[87] On another occasion he had described Thoth as a believer in the Copernican system.[88] Before that he had aligned himself with the German physician and alchemist Michael Maier (1568–1622) who had argued that, throughout history, all the true adepts of science had derived their knowledge from the Egyptian moon-god.[89]

Amongst many other curiosities, I discovered that Newton had been struck by the fact that 'there was a general tradition of deluge amongst ancient peoples'[90] and had shown considerable interest in the biblical view that Noah was the common ancestor of all humanity.[91] Moreover, despite his own devoutly held religious convictions, he seemed at times to have seen Christ as an especially gifted *man* and as an interpreter of God's master-plan, rather than as the Son of God.[92] What I found most fascinating of all, however, was that the really pivotal figure in Newton's theology, and in his conception of early science, had been none other than the prophet Moses, whom he had regarded as an adept in the mysteries of the universe, a master of alchemy, and a witness to the double revelation of God (as expressed in His word and in His works).[93]

Long centuries before our own enlightened era, Newton had believed, Moses understood that matter consisted of atoms, and that these atoms were hard, solid and immutable: 'gravity accrued to both atoms and to the bodies they composed; gravity was proportional to the quantity of matter in every body.'[94] Newton had also regarded the account of creation presented in Genesis – and attributed to Moses – as an allegorical description of an alchemical process:

> Moses, that ancient Theologue, describing and
> expressing ye most wonderful Architecture of this great
> world, tells us that ye spirit of God moved upon ye waters
> which was an indigested chaos, or mass created before by
> God.

Later, referring to the efforts of the alchemists, the great English
scientist had added:

> Just as the world was created from dark chaos through
> the bringing forth of the light and through the separation
> of the aery firmament and of the waters from the earth, so
> our work brings forth the beginning out of black chaos
> and its first matter through the separation of the elements
> and the illumination of matter.[95]

Last but not least, I thought it was not accidental that Newton's
favourite biblical passage[96] had been one that had hinted at the
existence of some form of covert knowledge available only to
initiates:

> And I will give thee the treasures of darkness, and hidden
> riches of secret places, that thou mayest know that I, the
> Lord, which call thee by thy name, am the God of
> Israel.[97]

I reasoned that if Newton had indeed had access to the same
'treasures of darkness' and to the same 'hidden riches' as Moses,
then this would imply – at the very least – the continuous
existence over a period of millennia of a clandestine sect or cult
structured to pass on an exclusive and privileged wisdom. This
sounded far-fetched; it was, however, by no means impossible.
On the contrary, knowledge and skills had frequently and
successfully been transferred down the generations – and from
one region of the world to another – without any concrete
evidence being available to document the process. For example,
Rhabdas, a mathematician who had lived in the city of Constantinople in the twelfth century AD, was known to have used a
method for deriving square roots that had existed only in ancient

Egypt more than two thousand years previously and that had not, otherwise, been employed elsewhere.[98] How, and from where, he had acquired this technique was not easy to explain. Similarly, I was very much aware that the transmission of esoteric information, coupled with the teaching and sharing of arcane rituals and ceremonies, had occurred for centuries within the various Masonic orders without any public record ever being available.

Charting the contours of a genuinely reticent sect was, therefore, a daunting undertaking. But what I found more daunting by far was the task of guessing the real nature of the science and technology that such a long-lived and secretive institution as the cult of Thoth might have protected and preserved – particularly if, as I suspected, that science and technology had originated in a historically remote and now utterly obliterated culture. As I wrote in my notebook:

> It would be a mistake to assume that our own twentieth-century machinery and inventions are any guideline; on the contrary, if an advanced society did exist at some archaic period, then its wisdom is likely to have been quite different from anything with which we are familiar, and its machines could reasonably be expected to have operated according to principles unknown to us.

A monstrous instrument

It was with such thoughts, as my research moved on, that I found myself drawn to the strange passages in the Old Testament books of Exodus and Deuteronomy which described the encounters between God and Moses on Mount Sinai. Amidst thunder and fire, electrical storms and clouds of smoke, Yahweh supposedly disclosed the blueprint of the Ark of the Covenant to the Hebrew magus and presented him with the stone Tablets of the Law inscribed with the Ten Commandments. Then the Ark itself was built by the artificer Bezaleel who slavishly followed the 'divine' plan, almost as though he knew that he was forging some monstrous instrument.

And this, I suspect, is what the Ark really was: a monstrous instrument capable of releasing fearful energies in an un-controlled and catastrophic manner if it was mishandled or misused in any way – an instrument that was not conceived in the mind of God, as the Bible teaches, but rather in the mind of Moses.

A master sorcerer in an era when sorcery and science were indistinguishable from one another, it is after all possible (and perhaps more than possible) that Moses could have had the technical knowledge – and therefore the ability – to design a device of this sort. There is absolutely no proof of this, of course. Nevertheless I think that only those with a pedantic and cavilling attitude to history would insist that the ancient wisdom traditions of Egypt could have contained no special skills or ideas of a technical nature on which the prophet might have drawn in order to imbue the Ark with the awesome powers attributed to it in the Old Testament.

Speculation on such matters is surely healthy and – for those readers who are interested in penetrating more deeply into the mystery – I offer the following hypotheses and conjectures as food for thought.

Motive and opportunity

Assume for a moment that Moses did indeed have the technical knowledge to create 'a monstrous instrument' capable of destroy-ing city walls (as in the case of Jericho[99]), striking people dead (as in the case of Uzzah and the 'men of Bethshemesh'[100]), inflicting cancerous tumours on those who approached it without proper protection (as in the case of the Philistines after the battle of Ebenezer[101]), and counteracting gravity (as in the case of the bearers whom, on one occasion, it 'tossed into the air and flung to the ground again and again'[102]).

If Moses could have made such a machine then it only remains to ask whether he had a motive to do so, and whether he had the opportunity.

I would like to suggest that he had ample motive. One in a long line of civilizing heroes who had been 'saved from water', there is evidence to suggest that his prime objective in life might not have been to establish the Jewish faith (although he certainly did that) but rather to civilize the Israelites – who, prior to the Exodus, were little more than an anarchic tribe of migrant labourers marooned in Egypt.

Suppose that the prophet decided to inspire (and thus mobilize) this primitive and almost ungovernable group of nomads by convincing them that he was going to lead them to the 'Promised Land' – Canaan – which he had enticingly depicted as 'a good land and a large . . . a land flowing with milk and honey'.[103] If so then he was far too wily a leader, and far too astute a judge of human frailty, to take what was basically a disorganized rabble straight there. He knew that they would face formidable foes when they eventually arrived; if they were to overcome these foes, therefore, he would first need to mould and shape them, bend them to his will, and impose some discipline upon them.

This reasoning appeals to me because it seems to offer a logical explanation for something that otherwise makes very little sense – namely the fact that the Israelites supposedly spent forty years wandering in the inhospitable wildernesses of the Sinai peninsula.[104] There were, at the time, at least two well known and much-frequented trade routes which normally enabled travellers to cross the deserts between Egypt and Canaan in just a few days.[105] It seems to me, therefore, that Moses's decision not to use these highways (and instead to inflict a lengthy period of hardship on his people) could only have been a deliberate and calculated strategy: he must have seen this as the best way to get the Israelites into shape for the conquest of the Promised Land.[106]

Such a strategy, however, would also have had its drawbacks – notably the problem of persuading the tribesmen to stick together in the desert and to put up with all the difficulties and austerities of nomadic life. This problem was truly a knotty one: the biblical account of the wanderings in the wilderness makes it painfully clear that Moses had a hard time trying to keep his people's confidence and to force them to obey him. It was true that they fell briefly into line whenever he worked some new miracle (and he was obliged to work many); on other occasions, however – and particularly when they faced adversity – they seethed with discontent, criticized him bitterly and sometimes rebelled openly against him.[107]

In such circumstances, is it not reasonable to suppose that the prophet might have seen the need to equip himself with some sort of portable 'miracle machine' to enthral and impress the Israelites whenever and wherever a bit of 'magic' was required? And wasn't that exactly what the Ark was – a portable miracle machine which Moses used to ensure that the people would obey him no matter how difficult the circumstances?

Examples of the sacred object being used in precisely this manner are not hard to find in the Bible. Indeed a dramatic change appears to have taken place in Moses's behaviour after the building of the Ark. Previously he had responded to the incessant demands and complaints of the Israelites with relatively minor acts of wizardry – striking a desert rock with his wand in order to make fresh water gush forth from it,[108] extracting potable water from a stagnant pool,[109] delivering food in the form of manna and quails,[110] and so on and so forth. Later, however, the prophet did not bother with conjuring tricks like these. Instead, whenever the people grumbled, rebelled against him, or dared to dispute his leadership in any way he simply turned the Ark on them – with predictably dreadful results.

On one fairly typical occasion he used it to inflict a disfiguring skin condition on his sister Miriam because she had questioned his authority.[111] The Bible calls this skin condition 'leprosy'.[112] When Miriam had been suitably chastened, however, her sores vanished. Since they had appeared in the first place immediately after she had been exposed to the mysterious cloud that sometimes issued forth from between the two cherubim mounted on the Ark's lid, it is most unlikely that they were actually caused by leprosy.[113] Might they not rather have been induced by some chemical or other contaminant released from the Ark itself?

Miriam was not the only person to have been affected in this way after incurring Moses's wrath. Moreover other dissidents not lucky enough to be members of the priestly family tended to be punished with even greater severity. A particularly interesting series of events occurred in response to a mutiny in which the ascendancy of Moses and Aaron was openly questioned:

Two hundred and fifty of the sons of Israel joined forces

against Moses and Aaron saying, You take too much on yourselves! The whole community and all its members are consecrated, and Yahweh lives among them, Why set yourselves higher than the community of Yahweh?[114]

Moses was at first so shocked by this insubordination that he 'fell upon his face'.[115] He quickly recovered, however, and proposed the following 'test': to find out whether the two hundred and fifty rebels were really as 'holy' as he was, he suggested that they should each fill a bronze censer with incense and that they should then come in before the Ark to burn this incense.[116] If this was done, he argued, it would allow Yahweh to 'choose the one who is the consecrated man'.[117]

The challenge was accepted: 'And they took every man his censer, and put fire in them, and laid incense thereon, and stood at the door of the Tabernacle . . . with Moses and Aaron.'[118] No sooner had this gathering taken place than 'the glory of Yahweh appeared'.[119] Then the deity supposedly gave his 'favourites' a three-second warning of what he was about to do: 'Yahweh spoke to Moses and Aaron. He said, "Stand apart from this assembly, I am going to destroy them here and now." '[120] At this, the prophet and the High Priest 'threw themselves face downward on the ground . . . And there came out a fire [from the Ark] and consumed the two hundred and fifty men that offered incense.'[121]

Afterwards,

the children of Israel spake unto Moses, saying, Behold, we die, we perish, we all perish . . . Whosoever cometh anything near unto the tabernacle of the Lord shall die: shall we be consumed with dying?[122]

They had, it seemed, learned a salutary lesson. Subdued by the powers of the Ark, they mounted no further rebellions of any significance. On the contrary, apart from a few low-key gripes and murmurs, they fell very much into line behind Moses and did exactly what he told them to do during the remainder of their sojourn in the wilderness.

So much, then, for motive. Moses clearly had great need of a portable miracle machine exactly like the Ark. Moreover, once he had equipped himself with that machine – if machine it indeed was – he showed no hesitation in using it.

Motive and ability alone, however, do not add up to a coherent case. The next question, therefore, is this: did he have the opportunity to prepare a proper blueprint for the Ark and to fabricate some sort of 'power-pack' for it – some sort of energy source by means of which it might be activated?

The answer is yes – ample opportunity. To understand why it is worth recalling the main events of Moses's life, in the order that they occurred:

1 He was born in Egypt.
2 He was cast adrift on the Nile in a basket made of papyrus reeds coated with bitumen and pitch.
3 He was 'saved from water' by the daughter of Pharaoh.
4 He was reared in the royal household where he learned 'all the wisdom of the Egyptians' – and became an adept in sorcery, and almost certainly a High Priest.[123]
5 At the age of forty,[124] according to the Bible, he heard that his own native people – the Israelites – were being oppressed by the Egyptians. Accordingly he left the court and went to find out what was happening to them. He discovered that they were living a life of bondage, forced to do hard labour day and night. Incensed at this cruel treatment, and at the arrogance of the Egyptians, he lost his temper, killed an overseer and then fled into exile.[125]
6 At the age of eighty[126] – i.e. forty years later – he returned from exile to lead the Israelites out of their captivity.

What happened during the missing forty years? The Bible is singularly unhelpful in answering this question, devoting just eleven verses to direct discussion of the entire period.[127] It does, however, make one thing abundantly clear: in all this great expanse of time the key event was Moses's encounter with Yahweh at the burning bush – an encounter that took place at the foot of Mount Sinai where, some time later, the Ark of the Covenant was to be built.

Long before Moses persuaded the Israelites to follow him across the Red Sea, is it not therefore probable that he had thoroughly familiarized himself with the fearsome wildernesses of the Sinai peninsula? The location of the burning bush incident leaves no room for doubt that he spent at least part of his forty-year exile in these remote and mountainous deserts. Indeed, it is even possible that he passed most or all of this period there – a view for which there is a degree of academic support. According to one learned Egyptologist, Moses could have spent as long as a quarter of a century in Sinai, living in a settlement on a mountain known as Serabit-el-Khadem barely fifty miles from Mount Sinai itself.[128]

In June 1989 I visited and climbed Serabit-el-Khadem, which stands in the austere and barren highlands of southern-central Sinai. On the flat top of the mountain, completely innocent of tourists, were the ruins of the settlement in which Moses was thought to have lived – ruins dominated by the obelisks, altars and graceful columns of what must once have been an extensive Egyptian temple. As a High Priest of the ancient Egyptian religion, I reasoned, Moses would have felt comfortable here – and if he had indeed fled the wrath of Pharaoh after killing an overseer as the Bible claimed, then he would have been relatively safe in this remote and obscure spot.

I decided to find out more about Serabit-el-Khadem and researched it in some depth after my initial visit. In the course of this work, two significant facts came to light.

First, I learned that the temple site which I had seen had been thoroughly investigated in 1904–5 by the great British archaeologist Sir William Flinders Petrie – and that he had unearthed fragments of several stone tablets there.[129] These tablets were inscribed with writing in a strange pictographic alphabet that, much later, was proved to have belonged to a Semitic-Canaanite language related to ancient Hebrew.[130]

Second, I discovered that the settlement at Serabit-el-Khadem had been an important centre for the *mining and manufacture* of copper and turquoise from roughly 1990 BC until 1190 BC.[131] These dates meant that there was no anachronism in the assumption that Moses might have sojourned here in the thirteenth century BC, just prior to the Exodus. And the evidence that an alphabet related to Hebrew had been in use on the site at about the same time looked like further corroboration of this view. What really interested me, however, was the point emphasized above, namely that Serabit had functioned as a sort of industrial and metallurgical complex and that the whole area had been extensively mined. It seemed to me that if Moses had indeed lived here for a lengthy period then he could hardly have failed to acquire knowledge of the minerals and metal ores of southern Sinai.

After my visit to Serabit-el-Khadem in June 1989 I drove my hired Jeep the fifty miles across the desert to Mount Sinai. In a sense the word 'desert' is a misnomer for this region, for although there are sandy expanses, the bulk of the countryside consists of steep and withered mountain ranges, red in colour, upon which almost nothing grows. The only patches of greenery are created by occasional oases in the valleys, and one such oasis, rich in date palms, stands at the foot of Mount Sinai. Here, in the fourth century AD, a small Christian chapel was erected on the supposed site of the burning bush. That chapel was greatly extended in subsequent years. By the fifth century it had become a substantial monastery under the patronage of the Coptic Church of Alexandria. In the sixth century the Roman Emperor Justinian massively fortified the monastery's walls so that it could better withstand the attacks of marauding bedouin tribes. Finally, in the eleventh century, the whole complex was dedicated to Saint Catherine.[132] It continues to be known as 'Saint Catherine's' today, and many of the structures built in the fifth and sixth centuries still stand.

Before embarking on the arduous 7,450-foot climb to the top of Mount Sinai I spent some time inside the ancient monastery. The main church contained several remarkable icons, mosaics and paintings, some of them almost 1,500 years old. In the gardens was a walled enclosure built around a large raspberry bush that was believed by the monks to be the original burning bush.[133] This it certainly was not – and, indeed, I was well aware that even Mount Sinai's claim to be *the* 'Mount Sinai' referred to in the Bible had by no means been conclusively proved. The fact was, however, that monastic traditions dating back at least to the fourth century AD had associated this particular peak with the 'mountain of God,' and had almost certainly done so on the basis of reliable sources of information now lost.[134] Moreover I knew that local tribal traditions concurred: the bedouin name for Mount Sinai was simply *Jebel Musa* – 'the mountain of Moses'.[135] Scholarly opinion also associated the biblical Mount Sinai with the peak bearing that name today – and the few dissenting voices did not favour a different *region* but rather other nearby peaks in the same range (for example Jebel Serbal).[136]

I must confess that after climbing Mount Sinai in June 1989 I was left in no doubt that this had indeed been the mountain to which Moses had brought the Israelites 'in the third month' after leaving Egypt. Pausing at the summit, I stood on a ledge which overlooked tumbled miles of worn and jagged uplands descending to sere plains in the far distance. There was a haze and a powder-blue stillness in the air – not silence, exactly, but stillness. Then a sudden wind whipped up, cool and dry at that altitude, and I watched an eagle soar heavenwards on a thermal, gliding briefly level with me before it disappeared from sight. I remained there alone for a while, in that pitiless and uncompromising place, and I remember thinking that Moses could hardly have chosen a more dramatic or a more appropriate location in which to receive the Ten Commandments from the hand of God.

But is that really what the Hebrew magus came to Mount Sinai to do? It seems to me that there is an alternative scenario. Could it not be that his true purpose all along had been to build the Ark of the Covenant *and to place inside it some great energy source, the raw substance of which he had known that he would be able to find on this particular mountain top?*

This is a highly speculative thesis – but it is speculation that we are indulging in here and there is room for a little imaginative licence. If Moses had known of the existence of some potent substance on the peak of Mount Sinai, then what might that substance have been?

One suggestion – put forward in a different context in Chapter 3 – is that the tablets of stone on which God supposedly wrote the Ten Commandments were in fact two pieces of a meteorite.

Resonant with echoes of Wolfram's Grail Stone (described as having been brought down from heaven by a troop of angels[137]), this intriguing possibility is taken seriously by several top-flight biblical scholars, who point to the worship of meteoric fragments in a number of ancient Semitic cultures[138] and add that:

> concealing tables of law within a closed container [seems] somewhat odd . . . Words of law engraved upon stone were surely meant to be publicly displayed . . . [it may therefore be] supposed that the Ark held not two tables of the law but a fetish stone, a meteorite from Mount Sinai.[139]

If this conjecture is correct then the field lies open to guess what element exactly the 'meteorite from Mount Sinai' might have consisted of. It is at any rate not beyond the bounds of reason to suppose that it might have been radioactive, or that it might have possessed some chemical characteristic that would have made it useful to Moses if his purpose had really been to manufacture a potent and durable source of energy for installation in the Ark.

The notion that he might have been manufacturing something on Mount Sinai is certainly not ruled out by the Scriptures. On the contrary, many passages in the relevant chapters of the book of Exodus are sufficiently peculiar and puzzling to allow just such an interpretation to be put on them.

The so-called 'theophany' – the manifestation of a deity to a mortal man – began immediately after the Israelites had 'camped before the mount'. Then 'Moses went up unto God, and the Lord called unto him out of the mountain.'[140]

At this early stage the Bible makes no mention of smoke or fire or any of the other special effects that were soon to be brought into play. Instead the prophet simply climbed the mountain and held a private conversation with Yahweh, a conversation that was not witnessed by anyone else. Significantly, one of the first instructions that he supposedly received from the deity was this:

Thou shalt set bounds unto the people round about,

saying, Take heed to yourselves that ye go not up into the
mount, or touch the border of it: Whoever touches the
mountain will be put to death . . . He must be stoned or shot
down by arrow . . . he must not remain alive.[141]

It goes almost without saying that Moses would have had a strong
reason to impose just such a rigorous and 'divinely ordained'
exclusion zone if he had indeed been planning to manufacture or
process some substance on Mount Sinai: the prospect of being
stoned or shot would certainly have deterred the curious from
venturing up to see what he was really doing there and thus would
have enabled him to preserve the illusion that he was meeting
with God.

At any rate, it was only after he had spent three days on the
mountain that the drama really began. Then:

In the morning . . . there were thunders and lightnings,
and a thick cloud upon the mount, and the voice of the
trumpet exceeding loud; so that all the people that was in
the camp trembled . . . And mount Sinai was altogether
on a smoke, because Yahweh had descended on it in the
form of fire. Like smoke from a furnace the smoke went
up.[142]

Initially it seems that Moses spent only part of his time isolated on
the peak, and that he was frequently in the camp. Soon, however,
God told him this:

Come up to me on the mountain and stay there while I
give you the stone tablets – the law and the
commandments – which I have written.[143]

This, then, was the prelude to what was to be the key event on
Sinai – Moses's acquisition of the two tablets of stone that he
would later place inside the Ark of the Covenant. The prophet's
ascent was accompanied by further special effects:

Moses went up into the mount, and a cloud covered the

mount. And the glory of Yahweh settled upon mount Sinai; for six days the cloud covered it, and on the seventh day Yahweh called to Moses from inside the cloud. To the eyes of the sons of Israel the glory of Yahweh seemed like a devouring fire on the mountain top. Moses went right into the cloud. He went up the mountain and stayed there for forty days and forty nights.[144]

Would an omnipotent God have required forty days and forty nights to deliver two stone tablets to His prophet? Such a lengthy period seems hardly necessary. If, however, Moses had *not* been receiving 'the tablets of the Testimony' at all, but instead had been manufacturing or refining some compact stone-like energy source to place inside the Ark, then he could well have needed that much time to finish the work.

From this perspective, the 'devouring fire' on the mountain top that the Israelites had interpreted as 'the glory of Yahweh' would really have been the infernal glow given off by whatever devices or chemical processes the prophet was using to achieve his objective. And although this hypothesis sounds far-fetched, it is surely not more so than the strange information concerning the tablets of stone that is contained in the Old Testament, in the Mishnah, in the Midrash, in the Talmud, and in the most archaic Jewish legends.

Tablets of stone?

The clearest descriptions of the tablets are contained in the Talmudic-Midrashic sources which yield the following information: (1) they were 'made of a sapphire-like stone'; (2) they were 'not more than six hands in length and as much in width' but were nevertheless enormously heavy; (3) though hard they were also flexible; (4) they were transparent.[145]

It was upon these peculiar objects that the Ten Commandments were supposedly written – by no lesser figure than Yahweh Himself, as the Bible is at pains to point out:

When He had finished speaking with Moses on the mountain of Sinai, He gave him the two tablets of the

Testimony, tablets of stone, inscribed by the finger of God
... And Moses turned and went down from the mount with
the two tablets of the Testimony in his hands, tablets
inscribed on both sides, inscribed on the front and on the
back. These tablets were the work of God, and the writing
on them was God's writing.[146]

Theologically, therefore, there can be no doubting the sanctity or
the significance of the prophet's burden: written upon by the very
finger of God, the two tablets were quite literally fragments of the
divine. From the biblical viewpoint nothing more precious had
ever been entrusted to mortal man. One would have thought that
Moses would have looked after them. He did not do so, however.
Instead, in a fit of pique, he broke these pure and perfect gifts.

Why did he do this incomprehensible thing? According to the
explanation given in Exodus it was because the perfidious
Israelites had lost hope that he would ever return after his forty
days on the mountain and had fashioned a golden calf, which they
were worshipping. Arriving in the camp Moses then caught them
in flagrante delicto offering sacrifices and dancing and prostrating
themselves before the idol. At the sight of this grotesque apostasy
the prophet's 'anger waxed hot and he threw down the tablets
that he was holding and broke them at the foot of the
mountain.'[147] He then disposed of the golden calf, had about
three thousand of the worst idolators executed, and restored
order.[148]

So much, then, for the official account of how and why the
original tablets of stone came to be broken. These items,
however, were clearly of vital importance and had to be replaced.
Accordingly God instructed Moses to return to the mountain top
to receive two new tablets. The prophet complied and 'stayed
there with Yahweh forty days and forty nights ... and he
inscribed on the tablets the words of the Covenant, the Ten
Commandments.'[149] Moses then climbed down the mountain
again bearing the tablets, exactly as he had done before. A close
study of the relevant biblical passages, however, does reveal a
single substantive and significant difference between his two
descents: on the second occasion 'the skin of his face shone';[150]
on the first there had been no mention of this odd phenomenon.

What could have caused the prophet's face to shine? The biblical scribes naturally assumed that it had been his proximity to God, and explained: 'the skin on his face was radiant after speaking with Yahweh.'[151] Yet on several previous occasions, dating back as far as the burning bush, Moses had stood close to Yahweh and had not suffered any such consequences. Indeed, a typical example had occurred just before he had embarked on his second forty-day expedition to Sinai. While still in the Israelite camp he had participated in a lengthy and intimate encounter with the deity, an encounter that had been held in a specially sanctified structure called the 'Tent of Meeting'.[152] There 'the Lord spake unto Moses face to face, as a man speaketh unto his friend,'[153] but there was no hint or suggestion that the prophet's skin had glowed as a result.

So what could have produced this effect? Is it not reasonable to suggest that it might have been the tablets of stone themselves? Oblique corroboration for precisely this suggestion exists in the Talmudic and Midrashic sources which insist that the tablets had been infused with 'Divine radiance'. When God handed them to Moses: 'He seized them by the top third, whereas Moses took hold of the bottom third, but one third remained open, and it was in this way that the Divine radiance was shed upon Moses' face.'[154]

Since this did not happen with the first set of tablets – the ones that Moses broke – it is legitimate to ask a question: why were things so different the second time around? Could the answer possibly be that Moses had discovered that the first set of tablets were technically imperfect as an energy source precisely because they *didn't* burn his face? This would explain why he broke them. He did, however, sustain burns from the second set. Perhaps this proved to him that whatever process he had used to manufacture them had worked – and made him confident that they would function properly when they were placed inside the Ark.

The idea that the glow or shine on Moses's skin might in fact have been caused by some sort of burn is of course purely speculative. There is no support for it in the Bible. Nevertheless, it seems to me to be a perfectly reasonable deduction – as reasonable as any other – from the small amount of evidence that is available there. The description of the prophet's descent from the mountain with the second set of tablets is limited to just seven verses in Chapter 34 of Exodus.[155] These verses, however, make it absolutely clear that his appearance was so gruesome when he arrived in the camp that all the Israelites were 'afraid to come nigh him'.[156] To spare their feelings 'he put a veil over his face'[157] – and ever afterwards, except when he was alone in his tent, he wore this veil.[158]

Does this not sound much less like the behaviour of a man who had been touched by the radiance of God than of a man burned – and burned badly – by some potent energy source?

A testament to lost truths

It would be possible to speculate endlessly about the true character of the Ark of the Covenant – and of its contents. I have gone as far as I wish to down this particular road. Readers who would like to go further, however, might find it interesting to consider first the materials from which the Ark was made. Huge quantities of gold seem to have been used – and gold, as well as being beautiful and noble, is also chemically non-reactive and exceptionally dense. In particular the 'mercy seat' – which served as the lid of the relic – was believed by one learned rabbi (who lived in the twelfth century AD) to have been a full hand-breadth thick.[159] Since a hand-breadth was traditionally measured from the tip of the thumb to the extended tip of the little finger, this means that the Ark was closed with a hulking slab of solid gold *nine inches* deep.[160] Why was it necessary to use so much of the precious metal? And was it an accident that Rabbi Shelomo Yitshaki who procured this information – as well as a great deal of other intelligence concerning the sacred relic – was born and spent most of his life in the city of Troyes in the heart of France's Champagne region?[161] That same city was the home of Chrétien de Troyes whose work on the Holy Grail, written seventy-five years after the rabbi's death, established the genre in which Wolfram von Eschenbach was soon to follow. And it was in Troyes as well that the rule of the Knights Templar was drawn up by Saint Bernard of Clairvaux. In this way the mysteries and the connections multiply.

Those who are curious might also wish to give some thought to the peculiar garments that the High Priests of ancient Israel wore when they approached the Ark.[162] If they did not wear these garments their lives were believed to be at risk.[163] Was this purely a matter of superstition and ritual? Or was protective clothing necessary for some reason that perhaps had to do with the nature of the Ark itself?

Related to this point is another – the curious coverings, consisting of two layers of cloth and one of leather, that the Ark had to be wrapped in before it could be transported[164] (apparently in order to prevent anyone from being killed as a result of accidentally touching it whilst it was on the move[165]). Even when these precautions had been fully complied with, however, the sacred relic still sometimes caused the death of its bearers. It did so with 'sparks'.[166] But what were these sparks? And were the wrappings – which were all made of non-conductive materials[167] – perhaps intended to serve as insulation?[168]

Also of some potential interest is the story of Nadab and Abihu, the two sons of Aaron who were struck down by the Ark soon after its installation in the Tabernacle (I have described this incident briefly in Chapter 12; according to the Scriptures a flame leapt out at them 'and devoured them and they died'[169]). Surprisingly, Moses completely ignored the normally lengthy Hebrew funeral procedures and instead ordered that the bodies should immediately be taken 'far away' out of the camp.[170] Why should he have done such a thing? What was it exactly that he feared?

Moving forward in time, I suggest that those who wish to learn more could do worse than examine the passages in the Bible which recount the dreadful afflictions that the Ark worked amongst the Philistines during the seven months that it spent in their hands after they had captured it at the battle of Ebenezer.[171] Again, I have described these events in Chapter 12, but I have also left much unsaid that could be said.

Many riddles, too, might be solved by a close study of what happened in the years after the Ark was returned to the Israelites by the Philistines and before King Solomon finally installed it in the Holy of Holies of his Temple in Jerusalem. I believe that an explanation exists for the miracles and the terrors that it worked during this period[172] – a rational explanation connected to its character as a man-made device and not to any divine or unearthly influences.

Indeed, my own investigations have led me to conclude that it may *only* be possible to understand the sacred relic properly when it is seen in this light – not as a repository of supernatural powers but as an artefact and as an instrument. No doubt this instrument was very different from any known to us today, but it was none the less the product of human ingenuity, devised by human hands to fulfil very human objectives. As such its magic and its mystery are not diminished for me. The gift of an ancient and secret science, I think of it as a key to the sealed and unremembered history of our species, a sign of our forgotten glory, and a testament to lost truths about ourselves.

And what else is the quest for the Ark or the Grail if it is not a quest for knowledge, a quest for wisdom and a quest for enlightenment?

Part V: Israel and Egypt, 1990
Where is the Glory?

Mediterranean Sea

ISRAEL
Jerusalem

JORDAN

IRAQ

IRAN

Cairo

Arabian Gulf

Nile

Aswan/
Elephantine

Red Sea

SAUDI ARABIA

Meroe

Atbara

YEMEN

Khartoum

Asmara

Gulf of Aden

Takazze

Axum

Blue Nile

Gondar

Lake
Tana

Lalibela

White Nile

SOMALIA

Addis Ababa

ETHIOPIA

UGANDA

KENYA

Kilometres

0   200   400

Chapter 14

The Glory is departed from Israel

In the mid-afternoon of Thursday 4 October 1990 I entered the old walled city of Jerusalem through the Jaffa Gate. After passing Omar Ibn el-Khatab Square, with its pleasant cafés and hawkers' stands, a bewildering maze of narrow streets paved with ancient cobble stones lay ahead of me.

A few years earlier this whole area would have been seething with shoppers and sightseers; now, however, it was almost deserted. The Palestinian *intifada*, and recent threats by Iraq to 'burn' Israel with Scud missiles, had been enough to drive virtually all foreigners away.

To my right, as I walked, was the Armenian Quarter and, to my left, the Christian Quarter dominated by the Church of the Holy Sepulchre. Within this great edifice was the Chapel of the Invention of the Cross which the victorious Muslim general Saladin – at the request of King Lalibela – had granted to the Ethiopian community of Jerusalem after the Crusaders had been expelled from the city in AD 1187.[1] In later years the Ethiopians had lost their privileges in the chapel. I knew, however, that they still occupied an extensive monastery on its roof.

I continued in an easterly direction through the silent and deserted alleys, many of which were covered with canvas awnings that cut out the glare and heat of the afternoon sun, creating a cool, almost subterranean atmosphere. A few forlorn shop-keepers sitting in their doorways made half-hearted attempts to sell me souvenirs that I did not want and bags of ripe oranges that I had no desire to carry.

To my right now, as I proceeded along the Street of the Chain, was the Jewish Quarter where gangs of Hasidic youths dressed in dark suits and incongruous fur hats roamed pugnaciously about, declaring by their body language that they were the masters of all they surveyed. To my left, filled to the brim with unhappiness, frustration and restless despair, was the Muslim Quarter. And straight ahead, rising up above the clutter of the old city like a golden symbol of hope, was the Dome of the Rock – the beautiful mosque erected by the Caliph Omar and his successors in the seventh century AD and regarded as the third most sacred place in the Islamic world.[2]

It was the Dome of the Rock that I had come to see, although not because of its significance to Muslims but because it had been built on the original site of the Temple of Solomon. Inside I knew that I would find a great stone, believed by orthodox Jews to be the *Shetiyyah* – the foundation-stone of the world. And on that stone, in the tenth century BC, amidst the 'thick darkness' of the Holy of Holies, the Ark of the Covenant had been placed by Solomon himself.[3] Like a man who seeks to conjure up an image of his long-departed lover by caressing some item of her clothing, I therefore hoped that by touching the *Shetiyyah* I might gain a deeper and more abiding sense of the lost relic that I sought.

This, however, was not my only purpose on that afternoon in October. Just a few hundred metres to the south of the Dome of the Rock I knew that I would also be able to visit another building of central importance to my quest – the Al-Aqsa Mosque, which the Knights Templar had used as their headquarters in the twelfth century AD. From this base, I suspected, they had sallied forth to conduct investigations of their own in the caverns beneath the *Shetiyyah* – where certain legends suggested that the Ark had been concealed shortly before the destruction of Solomon's Temple.[4]

It was to the Al-Aqsa Mosque that I went first, slipping off my shoes and entering the cool and roomy rectangular hall believed by Muslims to be the 'furthermost sanctuary', to which Muhammad was supposedly transported by angels on his famous Night Journey. Whatever place of prayer existed in the Prophet's lifetime (AD 570–632) had long since vanished, however, and I was confronted by a medley of different building styles, the oldest of which dated back to around AD 1035 and the most recent to the period 1938–42, when the Italian dictator Mussolini had donated the forest of marble columns that lay ahead of me and when King Farouk of Egypt had financed the restoration and repainting of the ceiling.[5]

The Templars, too, had left their mark on the great mosque. Taking up residence here in AD 1119 and not leaving until 1187 when they were driven out of Jerusalem by Saladin, they had been responsible, amongst other things, for the three magnificent central bays of the porch. Much of the other architecture that the knights had added had subsequently been destroyed. Their refectory, however, had survived (being incorporated into the nearby Women's Mosque), and the vast underground area which they had developed as stables for their horses (the so-called 'Stables of Solomon') were also in a good state of repair.[6]

As I carefully picked my way in stockinged feet amongst the Muslims who were already assembling for afternoon prayer I felt strangely light-headed but at the same time alert – keyed-up. The jumble of different eras and influences, the old mixed in with the new, Mussolini's marble columns, and the eleventh-century Islamic mosaics, had all conspired to confuse my perceptions. Currents of incense-laden air wafted through the spacious and light-filled interior, summoning up visions of the European knights who had lived and died here so long ago and who had named their strange and secretive order after the Temple of Solomon – the site of which, now occupied by the Dome of the Rock, was only two minutes' walk away.

The *raison d'être* of the Temple had been extremely simple. It had been conceived and designed as nothing more, and nothing less, than 'an house of rest for the Ark of the Covenant of the Lord'.[7] But the Ark, of course, had long since vanished, and the Temple, too, was gone. Utterly and completely destroyed by the Babylonians in 587 BC, the structure erected by Solomon had been replaced half a century later by the Second Temple – which, in its turn, had been razed by the Romans in AD 70. The site had then lapsed into disuse until the arrival of the Muslim armies in AD 638 when the Dome of the Rock had been built.[8] Throughout all these changes the *Shetiyyah* had remained in place. The sacred floor on which the Ark had once stood was therefore the single constant factor that had weathered all the storms of history, that had seen Jews and Babylonians and

Romans and Christians and Muslims come and go, and that still endured today.

Leaving the Al-Aqsa Mosque, and slipping on my shoes again, I now made my way up through the tree-lined precincts of the Temple Mount to the Dome of the Rock – the very name of which reflected its guardianship of the *Shetiyyah*. A large and elegant octagonal building faced with rich blue tiling, its dominant exterior feature was its massive golden dome (which, indeed, could be seen from many different parts of Jerusalem). To my eye, however, there was nothing overwhelming about this tall and perfect monument. On the contrary it conveyed a complex feeling of lightness and grace coupled with an under-stated but reassuring strength.

This first impression was enhanced and completed by the interior of the building, which quite literally took my breath away. The soaring ceiling, the columns and arches supporting the inner octagon, the various niches and recesses, the mosaics, the inscriptions – all these elements and many more melded together in a sublime harmony of proportion and design that gave eloquent expression to humanity's yearning for the divine and that proclaimed that yearning to be both noble and profound.

My glance had been drawn upwards when I entered – upwards into the cupola, the farthest reaches of which were lost in the cool darkness overhead. Now, however, as though attracted by some powerful magnetic force, I felt my attention tugged down again towards the very centre of the mosque where a huge tawny rock perhaps thirty feet across, flat in places, jagged in others, lay directly beneath the dome.

This was the *Shetiyyah* and, as I approached it, I was aware that my heart was beating more quickly than usual and that my breathing seemed laboured. It was not difficult to understand why the ancients had thought of this great boulder as the foundation-stone of the world or to see why Solomon had chosen it as the centrepiece of his Temple. Rough-textured and asymmetrical, it jutted out above the bedrock of Mount Moriah as solid and as unshakable as the earth itself.

A carved wooden railing surrounded the whole central area, but into one corner of this railing was set a shrine through which I was allowed to push my hand to touch the *Shetiyyah*. Its texture,

smoothed down by the caresses of countless generations of
pilgrims before me, was slick, almost glasslike, and I stood there,
lost in my own thoughts, drinking in through the pores of my
fingers the immense antiquity of this strange and wonderful
stone. Though it was perhaps a small victory, it nevertheless
meant a great deal to me to be in this place and to savour this
moment of quiet reflection at the source of the mystery that I
sought to solve.

Eventually I withdrew my hand and continued my circuit of the
Shetiyyah. At one side a stairway led down to a deep hollow
beneath the stone – a cave-like cist known to the Muslims as *Bir
el-Arweh*, the 'Well of Souls'. Here, according to the faithful, the
voices of the dead could sometimes be heard mingled with the
sounds of the rivers of paradise. As I entered, however, I could
hear nothing except the murmured prayers of the half-dozen or
so pilgrims who had preceded me and who were now slumped in
obeisance on the cold rock floor invoking in mellifluous Arabic
the name of Allah, the Compassionate, the Merciful – a deity
whose prophets, long before the time of Muhammad, had
included Abraham and Moses and who, in his absolute and
uncompromising *oneness*, was in no way different from Yahweh,
the God of the Ark.[9]

I already knew that a number of Jewish and Islamic legends
spoke of a sealed and secret passage beneath the Well of Souls
leading into the bowels of the earth, where the Ark had
supposedly been concealed at the time of the destruction of
Solomon's Temple – and where many believed that it rested still,
guarded by spirits and demons.[10] As noted in Part II, I suspected
that the Knights Templar could have been motivated to search
here for the Ark in the twelfth century AD after learning of these
legends. One variant of the tale that might particularly have
excited their interest purported to be an eyewitness account by a
certain 'Baruch' of an intervention by an 'angel of the Lord' only
moments before the Babylonian army broke into the Temple:

> And I saw him descend into the Holy of Holics, and
> take from it the veil, and the Holy Ark, and its cover, and
> the two tablets . . . And he cried to the earth in a loud
> voice, 'Earth, earth, earth, hear the word of the mighty

> God, and receive what I commit to you, and guard them
> until the last times, so that, when you are ordered, you may
> restore them, and strangers may not get possession of
> them . . .' And the earth opened its mouth and swallowed
> them up.[11]

If the Templars had indeed been inspired by this text to search
beneath the Well of Souls they would not, I was absolutely
confident, have found the Ark there. The so-called 'Apocalypse
of Baruch' (from which the above quotation is taken) might easily
have seemed to them like a genuinely ancient document dating
from the sixth century BC. The truth, however, as modern
scholarship had subsequently revealed, was that it was written in
the late first century AD and that it therefore could not possibly
have been an eyewitness account of the concealment of the
sacred relic, whether by an angel or by any other agency. On the
contrary it was, from beginning to end, a work of imaginative
fiction which, despite its eerie and evocative tone, possessed no
historical merit whatsoever.[12]

For this and other reasons, I felt sure that the Templars would
have been frustrated in their excavations beneath the Temple
Mount. But I also suspected that they had later learned of
Ethiopia's claim to be the last resting place of the Ark and that a
group of knights had ultimately gone there to investigate this
claim for themselves.[13]

I, too, was following the same trail that those knights had
stumbled upon so many centuries before, and I felt that it
pointed compellingly towards the sanctuary chapel in the sacred
city of Axum. Before attempting to make my own way into the
war-torn highlands of Tigray, however, I wanted to be absolutely
satisfied that there was no other country or place where the lost
relic could be. It was that desire that had brought me to the
original site of the Temple of Solomon on 4 October 1990. And
it was that desire that had drawn me to the *Shetiyyah*, on which the
Ark had once stood and from which it had vanished.

That was my starting point, but now I intended to use the rest
of my stay in Jerusalem to talk to religious and academic
authorities and to examine in the greatest possible depth all the
circumstances known to have surrounded the mysterious dis-

appearance of the relic. Only if I was still confident of the basic merit of the Ethiopian claim after I had completed that exercise would I finally commit myself to the Axum adventure. The January 1991 *Timkat* ceremonials at which I hoped that the object believed to be the Ark would be carried in procession were, however, less than four months away. I was therefore acutely aware that my time was running out.

What house can you build me?

The installation of the Ark in the Temple of Solomon, which – as I had already established – must have taken place around the year 955 BC,[14] was described in the first book of Kings:

> Then Solomon assembled the elders of Israel . . . And
> the priests brought in the Ark of the Covenant of the
> Lord to its place in the Temple . . . in the Holy of
> Holies . . . And it came to pass, when the priests were
> come out of the holy place, that the cloud filled the house
> of the Lord, so that the priests could not stand to minister
> because of the cloud: for the glory of the Lord had filled
> the house of the Lord. Then spake Solomon, 'The Lord
> said that he would dwell in the thick darkness. I have
> surely built thee a house to dwell in, , a settled place for
> thee to abide in forever . . . But will God indeed dwell on
> the earth? behold, the heaven and heaven of heavens
> cannot contain thee; how much less this house that I have
> builded?'[15]

According to the Scriptures, Solomon had later 'turned away his heart after other gods' and had worshipped with particular enthusiasm 'Ashtoreth the goddess of the Zidonians and . . . Milcom the abomination of the Amorites'.[16] Because of this tendency to apostasy I found it difficult to believe that the monarch whose legendary wisdom was said to have excelled 'all the wisdom of Egypt'[17] had ever really held Yahweh in especially high esteem. And for the same reason I did not think that he had been paying metaphysical tribute to the omnipotence and omnipresence of the God of Israel when he had expressed his doubts about the ability of the Temple to 'contain' the Ark. On the contrary, it seemed to me that when Solomon had uttered these curious words he had been giving voice to genuine fears of a pragmatic rather than of a spiritual nature. Might not the sacred relic still break free, even though it was anchored now to the very foundation-stone of the world? Might not the unpredictable energies pent up within it still be sufficiently potent and dangerous to burn through the thick darkness of the Holy of Holies and to destroy the great 'house' that had been erected around it?

There was, I felt, a real sense in which the Temple appeared to have been built less as an earthly palace for a dearly beloved but incorporeal deity than as a kind of *prison* for the Ark of the Covenant. Within the Holy of Holies, above the two cherubim that faced each other across the relic's golden lid, Solomon had installed two additional cherubim of giant size – grim guardians indeed, with wingspans of fifteen feet or more, all covered in gold.[18] Meanwhile the Holy of Holies itself – the purpose of which, the Bible stated explicitly, had been 'to contain the Ark of the Covenant of Yahweh'[19] – had been a perfect cube, foursquare and immensely strong. Measuring thirty feet long, by thirty feet wide, by thirty feet high,[20] its floor, its four walls and its ceiling had been lined with pure gold, weighing an estimated 45,000 pounds,[21] and riveted with golden nails.[22]

Nor was this golden cell the only feature of the Temple's construction that caught my attention. At least as interesting was the pedigree of the craftsman – a foreigner – who had been called in to complete all the other metalwork that Solomon had required:

> And Solomon sent for Hiram of Tyre; *he was the son of a widow* of the tribe of Naphtali . . . and he was filled with wisdom, and understanding, and cunning to work all works in bronze.[23]

The phrase emphasized above in italics had jumped out at me from the page as soon as I had set eyes upon it. Why? Because I knew that the very first mention in literature of the Grail hero Parzival had described him in almost exactly the same words as *'the son of the widowed lady'*.[24] Indeed, both Chrétien de Troyes, the founder of the genre, and his successor Wolfram von Eschenbach, had gone to great lengths to make it clear that Parzival's mother had been a widow.[25]

Could I be looking, I wondered, at yet another of the bizarre coincidences in which, through the use of dense and often deceptive symbolism, the fictional quest for the Holy Grail seemed to have been deliberately devised to serve as a cryptogram for the real quest for the lost Ark? I had long since satisfied myself that the Knights Templar had been key players in both and that, after the destruction of their order in the fourteenth century, many of their traditions had been preserved in Freemasonry. I was therefore intrigued to learn that Hiram of Tyre, who the Bible said had been called to Jerusalem by Solomon, was not only a widow's son like Parzival, but also a figure of immense significance to Freemasons – who knew him as 'Hiram Abiff', and who made reference to him in all their most important rituals.[26]

According to Masonic tradition Hiram was murderd by three of his assistants soon after he had completed the bronzework of the Temple. And this event was for some reason regarded as so laden with meaning that it was commemorated in the initiation ceremonies for Master Masons – in which each initiate was required to play the role of the murder victim. In one authoritative study I found this description of the relevant part of the ceremonial (which is still in regular use today):

> Blindfolded on the ground, the initiate hears the three
> murderers decide to bury him in a pile of rubble until
> 'low twelve' (midnight), when they will carry the body
> away from the Temple. To symbolise the burial of Hiram
> Abiff, the candidate is wrapped in a blanket and carried
> to the side of the room. Soon he hears a bell strike twelve
> times and is carried from the 'rubble' grave to a grave dug
> on the brow of a hill 'west of Mount Moriah' (the Temple
> Mount). He hears the murderers agree to mark his grave
> with a sprig of acacia, then set out to escape to Ethiopia
> across the Red Sea.[27]

Here, then, were more coincidences – a minor one in the form of the sprig of acacia (the same wood that was used to make the Ark), and a major one in the Masonic tradition that Hiram's murderers had intended to flee 'to Ethiopia'. I had no idea how much weight I should attach to such details but I could not rid myself of the feeling that they must in some way be relevant to my quest.

This suspicion deepened, furthermore, when I turned back to the Bible to find that one of the bronze items of Temple furniture that Hiram was said to have built was

> the Sea of cast metal, ten cubits from rim to rim, circular
> in shape and five cubits high; a cord thirty cubits long
> gave the measurement of its girth . . . It was a
> handsbreadth in thickness, and its rim was shaped like
> the rim of a cup, like a flower. It held two thousand
> baths.[28]

This 'Sea', I learned, had stood in the courtyard of the Temple. It had been a huge bronze basin, fifteen feet in diameter and seven and a half feet high. It had weighed around thirty tonnes when empty but had normally been kept full with an estimated 10,000 gallons of water.[29] Most authorities admitted frankly that they did not know what its function had been – although some thought that it had symbolized the 'primordial waters' referred to in the book of Genesis[30] and others believed that it had been used by the priests for their ritual ablutions.[31] I, however, found neither of these hypotheses satisfactory – and, of the two, the latter seemed the most improbable because the Bible stated quite plainly that Hiram had made ten smaller bronze basins for precisely this purpose (placed on wheeled stands, each basin held 'forty baths'[32]). After reviewing the evidence, therefore, I entered the following speculation in my notebook:

> Is it not possible that the bronze 'Sea' which Hiram made
> for the courtyard of Solomon's Temple was a throwback
> to the ancient Egyptian rituals on which the ceremonies
> of the Ark appear to have been closely modelled? In the
> festival of Apet at Luxor the 'Arks' containing effigies of

the gods were always carried to water.[33] And this, too, is
precisely what happens in Ethiopia today: at *Timkat* in
Gondar the *tabotat* are carried to the edge of a 'sacred lake' at
the rear of the castle.[34] So perhaps the bronze Sea was also a
kind of sacred lake?

According to the Bible, the other items fashioned by Hiram for
Solomon's Temple had included 'the ash containers, the scoops
and the sprinkling bowls'[35] and also

> two bronze pillars; the height of one pillar was eighteen
> cubits, and a cord twelve cubits long gave the
> measurement of its girth; so also was the second
> pillar . . . He set up the pillars in front of the vestibule of
> the sanctuary; he set up the right-hand pillar and named
> it Jachin; he set up the left-hand pillar and named it
> Boaz. So the work on the pillars was completed.[36]

Jachin and Boaz, I discovered, also featured in Masonic
traditions.[37] According to the 'old ritual' these two great pillars
had been hollow. Inside them had been stored the 'ancient
records' and the 'valuable writings' pertaining to the past of the
Jewish people.[38] And amongst these records, the Freemasons
claimed, had been 'the secret of the magical *Shamir* and the
history of its properties'.[39]

My curiosity was aroused by this mention of the 'magical
Shamir'. What had it been? Was it just a piece of Masonic arcana,
or was it referred to in the Bible?

After a painstaking search, I was able to confirm that the word
'Shamir' appeared only four times in the Old and New
Testaments[40] – thrice as a place name and once as the name of a
man. Clearly, therefore, none of these could have been the
'magical' Shamir, the secrets of which the Masons claimed had
been concealed in Hiram's bronze pillars.

I did find the information that I was looking for, however – not
in the Scriptures but in the Talmudic-Midrashic sources at my
disposal. Because Moses had commanded the Israelites not to
use 'any tool of iron' in the construction of holy places,[41]
Solomon had ordered that no hammers, axes or chisels should be

used to cut and dress the many massive stone blocks from which
the outer walls and courtyard of the Temple had been built.
Instead he had provided the artificers with an ancient device,
dating back to the time of Moses himself.[42] This device was
called the Shamir and was capable of cutting the toughest of
materials without friction or heat.[43] Also known as 'the stone that
splits rocks',[44]

> the Shamir may not be put in an iron vessel for
> safekeeping, nor in any metal vessel: it would burst such a
> receptacle asunder. It is kept wrapped up in a woollen
> cloth, and this in turn is placed in a lead basket filled with
> barley bran . . . With the destruction of the Temple the
> Shamir vanished.[45]

I was fascinated by this odd and ancient tradition, which also
claimed that the Shamir had possessed 'the remarkable property
of cutting the hardest of diamonds'.[46] I then found a collateral
version of the same story which added that it had been quite
noiseless while it was at work.[47]

All in all, I concluded, these characteristics (like many of the
characteristics of the Ark of the Covenant) sounded broadly
technological in nature, rather than in any way 'magical' or
supernatural. And I also thought it significant that this peculiar
device – again like the Ark – had been directly associated with
Moses. Finally it did not seem to me entirely irrelevant that the
Freemasons had maintained their own separate traditions about
it – traditions which stated that its secrets had been concealed
inside the two bronze pillars placed 'in front of the vestibule of
the sanctuary' by Hiram the widow's son.

Without knowledge of those long-lost 'secrets', I realized that I
could not hope to go any further with this line of inquiry. At the
same time, however, I felt that the story of the Shamir deepened
the mystery surrounding the real nature of the great stronghold
on the top of Mount Moriah that had been built and explicitly
dedicated as 'an house of rest for the Ark of the Covenant of the
Lord'. With its bronze pillars and its bronze 'Sea', its giant
cherubim and its golden inner shrine, Solomon's Temple had
clearly been a special place, wonderfully made, the focus of

superstition and religious dread, and the centre of Jewish faith and cultural life. How, then, could the Ark possibly have disappeared from it?

Shishak, Jehoash and Nebuchadnezzar

An obvious answer to the last question – which, if correct, would completely invalidate the Ethiopian claim – was that the Ark could have been taken by force from the Temple during one of the several military catastrophes that Israel suffered after the death of Solomon.

The first of these catastrophes occurred in 926 BC during the unsuccessful reign of Solomon's son Rehoboam.[48] Then, according to the first book of Kings, an Egyptian Pharaoh known as Sheshonq (or 'Shishak') mounted a full-scale invasion:

> In the fifth year of king Rehoboam . . . Shishak king of
> Egypt came up against Jerusalem: And he took away the
> treasures of the house of the Lord, and the treasures of
> the king's house; he even took away all.[49]

There was nothing in this tantalizingly brief account to suggest that Shishak's booty had *not* included the Ark of the Covenant. But if the Ark had indeed been captured just thirty years after Solomon had installed it in the Temple then it seemed to me that the scribes would have said so – and would in addition have lamented the loss of the precious relic. They had not even mentioned it, however[50] – which to my mind implied one of two things: *either* the Ark had been secretly removed before the arrival of the Egyptian army (perhaps during the reign of Solomon himself as Ethiopian tradition insisted); *or* it had remained *in situ* in the Holy of Holies throughout the invasion. But the notion that the Pharaoh could have taken it looked most implausible.

A further indication that this was so had been left by Shishak himself in the form of his vast triumphal relief at Karnak. I had already become quite familiar with that relief during my various visits to Egypt and I felt sure that it had made no mention of the Ark of the Covenant or, for that matter, of any siege or pillage of

Jerusalem.[51] On checking further I was now able to confirm that this impression had been correct. One authoritative study stated unequivocally that the majority of the towns and cities listed as having been sacked by Shishak had in fact been in the northern part of Israel:

> Jerusalem, target of Shishak's campaign according to the Bible, is missing. Although the inscription is heavily damaged, it is certain that Jerusalem was not included because the list is arranged into geographical sequences which allow no space for the name Jerusalem.[52]

What then could have happened at the holy city to explain the Scriptural assertion that Shishak had taken away 'the treasures of the house of the Lord, and the treasures of the king's house'?

The academic consensus, I discovered, was that the Pharaoh had surrounded Jerusalem but that he had never actually entered it; instead he had been 'bought off with the treasures of Solomon's temple and palace.'[53] These treasures, moreover, could not possibly have included the Ark, even if it had still been there in 926 BC; instead they would have consisted of far less sacred items, mainly public and royal donations dedicated to Yahweh. Such items, normally quite precious and made of silver and gold, were not stored in the Holy of Holies but rather in the outer precincts of the Temple in special treasuries that were always mentioned in the Old Testament conjointly with the treasuries of the king's house.[54] 'Occasionally,' as one leading biblical scholar put it,

> these treasuries were depleted either by foreign invaders or by the kings themselves when they were in need of funds. The treasuries thus constantly oscillated between a state of affluence and want . . . The invasion of Shishak [had], therefore, nothing to do with the Temple sanctums, and it would be entirely inaccurate to associate [it] with the disappearance of the Ark.[55]

Precisely the same caution, I discovered, also applied to the next occasion on which the Temple had apparently been looted.

This had happened at a time when the unified state that David and Solomon had forged had been split into two warring kingdoms – 'Judah' in the south (which included Jerusalem) and 'Israel' in the north. In 796 BC[56] Jehoash, the monarch of the northern kingdom, joined battle at Bethshemesh with his Judaean counterpart Amaziah:

> And Judah was put to the worse before Israel, and they fled every man to their tents. And Jehoash king of Israel took Amaziah king of Judah . . . at Bethshemesh, and came to Jerusalem, and brake down the wall of Jerusalem . . . And he took all the gold and silver, and all the vessels that were found in the house of the Lord, and in the treasuries of the king's house.[57]

Once again, this pillage of the Temple had not involved the Holy of Holies or the Ark of the Covenant. As one authority on the period explained:

> Jehoash did not even enter the Temple's outer sanctum, certainly not the inner one . . . The phrase 'the house of the Lord' mentioned in connection with Jehoash . . . is simply a shortened form of 'the treasuries of the house of the Lord'. This may be seen from the fact that the 'treasuries of the king's house' which are always contiguously mentioned with the 'treasuries of the house of the Lord' are also mentioned.[58]

So much then for Shishak and Jehoash. The reason that neither of them had claimed to have taken the Ark, and the reason that neither had been reported by the Bible to have done so, was now quite clear to me: they had got nowhere near the Holy of Holies in which the sacred relic had been kept and had helped themselves only to minor treasures of gold and silver.

The same, however, could not be said for Jerusalem's next and greatest invader, King Nebuchadnezzar of Babylon. He attacked and occupied the holy city not once but twice, and even on the first occasion, in 598 BC,[59] it was clear that he had penetrated deeply into the Temple itself. The Bible described this disaster in the following terms:

> The troops of Nebuchadnezzar king of Babylon marched on Jerusalem, and the city was besieged. Nebuchadnezzar . . . himself came to attack the city while his troops were besieging it. Then Jehoiachin king of Judah surrendered to the king of Babylon, he, his mother, his officers, his nobles and his eunuchs, and the king of Babylon took them prisoner. This was the eighth year of King Nebuchadnezzar. The latter carried off all the treasures of the house of the Lord, and the treasures of the king's house, and cut in pieces all the golden furnishings that Solomon king of Israel had made for the sanctuary of Yahweh.[60]

What had Nebuchadnezzar's booty consisted of? I already knew that the 'treasures of the house of the Lord, and the treasures of the king's house' could not have included any truly sacred objects such as the Ark. As noted above, these phrases had very specific and distinct meanings in the original Hebrew and referred only to dispensable items stored in the royal and priestly treasuries.

More significant by far was the statement that the Babylonian monarch had 'cut in pieces all the golden furnishings that Solomon king of Israel had made for the sanctuary of Yahweh.' The Hebrew word that the translators of the Jerusalem Bible had rendered as 'sanctuary' was, I discovered, *hekal* and its precise meaning was 'outer sanctum'.[61] In trying to envisage its location I found it useful to recall the basic layout of Ethiopian Orthodox churches which – as I had learned on my trip to Gondar in January 1990 – exactly reflected the tripartite division of the Temple of Solomon.[62] By co-ordinating this mental picture with the best scholarly research on the subject I was able to confirm beyond any shadow of a doubt that the *hekal* had corresponded to the *k'eddest* of Ethiopian churches.[63] This meant that the 'sanctuary of Yahweh' despoiled by Nebuchadnezzar had *not* been the Holy of Holies in which the Ark had stood but rather the antechamber to that sacred place. The Holy of Holies itself – the inner sanctum – had been known in ancient Hebrew as the *debir* and corresponded to the *mak'das* in which the *tabotat* were kept in Ethiopian churches.[64]

If the Ark had still been in the Temple at the time of Nebuchadnezzar's first attack, therefore – and that, as it turned out, was a very big if – then it was certain that the Babylonian king had not taken it. Instead he had contented himself with cutting 'in pieces' and carrying off the 'golden furnishings' that Solomon had placed in the *hekal*.[65] The other 'furnishings' that had been looted by Nebuchadnezzar – and the list was quite specific – were as follows:

> the lamp-stands, five on the right and five on the left in front of the *debir*, of pure gold; the floral work, the lamps, the extinguishers of gold; the basins, knives, sprinkling bowls, incense boats, censers, of pure gold; the door sockets for the inner shrine – that is, the Holy of Holies – and for the *hekal*, of gold.[66]

Of course, in this translation, the terms 'inner shrine', '*debir*' and 'Holy of Holies' were all used interchangeably to refer to the same sacred place – i.e. the place in which the Ark had been installed by Solomon so many centuries before.[67] Once I had satisfied myself that that was indeed the case, a single significant fact suddenly became clear to me: while not looting the Holy of Holies, Nebuchadnezzar had nonetheless removed its door-sockets. From this it was safe to deduce that the doors had been taken off their hinges and that the Babylonian monarch – or the soldiers who had carried out his orders – would thus have been able to look right into the *debir*.

I realized immediately that this was an important, indeed a crucial, finding. Gazing into the inner sanctum the Babylonians should immediately have been able to see the two giant cherubim, overlaid with gold, that Solomon had placed as sentinels over the Ark – and they should also have been able to see the Ark itself. Since they had shown no compunction in removing the gold from the furnishings of the *hekal* it therefore had to be asked why they had not immediately rushed into the *debir* to strip the far larger quantities of gold from its walls and from the cherubim, and why they had not taken the Ark as booty.

The Babylonians had demonstrated that they held the Jews – and their religion – in complete contempt.[68] There was thus no mileage in assuming that they might have refrained from looting the Holy of Holies out of some sort of altruistic desire to spare the feelings of the vanquished. On the contrary all the evidence suggested that if they had indeed been confronted by rich pickings like the Ark, and the gold overlay on the walls and on the cherubim, then Nebuchadnezzar and his men would unhesitatingly have helped themselves to the lot.

What made this even more probable was that it had been the normal practice of the Babylonians at this time to seize the principal idols or cult-objects of the peoples they had conquered and to transport them back to Babylon to place in their own temple before the statue of their god Marduk.[69] The Ark would have been an ideal candidate for this sort of treatment. Yet it had not even been stripped of its gold, let alone carried off intact. Indeed neither it nor the cherubim had been mentioned at all.

> The logical conclusion [I wrote in my notebook] is that the Ark and the gold-covered cherubim were no longer in the *debir* in 598 BC when the first Babylonian invasion took place – and, indeed, that the walls, floor and ceiling of the *debir* had also been stripped of their gold prior to that date. This would seem to lend at least *prima facie* support to the Ethiopian claim – since I have already established that Shishak and Jehoash did not get their hands on the Ark, or on the other precious contents of the *debir*, and since they were the only previous invaders to have acquired any sort of treasure from the Temple.

Of course the Babylonian assault on Jerusalem in 598 BC had not been the last that Nebuchadnezzar would mount – and the conclusion that I had just scribbled in my notebook would be proved completely false if there were any evidence to suggest that he had taken the Ark the *second* time that he sacked the holy city.

After the successful operation of 598 BC he had installed a puppet king, Zedekiah, on the throne.[70] This 'puppet', however, turned out to have ideas of his own and, in 589 BC, he rebelled against his Babylonian overlord.[71]

The response was instantaneous. Nebuchadnezzar marched on Jerusalem once again and laid siege to it, finally breaching its walls and overrunning it in late June or early July of the year 587 BC.[72] Slightly less than a month later:[73]

> Nebuzaradan, commander of the guard, an officer of the king of Babylon . . . burned down the Temple of Yahweh, the royal palace and all the houses in Jerusalem. The . . . troops who accompanied the commander of the guard . . . broke up the bronze pillars from the Temple of Yahweh, the wheeled stands and the bronze Sea that were in the Temple of Yahweh, and took the bronze away to Babylon. They took the ash containers, the scoops, the knives, the incense boats, and all the bronze furnishings used in worship. The commander of the guard took the censers and the sprinkling bowls, everything that was made of gold and everything made of silver. As regards the two pillars, the one Sea and the wheeled stands . . . there was no reckoning the weight in bronze in all these objects.[74]

This, then, was the detailed inventory offered in the Bible of all the objects and treasures broken up or carried off to Babylon after Nebuchadnezzar's second attack on the city. Once again, and significantly, the Ark of the Covenant was not included – and nor was the gold that Solomon had used to line the Holy of Holies and to overlay the great cherubim that had stood within that sacred place. Indeed absolutely nothing else was mentioned at all and it was clear that the bulk of the loot taken in 587 BC had consisted of bronze salvaged from the pillars and the 'Sea' – and also from the wheeled basins – that Hiram had made four centuries earlier.

A fact that argued very strongly in favour of the basic veracity of the list was that it was entirely consistent with the biblical account of what had previously been stolen from the Temple in 598 BC. On that occasion Nebuchadnezzar had left the bronze items in place but had removed the 'treasures of the house of the Lord, and the treasures of the king's house' and had also stripped off all the gold from the furnishings of the *hekal*. This was why, eleven years later, Nebuzaradan's haul of gold and silver had consisted only of a few censers and sprinkling bowls:[75] he had not been able to find anything more valuable for the simple reason that all the best items had been looted and taken to Babylon in 598 BC.

Since I had already satisfied myself that those items had not included the Ark, and since the relic had not been amongst the second lot of booty either, I felt increasing confidence in my conclusion that it must have disappeared at some stage *prior* to the Babylonian invasions. By the same token the other oft-cited explanation for the loss of the relic – namely that it must have been destroyed in the great fire that Nebuzaradan had started[76] – also looked increasingly untenable. If the Ark had indeed been taken away before 598 BC – perhaps to Ethiopia – then it would of course have escaped the destruction of the Temple.

But was it safe, from this chain of reasoning, to deduce that it *had* gone to Ethiopia? Certainly not. Researching the matter further I found that Judaic traditions offered several alternative explanations for what had happened – any of which, if sufficiently strong, might prove fatal to the Ethiopian case and all of which therefore had to be considered on their merits.

'Deep and tortuous caches . . .'

The first point that became clear to me was that the Jews as a people had only become conscious of the loss of the Ark – and conscious that this loss was a great mystery – at the time of the building of the Second Temple.

I was already aware that in 598 BC Nebuchadnezzar had sent into exile in Babylon a large number of the inhabitants of Jerusalem.[77] In 587 BC, after the burning of Solomon's Temple,

> Nebuzaradan, commander of the guard, deported the
> remainder of the population left behind in the city, the
> deserters who had gone over to the king of Babylon, and
> the rest of the common people . . . Thus Judah was
> deported from this land.[78]

The trauma of the banishment, the humiliations of the captivity, and the firm resolve that Jerusalem should never be forgotten, were soon to be immortalized in one of the most poignant and evocative pieces of poetry in the whole of the Old Testament:

> By the rivers of Babylon, there we sat down, yea, we wept, when we remembered Zion.
>
> We hanged our harps upon the willows in the midst thereof,
>
> For there they that carried us away captive required of us a song; and they that wasted us required of us mirth, saying, Sing us one of the songs of Zion.
>
> How shall we sing the Lord's song in a strange land?
>
> If I forget thee, O Jerusalem, let my right hand forget her cunning.
>
> If I do not remember thee, let my tongue cleave to the roof of my mouth; if I prefer not Jerusalem above my chief joy.[79]

This physical exile of an entire people was not to last for very long. Nebuchadnezzar had begun the process in 598 BC and had completed it in 587. Slightly less than half a century later, however, the empire that had expanded so dramatically under his rule was utterly crushed by Cyrus the Great, king of Persia, whose triumphant armies entered Babylon in 539 BC.[80]

This Cyrus, who has been described as 'one of the world's most astonishing empire-builders',[81] adopted an enlightened approach towards his subject peoples. There were others, like the Jews, who had also been held captive in Babylon. He made it his business to set them all free. Moreover, he permitted them to remove their confiscated idols and cult objects from the temple of Marduk and to carry these home with them.[82]

The Jews, of course, were unable to take full advantage of this latter opportunity, because their principal cult object, the Ark of the Covenant, had not been brought to Babylon in the first place. Nevertheless a large number of the lesser treasures that

Nebuchadnezzar had seized were still intact, and these the Persians handed over with all due ceremony to the appropriate Judaean officials. The Old Testament contained a detailed report of the transaction:

> King Cyrus took the vessels of the Temple of Yahweh which Nebuchadnezzar had carried away from Jerusalem and dedicated to the temple of his god. Cyrus king of Persia handed them over to Mithredath, the treasurer, who counted them out to Sheshbazzar, the prince of Judah. The inventory was as follows: thirty golden bowls for offerings; one thousand and twenty-nine silver bowls for offerings; thirty golden bowls; four hundred and ten silver bowls; one thousand other vessels. In all, five thousand four hundred vessels of gold and silver. Sheshbazzar took all these with him when the exiles travelled back from Babylon to Jerusalem.[83]

That return journey took place in 538 BC.[84] Then, in the spring of 537 BC, the Second Temple began to be built above the razed foundations of the First.[85] The work was finally completed around 517 BC,[86] and although this was a cause for great rejoicing there were also reasons for sorrow. The removal of the Ark of the Covenant from the First Temple – whenever it had occurred – had clearly been kept secret from the public (not a difficult task since no one but the High Priest was supposed to enter the Holy of Holies). Now, however, after the return from Babylon, it was impossible to disguise the fact that the precious relic had gone, and that it therefore could not be installed in the inner sanctum of the Second Temple. This great change was explicitly admitted in the Talmud, which stated: 'In five things the First Sanctuary differed from the Second: in the Ark, the Ark-cover, the Cherubim, the Fire, and the Urim-and-Thummim.'[87] The Urim and Thummim had been mysterious objects (here referred to collectively as a single object) that had possibly been used for divining and that had been kept in the breast-plate of the High Priest in the time of Moses. They were not present in the Second Temple. Neither was the celestial fire that had always been associated with the Ark of the Covenant.

And of course the Ark itself was also missing – together with its thick golden cover and the two golden cherubim that had been mounted upon it.[88]

The secret, therefore, was out: the most precious relic of the Jewish faith had vanished, apparently into thin air. Moreover the people knew that it had not been brought into captivity with them in Babylon. So where could it possibly have gone?

Almost at once theories started to circulate and, in the normal way of things, some of these theories quickly took on the character of revealed truths. The majority supposed that Nebuchadnezzar's looters had failed to find the Ark because, before their arrival, it had been carefully hidden somewhere within Mount Moriah itself, where the Second Temple now stood on the site previously occupied by the First. According to one post-exilic legend, for example, Solomon had foreseen the destruction of his Temple even while he was building it. For this reason he had 'contrived a place of concealment for the Ark, in deep and tortuous caches'.[89]

It was this tradition, I felt sure, that must have inspired the author of the Apocalypse of Baruch to suggest that the relic had been swallowed by the earth below the great 'foundation stone' known as the *Shetiyyah*. I knew, of course that no reliance could be placed on that relatively late and apocryphal work. Nevertheless I was aware that other accounts existed which likewise identified some secret cavern within the Temple Mount as the last resting place of the Ark.

Reinforcing the notion that that cavern might have been located directly beneath the Holy of Holies, the Talmud expressed the view that 'the Ark was buried in its own place.'[90] And this entombment, it seemed, had been the work of King Josiah, who had ruled in Jerusalem from 640 to 609 BC,[91] i.e. until just a decade before the first Babylonian seizure of the city. Near the end of his long reign, the story went, foreseeing 'the imminent destruction of the Temple', 'Josiah hid the Holy Ark and all its appurtenances, in order to guard them against desecration at the hands of the enemy.'[92]

This, I found, was quite a pervasive belief. Not all the sources, however, agreed that the place of concealment had been in the immediate vicinity of the Holy of Holies. Another parallel tradition, recorded in the Mishnah, suggested that the relic had been buried 'under the pavement of the wood-house, that it might not fall into the hands of the enemy.'[93] This wood-house had stood within the precincts of Solomon's Temple, but its precise location had been forgotten by the time that the Jews returned from their exile in Babylon and thus 'remained secret for all time'.[94] Nevertheless the Mishnah reported that a priest had once been working in the courtyard of the Second Temple and there, by accident, he had stumbled upon 'a block of pavement that was different from the rest':

> He went and told it to his fellow, but before he could
> make an end of the matter his life departed. So they knew
> assuredly that there the Ark lay hidden.[95]

An entirely separate account of the concealment of the relic was put forward in the second book of Maccabees (a work excluded from the Hebrew Bible, but included in the canon of the Greek and Latin Christian churches, and in the Apocrypha of the English Bible[96]). Compiled at some time between 100 BC and AD 70 by a Jew of Pharisaic sympathies (who wrote in Greek),[97] the opening verses of 2 Maccabees 2 had this to say about the fate of the Ark:

> The prophet Jeremiah . . . warned by an oracle [of the
> impending destruction of the Temple of Solomon], gave
> instructions for the tabernacle and the Ark to go with him
> when he set out for the mountain which Moses had
> climbed to survey God's heritage. On his arrival Jeremiah
> found a cave dwelling, into which he brought the
> tabernacle, the Ark and the altar of incense, afterwards
> blocking up the entrance.[98]

In the opinion of the scholars who produced the authoritative English translation of the Jerusalem Bible – from which the above quotation is taken – Jeremiah's supposed expedition to hide the Ark was nothing more than an inspirational fable devised by the author of the second book of Maccabees as part of a deliberate attempt to re-awaken the interest of expatriate Jews in the national homeland.[99] The editors of the *Oxford Dictionary of the Christian Church* likewise regarded the passage as being of no historical value.[100] And since it was written some five hundred years after the death of Jeremiah himself it could not even be said to be a particularly ancient tradition[101] – although its author had attempted to dress it up as such by claiming that he had based his account on a document found in 'the archives'.[102]

It was a fact, however, that the prophet Jeremiah (unlike the author of Maccabees) *had* lived at around the time of the destruction of Solomon's Temple – which meant that he could, just conceivably, have played some role in the concealment of the Ark. Moreover 'the mountain which Moses had climbed to survey God's heritage' – Mount Nebo[103] – was a known place that stood barely fifty kilometres to the east of Jerusalem as the crow flies.[104] Culturally appropriate because of its associations with the founder of Judaism, this venerated peak thus also looked like a feasible hiding place in terms of its geographical location.

The Maccabees story had therefore not been entirely dismissed by later generations of Jews; on the contrary, although never incorporated into the Jewish canon of Scripture, it had been substantially elaborated upon and embellished in the folklore – where, for example, the knotty problem of exactly how Jeremiah (who had been very much at odds with the priestly fraternity in the Temple[105]) had managed to get the sacred items out of the Holy of Holies and across the Jordan valley to Nebo was solved by providing him with an angel for a helper![106]

After looking back through all the Jewish traditions that I had surveyed concerning the last resting place of the Ark, I entered the following summary in my notebook:

Outside of the Talmud, the Mishnah, the Apocalypse of Baruch, the second book of Maccabees, and various rather colourful legends, there is nothing of any substance in Jewish tradition concerning the whereabouts of the Ark of the Covenant. Since it now seems certain that it was not looted by Shishak or Jehoash or Nebuchadnezzar, it therefore follows that the only alternatives to the claim that it is in Axum are (a) very sketchy, (b) historically dubious, and (c) lacking in any current vitality (by contrast

religious feeling in Ethiopia continues to be massively
focussed upon the belief that the relic is indeed there).

All this makes the Ethiopian case look more and more
credible. Nevertheless the Jewish 'alternatives' cannot be
dismissed out of hand simply because they seem to be a bit
flimsy.

ACTION: find out whether any archaeologists have
excavated at Mount Nebo, or in and around the Temple
Mount – which are the only two locations proposed by the
Jews as the last resting place of the Ark.

I wrote that note in my hotel room in Jerusalem on the night of
Saturday 6 October 1990. Two days later, on the morning of
Monday 8 October, I attempted to go back to take a second look
at the Temple Mount, and to visit some excavations that I knew
were in progress just outside the sacred precincts, perhaps a
hundred metres to the south of the Al-Aqsa Mosque. As I
approached, however – walking along the city wall from David's
Tower to the Dung Gate – the sound of gunfire and of people
screaming forewarned me that something had gone seriously
wrong.

Death on the Mount

What I had walked into subsequently came to be known as the
'Temple Mount massacre', and although it represented the
coming to a head of years of hatred between the Jews and the
Arabs of Jerusalem, its proximate cause was a demonstration by
an ultra-conservative Zionist group known as the 'Temple
Mount Faithful'. The large banner that they carried as they
marched up to the Moghrabi Gate bore a Star of David and a
provocative inscription in Hebrew which summarized the key
issue for all concerned. That inscription read:

TEMPLE MOUNT – THE SYMBOL OF OUR
PEOPLE IS IN THE
HANDS OF OUR ENEMIES

What the demonstrators hoped to do was to enter the Temple

Mount itself through the Moghrabi Gate, march up to the Dome
of the Rock, and there lay the cornerstone for a proposed Third
Temple. This ambition, obviously, was packed with political
dynamite: since work began on the construction of the Dome of
the Rock in the seventh century AD, the whole of the Temple
Mount area had been a sacred site of immense importance to
Islam as well as to Judaism. Moreover, much to the chagrin of
groups like the 'Temple Mount Faithful', it is the Muslims who
are in possession of that site – which has contained no Jewish
place of worship since the destruction of the Second Temple by
the Romans in AD 70. Wishing to defend this *status quo* – against
what must have looked to them like a genuine threat – an
estimated five thousand militant Arabs had gathered inside the
walls of the Temple Mount and had armed themselves with
stones which they planned to hurl down at the approaching
Zionists.

The atmosphere was thus highly charged with emotion when
the Temple Mount Faithful began their march on Monday 8
October. And what added enormously to the tension was the
location of the Moghrabi Gate through which they intended to
pass. Opening out into the main compound less than fifty metres
from the front porch of the Al-Aqsa Mosque, this gate is built into
the southern end of the Western Wall – the exposed exterior of
which, known as the 'Wailing Wall', is today the single most
important Jewish holy place. Dating back to Second Temple
times, it is part of a retaining buttress built by Herod the Great in
the late first century BC. It escaped demolition by the Romans in
AD 70 (because, said the Midrash, the 'Divine Presence' hovered
over it) and, in later years, it became a potent symbol of the
nationalist aspirations of the Jewish people scattered during the
diaspora. Even after the formation of the State of Israel it
continued to be administered by the Hashemite Kingdom of
Jordan and it was not until the Six Day War of 1967 that it was
finally incorporated into Israel proper. A large plaza was then
cleared in front of it and dedicated as a formal place of worship –
where, to this day, Jews from all over the world gather to lament
the fact that they have no Temple. To avoid a potentially
catastrophic confrontation with Islam, however, Jewish worship
in any form continues to be banned on the Temple Mount itself,

which remains under the exclusive control of the Muslims of Jerusalem and which directly overlooks the Wailing Wall.[107]

By choosing to try to enter the Temple Mount through the Moghrabi Gate, therefore, the Temple Mount Faithful were asking for trouble. Access was in fact denied to them by the Israeli police but, as they turned away, the five thousand Arabs who had gathered inside began to rain down showers of stones – not only on the heads of the zealots who had participated in the march but also on the large numbers of other Jews then making their devotions at the Wailing Wall. In this way something that had started life as an apparently symbolic demonstration was very rapidly transformed into a full-scale riot in which eleven Israeli worshippers and eight policemen were hurt, and in which twenty-one Arabs were shot dead and one hundred and twenty-five seriously injured.

By the time I arrived on the scene the worst of it was over: piles of stones lay amongst pools of blood at the base of the Wailing Wall; the wounded were being ferried away in ambulances; and the police – dressed in riot gear and armed to the teeth – appeared to be in full control. The Temple Mount itself, having just been stormed by the security forces, was off-limits. So too was the area of excavations immediately to the south that I had intended to visit. Hundreds of angry and excited Jews, a few of them proudly wearing blood-stained bandages, milled around in a decidedly bellicose mood and soon a wild celebration began in front of the Wailing Wall – although exactly why anyone should have rejoiced over the brutal killing of a score of Arab youths was something that I just could not understand.

Disgusted and depressed I eventually left the area, climbing up the steps that led into the Jewish Quarter of the old city and crossing into the Street of the Chain – along which I had walked a few days previously on my first visit to the Temple Mount. Here I saw further gratuitous violence as the police, carrying guns and truncheons, rounded up Palestinians whom they suspected of having been amongst the rioters. One young man, protesting his innocence in a high-pitched and terrified voice, was repeatedly punched and slapped; another ran at break-neck speed into a narrow alley where he was cornered and beaten before being dragged away.

Altogether, it had been a most unpleasant morning and it cast a blight over the rest of my stay in Jerusalem. This was so not only because of the human suffering that current events had now directly linked to the place where the Ark had once stood, but also because the Temple Mount and the excavations to the south of it remained sealed off by the security forces until long after I had left Israel. Despite these inauspicious omens, however, I was determined not to waste any of the few days remaining to me in that unhappy country, and I therefore continued with my investigation as best I could.

Digging up sacred places

The immediate question that I was seeking to answer was the one that I had jotted down in my notebook on the night of Saturday 6 October: had any efforts been made by archaeologists to dig at the Temple Mount, or at Mount Nebo, in order to test the Jewish traditions about the last resting place of the Ark?

I began with the excavations that I had tried unsuccessfully to visit on the morning of 8 October. Though I could not now gain access to them, I was able to meet with some of the archaeologists involved in them and to research their findings. What I learned was that proper digging had started here in February 1968 – some eight months after Israeli paratroopers had seized control of Jerusalem in the Six Day War. And although all the excavations were safely outside the sacred precincts of the Temple Mount they had been a focus of controversy from the very beginning. According to Meir Ben-Dov, Field Director of the dig, early opposition came from members of the Higher Muslim Council, who suspected a plot against their interests. 'The excavations are not in fact a scientific venture,' they complained, 'their Zionist objective is rather to undermine the southern wall of the Temple Mount, which is likewise the southern wall of the Al-Aqsa Mosque, as a way of destroying the mosque.'[108]

To Ben-Dov's surprise, Christians were at first almost equally unhelpful. 'They suspected', he explained, 'that the purpose of the excavation was to lay the groundwork for building the Third Temple and the whole business about an archaeological venture was just a cover for an invidious plot. All I can say is that until you actually hear these rumours with your own ears, they sound like the product of a demonic imagination. Yet more than once – whether in jest or otherwise – people whose exceptional intelligence and abilities as historians and archaeologists are beyond question have come straight out and asked me: "Don't you intend to reinstitute the Temple?" '[109]

The strongest opposition of all came from the Jewish religious authorities – whose agreement to the dig was required by the government before any work could begin. Professor Mazar of the Archaeological Institute of the Hebrew University led the negotiations with the Sephardi and Ashkenazi Chief Rabbis – both of whom turned him down flat when he first approached them in 1967:

> The Sephardi Chief Rabbi, Rabbi Nissim, explained his refusal by the fact that the area of our proposed dig was a holy place. When asked to elucidate his answer further, he intimated that we might prove that the Wailing Wall was not in fact the western wall of the Temple Mount. Besides, what point was there in taking the chance and conducting a dig for scientific purposes when they were irrelevant anyway? On the other hand the Ashkenazi Chief Rabbi, Rabbi Unterman, agonized over *halakhic* problems (questions of Jewish law). 'What will happen,' he mused aloud, 'if, as a result of the archaeological excavation, you find the Ark of the Covenant, which Jewish tradition says is buried in the depths of the earth?' 'That would be wonderful!' Professor Mazar replied in all innocence. But the venerable Rabbi told the learned Professor that *that* was precisely what he feared. Since the Children of Israel are not 'pure' from the viewpoint of Jewish religious law, they are forbidden to touch the Ark of the Covenant. Hence it is unthinkable to even consider excavating until the Messiah comes![110]

The rabbi's concern about the Ark was entirely orthodox. All Jews have indeed been considered to be in a condition of ritual impurity since the destruction of the Second Temple – a condition that is only supposed to end with the coming of the true Messiah.[111] Dogma of this sort thus represented a considerable obstacle in the path of the archaeologists. Nevertheless they managed in due course to win the rabbis over – and also to overcome the objections of the representatives of the other two monotheistic faiths descended from the Old Testament worship of Yahweh. The dig went ahead. Moreover, despite the location of the site *outside* the Temple Mount, a number of artefacts from the days of the First Temple were recovered. Predictably, though, no trace of the Ark of the Covenant was found, and the vast bulk of the discoveries proved to be from the later Second Temple, Muslim and Crusader periods.[112]

In summary, therefore, I could see that Meir Ben-Dov's excavations had certainly *not* vindicated the Jewish traditions about the concealment of the Ark. But neither had they conclusively disproved those traditions. Only one thing could do that, and that would be a thorough and painstaking dig on the Temple Mount itself.

My own feeling, as the reader will recall, was that such a dig *had* been carried out by the Knights Templar long centuries before the discipline of archaeology was ever invented, and that they, too, had failed to find the Ark. Nevertheless I still needed to know whether any excavations had been undertaken in modern times, and if so what had been found. I put these questions to Dr Gabby Barkai, an archaeologist at Jerusalem's Hebrew University who specializes in the First Temple period.

'Since modern archaeology emerged,' he told me bluntly, 'no effort has been made to dig inside the Temple Mount.'

'Why?' I asked.

'Because it's the ultimate sacred site. The Muslim authorities are utterly opposed to any kind of scientific investigations being undertaken there. It would be the worst kind of sacrilege from their point of view. So the Temple Mount remains a riddle for archaeology. Most of what we know about it is theoretical and interpretive. Archaeologically we only have the findings of Charles Warren. And Parker of course. He actually did dig inside the Dome of the Rock – in 1910 if I remember correctly. But he wasn't an archaeologist. He was a lunatic. He was looking for the Ark of the Covenant.'

I was not sure from this statement whether Barkai had described Parker as a 'lunatic' because he had looked for the Ark; or whether he had looked for the Ark because he had been a lunatic; or whether his lunacy had been manifestly apparent before he had started to dig inside the Dome of the Rock. This, however, seemed like an excellent opportunity to refrain from mentioning that I, too, was looking for the Ark. I therefore confined myself to asking the archaeologist where I might find out more about Parker – and about Charles Warren, the other name he had mentioned.

A couple of days of archive research followed, during which I learned that Warren had been a young lieutenant in Britain's Royal Engineers who had been commissioned by the London-based Palestine Exploration Fund to excavate the Temple Mount in the year 1867. His work, however, had been confined to much the same areas – outside and to the south of the sacred precincts – that were to be more thoroughly investigated a century later by Meir Ben-Dov and his colleagues.[113]

The difference was that Warren had very actively sought permission to excavate *inside* the Temple Mount as well. But all his efforts had been rebuffed by the Ottoman Turks who then administered Jerusalem. Moreover, on the one occasion when he had managed to cut a tunnel northwards and to burrow under the exterior walls, the sledgehammers and other tools used by his labourers had disturbed the prayers of the faithful going on above them in the Al-Aqsa Mosque. The result had been a hail of stones, a riot, and orders from Izzet Pasha, the governor of the city, that the dig should be suspended forthwith.[114]

Despite such difficulties, Warren had refused to be discouraged and had persuaded the Ottomans to let him go back to work again. He had subsequently made several other clandestine attempts to tunnel beneath the Temple Mount, where he had planned to 'locate and map all the ancient remains' that he might encounter.[115] But he was unable to realize this ambition and reached only the foundations of the exterior walls.[116] Of course he did not find the Ark of the Covenant – there was no evidence that it had ever been his intention to look for it anyway. His chief interest had been in the Second Temple period and in this context he did make many discoveries of lasting value to scholarship.[117]

The same could not be said for Montague Brownslow Parker, a son of the Earl of Morley, who had gone to Jerusalem in 1909 with the express intention of locating the Ark – and who had made no contribution to scholarship whatsoever.

Parker's expedition, later politely described by the renowned British archaeologist Kathleen Kenyon as 'exceptional by any standards',[118] was the brainchild of a Finnish mystic named Valter H. Juvelius, who in 1906 had presented a paper at a Swedish university on the subject of the destruction of King Solomon's Temple by the Babylonians. Juvelius claimed to have acquired reliable information about the hiding place – inside the Temple precincts – of 'the gold-encrusted Ark of the Covenant', and he also said that a close study that he had made of the relevant biblical texts had revealed the existence of a secret underground passage running into the Temple Mount from some part of the city of Jerusalem. After poring over the reports of Charles Warren's excavations, he had convinced himself that this secret passage would be found to the south of the Al-Aqsa Mosque, in the area that Warren had already dug. Proffering the lure of the US $200 million that he believed the Ark would be worth if it could be recovered, Juvelius therefore sought investors to finance an expedition which would locate and clear that passage in order to gain access to the treasure.[119]

His fund-raising efforts were not crowned with success until, in London, he encountered Montague Brownslow Parker, then aged thirty, and won his support for the venture. Milking his contacts in the British aristocracy and abroad, including members of Chicago's wealthy Armour family, Parker very quickly managed to raise the useful sum of $125,000. The expedition accordingly went ahead and, by August 1909, had established its headquarters on the Mount of Olives (which directly overlooks the Temple Mount).

Digging began immediately on the site that Warren had previously so painstakingly explored. Moreover Parker and Juvelius were not deterred by the fact that their illustrious predecessor had found nothing of enormous significance; on the contrary they proceeded with optimism – since they had by now hired an Irish clairvoyant to assist them in their search for the supposed 'secret tunnel'.

Time passed. There were the predictable protests from the faithful of all religious persuasions. And, as winter came, the weather turned foul, flooding the excavations with rivers of mud. Understandably, Parker was discouraged. He called a temporary halt and did not resume the dig again until the summer of 1910. Several months of frenetic activity then followed. The secret tunnel, however, still obstinately refused to reveal itself and, in the meantime, opposition to the whole project had grown decidedly more pronounced. By the spring of 1911 Baron Edmond de Rothschild, a Zionist and a member of the famous international banking family, had made it his personal mission to prevent the potential desecration of the holiest site of Judaism, and to this end had purchased a plot of land adjoining the excavations from which he could directly threaten Parker.

The young British aristocrat was rattled by this development. In April of 1911, therefore, he abandoned the search for the tunnel and resorted to more desperate means. Jerusalem was then still under the control of the Ottoman Turks and the governor of the city, Amzey Bey Pasha, was not a man known for his scrupulous honesty. A bribe of $25,000 secured his co-operation, and an additional though smaller sum persuaded Sheikh Khalil – the hereditary guardian of the Dome of the Rock – to admit Parker and his team to the sacred site and to turn a blind eye to whatever they did there.

The work, for obvious reasons, was carried out at dead of night. Disguised as Arabs, the treasure hunters spent a week excavating the southern part of the Temple Mount close to the Al-Aqsa Mosque – where Juvelius and the Irish clairvoyant both believed that the Ark had been buried. These efforts proved entirely fruitless, however, and in the small hours of the morning of 18 April 1911 Parker switched his attentions to the Dome of the Rock, and to the legendary caverns supposed to lie far below the *Shetiyyah*.

In those days the staircase leading down to the 'Well of Souls' had not yet been installed and Parker and his team had to lower themselves and their equipment by means of ropes fastened to the *Shetiyyah* itself. They then lit storm lanterns and began to hack away at the floor of the grotto in the hope that they might thus gain access to the lasting resting place of the Ark.

Disaster struck before they had even begun to establish whether other hollows lay beneath them. Though Sheikh Khalil, the hereditary guardian, had been bought off, another mosque attendant unexpectedly appeared (the story goes that he had decided to sleep on the Temple Mount because his own home was full of guests). Hearing the sound of digging from the Dome of the Rock he burst in, peered down into the Well of Souls and, to his horror, saw a number of wild-eyed foreigners attacking the holy ground with picks and shovels.

The reaction, on both sides, was dramatic. The shocked mosque attendant uttered a piercing howl and fled screaming into the night to rally the faithful. The Englishmen, wisely realizing that the game was up, also beat a hasty retreat. Not even bothering to return to their base camp, they left Jerusalem at once and made for the port of Jaffa – where, conveniently, a motor-yacht that they had chartered lay moored in the harbour. In this way they managed to cheat the hysterical mob that arrived at the Temple Mount only moments after their departure and that carried off the unfortunate Sheikh Khalil to an unspeakable fate.

Before morning there were full-scale riots in Jerusalem and Amzey Bey Pasha – who was rightly suspected of complicity – had been assaulted and insulted. His response was to close the Temple Mount and to issue orders that the treasure hunters should be apprehended on their arrival at Jaffa. No doubt he took this latter step in part to assuage his guilty conscience. However, rumours had spread that Parker had found and abducted the Ark of the Covenant, and Muslim and Jewish leaders were vociferous in their demands that the sacred relic must not be allowed to leave the country.

Alerted by telegraph, the Jaffa police and customs authorities arrested the fugitives, impounded all their belongings and made an extremely thorough search. They found nothing. Somewhat nonplussed by this they then locked the baggage up but allowed the Englishmen to row out to their yacht, in the salubrious surroundings of which, it had been agreed, the interrogation would continue. As soon as he and his colleagues were safely on board, however, Parker ordered the crew to weigh anchor.

A few weeks later he was back in England. He had failed to find the lost Ark, but he had succeeded in losing the entire $125,000 with which investors in the United States and Britain had entrusted him.[120] 'The whole episode, and excavations,' Kathleen Kenyon concluded many years later, 'did not redound to the credit of British archaeology.'[121]

British archaeologists, however, were not involved in the next attempt to find the Ark, which took place in the 1920s and which focussed on Mount Nebo where, according to the book of Maccabees, the prophet Jeremiah had concealed the sacred relic just before the destruction of Solomon's Temple.

The prime mover on this occasion was an eccentric American explorer who liked to dress up in flowing Arab robes and who, though male, went by the curious name of Antonia Frederick Futterer. After thoroughly surveying Mount Nebo (and also its neighbouring peak Mount Pisgah) he claimed – with truly awe-inspiring originality – to have found . . . a secret passage. This passage was blocked by a wall of some sort and Futterer did not attempt to break it down. When he examined it by flashlight, however, he discovered . . . an ancient inscription, which he faithfully copied and carried back to Jerusalem. There he made contact with a 'scholar' at the Hebrew University who helpfully deciphered the hieroglyphs for him. The message read:

HEREIN LIES THE GOLDEN ARK OF THE COVENANT

Unfortunately Futterer would not name the scholar who had produced this translation; nor, in the furore that followed, did anyone step forward to claim that honour; nor was Futterer subsequently able to produce the copy that he claimed to have made of the inscription; nor did he ever go back to Mount Nebo to retrieve the Ark from its alleged secret passage.[122]

Half a century later, however, a new champion emerged to pick up the baton that Futterer had dropped. That champion, too, was an American explorer, Tom Crotser by name, whose previous 'discoveries' had included the Tower of Babel, Noah's Ark, and the City of Adam. In 1981, by rather circuitous means, this gentleman acquired some papers that Futterer had left, papers which apparently included a sketch of the walled-up secret passage on Mount Nebo where the Ark of the Covenant was supposed to lie buried.[123]

Mount Nebo is located just inside the border of the modern state of Jordan and it was to that country that Crotser now flew, together with a group of zealous colleagues from an organization known as the 'Institute for Restoring History International' (headquarters: Winfield, Kansas).[124] Their mission, of course, was to salvage the Ark. To this end they spent four days sleeping rough on Mount Nebo – much to the consternation of the Franciscans of Terra Santa who own the summit, who guard the Byzantine church that was erected there over the supposed burial place of Moses, and who, for the past several decades, have conducted careful and professional archaeological excavations in the area.[125]

Needless to say, the Franciscans have never found the Ark, and nor did Crotser – at least not on Mount Nebo. After finishing there, however, he and his team moved on to neighbouring Mount Pisgah (which Futterer had also visited). On that peak they stumbled upon a gully which they were confident would give them access to the 'secret passage' identified in Futterer's sketch.

The fact that part of the floor of the gully was blocked by a length of tin sheeting only added to their excitement. On the night of 31 October 1981 they removed this flimsy obstacle and, sure enough, a passage stretched ahead of them. They followed the passage, which they said was about four feet wide and seven feet high, for a distance of some six hundred feet into the bowels of the earth. There they came across a wall exactly like the one that Futterer had described and, without further ado, they broke it down.

Beyond it was a rock-hewn crypt measuring roughly seven feet by seven feet and containing, according to Crotser, a gold-covered rectangular chest measuring sixty-two inches long, thirty-seven inches wide and thirty-seven inches high. Beside it, apparently, were carrying poles exactly matching the biblical description of the carrying poles of the Ark of the Covenant. And off to one side lay cloth-wrapped packages which Crotser assumed to be the cherubim that, in times gone by, had been mounted upon the mercy seat.

The Americans were certain that they had found the sacred relic. They did not remove it; neither did they touch it or open it; using flash-guns, however, they did take colour photographs of it. Then they left Jordan and returned to the USA where they immediately informed the press agency UPI about their discovery. The result was an internationally syndicated news story which, according to the journalist responsible, 'got more play than anything I wrote in my life.'[126]

So, had the Ark really been found? Obviously the photographs taken in the crypt were crucial evidence that might vindicate the sensational claim that the Americans had made – if suitably qualified biblical archaeologists were given the opportunity to study them. It was therefore difficult to understand why Crotser steadfastly refused to release these pictures to anyone. Few were convinced by his argument that God had instructed him to give them only to the London banker David Rothschild who, he said, was a direct descendant of Jesus Christ and had been chosen by the Lord to build the Third Temple – in which the Ark of the Covenant, retrieved from its hiding place, would occupy centre stage.[127]

A member of the same international banking family that had opposed Montague Parker's excavations at the Temple Mount in 1910, Rothschild icily declined to take delivery of the photographs – which Crotser still keeps in his home in Winfield, Kansas, which he still refuses to release, but which he will show to selected visitors.

In 1982, one such visitor was the respected archaeologist Siegfried H. Horn, a specialist on the Mount Nebo area and the author of more than a dozen scholarly books.[128] He spent some time closely examining Crotser's photographs which, unfortunately, seemed to have come out of the development process rather badly:

> All but two showed absolutely nothing. Of the two that registered images, one is fuzzy but does depict a chamber with a yellow box in the centre. The other slide is quite good and gives a clear view of the front of the box.[129]

Immediately after leaving Crotser's house, Horn (who is an

accomplished draughtsman) made a sketch of the box as he had observed it in the slide. Some parts of the yellow metal overlay appeared to him to be brass, not gold, and, moreover, were stamped with a diamond pattern that looked machine-worked. More damning by far, however, was the fact that a nail with a modern style of head could be seen protruding out of the upper right corner of the front of the box.[130] Horn concluded:

> I do not know what the object is but the pictures convinced me that it is not an ancient artefact but of modern fabrication with machine-produced decorative strips and an underlying metal sheet.[131]

From fictions to fact

After working my way steadily through the archaeological records in Jerusalem I was unable to trace any further references to expeditions that had sought to test the Judaic traditions about the last resting place of the Ark of the Covenant. And the scholars whom I talked to confirmed that the field was indeed a limited one: Charles Warren, and later Meir Ben-Dov and his team, had dug in the vicinity of the Temple Mount (though they were not looking for the Ark); Montague Brownslow Parker – not an archaeologist but a 'lunatic', as Gabby Barkai had described him – had dug inside the Temple Mount but had not found anything; Antonia Frederick Futterer had found, but not explored, a secret passage on Mount Nebo which he had believed to contain the Ark; and lastly Tom Crotser claimed to have found the Ark itself in that same passage – which, however, seemed to have migrated from Mount Nebo to Mount Pisgah in the fifty years since Futterer's visit.

And that was it. That, as the saying goes, was the boiling lot – with the sole exception of my own activities. And what was I doing? Well I was looking for the Ark, too, of course – a venture in which, I must confess, I was disconcerted to discover that I had been preceded only by Messianic visionaries and harebrained cranks.

My saving grace, I supposed, was that I had not the slightest interest in the building of the Third Temple and that I did not believe that the Ark had been buried beneath the Dome of the Rock or in Mounts Nebo or Pisgah. I realized that it would be practically impossible to *prove* that those locations concealed no further secrets; but I was now as satisfied as I ever would be that the lost relic had not gone to any of the places indicated in the Judaic traditions, that it had not been taken by the Egyptians or the Babylonians, and that it had not been destroyed either.

Its disappearance, therefore, looked more and more like a genuinely baffling mystery – 'one of the great mysteries of the Bible' as Richard Elliott Friedman, Professor of Hebrew and Comparative Religion at the University of California, had once described it.[132] All my work in 1989 and 1990 had strengthened my conviction that the solution to that mystery must lie in Ethiopia. And yet . . . And yet . . . the one problem that I had not confronted at all, at any stage of my research, was that Ethiopia's claim to possess the Ark seemed to rest on foundations that were every bit as flimsy as the Apocalypse of Baruch or the book of Maccabees.

To put matters plainly, I was beginning to feel that the *Kebra Nagast*'s bold assertions were not sufficiently reliable as a historical witness to justify a trip to the sacred city of Axum – a trip during which I would have to put my own life at risk. The insistence that the Queen of Sheba had been an Ethiopian and the linked pretence that she had borne a son to King Solomon who, in due course, had abducted the Ark from Jerusalem, had more the ring of preposterous fictions than of sober truths. To be sure, I had uncovered a great deal of evidence in Ethiopia – persuasive evidence – which did lend considerable support to the notion that the relic might really lie in the sanctuary chapel in Axum. And now I had satisfied myself that no other location could hope to present a more convincing case. That, however, was less a reflection of the strength of the *Kebra Nagast*'s account of how the Ark had got to Ethiopia than of the weakness of the alternatives.

Before finally committing myself to going to Axum, therefore, I felt that I needed to find a more convincing explanation than that offered in the *Kebra Nagast* of how 'the most important object in the world in the Biblical view'[133] could possibly have ended up in the heart of Africa. By the time that I finally left Jerusalem in mid-October 1990 I had found that explanation – as I shall recount in the next chapter.

Chapter 15

Hidden History

After a painstaking investigation, I had satisfied myself that Ethiopia's claim to be the last resting place of the lost Ark was not challenged by any particularly strong or striking alternative. That finding, however, had not been the only outcome of my research. As I wrote in my notebook:

> No one who has followed the story of the Ark from its construction at the foot of Mount Sinai until the moment of its deposition in Solomon's Temple would seriously dispute that it was an object of immense importance to the Jewish people. And yet the fact is that the Scriptures – so dominated by the presence of the relic *before* Solomon – seem to forget about it entirely *after* him. Its loss is formally recognized at the time of the construction of the Second Temple. The great mystery, however, to quote the words of Professor Richard Friedman, is that: 'There is no report that the Ark was carried away or destroyed . . . There is not even any comment such as "And then the Ark disappeared, and we do not know what happened to it," or "And no one knows where it is to this day." The most important object in the world, in the biblical view, simply ceases to be in the story.'[1]

Reviewing the evidence I had to ask myself: Why should this be? Why should the compilers of the Old Testament have allowed the Ark to vanish from the sacred texts – not with a bang, as one might have expected, but with a whimper?

The *Kebra Nagast*, I knew, did offer a clear answer to exactly this question. In Chapter 62 it described Solomon's grief after he had discovered that his son Menelik had abducted the relic from the Temple and carried it off to Ethiopia. When he had had time to collect his thoughts, however, the king turned to the elders of Israel – who were likewise loudly lamenting the loss of the Ark – and warned them to desist:

> Cease ye, so that the uncircumcised people may not boast themselves over us and may not say unto us, 'Their glory is taken away, and God hath forsaken them.' Reveal ye not anything else to alien folk . . .
>
> And . . . the elders of Israel made answer and said unto him, 'May thy good pleasure be done, and the good pleasure of the Lord God! As for us, none of us will transgress thy word, and we will not inform any other people that the Ark hath been taken away from us.' And they established this covenant in the House of God – the elders of Israel with their King Solomon unto this day.[2]

In other words, if the *Kebra Nagast* was to believed, there had been a massive cover-up. The Ark had been removed to Ethiopia during the lifetime of Solomon himself; all information about this tragic loss had, however, been suppressed, which was why no mention was made of it in the Scriptures.

There was, I thought, much to recommend this argument. It made a great deal of sense to suppose that the Jewish king would indeed have sought to keep from the common herd any knowledge of the loss of the Ark. But at the same time I had serious problems with some other aspects of the *Kebra Nagast* account – notably those concerning the Queen of Sheba's Ethiopian credentials, her alleged love affair with Solomon, the birth of their son Menelik, the notion that the latter had brought the Ark to Ethiopia, and the implication that this had happened in the tenth century BC:

1 There appeared to be no justification for the *Kebra Nagast*'s audacious claim that the Queen of Sheba had been an Ethiopian woman. It was not absolutely *impossible* that she might have been (in his *Antiquities of*

the Jews, for example, Flavius Josephus had described her as 'the queen of Egypt and Ethiopia'[3]). On balance, however, historical research did not suggest that she had started her journey in the Abyssinian highlands when, as the Bible put it, she had travelled to 'Jerusalem with a very great train, with camels that bare spices, and very much gold, and precious stones.'[4]

2 If the evidence linking the Queen of Sheba to Ethiopia was thin, then evidence for the very *existence* of her son Menelik was even thinner. I had known for some time that historians considered the supposed founder of Ethiopia's 'Solomonic' dynasty to be a purely legendary figure – and I had learnt nothing in two years of research to persuade me that they were mistaken about this rather crucial point.

3 In particular it seemed to be inconceivable that an advanced culture and a centralized monarchy of the kind described in the *Kebra Nagast* could have existed in the Abyssinian mountains in the tenth century BC. 'At the time when Solomon was reigning,' as E. A. Wallis Budge had put it, 'the natives of the country which we now call Abyssinia were savages.'[5] This was the orthodox view and my research had uncovered nothing that would enable me to refute it.

4 Even more fatal to any kind of literal acceptance of the *Kebra Nagast* was the evidence that I myself had collected in Ethiopia. Of all the many traditions that I had encountered in that country, by far the purest and most convincing had indicated that the Ark of the Covenant had been brought first of all to Lake Tana, where it had been concealed on the island of Tana Kirkos. Memhir Fisseha, the priest whom I had interviewed there (see Chapter 9), had told me that the relic had remained on the island for eight hundred years before it had finally been taken to Axum at the time of Ethiopia's conversion to Christianity. Since that conversion had occurred around AD 330, the implication of the strong folk memory preserved on Tana Kirkos was that the Ark must have arrived in Ethiopia in 470 BC or thereabouts – in

other words about five hundred years *after* Solomon,
Menelik and the Queen of Sheba.

These, of course, were not the only difficulties that I had with the
account given in the *Kebra Nagast*. Something else that bothered
me greatly, for example, was the practical question of how
Menelik and his companions could possibly have removed so
precious and so *heavy* an object as the Ark from the Temple of
Solomon without attracting the attention of the zealous Levites
who guarded the Holy of Holies.

And I had several other reservations too, all of which, together
with those listed above, had forced me to agree with the academic
experts that the *Kebra Nagast* was indeed a remarkable document
but that it had to be taken with a very large pinch of salt. This,
however, did not make me want to dismiss the great epic entirely.
On the contrary, in common with many other legends, I felt that
there was every possibility that its elaborate fictional superstruc-
ture might have been erected above a solid foundation of
historical truth. In short, while reluctantly rejecting the lovely
idea of the romance between Solomon and Sheba, and the
cheeky suggestion that the Ark had been stolen from the Temple
by their son Menelik, I saw no reason to conclude that the relic
might not have been brought to Ethiopia by some other means,
thus creating an enigma which the *Kebra Nagast* had much later
gone on to explain in its own peculiarly original and colourful
way. Indeed, I was satisfied that the social and cultural evidence
in Ethiopia itself very strongly supported that country's claim to
be the last resting place of the Ark. And, since I now also knew
that no other country or place had a stronger claim, I was more
inclined than ever to believe that the Ark really was there.

Nevertheless, the final pieces of the jigsaw puzzle remained to
be put in place. If the Queen of Sheba had not been Solomon's
lover, and if she had never borne him a son called Menelik as the
legends claimed, then who in fact *had* brought the Ark to
Ethiopia – and when, and under what circumstances?

The lady doth protest too much, methinks . . .

In my attempt to answer these questions I kept at the forefront of my mind the very acceptable notion, put forward in the *Kebra Nagast*, that the removal of the Ark of the Covenant from the Holy of Holies could have been the subject of a cover-up – of a conspiracy of silence involving the priestly elite and the king. But, if not Solomon, then *which* king?

Part of the definition of a 'cover-up', of course, is that it should be difficult to detect. I therefore did not expect that evidence of the sort that I was seeking would be easily extracted from the Old Testament. That great and complex book had guarded its secrets well for more than two thousand years and there was no reason to suppose that it would simply surrender them to me now.

I began by typing up every single mention of the Ark of the Covenant that had ever appeared in the Bible. Even with access to the best scholarship on the subject it was a hard task to track them all down, and when I had finished I had before me a document more than fifty pages long. Strikingly and significantly, only the last page contained references that related to the period after Solomon's death; all the others concerned themselves with the story of the Ark during the wanderings in the wilderness, the conquest of the Promised Land, the reign of King David, and the reign of King Solomon himself.

The Bible, as I was well aware, contains a hotch-potch of material produced by several different schools of scribes over hundreds of years. Many of the references to the Ark, I knew, were very old indeed; but others were relatively late. None of those in the first book of Kings, for example, were codified before the reign of Josiah (640–609 BC).[6] This meant that the account of the Ark's installation in Solomon's Temple in 1 Kings 8, although undoubtedly based on ancient oral and written traditions, had been the work of the priests who had lived long after the event. And exactly the same observation applied to all the relevant references in the book of Deuteronomy, since this, too, was a late document that dated only from the time of King Josiah.[7] Therefore, if the Ark had been secretly removed from the Holy of Holies before the destruction of the Temple in 587 BC, it seemed to me probable that the traces of any cover-up would be found in Kings and in Deuteronomy – if they were to be found anywhere – for in compiling these books the scribes would have had an opportunity to tamper with the facts in order to create the desired impression that 'the glory' had not departed from Israel.

On close examination of the texts I came across a passage in Chapter 8 of the first book of Kings that seemed somehow out of character, that jarred in a curious way with the rest of the description of the great ceremony that had surrounded the deposition of the Ark in the Holy of Holies. That passage read as follows:

> The priests brought in the Ark of the Covenant of the Lord to its place, the inner shrine of the house, the Most Holy Place, beneath the wings of the cherubim. The cherubim spread their wings over the place of the Ark; they formed a screen above the Ark and its poles. The poles projected and their ends could be seen from the Holy Place immediately in front of the inner shrine, but from nowhere else outside; *they are there to this day*.[8]

Why, I wondered, had the biblical scribe responsible for this passage found it necessary to assert that the carrying poles of the Ark could, in his day, still be seen projecting out of the inner shrine? What would have been the point of such a statement unless the relic had in fact *not* been there at the time that these words were written (approximately 610 BC according to the authorities[9])? The oddly defensive tone had, I thought, the ring of one of those emphatic declarations of innocence that guilty parties sometimes make in order to obscure the truth. In short, like the famous lady in Shakespeare's *Hamlet*, the author of 1 Kings 8 had aroused my suspicions by 'protesting too much'.[10]

I was pleased to discover that I was not alone in this intuition. In 1928 the leading biblical scholar Julian Morgenstern had also been struck by the strangeness of the words 'they are there to this day'. His conclusion, in an erudite paper published in the Hebrew Union College Annual, was that the scribe must have intended

> to convince his readers that the staves of the Ark, and therefore, of course, the Ark itself, were present in the innermost part of the Temple, even though they could

not be seen by the people at large, or, for that matter, by
anyone other than the High Priest, when he entered the
Holy of Holies once a year, on Yom Kippur . . . The fact that
[the scribe] seems to have felt compelled to insist in this
manner that the Ark was still present in the Temple in his
day . . . indicates that he must have had to contend with a
prevalent and persistent doubt of this, a doubt founded in all
likelihood upon actual fact.[11]

Nor was this all. The very next verse of the same chapter of the
book of Kings insisted:

There was nothing in the Ark except the two stone tablets
Moses had placed in it . . . the tablets of the covenant
which Yahweh had made with the Israelites when they
came out of the land of Egypt; *they are still there today*.[12]

And the book of Deuteronomy, written at the same time, said
almost exactly the same thing – the tablets of stone were placed in
the Ark by Moses, 'and there they have remained ever since'.[13]

Morgenstern's analysis of these words was that they 'must
have been inserted for some particular purpose'.[14] And, after
referring to the original Hebrew text, he concluded that this
purpose could only have been to provide

a direct and positive affirmation, *almost, it would seem, in
the face of a doubt or question*, that the tablets of the Ten
Commandments were still present in the Ark in the days
. . . of the author of this verse.[15]

Deuteronomy and the first book of Kings had, of course, dealt
with widely different periods of Israelite history. Crucially,
however – and the point is so important that it will bear repetition
– they had both been compiled at the same time. That time, as I
had already established, had been the reign of King Josiah, i.e.
from 640 to 609 BC.

My curiosity aroused, I turned to the typescript in which I had
set down all the biblical references to the Ark. I remembered that
there were very few in the whole of the Old Testament which

related to the period after the death of Solomon. Now I discovered that there were in fact only two: one had been written during Josiah's reign; the other quoted the words of Josiah himself; and both appeared on the last page of my document.

Josiah and Jeremiah

I had already come across Josiah in my research. When I had been investigating the antiquity of the religious customs of the black Jews of Ethiopia I had learned that it had been during his reign that the institution of sacrifice had finally and conclusively been centralized on Jerusalem and banned in all other locations (see Chapter 6). Since the Falashas themselves still practised sacrifice in Ethiopia (having altars in all their villages), I had concluded in my notebook that their ancestors

> must have been converted to Judaism at a time when it was still acceptable for those far away from the centralized national sanctuary to practise local sacrifice. This would suggest that the conversion took place before King Josiah's ban – i.e. no later than the seventh century BC.

My research had moved on into areas that I had not even dreamt of when I had originally written those words in 1989, and now I was confronted by a peculiarly interesting set of circumstances. Sitting in my hotel room in Jerusalem in October 1990 I therefore opened my notebook again and listed the following points:

- In 1 Kings 8 and Deuteronomy there are signs of efforts being made to convince people that the Ark was still in its place in the Temple; this looks like an attempt to cover up the truth – i.e. that the relic was in fact no longer there.
- The relevant passages were written in the time of King Josiah.
- From this I conclude that the Ark may have been removed from the Temple during Josiah's reign; it is more likely

by far, however, that its loss was discovered then but that it had actually occurred somewhat earlier. Why? Because Josiah was a zealous reformer who sought to emphasize the paramount importance of the Temple in Jerusalem – and because the *raison d'être* of the Temple was as 'an house of rest for the Ark of the Covenant of the Lord'. It is virtually inconceivable that such a monarch would have permitted the ultimate symbol of Judaism, the sign and the seal of Yahweh's presence on earth, to be taken out of the Holy of Holies. The logical deduction, therefore, is that the Ark must have been spirited away before Josiah came to power – i.e. before 640 BC.

- The religious customs of the Falashas include local sacrifice, a practice that was only conclusively banned during Josiah's reign. On the basis of this and other data it has been my opinion for some time that the ancestors of the Falashas must have migrated to Ethiopia before 640 BC.
- Surely these matters cannot be unconnected?

The chain of evidence looked convincing: the Ark was removed from the Temple before 640 BC; the ancestors of the Falashas migrated to Ethiopia before 640 BC; was it therefore not reasonable to assure that the ancestors of the Falashas might have taken the Ark with them?

This struck me as a fairly logical hypothesis. It did not, however, establish *when* before 640 BC the supposed migration from Jerusalem had taken place. Neither did it entirely rule out the possibility that the Ark could have been removed during Josiah's reign. Given the known religious integrity and traditionalism of that monarch the latter notion looked like a very long shot indeed. Nevertheless it had to be considered – if only because, as I already knew (see previous chapter), certain Jewish legends had furnished him with a valid motive. In the last years of his reign, those legends said, he had foreseen the destruction of the Temple by the Babylonians and had hidden 'the Holy Ark and all its appurtenances in order to guard them against desecration at the hands of the enemy.'[16] Moreover he was believed – possibly by miraculous means – to have concealed the relic 'in its own place'.[17]

I was now as satisfied as I ever would be that the Ark had not been buried in the Temple Mount – or anywhere else in the Holy Land. Nevertheless I still had to ask myself: was this possible? Could Josiah really have foreseen the fate of the Temple and taken steps to safeguard the Ark?

I looked into this scenario but concluded that, unless the Jewish king had possessed a truly remarkable gift of prescience, there was just no way that he could have predicted the events of 598–587 BC. He died in 609 BC, five years before Nebuchadnezzar – the author of Jerusalem's destruction – inherited the Babylonian throne.[18] Moreover, Nebuchadnezzar's predecessor Nabopolassar had shown little or no military interest in Israel and had concentrated instead on wars with Assyria and Egypt.[19]

The historical background to Josiah's reign therefore did not support the theory that he might have concealed the Ark of the Covenant. More damning by far, however, was the very last mention of the sacred relic in the Old Testament, which cropped up in a passage in the second book of Chronicles – a passage that described Josiah's campaign to restore traditional values to Temple worship:

> Josiah removed all the abominations throughout the
> territories belonging to the sons of Israel . . . And he set
> the priests in their charges, and . . . said unto the Levites
> that taught all Israel, which were holy unto the Lord, '*Put
> the Holy Ark in the house which Solomon the son of David
> king of Israel did build; it shall not be a burden upon your
> shoulders.*'[20]

It was immediately obvious to me that these few short verses, particularly the words emphasized in italics above, were of vital importance to my quest. Why? Quite simply because Josiah would have had no need to ask the Levites to put the Ark in the Temple if it had already been there. Two inescapable conclusions emerged from this: (1) The king himself could not have been responsible for the removal of the relic because he plainly thought that it had been taken by its traditional bearers, the Levites; and (2) the date of the Ark's disappearance from the Temple could now be fixed to some time before Josiah had made this little speech.

And when exactly had that speech been made? Happily the book of Chronicles provided a very precise answer to this question: 'in the eighteenth year of the reign of Josiah'[21] – in other words in 622 BC.[22] What Chronicles did not do, however, was give any indication at all that the Levites had complied with the king's order; indeed, far from the colourful ceremony that one might have expected to accompany any reinstallation of the Ark in the Temple, there was no follow-up – either in this book or in any other part of the Bible – to Josiah's strange command. On the contrary, it was clear that his words had fallen on deaf ears or on the ears of people who were not in a position to obey them.

Chronologically, as I have already observed, Josiah's speech contained the last reference to the Ark of the Covenant in the whole of the Old Testament. I now turned to examine the penultimate reference. This occurred in the book of Jeremiah, in a chapter composed by Jeremiah himself around the year 626 BC,[23] and took the form of a prophetic utterance addressed to the people of Jerusalem:

> And when you have increased and become many in the land, then – it is Yahweh who speaks – *no one will ever say again 'Where is the Ark of the Covenant of Yahweh?' There will be no thought of it, no memory of it, no regret for it, no making of another.* When that time comes, Jerusalem shall be called: 'The throne of Yahweh'; all nations will gather there in the name of Yahweh and will no longer follow the dictates of their own stubborn hearts.[24]

Like Josiah, I knew that Jeremiah had been credited in certain Jewish legends – and in the apocryphal book of Maccabees – with hiding the Ark (in his case on Mount Nebo immediately before the destruction of the Temple – see previous chapter). The words quoted above, however, had infinitely greater value as historical testimony than the legends or the Apocrypha because they had been spoken at a known date by a real person, Jeremiah himself.[25] Moreover, in the context of everything else that I had learned, there could be no doubt about the meaning of these words, or about their wider implications. To put matters as plainly as possible, they corroborated the impression given in

Josiah's speech that the Ark was no longer in the Temple by 622 BC – and they pushed back to at least 626 BC the likely date at which it had gone missing. I say at least to 626 BC because that, as noted above, was the year in which Jeremiah had uttered his prophecy. It was clear, however, that in doing so he had been responding, at least in part, to some prevalent and probably by then quite long-established anguish over the loss of the Ark. This was the only possible explanation for the verse which stated: 'And when you have increased and become many in the land, then . . . no one will ever say again "Where is the Ark of the Covenant of Yahweh?" ' Obviously if people had not been saying such things in 626 BC, and for some considerable while beforehand, then there would have been no need for Jeremiah to have made such a remark.

In reaching this judgment I was pleased to discover that I had the full support of one of the world's leading biblical scholars, Professor Menahem Haran of Jerusalem's Hebrew University. In his authoritative treatise on *Temples and Temple Service in Ancient Israel*, this learned academic had considered the passage in question and had reached the following conclusion:

> This verse follows upon words of consolation and itself contains a message of consolation and mercy. What the prophet promises here is that in the good days to come there will no longer be any need for the Ark – implying that its absence should no longer cause any grief. These words would, of course, be devoid of any significance if the Ark [had] still . . . been inside the Temple at the time.[26]

On this basis I felt that it was entirely safe to conclude that I would have to peer back into the period before 626 BC if I was to have any prospect of establishing the actual date on which the Ark had disappeared. Moreover I did not think that it would be at all fruitful to devote time to a close study of the earlier years of King Josiah's reign – i.e. from 626 BC back to 640 BC. As I already knew, that monarch had sought unsuccessfully to have the relic reinstalled in the Temple in 622 BC; it was therefore hardly likely that he would have been responsible for its removal in the first place. The guilty party must have been one of his predecessors – any one, in fact, of the fifteen kings who had ruled in Jerusalem since Solomon had placed the Ark in the Holy of Holies in 955 BC.[27]

Search and find

I was looking at a period of 315 years – from 955 BC down to Josiah's accession to the throne in 640 BC. In this time Jerusalem and the Temple had been at the centre of an enormously complex series of events. And although these events were described at great length in several books of the Bible, the Ark of the Covenant had not been mentioned once: between Solomon and Josiah, as I had previously established, the sacred relic had been enshrouded in a thick blanket of silence.

I resorted to a modern research tool to find out just how thick that ancient blanket really was. On the desk in my hotel room in Jerusalem was a computerized edition of the King James Authorized Version of the Bible that I had brought with me from England.[28] For the period that I was now interested in I knew that it would be useless to run a search-and-find programme on the words 'Ark' or 'Ark of the Covenant' or 'Ark of God' or 'Holy Ark' or any similar epithets: they simply did not appear. I did, however, have one other option, and that was to look for phrases that had been regularly associated with the Ark earlier in the Scriptures, and also for reports of afflictions of the type routinely caused by the Ark.

In the realm of afflictions I settled on the word 'leprous', because, in Chapter 12 of the book of Numbers Moses had punished Miriam for criticizing his authority by using the powers of the Ark to make her 'leprous'.[29] In the realm of phrases I chose 'between the cherubims', because the God of Israel had been believed to dwell 'between the cherubims' mounted on the Ark's golden lid and because, prior to the reign of Solomon, this formula had always been used in connection with the Ark and never in any other way.[30]

I started by running the word 'leprous'. My electronic Bible of course picked it up in Chapter 12 of the book of Numbers, which described what happened to Miriam. After that it occurred only twice more in the whole of the Scriptures: in the second book of Kings, where there was a plainly irrelevant reference to 'four leprous men' sitting by a gate in the northern Israelite city of Samaria;[31] and in the second book of Chronicles – where it cropped up in a passage that looked very relevant indeed.

That passage, in 2 Chronicles 26, described how King Uzziah – who had ruled Jerusalem from 781 to 740 BC[32] – 'transgressed against the Lord his God, and went into the Temple of the Lord to burn incense upon the altar of incense.'[33] At once the High Priest Azariah and some of his assistants rushed in after the monarch hoping to dissuade him from committing this act of sacrilege at the very entrance to the Holy of Holies:

> Then Uzziah was wroth, and had a censer in his hand to burn incense: and while he was wroth with the priests, the leprosy even rose up in his forehead before the priests in the house of the Lord, from beside the incense altar.[34]

It seemed that Uzziah had not actually entered the Holy of Holies (although the text was somewhat ambiguous on this point), but he had certainly stood very close to it. Moreover he had been holding a metal incense burner in his hand – and that, since the two sons of Aaron had been struck down at the foot of Mount Sinai for offering 'strange fire before the Lord',[35] had always been a dangerous thing to do within striking distance of the Ark.[36]

On this basis, therefore, I felt that there was at least a *prima facie* case for concluding that the 'leprous' sores on Uzziah's forehead had been caused by exposure to the Ark (and I was later to discover that others had thought so too – an illustration from an eighteenth-century English Bible reproduced in the present work clearly shows the unfortunate king standing beside the Ark at the very moment that he is 'smitten').

> *If* the monarch's affliction was caused by the Ark [I wrote in my notebook] then this means that it was still present in the Holy of Holies in 740 BC (Uzziah's reign ended in that year as a result of what had happened to him[37]). This narrows the field enormously, since the implication is that

the relic could only have been removed in the century
between that date and the beginning of Josiah's reign – i.e.
at some point between 740 BC and 640 BC.

Of course I was well aware that the Uzziah incident had little
value as historical evidence: it was a tantalizing hint – a clue if you
like – but it was quite impermissible to conclude from it that the
Ark had definitely still been in the Temple in 740 BC. I needed
something stronger if I was to be satisfied that that had indeed
been the case – and I found what I was looking for when I ran a
search for the phrase 'between the cherubims'.

As noted above, in biblical passages referring to the period
before the reign of Solomon, these words had been used
exclusively in connection with the Ark, and in no other way
whatsoever. Although it would be necessary to keep a close eye
on the context, I therefore felt that any recurrence of these words
after the deposition of the relic in the Temple in 955 BC would
constitute strong evidence that it had in fact still been present in
the Holy of Holies on the date – or dates – that the phrase had
been used.

Accordingly I programmed my computer to search for the
words 'between the cherubims'. A few seconds later I knew that
they had been cited only seven times in the entire post-
Solomonic period.

Two of these citations, in Psalm 80:1 and in Psalm 99:1,
clearly referred to the cherubim of the Ark. Unfortunately they
were impossible to date with any degree of accuracy:[38] there was
a small chance that they were pre-Solomonic, but the balance of
scholarly opinion held that the relevant verses were likely to have
been composed in the 'early years of monarchy'[39] – i.e. during
Solomon's lifetime or within a century or so of his death.

The words 'between the cherubims' also cropped up three
times in the book of Ezekiel,[40] which was a late work written after
the year 593 BC.[41] In this context, however, all the uses of the
phrase were irrelevant to my investigation because: (a) the
'cherubims' referred to had been seen by Ezekiel in a vision that
came to him while he sat in his house;[42] (b) they were described
as having 'four faces' and 'four wings' each, whereas the
cherubim of the Ark had each only one face and two wings;[43] and

(c) they were clearly living creatures of enormous size, not the relatively compact figurines of solid gold that had faced each other across the 'mercy seat'.[44] Indeed, at the end of Ezekiel's vision, his cherubims 'lifted up their wings and mounted up from the earth in my sight . . . and the sound of the cherubims' wings was . . . even . . . as the voice of the Almighty God when he speaketh.'[45]

In my hunt for references that might prove the continued presence of the Ark in the Jerusalem Temple at particular periods, therefore, Ezekiel's cherubims were of no consequence and could safely be ignored. This meant that out of all the occurrences of the phrase that I had instructed my computer to search for I was now left with only two that might be of any help to me at all. These appeared in Chapter 37 of the book of Isaiah and in Chapter 19 of the second book of Kings.[46] Both recounted the same event, both were of great importance, and both clearly and unambiguously referred to the Ark of the Covenant – though they did not mention it by name. This is what they said (the Isaiah version, the older of the two, is in the left-hand column; the Kings version is in the right-hand column):

Hezekiah went up unto the house of the Lord, and . . . prayed unto the Lord, saying, O Lord of Hosts, *God of Israel, that dwellest between the cherubims,* thou art the God, even thou alone, of all the kingdoms of the earth.[47]	Hezekiah went up into the house of the Lord, and . . . prayed before the Lord, and said, O Lord *God of Israel, which dwellest between the cherubims*, thou art the God, even thou alone, of all the kingdoms of the earth.[48]

As the reader will no doubt have observed, both passages not only spoke of the same event but also did so in almost exactly the same language. Indeed the verses in Kings came very close to being a verbatim repeat of the verses in Isaiah. Those verses, scholars were agreed, had been written by Isaiah himself.[49] And, since a great deal was known about the life, times and activities of this famous prophet, it was possible to put a fairly precise date on his account of Hezekiah's prayer to the God of Israel that dwelled 'between the cherubims'.

Isaiah was called to the prophetic office in 740 BC[50] – the very year in which King Uzziah had died after being smitten with leprous sores in the incident described earlier.[51] He then continued his ministry throughout the reigns of Jotham, Ahaz and Hezekiah (respectively 740–736 BC, 736–716 BC and 716–687 BC).[52] Of crucial significance to my investigation was a fact upon which academic opinion was unanimous: the verse in which my computer had flagged the phrase 'between the cherubims' had been written by Isaiah in 701 BC – the year in which the Assyrian King Sennacherib had tried and failed to capture Jerusalem.[53]

Indeed, it had been on Isaiah's direct advice that Hezekiah – the Judaean monarch – had refused to surrender the city to the Assyrians.[54] Sennacherib's response had been to send a letter threatening death and destruction, and Hezekiah had actually been carrying this letter[55] when he had gone up 'unto the house of the Lord, and . . . prayed unto the Lord, saying, O Lord of Hosts, God of Israel, that dwellest between the cherubims, thou art the God, even thou alone, of all the kingdoms of the earth.'

Hezekiah's prayer had continued as follows:

> Incline thine ear, O Lord, and hear; open thine eyes, O
> Lord, and see: and hear all the words of Sennacherib,
> which hath sent to reproach the living God. Of a truth,
> Lord, the kings of Assyria have laid waste all the nations
> and their countries. . . . Now therefore, O Lord our God,
> save us from his hand, that all the kingdoms of the earth
> may know that thou art the Lord, even thou only.[56]

Miraculously, the Lord complied. First he sent his prophet Isaiah to Hezekiah with this message:

> Thus saith the Lord concerning the king of Assyria, He
> shall not come into this city, nor shoot an arrow there,
> nor come before it with shields, nor cast a bank against it

. . . For I will defend this city to save it for mine own sake.[57]

Yahweh was as good as his word. That very night

> The angel of the Lord went forth, and smote in the camp
> of the Assyrians a hundred and fourscore and five
> thousand: and when they arose early in the morning,
> behold, they were all dead corpses. So Sennacherib king
> of Assyria departed.[58]

There could be no doubt about the historicity of these events: the
Assyrians *had* surrounded Jerusalem in 701 BC and they *had*
suddenly lifted their siege and fled.[59] Scholars believed that this
had happened because they had been afflicted by an outbreak of
bubonic plague.[60] Strangely, however, there was no evidence
that anyone in Jerusalem itself had gone on to contract this easily
transmissible disease. In the context of everything that I had learned
hitherto, therefore, I could not help but wonder whether the Ark
of the Covenant might not in some way have been involved in
Sennacherib's undoing. The mass slaughter that had taken place
did sound very much like the sort of 'miracle' that, in earlier
times, the relic had so frequently performed.[61]

But this was only an intuition, a hunch of my own. It had no
status whatsoever as evidence of the continued presence of the
Ark in the Temple in 701 BC. What *did* have that status was
Isaiah's pure and eloquent testimony that King Hezekiah had
prayed for his deliverance to the 'God of Israel, that dwellest
between the cherubims'. The monarch uttered this prayer inside
the Temple.[62] Moreover the full text of the first verse of the
passage containing this citation not only stated that he had
carried Sennacherib's threatening letter with him – as noted
above – but also added that he had 'spread it before the Lord'.[63]
In just such a fashion, though in an earlier era, 'Solomon . . .
came to Jerusalem and stood *before* the Ark of the Covenant of the
Lord . . . and offered peace offerings.'[64] In just such a fashion,
though in an earlier era, 'David and all the house of Israel played
before the Lord on all manner of instruments made of fir wood,
even on harps, and psalteries, and on timbrels, and on cornets,
and on cymbals.'[65] And in just such a fashion, though in an

earlier era, 'the Lord separated the tribe of Levi, to bear the Ark of the Covenant of the Lord, to stand *before the Lord* to minister unto him, and to bless his name.'[66]

To cut a long and convoluted story very short indeed, the fact that Hezekiah had spread Sennacherib's letter out *'before the Lord'*, and then had prayed to the 'God of Israel, that dwellest between the cherubims' made it quite certain that the Ark of the Covenant had been in the Holy of Holies at that time. There was no other way in which this passage could be interpreted. And because it did so effectively prove the continued presence of the relic within the Temple long after the reign of Solomon it also dealt a fatal blow to the *Kebra Nagast*'s claim that the Ark had been stolen by Menelik while Solomon was still alive.

I was not sure whether I should rejoice over this discovery or whether I should lament it. I always find it slightly depressing when a beautiful myth is discredited. And although I still hoped to vindicate the central contention of the *Kebra Nagast* – namely that the Ark had indeed gone to Ethiopia (although of course not by the hand of Menelik) – I had absolutely no idea how I was going to do this.

Rather dispiritedly, therefore, I turned back to the piles of research papers and books spread out all around me in my hotel room in Jerusalem. The good news, I supposed, was that my investigation had come a long way. I had satisfied myself that the Ark had not been removed from the Temple either during or after the reign of King Josiah, which had begun in 640 BC. Moreover it was now clear that it had still been in its place in the Holy of Holies in 701 BC, the date of Hezekiah's prayer. This left just sixty-one years in which it could have disappeared, and even that period could be narrowed down somewhat. Why? Because it seemed obvious that Hezekiah himself would not have allowed the sacred relic – before which he had prayed so efficaciously – to be carried off by anyone.

Hezekiah had died in 687 BC and Josiah had taken the throne in 640 BC. Between them there were only two monarchs – Manasseh (687–642 BC) and Amon (642–640 BC).[67] It followed that the loss of the Ark must have occurred during the reigns of one or other of these two kings.

The sin of Manasseh

As I immersed myself in the biblical texts once again it quickly became apparent that the guilty party could only have been Manasseh, who was castigated unmercifully by the scribes because:

> He did that which was evil in the sight of the Lord, after the abominations of the heathen . . . For he . . . reared up altars for Baal . . . and worshipped all the host of heaven, and served them. And he built altars in the house of the Lord . . . for all the host of heaven . . . And he made his son pass through the fire, and . . . used enchantments, and dealt with familiar spirits and wizards: he wrought much wickedness in the sight of the Lord to provoke him to anger . . . And he set a graven image of the grove that he had made in the house, of which the Lord said to David and to Solomon his son, In this house, and in Jerusalem, which I have chosen out of all the tribes of Israel, will I put my name for ever.[68]

What was this 'graven image of the grove' that Manasseh had made? And where exactly in the Temple had he put it?

To find an answer to the first question I temporarily abandoned the King James Authorized Version of the Bible (from which the above quotation is taken) and turned to the more modern Jerusalem Bible which informed me that the 'graven image of the grove' was in fact a 'carved image of Asherah', an arboreal pagan deity.[69] The answer to the second question was self-evident: the 'house' in which Yahweh had said that he would put his 'name for ever' was the Holy of Holies of the Temple – the *debir*, the dense golden cell that Solomon had 'designed . . . to contain the Ark of the Covenant of Yahweh.'[70]

The implications of what I had just learnt were enormous. Manasseh, who had done 'that which was evil in the sight of the Lord', had introduced an *idol* into the Holy of Holies of the Temple. In taking this momentous step backwards towards paganism it was inconceivable that he could have allowed the Ark of the Covenant to remain in its place – since the Ark was the sign and the seal of Yahweh's presence on earth and the ultimate symbol of the fiercely monotheistic Judaic faith. At the same time it was improbable that the apostatizing king would actually have *destroyed* the sacred relic: on the contrary, with his predilection for enchantments and wizardry, he would have regarded that as a most unwise thing to do. The most likely scenario, therefore, was that he would have ordered the Levites to remove the Ark from the Temple *before* he installed his 'Asherah' in the inner sanctum. And this would have been an order that they would have been more than happy to comply with: as faithful servants of Yahweh they would have done anything within their power to avoid the pollution of the object that they regarded as the 'footstool' of their God[71] – and they could hardly have imagined any worse pollution than for it to have to share the Holy of Holies with the graven image of some alien deity. As priests they would not have been in a position to prevail militarily against a powerful monarch like Manasseh; their best course of action would have been to bow to the inevitable and to carry the Ark away to a place of safety.

There were even indications in the Bible that the relic's enforced departure from the Temple might have resulted in some kind of mass public protest against the king – a protest that he had ruthlessly suppressed. This was only guesswork on my part, of course, but such a hypothesis did help to explain why Manasseh was said to have 'shed innocent blood . . . in such great quantity that he flooded Jerusalem from end to end.'[72]

At any rate, it was clear that the reign of this monarch had, in later years, come to be regarded as a blot, an aberration and an abomination. He had been succeeded by his son Amon in 642 BC and Amon had in turn been succeeded in 640 BC by Josiah, the zealous reformer who was famous (and beloved of the scribes) for having restored the traditional worship of Yahweh.

Why had Amon's tenure of the throne been so brief? Because, as the Bible explained, he had done

> that which was evil in the sight of the Lord, as his father
> Manasseh did. And he walked in all the way that his
> father walked in, and served the idols that his father
> served, and worshipped them . . . And the servants of

Amon conspired against him, and slew the king in his own
house . . . and the people of the land made Josiah his son
king in his stead.[73]

Josiah, however, had been only 'eight years old when he began to
reign'[74] and it was not until eight years after that, the Bible
reported, that he had shown the first signs of wanting to 'seek
after the God of David'.[75] Indeed the young monarch's passionate reaction against the sins of Manasseh and Amon did not
begin until the 'twelfth year' of his reign when – at the age of
twenty – he launched a campaign 'to purge Judah and Jerusalem
from . . . the carved images, and the molten images'.[76]

And he brought out the grove [Asherah] from the house
of the Lord, right out of Jerusalem, unto the brook
Kidron, and burned it in the brook Kidron, and stamped
it to small powder, and cast the powder thereof on the
common burying ground.[77]

A passionate reaction indeed! And, moreover, one that could be
dated: it had been in 628 BC, the twelfth year of Josiah's reign,
that Manasseh's loathsome idol had at last been rooted out of the
Holy of Holies. The Ark, however, had certainly not been
brought back in to replace it. As I already knew, Jeremiah had
been responding to public grief at the continued absence of the
relic two years later when he had prophesied that a time would
eventually come when people would no longer ask 'where is the
Ark of the Covenant of Yahweh' – a time when they would have
'no regret for it' and when they would not consider 'making
another'.

Four years after that Josiah himself had rather forlornly asked
the Levites to restore the Ark to the Temple, adding 'it shall not
be a burden for your shoulders'. That had been in 622 BC, the
eighteenth year of his reign, and it was no coincidence that it had
been in that very same year, having completed a lengthy
nationwide purge, that he had 'returned to Jerusalem' and issued
orders 'to repair the house of the Lord his God'.[78]

The repairs had been duly carried out by 'carpenters and
builders and masons'.[79] The great mystery, however, was that

the Levites had been unable to comply with Josiah's request that they should 'put the Holy Ark in the house which Solomon the son of David king of Israel did build.' I was now increasingly sure that the answer to that mystery must lie in Ethiopia – although I was not yet in a position to fathom out exactly how or why.

Meanwhile I sought academic support for my view that it must have been during the reign of Manasseh that the Ark had gone missing in the first place. I found that support in an authoritative treatise that I had already had occasion to consult several times before – Professor Menahem Haran's *Temples and Temple Service in Ancient Israel*. Here, in a brief section in the middle of the book, I read that:

> throughout the various changes that took place in the
> Kingdom of Judah, the Temple at Jerusalem never ceased to
> serve exclusively as a Temple of Yahweh . . . There was
> only one single period in its history when it was temporarily
> deprived of its original function and for a short while ceased
> to serve as a Temple to Yahweh . . . This occurred during
> the reign of Manasseh . . . who set up vessels for Baal . . . in
> the outer sanctum and introduced the image of Asherah
> into the inner sanctum of the Temple . . . This is the only
> happening which may explain the disappearance of the Ark
> and the cherubim . . . We are entitled to infer that the
> image of Asherah . . . was substituted for the Ark and the
> cherubim. Some fifty years afterwards, when Josiah
> removed the Asherah from the Temple and burnt it in the
> Kidron Valley, beating it to dust and desecrating even the
> dust, the Ark and the cherubim were no longer there.[80]

After making a number of telephone calls to the Hebrew University I managed to track down Professor Haran. I told him that I had read his book and that I was excited by his suggestion that the Ark of the Covenant might have been lost during the reign of Manasseh. Could he spare me half an hour or so to discuss the matter further? He replied that he would be only too happy to do so and invited me to visit him at his home in Jerusalem's Alfasi Street.

Haran proved to be an elderly but robust man, grey-haired and solidly built – the very image of the type of learned but eminently practical biblical scholar that one meets so often in Israel. I told him a little about my own research and then asked whether he was certain in his own mind that the Ark had indeed been removed from the Temple in Manasseh's time.

'Yes,' he replied with conviction, 'I am as certain of that as I can possibly be. This is why the Ark is not referred to in the long lists of Temple vessels and treasures that were later taken by the Babylonians. And I should add with all modesty that my views on this subject have never been refuted in scholarship.'

I took this opportunity to put a question that had been bothering me for some time: 'If the Ark *was* taken out as a result of Manasseh's idolatry then how do you account for the fact that the Scriptures make absolutely no mention of the loss?'

'I account for it in this way. To have to write down such a report would have filled the scribes with disgust – with such a horrible feeling – that definitely they would have averted from it. I therefore believe that they deliberately refrained from reporting the loss of the Ark. Even in what they did report of Manasseh's reign their feelings of utter *horror* do come through. Yet they could not bring themselves to indulge in a description of the occurrence itself.'

'Do you have any idea at all', I asked next, 'what could have happened to the relic after it was removed?'

Haran shrugged: 'On that I cannot speculate. It is impossible to prove. I can only say with confidence that the orthodox priests of Yahweh would under no circumstances have permitted the Ark of Yahweh to stay in the same place as the idol of Asherah.'

'So do you think they took it away somewhere? To a place of safety?'

Another shrug: 'As I say, I cannot speculate on such matters. However it is evident from our records, from the Holy Writ, that Jerusalem itself – in fact the whole country – was not a safe place for those who were loyal to the worship of Yahweh during Manasseh's time.'

'Are you referring to the passage in the book of Kings that talks about innocent blood being spilled?'

'Yes. 2 Kings 21:16. And not only that. Jeremiah also speaks obliquely of the same events when he says "your sword hath

devoured your prophets like a destroying lion". I have no doubt
that this was a reference to the acts of Manasseh and I infer from
it that certain prophets had opposed him and that for this they
were massacred. It is an interesting phenomenon, you know, that
you do not find any prophets at all during the reign of Manasseh
himself – Jeremiah came just afterwards and others, like Isaiah,
came just before. The gap was the result of persecutions and of a
sustained campaign against the worship of Yahweh.'

The Professor would not be pushed any further on this subject
and resolutely refused to indulge in what he obviously regarded
as idle speculation about *where* the Ark could have gone. When I
mentioned my theory that it might have been taken to Ethiopia he
looked at me blankly for about half a minute and then concluded:
'That seems rather far.'

A temple on the Nile

After interviewing Menahem Haran I returned to my hotel
feeling directionless and confused. Of course it had been exciting
to get his confirmation that the Ark had been lost during
Manasseh's reign. The trouble was, however, that I now seemed
to have arrived at the brink of a deep intellectual precipice.
Ethiopia was indeed 'rather far' from Jerusalem, and I could see
no good reason why the loyal priests of Yahweh who had carried
the sacred relic out of the Temple should subsequently have
taken it to such a distant place.

Moreover, the dates didn't fit. Manasseh had sat on the throne
in Jerusalem from 687 to 642 BC, but the Tana Kirkos traditions
asserted that the Ark had not arrived in Ethiopia until approximately 470 BC. So I was still two hundred years adrift.

As I chewed over this problem I realized that what I needed to
do was to talk to some Ethiopians. And what better place was
there in which to talk to Ethiopians than in the State of Israel?
After all, tens of thousands of Falashas – who claimed citizenship
under the terms of the Law of Return – had been airlifted here
over the past decade. Surely amongst them there must be some
elders, knowledgeable in the folk memory of their people, who
could help me to bridge the geographical and chronological abyss
that yawned before me?

Further enquiries at the Hebrew University produced the name of Shalva Weil, a social anthropologist who had specialized in far-flung Jewish communities and who was regarded as something of an expert on Falasha culture. I telephoned her at her home and, after introducing myself, asked her if she could recommend any member of the Falasha community in Jerusalem who might be able to speak with authority on the ancient traditions of the Ethiopian Jews.

'Your best bet', she replied without hesitation, 'would be Raphael Hadane. He's a priest, a very senior priest. He's been here for a few years. He's an elderly man and extremely knowledgeable. The only problem is he doesn't speak English so you should try to see him with his son.'

'Whose name is?'

'Yoseph Hadane. He came to Israel as a boy in the early 1970s and he's now a fully trained rabbi. He does speak fluent English so he'll be able to translate for you.'

Arranging the meeting took up most of my last two days in Jerusalem. Finally, however, I did manage to get together with the Hadane family at the Falasha Absorption Centre, which was located in a suburb called Mevasserit Zion to the west of the city. Here I found hundreds of Ethiopians, some newly arrived, others long-term residents, living in a somewhat ramshackle housing estate.

Raphael Hadane, the Falasha priest, was dressed in a traditional Abyssinian *shemma* and sported a considerable beard. His son, the rabbi, was clean-shaven and wore a smart business suit. For a long while we sat around drinking tea and exchanging pleasantries while children played at our feet and various assorted relatives came and went. One of these latter, as it happened, had been born and brought up in the village of Anbober, which I had visited in January 1990 on my trip to Gondar.

'Does Anbober really still exist?' he asked me rather plaintively. 'It's five years since I left home.'

'It does still exist,' I replied, 'or rather it *did* in January. The population seemed to be mainly women and children, though.'

'This is because the men emigrate first to prepare a place for their families. Did you talk to anyone there?'

I told them that I had interviewed the priest, Solomon Alemu, and this brought smiles of recognition from everyone around the table. 'They all know him well,' explained Rabbi Hadane. 'Ours is a small society . . . and close knit.'

Eventually I switched on my tape-recorder and began the interview with the rabbi's venerable father. Much of what he had to say about Falasha culture and religion was already very familiar. When I turned to what was now the central issue for me, however – i.e. exactly how and when Judaism had arrived in Ethiopia – he told me something that made me prick up my ears.

I had asked a leading question about Menelik and the Queen of Sheba – hoping, after the ritual repetition of the *Kebra Nagast* story, to pin the old man down on the matter of the date that Menelik's supposed journey had taken place. Hadane surprised me by dismissing the legend entirely: 'Some of us say that we are descended from the Israelites who accompanied Menelik, but personally I do not believe that. According to the traditions that I heard in my childhood, our ancestors were Jews who had first lived in Egypt before they came to Ethiopia.'

'But,' I interjected, 'the *Kebra Nagast* says that too. It says that Menelik and his companions travelled through Egypt.'

'That is not what I mean. After leaving Israel, our forefathers did not just travel through Egypt. They settled in that country for a very long time – for hundreds of years. And they built a temple there.'

I leaned forward over the tape-recorder: 'A temple? *Where* did they build this temple?'

'At Aswan.'

This, I thought, was very interesting. Solomon Alemu, the priest at Anbober, had also mentioned Aswan to me when I had interviewed him in January. At the time I had resolved to make a trip there. And I had in fact travelled quite widely in Egypt since doing that interview. I had not yet gone as far south as Aswan, however, and I was now beginning to wonder whether that might not have been a mistake. If there had indeed been a Jewish temple there, as Hadane had just indicated, then this was potentially a matter of great importance – because the function of the Temple in orthodox Judaism had been to house the Ark of the Covenant. If it was true that a temple had been built at Aswan, and if this had happened after the Ark had been removed from Jerusalem, then the implications were obvious.

Hadane was unable to be at all specific as to the date of this Aswan temple, however. All he could tell me was that it had endured 'for a long while' but that it had eventually been destroyed.

'Why was it destroyed?'

'There was a great war in Egypt. A foreign king who had captured many countries came to Egypt and destroyed all the temples of the Egyptians. But he did not destroy our temple. So when the Egyptians saw that only the Jewish temple was not destroyed they suspected we were on the side of the invader. Because of this they started to fight against us and they destroyed our temple and we were forced to flee.'

'And you went to Ethiopia?'

'Not straight away. Our forefathers passed first into Sudan, through Meroe, where they remained for a short while. But they were driven out by another war. Then they split into two parties: one group went following the Takazze river; the other group following the Nile. And in this way they arrived in Ethiopia, in Quara, close to Lake Tana. There we made our homes. There we became Ethiopians. And because we were far from Israel, though we had stayed in touch with Jerusalem all the time that we were in Egypt and in the Sudan, we now lost that contact and it became to us only a memory.'

I next asked Hadane whether there was any place in the Lake Tana area that the Falashas regarded as being particularly important or sacred.

'Three places,' he replied. 'The first, the most important, is Tana Kirkos, the second is Daga Stephanos, the third is Zegie.'

I raised my eyebrows: 'Why is Tana Kirkos the most important?'

'I do not know exactly. But all our people regard it as sacred.'

My last question was a specific one about the Ark: 'Ethiopian Christians say that they have the Ark of the Covenant at Axum – the original Ark of the Covenant that was supposed to have been brought from Jerusalem by Menelik, son of the Queen of Sheba and King Solomon. You've told me that you don't believe the Menelik story. But do you believe that the Christians have the Ark as they claim?'

'Our people believe, and I myself also believe, that the Ark of the Covenant is in Axum. As a matter of fact, some years ago, I and others of our spiritual leaders went from our home to Axum to try to see the Ark for ourselves. We were very interested in this tradition and we wanted to see the Holy Ark. So we went there, and we got to Axum, and to the church of Saint Mary. But we were told that it was forbidden for us to enter the chapel where the Ark is, because if we were to enter into there we would die. So we said, "OK. We will purify ourselves and then we will go in there and we will see." So we did that, we purified ourselves, but still the Christian priests would not permit us to enter the chapel. Because of that we had to return to our place without seeing it.'

'I've heard that it is brought out in public once a year, at the ceremony of *Timkat*. You would have had a better chance of seeing it if you had gone there at *Timkat*.'

Hadane laughed bitterly: 'I have heard that too. But I do not believe that the Christians would ever bring out the true Ark. They would not do that. They will never show it to anyone. They will use a replica instead. Do you know why? Because they took the Ark from us long, long ago, and they do not want to give it back. They are jealous of it. So therefore they keep it always concealed in its chapel, surrounded by bars, where no one may approach it other than the one who is appointed as its guardian.'

When I finally left the Falasha Absorption Centre at Mevasserit Zion and returned to downtown Jerusalem my head was literally buzzing with ideas and question. Of all the Ethiopian Jews whom I had talked to during the course of my research, Hadane had proved to be by far the most lucid and the most informative. The story of his attempt to see the Ark in Axum had intrigued me. And the special importance that he had accorded to the island of Tana Kirkos was surely of great significance in the light of what I myself had learnt there during my trip in November 1989. But what had interested me most of all about his answers was the reference that he had made to the existence, at some remote period in history, of a Jewish temple at Aswan. If there was any truth to this then I would certainly have to go to that Upper Egyptian town, which lay some two hundred kilometres to the south of Karnak and Luxor.

Back in my hotel room I dialled the number of Dr Shalva Weil, the social anthropologist who had put me in touch with Hadane.

'How did the interview go?' she asked breezily.

'Very well, thank you. Most helpful. I'm grateful to you for the contact.'

I paused awkwardly. I always feel slightly silly putting completely idiotic questions to academics. But there was no getting around this one. I had to ask: 'During our interview Hadane mentioned something to me about a temple – a Jewish temple – at Aswan in Egypt. I know what I'm going to say next is a bit nuts, but I've learnt not to dismiss folk-traditions completely without at least checking them out. Anyway, what I want to ask you is this: is there actually any possibility that such a temple could ever have existed?'

'Certainly it existed,' Dr Weil replied. 'It was a proper temple, dedicated to Yahweh. But it wasn't actually in Aswan proper. It stood on the island of Elephantine in the middle of the Nile. There are some archaeological excavations going on there right now, as a matter of fact.'

'And this island . . . I mean . . . is it far from Aswan?'

'Not more than two hundred metres in a straight line. It takes about five minutes to sail there in a *felucca*.'

'So effectively Hadane was right when he talked about a temple at Aswan?'

'Absolutely right, yes.'

'But does this temple have anything to do with the Falashas? Hadane said that it had been built by his forefathers.'

'It's possible, I suppose. Academics are divided on the issue. Most of us believe that the Falashas are the descendants of Jewish merchants and settlers who reached Ethiopia from south Arabia. But there is one respectable body of opinion which holds that they are descended from the Jews who fled from Elephantine.'

'Fled? Why?'

'Their temple was destroyed – some time in the fifth century BC I believe – and the Jewish community that had lived on the island vanished after that. It's a bit of a mystery, actually. They just melted away. But I'm not an expert . . . I can recommend some books if you like.'

I thanked Dr Weil for this offer, jotted down the short bibliography that she gave me, and said goodbye to her in a state of some excitement. It had been in the fifth century BC, according to the Tana Kirkos traditions, that the Ark of the Covenant had arrived in Ethiopia. Now I knew that a Jewish temple on the upper Nile had been destroyed in that same century. Was it not possible that that temple had been built two hundred years earlier to house the Ark after it had been removed from Jerusalem during the reign of Manasseh?

I intended to find out and left Israel the next day – not for London, as I had originally planned, but for Egypt.

Chapter 16

Door of the Southern Countries

Aswan is located on the east bank of the Nile at a point roughly equidistant from Israel and from the northern borders of Ethiopia. Well placed as a staging post between the African and Mediterranean worlds, its name was derived from the Greek word *Seyene*, which in turn was a corruption of the ancient Egyptian *Swenet*, meaning 'making business'.[1] In antiquity the town profited greatly from a rich two-way commerce in which manufactured goods flowed southwards from the high civilization of Egypt, and in which spices, aromatic substances, slaves, gold and ivory from sub-Saharan Africa were traded north. It was from this latter commodity, ivory, that the island in which I was interested had received its name, for Elephantine (which lies in the middle of the Nile directly opposite Aswan) had once been known simply as *Abu*, or Elephant Land.[2]

At the reception desk of the New Cataract Hotel in Aswan I enquired about Elephantine and particularly about its Jewish temple. Shalva Weil had already told me that it had been destroyed in the fifth century BC but she had also said that archaeologists were working there, so I hoped very much that there might be ruins to visit.

Mention of the word 'Jewish' did not elicit a favourable response from the hotel staff; despite the relatively positive diplomatic relationship that had been forged between Egypt and Israel in recent years I had forgotten how much bad blood and bitterness still divided the peoples of the two neighbouring countries. Finally, however, I did manage to extract the following intelligence from the front-desk manager: 'Many temples on Elephantine – Egyptian, Roman, maybe Jewish . . . I don't know.

You can go see, take a *felucca* ride, find out. Anyway there are archaeologists there, German archaeologists. Just ask for Mr Kaiser.'

Mr Kaiser, eh, I thought as I walked out of the lobby and into a fiercely hot day, a likely story!

Indiana Jones

After a short *felucca* ride to Elephantine I was shown to a building on the island's west bank where I was told 'the Germans' lived. I made my way to the front door, knocked, and was admitted by a Nubian manservant wearing a red *fez*. Without questioning me he led me along a corridor and into an interesting room, the walls of which were lined from floor to ceiling with wooden shelves loaded with broken fragments of pottery and other artefacts. Then he turned to go.

I coughed: 'Excuse me. Er . . . I'm looking for Mr Kaiser. Could you call him please?'

The servant paused, favoured me with an inscrutable stare and then left, still without saying anything.

Five minutes or so passed, during which I stood dithering in the middle of the floor, and then . . . Indiana Jones appeared in the doorway. Or, rather, not Indiana Jones himself but a Harrison Ford lookalike. Wearing a Panama hat at a jaunty angle, he was tall and muscular, ruggedly handsome, and gimlet-eyed. Clearly he had not shaved for several days.

I resisted a strong urge to exclaim, 'Mr Kaiser, I presume', and asked less theatrically: 'Are you Mr Kaiser?'

'No. My name is Cornelius von Pilgrim.' He advanced towards me, and, as I introduced myself, he extended a strong and suntanned right hand for me to shake.

'I'm visiting Elephantine', I explained, 'in connection with a project of mine. I'm interested in the archaeology of the temple here.'

'Ah ha.'

'Yes. You see I'm investigating a historical mystery . . . the . . . er . . . the loss of, I mean the disappearance of the Ark of the Covenant.'

'Ah ha.'

'Do you know what I mean by the Ark of the Covenant?'

By now Cornelius von Pilgrim's expression could only be described as glazed. 'No,' he replied curtly in answer to my question.

'You do speak English do you?' I asked. I wanted to be sure.

'Yes. Quite well.'

'Good. OK, then. The Ark. Now let's see. You know about Moses, right?'

A faint nod.

'And the Ten Commandments, carved on tablets of stone?'

Another nod.

'Well, the Ark of the Covenant was the chest made of wood and gold that the Ten Commandments were put in. And . . . er . . . I'm looking for it.'

Cornelius von Pilgrim did not seem to be overly impressed. Then he said, without the slightest trace of humour: 'Ah ha. Like Indiana Jones you mean?'

'Yes. That's exactly what I mean. Anyway, the reason why I'm in Elephantine is that I was told on good authority that there was a Jewish temple here. My theory is that the Ark, somehow, was taken to Ethiopia in ancient times. So naturally I'm wondering whether there is any possibility – or any archaeological evidence even – that it might have been brought here first before it went to Ethiopia. You see, I think it was removed from Jerusalem in the seventh century BC. So the question is – what happened in the intervening two hundred years?'

'You are wondering whether during those two centuries the Ark could have been kept in the Jewish temple on this island?'

'Absolutely. In fact I'm hoping that you and your team may have excavated the temple. If you have then I'd very much like to know what you found.'

Cornelius von Pilgrim removed his hat before demolishing my hopes. 'Yes,' he said after a rather lengthy pause, 'but on the site that you are interested in there's nothing to be seen. We'd thought there might be something left . . . beneath the ruins of the Roman temple that was later built on top of the Jewish one. But now we've dug down all the way through the foundations. And there's just nothing. Absolutely nothing at all. It's a fact that there was a substantial Jewish settlement here between the seventh and the fifth century BC but nothing remains of it now for archaeology except some of the houses of the people. That's all, I'm afraid.'

Trying to ignore the immense feeling of depression that had just washed over me I asked: 'If nothing remains of the temple then how do you know that it was ever there?'

'Oh. That is not a problem. That is not in doubt. For a while there was a great deal of correspondence between this island and the city of Jerusalem. These letters were written on ostraca – potsherds – and on papyrus scrolls. Many of them have been found and translated and a large number make specific reference to the Temple of Yahweh on Elephantine. The matter is well attested historically and because of this we do know, within a few metres, the exact site of the temple, we also know when the temple was destroyed – it was 410 BC – and finally we know that the later Roman temple was built in the place where the Jewish temple had previously stood. It is all very clear.'

'Why was the Jewish temple destroyed?'

'Look . . . I am not an expert in these matters. I specialize in the remains from the second millennium BC – well before your period. To find out more detailed information you will have to talk to a colleague of mine who has taken a special interest in the Jewish colony. He is Mr Achim Krekeler.'

'Is he here now?'

'Unfortunately not. He is in Cairo. But he will return tomorrow. Will you still be here tomorrow?'

'Yes. I mean . . . I don't have long. I have to get back to England. But I can wait until tomorrow.'

'Good. So I suggest then that you come back tomorrow, in the afternoon, say around three p.m., and you will see Mr Krekeler. Meanwhile, if you like, I would be happy to show you where the Jewish colony was . . . and the site of your temple.'

I took von Pilgrim up on this kind offer. As we walked I asked him under whose auspices the excavations on Elephantine were being conducted.

'We are from the German Archaeological Institute in Berlin,' he replied. 'We have been working here for a number of years.'

We had arrived at the foot of a low hill. On the slopes above us, spread out over a wide area, was a maze of rubble and masonry,

amidst which partially reconstructed dry-stone walls betrayed
the outlines of rooms, houses and streets. 'This', said von
Pilgrim, 'was the part of the old town of Elephantine where the
Jewish people lived.'

We began to climb, picking our way with care amongst the
crumbling ruins. By the time we reached the summit I was quite
out of breath – but I had also shaken off the mood of depression
that had assailed me earlier. Though I could not have explained
exactly why, I felt that there was something about this place which
was . . . *right* – something haunting and evocative that spoke of
ancient days and hidden histories.

Cornelius von Pilgrim had led me to the highest point on the
island of Elephantine. Now he gestured around us and said: 'The
Jewish temple was here, beneath where we are standing.'

I pointed to a massive, broken column that loomed just ahead
of us and to our right and asked what it was.

'Part of the Roman temple I told you about. As a matter of fact
there's evidence that quite a number of other temples stood here
at different periods, dedicated to the gods of the various foreign
powers that occupied Egypt in the first millennium BC. Often the
architects of these temples would re-use the materials from the
earlier buildings. This, I think, is why the Jewish temple so
completely disappeared. It was destroyed, knocked down, maybe
burnt, and then its masonry was broken up and incorporated into
the walls of the next temple.'

'I asked before why the Jewish temple was destroyed. You
didn't get round to telling me . . .'

'Broadly speaking we believe that there was a problem between
the members of the Jewish community and the Egyptian
residents of the island. You see there was an Egyptian temple
too . . .'

'On the same site?'

'No. The Jewish temple had been built more or less beside it.
The Egyptian temple was over there' – he gestured in the
direction of another pile of rubble – 'and some remains from it
have been found. It was dedicated to the god Khnum. He was a
ram-headed god. All his effigies show him with the head of a ram.
And we speculate from this that some serious tension may have
arisen between the Jewish priests and the Egyptian priests.'

'Why tension?'

'Well, it's obvious. It is known that the Jews here practised sacrifice and almost certainly they sacrificed rams. This would not have made the priests of Khnum very happy. So we guess that at a certain date they simply turned on the Jews and perhaps massacred them, or perhaps expelled them from the island, and then afterwards destroyed their temple.'

'And you said that that date was 410 BC?'

'Yes. That's right. But you must talk to Achim Krekeler for more details.'

The missing link?

I returned the next afternoon as von Pilgrim had suggested. Meanwhile I had spent a sleepless night and a restless morning thinking through everything that I had learned, working out the logic of events and trying to arrive at some tentative conclusions.

As a result of this process – even before my meeting with Krekeler – I was reasonably confident in my own mind that the Jewish temple on Elephantine might indeed prove to be the missing link in the chain of clues that I had assembled over the previous two years. If I was right, and if a group of Levites had left Jerusalem with the Ark of the Covenant during the reign of Manasseh, then they could hardly have chosen a better place of safety. Here they would have been far beyond the reach of the wicked Jewish king who had introduced an idol into the Holy of Holies. Moreover, since I had established the relationship between the ceremony of the Ark and the festival of Apet (held each year at Luxor just two hundred kilometres to the north – see chapter 12), it seemed to me that this Upper Egyptian island could also have been seen by the fugitive priests as a uniquely *appropriate* location: surrounded on all sides by the sacred waters of the river Nile, might they not have felt that they had returned to their roots?

All this was speculation. What was certain, however, was that a Jewish temple *had* been built here at approximately the right time to have sheltered the Ark after its removal from the Holy of Holies in Jerusalem. It was also certain that that same temple had subsequently been destroyed during the same century in which –

according to the Tana Kirkos traditions – the Ark had been brought to Ethiopia. All this, it seemed to me, added up to a compellingly suggestive series of events. And I was not greatly worried by the fact that the date of the Elephantine temple's destruction – 410 BC – was approximately sixty years *later* than the date that I had calculated for the Ark's arrival on Tana Kirkos (470 BC). Over the huge period of time between the fifth century BC and the twentieth century AD it seemed to me quite possible that the Ethiopian oral traditions on which I had based that calculation could have gone adrift by sixty years or so.

I was therefore in an optimistic frame of mind when I arrived back at the German Archaeological Institute's house for my meeting with Achim Krekeler. A stocky, friendly man in his mid-thirties who spoke good English, I found him poring over fragments of ancient papyrus which, he explained, had to be handled with great care because they were exceptionally brittle.

'And it's papyri like these that have provided the main evidence for the existence of the Jewish temple?'

'Yes, and for its destruction. After 410 BC a number of letters were sent to Jerusalem describing what had happened and seeking funds and permission for a possible reconstruction.'

'But the temple was never rebuilt, was it?'

'No, definitely not. In fact all the correspondence suddenly stopped around 400 BC. After that it seems that the Jewish people left Elephantine.'

'Do you know what happened to them?'

'No. Not really. But clearly they had been in trouble with the Egyptians for some time. Probably they were forced to leave.'

'And you don't know where they went?'

'No information on that has ever been found.'

At some length I explained to Krekeler my interest in the Ark of the Covenant and my feeling that it might have got to Ethiopia by way of Elephantine. I then asked whether he thought that there was any possibility at all that the sacred relic could have been brought to the island.

'Of course it is *possible*. Anything is possible. But I had always understood that the Ark was destroyed when the Temple in Jerusalem was burnt down by the Babylonians.'

'That's the orthodox theory. But I'm fairly sure that it was taken out quite some time before then – in the seventh century BC, during the reign of Manasseh. So one of the things that I'm hoping you'll be able to give me is a precise date for the building of the temple here in Elephantine.'

'I'm afraid there is no precise date. Opinions vary. But personally I would have no difficulty in accepting that it might have been built some time in the seventh century BC. Other scholars also share that view.'

'And do you have any idea what the temple would have looked like? I know you haven't recovered any material artefacts but I'm wondering whether there might have been any hints in the papyri?'

'A few. No sacred writings as such have yet been recovered. But we have found a fair amount of descriptive information about the exterior of the temple. From this we can say for certain that it had pillars of stone, five gateways also made of stone, and a roof of cedarwood.'

'Would it have had a Holy of Holies?'

'Presumably. It was a substantial building, a proper temple. But there is insufficient evidence to be certain whether there was a Holy of Holies or not.'

We continued to talk around the subject for another hour or so. Finally, however, Krekeler announced that his time was short as he was due to return to Cairo the next day and he had much to do. 'I can lend you two of the best academic publications on Elephantine,' he offered, 'as long as you promise to bring them back tomorrow. They summarize all the main findings of the research that has been done here by scholars from many different countries since the turn of the century.'

When I returned to my hotel I was carrying the weighty tomes that Krekeler had mentioned. They fully repaid the long night that I spent studying them.

The Ark in Elephantine

Here is what I learned about the Jewish Temple on Elephantine – the key facts of relevance to my quest, as I recorded them in my notebook:

1 The temple, as Krekeler told me, must have been a building of some considerable size. Quite a lot of information about its appearance survived in the papyri and the archaeologists have concluded that its dimensions were ninety feet long by thirty feet wide.[3] In old measurements this is, of course sixty cubits by twenty cubits.[4] Interestingly, the Bible gives exactly the same measurements for *Solomon's* Temple in Jerusalem.[5]

2 The Elephantine Temple was roofed with cedarwood;[6] so was Solomon's Temple.[7]

3 It seems, therefore, that Soloman's Temple must have provided the model for the Elephantine Temple. Since the former had originally been built to accommodate the Ark of the Covenant, is it not probable that the latter was as well?

4 Animal sacrifice was routinely practised at the Elephantine Temple – including the all-important sacrifice of a lamb as the opening rite of Passover week.[8] This is highly significant since it indicates that the Jewish community must have migrated to Elephantine *before* the reforms of King Josiah (640- 609 BC). Those reforms conclusively banned sacrifice at any location other than the Jerusalem Temple (a ban that was subsequently respected even by the exiles during the captivity in Babylon). On Elephantine, however, sacrifice continued to be an important ritual for the Jews in the sixth and fifth centuries BC.[9] Since those Jews were engaged in a regular correspondence with Jerusalem there can be no doubt that they would have known about Josiah's ban. Nevertheless, they continued to perform sacrifices. They must, therefore, have felt that they had some special authority so to do. It goes without saying that the presence of the Ark of the Covenant in their temple would have provided them with all the authority they needed.

5 In this connection it is worthy of note that the Elephantine Jews clearly thought that Yahweh resided physically in their temple: a number of papyri speak of

him – in no uncertain terms – as 'dwelling' there.[10] In ancient Israel (and during the wanderings in the wilderness) Yahweh was believed to reside wherever the Ark was;[11] indeed this belief only really changed after the loss of the Ark had been recognized.[12] When the Jews of Elephantine spoke of Yahweh as a deity who was physically present with them, therefore, it follows that they could well have been referring to the Ark.

6 The Elephantine Jews frequently spoke of the deity dwelling in their temple as 'the Lord of Hosts' or 'Yahweh of Hosts'.[13] Scholars recognize this phrase as an archaic one.[14] It was frequently used in connection with the Ark (e.g. in the period before Solomon's Temple was built 'the people sent to Shiloh that they might bring from thence the Ark of the Covenant of the Lord of Hosts.'[15]).

7 All the above factors lend credibility to the view that the Ark could have been lodged in the Elephantine Temple – and, indeed, that its presence on the island could have been the reason for the building of that Temple in the first place. Krekeler was right to tell me that no exact date of construction has yet been established. From the literature, however, it is clear that the scholars who analysed the papyri did a great deal of work on precisely this subject. They point out that by the early seventh century BC there was already a substantial Jewish population on the island of Elephantine, made up mainly of a garrison of mercenaries in the pay of the Egyptians. These Jewish soldiers, together with their families, would have constituted a viable social context for temple worship. On the basis of this and a great deal of other evidence, the considered opinion of the scholars is therefore that the Elephantine Temple must have been built by the year 650 BC.[16]

8 It is impossible to overstate the significance of this date. Why? Because it falls during the reign of Manasseh – the king who introduced an idol into the Holy of Holies of the Jerusalem Temple, thus causing the Ark to be removed (probably by priests who remained loyal to the traditional worship of Yahweh).

It was a difficult enough task to establish that the
sacred relic must indeed have been taken out at this
time[17] – but, having completed that task, I am
satisfied that there is no evidence in the Bible about
where it might have been *taken to* (even Professor
Menahem Haran was unable to put forward any
theories as to what could have happened to it after it
left Jerusalem).

9 The academic authorities who studied the
Elephantine papyri, and who arrived at the date of
650 BC for the construction of the Temple, were
clearly not aware that the Ark could have gone
missing from Jerusalem during the reign of Manasseh.
If they had been then they would certainly have put
two and two together. They were aware, however, of
the widespread outrage caused by that monarch's
'pagan innovations', and they concluded that this
outrage was the only possible explanation for the
otherwise inexplicable fact that a Jewish temple was
built on Elephantine:

> Manasseh's reign was accompanied by much
> bloodshed and it may be surmised that priests
> as well as prophets opposed his paganisation.
> Some of the priests fled to Egypt, joined the
> Jewish garrison at Elephantine, and there . . .
> erected the Temple.[18]

10 These are the words of Bezalel Porten, author of the
authoritative study *Archives from Elephantine*. Porten
nevertheless remains puzzled by the fact that a Jewish
temple could have been built at Elephantine at all,
because of the notion, deeply entrenched within
Judaism, 'that foreign soil was unclean and that,
therefore, no Temple to the Lord might be erected on
it.'[19] He points out that, after the destruction of
Solomon's Temple in Jerusalem, the Jews carried off
into exile in Babylon 'were counselled by Jeremiah to
settle down and *pray* (not sacrifice) to the Lord.' The
same author then adds: 'there is no evidence that any

Temple to YHWH was erected in Babylonia' and asks:
'With what justification, then, did the Jews at
Elephantine erect their temple?'[20]

11 It seems to me that the answer to Porten's rhetorical
    question is obvious: their justification was that they had
    brought with them from Jerusalem the Ark of the
    Covenant and that they now needed to build 'an house
    of rest' for it,[21] just as Solomon had done so long before.

Elephantine and the Falashas

When I returned to England I felt quite confident that I had at
last uncovered the real sequence of events underlying the
mystery of the lost Ark.

Seeking supporting evidence I went to the School of Oriental
and African Studies in London and acquired copies of the two
out-of-print volumes that Achim Krekeler had lent me, volumes
that I now wanted to examine much more thoroughly. I also
assembled other relevant sources, including *The History* of
Herodotus (because I had learned that the famous Greek scholar
had paid a visit to Elephantine around the year 450 BC[22]).

This further research effort proved fruitful. One thing that
had been bothering me, for example, was why Josiah – the
zealous traditionalist who had inherited the throne in Jerusalem
two years after Manasseh's death – had not sought to get the Ark
back from Elephantine. The answer to that question did not
prove difficult to find. As I had already established, Josiah's
reforms had not started until the twelfth year of his reign (when
he was twenty) and his restoration of the Temple had only begun
in the eighteenth year of his reign (622 BC).[23] By this time
relations between Judah and Egypt had deteriorated dramatically
– so much so, in fact, that Josiah was ultimately killed fighting the
Egyptians.[24] Even if he had known that the Ark had been taken to
Elephantine, therefore, he would not have been in a position to
enforce its return from a powerful country with which he was at
war.

Having satisfied myself on this point I then moved on to
consider the next stage of the lost history that I was attempting to
reconstruct – the journey of the Ark from Elephantine into

Ethiopia during the fifth century BC. My interview in Jerusalem with the Falasha priest Raphael Hadane had raised the intriguing possibility that the ancestors of Ethiopia's black Jews might have been migrants from Elephantine – because there could be no doubt that he had been speaking of that island when he had told me that his forefathers had built a temple at Aswan. Moreover the notion that the Falashas might have reached Ethiopia from Elephantine was supported by the findings of my own earlier research. In November 1989 I had been struck by the 'ethnographic fingerprint' of Falasha settlement around Lake Tana and – on the basis of this and other evidence – I had concluded that:

> the religion of Solomon could only have entered Ethiopia
> from the west – through Egypt and the Sudan along the
> ancient and well-travelled trade routes provided by the
> Nile and Takazze rivers.

For some time before reaching that conclusion I had been profoundly dissatisfied with the large body of academic opinion which held that the Falashas were the descendants of Jews from southern Arabia who had arrived in Ethiopia after AD 70 (see Chapter 6). Now, as I followed up the bibliography that the social anthropologist Shalva Weil had dictated to me in Jerusalem, I discovered that a number of other theories had been put forward to challenge the prevailing orthodoxy. Though repeatedly ridiculed by the masters of Ethiopian studies like Professor Edward Ullendorff,[25] some of the dissenting voices had suggested that the ancestors of the Falashas could well have been converted to Judaism by migrants from the Jewish colony on the island of Elephantine.[26] No doubt there had been extensive commercial and cultural contacts between Yemen and Ethiopia during this period; the reality was, however, that several quite substantial Jewish communities had been established in Egypt for hundreds of years before any Jews had settled in south Arabia. Given the profoundly Old Testament character of Falasha religion, therefore, logic suggested that the Jewish faith must have been carried south-eastwards from Egypt and into Ethiopia in a gradual process of 'cultural diffusion'.[27]

To be sure, there were no absolutely unassailable historical facts linking the Falashas to Elephantine. I did, however, come across a great many tantalizing clues and coincidences which seemed to me to be highly suggestive of such a link. All the evidence was circumstantial and none of it actually *proved* my theory that the Ark had reached Ethiopia in the fifth century BC after spending two hundred years in the Jewish Temple on Elephantine. Viewed in the context of everything else that I had learned, however – in Israel, in Egypt and in Ethiopia itself – my latest findings took on a different and entirely more persuasive aspect.

Set out below, as I recorded them in my notebook, are the principal conclusions that I reached and the evidence on which they were based:

1 The fact that the Jewish community at Elephantine practised sacrifice – and that it continued to do so long after King Josiah's reforms – is surely highly significant. One of the proofs of the antiquity of Judaism in Ethiopia is the extremely archaic character of Falasha religion, in which animal sacrifice of precisely the kind carried out at Elephantine plays a crucial role.[28] This adds weight to the hypothesis that the Falashas are the 'cultural descendants' of Jewish migrants from Elephantine and therefore provides strong support for the thesis that the Ark of the Covenant may have been brought to Ethiopia from that island.

2 In its heyday the Jewish Temple on Elephantine had its own well established priesthood. In the vowel-less language of the papyri these priests are referred to as KHN.[29] This word, of course, becomes *kahen* when the vowels 'a' and 'e' are added. Falasha priests are also called Kahen.[30]

3 One of the names given to the Jewish Temple on Elephantine was MSGD.[31] It meant 'place of prostration'.[32] To this day the Falashas in Ethiopia have no synagogues; neither do they have a temple; they do, however, call their simple houses of worship *Mesgid*[33] (i.e. MSGD with the vowels 'e' and 'i' added).

In this context it is also worthy of note that it was exactly in a prostrate position, knees to the ground, that King Solomon once prayed before the Ark of the Covenant of Yahweh.[34]

4 In his interview with me in Jerusalem Raphael Hadane said that the Jewish Temple built by his forefathers 'at Aswan' had been exempted from a great destruction that had been inflicted upon Egyptian temples by a 'foreign king':

> 'he did not destroy our temple. So when the Egyptians saw that only the Jewish temple was not destroyed they suspected that we were on the side of the invader. Because of this they started to fight against us and they destroyed our temple and we were forced to flee.'

In 525 BC a foreign king did invade Egypt and did indeed destroy many temples.[35] His name was Cambyses and he was the ruler of the expansionist Persian Empire that had been founded by his father Cyrus the Great. The Elephantine papyri preserve this recollection of him:

> when Cambyses came into Egypt he found this [Jewish] Temple built. They [the Persians] knocked down all the temples of the gods of Egypt, but no one did any damage to this Temple.[36]

The Persians remained in power in Egypt until very close to the end of the fifth century BC. During this period the Jews on Elephantine co-operated closely with them. It was after their protection had been effectively removed that the Jewish Temple on that island was finally destroyed.[37] Raphael Hadane's folk traditions about the origins of the Falashas are therefore borne out by established historical facts.

5 Hadane also reported that his people especially venerated the island of Tana Kirkos – the same island to which I was told the Ark had been brought in the fifth century BC. Moreover, Memhir Fisseha, the Christian priest whom I

interviewed on that island, told me that the Ark had been
kept there 'inside a tent' for eight hundred years before
being taken to Axum.[38] It seems to me hardly surprising
that a tent or 'tabernacle' might have been used on Tana
Kirkos to shelter the Ark. If my theory is correct then the
Jews who brought the relic there had just experienced the
destruction of their own Temple on Elephantine and
would have known also of the earlier destruction of
Solomon's Temple by Nebuchadnezzar. They could well
have decided that it was time to abandon formal temples
for ever and to return to the pure tradition of the desert
wanderings when the Ark had always been housed in a
tent.

6 Last but not least, Raphael Hadane told me that the
ancestors of the Falashas reached Ethiopia not only by
way of Aswan (i.e. Elephantine) but also that they passed
through the city of Meroe 'where they remained for a
short while'. These same two places were also named by
Solomon Alemu, the Falasha priest whom I interviewed at
the village of Anbober in January 1990. Can it be a
coincidence that, after being lost to history for more than
1,500 years, the ruins of Meroe were finally unearthed by
– guess who? Answer: they were discovered in 1772 by
the Scottish explorer James Bruce.[39]

The land of the Deserters

All this, I felt, very strongly suggested that I was on the right track
– and the fact that the site of ancient Meroe had been discovered
by none other than my old friend James Bruce only served to
quicken my enthusiasm for the chase. The Scottish explorer, I
was sure, had made his epic journey to Ethiopia in order to locate
the Ark of the Covenant (see Chapter 7). How appropriate
therefore that he should also have located the fabled city through
which the sacred relic had passed on its journey to the Abyssinian
highlands.

But had it really passed that way? There was still, it seemed to
me, one vital question that I had not yet satisfactorily answered:

why should the Jews of Elephantine have migrated to the *south* with the Ark of the Covenant after they left the island? Why not head north – back towards Israel, for example?

I found that there were several possible explanations for this, all of which could have played a role. For a start, by the fifth century BC, the Jews in Jerusalem had got used to living without the Ark. Solomon's Temple was long gone and a new one had been built to replace it. This Second Temple, furthermore, was administered by an entrenched priesthood which would definitely not have welcomed competitors from Elephantine.

By the same token, the Elephantine Jews would have felt alien and out of place in the theological environment afforded by Jerusalem in the fifth century BC. Religious thinking had moved on, God was no longer thought of as the quasi-corporeal deity who had dwelled 'between the cherubims', and the forms of worship in which the Ark had once occupied centre stage had been largely abandoned.

The return of the relic would, therefore, have led to many potentially catastrophic problems. It would have been quite obvious to the Elephantine priesthood that in order to avoid these problems they would have to stay away from Jerusalem. But where could they go instead? Clearly, they could not remain in Egypt, since the Egyptians had turned against them and destroyed their Temple. Nor, for the same reason, could they have been sure of safe passage if they had chosen to travel *north* in order to leave that country. A logical solution, therefore, would have been to turn towards the south. It was not without good reason that the Governor of Aswan and Elephantine was titled 'Governor of the Door of the Southern Countries'.[40] In order to take their precious relic to safety the Jews would only have needed to open that metaphorical 'door' and head off into those 'Southern Countries', which were known collectively as 'Ethiopia' – a Greek word meaning 'burnt faces' applied at that time to all areas in which dark-skinned people lived.[41]

The fugitives would by no means have been venturing forth into a terrifying *terra incognita*. On the contrary, there was direct evidence that members of the Jewish community had been involved in military expeditions far to the south as early as the sixth century BC.[42] Furthermore, I discovered well documented instances of *previous* migrations – migrations that had not necessarily involved Jews but that had seen large numbers of people from the Aswan area travelling and settling in 'the Southern Countries'. For example, Herodotus, the 'father of History', reported that four days' journey beyond Elephantine the river Nile ceased to be navigable:

> You will then disembark and travel along the bank for forty days, for there are sharp rocks in the Nile and many reefs through which you will be unable to sail. Having marched through this country in forty days, you will embark again in another boat and sail for twelve days, and then you will come to a great city, *the name of which is Meroe.* This city is said to be the mother of all Ethiopia . . . From this city, making a voyage of the same length of sailing as you did from Elephantine to the mother city of the Ethiopians, you will come to *the land of the Deserters* . . . These were two hundred and forty thousand Egyptians, fighter Egyptians, who revolted from the Egyptians and joined the Ethiopians . . . in the time of King Psammetichus. When these people had settled among the Ethiopians, the Ethiopians became more civilised, through learning the manner of the Egyptians. For four months of travel space, then, sailing and road, beyond its course in Egypt, the Nile is a known country. If you add all together, you will find that *it takes four months of journeying from Elephantine to these Deserters of whom I spoke.*[43]

I said earlier that the mass exodus of 'the Deserters' from Elephantine had not necessarily involved Jews, and I could find no proof that it had. Herodotus had stated very clearly, however, that this exodus had occurred in the time of the Pharaoh Psammetichus (595–589 BC[44]). I was therefore excited to learn from an impeccable source that 'Jews had been sent out as auxiliaries to fight in the army of Psammetichus against the King of the Ethiopians.'[45] On the basis of this well documented historical fact it did not seem unreasonable to conclude that there might indeed have been some Jews amongst the Deserters.

Another aspect of the Herodotus report which I found intriguing was that it made specific mention of Meroe – through which, according to Raphael Hadane, the forefathers of the Falashas had passed on their way to Abyssinia. Moreover, Herodotus had gone to considerable lengths to explain that his 'Deserters' had lived a full fifty-six days' sail *beyond* Meroe. If this journey had been made on the Atbara river, which flows into the Nile just to the north of Meroe (and into which, in turn, the Takazze also flows) then it would have brought the traveller as far as the borders of modern Ethiopia, and perhaps across those borders.[46]

Herodotus had written his report in the fifth century BC. It followed that if a group of Jews bearing the Ark of the Covenant had chosen to flee southwards from Elephantine in that same century then they would have passed through 'known country' almost all the way to Lake Tana. Moreover, simple logic suggested that the Abyssinian highlands could have been an attractive destination for them – cool and well watered, these green mountains would surely have looked like a Garden of Eden by comparison with the deserts of the Sudan.

Beyond the rivers of Cush

Could the fugitives from Elephantine have had foreknowledge of this 'garden beyond the wilderness'? Was it possible that in making their journey to the south they might not only have been travelling through 'known country' but also going towards a land in which they already had kin and co-religionists? As my research progressed I did find evidence to suggest that this was indeed possible and that Jews could well have ventured into Abyssinia at dates even earlier than the fifth century BC.

Part of this evidence was biblical. Though I knew that the use of the word 'Ethiopia' in the Scriptures could not automatically be assumed to refer to the country now going by that name, I also knew that there were circumstances in which it might have done. As noted above, 'Ethiopia' is a Greek word meaning 'burnt faces'. In the earliest Greek editions of the Bible, the Hebrew term 'Cush' was translated as 'Ethiopia' and was used to refer, as one leading authority put it, to 'the entire Nile Valley south of

Egypt, including Nubia and Abyssinia'.[47] What this meant was that biblical references to 'Ethiopia' might or might not refer to Abyssinia proper. Likewise, in English translations that had reverted to the use of the word 'Cush', Abyssinia might or might not have been implied.

In this context it seemed to me at least worthy of note that Moses himself had married an 'Ethiopian woman'[48] – according to an undeniably ancient verse in the book of Numbers. Added to this was the curious testimony of the Jewish historian Flavius Josephus – supported by several Jewish legends – which asserted that between his fortieth and eightieth years the prophet had lived for some time in 'Ethiopia'.[49]

Other passages in the Scriptures also referred to 'Ethiopia'/ 'Cush'. Many were plainly irrelevant to my interests. Some, however, were intriguing and raised the possibility that the scribes responsible for them had *not* had Nubia or any part of the Sudan in mind but rather the mountainous land in the Horn of Africa that we call 'Ethiopia' today.

One such, with which I was already familiar, occurred in the second chapter of the book of Genesis and referred to the rivers that flowed out of the Garden of Eden: 'And the name of the second river is Gihon; the same is it that compasseth the whole land of Ethiopia.'[50] A glance at a map showed me that there was a very real sense in which the Blue Nile, sweeping out from Lake Tana in a wide loop, did indeed compass 'the whole land of Ethiopia'. Moreover, as I had been aware for some time,[51] the twin springs regarded as the source of that great river are known to this day as *Giyon* by the Ethiopians themselves.[52]

Another interesting passage occurred in Psalm 68, described by Jon D. Levenson, Associate Professor of the Hebrew Bible in the Divinity School of the University of Chicago, as 'one of the oldest pieces of Israelite poetry'.[53] This psalm included a cryptic reference to the Ark of the Covenant[54] and also made the following strange prediction: 'Ethiopia shall soon stretch out her hands unto God.'[55] I could not help but wonder why Ethiopia had been given prominence in this way as a likely candidate for conversion to the religion of Israel. Unfortunately, there was nothing in the psalm itself which helped to answer this question. However, in a passage written somewhat later by the prophet Amos (whose ministry lasted from 783 to 743 BC[56]), there were indications that something so momentous had happened in Ethiopia/Cush that the inhabitants of that distant land were now to be regarded as being on a par with the 'Chosen People' of Israel. Three different translations of the same verse (Amos 9:7) help to illustrate what I mean:

Are ye not as children of the Ethiopians unto me, O children of Israel? saith the Lord. (King James Authorized Version)	Are not you and the Cushites all the same to me, sons of Israel? – it is Yahweh who speaks. (Jerusalem Bible)	Are not you Israelites like Cushites to me? says the Lord. (New English Bible)

While I realized that it would be possible to interpret this verse in another way – i.e. to understand from it that the children of Israel were no longer to be accorded any special privileges by Yahweh – it seemed to me that the more obvious reading also had to be considered. By the eighth century BC, when Amos was prophesying, was it not conceivable that there could already have been a flow of Hebrew migrants southwards through Egypt and into the highlands of Abyssinia? There was no proof for this admittedly wild speculation. It was an undeniable fact, however, that out of all the vast swathe of territory that Amos *could* have been referring to when he spoke of Ethiopia/Cush, only one specific area was known to have adopted the Judaic faith in antiquity (and, moreover, to have adhered to that faith right up until the twentieth century AD). That area, of course, lay in the vicinity of Lake Tana, the Falasha homeland since time immemorial.

The next biblical passage that caught my attention was in the book of Zephaniah, and had been written at some time between 640 and 622 BC[57] – i.e. during the reign of King Josiah. Again I found it helpful to view side by side three separate translations of the same verse (Zephaniah 3:10), which supposedly quoted the words of the Lord:

From beyond the rivers of Ethiopia my suppliants, even the daughter of my dispersed, shall bring mine offering. (King James Authorized Version)	From beyond the banks of the rivers of Ethiopia my suppliants will bring me offerings. (Jerusalem Bible)	From beyond the rivers of Cush my suppliants of the Dispersion shall bring me tribute. (New English Bible)

Since there was absolutely no doubt that this verse had been written before 622 BC – and thus well before the exile and captivity of the Israelites in Babylon – it was pertinent to ask the following questions:

1 When Zephaniah had referred to a 'dispersion' what event exactly had he been talking about?
2 Which part of biblical 'Cush' had he had in mind when he had envisaged the suppliants of the Lord bringing offerings 'from beyond the rivers of Ethiopia'?

In answer to the first question, I had to conclude that the prophet had been talking about some kind of voluntary popular migration, because there had been no enforced 'dispersion' of the Hebrews from the Holy Land prior to Zephaniah's time. As regards the second question, the reader will recall that the biblical term 'Cush' connoted 'the entire Nile Valley, south of Egypt, including Nubia and Abyssinia'. The verse quoted above, however, contained internal evidence which helped to narrow down the precise geographical area that Zephaniah had been speaking of. That evidence lay in the phrase variously translated as 'beyond the rivers of Ethiopia'. Since more than one river was involved, the Nile Valley as far south as Meroe could be ruled out. East of Meroe, however, flowed the Atbara, and beyond that the Takazze, while to the south (roughly parallel to the Atbara) the Blue Nile rushed down from Abyssinia. These, surely, were the rivers of Ethiopia, and beyond all of them lay Lake Tana. The possibility that the prophet had had the traditional area of Falasha settlement in mind when he had written this intriguing verse could not, therefore, be entirely dismissed.

My feeling that there might be something to this speculation strengthened when I ran a computer check and discovered that the phrase 'beyond the rivers of Ethiopia/Cush' had only been used on one other occasion in the entire Bible. The King James Authorized Version translated the relevant passage (from Chapter 18 of the book of Isaiah) as follows:

Woe to the land shadowing with wings, which is beyond the rivers of Ethiopia: That sendeth ambassadors by the sea, even in vessels of bulrushes upon the waters, saying, Go, ye swift messengers, to a nation scattered and peeled, to a people terrible from their beginning hitherto; a nation meted out and trodden down, whose land the rivers have spoiled![58]

The other translations of the same passage, which I reproduce below side by side, added further shades of meaning to an already rich and haunting message:

Country of whirring wings beyond the rivers of Cush, who send ambassadors by sea, in papyrus skiffs over the waters. Go, swift messengers to a people tall and bronzed, to a

There is a land of sailing ships, a land beyond the rivers of Cush which sends its envoys by the Nile, journeying on the waters in vessels of reed. Go, swift messengers, go to a people tall and smooth-

nation always feared, a people mighty and masterful, in the country criss-crossed with rivers. (Jerusalem Bible)	skinned, to a people dreaded near and far, a nation strong and proud, whose land is scoured by rivers. (New English Bible)

Falling as it did in Chapter 18 of the book of Isaiah, it was certain that this passage had been written by Isaiah himself.[59] This meant, of course, that it could be accurately dated to his lifetime which, as I already knew,[60] had been a long one, spanning the reigns of Jotham, Ahaz and Hezekiah (respectively 740–736 BC, 736–716 BC and 716–687 BC[61]). In fact, the prophet had almost certainly survived into the reign of Manasseh, the monarch whose idolatry, I was now quite certain, had led to the removal of the Ark of the Covenant from the Holy of Holies of the Jerusalem Temple. I was therefore interested to learn of a strong and ancient Jewish tradition which held that Isaiah had died a martyr at the hands of Manasseh himself.[62]

What I found even more interesting was the way in which the prophet had spoken of the mysterious land that lay 'beyond the rivers of Cush'. The King James Authorized Version of the Bible suggested that he had cursed this land but the more recent translations conveyed no such impression. All three renderings, however, did agree on its geographical character: not only was it located 'beyond' rivers, but also it was itself 'spoiled', or 'scoured', or 'criss-crossed' by rivers.

In my view, this information made it virtually certain that Isaiah had been referring to Abyssinia and to the area of traditional Falasha settlement there. The high country around Lake Tana is indeed 'criss-crossed' by rivers (which also spoil and scour it by carrying away huge quantities of its precious top-soil). There were other clues as well:

1 The inhabitants of the land were said to be tall and 'peeled', or 'smooth-skinned', or – in the authoritative Jerusalem Bible translation – 'bronzed'. This, I thought, was a description that could easily be applied

to modern Ethiopians, whose glowing, chestnut-brown complexions are quite distinct from the 'black', negroid skin tones found in other African countries.

2 The land was curiously described as 'shadowing with wings' (or more directly as a 'country of whirring wings'). This, I felt, might very well be a reference to the giant locust swarms that, every decade or so, lay waste Ethiopia, overshadowing the fields of the peasants and filling the air with a dry whirring sound that sends shivers down the spine.

3 Finally Isaiah had made specific mention of the fact that the messengers of the land travelled in 'vessels of bulrushes' or in 'papyrus skiffs', or in 'vessels of reed'. To this day, as I was very well aware, those who dwell around the vast inland sea of Lake Tana make extensive use of papyrus-reed boats known as *tankwas*. [63]

All in all, therefore, I felt that the biblical data did lend a considerable degree of credibility to the view that some kind of relationship might have been established between Israel and the Abyssinian highlands at a very early date. Moses's Ethiopian wife, Isaiah's 'people tall and bronzed', and Zephaniah's 'dispersed' suppliants – who would return to Jerusalem 'from beyond the rivers of Cush' – all made it very difficult to resist the suspicion that Hebrews had been travelling to Ethiopia, and probably settling there, long before the fifth century BC. If, as I suspected, the Jewish priests of Elephantine had brought the Ark of the Covenant to the island of Tana Kirkos in that same century then it followed that they would have been coming to a land in which their co-religionists had already established a secure foothold.

Waves of migration?

Outside the Bible was there any evidence at all which might support this hypothesis? I felt that there was. The research that I myself had conducted in Ethiopia during 1989–90, for example, had already raised the possibility that there might have been successive waves of Hebrew migration over an immense span of time extending back into the remotest antiquity. Most strongly suggestive of this had been the long interview that I had conducted with Wambar Muluna Marsha, High Priest of the 'Hebraeo-Pagan' Qemant (see Chapter 11). He had told me that Anayer, the founder of his religion, had come to the Lake Tana area from 'the land of Canaan'. When I had made a closer examination of Qemant religion I had established that it contained a peculiar mixture of pagan and Jewish practices – the latter reflected particularly in the distinctions between 'clean' and 'unclean' foods – coupled with a reverence for 'sacred groves' which bore a close resemblance to the very earliest forms of Judaism (the patriarch Abraham had 'planted a grove in Beersheba,' and had 'called there on the name of the Lord'.[64] Such tendencies had probably been quite widespread during the early period of Israelite settlement in Canaan, and had enjoyed a brief resurgence during Manasseh's reign, but had been thoroughly and finally stamped out by King Josiah in the seventh century BC.

The implication was that the forefathers of the Qemant must have migrated to Ethiopia from Canaan at a very early date. By contrast the Falashas looked like the descendants of slightly more recent migrants. Their religion included certain practices also banned by King Josiah – notably animal sacrifice at local shrines – but otherwise looked like a rather pure form of Old Testament Judaism (and was certainly not adulterated with any obviously pagan beliefs).

Neighbours in the mountains and valleys around Lake Tana, the Qemant and the Falashas maintained that they were related to each other (Wambar Muluna Marsha had told me that the founding family of his religion and the founding family of the Falasha religion had travelled 'on the same journey' and had discussed a possible marriage alliance – which they had ultimately failed to make).

Such folklore, as I subsequently established, did reflect an ethnographic truth. The Falashas and the Qemant were indeed relatives: both were sub-sections of the great Agaw tribe of western central Ethiopia[65] – an ethnic group considered to represent the oldest stratum of population in the Horn of Africa.[66] Because of this, the mother-tongue of both peoples was a dialect of Agaw, classified, interestingly enough, as belonging to the 'Cushitic' group of languages.[67] Semitic tongues related to Hebrew and Arabic (for example, Amharic and Tigrigna) were also present in Ethiopia but were *not* spoken (except as second languages) either by the Falashas or by the Qemant.

The explanation for this anomaly, and the deductions that flowed logically from it, seemed to me to be obvious. I wrote in my notebook:

> The first small bands of Hebrews must have begun to migrate from Israel to Ethiopia a very long time ago. I suspect that this process started as early as the tenth century BC (perhaps even earlier) and that it continued at least until the end of the fifth century BC. On their arrival in the Lake Tana area the migrants would have found themselves amongst the oldest-established inhabitants of Ethiopia – such as the Agaw – and would have intermarried with them, thus gradually losing their own distinct ethnic identity. At the same time, however, they would have passed on the Judaic faith and culture that they had brought with them. In this fashion, by say the second or first century BC, there would have been no more 'Hebrews' as such living in Ethiopia, only 'Hebraized' or 'Judaized' peoples who to all other intents and purposes would have looked like native Ethiopians and who would, of course, have spoken a native Ethiopian language (Hebrew having long since been forgotten). The modern descendants of these 'Hebraized' or 'Judaized' peoples are the Qemant and the Falashas – the black Jews of Ethiopia – and their mother-tongue, a dialect of Agaw, is indeed a native Cushitic language.
>
> And what about the 'Semitic' peoples of Ethiopia such as the politically dominant Christian Amharas? Almost certainly they are, as the ethnographers maintain, the descendants of Sabaean/South Arabian settlers who moved into the highlands in separate and somewhat later waves of immigration. Judaism in one form or another was probably quite well established amongst indigenous Agaw groups by the time that these Sabaean conquerors

arrived – which would explain why their cultures, too, were gradually 'Judaized' and why Judaic elements survive to this day in the curiously Old Testament character of Abyssinian Christianity.

'There were always Jews in Ethiopia, from the beginning,' wrote the Portuguese Jesuit Balthaza Tellez in the seventeenth century.[68] In this judgement he was, I suspect, far closer to the truth than those modern scholars who ascribe a relatively late date to the arrival of Judaism – and who seem to be completely blind to all the evidence that runs contrary to their own prejudices.

The mysterious 'BRs'

While possessing the merit of explaining a great deal that hitherto had never been properly explained, I was well aware of a potential weakness in the theory that I had just outlined in my notebook: might it not reflect my *own* prejudices rather than the facts? To be sure, it was a *fact* that the Falashas practised an archaic form of Judaism; likewise it was a *fact* that Qemant religion contained many ancient Hebraic elements; and in a similar fashion it was a *fact* that the Christianity of the Ethiopian Orthodox Church was riddled through and through with practices that were unmistakably Judaic in origin. But from all this was it legitimate to conclude that there had been waves of Hebrew immigration into Ethiopia for hundreds of years before the fifth century BC – when, as I believed, the Ark of the Covenant had been brought from the island of Elephantine on the upper Nile to the island of Tana Kirkos? If I was right, and if there had indeed been prior Hebrew settlement in that area, then there would no longer be any mystery about why Ethiopia (rather than some other country) had been chosen as the last resting place of the Ark.

But was I right? Thus far the evidence that I had gathered in support of my evolving theory had taken two distinctly different forms: (1) social and ethnographic data about the Falashas and the Qemant, notably concerning their religious beliefs, their folklore and their relationships to one another; (2) clues, scattered throughout the Old Testament, which seemed to bear witness to some kind of sustained Hebrew migration to Abyssinia in the first half of the first millennium BC. If there had really been such a migration, however, then surely there would be proof of it outside the Bible and outside the observed peculiarities of Falasha and Qemant culture? The impressionistic material that I had already gathered was strongly suggestive, but what I really needed in order to make a complete case was tangible archaeological or documentary evidence of Hebrew settlement in Ethiopia prior to the fifth century BC.

I had never come across such evidence and I knew that I was swimming against the current of scholarly opinion in seeking for it now. Nevertheless I put out feelers to my contacts in the academic world in an attempt to discover whether there was anything of importance that I might have missed.

Not long afterwards I received through the mail a paper written in French by a certain Jacqueline Pirenne and published in 1989 by the Université des sciences humaines de Strasbourg.[69] The paper had been sent to me by a professor of Egyptology at a major British university. In his covering note who said:

> Just a line to enclose a photocopy of an article by Jacqueline Pirenne, given at a recent conference in Strasburg.
>
> Frankly, from a scholarly point of view, I consider she's gone 'way over the top'; she's undoubtedly a very able person, knows her ancient Arabian documentation, but has (for not a few of us) improbable ideas on anc. Arabian chronology & script origin. This essay is fascinating, but more fiction than history, I fear. (Beeston, I gather, criticised it heavily at a recent meeting of the Seminar for Arabian Studies; he's pre-eminently sane, though no more infallible than the rest of us.)

I naturally wondered why the professor should have thought that a paper by someone who knew her 'ancient Arabian documentation' could possibly be of any relevance to my own research. After I had had the paper translated into English, however, I could see exactly why he had thought that, and I was also able to understand why members of the academic establishment had reacted with hostility to Jacqueline Pirenne's views.

To strip a rather complex thesis down to its bare essentials, the main thrust of her argument was that scholars who had examined the historical relationship between Ethiopia and South Arabia had been completely wrong: far from Sabaean influences reaching Ethiopia *from* the Yemen, as had previously been supposed, the flow had in fact been in the opposite direction, in other words from Ethiopia to South Arabia:

> The Sabaeans . . . arrived first of all in Ethiopian Tigray and entered Yemen via the Red Sea coast . . . This conclusion, which is the absolute contrary to all recognized views, is the only one . . . to explain the facts and do them justice.[70]

Pirenne then went on to demonstrate that the original homeland of the Sabaeans had been in north-west Arabia but that large numbers of them had emigrated from there to Ethiopia ('via the Hammamat river bed and along the Nile') in two separate waves, the first around 690 BC and the second around 590 BC. Why had they emigrated? In order to avoid paying tribute to the Assyrian invader Sennacherib on the first occasion and in order to avoid paying tribute to the Babylonian conqueror Nebuchadnezzar on the second.

This thesis was not as far-fetched as it sounded: during their respective campaigns Sennacherib and Nebuchadnezzar had not confined themselves to their famous attacks on Jerusalem; it was a fact that they had also pressed on into north-west Arabia, where they might indeed have encountered and displaced Sabaean tribes. This much I already knew. I did not feel, however, that I was in a position either to condemn or condone the rest of Pirenne's argument, namely that her fugitive Sabaeans had reached Ethiopia by following the Nile Valley and then had migrated onwards from there across the Red Sea and into the Yemen.

Nor was this argument, interesting though it was, central to Pirenne's importance for my own investigation. What caught my eye, and finally convinced me that I was on the right track, was her analysis of a Sabaean inscription found in Ethiopia and dated to the sixth century BC. Translated by the linguist R. Schneider and originally published in an obscure paper entitled 'Documents épigraphiques de l'Ethiopie',[71] this inscription honoured a Sabaean monarch who described himself as a 'noble fighter king' and boasted that in the empire he had established in the north and west of Ethiopia, he had reigned 'over Da'amat, the Sabas, and over the 'BRs, the whites and the blacks.'[72] Who were the 'BRs, Pirenne asked:

> R. Schneider did not venture any interpretation . . . but the term, witnessed in Assyrian inscriptions – the *Abirus* – may be attributed to the Hebrews . . . It is natural that Hebrews would have emigrated at the same time as the second wave of Sabaeans, since the first capture of Jerusalem by Nebuchadnezzar . . . followed by deportation to Babylon, was in 598 BC, whereas the attacks of the same Nebuchadnezzar against the Arabs were in 599–598 BC . . . Identification of the 'BRs as 'Hebrews' who arrived [in Ethiopia] with the second wave of Sabaeans explains . . . the existence of the Falashas, black but Jewish . . . They are the descendants of these 'Hebrews' who arrived in the sixth century BC.[73]

What Pirenne had not given any consideration to was the possibility that the 'BRs' – a standard way of writing the word 'Hebrews' (i.e. *ABIRUS*) in early alphabets lacking in vowels – might have arrived in Ethiopia *before* any of the Sabaean incursions. She had simply deduced, because the inscription that mentioned them had been dated to the sixth century BC, that they must have migrated in that century. On the basis of my own research, however, I now felt very confident in concluding that the 'BRs' over whom the Sabaean conquerors had claimed suzereinty could well have been in Ethiopia for some considerable while before that – and, moreover, that their numbers were still being added to at that time (and afterwards) by the arrival via the Nile Valley of more small bands of Hebrew immigrants.

This latter point was still in the realm of theory; Jacqueline Pirenne's gift to me, however, lay in the fact that she had drawn my attention to definite archaeological and documentary proof of the existence in Ethiopia, in the sixth century BC, of a people called the 'BRs'. Academics might argue until eternity about who these 'BRs' really were, but I myself was no longer in any doubt:

- they had been Hebrews who, at that early stage, had not yet submerged their identity with that of the indigenous Agaw amongst whom they had settled;
- they had worshipped a God called YHWH;
- in consequence, when the Ark of the Covenant of Yahweh was brought from Elephantine to Ethiopia in the fifth century BC there was a very real sense in which it could be said to have arrived in a receptive and appropriate resting place.

A chapel of mischance

There remained very little more for me to do. Throughout a long and circuitous historical investigation I had been trying to satisfy myself that there might be genuine merit to Ethiopia's claim to possess the lost Ark.

I had done that now. I was well aware that scholars might dispute my findings, and the conclusions that I had drawn from them – but, really, the approval of the 'experts' and the 'authorities' was not what I had sought during 1989 and 1990. Instead my goal had been an inner one in which I alone had been the judge and final arbiter of all the evidence and of all the arguments.

The central issue had been simple: to journey to the ancient Tigrayan city of Axum, and to the sanctuary chapel in which the Ark was supposed to lie, I would have to be prepared to accept physical risks and also to overcome a profound spiritual unease at the thought of putting myself into the hands of the TPLF – armed rebels who had good cause to hate me because of the cosy links that I had hitherto enjoyed with the very government that they were shedding blood to overthrow. I had not been prepared to accept those risks, or to struggle to master my own fears, unless I could first convince myself that in so doing I would be embarking on an adventure that was neither foolish nor quixotic but rather one that I could believe in and to which I could commit myself.

I now did believe that there was a very high degree of probability that the Ark might indeed lie in Axum, and I was therefore prepared to commit myself absolutely to the last stage of my quest – the journey to 'the sacred city of the Ethiopians' with all the risks and dangers and difficulties that that would entail.

This was not a decision that I had arrived at lightly; on the contrary, over the previous months, I had determinedly sought out every excuse that might possibly have justified the abandonment of the whole chancy project. Instead of finding such excuses, however, I had only stumbled upon more and more clues that appeared to point unerringly in the direction of Axum.

I had looked for alternative resting places for the Ark, but none of those that legend or tradition offered had seemed in the least bit likely. I had looked for proofs that the relic might have been destroyed, but no such proofs existed. I had established that the *Kebra Nagast*'s claims about Solomon, Sheba and Menelik could not literally be true – only to discover that these same claims might well serve as a complex metaphor for the truth. Certainly, the Ark of the Covenant could not have gone to Ethiopia in the era of Solomon; but it was entirely plausible that it might have made that journey later, at the time of the destruction of the Jewish Temple that had stood on the island of Elephantine in the upper Nile.

All in all, therefore, whatever the academics might think, I knew that I had reached the end of a long personal road and that I could not any more put off or avoid the final reckoning: if I was to preserve any sense of my own integrity, if I was not in later years to feel dishonoured and ashamed, then I would have to do my level best to reach Axum – no matter the risks that I would have to run, no matter the demons of self-interest and cowardice that I would have to overcome. It was a cliché – perhaps one of the oldest clichés known to man – but it seemed to me that what really counted was not so much that I should attain the sacred city but rather that I should try to get there, not so much that I should actually find the Ark but rather that I should find within myself sufficient reserves of character to make the attempt.

I was, in my own eyes, far from being an Arthurian knight clad in shining armour. Nevertheless, at this moment in my life, I had no difficulty in understanding why Sir Gawain, on his way to the perils that awaited him at the Green Chapel, had chosen to ignore the siren song of the squire who had sought to dissuade him from completing his quest and who had warned him:

> 'if you come there you'll be killed . . . therefore good Sir Gawain . . . ride by another route, to some region remote! Go in the name of God, and Christ grace your fortune! And I shall go home again and undertake to swear solemnly, by God and his saints as well, stoutly to keep your secret, not saying to a soul that you ever tried to turn tail.'[74]

After considering his position, Gawain had replied:

> 'It is worthy of you to wish for my well being, man, and I believe you would loyally lock it in your heart. But however quiet you kept it, if I quit this place, fled . . . in the fashion you propose, I should become a cowardly knight with no excuse whatever . . . I *will* go to the Green Chapel, to get what Fate sends.'[75]

With just such resolve, though with less chivalry, I was now determined that I must go to my own 'chapel of mischance'[76] to find there whatever Fate might send me. And, like Sir Gawain, I knew that I would have to make that journey at the dawn of a New Year – for the solemn feast of *Timkat* fast approached.

Part VI: Ethiopia, 1990-91
The Waste Land

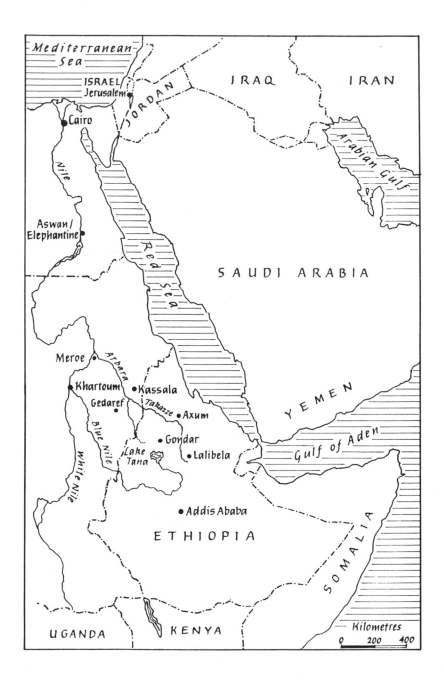

Chapter 17

Supping with Devils

After my trips to Israel and Egypt I returned to England in October 1990 with my mind made up: I would have to go to Axum, and the optimum time to travel there would be in January 1991. If I could arrive before the 18th of that month then I would be able to participate in the *Timkat* ceremony, during which I hoped that the Ark itself would be carried in public procession.

Raphael Hadane, the Falasha priest whom I had interviewed in Jerusalem, had doubted whether the genuine article would actually be used: 'I do not believe that the Christians would ever bring out the true Ark,' he had told me, 'they would not do that. They will never show it to anyone. They will use a replica instead.' Coming as it had from a man who had himself journeyed to Axum in the hope of seeing the sacred relic, this warning bothered me a great deal. Nevertheless I saw no alternative but to go ahead with my plan – and that meant confronting my own fears.

With Ethiopia's civil war continuing to go against the government there would no longer be any doubt that I would have to put myself into the hands of the Tigray People's Liberation Front if I was serious about getting to Axum. Over the years I knew that they had taken dozens of foreigners into the areas they controlled without the slightest harm coming to anyone. I, however, was terribly afraid that harm might come to me. Why?

The answer to this question lay in the close links that I had established with the Ethiopian regime over the period 1983–9. At the end of 1982 I had abandoned journalism, my former occupation, and had set up a publishing company of my own, the purpose of which was to produce books and other documentation for a wide range of clients, including a number of African governments. One of my earliest deals had been with the Ethiopian Tourism Commission; indeed, as reported in Chapter 1, it had been that deal that had taken me to Axum in the first place, way back in 1983.

The result had been a coffee-table book[1] which had been liked by senior members of the Ethiopian government and which had led to the commissioning of several similar projects. In the process I had met and got to know many powerful people: Shimelis Mazengia, the Head of Ideology, other Politburo and Central Committee activists including Berhanu Bayih and Kassa Kebede, and last but by no means least Ethiopia's so-called 'Red Emperor', President Mengistu Haile Mariam himself – the military strong-man who had seized control of the country in the mid 1970s and whose reputation for ruthless suppression of dissent was virtually without parallel anywhere in Africa.

There is a sense in which when you work closely with people you gradually begin to see things their way. This happened to me during the 1980s and, by the second half of the decade, I was one of the Ethiopian government's staunchest supporters. Though I never approved of that government's use of domestic repression, I managed quite successfully to persuade myself that particular initiatives taken by it were justified and helpful. Notable amongst these was the policy of resettlement inaugurated in 1984–5 with the goal of moving more than a million peasants from famine-stricken Tigray (then still under government control) to virgin lands in the south and west of the country. At the time I was convinced that this 'was necessary' because vast areas of the north had become 'uninhabitable wastelands on the verge of total, irreversible ecological collapse.'[2] The political leaders of the TPLF, however, looked at resettlement in quite a different way, seeing it as a grave threat to the rebellion that they were then desperately attempting to consolidate. The real aim underlying this 'sinister' policy, they were convinced, was to deprive them of vital grass-roots support in their own home region (since, obviously, every peasant removed from Tigray represented one less potential recruit for the Front).

By backing resettlement, therefore – and I did so publicly on a number of occasions – I had worked directly and explicitly against the interests of the TPLF. Moreover I had identified myself closely with the Ethiopian government in other ways as well. After several meetings with President Mengistu, for example, I had been asked to profile him for the BBC World Service. That profile, aired in 1988, had portrayed him in a far more favourable light than most people believed he deserved. What I had said had been a genuine expression of my own views – having got to know the man quite well I had concluded that his character had a great deal more depth and subtlety to it than he had ever before been given credit for. The end result, however, had been to make me vastly unpopular with his legions of critics and to give the TPLF further reason to conclude that I was firmly in the government's camp.

Finally, in 1988 and the early part of 1989, my involvement with the Addis Ababa regime had taken on a whole new dimension. In a bizarre series of journeys spread out over a period of more than a year I had carried messages back and forth between Ethiopia and neighbouring Somalia, where another African dictator with whom I was on friendly terms, President Mohamed Siyad Barre, was then still in power. The purpose of these trips had been to lend support to a faltering diplomatic peace process between the two countries, and my main role had been to reassure each head of state that his opposite number was in fact serious about negotiating and subsequently respecting a proper treaty.

At the time I had thought that what I was doing was honourable, worthwhile and manifestly in a good cause. Moreover it had flattered my ego to play the part of 'honest broker' between opponents as powerful and as dangerous as Mengistu and Barre. Such psychological inducements, however, had completely blinded me to the downside of my activities – the extent to which the close personal relationships that I was obliged to build with these cruel and calculating men might corrupt and compromise my own character. There is an old proverb which recommends that anyone planning to sup with the devil should use a long spoon. During my little burst of amateur diplomacy in 1988 and 1989 I supped with two devils – and unfortunately I neglected to use a spoon at all.

Did I emerge from the experience tainted in any way? The

honest answer to that question is a resounding Yes. Certainly I did. I could also add that I regret my actions and that, if I had my time over again, I surely would not allow myself to be lured by flattery and personal ambition into such vile company.

The fact was, however, that I now had to live with the consequences of my own mistakes. One of these consequences was that the Ethio-Somali peace process in which I had played a part had involved an agreement by both sides to cut off all the finance and arms that they had hitherto provided to each other's rebel groups. This naturally affected the interests of the TPLF who, over a period of several years, had built up a substantial support-office in Mogadishu, the Somali capital. Once again, therefore, I had demonstrated myself to be an enemy of the Tigrayan cause and a friend to Mengistu Haile Mariam, the dictator whom they regarded as the very incarnation of evil.

This was the background against which, with considerable trepidation, I made my first overtures to the TPLF's London office in November 1990. I expected that the most likely result was that they would flatly refuse my request to go to Axum. Alternatively, however, paranoia and a guilty conscience had conspired to produce a different and even more worrying scenario in my own mind: the guerillas would agree to take me to the sacred city; then, after I had crossed the border from Sudan into Tigray, they would arrange a fatal 'accident'. Melodramatic and even absurd though this fear might seem, it was very real to me.

Quest or cover story?

The response of the TPLF to my initial approach was underwhelming. Yes, they knew who I was. Yes, they were surprised that I should want to go to Axum. But no, they did not object to my plans.

There was a problem, however. A visa would be required from the government of the Sudan before I could even fly to Khartoum. An internal travel permit from that same government would also be necessary to enable me to cross the hundreds of kilometres of desert between Khartoum and the Tigrayan frontier.

Unfortunately neither visas nor permits were readily forth-coming for British citizens in the closing months of 1990. By then a major conflict in the Arabian Gulf looked unavoidable, and Sudan had thrown in its lot with Iraq. Britain, by taking the American side, had therefore rendered its nationals virtually *persona non grata* in Khartoum.

Didn't the TPLF have ways to get around that ban? Yes, they told me, they did. However, they reserved their efforts for visitors who were their friends or for visitors who could actively assist their cause. Since I was not a friend, and since I did not appear to be offering them anything that was to their immediate advantage, I would have to make my own arrangements with the Sudanese authorities. If I succeeded with that and if I could get myself as far as the frontier town of Kassala, then the TPLF would take me across the border from there and would allow me to proceed to Axum.

My contacts with the Sudanese Embassy in London only added to my growing sense of futility and depression. As a writer I was obliged to lodge my visa request with the Information Counsellor, Dr Abdel Wahab El-Affendi, who turned out to be a dapper young fellow in a suit. He told me, very politely, that I should abandon hope at once: in the present political climate there was absolutely no chance that I would be permitted to enter Sudan and even less that I would be allowed to travel internally from Khartoum to Kassala.

'Would it help if the TPLF supported my case?' I asked.

'Certainly. Will they?'

'Er . . . not at the moment. They have other priorities.'

'Well, there you are,' sighed Dr Affendi with the air of a man who has just proved his point, 'you're wasting your time.'

I asked: 'Would you mind forwarding my application to Khartoum anyway?'

The Information Counsellor smiled broadly and turned both his hands palms upwards in an eloquent gesture of insincere apology: 'I will be happy to do that, but I assure you that no good will come of it.'

Throughout the month of November I stayed in touch with Dr Affendi by telephone. He had no news for me. And after my first discussion with the TPLF on 2 November I went back to see them again on the 19th, this time for a meeting with Tewolde Gebru, their head of mission. During that meeting I had the sense that my motives were being skilfully probed by a clever negotiator whose aim was to find out whether I could be taken at face value or whether my real reason for wanting to go to Axum might not have more to do with the military ambitions of the Addis Ababa regime.

Of course, *I knew* that I was only interested in the Ark of the Covenant. Not for the first time, however, it occurred to me that my so-called 'quest' could easily look to the TPLF like the cover story of a spy. I was therefore not sure whether I should be elated or alarmed when, at the end of our conversation, Tewolde told me that he would ask the Front's Khartoum office to facilitate my visa and travel permit applications.

A deal

During the next three weeks I heard nothing further from the TPLF or from the Sudanese Embassy in London. A stalemate seemed to have set in and I began to realize that I was going to have to do something to force the pace.

The idea that I finally came up with was very simple. It was clear that an intense propaganda campaign was being waged alongside the war on the ground in Ethiopia. As part of this campaign the government had accused the TPLF – probably wrongly – of looting and burning churches. I therefore decided that I might have a chance of securing the rebels' co-operation if I could offer them the prospect of a television news report about religious freedom in Tigray under their administration – a report in which they would be given the opportunity to refute the allegations that had been levelled against them.

I did not want to make a public statement in the media in favour of the TPLF – partly because of a residual sense of loyalty to people in the government like Shimelis Mazengia who had helped me over the years, and partly because I found the prospect of a complete *volte face* distasteful. It was true that my views on Ethiopia's political problems had already changed, and that they were still changing. Nevertheless to stand up and support the TPLF now just because I needed to get to Axum was precisely the sort of behaviour that, in recent months, I had come to despise most in myself.

The solution that I had thought up to get around this problem was, however, almost equally devious. I would not make or present the television news report on Tigray. I would get someone else to do it for me.

The person whom I had in mind was an old friend, a former BBC producer named Edward Milner who had gone freelance some years previously. He had recently come back from the South American country of Colombia where he had filmed a special report for Britain's Channel 4 News. I therefore thought there was a good chance that he might be interested in doing a story on Tigray for the same outlet. Of course there could be no question of steering him in any particular direction. I knew him to be a man of integrity and I knew that he would insist on complete editorial freedom to film and report exactly what he saw in the field. Nevertheless I thought that the TPLF might show more interest in my application to go to Axum if, by this device, I could connect my own proposed trip to an important piece of television coverage. All rebel groups, in my experience, are keen on publicity and I did not think that the TPLF would prove to be any exception.

Accordingly, on Monday 10 December, I telephoned Tewolde Gebru again. When I had met him on 19 November he had told me that he would request the Front's Khartoum office to facilitate my visa and travel permit applications. I now asked him if there had been any progress on this.

'None at all,' he replied. 'Our people in Sudan are very busy and your case isn't really a priority for them.'

'Would it make a difference if I was able to offer you some television coverage?'

'Depends what it would be about.'

'It would be about the whole issue of religious freedom in Tigray – and about the relationship between the TPLF and the church. You may be winning the war on the ground but it seems to me that you're losing the propaganda war . . .'

'What makes you say that?'

'I'll give you an example. You've been accused recently of looting and burning churches, right?'

'Yes.'

'Which presumably has done you some harm?'

'Actually it has done us a great deal of harm both with the people and internationally.'

'And is it true?'

'No. Not true at all.'

'Nevertheless it's been said – and once mud of that sort has been thrown it tends to stick.' I played my trump card: 'It's quite obvious that it's part of a well planned government propaganda campaign against you. Listen, let me quote you something from a report in *The Times* of 19 October.' I had in front of me a clipping that my research assistant had given me. 'The Ethiopian government', I now read, 'particularly wants church support in its struggle against further disintegration of the state. President Mengistu said recently: "Our nation is the product of the process of history and it has existed for thousands of years. This is proved by existing historical relics." Ironically, the President also wants to contrast his liberalizing regime with what is perceived as the continuing communism and anti-clericalism of the secessionist movements . . .'

'I am familiar with that report,' Tewolde interjected. 'Any liberalization that Mengistu is doing is just a cynical measure designed to win popular support now that he sees that he cannot defeat us on the battlefield.'

'But that's not really the issue. The point is that you need to do something about your anti-clerical image. A proper news story televised nationally here in Britain would help you a lot. If we filmed that story at *Timkat* – which is when I want to be in Axum – then the processions and the whole atmosphere would help to demonstrate that the TPLF aren't against the church and that you are the responsible guardians of the most precious historical relic of all.'

'You could be right.'

'So shall I go ahead and see if I can organize some television coverage?'

'That would be a good idea.'

'And if I succeed do you think you'll be able to arrange the visas and permits in time?'

'Yes. I think I can guarantee that.'

The eleventh hour

After finishing with Tewolde I got straight on the phone to my friend Edward Milner, explained the situation to him and asked whether he was interested in offering the Tigray story to Channel 4 News.

He was interested and, by Wednesday 12 December, had secured a written commitment from the channel which we faxed to the TPLF together with Ed's passport details. We also sent a covering letter saying that we would have to leave for Tigray no later than Wednesday 9 January 1991 – well ahead of *Timkat*.

Two more weeks went by and still we had heard nothing definite from the TPLF. The visas and permits, although now forcefully requested, had simply not come through. 'Check with me immediately after the New Year,' Tewolde advised.

By Friday 4 January 1991 I had given up hope entirely and was beginning to experience an odd mixture of regret and relief: the former because I had failed to complete my quest; the latter because I had at least satisfied my own sense of honour by trying my best – and because I now seemed to be safe from all the dangers, real or imaginary, that the journey into Tigray had threatened. Then, late in the afternoon, Tewolde called: 'You can go ahead,' he announced, 'everything is arranged.'

Ed and I flew to Khartoum on 9 January as scheduled. From there an overland trek of less than a week would bring us to the sacred city of Axum.

Chapter 18

A Treasure Hard to Attain

Ed Milner and I disembarked from the KLM Airbus that had carried us to Khartoum and stepped out into the moist embrace of an African night. We had no visas, only reference numbers given to us by the TPLF in London. These, however, were clearly known to the immigration officer who handled our arrival and who retained our passports while we went to collect our luggage.

Married to a lovely Thai wife, and with two beautiful children, Ed was best man at my wedding and is one of my oldest friends. Short and stockily built with dark hair and angular features, he is also a consummate television professional – a veritable one-man band who produces and directs, shoots film and records sound all by himself. These special skills, quite apart from his contacts at Channel 4, had made him an ideal choice for this trip, for while I had needed to offer the TPLF a news story I had not wanted my own work in Axum to be complicated by the presence of a large film crew.

Ed's full name is John Edward Douglas Milner. In the arrivals hall at Khartoum Airport, therefore, we naturally pricked up our ears when we heard these words over the tannoy: 'John Edward, John Edward, John Edward. Will Mr John Edward please report to Immigration Office immediately.'

Ed complied and then disappeared. Half an hour later I had collected all our luggage and had been handed my passport duly stamped by immigration. A further half an hour passed, then an hour, then an hour and a half. Finally, well after midnight, with all the other passengers cleared through customs and the airport virtually deserted, my colleague surfaced again looking perplexed but cheerful. 'For some reason,' he explained, 'the name John Edward appears on the police blacklist. I've tried to make it clear to them that I'm John Edward *Milner* but they don't seem to get the point. They've kept my passport. I have to come back tomorrow morning to pick it up.'

The TPLF had sent a car to the airport to meet us. Its driver, who spoke no English, whisked us through the deserted streets of Khartoum, stopping every few minutes at road blocks manned by loutish, heavily armed soldiers who illiterately examined the *laissez passer* that he carried.

I had been in the Sudan before – indeed, between 1981 and 1986 I had visited the country regularly. I was immediately aware, however, that much had changed since then. For a start it was clear from the road blocks that there was now a strictly enforced curfew, something that would have been unheard of in the old days. Also, though I couldn't quite put my finger on it, the atmosphere felt different. There was an eerie quality about the blackened buildings, the litter-strewn alleyways, and the roaming packs of stray dogs. Always a mess, Khartoum tonight felt ugly and out-of-joint in a way that was entirely new to me.

We had arrived in the centre of the city and presently we turned right on to the Shariah-el-Nil, just to the north of the imposing Victorian palace where, in the year 1885, General Charles Gordon was killed by the Mahdi's dervishes.

Shariah-el-Nil means 'Nile Street' or 'Nile Way' and we were, indeed, now driving alongside that great river. Overhead a canopy of Neem trees blotted out the stars while to our right, glimpsed between the thick trunks and hanging branches, the Nile itself could be seen flowing sedately towards distant Egypt.

On our left we passed the vacant terrace of the Grand Hotel, once an elegant meeting place, now looking rather seedy and run-down. Soon afterwards we came to a last check-point at a roundabout, and here the driver was once again obliged to produce his *laissez passer*. Then we were waved on to the spit of land at the confluence of the Blue and White Niles where the Khartoum Hilton stands. As we pulled into the hotel's well lit courtyard I was looking forward very much indeed to two or perhaps three double vodkas, tonic and a bucket of ice. When I later attempted to order these items from room service, however,

I was reminded of an important fact that I had forgotten: since the adoption of Islamic law in the mid-1980s, alcohol had been banned in the Sudan.

The next morning, Thursday 10 January, Ed and I took a taxi to the offices of the Relief Society of Tigray, where the TPLF in London had told us to report to make the final arrangements for our trip. Our names, we noticed, were scrawled in chalk on a blackboard in an upstairs room; however no one there seemed to know anything else about us. Neither was it immediately possible to make contact with Haile Kiros, TPLF head of mission in Khartoum: always unreliable, the city's telephone system appeared to have broken down entirely that morning.

'Can't we just drive over to the TPLF office?' I asked one of the REST officials.

'No. Better you stay here. We will find Haile Kiros for you.'

By mid-morning there was no news. We decided that I should stay put to wait for Haile Kiros and that Ed should go to the airport in the taxi to collect his passport. He did this. Two hours later, however, he had failed to return and there was still no sign of the TPLF official, or indeed of anyone who appeared to be even remotely interested in me or my plans to get to Axum.

The silver lining to this particular cloud, I reflected, was that such a laid-back attitude did not lend credibility to my paranoid fancies that I might be murdered in Tigray. Indeed, a much more realistic prospect was beginning to suggest itself to me, namely that all concerned could turn out to be too comatose and slow-moving to get me to Tigray at all.

I looked at my watch and found that it was after one o'clock. In less than an hour, I remembered, all offices in Khartoum would close down for the day, probably including those of REST and the TPLF. Tomorrow, Friday, was the Islamic sabbath. It was therefore clear that nothing very much was going to happen before Saturday 12 January.

And where was Ed? Perhaps he had gone directly back to the Hilton. I tried to telephone the hotel but of course could not get through. Feeling increasingly irritated I wrote a note for Haile Kiros giving him my room number and asking him to contact me. I then handed this note to one of the friendly young people manning the REST office and walked out on to the street in search of a taxi.

First I went back to the Hilton, but Ed was not there. Then, just in case, I went to REST again, but he was not there either. Finally I ordered my driver to take me to the airport – where, with much patient inquiry, I managed to establish that my colleague had been detained and was being 'interviewed' by the police.

Could I go in and see him?

No.

Could I get any further information at all?

No.

When might he reappear?

'Today, tomorrow, maybe Saturday,' explained the English-speaking businessman who had kindly assisted me. 'Nobody knows. Nobody will say. It is the National Security Police who are holding him. Very bad men. Very impossible for you to do anything.'

By now genuinely concerned, I hurried over to the airport information kiosk which – amazingly – was open. There, not without some difficulty, I obtained the telephone number of the British Embassy. Then I found a public telephone which actually worked and, moreover, was free of charge. Unfortunately, however, no one answered at the other end.

Two minutes later I was in my taxi again. The driver did not know where the Embassy was – although he had claimed otherwise – and eventually located it by a curious process of trial and error which took slightly more than an hour.

I spent what was left of the afternoon back at the airport with two British diplomats whom I had found drinking illegal substances at the Embassy club. These officials, however, were no more successful than I had been in establishing why – or even where – Ed was being held. Their efforts, moreover, were complicated by the fact that Yasser Arafat, leader of the Palestine Liberation Organization, had just arrived in a Libyan jet to discuss the Gulf crisis with Sudan's military dictator, General Omar el-Bashir. Bristling with automatic weapons, platoons of soldiers roamed around giving vent to patriotic anti-Western feelings and generally making life unpleasant for everyone. Neither were my two diplomats in a particularly good mood. 'All

British citizens have been warned to stay away from this bloody country,' one of them reminded me with a faint note of accusation in his voice. 'Now perhaps you can see why.'

Around nine that evening, with Ed still not rescued, I was dropped back at the Hilton for dinner. Then, just after ten, to my great relief he appeared in the lobby looking a little grimy and tired but otherwise none the worse for wear.

He held up his hands as he sat down at my table. They were covered with black ink. 'I've been finger-printed,' he explained. He then attempted – fruitlessly – to order a large gin and tonic. Finally, with only minimal disgruntlement, he settled for a warm non-alcoholic beer.

On the road

As it turned out, Ed had not been held by the dreaded National Security Police but by the Sudanese branch of Interpol. Apparently the name 'John Edward' was one of the half dozen or so aliases used by an internationally wanted drugs dealer. Ed's fate had been sealed when the investigating officers had noticed that his passport contained a visa stamp for Colombia, the cocaine capital of the world. The fact that he had been there to film a news story for Channel 4 had not impressed the Sudanese detectives at all, nor had his distinct non-resemblance to the photograph of the wanted man that had been wired by Interpol. Fortunately a set of fingerprints had been sent as well and, rather late in the evening, someone had the bright idea of comparing Ed's fingerprints with these. His release had followed shortly afterwards.

The next day we told the story to Haile Kiros, the TPLF representative, who turned up at the Hilton in the middle of the afternoon. Though it had been rather worrying at the time, it was risible in retrospect and the three of us had a good laugh about it.

We then began to discuss the logistics of the trip to Axum and, as we did so, I found myself watching Haile Kiros closely. I could detect absolutely nothing in his demeanour, however, to suggest that he might wish me any harm whatsoever. On the contrary, he was an affable, easy-going, sophisticated individual who was clearly devoted to the cause of overthrowing the Ethiopian government but otherwise appeared to be entirely without malice. As we talked it began to dawn on me just how badly I might have got things out of perspective in the preceding months. Confronted with the friendly reality of Haile Kiros, all the fears and anxieties that I had suffered at the prospect of putting myself into the hands of the rebels looked unwarranted and all the dark imaginings that I had admitted into my life seemed absurd.

On the morning of Saturday 12 January we were joined by a TPLF official whom I was only ever to know by the single name of 'Hagos'. Lean and slightly built, with a complexion scarred by childhood smallpox, he explained that he had been assigned to accompany us to Axum – where he had been born – and to return with us from there when our work was complete. Meanwhile, here in Khartoum, he would facilitate our travel warrants to the border and would also help us to hire a vehicle for the journey.

By noon we had completed the paperwork and by the early evening we had done a deal with an Eritrean businessman resident in the Sudan who agreed to provide us with a sturdy Toyota Landcruiser, an even sturdier driver named Tesfaye, and six jerry-cans for spare fuel. At US$200 per day the rental seemed to me a bargain: I knew, you see, that much of our journey would have to be made by night on precarious mountain tracks so as to avoid the unwelcome attentions of the Ethiopian government aircraft that still patrolled the daytime skies above the rebel province of Tigray.

The next morning, Sunday 13 January, we left Khartoum just before dawn. Ahead of us lay hundreds of kilometres of Sudanese desert into which we now motored at high speed. Tesfaye, our driver, was a piratical-looking character with woolly hair, tobacco-yellow teeth, and a wandering eye; he handled the Landcruiser with masterful confidence, however, and clearly knew the route well. Beside him in the front of the vehicle, keeping his own counsel, sat Hagos. Ed and I occupied the rear bench and said little to each other as the sun of a white-hot day gradually rose to greet us.

We were aiming for the frontier town of Kassala where, that evening, a convoy of lorries operated by the Relief Society of Tigray would be marshalling to cross the border. Our plan was to join that convoy and ride with it as far as we could in the direction of Axum. 'It is safer to travel in a large group,' Hagos explained, 'in case anything goes wrong.'

The journey from Khartoum to Kassala helped me to realize just how drear and empty the landscapes of the Sudan really were. All around us, in all directions, an arid plain stretched away towards the horizon, making me aware, as I had never been before, of the soft relentless curve of the planet's surface.

Then, as the day soared towards noon, we began to pass the desiccated corpses of sheep, goats, cattle and – finally and alarmingly – of camels as well. These were the first casualties of a great famine in which people, too, would soon perish – but which the government of the Sudan had thus far refused even to acknowledge, let alone to seek to remedy. This, I thought, was surely an act of fatal arrogance on its part – the callous folly of yet another African dictatorship obsessed with maintaining its own prestige and power at the price of immense human suffering.

But I had supported just such dictatorships in the past, hadn't I? And even now I could hardly be said to have severed all my links with them. So who was I to judge? Who was I to feel regret? And by what right did I seek now to empathize with the dispossessed?

Kassala

Shortly before two that afternoon we crossed the silt-laden stream of the Atbara river near its confluence with the Takazze and I realized, almost with a sense of shock, how rapidly and how remorselessly the great distance that had once separated me from Axum was now being narrowed. Only a month before, that distance had looked impossible to bridge – a chasm deep and wide raging with nameless dreads. It therefore seemed almost a miracle that I was here and that I had been allowed to set my eyes upon the very rivers that I felt sure the Hebrew migrants had followed when they had brought the Ark of the Covenant into Ethiopia – the mighty rivers that scoured the land shadowing with wings, that poured down into the thirsty deserts of the Sudan, that merged with the Nile, and that flowed on past Elephantine and Luxor, past Abydos and Cairo, to spend themselves at last in the Mediterranean Sea.

Soon after three p.m. we arrived in Kassala, which was built around an oasis of date palms and dominated by a weird granite outcropping which reared up more than 2,500 feet above the surrounding plain. That red and withered hill, I realized, though it appeared to be isolated, was in fact the first harbinger of the great highlands of Ethiopia.

I felt a thrill of excitement at the knowledge that the border was now so close – just a few kilometres away – and looked around with renewed interest at the turbulent frontier town through which we were driving. Everywhere, oblivious to the enervating heat, crowds of people milled about, filling the dusty streets with bright colours and loud sounds. Here a group of quick and subtle highlanders, down from Abyssinia to barter the trade of the mountains for the trade of the desert, stood arguing with a stall-keeper; there a fuzzy haired nomad sat astride his grumbling camel and gazed at the world with arrogant eyes; here a Muslim holy man, dressed in rags, bestowed benedictions upon those who would pay him and curses upon those who would not; there a child, squealing with glee, pursued a makeshift hoop with an outstretched stick . . .

Hagos directed Tesfaye to drive us to a small, flat-roofed house on the outskirts of town. 'You have to stay here,' he explained, 'until it is time for us to cross the border. The Sudanese authorities are a little unpredictable at the moment. So it's better that you keep your heads down and remain indoors. That way there will be no chance of any problem.'

'Who lives here?' I asked as we climbed down from the Landcruiser.

'This is a TPLF house,' Hagos explained, showing us into a clean courtyard around which a number of rooms were arranged. 'Rest, get a little sleep if you can. It's going to be a long night.'

Across the border

At five that evening we were driven to a huge, open, dusty expanse of ground littered with the bones of slaughtered quadrupeds. Swarms of blowflies buzzed around and here and there, amongst the mouldering vertebrae and the fusty shoulder-blades, lay little piles of stinking human faeces. To my right, thoughtfully arranging itself between Kassala's great granite butte and the town itself, the sun descended the sky in a surreal extravaganza of tangerine and magenta. The whole collage, I thought, looked like some existentialist vision of the end of all flesh.

'Where exactly are we?' I asked Hagos.

'Oh . . . this is where the convoy assembles before crossing the border,' explained the TPLF official. 'We will wait maybe half an hour, maybe an hour. Then we will go.'

Ed immediately climbed down out of the Landcruiser and went off with his tripod and video camera to find a vantage point from which to film the lorries arriving. His story for Channel 4 would focus not only on religious issues, as I had told the TPLF, but also on the burgeoning famine in Tigray.

While he was making his preparations I wandered pensively about, warding off flies and looking for somewhere to sit down and complete my notes for the day. The charnel house atmosphere, however, had thoroughly disconcerted me. Besides, with the sun now resting on the horizon, the gloaming was already too deep to write in.

A coolness also had filled the air, an unexpected chill after the heat of the afternoon, and a keen wind sang amongst the derelict buildings that ringed the marshalling ground. People walked to and fro – shadowy figures of men and women who seemed to have come here from nowhere with nowhere to go. Meanwhile small groups of ragged children had gathered to play amidst the rubbish and the bones, their high-pitched giggles mingled with the lowing of a passing herd of cattle.

And then I heard the rumble of approaching vehicles accompanied by a crashing of gears. Looking back in the direction from which these sounds were coming I saw a glimmer of headlights, then a dazzling beam. Finally, out of the murk, the mammoth shapes of perhaps twenty Mercedes lorries materialized. As they rolled past me I could see that each one was loaded up with hundreds of sacks of grain, loaded so heavily that the suspension sagged and the chassis groaned.

The trucks pulled to a halt in parallel files in the centre of the open ground and there, in twos and threes, their number was augmented by others snaking out from town. Soon the evening air was filled with billowing clouds of dust and the sounds of revving engines. And then, as though on a signal – though none was given – the whole convoy started to move.

I ran back to the Landcruiser where Ed, helped by Hagos, was hurriedly stowing his camera equipment. Then we all jumped into the vehicle and set off in pursuit of the lorries' tail-lights. The trail that we were following, I could see, was deeply rutted and grooved and I wondered how many convoys over how many years had passed this way bearing food for people made hungry by the folly and wickedness of their own government.

In our faster car we soon overtook the last of the trucks, and we passed perhaps a dozen more before Tesfaye – who was clearly enjoying the role of safari-rally driver – slotted us into position in the middle of the convoy. All around us now the dust and sand that the vehicles were throwing up created a wild and turbulent agitation, sometimes reducing the visibility to just a few feet. Straining my eyes to peer out of the windows at the night as it rushed by, I experienced a sensation of tremendous momentum coupled with a feeling of inevitability. I was on my way, going wherever I would go, to get whatever Fate would send. And I thought: *this is where I want to be; this is what I want to do*.

Shortly before seven we arrived at the border and halted at a Sudanese army check-point – just a collection of mud huts in the middle of a bleak and furrowed plain. Carrying hurricane lanterns, a few uniformed men emerged out of the darkness and began to check documents and identities. Then, one by one, the lorries ahead of us were waved through.

When our turn came Hagos was ordered out of the car by an officer who questioned him closely, making frequent gestures towards the back seat – where Ed and I were doing our best not to look conspicuous. At one point our passports were produced and minutely examined under the headlights. Then suddenly the officer seemed to lose interest in us and walked off to harass the occupants of the next lorry in the queue.

Hagos climbed back into the Landcruiser and slammed the door.

'Any problems?' I asked nervously.

'No. None at all,' replied the TPLF official. He turned and

gave me a broad smile: 'Don't worry. They are not going to arrest Ed again. Everything is in order. We can go.'

He said something in Tigrigna to Tesfaye who happily released the handbrake and gunned the engine. Then we rolled forward across the border and on into Ethiopia – though not yet into Tigray. Our route, I knew, would take us first through territory controlled by the Eritrean People's Liberation Front, a guerilla movement older than the TPLF which had been fighting for the independence of Eritrea for almost thirty years and which now, in early 1991, was nearer than ever before to achieving its objective. As we drove I asked Hagos about the links between the two rebel groups.

'We co-operate closely,' he explained. 'But the EPLF is campaigning to create a separate Eritrean state whereas we in the TPLF do not seek to secede but only to make it possible for a democratic government to be elected in Ethiopia.'

'And to do that you have to overthrow Mengistu?'

'Certainly. He and his Workers' Party are the main obstacles to freedom in our country.'

We drove on for about half an hour, during which we saw no sign of the rest of the convoy. Then suddenly lights appeared in front of us and we pulled to a halt amongst parked lorries in what seemed to be a broad valley surrounded by low hills.

'Why are we stopping?' I asked Hagos.

'We will wait for the other vehicles behind us to catch up. Also we will collect some TPLF fighters who will travel with us as guards for the convoy.'

Without further explanation Hagos then got out of the Landcruiser and disappeared. Ed grabbed his camera and a hand-held light and walked off too.

A moment later I decided that I might as well stretch my legs and have a look around. Stepping down into the velvety coolness of the night, I stood for a while quite close to the vehicle gazing up at the sky. I was aware of the faint effulgence shed by the clusters of stars and the crescent moon above me, and I could just make out the silhouettes of the nearby trucks, their headlights now extinguished. Off to my right, almost lost in deep shadow, was a grove of acacia thorn trees. Further away a white rock at the top of a hill reflected a delicate incandescence.

Gradually my eyes adjusted and I was able to see more and more of what was going on around me. Groups of fierce and brigandish-looking men stood here and there or crouched down on the ground talking in low voices. And whereas there had been no guns in evidence while we were still inside the Sudan, everyone now appeared to be armed with automatic weapons.

Feeling slightly apprehensive, I walked amongst the parked lorries and, after a few moments, came across Hagos, who was conversing with several TPLF fighters dressed in battle fatigues. As I approached I was startled to hear the harsh metallic clunk of an AK47 assault rifle being cocked and I thought: *I'm going to get shot and it's going to be now.*

But instead Hagos welcomed me and introduced me to the other men. I had even been wrong about the noise I had heard – which turned out to have been produced by a weapon being expertly stripped and cleaned. Not for the first time I experienced a sense of shame at the self-inflicted terrors that I had endured in the months before setting out on this trip. And I resolved that henceforward I would trust the rebels – who, after all, had also been obliged to trust me.

It was quite some time before we were back on the road: one of the lorries that had passed through the border post behind us had punctured a tyre and it seemed to be a matter of policy to keep the convoy together. Eventually, however, we set off and drove for perhaps another two hours.

Then – and I don't think it was later than eleven p.m. – we stopped again. We seemed, though I could not be sure, to be in the middle of a vast plain. Here all the vehicles arranged themselves side by side into a straight rank and doused their headlights.

'We won't be going any further tonight,' Hagos announced after a moment's silence.

'Why not?' I asked.

'There is shelter nearby and we will have to spend tomorrow there. The next safe place is too far ahead for us to reach before sunrise.'

And with that, cradling an AK47 that he had somehow acquired, the TPLF official fell asleep.

Breakfast at Tessenei

I slept, too – though rather badly – with my feet and shins stuck out of the open side-window of the Landcruiser. Then, after a few hours of troubled dreams and restless discomfort, I was awakened by the asthmatic sounds of engines turning over and the smell of diesel smoke.

We did not drive far. Less than a kilometre away there was a copse of tall, thickly leaved trees under which the entire convoy proceeded to conceal itself. I watched with amazement as canvas tarpaulins were produced and draped over all the vehicles, including our own. 'To cut out reflections,' Hagos explained. 'From the air we will be almost invisible unless any shining metal attracts the MiGs.' He then added that even the most careful attempts at camouflage could not guarantee our safety: 'Sometimes the pilots just bomb and strafe woodland like this on the off-chance that relief trucks will be taking cover there.'

The sun had risen while the convoy was being hidden and, in the pale light of the early morning, like a salutary lesson, I could see the blackened and burnt-out hulks of three Mercedes lorries. 'They hit those a few weeks ago,' said Hagos. 'It was just bad luck.' He then broke a leaf-covered branch from one of the trees and walked out onto the sandy plain behind us. There he joined Tesfaye and several of the other drivers who were methodically engaged in brushing over the criss-crossed network of tyre tracks leading to the copse.

At around eight in the morning all was done and Hagos proposed that we walk into the nearby Eritrean town of Tessenei.

'How far is that?' I asked.

'Not far. Half an hour or so. We should be quite safe. The MiGs are mainly interested in high-value targets like trucks. They don't usually shoot up small groups of people out in the open.'

'And what about the towns?'

'Sometimes they attack the towns if they see any vehicles or any large public gathering. Tessenei has been bombed many times.'

The walk was a pleasant one, along an earth path through little clumps of scrub vegetation amidst which brightly coloured birds darted prettily to and fro. Looking around I could see that we were in rising country and, in the far distance, I thought that I could just make out the hazy silhouettes of lofty mountains.

Tessenei itself was surrounded by eroded granite hills in a boulder-strewn valley. Not a single car moved on the largely unpaved streets but there were people everywhere: children playing, an old woman leading a heavily laden donkey, three attractive teenage girls who covered their faces and fled giggling as we approached, and large numbers of armed men – all of whom greeted us with warm smiles and cheerful waves.

The town, frankly, was a mess. Most of the poor, flat-roofed buildings showed signs of house-to-house fighting – gaping holes blown through walls, façades cratered by machine-gun bullets, collapsed masonry. Above us, to our right, was the hospital, completely gutted. Underfoot, everywhere we walked, were countless spent shell cases that formed a glittering, clinking carpet.

I asked Hagos: 'What happened here?'

'A few years ago, when the government seemed to be winning the war, Tessenei was one of the last strongholds of the EPLF. In fact the Ethiopian army seized the town several times, but the EPLF always got it back again. There was a great deal of heavy fighting – very brutal, very bloody. But now the front line is far away and it is peaceful here – except for the bombing.'

A few minutes later Hagos led us into a small hotel which consisted of perhaps twenty rooms arranged in a square around an earthen courtyard. Here, under a canopy of camouflage netting, several groups of Eritreans were sitting at tables drinking cups of coffee and conversing light-heartedly. A waitress bustled to and fro and a promising aroma of cooking filled the air.

There was, I decided, a rather *décontracté*, boulevard atmosphere about this little scene which contrasted remarkably with the devastation outside. People, clearly, could adapt to almost any circumstances – no matter how grim – and find a way to make life bearable.

As though reading my thoughts, Hagos said to me as we sat down: 'They don't have much, but at least they are free now. And conditions are getting better every day.'

Evidence that this was indeed so soon arrived in the form of a breakfast of fried eggs and a six-pack of Dutch beer.

'Where on earth did they get this from?' I spluttered as I opened my first can.

'Since the EPLF took back the port of Massawa from the government last year there has been beer in Eritrea,' explained Hagos with a smile. He opened a can for himself and took a long swig, then added: 'It is a great luxury after Khartoum, is it not?'

In this fashion, drinking beer and chatting with half the population of Tessenei – who had by now trooped into the hotel to see the foreigners – we whiled away most of the morning. At noon we tuned in to Ed's short-wave radio and listened to the increasingly gloomy news from the Arabian Gulf. It was now Monday 14 January and the UN deadline for the withdrawal of Iraqi troops from occupied Kuwait was due to expire at midnight on the 15th.

We then slept for a few hours, awoke at four p.m., and walked out to rejoin the convoy in time for its scheduled departure at six.

The magic and the marvels

That night's journey seemed to go on for ever, although in reality it only lasted for eleven hours. Full darkness had fallen by the time we left Tessenei. Tesfaye manoeuvred us into his favourite spot in the middle of the convoy and then, amidst the now familiar clouds of dust, we began an epic drive through the western foothills of Ethiopia's great central escarpment and then up into the mountains beyond.

Around one in the morning we stopped to refill the Land-cruiser's tank from the reeking jerry-cans that we had brought with us. Stiff and cramped, bruised from the pounding I had taken on the bumpy and rutted tracks, I stepped down from the vehicle while this operation was under way and watched the lorries that had been behind us roll by one by one, their headlights blazing, air brakes hissing.

When the last of them had gone past and disappeared I took a deep breath, and gazed up at the constellations overhead and felt grateful to whatever good fortune it was that had allowed me to be here. Then we were back on the road, back amongst the potholes and the gullies, lurching forward to catch up with the convoy.

Soon I became aware, as I had not been before, that we were ascending increasingly precipitous gradients, winding around hairpin bends that seemed to hang suspended over empty space, powering forward across bleak stretches of plateau, and then climbing again. And I had the sense of great distances being covered and of profound changes in the terrain.

I knew that at some point in the past few hours we had crossed over the border from Eritrea into Tigray. And gradually, though my body ached from the unremitting pummelling that it was taking, I found myself slipping into a dream-like state in which everything that had happened to me during the past two years, the strange twists and turns of my quest, the dead-ends, and the moments of discovery, seemed to merge into a single continuous and coherent form. And I understood, all at once and with boundless clarity, that the search which had obsessed me for so long would amount to just a poor and meaningless adventure if it had been motivated only by avarice and ambition. Lying in the remote darkness of its sanctuary, the Ark of God might glitter with ancient gold, but its real value did not lie in that. Neither did it matter that it was an archaeological treasure beyond price. Indeed nothing about it that could be measured, or calculated, or evaluated, or costed out had the slightest significance, and if I had ever set my eyes on these things (and I knew in my heart that I had) then the error that I had committed verged on desecration – not of the object sought, but of the seeker, not of the the Holy Ark, but of myself.

And where, if not in the material world, did the true value of the relic lie? Why . . . in its mystery, of course, and in its enchantment, and in the hold that it had exercised upon human imaginations in many different lands across all the long and weary centuries. These were the enduring things – the magic and the marvels, the inspiration and the hope. Better to hold fast to them than to ephemeral prizes; better to aspire with a certain nobility and to win nothing than to succeed and later be ashamed.

Lonely road

Just before dawn, exhausted, grey from head to toe with the fine, powdery grime of the road, we pulled into a small town where not a single light flickered, not a single person stirred.

Here Hagos beat unmercifully on a locked door until it was opened. Then we unloaded Ed's camera equipment and other luggage that we might need during the day and went inside while Tesfaye drove off to hide the Landcruiser somewhere.

We found ourselves in a half-covered, half-open courtyard where people lay sleeping on rudimentary beds. Some of these beds, fortunately, were empty and Ed, Hagos and I quickly acquired three of them. I then wrapped myself in a sheet, closed my eyes and fell instantly asleep.

A few hours later, when I awoke in full daylight, my two companions had disappeared and a dozen Tigrayans were sitting around staring at me with keen interest. I said good morning to them, got up with as much dignity as I could muster, washed my face in a dribble of water from a tap attached to a metal barrel, and then sat down to write my notes.

Soon Ed and Hagos came back – they had been filming the distribution of some of the food brought by the convoy. I asked where we were.

'This is Cherero,' Hagos replied. 'It's an important town in this part of Tigray. Also it is the destination of the convoy. All the trucks have unloaded here.'

'How far is it to Axum?'

'One more night of driving. But it is somewhat unsafe for us to proceed alone. It may be advisable for us to wait here until another convoy assembles.'

I looked at the date indicator on my watch. It was Tuesday 15 January – just three days away from the start of *Timkat*.

'Do you think we'll have to wait long?' I asked.

'Two, three days maybe. Or maybe we will be lucky and have the chance to leave tonight.'

'Why do you say that it's unsafe for us to proceed on our own?'

'Because the government sends saboteurs into Tigray from their garrison at Asmara. They send out small teams to ambush vehicles moving on the roads. A Landcruiser like ours with just a few people in it would make a good target for such an attack.'

'What about the convoys? Aren't they subject to attack too?'

'No. Almost never. Too many lorries. Too many guards.'

The day passed long and slow, hot, boring and sticky. Then, as evening came down, Hagos, who had been out and about for several hours, announced that no convoy would be leaving that night. 'I advise', he said, 'that we stay – at least until tomorrow.'

Seeing the look of horror that this remark had induced on our faces he then added: 'But of course, it is up to you.'

Ed and I had already made up our minds on this point, which we had discussed between ourselves at some length during the afternoon. We therefore told the TPLF official that we would like to press on – unless he thought it completely foolhardy for us to do so.

'No. It is OK. I understand that you want to get to Axum before *Timkat*. The danger is not very great. But I will see if we can bring one other TPLF fighter with us in case there is any trouble.'

At dusk we set off again. On the front bench beside Hagos was the guard he had promised – a teenage boy with startlingly white teeth, an extravagant Afro, an AK47, and three or four magazines of spare ammunition. He was a cheerful sort of fellow who laughed a great deal and insisted on playing Tigrayan war songs at maximum volume on the Landcruiser's stereo as we drove through the night. But I couldn't help feeling that all his energy and bravado would not be sufficient to keep the bullets at bay if anyone decided to shoot us up – from the cover, say, of that bush over there, or of that clump of trees, or from behind that boulder even.

I was amazed at how *different* it felt to be travelling alone like this, unescorted, with no great rumbling lorries in front of us and none behind. Before we had seemed part of some prodigious and invincible army relentlessly beating down the barriers of darkness, driving away the shadows with a barrage of light. Now we were small, vulnerable, forsaken. And as we wound our way amongst the withered trees of the mountain slopes I was conscious of the immensity of these wild lands and of their bleak and implacable hostility.

We climbed for several hours, the engine labouring under the stress, the outside air temperature dropping steadily. Then suddenly we emerged at the top of a narrow pass to find armed men blocking our path.

I muttered some expletive but Hagos reassured me: 'Nothing to worry about. There is a TPLF camp here, guarding the road. These are our people.' Opening his door, he exchanged words and handshakes with the rebels who had now surrounded the Landcruiser. Then we were waved through an improvised barrier and emerged moments later on to a windswept plateau where campfires flickered amongst wooden huts.

We paused for half an hour to drink tea and then we were on the move again, edging forward through the lonely night. Behind us, one by one, the lights of the camp disappeared and were replaced by shadows.

Time passed. I dozed, then awoke again to find that we were skirting the lip of an immense valley: to our left the mountainside, stony and close, to our right a plunging abyss defined by the road's ragged edge. And then, out of the inky blackness that filled the chasm's floor, a brilliant firefly soared up towards us, a speck of pure energy pulling behind it a ghostly, luminescent trail. In a fraction of a second this glowing apparition had reached us. It streaked directly across our path, narrowly missing the front windscreen of the car, and then extinguished itself against the embankment.

As this happened Tesfaye jammed on the brakes and switched off all the Landcruiser's lights. Meanwhile Hagos and the guard whom we had brought with us from Cherero leaped out and rushed to the rim of the precipice clutching their AK47s.

The two men, I thought, looked lithe and dangerous, businesslike and unafraid. They seemed to move in harmony together, as though they were completing some manoeuvre for which they had been well trained.

'What on earth's going on?' asked Ed, who had been awakened from a deep sleep by the dramatic, skidding stop of the vehicle.

'I'm not sure,' I replied, 'but I rather think we've just been shot at.'

I was about to suggest that it might be in our interests to get out of the car when Hagos and his companion came running back towards us. They clambered up on to the front bench, slammed the door behind them and ordered Tesfaye to proceed.

'I assume that was a tracer bullet we saw,' I remarked a few moments later.

'Yes,' replied Hagos matter-of-factly. 'Someone down in the valley fired off a few rounds at us.'

'But there was only one.'

'No, no. We only *saw* one. Several shots would have been fired – a short burst. The normal practice is to load a round or two of tracer at the top of each magazine to enable the gunner to correct his aim. The rest of the bullets are of the ordinary type.'

'Charming,' remarked Ed.

We drove on in silence for a while, then I asked Hagos: 'Who do you think shot at us?'

'It would have been government agents. As I told you, they are constantly sending such people into Tigray to cause trouble. At night they cannot bomb us from the air so they make use of these sabotage squads in order to disrupt the traffic moving on the roads. Sometimes they succeed . . .'

Another question had occurred to me: 'Why didn't they carry on firing? We were sitting ducks up there.'

'Too dangerous for them. Since they missed us with the first burst and since they were not very close to us, they would have been unwise to continue with the attack. There are a lot of TPLF fighters in this area. A prolonged exchange of fire would have attracted attention.'

'Oh . . . I see.'

I rested my head wearily against the side window of the Landcruiser and thought how easily life could be stolen by a mindless bullet and how fragile we all were beneath our bluster and conceit.

At around three that morning, picking up speed on a metalled road, we drove by a field in which a tank lay derelict, its turret blown askew, its gun-barrel drooping impotently. Then, to our left, I saw the hulking ruins of an ancient building bathed in starlight. I was overtaken by an acute, almost poignant, sense of *déjà vu* and I asked: 'Where are we?'

'We are coming into Axum,' answered Hagos. 'We have just passed the Queen of Sheba's palace.'

A few minutes later we entered the small town, turned right and left through the narrow streets, and then pulled to a halt in front of a walled enclosure draped with creeping vines and tropical flowers. While the others knocked on the gate to gain admission, I slipped unnoticed around the side of the Land-cruiser, dropped to my knees and kissed the ground. It was, I knew, an extravagant and sentimental gesture. But somehow it felt right.

Strategy

In the morning I was awakened by bright sunlight streaming through the uncurtained window of the room that had been assigned to me. In the small hours, when we had arrived, everything had been in darkness, for there was no electricity in Axum. But now, as I stepped outside, I could see that we were lodging in a pleasant little guest house built around a patch of green lawn.

I ambled over to a terrace where some chairs were arranged. There, in a corner, a kettle was boiling promisingly on a stove fashioned out of a large oil can. Nearby was a kitchen in which two women, whom I judged to be mother and daughter, were chopping vegetables.

I was greeted with smiles and was almost immediately provided with a cup of sweet, scented tea. Then I sat down and collected my thoughts while I waited for the others to wake up.

The date was now Wednesday 16 January 1991. During the night that had just passed, the UN deadline for the withdrawal of Iraqi troops from Kuwait had expired – and I wondered, in a rather abstract way, whether World War III had broken out. Meanwhile, in just two days' time, the *Timkat* ceremonies were due to begin here in Axum and I needed to have a strategy worked out before then.

I found myself curiously reluctant to march straight round to the Saint Mary of Zion church and to the sanctuary chapel. Strangely, having come all this way, those few final steps seemed the hardest of all to take. This was partly natural diffidence, partly superstitious dread, and partly because I felt that an early visit to the church of Saint Mary of Zion would alert the priests to my presence and would probably ensure that the true Ark would *not* on this occasion be carried out in the *Timkat* processions. It therefore seemed logical that I should hold back and keep a low profile until the beginning of the ceremony. Then, in the scrum of wild dancing that I knew would occur, I might find some opportunity to get close to the relic and to take a proper look at it.

There was, however, an argument against this strategy. Ever since my discussion in Jerusalem with the Falasha elder Raphael Hadane I had become aware that the real Ark might *never* be used in the *Timkat* processions – that a replica might be substituted for it while the genuine article remained safely inside the chapel. If this was so then clearly the sooner I introduced myself to the Axum priests the better. I would have nothing to gain by waiting and nothing to lose by being open and above board. Quite the contrary, in fact, because only by talking to the clergymen at great length would I have any chance of persuading them that I did not represent a threat, that I was sincere, and that I was a worthy candidate for admission into the presence of the Ark.

For these reasons, faced with irrevocable decisions that had to be made right away, I was in something of a quandary as I sat drinking my tea on that morning of 16 January.

In a little while a bleary-eyed Ed appeared from his room, clutching a short-wave radio to his ear.

'Has the war started?' I shouted.

'Well no, actually. It hasn't. The deadline's passed but there are no reports of any fighting at all. Now what about some tea? Or coffee? Coffee will do. And some breakfast. Is there any of that around?'

While Ed was being catered for, Hagos also arrived – though not from his room. He had obviously been into town already because, in tow behind him, was a venerable bearded old fellow in flowing vestments.

'This is my father,' explained the TPLF official, making polite introductions all round. 'He is a priest at Saint Mary of Zion church. I told him about your interest in the Ark of the Covenant and he said that he would like to meet you.'

An honour and a burden

I had, of course, talked to Hagos about my quest on several occasions during our long journey from Khartoum. I had learnt before we set out that he was a native of Axum but it had not occurred to me for a moment that he might have any connections with the church, let alone that his father would actually turn out to be a priest. Perhaps if I had known that I would have been more guarded in my remarks – but then again perhaps not. I had liked Hagos from the beginning and had not wanted to keep anything from him.

The end result was that any element of surprise that I might have retained had been removed, not out of design or malice on anyone's part but as the result of a pure fluke. I decided, therefore, that there was no longer any point in attempting to be guarded or cloak-and-dagger about what I was here to do. Better by far to put all my cards on the table and accept the consequences, whether positive or negative.

I had a long discussion with Hagos's father, who seemed intrigued by the notion that a foreigner should have come all this way in the hope of seeing the Ark of the Covenant.

'And will I see it?' I asked. 'During the *Timkat* ceremonies? Do they use the real Ark or do they use a replica?'

Hagos translated my question. There was then a pregnant pause which the old man eventually broke with this reply: 'On such matters I am not qualified to speak. You must talk to my superiors.'

'But you know the answer, don't you?'

'I am not qualified to speak. It is not my responsibility.'

'Whose responsibility is it?'

'First and foremost you must meet the *Nebura-ed*, the most senior of all the priests in Axum. Without his blessing you will be able to do nothing. If he grants his permission then you must also talk with the guardian of the Ark . . .'

'I was here before,' I interrupted, 'in 1983, and I met the guardian then. Is he still alive do you know? Or has someone else taken over from him?'

'Unfortunately that one died, four years ago. He was very old. He named his successor to replace him and this new man is now at his post.'

'And he always stays at the chapel where the Ark is kept?'

'It is his burden that he may never leave the Ark. Do you know that his predecessor, the guardian whom you met, attempted to run away when he was told that he had been appointed?'

'No,' I replied, 'I didn't know that.'

'Yes. He fled outside Axum, into the mountains. Other monks were sent after him to catch him. When they brought him back he still wanted to escape. He had to be chained at the chapel for many months before he fully accepted his responsibility.'

'Chained, you say?'

'Yes. Chained inside the chapel.'

'I'm surprised.'

'Why?'

'Because it sounds like he really didn't want the job. I would have thought it was a great honour to be appointed as guardian of the Ark.'

'An honour? Yes, certainly. But it is also a heavy burden. After he takes up his post the chosen monk has no life outside the Ark. He exists to serve it, to burn incense round about it, to be before it constantly.'

'And what would happen if it were ever taken out of the chapel – during *Timkat*, for example? Would the guardian go with it?'

'He must stay close to it at all times. But you should speak to others about these matters. I am not qualified . . .'

I put several other close questions about the Ark, but all of them produced the same response from the old man – such matters were not his business, he couldn't say, I would have to talk to someone more senior. Interestingly, however, he did tell me that government officials had come to Axum shortly before the town was captured by the TPLF and had attempted to remove the relic.

I asked: 'How? I mean, what did they do? Did they try to go into the chapel?'

'Not at first. They wanted to persuade us that the Ark should go with them to Addis Ababa. They said that there was fighting coming and that it would be safer there.'

'And what happened?'

'When they became forceful and aggressive we resisted them. They called soldiers, but we resisted them. The whole town heard what they were trying to do and there were demonstrations in the streets. Eventually they returned to Addis Ababa empty-handed. Soon afterwards, thanks be to God, Axum was liberated.'

I was aware that the father of a guerilla fighter was likely to be biased in favour of the TPLF. Nevertheless I asked: 'Since the government forces left, have things improved here for the clergy, or have they got worse?'

'Definitely things are better. In fact the situation in the churches is very good. We go to the church to pray when we like –as much as we like, day, night, evening, whenever we wish. Before, under the government, due to the curfew that they had imposed, we were not allowed to go to the church at night, or to go home from the church at night. If we went out from the church, even for fresh air, they came and took us to prison. But we don't have to fear now. We can sleep safe in our homes and go to church every day like normal people, and feel safe. We don't have to spend the night in the church for fear that we might be caught walking home at night. During the government's time we never felt relaxed when we attended services. There was always fear, not knowing what might happen to us or the church. Now we practise our faith in peace.'

Croix pattée

Hagos's father eventually left, promising that he would arrange a meeting for me with the *Nebura-ed*, the chief priest of the Saint Mary of Zion church. He did not advise that I should attempt to contact the guardian of the Ark before this meeting had taken place: 'That might cause some bad feeling. Things should be done in the proper order.'

Although this strategy seemed to me to be full of potential pitfalls, I realized that I had little choice but to go along with it. I therefore decided, while waiting for an appointment with the *Nebura-ed*, that I would explore some of the archaeological sites which I had visited all too briefly in 1983 – and others that I had not been able to see at all.

I remembered that there was supposed to be an ancient carving of a lioness on a rock face near the quarries where

Axum's famous stelae had been cut in pre-Christian times. That carving had been out of bounds in 1983 because it had been located beyond the area controlled by the military garrison. Now, however, it was accessible.

While Ed went off with another TPLF official to film various sequences for his Channel 4 news story, I persuaded Hagos to take me to the quarries in the Landcruiser. This was a risky thing to do because of the danger of an air strike. However, we would be driving less than five kilometres and would be able to conceal the vehicle when we arrived.

We set off out of town past the so-called Queen of Sheba's palace and soon came to a rock-strewn hillside. We parked in a gully, covered the Landcruiser with its camouflage tarpaulin, and then began to hike up the scree.

'What do you think of my chances of persuading the priests to let me into the chapel to see the Ark?' I asked as we walked.

'Oh ... they will not allow you to do that,' replied Hagos confidently. 'Your only opportunity will be during *Timkat*.'

'But do you think they really do bring the Ark out at *Timkat*? Or do you think they use a replica?'

A shrug: 'I don't know. During my childhood I believed, and all my friends believed, that it was the true Ark rather than a replica which was carried at *Timkat*. We never questioned that fact. It was not even an issue for us. But now I am not so sure . . .'

'Why?'

'It does not seem logical.'

Hagos would be drawn no further on this subject and for the next fifteen minutes or so we climbed strenuously in complete silence. Then he pointed out a giant boulder across a ridge: 'Your lioness is there,' he said.

I had noticed that he had developed a slight limp. 'What happened to your leg?' I asked. 'Did you sprain it?'

'No. I was shot.'

'Oh. I see.'

'It happened a few years ago, in a battle with government forces. The bullet passed through my shin, shattering the bone. Since then I have not been fit enough to participate in active service.'

We had come now to the boulder and Hagos led me round its

side. There, although partially occluded by deep shadow, I could quite clearly make out the gigantic silhouette of a charging lioness carved in low relief. It was extensively eroded. Nevertheless it conveyed a lifelike sense of ferocity and sinuous grace.

I knew that Theodore Bent, a British traveller and amateur archaeologist who had visited Axum in the nineteenth century, had also seen this carving – which he had later described as 'a very spirited work of art, measuring 10 ft. 8 in. from the nose to the tail. The running attitude is admirably given, and the sweep of the hind legs shows that the artist had thorough command of his subject.' Bent had then added: 'A few inches from the nose of the lioness is a circular disk with rays, probably intended to represent the sun.'[1]

I now examined this 'circular disk with rays', which turned out to consist of two pairs of elliptical incisions cut into the bare rock. If these incisions had been arranged around a watch-face then the top pair would have pointed, respectively, to 10 o'clock and 2 o'clock and the bottom pair to 4 o'clock and 8 o'clock. I therefore found it easy to understand Bent's interpretation of the device: at first glance it did indeed look like a series of spokes – or rays – emanating outwards from a disk-shaped centre.

It was far from being that, however. Indeed the 'circular disk' that the traveller had described was an illusion. If he had bothered to trace the *complete* shape defined by the spaces between the elliptical incisions he would have found that the result was not a representation of the sun at all but of a *croix pattée* with arms that widened out from the centre point – in other words, a perfect Templar cross.

'Hagos,' I said, 'am I seeing things or is that a cross?'

As I asked this question I ran my fingers around the outline that had immediately been so apparent to me.

'It is a cross,' affirmed the TPLF official.

'But it shouldn't be there. The lioness is definitely pre-Christian – so how come there's this Christian symbol beside it?'

'Who knows? Maybe someone added it later. There are other crosses, just like this one, at the site of King Kaleb's palace.'

'If you don't mind,' I said, 'I think I would very much like to go and see them.'

The work of angels

I had visited Kaleb's palace in 1983 and I knew that the ruins dated to the sixth century AD, the early part of the Christian era in Axum. I remembered that it was a hill-top fortress with deep dungeons and chambers beneath.[2] I did not, however, remember seeing any crosses there.

Now, as we drove back into town, I looked forward impatiently to exploring the palace again. In 1983 the Templars had held no significance for me. My more recent research, however, had raised the possibility that a contingent of knights could have come from Jerusalem to Ethiopia in search of the Ark of the Covenant at the time of King Lalibela (AD 1185–1211) and could later have served as bearers for the Ark itself.[3] The reader will recall that I had found what looked like striking support for this theory in an eyewitness account given by the thirteenth-century Armenian geographer Abu Salih – an account that had spoken of the Ark being carried in Axum by men who were 'white and red in complexion with red hair'.[4]

If those men had indeed been Templars, as I very strongly suspected, then it was reasonable to suppose that they might have left some mementos of their order behind in Axum. It therefore seemed to me at least possible that the oddly out-of-place *croix pattée* on the rock beside the carved lioness could have been put there by a Templar artist.

This particular type of cross, as I knew very well, was not one that was common or popular in Ethiopia: indeed in all my years of travels in that country the only place in which I had ever seen one had been on the ceiling of the rock-hewn church of Beta Maryam in the town of Lalibela – a town that had been the capital of the very king who I believed had brought the Templars to Ethiopia in the first place.[5] Now I had found another *croix pattée* on the outskirts of Axum and, if Hagos was right, I was about to see several more in the ruins of King Kaleb's palace – a structure that could well have been still standing and inhabited in the thirteenth century.

After driving past the grass area where the majority of Axum's great stelae were located, we skirted the huge and ancient reservoir known as the Mai Shum. In local tradition, I remembered, this was supposed to have been the Queen of Sheba's pleasure bath. Since the coming of Christianity, however, it had been used for the curious baptismal rituals associated with *Timkat*. Here, in two days' time, the Ark was supposed to be brought in procession at the start of the ceremonies that I had come to witness.

Leaving the Mai Shum behind us, we motored about half way up the steep and broken path leading to the site of King Kaleb's palace and completed the journey on foot after first camouflaging the car. Hagos then led me into the ruins where he poked around for a while amongst the rubble before finally exclaiming in triumph: 'Here! Over here! I think this is what you want to see.'

I hurried to join him and saw that he had retrieved a block of sand-coloured stone about two feet square and six inches thick. Out of it had been carved four elliptical holes of precisely the same shape and disposition as the elliptical incisions near the carving of the lioness. In this case, however, because the holes passed right through the block, there could be no ambiguity at all about the shape of the remaining stone: it formed another perfect Templar cross.

'When I was a child,' mused Hagos, 'I and my friends used to play up here. In those days there were many blocks like this lying around. I expect that all the other ones must have been removed since then.'

'Where would they have been taken?'

'The townspeople constantly re-use the stones from the ruins to build or repair their own homes. So we're lucky to have found this block intact . . . But there are other crosses, just the same shape as this one, in the cellars under the palace.'

We made our way down a flight of stairs into the dark dungeons that I had visited in 1983. Then, by flashlight, I had been shown a number of empty stone coffers which the Axumites believed had once contained great riches in gold and pearls. Now, producing a box of matches, Hagos showed me a Templar cross carved into the end of one of these coffers.

'How did you know that was there?' I asked in amazement.

'Everyone in Axum knows. As I said, I used to play in these ruins when I was a boy.'

He then led me into the next chamber, struck a match, and

showed me two more Templar crosses – one, rather crudely formed, on the far wall and another, beautifully executed, high up on the longer side wall.

Until the flame guttered out I stood gazing up at these crosses lost in thought. I knew that I might never be able to prove my hypothesis to the complete satisfaction of archaeologists or historians, but I now felt certain in my own heart that the Templars had indeed been here. The *croix pattée* had been their characteristic emblem, worn on their shields and on their tunics. It was entirely in keeping with everything else that I had learnt about them that some of their number should have come down here, into the obscure darkness of these dungeons, to leave that emblem on the walls – as a kind of puzzle perhaps, or as a sign, for future generations to wonder over.

'Are there any traditions', I asked Hagos, 'about who carved these crosses here?'

'Some of the townspeople say that they were the work of angels,' replied the TPLF official, 'but of course that is nonsense.'

A bearer of bad news

I did not hear from Hagos's father until after night had fallen, and when I did the news was bad. He came round to the little guest house in which we were staying shortly after seven that evening to tell me that the *Nebura-ed* was out of town.

My first reaction, which I did not voice, was that it was extremely unlikely that the chief priest of the Saint Mary of Zion church would be absent at this time of year. With *Timkat* just around the corner, and many preparations to make, his presence would surely be required in Axum.

'How unfortunate,' I said. 'Where's he gone?'

'He has gone to Asmara . . . for consultations.'

'But Asmara is still in government hands. How can he go there?'

'The *Nebura-ed* may go anywhere.'

'And will he be back before *Timkat*?'

'I am told that he will not return for several days. His deputy will stand in for him during the *Timkat* ceremonies.'

'So what does this mean for my work? Will I be able to talk to the guardian of the Ark, for example? There are so many questions that I have to ask.'

'Without the permission of the *Nebura-ed* you will be able to do nothing.'

Hagos's father was clearly an innocent messenger, so I had no right or reason to feel furious with him. Nevertheless it seemed obvious that the information he had just delivered was part of a strategy to prevent me from learning more about the Ark. Though they would probably be polite and friendly towards me as individuals, the plain fact was that the monks and priests of Axum would not co-operate with my investigation without the permission of the *Nebura-ed*. Sadly, however, the *Nebura-ed* was absent. Therefore I could not obtain his permission. Therefore I would not be able to find out anything of any significance from anyone; nor would I be able to do any of the things that I had come so many miles to do. In this classically Abyssinian fashion, I would be neutralized without anyone actually having to refuse me anything. The clergymen would not have to be boorish or rude; on the contrary they would only need to shrug and tell me with deep regret that this or that could not be done without the sanction of the *Nebura-ed*, and that – on this or that matter – they themselves were not qualified to speak.

'Is there any way,' I asked, 'that we can get a message to the *Nebura-ed* – about my work here?'

'While he is in Asmara?' laughed Hagos's father. 'Impossible.'

'OK then. What about the deputy chief priest? Can't he give me the permission I need?'

'I do not think so. To give you that permission he would first have to obtain the permission of the *Nebura-ed*.'

'In other words he would have to get permission to give me permission?'

'Exactly.'

'But can't I at least try? Can't I even *meet* the deputy and explain to him why I'm here? Who knows? He might be willing to help me.'

'Perhaps,' said Hagos's father. 'At any rate I will talk to the deputy tonight and I will bring you his answer tomorrow.'

Sanctuary of the Ark

The next morning, Thursday 17 January 1991, we were all up and about before dawn. Ed had wanted to shoot some general views at sunrise and Hagos had suggested that the summit of one of the several stony hills behind the town would provide the best vantage point.

Accordingly, at four-thirty a.m. we rousted Tesfaye, our driver, out of the bed that he been sharing with a local prostitute virtually non-stop since our arrival. On the road before five, we shoved the aerial of Ed's short-wave radio out of the window. The reception was bad, fogged with static. Nevertheless we managed to unscramble enough of the broadcast to understand that war had finally broken out in the Gulf, that American bombers had flown hundreds of sorties against Baghdad during the night, and that massive devastation had been caused. Apparently the Iraqi airforce had not managed to send up a single fighter in response.

'Sounds like it's all over,' commented Ed with a certain amount of satisfaction.

'I doubt that,' said Hagos. 'We will have to wait and see.'

We sat in silence for a while, listening to the continuing reports, as Tesfaye manoeuvred us up the steep track towards the summit we were heading for. The sky was still almost completely dark and he was perhaps dreaming of the humid pleasures he had so recently been enjoying; at any rate he managed to half roll the vehicle at one point and only just avoided driving us over the edge of a small cliff.

Ed, Hagos and I took this as our cue to get out. Leaving Tesfaye to deal with the camouflage tarpaulin we then walked the rest of the way to the summit.

It was a short hike through the litter of an old battlefield. 'This was where the last part of the Ethiopian army garrison held out when we took Axum from them,' explained Hagos. 'They were tough fighters, from the Seventeenth Division. We over-ran them in eight hours.'

All around us were smashed military lorries, burnt-out armoured personnel carriers and gutted tanks. And, as the sun began to come up, I noticed that huge amounts of munitions were still lying underfoot. Most of the debris consisted of spent shells and chunks of shrapnel. There were also several 81mm mortar bombs, rusty but unexploded, which nobody had bothered to remove.

Eventually we reached the summit, upon which perched the twisted and blackened wreckage of a barrack block. There beneath the crimson sky of morning, I stood and gazed gloomily down on the town of Axum.

Behind me was the devastated ruin of a building. Its corrugated aluminium roof, still partially intact, creaked and groaned eerily in the cold dawn breeze. On the ground in front of me was a soldier's helmet, split across the brow by some anonymous projectile. Further off, in a crater, lay a soldier's rotting boot.

The light was stronger now and far below I could see the garden in the centre of Axum where the main collection of giant stelae stood. Beyond, across a deserted square, set back in a secluded compound, rose the battlements and towers of the great church of Saint Mary of Zion. And by the side of that imposing edifice, surrounded by barbed iron railings, sat a squat grey granite chapel, windowless and barred, with a dome of green copper. This was the sanctuary of the Ark, near and yet far away, approachable and yet unapproachable. Within it lay the answer to all my questions, proof or disproof of all my work. Accordingly I looked down at it with longing and respect, with hope and agitation, with impatience but also with uncertainty.

Men of straw

We returned to the guest house for breakfast. And there we sat until mid-morning surrounded by a group of unusually sombre and pensive Tigrayans – all of whom had come to hear the news that boomed and crackled out of Ed's short-wave radio and that Hagos solemnly translated for them. Looking around at the faces, young and old, handsome and plain, I was struck by the poignancy of this intense interest in a distant war. Perhaps it provided a distraction from the home-grown conflict that had killed and maimed so many in this little town. Perhaps it arose from feelings of sympathy at the thought of the savage bombing that others were now enduring.

Taking in the nuances of this scene, I realized that such freedom of association would have been quite impossible for the browbeaten and terrorized townsfolk in the days when the Ethiopian government still ruled in Axum. And it seemed to me, though there was great poverty, though the schools were closed, though people could not move openly for fear of air strikes, though farmers could hardly plough their fields, and though famine threatened, that things were better here – far better – than they had been before.

Around eleven a.m., after Ed's filming schedule for the day had been worked out, Hagos and I walked into town in the direction of the main stelae park. At one point we passed a handpainted TPLF mural which depicted President Mengistu as a ravening demon with a blood-stained swastika on his cap and lines of armed soldiers marching out of his mouth. Half a dozen MiGs circled above his head and he was surrounded by tanks and artillery. The caption proclaimed in Tigrigna: 'We will never kneel before the dictator Mengistu.'

We walked on through the pot-holed streets of Axum, past poor market stalls and empty shops, amongst the simple houses, encountering on our way a constant stream of pedestrians – monks and nuns, priests, urchins, dignified elders, peasants in from the countryside, townsfolk, a woman carrying a huge earthen pot of water, groups of teenage boys trying to look stylish like teenagers everywhere. And I thought: *a few years ago I would have been quite happy to stand by while the government took all these people away to resettlement camps.*

'Hagos,' I said, 'things are so different in Axum since you expelled the government troops. I can't quite put my finger on it, but the atmosphere's completely changed.'

'It is because no one is afraid any more,' the TPLF official replied a moment later.

'Not even of the bombing and the air raids?'

'We fear those things, of course. But they are more of a nuisance than a terror – and we have found ways to avoid them. In the past, when the government was here, we could not avoid the cruelty of the garrisons, the tortures, the random arrests. That was the terror that oppressed us for so long. Yet when we confronted it, do you know what happened?'

'No. Not exactly.'

'We discovered that it had been spread by men of straw and that freedom had always been within our grasp.'

We had reached the garden of the stelae. As I walked amongst the great monoliths, I marvelled at the artistry and at the sheer skill of the forgotten culture that had conceived them. And I remembered that in 1983 the guardian monk had told me that they had been raised up by the Ark – by 'the Ark and the celestial fire'.

At the time I had not known what to make of the old man's words: now, with all I had learned, I knew that he could have been telling the truth. In its history the sacred relic had worked many great miracles: the erection of a few hundred tons of stone would surely not have been beyond its powers.

Miracle made real

That afternoon at four Hagos's father came to the guest house to report that the deputy chief priest would see us. He said that for reasons of protocol he could not accompany us there but gave us precise directions as to where we should go.

Hagos and I then walked over to the Saint Mary of Zion church and entered into a warren of small dwellings built around the rear of the compound. Passing under a low arch we came to a gateway. We knocked and were admitted to a garden where, on a bench, sat an elderly man dressed in black robes.

When he saw us approaching he murmured a quiet command. Hagos turned to me and said: 'You must stay here. I will talk on your behalf.'

An earnest conversation then ensued. Watching it from a distance I felt . . . impotent, paralysed, nullified, invalidated. I considered rushing forward and passionately pleading my case. But I knew that my entreaties, however heartfelt, would fall on ears tuned only to the rhythms of tradition.

Eventually Hagos came back. 'I have told the deputy everything,' he explained. 'He says that he will not talk to you. He says that on a matter as important as the Ark only the *Nebura-ed* and the guardian monk are qualified to speak.'

'And I assume that the *Nebura-ed* is still away?'

'Still away. Yes. But I have good news. The deputy has accepted for you to talk to the guardian.'

A few minutes later, having followed a maze of dusty paths, we came to the Saint Mary of Zion church. Passing in front of it we arrived at the metal railings that surrounded the sanctuary chapel. I stood for a while, staring through these railings. I calculated that with an energetic climb and a short dash I could reach the locked door of the building in about ten seconds.

Half joking, I mentioned this idea to Hagos, who responded with a look of genuine horror.

'Don't think of it,' he cautioned. He gestured back in the direction of Saint Mary of Zion where half a dozen tall young deacons were loitering. 'As a foreigner you command great respect. But if you were to commit such sacrilege you would certainly be killed.'

'Where do you suppose the guardian is?' I now asked.

'He is inside. He will join us when he is ready.'

We waited patiently until the sun was low in the sky. Then, as the darkness deepened, the guardian appeared. He was a tall, heavily built man, perhaps twenty years younger than his predecessor. Like his predecessor, his eyes were occluded with cataracts. Like his predecessor he wore thick robes redolent of incense.

He showed no inclination to invite us in but approached and shook hands with us through the railings.

I asked his name.

In a gravelly voice he replied simply: 'Gebra Mikail.'

'Please tell him', I said to Hagos, 'that my name is Graham Hancock and that I have spent the last two years studying the history and traditions of the Ark of the Covenant. Please tell him that I have come all the way from England, a journey of more than seven thousand kilometres, in the hope that I will be allowed to see the Ark.'

Hagos relayed this message. When he had finished the guardian said: 'I know. I have been informed of this already.'

'Will you allow me to enter the chapel?' I asked.

Hagos translated the question. There was a long pause, and then the expected answer: 'No, I cannot do that.'

'But,' I protested lamely, 'I have come to see the Ark.'

'Then I regret that you have wasted your journey. Because you will not see it. You should have known this if, as you say, you have studied our traditions.'

'I knew it, and yet I hoped.'

'Many hope. But other than myself no one may visit the Holy Ark. Not even the *Nebura-ed*. Not even the Patriarch. It is forbidden.'

'This is a great disappointment for me.'

'There are worse things in life than disappointment.'

I asked: 'Can you at least tell me what the Ark looks like? I think that I could go away content if you would tell me that.'

'I believe that the Ark is well described in the Bible. You can read there.'

'But I want you to tell me in your own words what it looks like. I mean the Ark that rests here in the sanctuary. Is it a box made of wood and gold? Does it have two winged figures on its lid?'

'I will not speak about such matters . . .'

'And how is it carried?' I continued. 'Is it carried on poles? Or in some other way? Is it heavy or light?'

'I have said that I will not speak about such matters, and therefore I will not speak.'

'And does it perform miracles?' I persisted. 'In the Bible the Ark was described as performing many miracles. So here in Axum does it also perform miracles?'

'It performs miracles. And it is in itself . . . miracle. It is miracle made real. And that is all that I will say.'

With this the guardian thrust his hand through the bars again and clenched my own hand firmly for a moment as though in farewell.

'I have another question,' I said insistently. 'Just one more question . . .'

A faint, affirmative nod.

'Tomorrow evening', I continued, 'is the beginning of *Timkat*. Will the true Ark be brought out then, for the procession to the Mai Shum, or will a replica be used?'

As Hagos translated my words into Tigrigna the guardian listened, his face impassive. Finally he replied: 'I have already said enough. *Timkat* is a public ceremony. You may attend it and see for yourself. If you have studied as you have claimed, even though it may only have been for two years, I think that you will be able to know the answer to your question.'

And with that he turned away and slipped into the shadows and was gone.

The secret behind the signs

The object that was carried to the Mai Shum reservoir when the *Timkat* ceremonies began late in the afternoon of Friday 18 January 1991 was a bulky rectangular chest over which was draped a thick blue cloth embroidered with an emblem of a dove. And I remembered that in Wolfram's *Parzival* the dove, too, had been the emblem of the Grail.[6] Yet I knew, beyond any shadow of a doubt, that what I was looking at was neither Grail nor Ark. Rather it was in itself an emblem and a symbol, a token and a sign.

As the Falasha priest Raphael Hadane had warned me months before, the sacred relic kept in the sanctuary chapel remained there – jealously guarded in the Holy of Holies. What was brought out in public procession was therefore merely a replica of it – a replica, however, that was quite different in form from the familiar flat *tabotat* that I had seen paraded during the previous year's celebrations at Gondar, and that did indeed accord with the shape and dimensions of the biblical Ark.

How, then, can I be so sure that it was a replica? The answer is simple. Not for a single moment during the whole of the two-day ceremony did Gebra Mikail, the guardian monk, leave the sanctuary chapel. Late in the afternoon of the 18th, as the procession carrying the cloth-wrapped chest moved away in the direction of the Mai Shum, I saw him sitting there behind the iron bars, leaning against the grey granite wall of the squat building, seemingly lost in contemplation. He did not even look up as the priests departed, and it was plain that the object which they bore aloft held no special importance for him.

Then, when they were gone, he disappeared inside the chapel. Moments later I heard his slow arrhythmic chant. And had I been permitted to move closer I knew that I would have recognized the sweet savour of frankincense.

For what was Gebra Mikail doing, there in the thick darkness, if not offering up a fragrance pleasing to the Lord before the Holy

Ark of His Covenant? And why else should he, who had been selected from amongst all his brethren to fulfil a precious trust, have stayed closed within the sanctuary until morning, if the sacred and inviolable relic that he had forfeited his own freedom to guard had not remained there with him?

In this way I believe at last that I did glimpse the secret behind the symbol, the glorious enigma proclaimed in so many wondrous signs – proclaimed and yet not revealed. For the Ethiopians know that if you want to hide a tree you must place it in a forest. And what else are the replicas that they venerate in twenty thousand churches if not a veritable forest of signs?

At the heart of that forest lies the Ark itself, the golden Ark that was built at the foot of Mount Sinai, that was carried through the wilderness and across the river Jordan, that brought victory to the Israelites in their struggle to win the Promised Land, that was taken up to Jerusalem by King David, and that – around 955 BC – was deposited by Solomon in the Holy of Holies of the First Temple.

From there, some three hundred years later, it was removed by faithful priests who sought to preserve it from pollution at the hands of the sinner Manasseh and who bore it away to safety on the far-off Egyptian island of Elephantine. There a new temple was built to house it, a temple in which it remained for two further centuries.

When the temple was destroyed, however, its restless wanderings resumed again and it was carried southward into Ethiopia, into the land shadowing with wings, into the land criss-crossed by rivers. Having come from one island it was taken to another –to green and verdant Tana Kirkos – where it was installed in a simple tabernacle and worshipped by simple folk. For the eight hundred years that followed it stood at the centre of a large and idiosyncratic Judaic cult, a cult whose members were the ancestors of all Ethiopian Jews today.

Then the Christians came, preaching a new religion, and – after converting the king – they were able to seize the Ark for themselves. They took it to Axum and placed it in the great church that they had built there, a church dedicated to Saint Mary the Mother of Christ.

Many more years then went by and – as the weary centuries

passed – the memory of how the Ark had really come to Ethiopia grew blurred. Legends began to circulate to account for the now mysterious and inexplicable fact that a small city in the remote highlands of Tigray appeared to have been selected – presumably by God Himself – as the last resting place of the most precious and prestigious relic of Old Testament times. These legends were eventually codified and set down in writing in the form of the *Kebra Nagast* – a document containing so many errors, anachronisms and inconsistencies that later generations of scholars were never able to see their way through to the single ancient and recondite truth concealed beneath the layers of myth and magic.

That truth, however, *was* recognized by the Knights Templar, who understood its earth-shaking power and who came to Ethiopia in pursuit of it. It was, moreover, expressed by Wolfram von Eschenbach in his story of *Parzival*, where the Holy Grail – 'the consummation of heart's desire' – served as an occult cryptogram for the Holy Ark of the Covenant.

In Wolfram's text the heathen Flegetanis was said to have penetrated the hidden mysteries of the constellations and to have declared in a reverential voice that there was indeed 'a thing called the Gral'. He declared also that this perfect thing, this spiritual thing, was guarded by a Christian progeny bred to a pure life. And he concluded his soothsaying with these words: 'Those humans who are summoned to the Gral are ever worthy.'[7]

So too those humans who are summoned to the Ark – for Ark and Grail are one and the same. I, for my part, however, was never worthy enough. I knew it even as I traversed the waste land. I knew it as I approached the sanctuary chapel. I know it still. And yet . . . And yet . . . 'my heart is glad, and my very soul rejoices, and my flesh also shall rest in hope.'

Datta. Dayadhvam. Damyata.
Shantih shantih shantih

References

Chapter 1 Initiation

1 For example, see Julian Morgenstern, 'The Book of the Covenant', *Hebrew Union College Annual*, vol. V, 1928, reprinted by KTAV Publishing House Inc., New York, 1968, p. 118: 'the Ark itself came in popular thought and speech to be identified with the deity; the Ark itself was to all extents and purposes the deity.' The direct identification of the Ark with God is well illustrated in the following passage from Numbers 10:35: 'And it came to pass, when the Ark set forward, that Moses said, Rise up, Lord, and let thine enemies be scattered and let them that hate thee flee before thee' (King James Authorized Version). The Jerusalem Bible translation of the same verse, which makes use of Yahweh, the name of God, reads: 'And as the Ark set out, Moses would say, Arise, Yahweh, may your enemies be scattered and those who hate you run for their lives before you.' *The Interpreter's Dictionary of the Bible* comments: 'The Ark is not only seen as the leader of Israel's host, but is directly addressed as Yahweh. There is virtually an identification of Yahweh and the Ark ... there is no doubt that the Ark was interpreted as the extension or embodiment of the presence of Yahweh' (*The Interpreter's Dictionary of the Bible: An Illustrated Encyclopaedia*, Abingdon Press, Nashville, 1962, pp. 222–3.

2 See Exodus 37:1, which gives the dimensions of the Ark as follows: 'two cubits and a half was the length of it, and a cubit and a half the breadth of it, and a cubit and a half the height of it.' The measurements in feet and inches are extrapolated from the ancient cubit, which was eighteen inches. See Dr J. H. Hertz (ed.), *The Pentateuch and the Haftorahs*, Soncino Press, London, 1978, p. 327. The Jerusalem Bible, footnote (b), p. 87, concurs (*Jerusalem Bible*, Eyre & Spottiswoode, London, 1968).

3 Exodus 37:7–9.

4 I Chronicles 28:2.

5 Richard Elliott Friedman, *Who Wrote the Bible?*, Jonathan Cape, London, 1988, p. 156.

6 *The Interpreter's Dictionary of the Bible*, op. cit., p. 222.

7 The phrase is taken from J. Theodore Bent's nineteenth-century book on Axum, *The Sacred City of the Ethiopians: Travel and Research in Abyssinia in 1893*, Longmans, Green, London, New York and Bombay, 1896.

8 Eritrea was in fact decolonized in 1952. For the next ten years it was federated with Ethiopia but kept its own separate identity. In 1962, after what was widely believed to be a rigged referendum, the federal relationship was dissolved and Ethiopia took over full control of the territory, which thenceforward was governed directly from Addis Ababa. Haile Selassie argued that apart from the brief colonial interlude Eritrea had always been an integral part of Ethiopia and should remain so. Many Eritreans, however, felt differently.

9 G. W. B Huntingford (ed.), *The Periplus of the Eritrean Sea*, Hakluyt Society, London, 1980.

10 Reported in A. H. M. Jones and Elizabeth Monroe, *A History of Ethiopia*, Oxford University Press, 1955, pp. 32–3.

11 J. W. McCrindle (trans. and ed.), *The Christian Topography of Cosmas, an Egyptian Monk*, Hakluyt Society, London, 1898.

12 The Rufinius history of the conversion of Ethiopia to Christianity is reported at length in A. H. M Jones and Elizabeth Monroe, *A History of Ethiopia*, op. cit., pp. 26–7. See also Graham Hancock, Richard Pankhurst, Duncan Willetts, *Under Ethiopian Skies*, Editions HL, London and Nairobi, 1983, pp. 34–5.

13 Reported by Richard Pankhurst, writing in Hancock, Pankhurst and Willetts, *Under Ethiopian Skies*, op. cit.

14 For a full account of the findings of this dig see S.C. Munro-Hay, *Excavations at Axum: An Account of Research at the Ancient Ethiopian Capital directed in 1972–74 by the Late Dr Neville Chittick*, Royal Geographical Society, London, 1989.

15 Another tradition says that the coffers are in fact *coffins* and that they once contained the bodies of Kaleb and Gebre-Maskal.

16 C. F. Beckingham and G. W. B Huntingford (eds), *The Prester John of the Indies: A True Relation of the Lands of Prester John, being the Narrative of the Portuguese Embassy to Ethiopia in 1520 written by Father Francisco Alvarez*, Cambridge, published for the Hakluyt Society at the University Press, 1961, vol. I, pp. 151–3.

17 Ibid., footnote 2, p. 151.

18 Ibid., pp. 145–8.

Chapter 2 **Disenchantment**

1 From Article II of the 1955 (revised) Constitution.
2 Aymro Wondemagegnehu and Joachim Motovu, *The Ethiopian Orthodox Church*, The Ethiopian Orthodox Mission, Addis Ababa, 1970, p. 48.
3 Ibid., p. 46.
4 Ibid., p. 152.

Chapter 3 **The Grail Cipher**

1 The book was published in 1990. Carol Beckwith, Angela Fisher, Graham Hancock, *African Ark: Peoples of the Horn*, Collins Harvill, London, 1990.
2 William Anderson, *The Rise of the Gothic*, Hutchinson, London, 1985, p. 34. And see in general pp. 33–7.
3 For a chronology see *Chartres: Guide of the Cathedral*, Editions Houvet-la-Crypte, Chartres, pp. 12–13.
4 John James, *Medieval France: A Guide to the Sacred Architecture of Medieval France*, Harrap Columbus, London, 1987, p. 71.
5 Malcolm Miller, *Chartres: The Cathedral and the Old Town*, Pitkin Pictorials, Norwich, UK, pp. 13 and 18. See also *Chartres: Guide of the Cathedral*, op. cit., Foreword written by Etienne Houvet, custodian of the cathedral, p. 3.
6 *Chartres: Guide of the Cathedral*, op. cit., p. 53.
7 Sir E. A. Wallis Budge, *The Queen of Sheba and her Only Son Menelik: being the 'Book of the Glory of Kings' (Kebra Nagast)*, Oxford University Press, 1932, p. 29. In a conversation with Solomon the Queen of Sheba is quoted as saying: 'From this moment I will not worship the sun, but will worship the creator of the sun, the God of Israel . . . because of this I have found favour with thee, and before the God of Israel, my Creator.'
8 1 Kings 10:1–13; 1 Chronicles 9:1–12.
9 For a good résumé of the scholarly conventional wisdom see H. St John Philby, *The Queen of Sheba*, Quartet Books, London, 1981.
10 Malcolm Miller, *Chartres Cathedral: Illustrating the Medieval Stained Glass and Sculpture*, Pitkin Pictorials, Norwich, UK, p. 14. See also *Chartres: Guide of the Cathedral*, op. cit., pp. 37–47.
11 Genesis 14:18; Psalm 110:4.
12 Malcolm Miller, *Chartres Cathedral: Illustrating the Medieval Stained Glass and Sculpture*, op. cit., p. 20.
13 *Chartres: Guide of the Cathedral*, op. cit., p. 42.
14 See Exodus 37:1 and Chapter 1, note 2 above.
15 *Chartres: Guide of the Cathedral*, op. cit., p. 40.
16 Louis Charpentier, *The Mysteries of Chartres Cathedral*, RILKO,

London, 1983 (originally published by Robert Laffont, Paris, 1966), p. 70.

17 *Chartres: Guide of the Cathedral*, op. cit., p. 37.

18 Louis Charpentier, *The Mysteries of Chartres Cathedral*, op. cit., p. 68, photographic section between pp. 32 and 33, and p. 113.

19 See, for example, Robert Graves, *The White Goddess*, Faber & Faber, London and Boston, 1988 edn, p. 161.

20 Hebrews 7.

21 Louis Charpentier, *The Mysteries of Chartres Cathedral*, op. cit., p. 113.

22 See D. D. R. Owen (trans.), *Chrétien de Troyes: Arthurian Romances*, J. M. Dent, London, 1988, Introduction, p. x.

23 Sir Thomas Malory, *Le Morte d'Arthur*, Penguin Classics, London, 1988 – see half-title page.

24 See Edwin H. Zeydel (trans. and ed.), *The Parzival of Wolfram von Eschenbach*, University of North Carolina, Chapel Hill, 1951, p. 14. See also Wolfram von Eschenbach, *Parzival*, Penguin Classics, London, 1980, Introduction, p. 8.

25 Sir Thomas Malory, *Le Morte d'Arthur*, op. cit., pp. 190 and 213.

26 Wolfram von Eschenbach, *Parzival*, op. cit., p. 239.

27 Lady Flavia Anderson, *The Ancient Secret: Fire from the Sun*, RILKO, London, 1987, p. 15.

28 Ibid.

29 Chrétien de Troyes, *Arthurian Romances*, op. cit., p. 417.

30 Ibid., pp. 417–18.

31 Ibid., p. 459.

32 Emma Jung and Marie-Louise von Franz, *The Grail Legend*, Coventure, London, 1986, pp. 29 and 116. (Originally published by Walter Verlag, Olten, 1980, and in the USA by Sigo Press, Boston, 1970.) See also A. M. Hatto's Foreword to Wolfram's *Parzival*, op. cit., p. 7. Old Catalan *grazal* and Provençal *grasal* both also meant 'vessel, cup or bowl of wood, earthenware or metal'.

33 The word 'holy' appears in no less than thirty books of the Old Testament.

34 John Matthews, *The Grail: Quest for the Eternal*, Thames & Hudson, London, 1987, p. 12.

35 See F. L. Cross and E. A. Livingstone (eds), *The Oxford Dictionary of the Christian Church*, Oxford University Press, 1988, p. 162.

36 William Anderson, *The Rise of the Gothic*, op. cit., p. 65.

37 For a discussion see M. Kilian Hufgard, 'Saint Bernard of Clairvaux', *Medieval Studies*, vol. II, Edwin Mellen Press, 1989, p. 143: 'It would be impossible to calculate the full extent of Bernard's influence on the iconography of the early Gothic cathedrals.'

38 See John Matthews, *The Grail: Quest for the Eternal*, op. cit., p. 12.

39 For a discussion see Bodo Mergell, *Der Graal in Wolframs Parsifal*, Halle, 1952. See also *Encyclopaedia Britannica*, Micropaedia, 15th edn, 1991, vol. V, pp. 408–9, which states that the *Queste del Saint Graal* 'was clearly influenced by the mystical teachings of Saint Bernard of Clairvaux'.

40 An excellent discussion of this symbolism is contained in John Matthews, *The Grail: Quest for the Eternal*, op. cit., pp. 14–17.

41 F. L. Cross and E. A. Livingstone (eds), *The Oxford Dictionary of the Christian Church*, op. cit., p. 827.

42 John Matthews, *The Grail: Quest for the Eternal*, op. cit., p. 15.

43 Ibid., p. 15.

44 M. Kilian Hufgard, 'Saint Bernard of Clairvaux', op. cit., p. 141.

45 F. L. Cross and E. A. Livingstone (eds), *The Oxford Dictionary of the Christian Church*, op. cit., pp. 42–3 and 87–8.

46 Helen Adolf, 'New Light on Oriental Sources for Wolfram's *Parzival* and other Grail Romances', *Publications of the Modern Languages Association of America*, vol. 62, March 1947, pp. 306–24.

47 Ibid., p. 306. 'I am indebted', wrote Adolf, 'to the pioneers in this field, to Veselovskij and Singer, founders of the Ethiopian theory.' A. N. Veselovskij had written several works on the origin of the Grail legend which had been published in Russia between 1886 and 1904; S. Singer had been a German academic writing at about the same time. Details of their works are to be found in Adolf's Bibliography, p. 324.

48 Ibid., p. 306.

49 See, for example, Chrétien de Troyes, *Arthurian Romances*, op. cit., Introduction by D. D. R. Owen, p. ix–xviii. See also Jessie L. Weston, *From Ritual to Romance*, Cambridge University Press, 1920, particularly Chapter 6 where she specifically rejects the cauldrons of Celtic mythology as being the prototypes for the Grail, adding 'these special objects belong to another line of tradition altogether' (pp. 69–70). She also rejects the other common derivation in the Cup of the Last Supper and the Lance of Longinus (p. 68). It was Jessie Weston's scholarly book that largely inspired T. S. Eliot's poem *The Waste Land*. See T. S. Eliot, *Selected Poems*, Faber & Faber, London, 1961, p. 68.

50 Wolfram von Eschenbach, *Parzival*, op. cit., p. 410.

51 Wolfram von Eschenbach, *Parzival*, op. cit. See in particular Foreword, pp. 7–8. A typical example of the close correspondences between the two texts is to be found in the near-identical descriptions of the Grail procession and of the subsequent disappearance of the Grail castle (Wolfram, pp. 123–31; Chrétien, pp. 415–22). The *Encyclopaedia Britannica*, 11th

(1910) edn, confirms that *Parzival* was 'beyond all doubt' a rendering of a 'French original' (entry under 'Wolfram von Eschenbach', p. 775). See also Margaret Fitzgerald Richey, *The Story of Parzival and the Grail, As Related by Wolfram von Eschenbach*, Basil Blackwell & Mott, Oxford, 1935, pp. 10–11: 'the external resemblances [between Wolfram's account and Chrétien's] are so close, not only in the ordering of the episodes but also in points of detail, that many scholars regard Chrétien's poem as the one specific basis of Wolfram's.'

52 Helen Adolf, 'New Light on Oriental Sources for Wolfram's *Parzival*', op. cit., p. 307.

53 For confirmation of the use of stone 'white and beautiful like marble' in the most precious *tabots* see C. F. Beckingham and G.W.B. Huntingford (eds), *The Prester John of the Indies: A True Relation of the Lands of Prester John, being the Narrative of the Portuguese Embassy to Ethiopia in 1520 written by Father Francisco Alvarez*, Cambridge, published for the Hakluyt Society at the University Press, 1961, vol. II, p. 543.

54 Helen Adolf, 'New Light on Oriental Sources for Wolfram's *Parzival*', op. cit., p. 309.

55 Wolfram von Eschenbach, *Parzival*, op. cit., for example p. 240. Another even more specific example of the Grail's legislative function occurs on p. 406.

56 Ibid., p. 246.

57 Judges 20:27–8.

58 1 Samuel 3:1–11.

59 1 Chronicles 28. Note in particular verse 19.

60 Wolfram von Eschenbach, *Parzival*, op. cit., p. 243.

61 Louis Ginzberg, *The Legends of the Jews*, The Jewish Publication Society of America, Philadelphia, 1911, vol. III, pp. 128–9.

62 Wolfram von Eschenbach, *Parzival*, op. cit., p. 232. Emphasis added.

63 *The Jewish Encyclopaedia*, Funk & Wagnells, New York, 1925, vol. II, p. 107. See also Menahem Haran, *Temples and Temple Service in Ancient Israel*, Clarendon Press, Oxford, 1978, reprinted by Eisenbrauns, Winona Lake, Indiana, 1985, p. 246. Haran states the scholarly view that 'the Ark held not the two tables of the law but . . . a meteorite from Mount Sinai'.

64 For a discussion see Emma Jung and Marie-Louise von Franz, *The Grail Legend*, op. cit., p. 148, footnote 28.

65 Jennifer Westwood (ed.), *The Atlas of Mysterious Places*, Guild Publishing, London, 1987, p. 74.

66 Ibid.

67 For a lengthy and very scholarly discussion of these links see two papers by Julian Morgenstern: 'The Book of the Covenant',

Hebrew Union College Annual, vol. V. 1928; and 'The Ark, the Ephod and the Tent of Meeting', *Hebrew Union College Annual*, vol. XVII, 1942–3; both reprinted by KTAV Publishing House, New York, 1968. In 'The Book of the Covenant', p. 118, Morgenstern writes: 'The most natural assumption is that the Ark contained a *betyl* . . .This conception was, of course, common amongst the primitive Semites, and the evidence is ample that it was current in ancient Israel.'

68 W. H. Roscher, *Lexikon der griechischen und römischen Mythologie*, 1884, cited in Emma Jung and Marie-Louise von Franz, *The Grail Legend*, op. cit., p. 148.

69 Wolfram von Eschenbach, *Parzival*, op. cit., p. 239.

70 See, for example, Emma Jung and Marie-Louise von Franz, *The Grail Legend*, op. cit., pp. 149 and 157.

71 John Matthews, *The Grail: Quest for the Eternal*, op. cit., p. 17. Emma Jung and Marie-Louise von Franz also suggest a similar derivation: *The Grail Legend*, op. cit., p. 148.

72 Wolfram von Eschenbach, *Parzival*, op. cit., e.g. pp. 225, 240.

73 Ibid., pp. 126–7.

74 *Tan. Terumah*, XI; also, with slight variations, *Yoma* 39b. Cited in *The Jewish Encyclopaedia*, vol. II, op. cit., p. 105.

75 I Kings 8:12.

76 Zev Vilnay, *Legends of Jerusalem: The Sacred Land*, The Jewish Publication Society of America, Philadelphia, 1973, vol. I, pp. 11–12.

77 E.g., Exodus 40:20–38.

78 Chrétien de Troyes, *Arthurian Romances*, op. cit., p. 417.

79 Ibid.

80 Exodus 37:1–2.

81 Exodus 37:6.

82 Exodus 34:29–30. This is the Jerusalem Bible translation, direct from Hebrew, rather than through Greek in the case of the King James Authorized Version (*The Jerusalem Bible*, Eyre & Spottiswoode, London, 1968). The King James Version has the two verses as follows: 'And it came to pass, when Moses came down from Mount Sinai with the two tables of testimony in Moses' hand, when he came down from the mount, that Moses wist not that the skin of his face shone while he talked with him. And when Aaron and all the children of Israel saw Moses, behold, the skin of his face shone; and they were afraid to come nigh him.'

83 Wolfram von Eschenbach, *Parzival*, op. cit., p. 125.

84 Ibid., p. 125.

85 Ibid., p. 125.

86 Ibid., pp. 125 and 401.

87 Ibid., p. 239.

88 Ibid., p. 389.

89 1 Chronicles 15:2. Similarly see Deuteronomy 10:8.

90 Sir E. A. Wallis Budge, *Kebra Nagast*, op. cit.

91 Ibid., p. 98.

92 Ibid., p. 79.

93 Ibid., p. 95.

94 In his translation, Sir E. A. Wallis Budge used a variety of different words and phrases to refer to the Ark of the Covenant – e.g. 'Zion', 'Heavenly Zion', 'Tabernacle of His Law', 'Tabernacle of His Covenant', 'Tabernacle of the Law of God'. He makes clear at several points that these terms are all completely interchangeable and that they refer to exactly the same thing. For example, in his Introduction (p. xvii), he speaks of 'the Tabernacle of the Law of God, i.e. the Ark of the Covenant'. Likewise, within the main body of the translation, there are several points, cross-referenced to biblical passages, at which this interchangeability of terms for the Ark (including 'Zion' and 'Heavenly Zion') is unequivocally spelled out – e.g. pp. 14–15 and 178. For purposes of clarity in my own text, and with apologies to Budge, I have adopted the policy of simplifying this confusing terminological spaghetti. In all my quotations from the *Kebra Nagast* the familiar epithets 'Ark of the Covenant', 'Ark of His Covenant', 'Ark of God', 'Ark of the Lord', and just plain 'Ark' will be used.

95 Sir E. A. Wallis Budge, *Kebra Nagast*, op. cit., p. 169.

96 Ibid. pp. 94–5.

97 Wolfram von Eschenbach, *Parzival*, op. cit., p. 393.

Chapter 4 A Map to Hidden Treasure

1 Wolfram von Eschenbach, *Parzival*, Penguin Classics, London, 1980, p. 22.

2 Ibid., p. 17.

3 Ibid., p. 22.

4 See, for example, H. St John Philby, *The Queen of Sheba*, Quartet Books, London, 1981, pp. 58–60.

5 Wolfram von Eschenbach, *Parzival*, op. cit., p. 30.

6 Ibid., p. 27.

7 Ibid., p. 24.

8 Ibid., p. 34.

9 Ibid., p. 39.

10 Ibid.

11 Ibid.

12 Ibid., p. 56.
13 Ibid., p. 40.
14 Ibid., p. 66.
15 The complex tangle of relationships in *Parzival* requires some unravelling. On pp. 439–47 of the Penguin Classics edition, Professor A. T. Hatto provides a useful glossary of personal names. Feirefiz is described on p. 440 as 'Parzival's infidel half-brother; son of Gahmuret and his first wife Belacane'.
16 Sir E. A. Wallis Budge, *The Queen of Sheba and her Only Son Menelik: being the 'Book of the Glory of Kings' (Kebra Nagast)*, Oxford University Press, 1932, p. 35.
17 Ibid., p. 37.
18 Ibid., p. 38.
19 See Chapter 3, note 94 above.
20 Sir E. A. Wallis Budge, *Kebra Nagast*, op. cit., p. 102. For a further example of the emphasis on skin colour in the *Kebra Nagast* see p. 156.
21 Wolfram von Eschenbach, *Parzival*, op. cit., Professor A. T. Hatto's footnote to p. 40.
22 A. N. Veselovskij, 'On the Problem of the Origin of the Grail Legend', *Zurnal [Journal] of the [Russian] Ministry for the Enlightenment of the People*, Moscow, February 1904, p. 452. See also Helen Adolf, 'New Light on Oriental Sources for Wolfram's *Parzival* and other Grail Romances', *Publications of the Modern Languages Association of America*, vol. 62, March 1947, p. 310.
23 Sir E. A. Wallis Budge, *Kebra Nagast*, op. cit., p. 46.
24 Dr E. Littman (trans. and ed.), *The Legend of the Queen of Sheba in the Tradition of Axum*, Bibliotheca Abessinica (Studies Concerning the Languages, Literature and History of Abyssinia), vol. I, Princeton University Library, 1904, p. 9.
25 See Chapter 3 above.
26 Wolfram von Eschenbach, *Parzival*, op. cit., pp. 406–7.
27 Ibid., p. 408.
28 See, for example, C. F. Beckingham and G. W. B. Huntingford (eds), *The Prester John of the Indies: A True Relation of the Lands of Prester John, being the Narrative of the Portuguese Embassy to Ethiopia in 1520 written by Father Francisco Alvarez*, Cambridge, published for the Hakluyt Society at the University Press, 1961.
29 Wolfram von Eschenbach, *Parzival*, op. cit., p. 408.
30 Linda B. Parshall, *The Art of Narration in Wolfram's 'Parzival' and Albrecht's 'Jüngerer Titurel'*, Cambridge University Press, 1981, p. 1.
31 Henry and Mary Garland, *The Oxford Companion to German Literature*, Oxford University Press, 1986, p. 892.

32. Dorothy Reich, *A History of German Literature*, Blackwood, Edinburgh and London, 1970, p. 95.

33. Linda B. Parshall, *The Art of Narration in Wolfram's 'Parsival' and Albrecht's 'Jüngerer Titurel'*, op. cit., p. 1.

34. No English translation exists of *Der Jüngerer Titurel*. That it depicts the last resting place of the Holy Grail as being 'the land of Prester John' is, however, not in dispute. Readers who wish to follow the matter further, and who read German, are referred to K. A. Hahn, *Titurel*, Leipsig, 1842. See also Werner Wolf and Kurt Nyholm's edited edition in several volumes in the Deutsche Texte des Mittelalters (DTM) series, originally published by the Academy of Sciences of the GDR, Berlin, 1955–84.

35. Wolfram von Eschenbach, *Parsival*, op. cit., p. 408.

36. Ibid., p. 408.

37. Ibid., p. 373.

38. Ibid., p. 377.

39. See *Encyclopaedia Britannica*, 11th (1910) end, p. 304. See also Sergew Hable-Selassie, *Ancient and Medieval Ethiopian History to 1270*, Haile-Selassie I University, Addis Ababa, 1972, pp. 254–5.

40. Ibid.

41. Ibid.

42. Ibid., p. 261.

43. Ibid. and *Encyclopaedia Britannica*, op. cit., p. 305.

44. *Encyclopaedia Britannica*, op. cit., p 305

45. For a discussion see Irmgard Bidder, *Lalibela: the Monolithic Churches of Ethiopia*, M. DuMont, Cologne, p. 11.

46. See Chapter 1 above for full details.

47. Helen Adolf, 'New Light on Oriental Sources', op. cit., p. 306.

48. E. A. Wallis Budge, *A History of Ethiopia*, London, 1928, p. 178.

49. Extract from *The Travels of Marco Polo*, quoted in Henry Salt, *A Voyage to Abyssinia* Frank Cass and Co., London, 1967, Appendix V.

50. *Encyclopaedia Britannica*, op. cit., p. 306.

51. C. F. Beckingham and G. W. B. Huntingford (eds), *The Prester John of the Indies*, op. cit., see p. 5.

52. Ibid., e.g. p. 296.

53. *Encyclopaedia Britannica*, op. cit., p. 306.

54. Ibid., p. 306.

55. Ibid., p. 306.

56. Ibid., p. 304.

57. Ibid., p. 306 (emphasis added).

58. David Buxton, *The Abyssinians*, Thames & Hudson, London, 1970, p. 45.

59. See Chapter 3 above.

60. John Matthews, *The Grail: Quest for the Eternal*, Thames & Hudson, London, 1987, p. 69.

61 *Encyclopaedia Britannica*, op. cit., p. 591.

Chapter 5 White Knights, Dark Continent

1 Emma Jung and Marie-Louise von Franz, *The Grail Legend*, Coventure, London, 1986, pp. 10–11. (Originally published by Walter Verlag, Olten, 1980, and in the USA by Sigo Press, Boston, 1970.)

2 Wolfram von Eschenbach, *Parzival*, Penguin Classics, London, 1980, p. 232. See also p. 213.

3 Ibid., p. 410.

4 Ibid., p. 233.

5 Ibid., p. 214.

6 See Jessie L. Weston's translation of *Parzival*, David Nutt, London, 1894, 'Excursus A: Wolfram's Source', pp. 191–2. See also Emma Jung and Marie-Louise von Franz, *The Grail Legend*, op. cit., p. 152.

7 Ibid.

8 See, for example, *The Hutchinson Encyclopedia*, Hutchinson, London, 1988, p. 481.

9 See in particular F. Kampers, *Das Lichtland der Seelen und der Heilige Gral*, Cologne, 1916, pp. 20–7. See also Emma Jung and Marie-Louise von Franz, *The Grail Legend*, op. cit., p. 152. That great authority on *Parzival*, Jessie Weston, concurs. See 'Excursus A' to her translation of *Parzival*, op. cit., particularly p. 191, last paragraph.

10 Emma Jung and Marie-Louise von Franz, *The Grail Legend*, op. cit., p. 152.

11 Wolfram von Eschenbach, *Parzival*, op. cit., for example pp. 228, 393 and 406.

12 Ibid., p. 241.

13 Ibid. Professor A. T. Hatto's 'Introduction to a Second Reading', p. 438.

14 Margaret Fitzgerald Richey, *The Story of Parzival and the Graal, As Related by Wolfram von Eschenbach*, Basil Blackwell & Mott, Oxford, 1935, p. 198.

15 Ibid., p. 211. See also p. 198: 'This identification with the Templars is very striking, and what else is told in connection in the text of *Parzival* agrees with the character of that Order.'

16 Louis Charpentier, *The Mysteries of Chartres Cathedral*, RILKO, London, 1983, p. 68.

17 As, for example, in Gaetan Delaforge, *The Templar Tradition in the Age of Aquarius*, Threshold Books, Vermont, 1987, p. 68.

18 The principal source for discussion of Wolfram's visit to the Holy

Land is Karl Bertau, *Deutsche Literatur im europäischen Mittelalter*, C. H. Beck, Munich, 1974.

19 1 Chronicles 28:2. The words are those of Solomon's father, King David, who had hoped to build the Temple for the Ark, but who had been instructed by God to leave this task to Solomon.

20 William of Tyre, *A History of Deeds done Beyond the Sea* (E. Babcock and A. C. Krey trans.), Octagon Books, New York, 1986, vol. I, pp. 524–5.

21 *Encyclopaedia Britannica*, 11th edn, 1910, p. 593.

22 Edward Burman, *The Templars: Knights of God*, Aquarian Press, Wellingborough, 1986, p. 21.

23 John J. Robinson, *Born in Blood*, Century, London, 1990, p. 66. Originally published in the USA in 1989 by M. Evans.

24 *Encyclopaedia Britannica*, Micropaedia, 15th edn, 1991, vol. III, p. 133. The city was sold to the King of France in 1286.

25 Edward Burman, *The Templars*, op. cit., p. 27. Saint Bernard's mother, Aleth, was André de Montbard's sister.

26 Interestingly, it is thought possible that Saint Bernard himself provided the model for Sir Galahad, the hero of the Cistercian *Queste del Saint Graal*. See Edward Burman, *The Templars*, op. cit., p. 30. See also *Encyclopaedia Britannica*, Micropaedia, 15th edn, 1991, vol. V, pp. 79–80 and 408–9.

27 John J. Robinson, *Born in Blood*, op. cit., p. 66.

28 Edward Burman, *The Templars*, op. cit., p. 21.

29 Chrétien de Troyes, *Arthurian Romances*, J. M. Dent, London, 1988, D. D. R. Owen's Introduction, p. ix.

30 Steven Runciman, *A History of the Crusades*, Penguin Books, London, 1987, vol. II, p. 157.

31 Ibid. See also *Encyclopaedia Britannica*, 11th edn, 1910, p. 591. Then, as now, the Mosque of Omar, better known as the Dome of the Rock, stood over the site of Solomon's Temple. See also F. L. Cross and E. A. Livingstone (eds), *The Oxford Dictionary of the Christian Church*, Oxford University Press, 1988, p. 1345.

32 Steven Runciman, *A History of the Crusades*, op. cit., vol. II, p. 157.

33 John G. Robinson, *Born in Blood*, op. cit., p. 66.

34 Steven Runciman, *A History of the Crusades*, op. cit., vol. II, p. 157.

35 Meir Ben-Dov, *In the Shadow of the Temple: The Discovery of Ancient Jerusalem*, Harper & Row, New York, 1985 and Keter Publishing House, Jerusalem, 1985, p. 347.

36 Ibid.

37 Zev Vilnay, *Legends of Jerusalem: The Sacred Land*, Jewish Publication Society of America, Philadelphia, vol. I, 1973, p. 11.

38 See Professor Richard Elliott Friedman, *Who Wrote the Bible?*,

Jonathan Cape, London, 1988, Chapter 1, pp. 155–6, quoted in Chapter 1, p. 7 above.

39 Zev Vilnay, *Legends of Jerusalem*, op. cit., p. 11.

40 Ibid., pp. 123 and 324, note 136. See also N. A. Silberman, *Digging for God and Country*, Alfred A. Knopf, New York, 1982, p. 186. See also 'The Syriac Apocalypse of Baruch' in H. F. D. Sparks (ed.), *The Apocryphal Old Testament*, Clarendon Press, Oxford, 1989, pp. 843 and 844.

41 Malcolm Barber, 'The Origins of the Order of the Temple', *Studia Monastica*, vol. XII, 1970, pp. 221–2.

42 Jean Richard, *Le Royaume Latin de Jerusalem*, Presses Universitaires de France, Paris, 1953, p. 105.

43 Ibid.

44 Emma Jung and Marie-Louise von Franz, *The Grail Legend*, op. cit., pp. 131 and 126.

45 See the essay on relics in John James, *Medieval France: A Guide to the Sacred Architecture of Medieval France*, Harrap Columbus, London, 1987, pp. 36–40.

46 Ibid., p. 39.

47 Gaetan Delaforge, *The Templar Tradition in the Age of Aquarius*, op. cit., p. 68.

48 Ibid.

49 F. L. Cross and E. A. Livingstone (eds), *The Oxford Dictionary of the Christian Church*, op. cit., p. 162.

50 Edward Burman, *The Templars*, op. cit., p. 23.

51 F. L. Cross and E. A. Livingstone (eds), *The Oxford Dictionary of the Christian Church*, op. cit., pp. 162 and 1345.

52 Ibid., p. 162.

53 Ibid., pp. 162 and 1345. See also *Encyclopaedia Britannica*, 11th edn, 1910, p. 591.

54 F. L. Cross and E. A. Livingstone (eds), *The Oxford Dictionary of the Christian Church*, op. cit., pp. 1345–6.

55 For a discussion of the financial activities of the Templars see Edward Burman, *The Templars*, op. cit., pp. 74–97.

56 F. L. Cross and E. A. Livingstone (eds), *The Oxford Dictionary of the Christian Church*, op. cit., p. 162: 'In the disputed election which followed the death of Pope Honorious II in 1130 Bernard sided with Innocent II against the antipope, Anacletus, and was eventually successful in securing Innocent's victory.'

57 In the Papal Bull *Omne Datum Optimum*. See Edward Burman, *The Templars*, op. cit., p. 41.

58 S. Howarth, *The Knights Templar*, London, 1982, p. 194.

59 Ibid., pp. 193–5.

60 C. N. Johns, 'Excavations at Pilgrim's Castle, Atlit, 1932',

Quarterly of the Department of Antiquities in Palestine, vol. III, no. 4, 1933, pp. 145–64.

61 John Wilkinson, Joyce Hill and W. F. Ryan (eds), *Jerusalem Pilgrimage 1099–1185*, Hakluyt Society, London, 1988, p. 294.

62 Ibid.

63 Meir Ben-Dov, *In the Shadow of the Temple*, op. cit., p. 346.

64 John Wilkinson, Joyce Hill and W. F. Ryan (eds), *Jerusalem Pilgrimage 1099–1185*, op. cit., p. 294.

65 Louis Charpentier, *The Mysteries of Chartres Cathedral*, op. cit., p. 70.

66 For a general discussion see M. Kilian Hufgard, 'Saint Bernard of Clairvaux', *Medieval Studies*, vol. II, Edwin Mellen Press, 1989. See in particular pp. 140–1 and 143–50.

67 Quoted in Robert Lawlor, *Sacred Geometry: Philosophy and Practice*, Thames & Hudson, London, 1989, p. 10.

68 Ibid.

69 M. Kilian Hufgard, 'Saint Bernard of Clairvaux', op. cit., pp. 148–9.

70 Ibid., p. 139.

71 Ibid., p. 129.

72 Sergew Hable-Selassie, *Ancient and Medieval Ethiopian History to 1270*, Haile-Selassie I University, Addis Ababa, 1972, pp. 265–7.

73 *Encyclopaedia Britannica*, 11th edn, 1910, p. 306. See also A. H. M. Jones and Elizabeth Monroe, *A History of Ethiopia*, Clarendon Press, Oxford, 1966, p. 53: 'There can be little doubt that the King, whose envoy had discourse with Master Philip, was the King of Abyssinia, who was the only Christian King in the Near East who could have sent such an embassy.'

74 Sergew Hable-Selassie, *Ancient and Medieval Ethiopian History to 1270*, op. cit., pp. 239–87.

75 See David Buxton, *The Abyssinians*, Thames & Hudson, London, 1970, pp. 44 ff. See also Jean Doresse, *Ancient Cities and Temples of Ethiopia*, Elek Books, London, 1959, p. 92, and Sergew Hable-Selassie, *Ancient and Medieval Ethiopian History to 1270*, op. cit., pp. 225–32.

76 See Wolf Leslau, *Falasha Anthology*, Yale University Press, New Haven and London, 1979, Introduction, pp. xx–xi.

77 Richard Pankhurst, *An Introduction to the Economic History of Ethiopia from Early Times to 1800*, Lalibela House/Sidgwick & Jackson, London, 1961.

78 Sergew Hable-Selassie, *Ancient and Medieval Ethiopian History to 1270*, op. cit., p. 265.

79 A good summary of this legend is given by Professor Richard

Pankhurst in Graham Hancock, Richard Pankhurst and Duncan Willetts, *Under Ethiopian Skies*, Editions HL, London and Nairobi, 1983, pp. 58–9. For further details, see J. Perruchon, *Vie de Lalibela, roi d'Ethiopie*, Paris, 1892, and *Gedle Lalibela* (Amharic translation from *Ge'ez*), Haile-Selassie I University, Addis Ababa, 1959.

80 Sergew Hable-Selassie, *Ancient and Medieval Ethiopian History to 1270*, op. cit., see in particular pp. 265 and 266. Lalibela's sojourn in Jerusalem in also reported in Jean Doresse, *Ancient Cities and Temples of Ethiopia*, op. cit., p. 113.

81 Sergew Hable-Selassie, *Ancient and Medieval Ethiopian History*, op. cit., p. 265.

82 Ibid.

83 See David Buxton, *The Abyssinians*, op. cit., p. 44. See also Irmgard Bidder, *Lalibela: the Monolithic Churches of Ethiopia*, M. DuMont, Schauberg, Cologne, pp. 14 and 108.

84 Sergew Hable-Selassie, *Ancient and Medieval Ethiopian History*, op. cit., pp. 272–3. See also Jean Doresse, *Ancient Cities and Temples of Ethiopia*, op. cit., p. 113.

85 Sergew Hable-Selassie, *Ancient and Medieval Ethiopian History*, op. cit., p. 112.

86 Ibid., p. 262.

87 David Buxton, *The Abyssinians*, op. cit., p. 45.

88 A. H. M. Jones and Elizabeth Monroe, *A History of Ethiopia*, op. cit., p. 53. In October 1990 I visited the Ethiopian monastery on the roof of the Chapel of the Invention of the Cross.

89 A good account of the restoration of the Solomonic dynasty is given in Richard Pankhurst, *An Introduction to the Economic History of Ethiopia*, op. cit., pp. 60–71.

90 *Encyclopaedia Britannica*, op. cit., p. 594.

91 For example see Helen Adolf, 'New Light on Oriental Sources for Wolfram's *Parzival* and Other Grail Romances', *Publications of the Modern Languages Association of America*, vol. 62, March 1947, p. 308.

92 An English translation of the letter is given in full in Sergew Hable-Selassie, *Ancient and Medieval Ethiopian History*, op. cit., pp. 255–61.

93 Ibid.

94 Ibid.

95 Sir E. A. Wallis Budge (trans. and ed.), *The Bandlet of Righteousness: An Ethiopian Book of the Dead*, Luzac, London, 1929. See, for example, pp. 41 ff.

96 This conflict, and its implications, are discussed in Chapter 6 below.

97 Full text of the letter in Sergew Hable-Selassie, *Ancient and Medieval Ethiopian History*, op. cit., pp. 255–61.

98 Ibid.

99 Irmgard Bidder, *Lalibela*, op. cit., p. 29.

100 Wolfram von Eschenbach, *Parzival*, op. cit., for example pp. 406, 393 and 241.

101 Ibid., p. 406.

102 Ibid., p. 251.

103 Ibid., p. 252.

104 Ibid., p. 252, footnote.

105 An independent state from AD 1056 until it passed to the Habsburgs in the thirteenth century, Styria was annexed by Hitler in 1938 and is now an alpine province of south-east Austria (capital Graz). Slovenes are included amongst the inhabitants of the province – and Wolfram mentions Slovenes after referring to 'the Rohas'. This insertion of a deliberate ambiguity into his text, leaving room for two or more possible interpretations, is the sort of technique that Wolfram repeatedly employs in his encoding of vital information. In this way he veils the truth he wishes to convey in an alternative meaning that most will accept as the only possible meaning of his words.

106 For details of the Templar *croix pattée* see Andrea Hopkins, *Knights*, Collins & Brown, London, 1990, pp. 72–91.

107 UNESCO was involved in the restoration of some of the Lalibela churches in the 1960s and subsequently adopted them as a world heritage site. They are described as 'A remarkable coupling of engineering and architecture and a unique artistic achievement.' See *A Legacy for All: The World's Major Natural, Cultural and Historic Sites*, UNESCO, Paris, 1982, p. 74.

108 See, for example, D. R. Buxton, 'The Christian Antiquities of Northern Ethiopia', *Archaeologica*, no. 92, 1947, p. 23.

109 C. F. Beckingham and G. W. B Huntingford (eds), *The Prester John of the Indies: A True Relation of the Lands of Prester John, being the Narrative of the Portuguese Embassy to Ethiopia in 1520 written by Father Francisco Alvarez*, Cambridge, published for the Hakluyt Society at the University Press, 1961, vol. I. pp. 11–13.

110 Ibid., p. 223.

111 Ibid., p. 226.

112 Ibid., p. 227.

113 Wolfram von Eschenbach, *Parzival*, op. cit., p. 406.

114 Ibid., p. 406.

Chapter 6 **Resolving Doubts**

1 Le R. P. Dimotheos, *Deux ans de séjour en Abyssinie: ou vie morale, politique et religieuse des Abyssiniens,* Jerusalem, 1871, p. 137.
2 Ibid., p. 141.
3 Ibid., p. 141.
4 Ibid., p. 143.
5 As noted in Chapter 1 above, the sanctuary chapel was built by the late Emperor Haile Selassie in 1965.
6 Again, see Chapter 1 above.
7 Le R. P. Dimotheos, *Deux ans de séjour en Abyssinie,* op. cit., p. 141.
8 Ibid., p. 141.
9 Sergew Hable-Selassie, *Ancient and Medieval Ethiopian History to 1270,* Haile-Selassie I University, Addis Ababa, 1972.
10 See Chapter 3 above.
11 Exodus 37:1–2.
12 B. T. Evetts (trans. and ed.), Abu Salih, *Churches and Monasteries of Egypt and some Neighbouring Countries,* Oxford, 1895.
13 Ibid., p. 287.
14 Ibid., p. 288.
15 Numbers 4:5–6.
16 For a short summary of the place of Amharic and other northern Ethiopic languages within the Semitic language group as a whole see Edward Ullendorff, *The Ethiopians: an Introduction to Country and People,* Oxford University Press, London, 1973, Chapter 6, 'Languages', pp. 111 ff. Arabic is also a Semitic language, and Amharic has the second largest number of speakers of any Semitic language after Arabic.
17 See, for example, Julian Morgenstern, 'The Ark, the Ephod and the Tent of Meeting' in *Hebrew Union College Annual,* vol. XVII, 1942–3, KTAV Publishing House, New York, 1968, p. 249.
18 See for example Edward Ullendorff, 'Hebraic-Jewish Elements in Abyssinian (Monophysite) Christianity', *Journal of Semitic Studies,* vol. I, no. 3, 1956, p. 233, footnote 6. He says that *tabot* is 'derived from the Jewish Pal. Aramaic *tebuta* (*tebota*) which in turn is a derivation from Hebrew *tebah*.'
19 See Genesis 6:7 ff. The first reference to Noah's Ark as *tebah* comes in verse 14 of this chapter.
20 See Exodus 2:3. For confirmation that *tebah* is used in the Bible to refer to the Ark of Noah and also to Moses's Ark of bulrushes see Bruce Metzger, David Goldstein, John Ferguson (eds), *Great Events of Bible Times: New Perspectives on the People, Places and History of the Biblical World,* Guild Publishing, London, 1989, p. 12.
21 E. A. Wallis Budge, *The Queen of Sheba and her Only Son Menelik:*

being the 'Book of the Glory of Kings' (Kebra Nagast), Oxford
University Press, 1932, pp. 14–15.

22 Ibid., p. 14.

23 Edward Ullendorff, 'Hebraic-Jewish Elements in Abyssinian
(Monophysite) Christianity', op. cit., p. 234. Ullendorff also
advances the same argument in his excellent *Ethiopia and the Bible:
The Schweich Lectures 1967*, published for the British Academy by
Oxford University Press, 1988, p. 84.

24 Edward Ullendorff, 'The Queen of Sheba in Ethiopian
Tradition', in James B. Pritchard (ed.), *Solomon and Sheba*,
Phaidon Press, London, 1974, p. 108.

25 *Kebra Nagast*, op. cit., Introduction, p. xlii.

26 Jean Doresse, *Ancient Cities and Temples of Ethiopia*, Elek Books,
London, 1959, p. 21.

27 A. H. M. Jones and Elizabeth Monroe, *A History of Ethiopia*,
Clarendon Press, Oxford, 1966, p. 16.

28 *Kebra Nagast*, op. cit., p. 29.

29 See Chapter 2 above.

30 Edward Ullendorff, *Ethiopia and the Bible*, op. cit., p. 18.

31 Ibid., pp. 117 and 17–21.

32 Ibid., pp. 16–17.

33 For an informative account of the negative impact of Christian
missionary activity on Falasha culture, see David Kessler, *The
Falashas: The Forgotten Jews of Ethiopia*, Schocken Books, New
York, 1985.

34 Date from *The Jerusalem Bible*, Eyre & Spottiswoode, London,
1968, Chronological Table, p. 345.

35 J. M. Flad, *Falashas of Abyssinia*, London, 1869, p. 3.

36 For a good and up-to-date reference on Jewish festivals see
Geoffrey Wigoder (ed.), *The Encyclopaedia of Judaism*, Jerusalem
Publishing House, Jerusalem, 1989. For Hanukkah see p. 319.

37 Ibid., p. 576. See also J. S. Trimingham, *Islam in Ethiopia*, Frank
Cass, London, 1965, pp. 20–1. This scholarly and meticulously
researched book, first published in 1952, contains a
recommendable general round-up on Ethiopia, 'The Region and
its Folk', pp. 1–31.

38 Henry A. Stern, *Wanderings among the Falashas in Abyssinia*,
London, 1862. Reprinted by Frank Cass, London, 1968, p. 188.

39 Ibid., pp. 188–9.

40 In fact a few years later Stern was punished, on the order of the
Ethiopian Emperor Tewodros who had him flogged within an
inch of his life (though not because he had interfered with the
Falashas). Stern was imprisoned, along with several other
Europeans, and was eventually rescued by the Napier expedition

to the citadel of Magdala which cost the British taxpayer several million pounds.

41 Date from *The Jerusalem Bible*, op. cit., Chronological Table, p. 343.

42 Leviticus 17:8–9.

43 See Geoffrey Wigoder (ed.) *The Encyclopaedia of Judaism*, op. cit., p. 615.

44 F. L. Cross and E. A. Livingstone (eds), *The Oxford Dictionary of the Christian Church*, Oxford University Press, 1988, p. 1221.

45 Ibid.

46 Ibid. See also Geoffrey Wigoder (ed.), *The Encyclopaedia of Judaism*, op. cit., pp. 618 and 693.

47 Ibid., pp. 481–3 and 695–6.

48 '[The Falashas] are . . . the only Jews in the world whose worship is focussed upon sacrifice on the altar', J. S. Trimingham, *Islam in Ethiopia*, op. cit., p. 21.

49 See, for example, David Kessler, *The Falashas*, op. cit., p. 69 and Wolf Leslau, *Falasha Anthology*, Yale University Press, New Haven and London, 1979, pp. xxvi ff.

50 James Bruce, *Travels to Discover the Source of the Nile in the years 1768, 1769, 1770, 1771, 1772 and 1773*, Edinburgh, 1790, vol. I, p. 500.

51 For Bruce's views on this subject, see for example *Travels*, vol. II, p. 293 in which he describes Judaism as being the religion of Ethiopia 'long before Christianity'.

52 Before the sack of Magdala the manuscript was seen by Flad and translated for him by the Emperor's librarian. See J. M. Flad, *Falashas of Abyssinia*, op. cit., p. 4.

53 James Bruce, *Travels*, op. cit., vol. I, p. 485.

54 Ibid.

55 See, for example, A. H. M. Jones and Elizabeth Monroe, *A History of Ethiopia*, op. cit., p. 30. See also Jean Doresse, *Ancient Cities and Temples of Ethiopia*, op. cit., pp. 85–6.

56 *Kebra Nagast*, op. cit., pp. 225 ff.

57 For confirmation of the Falashas' own use of the term *Beta Israel*, see for example Wolf Leslau, *Falasha Anthology*, op. cit., Introduction, p. ix. The word 'Falasha' itself is derived from an ancient Ethiopic term meaning 'Immigrant' or 'Stranger'.

58 See note 94 to Chapter 3 above. For the use of 'Zion' as an epithet or synonym for the Ark of the Covenant in the *Kebra Nagast* see Sir E. A. Wallis Budge, *Kebra Nagast*, op. cit., for example, pp. 14–15 and 178–79. See also p. 223.

59 *Kebra Nagast*, op. cit., p. 227.

60 Ibid., pp. 226 and 227.

61 A full translation of Eldad's treatise is given in Elkan Adler, *Jewish Travellers*, London, 1930. See p. 11.

62 For a discussion, see *The Jewish Encyclopaedia*, Funk and Wagnalls Co., New York, 1925, vol. V, pp. 90–1. See also *The Universal Jewish Encyclopaedia*, vol. IV. p. 46.

63 Date from *The Jerusalem Bible*, op. cit., Chronological Table, p. 344.

64 Quoted in Elkan Adler, *Jewish Travellers*, op. cit., p. 13.

65 See for example David Kessler, *The Falashas*, op. cit., p. 68 ff. See also *Encyclopaedia Judaica*, vol. VI, which Kessler cites extensively. See also Geoffrey Wigoder (ed.), *The Encyclopaedia of Judaism*, op. cit., pp. 568–70, and Wolf Leslau, *Falasha Anthology*, op. cit., Introduction, p. xxiii.

66 Quoted in Elkan Adler, *Jewish Travellers*, op. cit., p. 12.

67 Ibid., p. 11.

68 Benjamin of Tudela's book of travels is translated in Elkan Adler, *Jewish Travellers*, op. cit., see p. 60.

69 R. L. Hess, 'An Outline of Falasha History', *Journal of Ethiopian Studies*, no. 6, Addis Ababa, 1967. See also Elkan Adler, *Jewish Travellers*, op. cit., p. 153.

70 S. Mendelssohn, *The Jews of Africa*, London, 1920.

71 Joseph Halévy, *La Guerre de Sarsa-Dengel contre les Falachas*, Paris, 1907.

72 Ibid. *Adonai* is, of course, one of the Hebrew names of God.

73 Ibid.

74 James Bruce, *Travels*, op. cit., vol. II, p. 293.

75 Ibid., vol. I, p. 486.

76 Joseph Halévy, *Travels in Abyssinia*, London, 1877.

77 Reported in David Kessler, *The Falashas*, op. cit. – to whose account I am greatly indebted.

78 *The Falashas: The Jews of Ethiopia*, Minority Rights Group Report no. 67, London, July 1985.

79 See Chapter 2 above.

80 Wolfram von Eschenbach, *Parzival*, Penguin Classics, London, 1980, p. 125.

Chapter 7 A Secret and Never-Ending Quest

1 For the adoption of Christianity by the Roman Empire under Constantine see, for example, J. M. Roberts, *The Pelican History of the World*, Penguin, London, 1981, pp. 281–4. For details on the civilization, power and prosperity of the Axumite Empire see Chapter 1 above.

2 Edward Gibbon, *The History of the Decline and Fall of the Roman Empire*, London, 1788.

3 See Chapter 4 above for a discussion.
4 See, for example, Edward Burman, *The Templars: Knights of God*, Aquarian Press, Wellingborough, 1986. See also Malcolm Barber, *The Trial of the Templars*, Cambridge University Press, 1989.
5 Malcolm Barber, *The Trial of the Templars*, op. cit., page 45.
6 See F. L. Cross and E. A. Livingstone (eds), *The Oxford Dictionary of the Christian Church*, Oxford University Press, 1988, pp. 117 and 119.
7 Ibid., p. 300.
8 Malcolm Barber, *The Trial of the Templars*, op. cit., p. 2.
9 Ibid., p. 3.
10 James Bruce, *Travels to Discover the Source of the Nile in the years 1768, 1769, 1770, 1771, 1772 and 1773*, Edinburgh, 1790, vol. I, p. 528.
11 Ibid., p. 530.
12 Ibid., p. 530. Interestingly, the notion that Ethiopia might take steps to interrupt the flow of the Nile to the disadvantage of Egypt is still in circulation. In January 1990, for instance, aware of the close military and economic co-operation that was then being developed between Ethiopia and Israel, the Egyptian government officially warned Ethiopia and Israel not to 'tamper' with the Blue Nile. See *The Independent*, London, 6 January 1990, p. 16.
13 See Edward Burman, *The Templars*, op. cit., p. 123.
14 James Bruce, *Travels*, op. cit., vol. I, p. 530.
15 Ibid., p. 532.
16 For a discussion, see Chapter 5 above.
17 James Bruce, *Travels*, op. cit., vol. I, p. 528.
18 B. T. Evetts (trans. and ed.), Abu Salih, *Churches and Monasteries of Egypt and some Neighbouring Countries*, Oxford, 1895.
19 Ibid., p. 288. Emphasis added.
20 This rendering of 'blond hair' instead of 'red hair' is given in a direct translation from the original made by that great linguist Professor Edward Ullendorff in his *Ethiopia and the Bible: The Schweich Lectures 1967*, published for the British Academy by the Oxford University Press, 1988, p. 26.
21 Secrecy was enshrined within the rule that governed the Templar order, and betrayal of secrets was punishable by expulsion or worse. See for example Edward Burman, *The Templars*, op. cit., p. 46. See also John J. Robinson, *Born in Blood*, Century, London, 1990, p. 77.
22 O. G. S. Crawford (ed.), *Ethiopian Itineraries circa 1400–1524*, Cambridge University Press for the Hakluyt Society, 1958, p. 212.
23 Ibid., pp. 213 and 214.

24 Extract from Foresti's chronicle translated in Ibid., p. 215.

25 Ibid., p. 212.

26 Ibid., pp. 214–15.

27 The significance of the data is indeed that it confirms a meeting with Pope Clement V *somewhere* in 1306. That meeting may not necessarily have taken place in Avignon - which anyway was not part of France at that time and which did not become the official seat of the Pope until the year 1309. Between 1305 (the date of his coronation in Lyons) and March of 1309, when he officially took up residence in Avignon, Clement V had an itinerant existence, travelling around France and basing himself temporarily in various cities. It is possible that he did meet with the envoys in Avignon: even though he had not yet established his official seat there in 1306 he could well have been temporarily in residence at the time. Alternatively the envoys may have travelled to meet him elsewhere in France. Foresti's abstract from the original chronicle was made nearly two hundred years after that chronicle was written. It may be surmised that the original did not even state where in France the meeting between the envoys and the Pope took place. If so Foresti may be excused for jumping to the conclusion that the venue was Avignon since that was the Pope's official seat for most of his period in office. Foresti may simply not have known that he did not move there officially until 1309. At any rate, establishing the precise venue of the meeting is a matter of minor significance. The point is that a meeting did take place. For a discussion of these issues see E. Ullendorff and C. F. Beckingham, *The Hebrew Letters of Prester John*, Oxford University Press, 1982, pp. 6–7.

28 This is confirmed, for example, in Richard Pankhurst, *An Introduction to the Economic History of Ethiopia from Early Times to 1800*, Lalibela House/Sidgwick & Jackson, London, 1961, pp. 64–5. See also Sir E. A. Wallis Budge, *The Queen of Sheba and her Only Son Menelik: being the 'Book of the Glory of Kings' (Kebra Nagast)*, Oxford University Press, 1932, Introduction, p. xxxvii.

29 *Kebra Nagast*, op. cit., Introduction, pp xvi and xxli.

30 Mordechai Abir, *Ethiopia and the Red Sea*, Cass, London, 1980, p. 47.

31 Malcolm Barber, *The Trial of the Templars*, op. cit., pp. 47–8.

32 Ibid., p. 48.

33 Possibly as many as twenty-four knights. See Malcolm Barber, *The Trial of the Templars*, op. cit., p. 46.

34 See, for example, John J. Robinson, *Born in Blood*, op. cit., p. 138.

35 See Malcolm Barber, *The Trial of the Templars*, op. cit., pp. 193–220.

36 Ibid., p. 203.

37 See John J. Robinson, *Born in Blood*, op. cit., pp. 150–1.

38 Ibid., pp. 150–1.

39 Ibid., p. 153. See also O. A. Haye, *The Persecution of the Knights Templars*, Edinburgh, 1865, p. 114.

40 The Monymusk Reliquary, which may now be seen at the National Museum of Antiquities, Queen Street, Edinburgh. It is said to have been modelled on the Temple of Solomon. For accounts of its role at Bannockburn see article by David Keys in *The Independent*, London, 29 July 1989, p. 38. See also *Robert the Bruce*, Pitkin Pictorials, London, 1978, p. 15.

41 The oldest Masonic documents, the *Old Charges*, date back no earlier than the mid-1300s, i.e. just after the suppression of the Templars. See, for example, Alexander Horne, *King Solomon's Temple in Masonic Tradition*, Aquarian Press, Wellingborough, 1972, p. 25.

42 Kenneth Mackenzie, *The Royal Masonic Cyclopaedia*, Aquarian Press, Wellingborough, 1987 (first published 1877). See pp. 84 and 420–1.

43 Ibid. See pp. 593–4 and 719–22.

44 Ibid., p. 325.

45 It was in 1717, after four centuries of complete secrecy, that Freemasonry first officially declared its existence.

46 Kenneth Mackenzie, *The Royal Masonic Cyclopaedia*, op. cit., pp. 719–22.

47 John J. Robinson, *Born in Blood*, op. cit.

48 Ibid., p. 137.

49 Hyginus Eugene Cardinale (ed.), *Orders of Knighthood, Awards and the Holy See*, Van Duren Publishers, 1985, p 27.

50 Ibid., pp. 27 and 207–8.

51 Ibid., p. 27. Papal confirmation took the form of the granting of a constitution: *Ad ea ex quibus*.

52 A small and intrepid group of Dominican friars went to Ethiopia as evangelists in the fourteenth century (and it is a matter of some interest that they were sent by the same Pope, John XXII, who had granted confirmation to the Order of Christ). Somewhat later, in the fifteenth century, a Venetian painter named Nicholas Brancaleone was attached to the court of Emperor Baeda Mariam.

53 Zurara, quoted in Edgar Prestage, *The Portuguese Pioneers*, Adam & Charles Black, London, 1933, p. 158.

54 Ibid., p. 27.

55 Ibid., pp. 215–16.

56 Ibid., pp. 165–6.

57 Ibid., pp. 168–70.

58 Ibid., p. 170.

59 Ibid., p. 30.

60 Ibid., pp. 32 and 212–13.

61 Ibid., p. 27: 'Henry was a crusader by disposition.'

62 Ibid., pp. 27 and 160.

63 Ibid., p. 29.

64 Wolfram von Eschenbach, *Parzival*, Penguin Classics, London, 1980, p. 232.

65 Edgar Prestage, *The Portuguese Pioneers*, op. cit., pp. 161 and 155.

66 Ibid., p. 154.

67 Ibid., p. 170.

68 Ibid.

69 Ibid.

70 Ibid.

71 *Encyclopaedia Britannica*, Micropaedia, 15th edn, 1991, vol. V, p. 100.

72 Edgar Prestage, *The Portuguese Pioneers*, op. cit., pp. 251–2.

73 Ibid., p. 257.

74 Ibid.

75 Ibid., see Chapter XII.

76 A useful account of Covilhan's journey to Ethiopia is provided by James Bruce in *Travels*, op. cit., vol. II, pp. 103–13. See also Edgar Prestage, *The Portuguese Pioneers*, op. cit., pp. 214–21.

77 Edgar Prestage, *The Portuguese Pioneers*, op. cit., p. 216.

78 A. H. M. Jones and Elizabeth Monroe, *A History of Ethiopia*, Clarendon Press, Oxford, 1966, p. 62.

79 C. F. Beckingham and G. W. B. Huntingford (eds), *The Prester John of the Indies: A True Relation of the Lands of Prester John, being the Narrative of the Portuguese Embassy to Ethiopia in 1520 written by Father Francisco Alvarez*, Cambridge University Press for the Hakluyt Society, 1961, vol. I, p. 227.

80 Ibid., p. 226.

81 Captain Sir Richard F. Burton, *First Footsteps in East Africa*, London, 1894, reprinted Darf Publishers, London, 1986, vol. II, p. 5.

82 Ibid., p. 6. See also James Bruce, *Travels*, op. cit., vol. II, pp. 162–72, and A. H. M Jones and Elizabeth Monroe, *History of Ethiopia*, op. cit., pp. 82–3.

83 Jean Doresse, *Ancient Cities and Temples of Ethiopia*, Elek Books, London, 1959, p. 127.

84 James Bruce, *Travels*, op. cit., vol. II, p. 164.

85 A. H. M. Jones and Elizabeth Monroe, *History of Ethiopia*, op.cit., p. 83.

86 James Bruce, *Travels*, op. cit., vol II, p. 173.

87 Quoted in Philip Carman, *The Lost Empire: the Story of the Jesuits in Ethiopia*, Sidgwick & Jackson, London, 1985, p. 8.

88 Edward Gibbon, *The History of the Decline and Fall of the Roman Empire*, op. cit.

89 The best overall account of Don Christopher's mission is given by Bruce, *Travels*, op. cit., vol. II, pp. 181 ff. Sir Richard Burton, *First Footsteps*, op. cit., pp. 6–11, also contains useful material. In addition, the campaign is well covered in all the general histories.

90 James Bruce, *Travels*, op. cit., vol. II, p. 185.

91 Reported in *The Itinerario of Jeronimo Lobo*, The Hakluyt Society, London, 1984, pp. 206–7.

92 James Bruce, *Travels*, op. cit., vol. II, pp. 187–8.

93 Ibid., pp. 190–1.

94 Ibid., p. 418.

95 A. H. M. Jones and Elizabeth Monroe, *History of Ethiopia*, op. cit., p. 108. Professor Edward Ullendorf, *The Ethiopians*, Oxford University Press, 1973, p. 76. The tradition of the Ark's sojourn on Lake Tana during and after the Gragn campaigns is well known in Ethiopia and was repeated to me in an interview with the Head of the Ethiopian Orthodox Church in Britain, Archpriest Solomon Gabre Selassie. The answers to the questions that I addressed to the archpriest were given to me in writing on 12 July 1989.

96 James Bruce, *Travels*, op. cit., vol. II, p. 409. Philip Carman, *The Lost Empire*, op. cit., p. 156.

97 James Bruce, *Travels*, op. cit., vol. I, pp. 481–2.

98 Professor Edward Ullendorff, 'James Bruce of Kinnaird', *Scottish Historical Review*, T. Nelson, Edinburgh, 1953, p. 129.

99 James Bruce, *Travels*, op. cit., vol. III, p. 598.

100 See, for example, discussion in Alan Moorehead, *The Blue Nile*, Penguin Books, London, 1984, pp. 34–5. See also Professor Edward Ullendorff, 'James Bruce of Kinnaird', op. cit., pp. 133–6.

101 For Bruce's comments on Paez see, for example, *Travels*, op. cit., vol. II, pp. 244, 245, 266, 344, and vol. III, p. 617. Likewise an extensive treatise on Lobo's book (which had been translated into English by Dr Samuel Johnson in 1735 as *A Voyage to Abyssinia*) appears in vol. III of *Travels*, pp. 133–41. See also vol. III, p. 426 for a further comment on Lobo.

102 Indeed he not only failed to give them credit for their achievements but also blatantly plagiarized their accounts. Here, for example, is Paez on his own visit to the twin springs which lie to the south of Lake Tana and which are regarded as the source of the Blue Nile: 'On April 21 in the year 1618, being here together with the king and his army, I ascended the place and observed everything with great attention; I discovered first two

round fountains, each about four palms in diameter, and saw, with the greatest delight, what neither Cyrus, the king of the Persians, nor Cambyses, nor Alexander the Great, nor the famous Julius Caesar, could ever discover. The two openings of these fountains have no issue in the plain at the top of the mountain, but flow from the foot of it. The second fountain lies abut a stone cast west from the first' (quoted in Alan Moorehead, *The Blue Nile*, op. cit., p. 34).

Jeronimo Lobo reached the source some twelve years after Paez, around the year 1630. Here is his description: 'The source of this famous river, the object of so much searching but hidden for so long, is discovered . . . on a very gradual slope made by a certain mountain, seeming rather more like a rather irregular field than a mountain slope with quite an expanse of open, flat ground, where one can see for a fair distance. In this gradually rising plain, one discovers, in the driest part of summer, two circular pools or wells of water, which we can more appropriately call pits four spans in width and separated from each other by a distance of a stone's throw . . . The whole plain, especially the part near the said wells . . . is swollen and undermined with water . . . and the reason it does not swallow up anyone who walks on it is that, since all the land is green and this part has many various grasses and herbs, the roots are so intertwined that . . . they can support anyone who walks on the field' (*The Itinerario of Jeronimo Lobo*, op. cit., p. 228).

Bruce's own 'discovery' was made on 4 November 1770 (a century and a half after Paez and Lobo) and was preceded by his guide pointing out to him a 'hillock of green sod . . . in [which] the two fountains of the Nile are to be found . . . Throwing off my shoes, I ran down the hill towards the little island of green sods, which was about two hundred yards distant; the whole side of the hill was thick grown over with flowers, the large bulbous roots of which appearing above the surface of the ground . . . occasioned two very severe falls before I reached the brink of the marsh; I after this came to the island of green turf . . . and I stood in rapture over the principal fountain which rises in the middle of it.

'It is easier to guess than to describe the situation of my mind at that moment – standing in that spot which had baffled the genius, industry, and inquiry of both ancients and moderns for the course of near three thousand years. Kings had attempted this discovery at the head of armies, and each expedition was distinguished from the last only by the difference of the numbers which had perished, and agreed alone in the disappointment which had uniformly, and without exception, followed them all . . . Though a mere private Briton I triumphed here, in my own mind, over kings and their armies' (James Bruce, *Travels*, op. cit., vol. III, pp. 596–7).

    As I read and re-read Bruce's description I could not help but feel that it was a kind of bastardized pastiche of the earlier experiences of Paez and Lobo (mixing the intertwined roots and swollen green marshes of the latter with the former's allusions to kings and conquerors). Moreover, as I have already stated, it cannot be denied that the Scottish traveller was thoroughly familiar with the writings of both his predecessors.

103 Alan Moorehead, *The Blue Nile*, op. cit., p. 49. Professor Edward Ullendorff, in his paper 'James Bruce of Kinnaird', op. cit., describes Bruce as 'one of the great universal *savants* and men of action of the eighteenth century' and quotes the comment of the brothers d'Abbadie, the French explorers, who said that they had consulted the *Travels* as a daily text-book and 'had never discovered a mis-statement, and hardly even an error of any considerable importance'.

104 James Bruce, *Travels*, op. cit., vol. III, p. 615.

105 Ibid., p. 131.

106 Reported in 'the Annals of Emperor Iyasu I' in I. Guidi (ed.), *Annales Iohannis I, Iyasu I, Bakaffa*, Paris, 1903, pp. 151–9. See also Jean Doresse, *Ancient Cities and Temples of Ethiopia*, op. cit., p. 180. See also R. Basset, 'Etudes sur l'histoire d'Ethiopie', *Journal Asiatique*, Octobre-Novembre-Décembre 1881, p. 297.

107 I subsequently learned from Professor Richard Pankhurst (conversation in Addis Ababa Tuesday 4 December 1990) that Bruce had in fact *owned* copies of the two principal documents of Iyasu's life, the full chronicle and the abbreviated chronicle. Both these documents tell the story of the king going into the Holy of Holies and opening the Ark. In his *Travels* Bruce gave a potted history of all the solar eclipses and comets that had been seen in Ethiopia during the few centuries prior to his own visit. In this potted history he drew extensively on Iyasu's abbreviated chronicle, which had mentioned a sighting of Richaud's Comet in 1689. As Pankhurst put it: 'The point is this. After describing the comet, the abbreviated chronicle goes on *in the very next paragraph* to report Iyasu's encounter with the Ark in 1690. So Bruce *must* have known about it. That being so, his suggestion that the relic had been destroyed by the Muslims in the early 1500s does indeed look suspicious.'

108 James Bruce, *Travels*, op. cit., vol. I, pp. 365–492.

109 Ibid., vol. I, pp. 471–3.

110 Ibid., vol. I, p. 472.

111 Ibid., vol. I, pp. 472–3. See also pp. 444–6.

112 Ibid., vol. I, p. 475.

113 Ibid., vol. I, p. 476.

114 Ibid., vol. I, pp. 471 and 478.

115 Ibid., vol. III, pp. 128–33. E.g.: 'On the 18th, in the morning, we . . . came into the plain wherein stood Axum' (p. 128); and: 'On the 19th of January, I found the latitude of Axum to be 14° 6′ 36″ north . . .' (p. 133).

116 See Chapter 1 above.

117 The tradition of the original Ark being brought out only at *Timkat* is also confirmed, for example, in Ruth Plant, *Architecture of the Tigré, Ethiopia*, Ravens Educational and Development Services, Worcester, 1985, p. 206: 'It is said that the original Ark of the Covenant, brought by Menelik I from Jerusalem, is held in the Treasury. Only one monk is allowed to see it, although the casket is led in procession at the time of *Timkat*.'

118 Professor Edward Ullendorff, 'James Bruce of Kinnaird', op. cit., p. 141.

119 Ibid., p. 141.

120 Ibid., p. 141.

121 James Bruce, *Travels*, op. cit., vol. I, pp. 483–4.

122 Alan Moorehead, *The Blue Nile*, op. cit., p. 31.

123 *Kebra Nagast*, op. cit., Budge's Introduction, pp. xxxii and xxxiii.

124 Around the third to second centuries BC. See R. H. Charles (trans.), *The Book of Enoch*, Society for the Propagation of Christian Knowledge, London, 1987, Introduction, p. xiii.

125 H. F. D. Sparks (ed.). *The Apocryphal Old Testament*, Clarendon Paperbacks, Oxford, 1989, p. 170: 'Among the Ethiopic manuscripts that Bruce brought back were three containing what is now known as "1 Enoch" or "Ethiopian Enoch". One of these manuscripts (now in the Bodleian Library at Oxford) contained "1 Enoch" only; the second (also in the Bodleian) contained "1 Enoch" followed by Job, Isaiah, "the Twelve", Proverbs, Wisdom, Ecclesiastes, Canticles and Daniel; the third (now in the Bibliothèque Nationale in Paris) is a transcript of the second.'

126 Kenneth Mackenzie, *The Royal Masonic Cyclopaedia*, op. cit., pp. 200–2.

127 Ibid.

128 Major F. B. Head, *The Life of Bruce, the African Traveller*, London, 1836.

129 J. M. Reid, *Traveller Extraordinary: The Life of James Bruce of Kinnaird*, Eyre & Spottiswoode, London, 1968.

130 Elgin occupied the position of Grand Master Mason of Scotland, 1961–5. *Debretts Illustrated Peerage*, Macmillan, London, 1985, p. 412.

Chapter 8 **Into Ethiopia**

1 For further details see Chapter 12 below.
2 Richard Pankhurst, writing in Graham Hancock, Richard Pankhurst and Duncan Willetts, *Under Ethiopian Skies*, Editions HL, London and Nairobi, 1983, p. 24. See also Yuri Elets, *Emperor Menelik and his War with Italy*, Saint Petersburg, 1898.

Chapter 9 **Sacred Lake**

1 James Bruce, *Travels to Discover the Source of the Nile in the Years 1768, 1769, 1770, 1771, 1772 and 1773*, Edinburgh, 1790, vol. III, pp. 425–7.
2 E.g. Sergew Hable-Selassie, *Ancient and Medieval Ethiopian History to 1270*, Addis Ababa, 1972, p. 26.
3 See note 102 to Chapter 7 above.
4 See, for example, Alan Moorehead, *The Blue Nile*, Penguin Books, London, 1984, pp. 12–13 and 34. See also Major R. E. Cheesman, *Lake Tana and the Blue Nile: An Abyssinian Quest*, Macmillan, London, 1936.
5 Alan Moorehead, *The Blue Nile*, op. cit., p. 17.
6 For a further discussion see, for example, Lucie Lamy, *Egyptian Mysteries*, Thames & Hudson, London, 1981, pp. 7–8.
7 H. L. Jones (ed.), *The Geography of Strabo*, Loeb Library, London, 1940.
8 E. L. Stevenson, *Geography of Claudius Ptolemy*, New York, 1932.
9 Aeschylus, Fragment 67, quoted in Jean Doresse, *Ancient Cities and Temples of Ethiopia*, Elek, London, 1959.
10 For a discussion see Edward Ullendorff, *Ethiopia and the Bible*, Oxford University Press, 1988, p. 2.
11 James Bruce, *Travels*, op. cit., vol. III, p. 387.
12 See for example Gaalyah Cornfeld, *Archaeology of the Bible Book by Book*, Harper & Row, San Francisco, 1976, pp. 25 and 118.
13 Leviticus 4:6.
14 Leviticus 5:9.
15 Herbert Danby DD (trans.), *The Mishnah*, Oxford University Press, 1933, pp. 166, 167 and 168.
16 Ibid., p. 168.

Chapter 10 **Ghost in a Maze**

1 E. A. Wallis Budge, *The Queen of Sheba and Her Only Son Menelik, being the 'Book of the Glory of Kings' (Kebra Nagast)*, Oxford University Press, 1932, p. 145.
2 Which had supposedly taken place during the reign of Solomon in

Jerusalem, i.e. in the tenth century BC. Axum was not founded until some eight hundred years later. See S. C. Munro-Hay, *Excavations at Axum*, British Institute in Eastern Africa, London, 1989, pp. 19–24.

3 E.g. the guardian monk. See Chapter 1 above. E. A. Wallis Budge also (wrongly) makes the assumption that Menelik's destination with the Ark was Axum. In the Introduction to his English translation of the *Kebra Nagast* he states: 'The Tabernacle of the Law of God, i.e. the Ark of the Covenant, had been brought from Jerusalem to Axum by Menelik, Solomon's firstborn son, according to the Ethiopians.' Many Ethiopians do say this. It is significant, however, that the *Kebra Nagast* makes no such claim and only specifies 'Debra Makeda' as the place to which the Ark was brought. For the Budge passage quoted above see *Kebra Nagast*, op. cit., Introduction, p. xvii.

4 Major R. E. Cheesman, *Lake Tana and the Blue Nile: An Abyssinian Quest*, Frank Cass, London, 1968 (first published 1936), pp. 174–5 and 179. Cheesman, who visited Tana Kirkos in the early 1930s, was also told of the Ark traditions on the island (see pp. 174–80). This is the only other reference to these traditions that I have been able to find in the literature – a reflection of the extreme isolation of Tana Kirkos and of the fact that the island has never been the subject of a proper scholarly or archaeological study.

5 Wolfram von Eschenbach, *Parzival*, Penguin Classics, London, 1980. See, for example, pp. 132 and 392–405.

6 Margaret Fitzgerald Richey, *The Story of Parzival and the Grail as Related by Wolfram von Eschenbach*, Basil Blackwell & Mott, Oxford, 1935, p. 198. Another interpretation of the meaning of *Munsalvaesche* is 'wild' or 'savage' mountain. See, for example, footnote by Professor A. T. Hatto to Wolfram von Eschenbach, *Parzival*, op. cit., p. 123.

7 Psalm 130:3–7. Emphasis added.

8 See for example *The New Collins Thesaurus*, Collins, London and Glasgow, 1984, p. 594.

9 Wolfram von Eschenbach, *Parzival*, op. cit., p. 121.

10 Ibid., pp. 120–1.

11 Confirmation of this fact is available in a wide range of sources, for example in the survey of Christian and Jewish Ethiopian customs provided by J. S. Trimingham in his authoritative *Islam in Ethiopia*, Frank Cass, London, 1976, p. 26. See also David Kessler, *The Falashas: The Forgotten Jews of Ethiopia*, Schocken Books, New York, 1985, p. 68.

12 1 Kings 9:26: 'And king Solomon made a navy of ships in

Ezion-geber, which is beside Elath, on the shore of the Red sea, in the land of Edom.' For the identification of Ezion-geber with modern Elat see, for example, Gaalyah Cornfeld, *Archaeology of the Bible Book by Book*, Harper & Row, San Francisco, 1976, pp. 110–11.

13 *Kebra Nagast*, op. cit., pp. 77–8: 'And they loaded the wagons, and the horses, and the mules in order to depart . . . And as for the wagons, no man hauled his wagon . . . and whether it was men, or horses, or mules, or loaded camels, each was raised above the ground to the height of a cubit; and all those who rode upon beasts were lifted up above their backs to the height of one span of a man, and all the various kinds of baggage which were loaded on the beasts, as well as those who were mounted on them, were raised up to the height of one span of a man, and the beasts were lifted up to the height of one span of a man. And everyone travelled in the wagons . . . like an eagle when his body glideth above the wind.'

14 See for example *Biblical Archaeology Review*, May/June 1988, p. 31.

15 *Kebra Nagast*, op. cit., p. 78.

16 I later confirmed that the Takazze was frequently referred to by Ethiopians as 'the Nile' and vice versa – for example, in Axumite texts of the fourth century and many later documents. For a discussion see L. P. Kirwan, 'The Christian Topography and the Kingdom of Axum', *Geographical Journal*, London, vol. 138, part II, June 1972, pp. 172–3.

17 I later learned that this same route was much more than just plausible. Throughout recorded history it had been greatly favoured by merchants and by pilgrims travelling between Ethiopia and Jerusalem. See O. G. S Crawford, *Ethiopian Itineraries*, Cambridge University Press for the Hakluyt Society, London, 1958.

18 James Bruce, *Travels to Discover the Source of the Nile in the Years 1768, 1769, 1770, 1771, 1772 and 1773*, Edinburgh, 1790, vol. III, p. 252.

19 J. M. Flad, *Falashas of Abyssinia*, London, 1869, p. 10.

20 See, for example, *The Falashas: The Jews of Ethiopia*, Minority Rights Group Report Number 67, London, 1985. See also David Kessler, *The Falashas*, op. cit., p. 10, and Professor Edward Ullendorff, 'Hebraic-Jewish Elements in Abyssinian (Monophysite) Christianity', *Journal of Semitic Studies*, vol. I, no. 3, 1956, p. 254.

21 David Kessler, *The Falashas*, op. cit., p. 92.

22 In general for historical detail on trade and pilgrimage routes

between Ethiopia and Jerusalem through Egypt and the Sudan see
Ethiopian Itineraries, op. cit.

Chapter 11 **And David danced before the Ark...**

1 F. L. Cross and E. A. Livingstone (eds), *The Oxford Dictionary of the Christian Church*, Oxford University Press, 1988, p. 465.
2 Ibid.
3 See, for example, Richard Pankhurst, *A Social History of Ethiopia*, Institute of Ethiopian Studies, Addis Ababa University, 1990, pp. 41 and 193.
4 The absolute non-recognition by Coptic Christians of the unique *tabot*/Ark traditions of Ethiopia was forcefully confirmed in June 1989 in an interview in London with Bishop Serabion and Father Bishoi Boushra of the Coptic Orthodox Church. The interview was carried out on my behalf by Caroline Lasko, a freelance researcher.
5 Aymro Wondmagegnehu and Joachim Motovu, *The Ethiopian Orthodox Church*, The Ethiopian Orthodox Mission, Addis Ababa, 1970, pp. 11–14.
6 *The Independent*, London, 20 November 1990, p. 11.
7 Ibid. See also *The Falashas: The Jews of Ethiopia* (Minority Rights Group Report No. 67), Minority Rights Group, London, 1985, pp. 12–13.
8 Frederick C. Gamst, *The Qemant: A Pagan-Hebraic Peasantry of Ethiopia*, Holt, Rinehart & Winston, New York, 1969.
9 Ibid., p. 4.
10 Ibid., p. 122.
11 Genesis 12:9–10.
12 Genesis 41:27.
13 Leviticus 11:3–4, 7: 'Whatsoever parteth the hoof, and is cloven footed, and cheweth the cud, among the beasts, that shall ye eat. Nevertheless these shall ye not eat of them that chew the cud, or of them that divide the hoof: as the camel, because he cheweth the cud, but divideth not the hoof; he is unclean to you . . . And the swine, though he divide the hoof and be cloven footed, yet he cheweth not the cud; he is unclean to you.'
14 See Deuteronomy 14:21: 'Ye shall not eat of anything that dieth of itself.' See also Leviticus 17:13–14: 'And whatsoever man there be of the children of Israel . . . which hunteth and catcheth any beast or fowl that may be eaten; he shall even pour out the blood thereof . . . For it is the life of all flesh; the blood of it is for the life thereof: therefore I said unto the children of Israel, Ye shall eat the blood of no manner of flesh: for the life of all flesh is the blood thereof.'
15 Exodus 23:19 and 34:26; Deuteronomy 14:21.

16 Compare Exodus 35:2–3: 'Six days shall work be done, but on the
    seventh day there shall be to you an holy day, a Sabbath of rest to the
    Lord: whosoever doeth work therein shall be put to death. Ye shall
    kindle no fire throughout your habitations upon the Sabbath day.'

17 Genesis 21:33.

18 In his *Archaeology of the Bible Book by Book* (Harper & Row, San
    Francisco, 1976, p. 65), Gaalyah Cornfeld puts it this way: 'Altars
    were the focal point of both high places, *bamoth*, and temples. The
    bamoth were essentially Canaanite sites of worship, but were
    acceptable also in earlier Israelite religion. They were usually open
    areas, with sacred trees and stone pillars, *masseboth*, associated with
    the altar.'

19 See, for example, Judges 6:25, 1 Kings 16:33; 2 Kings 21:3; 2
    Kings 23:15; Isaiah 27:9.

20 2 Kings 23:7.

21 *The Falashas: The Jews of Ethiopia* (Minority Rights Group Report
    No. 67), op. cit., p. 9.

22 Geoffrey Wigoder (ed.), *The Encyclopaedia of Judaism*, Jerusalem
    Publishing House, Jerusalem, 1989, p. 684.

23 Ibid., p. 548.

24 Leviticus 15:19: 'If a woman have an issue [of] blood . . . she shall be
    put apart seven days: and whosoever toucheth her shall be unclean
    until the even.'

25 'And in the eighth day the flesh of his foreskin shall be
    circumcised', Leviticus 12:3.

26 Leviticus 1:9.

27 See Professor Edward Ullendorff, 'Hebraic-Jewish Elements in
    Abyssinian (Monophysite) Christianity', *Journal of Semitic Studies*,
    vol. I, no. 3, London, 1956, pp. 249–50. Ullendorff states: 'The
    date of circumcision on the eighth day is shared . . . by Jews and
    Ethiopians only. This is the more remarkable because members of
    the Coptic Church in Egypt [which was responsible for Ethiopia's
    conversion] are circumcised at an age between six and eight years,
    and Gallas, Muslims and other influences in Ethiopia, with widely
    varying dates, would all combine to shake the Ethiopian
    confidence in the eighth day. Yet this date has been steadfastly
    maintained, no doubt under the influence of the Pentateuchal
    injunction . . . I have no doubt that the maintenance of
    circumcision among Abyssinians is part of those elements of
    Hebraic-Jewish lore which have been so tenaciously preserved in
    that part of Africa.'

28 Ibid., pp. 243–4.

29 Ibid., pp. 245–6. See also Geoffrey Wigoder (ed.), *The
    Encyclopaedia of Judaism*, op. cit., pp. 192–4 and 604–6.

30 Professor Edward Ullendorff, 'Hebraic-Jewish Elements', op. cit., pp. 242–3 and 247, note 3.

31 See in particular Exodus 19:15 and Leviticus 20:18.

32 Genesis 32:32: 'Therefore the children of Israel eat not of the sinew which shrank, which is upon the hollow of the thigh.'

33 Professor Edward Ullendorff, 'Hebraic-Jewish Elements' op. cit., p. 242.

34 Ibid., p. 236. I am greatly indebted to Professor Ullendorff's paper for alerting me to these correspondences.

35 Exodus 28:4.

36 Ibid.

37 Ibid. See also Exodus 28:17–21.

38 Archbishop David Matthew, *Ethiopia*, London, 1947, p. 12.

39 Professor Edward Ullendorff, 'Hebraic-Jewish Elements', op. cit., p. 235.

40 Ibid., pp. 235–6.

41 This also was the view of the Scottish traveller James Bruce, who argued that Frumentius and other Christian missionaries who came to Ethiopia in the fourth century AD, 'finding Jewish traditions confirmed in the country, chose to respect them rather than refute them. Circumcision, the doctrine of clean and unclean meats, and many other Jewish rites and ceremonies are therefore part of the religion of the Abyssinians at this day.' James Bruce, *Travels to Discover the Source of the Nile in the Years 1768, 1769, 1770, 1771, 1772, and 1773*, 3rd edn, Edinburgh, 1813, vol. III, p. 13.

42 Professor Edward Ullendorff, 'Hebraic-Jewish Elements', op. cit., p. 227 (emphasis added).

43 Ibid., p. 251.

44 Leviticus 16:2–13.

45 Leviticus 16:13.

46 Professor Edward Ullendorff, 'Hebraic-Jewish Elements', op. cit., p. 238, quoting Isenberg's *Dictionary of the Amharic Language*, London, 1841, p. 112.

47 The *begegna* is a hand-held, ten-stringed wooden harp, today found only in Ethiopia and said to be descended from the biblical Harp of David. See Tesfaye Lemma, *Ethiopian Musical Instruments*, Addis Ababa, 1975, p. 10.

48 2 Samuel 6:5–16.

49 Wolfram von Eschenbach, *Parzival*, Penguin Classics, London, 1980, p. 121.

50 And throughout the Pharaonic period. See Adolf Erman, *Life in Ancient Egypt*, Dover Publications, New York, 1971, pp. 279, 296, 390.

51 II Chronicles 5:12–13. See also 1 Kings 8:11.

52 II Chronicles 6:41 (Jerusalem Bible translation, Eyre & Spottiswoode, London, 1968, p. 464).

53 *Sir Gawain and the Green Knight*, translated by J. R. R. Tolkien and edited by Christopher Tolkien, Unwin Paperbacks, London, 1988, pp. 26 and 21.

Chapter 12 **Magic . . . or Method?**

1 Date from *The Jerusalem Bible*, Eyre & Spottiswoode, London, 1968, 'Chronological Table', p. 343.

2 These dimensions in feet and inches are extrapolated from the ancient cubit which measured approximately eighteen inches. See Dr J. H. Hertz (ed.), *The Pentateuch and the Haftorahs*, Soncino Press, London, 1978, p. 327. The Jerusalem Bible, footnote (b), p. 87, concurs.

3 The translation given here is from the Jerusalem Bible. The King James Authorized Version states 'corners' instead of 'supports' in Exodus 25:12.

4 Exodus 25:10–22.

5 Exodus 31:2–4.

6 Exodus 37:1–9.

7 'I came down from the mountain and put the tablets in the Ark', Deuteronomy 10:5, supposedly quoting Moses's own words. See also Exodus 40:20, 'He [Moses] took the Testimony and placed it inside the Ark. He set the shafts to the Ark and placed the throne of mercy on it.'

8 Exodus 40:21: 'He [Moses] brought the Ark into the Tabernacle and put the screening veil in place; thus he screened the Ark of Yahweh, as Yahweh had directed Moses.'

9 Leviticus 10:1.

10 Ibid.

11 Leviticus 10:2. The full passage reads: 'And there went out fire from the Lord and devoured them and they died there before the Lord' (King James Authorized Version). The Jerusalem Bible translation of the same, which makes use of 'Yahweh' (YHWH), the mystical name of God, reads as follows: 'Then from Yahweh's presence a flame leaped out and consumed them and they perished in the presence of Yahweh.' It is important to stress that in this and other similar contexts the Bible is actually and quite explicitly referring to the Ark when it speaks of 'the Lord' and/or 'before the Lord', or of 'Yahweh' and/or 'in the presence of Yahweh'. This is best illustrated by the following passage from Numbers 10:35: 'And it came to pass, when the Ark set forward,

that Moses said, Rise up, Lord, and let thine enemies be scattered
and let them that hate thee fall before thee' (King James
Authorized Version). The Jerusalem Bible translation of the same
verse reads: 'And as the Ark set out, Moses would say, Arise,
Yahweh, may your enemies be scattered and those who hate you
run for their lives before you.' *The Interpreter's Dictionary of the
Bible* comments: 'The Ark is not only seen as the leader of Israel's
host, but is directly addressed as Yahweh. There is virtually an
identification of Yahweh and the Ark . . . there is no doubt that
the Ark was interpreted as the extension or embodiment of the
presence of Yahweh.' *The Interpreter's Dictionary of the Bible: An
Illustrated Encyclopaedia*, Abingdon Press, Nashville, 1962, pp.
222–3.

12 Leviticus 16:1–2, amalgam of King James Authorized Version
and Jerusalem Bible translations.

13 Louis Ginzberg, *Legends of the Jews*, Jewish Publication Society of
America, Philadelphia, 1911, vol. III, p. 210.

14 Ibid. Compare Exodus 40:35.

15 The Ark was installed in the Tabernacle on the first day of the
first month of the second year after the Israelites had fled Egypt
(Exodus 40:17). It was on the eighth day of the same month that
the priests were invested and the deaths of Nadab and Abihu
occurred (Leviticus 9:1 *et seq.*). The entry of Moses into the Holy
of Holies to which I am referring here took place soon after, and
indeed in the same month, since this entry is described in Chapter
7 of the book of Numbers and since Chapter 9 of the same book
is still set 'in the first month of the second year' – clearly an
eventful period (Numbers 9:1).

16 Numbers 7:89.

17 Louis Ginzberg, *Legends of the Jews*, op. cit., vol. III, p. 210.

18 Ibid., vol. III, p. 157. See also *The Jewish Encyclopaedia*, Funk &
Wagnells, New York, 1925, vol. II, p. 105.

19 Numbers 10:33, 35–6, Jerusalem Bible translation.

20 Louis Ginzberg, *Legends of the Jews*, op. cit., vol. III, p. 228.

21 Julian Morgenstern, 'The Book of the Covenant', in *Hebrew Union
College Annual*, vol. V, 1928, reprinted by KTAV Publishing
House, New York, 1968, p. 20, footnote 25. See also *The Jewish
Encyclopaedia*, op. cit., vol. II, p. 105.

22 E.g. during the crossing of the Jordan. See *The Jewish
Encyclopaedia*, op. cit., vol. II, p. 105.

23 Ibid. And see also Louis Ginzberg, *Legends of the Jews*, op. cit.,
vol. III, p. 194.

24 Louis Ginzberg, *Legends of the Jews*, op. cit., vol. III, p. 395.
Another legend, supported by Midrashic commentaries, says that

during the wilderness wanderings: 'The Ark gave the signal for breaking camp by soaring high and then swiftly moving before the camp at a distance of three days' march' (Ibid., vol. III, p. 243).

25 Julian Morgenstern, 'The Book of the Covenant', op. cit., pp. 27–8: 'The oldest Biblical references to the Ark agree absolutely in representing it as discharging two specific functions, that of choosing the way it wished to go, and that of going into battle with the army of Israel and giving it victory over its enemies . . . These two important functions the Ark was able to discharge, all the evidence indicates, because of a *positive divine power resident in it.* And all these earliest sources agree in identifying this divine power with Yahweh' (emphasis added). For further corroboration of the frequency with which the Ark was taken into battle see Louis Ginzberg, *Legends of the Jews*, op. cit., vol. III, pp. 284 and 409; vol. IV, p. 143.

26 *The Jewish Encyclopaedia*, op. cit., vol. II, p. 106.

27 Numbers 14:44–5 (amalgam of King James Authorized Version and Jerusalem Bible translations).

28 Exodus 16:35. There has been a great deal of scholarly debate about whether the Israelites really did spend forty years in the desert (making Moses approximately 120 years old when the wanderings ended) or whether the period was shorter than this. Likewise the vast numbers of the Israelites given in the Bible (600,000 men on foot, plus their families) have been hotly disputed on ecological grounds – since Sinai could never have sustained such a population. Both these points are irrelevant to my argument. For the record, however, I suspect that the Israelites spent a good deal less than forty years in the wilderness: *four* years sounds far more likely. And I suspect that their numbers were small – a few hundreds or thousands at the most.

29 Numbers 31:2–11.

30 Numbers 22:1.

31 Numbers 20:28.

32 Numbers 20:24–8.

33 Numbers 27:12–23.

34 Deuteronomy 34:4–6, 10–12.

35 Deuteronomy 31:14–15.

36 Joshua 3:3–4 (King James Authorized Version translation). Emphasis added.

37 Joshua 3:6, 14–17; Joshua 4:18, 21, 23.

38 Joshua 6:11, 13–16, 20–1.

39 E.g. Joshua 7:3 ff. which tells of battle being started without the Ark and of the resulting defeat; Joshua 7:6 which inserts the Ark back into the narrative; and Joshua 8:1 ff. which tells of the

ultimate Israelite victory. See also Joshua 10:10 ff., which almost
certainly recounts the participation of the Ark in another
significant victory. Similarly Joshua 10:29–30 ff., especially verse
42.

40 See, for example, Joshua 18:1–10; 19:51; 21:2; 22:9; Judges
18:31; 21:19; and 1 Samuel 1:3–9 and 24; 3:21.

41 See Julian Morgenstern, 'The Ark, the Ephod and the Tent of
Meeting', *Hebrew Union College Annual*, vol. XVII, 1942–3,
reprinted by KTAV Publishing House, New York, 1968, pp.
235–6: 'It [the Ark] was not carried into ordinary battles.'

42 1 Samuel 4:1–2 (amalgam of King James Authorized Version and
Jerusalem Bible translations).

43 1 Samuel 4:3 (Jerusalem Bible translation).

44 1 Samuel 4:4–5 (King James Authorized Version translation).

45 1 Samuel 4:6–9 (Jerusalem Bible translation).

46 1 Samuel 4:10–11.

47 1 Samuel 4:13, 15–17 (King James Authorized Version
translation); and 1 Samuel 4:18–19 (Jerusalem Bible translation).

48 *Encyclopaedia Britannica*, 15th edn, 1991, vol. XIV, p. 786.

49 1 Samuel 4:22.

50 1 Samuel 5, complete text.

51 1 Samuel 6:1.

52 1 Samuel 6:2 (Jerusalem Bible translation).

53 1 Samuel 6:7 (King James Authorized Version translation).

54 1 Samuel 6:12 (King James Authorized Version translation).

55 1 Samuel 6:13–14, 19 (King James Authorized Version
translation).

56 See for example 1 Samuel 6:19, Jerusalem Bible translation. See
also the same verse in the *New English Bible*, Oxford and
Cambridge University Presses, 1970, p. 308, and in the *Holy
Bible: New International Version*, The Bible Societies/ Hodder &
Stoughton, UK, 1988. This latter states: 'But God struck down
some of the men of Bethshemesh, putting seventy of them to
death because they had looked into the Ark of the Lord.' See also
Handbook to the Bible, Lion Publishing, London, 1988, p. 234.

57 Two of the biblical translations (Jerusalem Bible and New English
Bible) imply that the men were killed because they had not
rejoiced when they saw the Ark of Yahweh; the King James
Authorized Version and the New International Version, on the
other hand, specifically say that they were killed because they
looked into the Ark. This latter interpretation is supported in the
Handbook to the Bible, op. cit., p. 234 and by Julian Morgenstern
in 'The Ark, the Ephod and the Tent of Meeting', op. cit., p. 241.

58 1 Samuel 6:20 (New English Bible translation).

59 1 Samuel 6:15.
60 1 Samuel 7:1. A Christian church dedicated to 'the Virgin Mary Ark of the Covenant' now stands at Kiriath-Jearim. See Chapter 3 above.
61 1 Samuel 7:1. The Jerusalem Bible states that a certain Eleazar was appointed 'to guard the Ark of Yahweh'. The New English Bible states that he was its 'custodian'.
62 Julian Morgenstern, 'The Ark, the Ephod and the Tent of Meeting', op. cit., p. 241, footnote 143.
63 See Jerusalem Bible, op. cit., Chronological Table, p. 343.
64 2 Samuel 6:3–4; 6–7.
65 2 Samuel 6:9–10 (New English Bible translation).
66 2 Samuel 6:10 (New English Bible translation).
67 2 Samuel 6:11 (Jerusalem Bible translation).
68 Louis Ginzberg, The Legends of the Jews, op. cit., vol. VI, p. 275.
69 2 Samuel 6:12 (King James Authorized Version translation).
70 E.g. 1 Chronicles 15:15.
71 2 Samuel 6:15.
72 2 Samuel 6:5.
73 1 Chronicles 16:1. See also 1 Chronicles 17:45.
74 1 Chronicles 28:2.
75 Jerusalem Bible, op. cit., Chronological Table, p. 344.
76 1 Kings 6:38 states that the Temple took eleven years to build.
77 1 Kings 8:1, 3, 4, 5, 6 (amalgam of King James Authorized Version and Jerusalem Bible translations).
78 Some details of what is known about this mysterious disappearance are given in Chapter 1 above. The phrase 'thick darkness' is from 1 Kings 8:12.
79 See for example Professor Richard Elliott Friedman, Who Wrote the Bible?, Johnathan Cape, London, 1988, p. 156.
80 As in the case of Moses's insubordinate sister Miriam. See Numbers 12. This incident is discussed further in Chapter 13 below.
81 Exodus 12:40.
82 The date of the Exodus, which Moses led in his old age, is generally put at between 1250 and 1230 BC (see, for example, Jerusalem Bible, op. cit., Chronological Table, p. 343). For a discussion of the dates of Tutankhamen's short rule see Christiane Desroches-Noblecourt, Tutankhamen: Life and Death of a Pharaoh, Penguin, London, 1989, p. 105.
83 Christiane Desroches-Noblecourt, Tutankhamen, op. cit., pp. 15 and 20.
84 Exodus 25:11.
85 Christiane Desroches-Noblecourt, Tutenkhamen, op. cit., p. 131.

See also Nicholas Reeves, *The Complete Tutankhamun*, Thames & Hudson, London, 1990, pp. 102 and 104. It is interesting to note that the sarcophagus itself also bore images of these tutelary deities in high relief – see page 105.

86 Exodus 25:18.

87 For a discussion see Geoffrey Wigoder (ed.), *The Encyclopaedia of Judaism*, Jerusalem Publishing House, Jerusalem, 1989, pp. 157–8.

88 Christiane Desroches-Noblecourt, *Tutankhamen*, op. cit., p. 185.

89 Ibid., p. 185. See also John Anthony West, *Ancient Egypt*, Harrap Columbus, London, 1989, p. 268, and Jill Kamil, *Luxor*, Longman, London and New York, 1989, p. 28.

90 Alan Moorehead, *The Blue Nile*, Penguin, London, 1984, p. 17.

91 I Chronicles 15:15, Jerusalem Bible translation. The King James Authorized Version reads: 'And the children of the Levites bare the Ark of God upon their shoulders with the staves thereon, as Moses commanded.'

92 See, for example, Edward Ullendorff, 'Hebraic-Jewish Elements in Abyssinian (Monophysite) Christianity', *Journal of Semitic Studies*, vol. I, no. 3, 1956, p. 223, footnote 6. Ullendorff says that *tabot* is 'derived from the Jewish Pal. Aramaic *tebuta* (*tebota*) which in turn is a derivation from the Hebrew *tebah*.'

93 E. A. Wallis Budge, *The Queen of Sheba and her Only Son Menelik: being the 'Book of the Glory of Kings' (Kebra Nagast)*, Oxford University Press, 1932, pp. 14–15.

94 Ibid., p. 14.

95 I am grateful to Dr Kitchen for his help and advice at various stages of this project. I first came into contact with him after he met and was interviewed on 12 June 1989 by Caroline Lasko (a freelance researcher then working with me). He subsequently was kind enough to be available for further meetings and to write to me on various salient points. For his authoritative views on the ancient Egyptian origins of many aspects of early Judaism the reader is referred to his paper 'Some Egyptian Background to the Old Testament', *Tyndale House Bulletin*, no. 5–6, Cambridge, April 1960. As regards the Ark of the Covenant and its relationship to the arks from Tutankhamen's tomb, see in particular pp. 10–11.

96 E. A. Wallis Budge, *From Fetish to God in Ancient Egypt*, Oxford University Press, 1934, p. 40.

97 A. H. Sayce, *Fresh Light from the Ancient Monuments*, Religious Tract Society, London, 1884, p. 67. See also p. 68.

98 Christiane Desroches-Noblecourt, *Tutankhamen*, op. cit., p. 186. See also Shalom M. Paul and William G. Dever (eds), *Biblical*

Archaeology, Keter Publishing House, Jerusalem, 1973, part III, p. 252: 'Some scholars have compared the Ark to the chests (*the lower part of which was generally boat-shaped*) which were brought out of the temple by the Egyptian priests at festivals, and on which statues of the gods were placed.' Emphasis added.

99 Julian Morgenstern, 'The Book of the Covenant', op. cit., p. 121.

100 J. A. West, *Ancient Egypt*, op. cit., p. 236.

101 Ibid.

102 Ibid.

103 Lady Flavia Anderson, *The Ancient Secret: Fire from the Sun*, RILKO Books, London, 1987, pp. 113–14.

104 I made the following entry in my notebook: 'The arks carried in the Apet ceremonies – though later transformed into chests – initially took the form of boats. It is therefore not difficult to see how the word *tebah* came to be used in biblical Hebrew for the ark of Noah and for Moses's ark of bullrushes. That a different name (*'Aron*) was subsequently used for the Ark of the Covenant could simply be a function of the fact that the Ark itself had *disappeared* from Jerusalem by the time that the books of the Old Testament came to be officially codified – and that the biblical scribes, setting down the oral history of the Jewish people, had been confused or uncertain about some of the key details of the religious tradition from which the lost relic had hailed. If my theory is correct, of course, it was not "lost" at all, but instead had been taken to Ethiopia – where its original name (*Tapet* or *Tabot*) has continued to be used right up to the present day.'

I later discovered that the Scottish explorer James Bruce had considered similar issues in vol. I of his *Travels*. He passed through Luxor (then known to Europeans as Thebes) on his way to Ethiopia and speculated that the name 'Thebes' must have been derived from 'Theba, which was the Hebrew name for the Ark when Noah was ordered to build it – Thou shalt "make thee an Ark (Theba) of gopher-wood". The figure of the temples in Thebes do not seem to be far removed from the idea given us of the Ark.' Though he did not proceed, as I had done, to link *Tapet* (the ancient Egyptian name for Thebes) to *Tabot*, I was intrigued that he followed this particular linguistic trail. It further convinced me that his principal aim in going to Ethiopia had been to search for the Ark of the Covenant and not, as he pretended, to discover the source of the Nile. See James Bruce, *Travels to Discover the Source of the Nile in the Years 1768, 1769, 1770, 1771, 1772 and 1773*, Edinburgh, 1790, vol. I. pp. 394–5.

105 Geoffrey Wigoder (ed.), *Encyclopaedia of Judaism*, op. cit., p. 504.

106 *Jerusalem Bible*, op. cit., Chronological Table, p. 343.

107 Josephus, *Jewish Antiquities*, translated by H. St J. Thackeray, Heinemann, London, 1930, vol. IV, books I–IV, p. 253.

108 Ibid., pp. 257–9.

109 Acts 7:22.
110 Philo Judaeus, *De Vita Mosis*, translated by F. H. Colson, Heinemann, London, 1935, vol. VI, pp. 287–9.
111 This is attested to at some length in both Philo and Josephus, op. cit.
112 What we know about the life of Moses confirms that 'he had studied the various branches of Egyptian magic', E. A. Wallis Budge, *From Fetish to God*, op. cit., p. 8.
113 'All the pharaohs were magicians as part of their office', C. Jacq, *Egyptian Magic*, Bolchazy-Carducci Publishers, Chicago, 1985, p. 12. And see in general pp. 9–13.
114 Acts 7:22.
115 Luke 24:19.
116 That knowledge of words of power is indeed referred to in the phrase 'mighty in words' – rather, say, than oratory – becomes clear when we remember that Moses later told Yahweh, 'never in my life have I been a man of eloquence.' The deity replied that the prophet should use his half-brother Aaron as his mouthpiece: 'I know that he is a good speaker.' Exodus 4:10–17.
117 E. A. Wallis Budge, *Egyptian Magic*, Kegan Paul, Trench, Trübner, London, 1901, p. 5.
118 Josephus, op. cit., footnote c, pp. 276–7. See also *Jerusalem Bible*, op. cit., footnote 3a, p. 63.
119 Exodus 3:2.
120 Exodus 3:7–10.
121 Exodus 3:13.
122 J. G. Frazer, *The Golden Bough: A Study in Magic and Religion*, Macmillan, London, 1987 edn, p. 261.
123 Exodus 3:14 and Exodus 3:6.
124 See Irving M. Zeitlin, *Ancient Judaism*, Polity Press, Cambridge, 1984, pp. 58–9. See also *Handbook to the Bible*, Lion Publishing, London, 1988, p. 157. The meaning of the Hebrew verb 'to be' goes beyond 'to exist' and conveys the notion 'to be actively present'. For a fuller discussion see F. L. Cross and E. A. Livingstone (eds), *The Oxford Dictionary of the Christian Church*, Oxford University Press, 1988, p. 1354. See also Geoffrey Wigoder (ed.), *The Encyclopaedia of Judaism*, op. cit., pp. 289–90.
125 E.g. Exodus 4:20; Exodus 17:9.
126 Exodus 4:2.
127 Exodus 4:3–4.
128 E. A. Wallis Budge, *Egyptian Magic*, op. cit., p. 5, and *From Fetish to God*, op. cit., pp. 119 and 129.
129 Exodus 7:11–12.
130 Exodus 7:20–2.

131 Exodus 8:1–7.
132 Exodus 8:16–19.
133 Exodus 8:21–32.
134 Exodus 9:1–7.
135 Exodus 9:8–11.
136 Exodus 10:1–20; Exodus 10:21–3.
137 Exodus 12:23–30.
138 Exodus 12:31–3.
139 Exodus 14:21–2.
140 Exodus 14:23.
141 Exodus 14:7–9.
142 Budge, *Egyptian Magic*, op. cit., p. 10.
143 Budge, *From Fetish to God*, op. cit., p. 8.
144 Ibid., p. 43: 'It is impossible to think that the highest order of the priests did not possess esoteric knowledge which they guarded with the greatest care.'
145 See, for example, Lucie Lamy, *Egyptian Mysteries*, Thames & Hudson, London, 1981, p. 86.
146 Luciano Canfora, *The Vanished Library: A Wonder of the Ancient World*, Hutchinson, London, 1989, p. 21.
147 Herodotus, *The History*, David Green (trans.), University of Chicago Press, Chicago and London, 1988, p. 132.
148 W. B. Emery, *Archaic Egypt*, Penguin, London, 1961, p. 206.
149 See the paper 'Mathematics and Astronomy' in J. R. Harris (ed.), *The Legacy of Egypt*, Oxford University Press, 1971.
150 This may be deduced from measurement of a variety of ancient Egyptian structures. Sir William Flinders Petrie, the nineteenth-century archaeologist (who was highly sceptical in general of theories suggesting advanced knowledge in ancient Egypt) was satisfied that the proportions of the Great Pyramid at Giza (*c.* 2550 BC) 'expressed the transcendental number *pi* with very considerable precision'. See A. J. West, *The Traveller's Key to Ancient Egypt: A Guide to the Sacred Places of Ancient Egypt*, Harrap, London, 1987, p. 90.
151 Reported in *Mystic Places*, Time-Life Books, Amsterdam, 1987, p. 65.
152 See R. El-Nadoury, 'The Legacy of Pharaonic Egypt', in *General History of Africa II*, UNESCO, Paris, 1981.
153 See the paper on 'Medicine' in J. R. Harris (ed.), *The Legacy of Egypt*, op. cit.
154 See Chapter 5 above.
155 Quoted in Robert Lawlor, *Sacred Geometry: Philosophy and Practice*, Thames & Hudson, London, 1982.

156 See William Anderson, *The Rise of the Gothic*, Hutchinson, London, 1985, p. 65.
157 Dates from J. A. West, *Ancient Egypt*, op. cit., pp. 249–50.
158 Ibid., pp. 249–50.
159 Ibid., p. 252.
160 Ibid., p. 424.
161 J. R. Harris, 'Technology and Materials', in *The Legacy of Egypt*, op. cit., p. 103.
162 J. A. West, *Ancient Egypt*, op. cit., p. 251.
163 Ibid., p. 109.
164 Quoted in ibid., p. 40.
165 Ibid., pp. 112–23, for all measurements and weights. See also A. J. Spencer, *The Great Pyramid*, P. J. Publications, London, 1989.
166 A. Abu Bakr, 'Pharaonic Egypt', in the *UNESCO General History of Africa II*, op. cit.
167 *Mystic Places*, op. cit., pp. 49–50.
168 Ibid., p. 62.
169 Ibid., p. 62. For a full and up-to-date presentation of the pyramidologists' point of view see Peter Lemesurier, *The Great Pyramid Decoded*, Element Books, Dorset, UK, 1989.
170 Peter Lemesurier, *The Great Pyramid Decoded*, op. cit., p. 7.
171 *Mystic Places*, op. cit., p. 59, and Lemesurier, op. cit., p. 3. In fact, as Lemesurier points out, the alignment is fractionally off true – by nearly five minutes of arc, or one-twelfth of a degree. But this would be to ignore the astronomical evidence that the cause even of this minute error is to be found in the gradual movement of the earth's own axis rather than in any inaccuracy on the part of the building's original surveyors.
172 See *Mystic Places*, op. cit., p. 47; J. A. West, *Ancient Egypt*, op. cit., p. 123; and A. J. Spencer, *The Great Pyramid*, op. cit.
173 Herodotus, op. cit., 2. 125, p. 186.
174 Quoted in J. A. West, *Ancient Egypt*, op. cit., p. 107.
175 Ibid., Introduction, p. xi. As well as the sheer magnitude of the task involved in building the Great Pyramid, other factors also contributed to my deepening suspicion that the ancient Egyptians must have known something that modern civilization did not. In the late nineteenth century, for example, Sir William Flinders Petrie, certainly the most eminent archaeologist of his generation, spent months at Giza carefully measuring the edifice – principally with a view to demolishing some of the wilder speculations of the pyramidologists. This he largely succeeded in doing (he claimed subsequently that he had provided 'the ugly little fact which killed the beautiful theory'). However, even he was forced to admit on several occasions that some of the achievements of the pyramid's

builders were quite baffling. Commenting on the precision with which the 115,000 ten-ton casing blocks were laid around the core masonry, he wrote: 'Merely to place such stones in exact contact would be careful work, but to do so with cement in the joint seems almost impossible; it is to be compared to the finest opticians' work on a scale of acres.' Petrie's remark is quoted in J. A. West's *Ancient Egypt*, op. cit., p. 90.

Chapter 13 **Treasures of Darkness**

1 Garth Fowden, *The Egyptian Hermes: A Historical Approach to the Late Pagan Mind*, Cambridge University Press, 1987, pp. 22–3.
2 See *New Larousse Encyclopaedia of Mythology*, Hamlyn, London, 1989, p. 28.
3 Ibid., p. 27. See also E. A. Wallis Budge, *Egyptian Magic*, Kegan Paul, Trench, Trübner, London, 1901, p. xi: 'the world itself came into existence through the utterance of a word by Thoth.' Soon after I had learned this it occurred to me that the whole concept was eerily analogous to the well known biblical passage which stated: 'In the beginning was the word, and the word was with God, and the word was God. He was with God in the beginning. Through him all things came to be, not one thing had its being but through him' (John 1:1–3). Intrigued by this coincidence I looked further and discovered, to my considerable surprise, that the Judaeo-Christian Scriptures allowed a number of other close parallels to be drawn between Thoth, the pagan moon-god of the Egyptians, and Yahweh, the God of Moses. One of the most striking of these concerned the Ten Commandments given to Moses on Mount Sinai and supposedly inscribed on the tablets of stone that were contained within the Ark of the Covenant: 'Thou shalt have no other gods before me. Thou shalt not make unto thee any graven image . . . Thou shalt not take the name of the Lord thy God in vain . . . Remember the sabbath day and keep it holy . . . Honour thy father and thy mother . . . Thou shalt not kill . . . Thou shalt not commit adultery . . . Thou shalt not steal . . . Thou shalt not bear false witness . . . Thou shalt not covet thy neighbour's wife.' (Exodus 20:3–17).

I had always thought that this exacting legal code was unique to early Judaic culture. This assumption, however, was overturned when I found the following remarkably similar formulae in Chapter CXXV of the ancient Egyptian *Book of the Dead* – a chapter which consisted of a series of negative confessions that the soul of the deceased was obliged to make before Thoth in his capacity as divine judge and scribe: 'Not have I despised god . . .

Not have I killed . . . Not have I fornicated . . . Not have I despoiled the things of the god . . . not have I defiled the wife of a man . . . Not have I cursed god . . . Not have I borne false witness' (see E. A. Wallis Budge, *The Egyptian Book of the Dead: The Papyrus of Ani*, British Museum Publications, London, 1895, pp. 195–204). Perhaps the most striking parallel of all, however, occurred in a rubric to one part of the *Book of the Dead* which stated: 'This chapter was found on an alabaster brick, under the feet of the Majesty of this venerable place, the God Thoth, and it was written by the God himself.' I already knew, of course, that the Ark of the Covenant had frequently been referred to in the Bible as the 'footstool of God' (e.g. 1 Chronicles 28:2) and that it had contained the stone Tablets of the Law written by Yahweh's own finger. I could therefore only conclude that the match between the thinking and behaviour of Yahweh and Thoth – and also between the *beliefs* that people had held about the two deities – was much too close to be entirely fortuitous. Neither, I reasoned, was it possible that the biblical passages had influenced the writers of the *Book of the Dead* since, of the two documents, the latter was by far the most ancient (some of its contents, I knew, went back as far as the fourth millennium BC; the most archaic sections of the Bible, by contrast, were at least 2,000 years younger).

4 Garth Fowden, *The Egyptian Hermes*, op. cit., p. 33.
5 Ibid., p. 23. See also E. A. Wallis Budge, *From Fetish to God in Ancient Egypt*, Oxford University Press, 1934, pp. 121–2, and the *New Larousse Encyclopaedia of Mythology*, op. cit., p. 27.
6 *New Larousse Encyclopaedia of Mythology*, op. cit., p. 27.
7 John Anthony West, *The Traveller's Key to Ancient Egypt: a Guide to the Sacred Places of Ancient Egypt*, Harrap Columbus, London, 1987, pp. 74–5.
8 E. A. Wallis Budge (trans.), *The Egyptian Book of the Dead*, op. cit., Introduction, p. cxviii.
9 E. A. Wallis Budge, *From Fetish to God*, op. cit., p. 157. See also M. V. Seton-Williams, *Egyptian Legends and Stories*, Rubicon Press, London, 1990, p. 16.
10 This story is to be found in its fullest form in Plutarch, *De Iside et Osiride*. See M. V. Seton-Williams, op. cit., pp. 24–9. See also E. A. Wallis Budge, *From Fetish to God*, op. cit., pp. 177 ff.
11 W. B. Emery, *Archaic Egypt*, Penguin, London, 1987, p. 192.
12 E. A. Wallis Budge (trans.), *The Egyptian Book of the Dead*, op. cit., Introduction, pp. xii and xiii.
13 W. B. Emery, *Archaic Egypt*, op. cit., p. 38. Emphasis added.
14 Ibid., p. 175–91.

15 Ibid., pp. 177 and 31.
16 Ibid., p. 26.
17 Instructions given to Sin on the day of creation by Marduk, chief figure in the Mesopotamian pantheon. Quoted in the *New Larousse Encyclopaedia of Mythology*, op. cit., p. 57.
18 Ibid.
19 E. A. Wallis Budge, *From Fetish to God*, op. cit., p. 155
20 W. B. Emery, *Archaic Egypt*, op. cit., p. 31.
21 This is Emery's view also. See ibid., p. 122–3.
22 Plato, *Timaeus and Critias*, Penguin Classics, London, 1977, p. 39.
23 Ibid., pp. 35–8 and 137–8.
24 Ibid., p. 38.
25 Ibid. See 'Appendix on Atlantis' by Sir Desmond Lee, p. 158.
26 Ibid., p. 158.
27 Ibid., p. 40.
28 See Edmond Sollberger, *The Babylonian Legend of the Flood*, British Museum Publications, London, 1962. See also *The Epic of Gilgamesh*, Penguin Classics, London, 1960.
29 Peter Marshall, *Journey Through the Maldives*, Camerapix Publishers International, London, 1991, p. 191.
30 See *Encyclopaedia Britannica*, 15th edn, 1991, Micropacdia, vol. IV, pp. 441–2.
31 See Chapter CLXXV of the *Book of the Dead* where Thoth (in his capacity as universal demiurge) resolves to send a flood to punish sinful humanity: 'They have fought fights, they have upheld strifes, they have done evil, they have created hostilities, they have made slaughter, they have caused trouble and oppression . . . [Therefore] I am going to blot out everything which I have made. This earth shall enter into the watery abyss by means of a raging flood, and will become even as it was in primeval time' (from the Theban Recension of the *Book of the Dead*, quoted in E. A. Wallis Budge, *From Fetish to God*, op. cit., p. 198). This compares intriguingly with Chapter 6 of Genesis: 'And God saw that the wickedness of man was great in the earth, and that every imagination of the thoughts of his heart was only evil continually. And it repented the Lord that he had made man on the earth, and it grieved him at his heart . . . And God said, The end of all flesh is come before me; for the earth is filled with violence . . . And behold I, even I, do bring a flood of waters upon the earth to destroy all flesh wherein is the breath of life from under heaven; and everything that is in the earth shall die' (Genesis 6:5–17).
32 E. A. Wallis Budge, *From Fetish to God*, op. cit., pp. 197–8.
33 Good summaries of the Plutarch account are given in M. V.

Seton-Williams, *Egyptian Legends and Stories*, op. cit., pp. 24–9; and in E. A. Wallis Budge, *From Fetish to God*, op. cit., pp. 178–83.

34 See in particular E. A. Wallis Budge, *From Fetish to God*, op. cit., p. 182. The Plutarch story has the coffer floating across the Mediterranean to 'Byblos' near modern Beirut. Budge dismisses this as a mistranslation, pointing out that *byblos* was simply a name for the papyrus plant.

35 Ibid., p. 180.

36 Josephus, *Jewish Antiquities*, translated by H. St J. Thackeray, Heinemann, London, 1930, vol. IV, books I–IV, p. 263.

37 Philo, *Life of Moses*, translated by F. H. Colson, Heinemann, London, 1935, vol. VI, p. 285.

38 E. A. Wallis Budge, *From Fetish to God*, op. cit., pp. 181–2.

39 Samuel Noah Kramer, *The Sumerians: Their History, Culture and Character*, University of Chicago Press, 1963. See also John Oates, *Babylon*, Thames & Hudson, London, 1979.

40 *New Larousse Encyclopaedia of Mythology*, op. cit., pp. 58–60.

41 Jonah 2:10; 3:2.

42 Genesis 6:19.

43 Genesis 6:14.

44 Genesis 9:1.

45 Luke 24:19.

46 John 3:5.

47 Mark 1:9–11.

48 See E. A. Wallis Budge, *Egyptian Magic*, Kegan Paul, Trench, Trübner, London, 1901.

49 J. A. West, *Ancient Egypt*, op. cit., p. 8.

50 Thor Heyerdahl, *The Ra Expeditions*, Book Club Associates, London, 1972, p. 17. Heyerdahl adds, without much further comment, that the pyramid boat had clearly been built 'to a pattern created by shipbuilders from a people with a long, solid tradition of sailing on the open sea' (p. 16).

51 J. A. West, *Ancient Egypt*, op. cit., pp. 132–3. See also A. J. Spencer, *The Great Pyramid*, P. J. Publications, London, 1989.

52 Christiane Desroches-Noblecourt, *Tutankhamen*, Penguin, London, 1989, pp. 89, 108, 113 and 283.

53 A. J. Spencer, *The Great Pyramid*, op. cit.

54 See, for example, W. B. Emery, *Archaic Egypt*, op. cit., p. 68.

55 *General History of Africa*, UNESCO, Paris, 1981, p. 84–107.

56 For further discussion see W. B. Emery, *Archaic Egypt*, op. cit., particularly Chapter 4; Lucy Lamy, *Egyptian Mysteries*, Thames & Hudson, London, 1981, p. 68; and *UNESCO General History of Africa*, op. cit.

57 J. A. West, *Ancient Egypt*, op. cit., p. 158. The Greeks later appropriated Imhotep, under the Hellenized name Asclepius, as the founder of the science of medicine.

58 E. A. Wallis Budge, *From Fetish to God*, op. cit., p. 161.

59 Garth Fowden, *The Egyptian Hermes*, op. cit., p. 33.

60 Ibid., p. 23.

61 J. A. West, *Ancient Egypt*, op. cit., p. 12.

62 Ibid., p. 340.

63 Ibid., p. 343.

64 *The Jewish Encyclopaedia*, Funk & Wagnells, New York, 1925, vol. II, p. 497.

65 *Collins English Dictionary*, Collins, London, 1982, p. 261; emphasis added.

66 Malcolm Barber, *The Trial of the Templars*, Cambridge University Press, 1989, p. 62. See also pp. 61, 67, 69, 100, 101, 147, 163–4, 167, 175, 178, 182–3, 185–8, 210, 249.

67 G. Legman, *The Guilt of the Templars*, Basic Books, New York, 1966, p. 85.

68 See H. J. Schonfield, *The Essene Odyssey*, Element Books, London, 1984, pp. 162–5. The code is known as the Atbash cipher. See in particular p. 164.

69 Ibid., p. 164.

70 E. A. Wallis Budge, *The Gods of the Egyptians*, Methuen, London, 1904, vol. I, p. 415.

71 Ibid., p. 414.

72 Ibid., p. 414.

73 David Stevenson, *The Origins of Freemasonry*, Cambridge University Press, 1990, p. 85. The Masons had venerated Thoth in his later incarnation as Hermes, the Greek god of wisdom. As Stevenson explains: 'The Greeks had identified their god Hermes with the Egyptian god Thoth, scribe to the gods, and himself a god of wisdom' (ibid., p. 83).

74 Ibid., p. 85 (with Thoth again in his incarnation as Hermes).

75 In *De Revolutionibus*. For a discussion see Timothy Ferris, *Coming of Age in the Milky Way*, Bodley Head, London, 1988, p. 65.

76 From *The Harmonies of the World*, quoted in Timothy Ferris, *Coming of Age in the Milky Way*, op. cit., p. 79.

77 The quotation is from Newton's *Principia*, cited in Richard S. Westfall, *Never at Rest: a Biography of Isaac Newton*, Cambridge University Press, 1980, p. 435.

78 Ibid., p. 434.

79 John Harrison, *The Library of Isaac Newton*, Cambridge University Press, 1978.

80 Frank Manuel, *The Religion of Isaac Newton*, Oxford University Press, 1974, p. 86.
81 Gale E. Christianson, *In the Presence of the Creator: Isaac Newton and His Times*, Collier Macmillan, London, 1984, p. 262.
82 Richard S. Westfall, *Never at Rest*, op. cit., p. 346.
83 Gale E. Christianson, op. cit., pp. 256–7.
84 Ibid., p. 257.
85 Richard S. Westfall, *Never at Rest*, op. cit., p. 250.
86 John Maynard Keynes, 'Newton the Man', in *Newton Tercentenary Celebrations*, Cambridge University Press, 1947, pp. 27–9.
87 Gale E. Christianson, *In the Presence of the Creator*, op. cit., p. 362.
88 Ibid.
89 Ibid., p. 222
90 Yahuda Manuscript Collection, Jewish National and University Library, Jerusalem, MS 16.2, pp. 48, 50 and 74.
91 Richard S. Westfall, *Never at Rest*, op. cit., p. 355.
92 Ibid., p. 356. See also Gale E. Christianson, *In the Presence of the Creator*, op. cit., p. 255.
93 See Gale E. Christianson, *In the Presence of the Creator*, p. 256.
94 Piyo Rattansi, 'Newton and the Wisdom of the Ancients', in John Fauvel, Raymond Flood *et al.* (eds), *Let Newton Be! : A New Perspective on his Life and Works*, Oxford University Press, 1988, pp. 188 and 195.
95 Quoted by Jan Golinski in ibid., pp. 159–60.
96 Gale E. Christianson, *In the Presence of the Creator*, op. cit., p. 222.
97 Isaiah 45:3.
98 J. A. West, *Ancient Egypt*, op. cit., p. 33.
99 Joshua 6:11–21.
100 1 Samuel 6:13–19.
101 1 Samuel 5.
102 Louis Ginzberg, *The Legends of the Jews*, The Jewish Publication Society of America, Philadelphia, 1911, vol. III, p. 194.
103 Exodus 3:8.
104 Exodus 16:35. See Chapter 12, note 28 above.
105 The shortest route was the 'Way of the Sea' (known to the Egyptians as the 'Way of Horus' and to the Bible as the 'Way of the Land of the Philistines'). Slightly longer, but also quickly traversed, was the more southerly 'Way of Shur'. See Itzhaq Beit-Arieh, 'The Route Through Sinai', *Biblical Archaeology Review*, May/June 1988, p. 31.
106 Indeed, this is hinted at in the Bible. According to Exodus 13: 'When Pharaoh had let the people go . . . God led them not through the way of the land of the Philistines, although that was near; for God said, Lest peradventure the people repent when they

see war, and they return to Egypt. But God led the people about, through the way of the wilderness' (Exodus 13:17–18).

107 E.g. Exodus 14:9–12; Exodus 14:31; Exodus 15:22–4; Exodus 15:25; Exodus 16:2–3; Exodus 16:4–36; Exodus 17:1–4; Exodus 17:6–7.

108 Exodus 17:6–7.

109 Exodus 15:25.

110 Exodus 16:4–36.

111 Numbers 12:1–2, and in general Numbers 12.

112 Numbers 12:10.

113 Numbers 12:10.

114 Numbers 16:2–3.

115 Numbers 16:4.

116 Numbers 16:5–7, 17. See also 16:39 (King James Authorized Version translation) or 17:4 (Jerusalem Bible translation) for confirmation that the censers were brazen/bronze. There can be no doubt that the phrases 'put fire therein and put incense in them *before the Lord*' (King James Authorized Version) and 'fill them with fire and . . . put incense in them *before Yahweh*' ('Jerusalem Bible translation) explicitly and unambiguously mean that they were to burn incense before the Ark. See Chapter 12, note 11, above for a full explanation of why this is. See also note 121 below.

117 Numbers 16:7.

118 Numbers 16:18.

119 Numbers 16:19.

120 Numbers 16:20–1.

121 Numbers 16:22 and 35 (amalgam of King James Authorized Version and Jerusalem Bible translations). Numbers 16:35 in fact states 'there came out a fire from the Lord' (King James Authorized Version translation). The Jerusalem Bible translation says 'a fire came down from Yahweh'. See Chapter 12, note 11 above for a full explanation of why the work is implied. It is worth adding with reference to this passage that the Israelites did not accept that it had been 'the Lord' who had blasted the hapless rebels. Instead they pinned the blame fairly and squarely on the man who controlled the Ark. Numbers 16:41 states: 'All the congregation of the children of Israel murmured against Moses . . . saying *You* have brought death to the people' (amalgam of King James Authorized Version and Jerusalem Bible translations). The latter is doubly logged as Numbers 17:6. (Emphasis added.)

122 Numbers 17:12–13 (King James Authorized Version translation). In the Jerusalem Bible the same passage is logged under Numbers 17:27–8.

123 See Chapter 12 above for a full discussion.

124 Acts 7 :23–4.

125 Exodus 2:12–15.

126 Exodus 7:7.

127 Exodus 2: 15–25

128 Ahmed Osman, *Moses: Pharaoh of Egypt*, Grafton Books, London, 1990, p. 171. Osman identified Moses with Pharaoh Akhenaten who briefly introduced a version of monotheism into Egypt before being overthrown.

129 A good summary account of Flinders Petrie's expedition to Serabit-el-Khadem is given in Werner Keller, *The Bible as History*, Bantam Books, New York, pp. 126–9. See also William M. Flinders Petrie, *Researches in Sinai*, Dutton, New York, 1906.

130 Itzhaq Beit-Arieh, 'The Route Through Sinai', op. cit., p. 33. See also William F. Albright, *The Proto-Sinaitic Inscriptions and their Decipherment*, Harvard University Press, 1969; Frank Moore Cross, 'The Evolution of the Alphabet', *Eretz-Israel*, vol. 8, 1967, p. 12; Joseph Naveh, *Early History of the Alphabet*, Hebrew University, Jerusalem, 1982.

131 Itzhaq Beit-Arieh, 'The Route Through Sinai', op. cit., p. 33.

132 For further details see, for example, Aviram Perevolotsky and Israel Finkelstein, 'The Southern Sinai Route in Ecological Perspective', *Biblical Archaeology Review*, July/August 1985, pp. 27 and 33. See also *Egypt: Insight Guide*, APA Publications, Singapore, 1989, pp. 243–6

133 Again for further details see Perevolotsky and Finkelstein, 'The Southern Sinai Route in Ecological Perspective', op. cit., p. 27.

134 Ibid., p. 33.

135 Ibid., pp. 27 and 33. See also *Egypt: Insight Guide*, op. cit., pp. 243–6, and Itzhaq Beit-Arieh, 'The Route Through Sinai', op. cit.

136 Itzhaq Beit-Arieh includes a helpful chart of other contenders for the role of Mount Sinai in his paper 'The Route Through Sinai', op. cit., p. 37. He concludes that the Exodus almost certainly did follow the southern route through Sinai leading to Mount Sinai as it is presently identified. The same conclusion is drawn in *The Times Atlas of the Bible*, Guild Publishing, London, 1987, p. 56.

137 Wolfram von Eschenbach, *Parzival*, Penguin Classics, London, 1980, p. 232

138 See Julian Morgenstern, 'The Book of the Covenant', *Hebrew Union College Annual*, vol. V, 1928; and 'The Ark, the Ephod and the Tent of Meeting', *Hebrew Union College Annual*, vol. XVII, 1942–3; both reprinted by KTAV Publishing House, New York, 1968. See also Chapter 3 above.

139 Menahem Haran, *Temples and Temple Service in Ancient Israel*,

Oxford, Clarendon Press, 1978; reprinted 1985 by Eisenbrauns, Winona Lake, Indiana, USA, p. 246.

140 Exodus 19:3.

141 Exodus 19:12–13 (Jerusalem Bible translation).

142 Exodus 19:16, 18 (amalgam of Jerusalem Bible and King James Authorized Version translations).

143 Exodus 24:12.

144 Exodus 24:15–18 (amalgam of Jerusalem Bible and King James Authorized Version translations).

145 See Louis Ginzberg, *The Legends of the Jews*, op. cit., vol. III, pp. 118–19.

146 Exodus 31:18; 32:15–16.

147 Exodus 32:19. The well known golden calf incident begins at Exodus 32:1.

148 Exodus 32:28.

149 Exodus 34:28.

150 Exodus 34:29.

151 Exodus 34:29 (Jerusalem Bible translation).

152 Exodus 33:7, Jerusalem Bible translation: 'Moses used to take the Tent and pitch it outside the camp. He called it The Tent of Meeting.'

153 Exodus 33:11.

154 Louis Ginzberg, *The Legends of the Jews*, op. cit., vol. III, p. 119.

155 Exodus 34:29–35.

156 Exodus 34:30.

157 Exodus 34:33.

158 Exodus 34:34–5.

159 See Moshe Levine, *The Tabernacle: Its Structure and Utensils*, Soncino Press, Tel Aviv, 1969, p. 88.

160 See, for example, *The Oxford Reference Dictionary*, Guild Publishing, London, 1988, p. 793, which gives the measure of a span or hand-breadth as nine inches. See also *The Oxford Library of Words and Phrases*, Guild Publishing, London, 1988, vol. III, p. 451.

161 Rabbi Shelomo Yitshaki was born at Troyes in AD 1040 and died in the year 1105. He is generally referred to as Rashi (an acronym based on his full title and name). See Geoffrey Wigoder (ed.), *The Encyclopedia of Judaism*, Jerusalem Publishing House, Jerusalem, 1989, p. 583.

162 Exodus 39:1–32.

163 See, for example, Exodus 28:43 and Leviticus 10:6.

164 Numbers 4:5–6 and 15: 'When the camp is broken, Aaron and his sons [Eleazar and Ithamar] are to come and take down the veil of the screen. With it they must cover the Ark . . . On top of this

they must put a covering of fine leather, and spread over the whole a cloth all of violet. Then they are to fix the poles to the Ark . . . [Then] the sons of Kohath are to come and take up the burden, but without touching any of the sacred things; otherwise they would die.'

165 Ibid.

166 Louis Ginzberg, *The Legends of the Jews*, op. cit., vol. III, p. 228: 'The most distinguished among the Levites were the sons of Kohath, whose charge during the march through the desert was the Holy Ark. This was a dangerous trust, for out of the staves attached to it would issue sparks that consumed Israel's enemies, but now and then this fire wrought havoc among the bearers of the Ark.'

167 See passage quoted in note 164 above which specifies that the 'veil of the screen', a layer of leather and a layer of cloth were used to wrap the Ark. When the Tabernacle was pitched and at rest, the 'veil of the screen' hung in the entrance to the Holy of Holies. It was made of 'blue, and purple, and scarlet, and fine twined linen of cunning work' (Exodus 26:31). Unusually for such an important accessory, it did not contain any gold – and neither, of course, did the 'covering of fine leather' or the 'cloth of violet'. In other words before the Ark was moved it was first thoroughly wrapped and insulated by several layers of non-conductive materials.

168 The view that the Ark was dangerous to carry for some possibly electrical reason is supported by the Jewish tradition quoted in note 166 above. The same tradition adds further credibility to this notion when it states that the Kohathites, rather than behaving as though they were honoured by being given the job of carrying the Ark – as one might have expected if it was indeed nothing more than a symbol of their God – in fact tried to avoid the duty, 'each one planning cautiously to shift the carrying of the Ark upon another.' Louis Ginzberg, *Legends of the Jews*, op. cit., vol. III, p. 228.

169 Leviticus 10:2. The full passage reads: 'And there went out the fire from the Lord and devoured them and they died there before the Lord' (King James Authorized Version). The Jerusalem Bible translation of the same verse reads: 'Then from Yahweh's presence a flame leaped out and consumed them and they perished in the presence of Yahweh.' See Chapter 12, note 11 above for an explanation of why the Ark is implied.

170 Leviticus 10:4–5 (Jerusalem Bible translation).

171 1 Samuel 5.

172 E.g. the slaying of Uzzah by what sounds like some kind of electrical discharge. See 2 Samuel 6:3–7.

Chapter 14 The Glory is departed from Israel

1 See Chapter 5 above.

2 Mecca and Medina are the first two. For details as to the date of construction of the Dome of the Rock see Dan Bahat, *Carta's Historical Atlas of Jerusalem*, Carta, Jerusalem, 1989, p. 44–9.

3 See Chapter 12 above. See also Zev Vilnay, *Legends of Jerusalem: The Sacred Land*, vol. I, Jewish Publication Society of America, Philadelphia, 1973, pp. 11–12.

4 See Chapter 5 above, and later parts of this chapter, for further details.

5 For further details see Jerome Murphy-O'Connor, *The Holy Land*, Oxford University Press, 1986, pp. 84–6.

6 See Chapter 5 above.

7 1 Chronicles 28:2.

8 For a good concise history of the successive stages of building and destruction on the Temple Mount see *Carta's Historical Atlas of Jerusalem*, op. cit. As regards archaeological confirmation that the Dome of the Rock does indeed stand over the site of the original Temple of Solomon, see Kathleen Kenyon, *Jerusalem: Excavating 3,000 Years of History*, Thames & Hudson, London, 1967, p. 55: 'From the present structure back to Solomon there is no real break. One can therefore be certain of the site of Solomon's Temple.' See also Kathleen Kenyon, *Digging up Jerusalem*, Benn, London, 1974, p. 110.

9 Islam also accepts Jesus Christ as a prophet. Muhammad is regarded as exceptional because he was the last of the prophets – the last of the messengers sent by God to teach and enlighten humankind and whose honour it therefore was to complete the divine message. There can be no serious dispute that the God worshipped by the Jews, Christians and Muslims is, in essence, the same deity. The *oneness* of this God is accepted by all three faiths although Muslims believe that Christians are confused by such notions as the Trinity and the divinity of Christ. An Arabic inscription within the Dome of the Rock reads as follows: 'O you People of the Book, overstep not bounds in your religion, and of God speak only the truth. The Messiah, Jesus, son of Mary, is only an apostle of God, and his word which he conveyed into Mary, and a Spirit proceeding from him. Believe therefore in God and his apostles, and say not Three. It will be better for you. God is only one God. Far be it from his glory that he should have a son.'

10 See Zev Vilnay, *Legends of Jerusalem*, op. cit., pp. 123 and 324, footnote 136. See also Neil Asher Silberman, *Digging for God and Country: Exploration, Archaeology and the Secret Struggle for the Holy Land 1799–1917*, Knopf, New York, 1982, p. 186.

11 Quoted from 'The Syriac Apocalypse of Baruch' in H. F. D. Sparks

(ed.), *The Apocryphal Old Testament*, Clarendon Press, Oxford, 1989, pp. 843–4.

12 Ibid.; see 'Introduction to the Syriac Apocalypse of Baruch', particularly p. 837.

13 See Chapter 5 above.

14 See Chapter 12 above.

15 1 Kings 8:1, 6, 10–11, 27.

16 1 Kings 11:4–5.

17 1 Kings 4:30.

18 Each wing measured five cubits (about seven and a half feet). See 2 Chronicles 3:11 and 1 Kings 6:24. According to the Jerusalem Bible translation, the cherubim were made of olive wood plated with gold.

19 1 Kings 6:19 (Jerusalem Bible translation).

20 Twenty cubits, by twenty cubits, by twenty cubits. See 1 Kings 6:20.

21 2 Chronicles 3:8 states that 600 talents of fine gold were used to overlay the walls, floor and ceiling of the Holy of Holies. An ancient talent weighed approximately 75 pounds, therefore 600 talents would have weighed 45,000 pounds – more than twenty tonnes. For further details, and academic support for the amounts of gold specified in the Bible as having been used in King Solomon's Temple, see Professor Alan R. Millard, 'Does the Bible Exaggerate King Solomon's Golden Wealth?', *Biblical Archaeology Review*, May/June 1989, pp. 21–34. See also 1 Kings 6:20, 22 and 30.

22 2 Chronicles 3:9.

23 1 Kings 7:13–14 (amalgam of King James Authorized Version and Jerusalem Bible translations).

24 Chrétien de Troyes, *Arthurian Romances* (translated by D. D. R. Owen), Dent, London, 1987, p. 375; emphasis added.

25 Wolfram von Eschenbach, *Parzival*, Penguin Classics, London, 1980. See in particular pp. 62–7 and 70–1.

26 See Kenneth Mackenzie, *The Royal Masonic Cyclopaedia*, Aquarian Press, Wellingborough, 1987 (first published 1877), pp. 316–17. See also Alexander Horne, *King Solomon's Temple in the Masonic Tradition*, Aquarian Press, Wellingborough, 1988, pp. 262–8 and 272–9. See also John J. Robinson, *Born in Blood*, Century, London, 1990, pp. 217–18. Hiram of Tyre, the bronzeworker and skilled craftsman, is of course not to be confused with *King* Hiram of Tyre who supplied Solomon with cedarwood for the construction of the Temple, and who also sent him a number of skilled artisans to assist with the work.

27 John J. Robinson, *Born in Blood*, op. cit., p. 219.

28 1 Kings 7:23, 26.
29 See Shalom M. Paul and William G. Dever (eds), *Biblical Archaeology*, Keter Publishing House, Jerusalem, 1973, part III, p. 257.
30 Bruce Metzger, David Goldstein, John Ferguson (eds), *Great Events of Bible Times*, Guild Publishing, London, 1987, p. 89.
31 Shalom M. Paul and William G. Dever, *Biblical Archaeology*, op. cit., p. 257.
32 1 Kings 7:38.
33 See Chapter 12 above.
34 See Chapter 11 above.
35 1 Kings 7:40, 45.
36 1 Kings 7:15, 21-2.
37 Kenneth Mackenzie, *The Royal Masonic Cyclopaedia*, op. cit., pp. 349-50. See also David Stevenson, *The Origins of Freemasonry*, Cambridge University Press, 1990, pp. 143-52.
38 Alexander Horne, *King Solomon's Temple in Masonic Tradition*, op. cit., p. 219.
39 Ibid.
40 Joshua 15:48; Judges 10:1; Judges 10:2; Chronicles 24:24.
41 E.g. Deuteronomy 27:5: 'And there shalt thou build an altar unto the Lord thy God, an altar of stones: thou shalt not lift up any iron tool upon them.' See also Joshua 8:31.
42 Moses was said to have used the Shamir in the desert to engrave writing on the precious stones worn in the breastplate of the High Priest. See Louis Ginzberg, *The Legend of the Jews*, Jewish Publication Society of America, Philadelphia, 1909, vol. I, p. 34, and vol. IV, p. 166.
43 Ibid., vol. I, p. 34.
44 Ibid., vol. IV, p. 166.
45 Ibid., vol. I, p. 34. On the vanishing of the Shamir see also Herbert Danby (trans.), *The Mishnah*, Oxford University Press, 1989, p. 305.
46 Louis Ginzberg, *Legends of the Jews*, op. cit., vol. I, p. 34.
47 From Islamic traditions about the Shamir, reported in Alexander Horne, *King Solomon's Temple in the Masonic Tradition*, op. cit., p. 165.
48 *Jerusalem Bible*, Eyre & Spottiswoode, London, 1968, Chronological Table, p. 344.
49 1 Kings 14:25-6.
50 The only objects specifically mentioned are the 'shields of gold which Solomon had made', 1 Kings 14:26.
51 For further details see Professor Kenneth A. Kitchen, 'Shishak's Military Campaign in Israel Confirmed', *Biblical Archaeology*

Review, May/June 1989, pp. 32–3. See also Bruce Metzger, David Goldstein, John Ferguson (eds), *Great Events of Bible Times*, op. cit., pp. 94–5.

52 Ibid., p. 95.

53 Ibid., p. 94. This view is also expressed with great authority by Professor Menahem Haran of Jerusalem's Hebrew University in his book *Temples and Temple Service in Ancient Israel*, Clarendon Press, Oxford, 1978, reprinted (with corrections) by Eisenbrauns, Winona Lake, Indiana, 1985, p. 286: 'It may be concluded that the Egyptian army bypassed Jerusalem in the north, proceeding from Aijalon to Beth-horon and Gibeon and from there north-eastwards to Zemaraim and down into the Jordan Valley at Succoth. Shishak's campaign seems to have been mainly directed against the Northern Kingdom. Only one section of his army seems to have overrun the Negeb as far as Arad, without advancing towards the Judean hills. It is thus not impossible that the temple treasuries and those of the king's house with "all the shields of gold which Solomon had made" were handed over to Shishak by Rehoboam himself. He thereby succeeded in diverting the Egyptian army from his land. This would be the meaning of his words "he took away" used with reference to Shishak. The story in 1 Kgs 14:25–6 only mentions one particular part of Shishak's route, highlighting it as viewed from Jerusalem.'

54 Professor Menahem Haran, *Temples and Temple Service in Ancient Israel*, op. cit., p. 284.

55 Ibid., pp. 284–5. Examples in the Bible of Judaean kings who emptied the treasuries for their own purposes include Ahaz and Hezekiah. See 2 Chronicles 28:24 and 2 Kings 18:15–16.

56 *Jerusalem Bible*, op. cit., Chronological Table, p. 344. The reign of Jehoash (Joash) is given as 798–783 BC. 2 Kings 14:1 states that the conflict between Jehoash and Amaziah took place in the second year of the reign of Jehoash – hence the date 796 BC.

57 2 Kings 14:12–14. The King James Authorized version states 'in the treasures of the king's house'. However, the more accurate and recent translations of the Jerusalem Bible and the New English Bible state, respectively, 'the treasury of the royal palace' and 'the treasuries of the royal palace'. It is clear that the translation 'treasury' or 'treasuries' is the correct one here.

58 Professor Menahem Haran, *Temples and Temple Service in Ancient Israel*, op. cit., pp. 277 and 285, footnote 19.

59 According to the authoritative chronology provided in the *Jerusalem Bible*, op. cit. See Chronological Table, p. 346. See also translation of the second book of Kings, pp. 423–4.

60 2 Kings 24:10–13 (amalgam of King James Authorized Version and Jerusalem Bible translations).

61 Professor Menahem Haran, *Temples and Temple Service in Ancient Israel*, op. cit., p. 287. The King James Authorized Version of the Bible wrongly translated the word *hekal* with the general term 'temple', thus causing much confusion to subsequent generations of scholars who did not have access to the original Hebrew. The *hekal* was a specific part of the Temple – the outer sanctum which formed the ante-chamber to the Holy of Holies.

62 For details see Chapter 11 above.

63 See Professor Edward Ullendorff, 'Hebraic-Jewish Elements in Abyssinian (Monophysite) Christianity', in *Journal of Semitic Studies*, vol. I, no. 3, 1956, p. 235.

64 Ibid., pp. 235–6: 'The outside ambulatory of the three concentric parts of the Abyssinian church (which is either round, octagonal, or rectangular) is called *k'ene mahlet*, i.e. the place where hymns are sung and where the *debtara* or cantors stand. This outer part corresponds to the *haser* of the Tabernacle or the *ulam* of Solomon's Temple. The next chamber is the *k'eddest* where communion is administered to the people; and the innermost part is the *mak'das* where the *tabot* rests and to which only priests have access. In some parts of Abyssinia, especially the north, the *k'eddest* (the *qodes* of the Tabernacle of *hekal* of Solomon's Temple) is called *'enda ta'amer*, "place of miracle", and the *mak'das* is named *k'eddusa k'eddusam* (the *qodes haqqodasim* of the Tabernacle and the *debir* of the Temple). This division into three chambers applies to all Abyssinian churches, even the smallest of them.'

65 This, as I subsequently established, had not been quite the act of senseless vandalism that the English version of the text implied: the phrase 'cut in pieces' was a translation of the Hebrew *way-e-qasses*, which did suggest cutting up but also connoted the stripping of metal plates from overlaid objects. Such a nuance made sense because the Bible stated unambiguously that the 'golden furnishings' that had stood in the *hekal* had included the 'altar' and the 'table of the showbread' – both of which had been made of wood overlaid with gold. For a discussion see Professor Menahem Haran, *Temples and Temple Service in Ancient Israel*, op. cit., p. 287, footnote 23.

66 1 Kings 7:49–50 (Jerusalem Bible translation).

67 If this is not already patently obvious to the reader, then it is made clear in the Jerusalem Bible's translation of 1 Kings 8:6 which reads as follows: 'The priests brought up the Ark of the Covenant of Yahweh to its place, in the *debir* of the Temple, that is, in the Holy of Holies, under the cherubs' wings.'

68 As is demonstrated by their treatment of King Jehoiachin (2

Kings 24:11–12), their deportation of large numbers of the inhabitants of Jerusalem (2 Kings 24:14–16), and their despolation of the Temple of Yahweh (2 Kings 24:13).

69　Research notes provided to the author by David Keys, Archaeology Correspondent of *The Independent*, London.

70　2 Kings 24:17.

71　2 Kings 25:1.

72　2 Kings 25:1–3. For the dates of these events I have relied on the Chronological Table in the *Jerusalem Bible*, op. cit., p. 346. There is a small margin of error in the dates allocated. Some archaeologists put the ending of the siege and final destruction of the Temple at 586 BC – e.g. see Kathleen Kenyon, *Jerusalem: Excavating 3,000 Years of History*. op. cit., p. 55.

73　2 Kings 25:8. It is important to stress that the academics disagree as to whether these events took place in 587 or 586 BC.

74　2 Kings 25:8–10, 13–16. A parallel inventory, which does not contradict this one in any way, and which also makes no mention of the Ark, may be found in Jeremiah 52:17–23.

75　The view that the gold and silver items taken by Nebuzaradan consisted only of relatively minor utensils is given additional weight by the text of the parallel list in Jeremiah 52:17–23 which, in verse 19, states explicitly that commander of the guard 'took the bowls, the censers, the sprinkling bowls, the ash containers, the lamp-stands, the goblets and the saucers: everything that was made of gold and everything of silver' (Jerusalem Bible translation). See also Jeremiah 27:18–22 which refers to the objects *not* taken by Nebuchadnezzar in 598 BC and prophesies that they will be taken after the second conquest of the city: 'But if they be prophets, and if the word of the Lord be with them, let them now make intercession to the Lord of Hosts, that the vessels which are left in the house of the Lord, and in the house of the king of Judah, and at Jerusalem, go not to Babylon. For thus saith the Lord of hosts concerning the pillars, and concerning the Sea, and concerning the bases, and concerning the residue of vessels that remain in the city, which Nebuchadnezzar king of Babylon took not when he carried away captive Jeconiah . . . king of Judah from Jerusalem to Babylon . . . Yea, thus saith the Lord of Hosts, the God of Israel, concerning the vessels that remain in the house of the Lord, and in the house of the king of Judah and of Jerusalem; They shall be carried to Babylon, and there shall they be until the day that I visit them, saith the Lord; then will I bring them up, and restore them to this place.'

76　E.g., Kathleen Kenyon, *Royal Cities of the Old Testament*, Barne & Jenkins, London, 1971, p. 148: 'Probably the Ark vanished in the burning of the Temple, though there is no actual reference to it subsequent to its deposit in the Holy of Holies in the time of Solomon.'

77 2 Kings 24:15–16.
78 2 Kings 25:11, 21.
79 Psalm 78:1–6.
80 *Jerusalem Bible*, op. cit., Chronological Table, p. 346.
81 Peter Calvocoressi, *Who's Who in the Bible*, Penguin, London, 1988, p. 45.
82 Ibid.
83 Ezra 1:7–11.
84 *Jerusalem Bible*, op. cit., Chronological Table, p. 346.
85 Ibid. See also Ezra 3:8; 5:16.
86 The *Jerusalem Bible* Chronological Table, op. cit. gives a completion date of 515 BC. The *Encyclopaedia of Judaism* proposes the slightly earlier dates of 520–517 BC. See Geoffrey Wigoder (ed.), *The Encyclopedia of Judaism*, Jerusalem Publishing House, Jerusalem, 1989, p. 694.
87 *Hebrew-English Edition of the Babylonian Talmud*, Soncino Press, London, Jerusalem, New York, 1974, *Tractate Yoma*, 21b.
88 See also Louis Ginzberg, *Legends of the Jews*, op. cit., vol. VI, p. 442: 'The following five things were in the First Temple only: the heavenly fire, the holy oil of anointing, the Ark, the Holy Spirit, and the Urim and Thummim.' Biblical references to the Urim and Thummim can be found in Exodus 28:30; Leviticus 8:8; Ezra 2:63; and Nehemiah 7:65.
89 Zev Vilnay, *Legends of Jerusalem*, op. cit., vol. I, p. 123. See also Louis Ginzberg, *Legends of the Jews*, op. cit., vol. VI, p. 378: 'Solomon, at the erection of the Temple, provided a secret place to be used later for "hiding" holy objects.'
90 *Hebrew-English Edition of the Babylonian Talmud*, op. cit., *Tractate Yoma*, 53b.
91 Dates from the *Jerusalem Bible*, op. cit., Chronological Table, p. 345.
92 Louis Ginzberg, *Legends of the Jews*, op. cit., vol. IV, p. 282. See also *Hebrew-English Edition of the Babylonian Talmud*, op. cit., *Tractate Yoma*, 52b. See also C. Roth and G. Wigoder (eds), *The New Standard Encyclopaedia of Judaism*. W. H. Allen, London, 1970, p. 158.
93 Louis Ginzberg, *Legends of the Jews*, op. cit., vol. III, p. 158.
94 Ibid.
95 Herbert Danby (trans.), *The Mishnah*, op. cit., p. 158. See also Zev Vilnay, *Legends of Jerusalem*, op. cit., p. 122.
96 See entry on the Books of Maccabees in F. L. Cross and E. A.

Livingstone (eds), *The Oxford Dictionary of the Christian Church*, Oxford University Press, 1988, p. 855.

97 Ibid. In its 'Introduction to the Books of Maccabees' the *Jerusalem Bible*, op. cit., concludes that Maccabees was probably written around 63 BC.

98 2 Maccabees 2:1, 4–5.

99 *Jerusalem Bible*, op. cit., p. 605, footnote 2a and 'Introduction to the Books of Maccabees', p. 569.

100 F. L. Cross and E. A. Livingstone (eds), *The Oxford Dictionary of the Christian Church*, op. cit., p. 855.

101 Jeremiah was born around 650 BC. The exact date of his death is not known; however it is thought to have occurred within a decade of the destruction of Solomon's Temple. See F. L. Cross and E. A. Livingstone (eds), *The Oxford Dictionary of the Christian Church*, op. cit., pp. 730–1. See also Peter Calvocoressi, *Who's Who in the Bible*, op. cit., pp. 101–2.

102 2 Maccabees 2:1, 4.

103 See Deuteronomy 34:1.

104 Mount Nebo is on the eastern side of the Dead Sea, in the modern state of Jordan, overlooking Jerusalem and Jericho.

105 Because he foretold – and welcomed – the destruction of the Temple by Nebuchadnezzar, whom he saw as God's chosen instrument for chastising Judah, 'He was frequently in personal danger from his own people, physically assaulted and for several years in hiding' (Peter Calvocoressi, *Who's Who in the Bible*, op. cit., p. 101). See also F. L. Cross and E. A. Livingstone (eds), *The Oxford Dictionary of the Christian Church*, op. cit., p. 730: Jeremiah faced 'the hostility of the official representatives of the Jewish religion'.

106 Louis Ginzberg, *Legends of the Jews*, op. cit., vol. IV, p. 320: 'The Holy Ark, the altar of incense, and the holy tent were carried by an angel to the mount whence Moses before his death had viewed the land divinely assigned to Israel. There Jeremiah found a spacious cave in which he concealed these sacred utensils.'

107 For further details on the Wailing Wall and on the current politico-religious status of the Temple Mount the reader is referred to the appropriate entries in Geoffrey Wigoder (ed.), *The Encyclopedia of Judaism*, op. cit., pp. 696–7 and 727–9.

108 See Meir Ben-Dov, *In the Shadow of the Temple: the Discovery of Ancient Jerusalem*, Harper & Row, New York, 1985, p. 24.

109 Ibid., p. 25.

110 Ibid., pp. 19–20.

111 See Geoffrey Wigoder (ed.), *The Encyclopedia of Judaism*, op. cit., p. 695 and 481–3.

112 Meir Ben-Dov, *In the Shadow of the Temple*, op. cit. See in particular Chapter 2, 'Remains from the Kingdom of Judah'. The rest of this excellent book, from p. 57 forward, is devoted to the finds relating to other periods.

113 Ibid., pp. 16–18. See also Neil Asher Silberman, *Digging for God and Country: Exploration, Archaeology and the Secret Struggle for the Holy Land, 1799–1917*, Knopf, New York, 1982, pp. 89–99.

114 Neil Asher Silberman, *Digging for God and Country*, op. cit., pp. 89–99.

115 Ibid., p. 93.

116 Ibid., pp. 94–7.

117 Meir Ben-Dov, *In the Shadow of the Temple*, op. cit., p. 18.

118 Kathleen Kenyon, *Digging up Jerusalem*, op. cit., p. 31.

119 See Neil Asher Silberman, *Digging for God and Country*, op. cit., pp. 180–8. In general I am indebted to this useful and informative work for the account of the Parker expedition that follows.

120 Ibid.

121 Kathleen Kenyon, *Digging up Jerusalem*, op. cit., p. 30.

122 See 'Tom Crotser has found the Ark of the Covenant – or has he?', *Biblical Archaeology Review*, May/June 1983, pp. 66–7.

123 Ibid., pp. 66–7.

124 Ibid., p. 66.

125 Ibid., p. 67.

126 Ibid., p. 68, quoting UPI reporter Darrell Day.

127 Ibid., p. 68.

128 Ibid., p. 68.

129 Ibid., p. 68.

130 Ibid., pp. 68–9.

131 Ibid., p. 69.

132 Richard Elliott Friedman, *Who Wrote the Bible?*, Jonathan Cape, London, 1988, p. 156.

133 Ibid.

Chapter 15 **Hidden History**

1 Richard Elliott Friedman, *Who Wrote the Bible?*, Jonathan Cape, London, 1988, p. 156.

2 Sir E. A. Wallis Budge, *The Queen of Sheba and her Only Son Menelik: being the 'Book of the Glory of Kings' (Kebra Nagast)*, Oxford University Press, 1932, pages 99 and 100. See Chapter 3, n. 94 above.

3 Josephus, *Jewish Antiquities*, Loeb Classical Library (Heinemann), London, 1934, books V–VIII, p. 665.

4 1 Kings 10:2.

5 E. A. Wallis Budge, *A History of Ethiopia, Nubia and Abyssinia*, London, 1928, Preface.

6 See David L. Edwards, *A Key to the Old Testament*, Fount Paperbacks, London, 1989, pp. 209–11, in particular p. 210.

7 Ibid. See also Richard Elliott Friedman, *Who Wrote the Bible?*, op. cit., p. 146.

8 1 Kings 8:6–8 (emphasis added). New English Bible translation, Oxford and Cambridge University Presses, 1970, p. 384.

9 See David L. Edwards, *A Key to the Old Testament*, op. cit., p. 210.

10 William Shakespeare, *Hamlet*, Act III, Scene 2, line 25.

11 Julian Morgenstern, 'The Book of the Covenant', in *Hebrew Union College Annual*, vol. V, 1928, reprinted by KTAV Publishing House, New York, 1968, p. 29, footnote 37.

12 1 Kings 8:9 (Jerusalem Bible translation).

13 Deuteronomy 10:5 (New English Bible translation). The Jerusalem Bible translation states: 'and there they stayed'; the King James Authorized Version states: 'and there they be'.

14 Julian Morgenstern, 'The Book of the Covenant', op. cit., p. 29, footnote 37.

15 Ibid. Emphasis added.

16 Louis Ginzberg, *Legends of the Jews*, Jewish Publication Society of America, Philadelphia, 1909, vol. IV, p. 282.

17 *Hebrew-English Edition of the Babylonian Talmud*, Soncino Press, London, Jerusalem, New York, 1974, *Tractate Yoma* 53b.

18 John Oates, *Babylon*, Thames & Hudson, London, 1988, p. 128.

19 Ibid., pp. 126–9.

20 2 Chronicles 34:33 (Jerusalem Bible translation); 2 Chronicles 35:2–3 (King James Authorized Version translation).

21 2 Chronicles 35:19 (cf. 2 Chronicles 35:1–3).

22 This date is arrived at by simple mathematics. since it is known that Josiah came to power in 640 BC (see *Jerusalem Bible*, Eyre & Spottiswoode, London, 1968, Chronological Table, p. 345), the eighteenth year of his reign must therefore have been 622 BC.

23 Jeremiah began his prophetic ministry in 626 BC – see Geoffrey Wigoder (ed.), *The Encyclopaedia of Judaism*, Jerusalem Publishing House, Jerusalem, 1989, p. 380. I attribute the date of 626 BC to the verses quoted because they are recognized by leading biblical scholars as being amongst 'Jeremiah's earliest prophecies'. See Menahem Haran, *Temples and Temple Service in Ancient Israel*, Clarendon Press, Oxford, 1978, reprinted in 1985 by Eisenbrauns, Winona Lake, Indiana, p. 281.

24 Jeremiah 3:16–17 (Jerusalem Bible translation).

25 Jeremiah's authorship of the book of Jeremiah is not in doubt – although he probably dictated it to an amanuensis. See, *inter alia*,

Geoffrey Wigoder (ed.), *The Encyclopaedia of Judaism*, op. cit., pp. 380–1; *Jerusalem Bible*, op. cit., Introduction to the book of Jeremiah, p. 1067; F. L. Cross and E. A. Livingstone (eds), *The Oxford Dictionary of the Christian Church*, Oxford University Press, 1988, pp. 730–1.

26 Menahem Haran, *Temples and Temple Service in Ancient Israel*, op. cit., p. 281.

27 See *Jerusalem Bible*, op. cit., Chronological Table, pp. 344–5. The fifteen kings between Solomon and Josiah were Rehoboam, Abijah, Asa, Jehosophat, Jehoram, Ahaziah, Athaliah, Joash, Amaziah, Uzziah, Jotham, Ahaz, Hezekiah, Manasseh and Amon.

28 *The Holy Bible, King James Version* (Electronic First Edition, KJ21), Franklin Computer Corporation, New Jersey, 1989. Throughout my research I made exhaustive use of this marvellous investigative instrument.

29 See Numbers 12:10 and discussion in Chapter 13 above.

30 The occurrences were: Exodus 25:22, Numbers 7:89; 1 Samuel 4:4; 2 Samuel 6:2; and 1 Chronicles 13:6.

31 2 Kings 7:3.

32 *Jerusalem Bible*, op. cit., Chronological Table, p. 345.

33 2 Chronicles 26:16.

34 2 Chronicles 26:19.

35 See Leviticus 10:1–2.

36 See Chapters 12 and 13 above for a fuller discussion.

37 2 Chronicles 26:21–3.

38 Geoffrey Wigoder (ed.), *The Encyclopedia of Judaism*, op. cit., p. 575: 'the precise dating of individual psalms is impossible.'

39 F. L. Cross and E. A. Livingstone (eds), *The Oxford Dictionary of the Christian Church*, op. cit., p. 1139. See also Geoffrey Wigoder (ed.), *The Encyclopedia of Judaism*, op. cit., pp. 574–6; and Stephen Bigger (ed.), *Creating the Old Testament: The Emergence of the Hebrew Bible*, Blackwell, Oxford, 1989, pp. 254–8.

40 Ezekiel 10:2; Ezekiel 10:6; Ezekiel; 10:7.

41 For the dating of Ezekiel see 'The Book of the Prophet Ezekiel', *The Cambridge Bible Commentary*, Cambridge University Press, 1974, Historical Table, p. xi.

42 Ezekiel 8:1–3: 'the spirit lifted me up between the earth and the heaven, and brought me in the visions of God to Jerusalem.'

43 Ezekiel 10:20–2, especially 21.

44 Ezekiel 10:1, 15, 20.

45 Ezekiel 10:19, 5.

46 Isaiah 37:16; 2 Kings 19:15.

47 Isaiah 37:14–16.

48 2 Kings 19:14–15.

49 Biblical scholars are unanimous that chapters 1–39 of the book of
   Isaiah, including this chapter of course, were written by Isaiah
   himself. See Geoffrey Wigoder (ed.), *The Encyclopedia of Judaism*,
   op. cit., p. 369. See also *Jerusalem Bible*, op. cit., 'Introduction to
   Isaiah', p. 970. See also Peter Calvocoressi, *Who's Who in the
   Bible*, Penguin, London, 1988, pp. 87–8. Some of the later
   chapters in Isaiah, from 40 onwards, were certainly written later.
   The antiquity of chapter 37, however, the one in which the
   reference to 'between the cherubims' crops up, is not in doubt.
   Moreover since the chapter refers to a known historical event –
   Sennacherib's invasion – it can be dated fairly precisely to 701 BC
   (see *Jerusalem Bible*, Chronological Table, p. 345; and F. L. Cross
   and E. A. Livingstone (eds), *Oxford Dictionary of the Christian
   Church*, op. cit., p. 715.
50 See *Jerusalem Bible*, op. cit., 'Introduction to the Book of Isaiah', p.
   970. See also F. L. Cross and E. A. Livingstone (eds), *The Oxford
   Dictionary of the Christian Church*, op. cit., p. 715.
51 Isaiah 6:1–3, and *Jerusalem Bible*, op. cit., p. 970.
52 *Jerusalem Bible*, op. cit., Chronological Table, p. 345, for dates.
53 F. L. Cross and E. A. Livingstone (eds), *The Oxford Dictionary of
   the Christian Church*, op. cit., p. 715. See also *Handbook to the
   Bible*, Lion Publishing, London, 1988, p. 376. See also the
   Encyclopedia of Judaism, op. cit., p. 369. 'Modern scholars maintain
   that the book of Isaiah is a composite work written by more than
   one prophet, and that only chapters 1–39 are the words of Isaiah.'
   The verse quoted above falls safely within this range, in chapter 37
   of Isaiah.
54 Isaiah 37:6–7. See also *Handbook to the Bible*, op. cit., p. 376; *The
   Encyclopedia of Judaism*, op. cit., p. 369.
55 Isaiah 37:14.
56 Isaiah 37: 17–20.
57 Isaiah 37:33, 35.
58 Isaiah 37:36–7.
59 See, for example, Paul Johnson, *A History of the Jews*, Weidenfeld
   & Nicolson, London, 1988, p. 73.
60 Ibid.
61 See Chapters 12 and 13 above.
62 Isaiah 37:14. 'The house of the Lord' is of course a synonym for
   the Jerusalem Temple (compare Jerusalem Bible translation of the
   same verse).
63 Isaiah 37:14.
64 1 Kings 3:15.
65 2 Samuel 6:5.
66 Deuteronomy 10:8.

67 Dates from *Jerusalem Bible*, op. cit., Chronological Table, p. 345.

68 2 Kings 21: 2–7.

69 *Jerusalem Bible*, op. cit., p. 419. See also Irving M. Zeitlin, *Ancient Judaism*, Polity Press, Cambridge, 1986, p. 173.

70 1 Kings 6:19 (Jerusalem Bible translation). With specific reference to the Ark, Solomon had asked: 'But will God indeed dwell on the earth? behold, the heaven and heaven of heavens cannot contain thee: how much less this house that I have builded? Yet have thou respect unto the prayer of thy servant, and to his supplication, O Lord my God, to hearken unto the cry and to the prayer, which thy servant prayeth before thee today: that thine eyes may be open towards *this house* night and day, even toward *the place of which thou hast said, "My name shall be there".*' 1 Kings 8:27–9. See also 2 Samuel 6:2: 'the Ark of God, whose *name* is called by the *name* of the Lord of Hosts that dwelleth between the cherubims.' (Emphasis added.)

71 E.g. see 1 Chronicles 28:2.

72 2 Kings 21:16 (Jerusalem Bible translation).

73 2 Kings 21:20–1, 23–4.

74 2 Kings 22:1.

75 2 Chronicles 34:3.

76 2 Chronicles 34:3.

77 2 Kings 23:6 (amalgam of King James Authorized Version and Jerusalem Bible translations).

78 2 Chronicles 34:7–8.

79 2 Kings 22: 6.

80 Professor Menahem Haran, *Temples and Temple Service in Ancient Israel*, op. cit., pp. 277, 278, 288, 281.

Chapter 16 **Door of the Southern Countries**

1 Jill Kamil, *Upper Egypt*, Longman, London and New York, 1989, p. 35.

2 Ibid., p. 36.

3 Bezalel Porten, *Archives from Elephantine: the Life of an Ancient Jewish Military Colony*, University of California Press, Berkeley, Los Angeles, 1968, p. 110. 'The length of the Temple was at least sixty cubits. A width of approximately twenty cubits may be inferred from the presence of two buildings lying northeast of the Temple.' An ancient cubit measured eighteen inches – see Dr J. H. Hertz (ed.), *The Pentateuch and the Haftorahs*, Soncino Press, London, 1978, p. 327. The *Jerusalem Bible*, footnote (b) p. 887, concurs (*Jerusalem Bible*, Eyre & Spottiswoode, London, 1968).

4 Bezalel Porten, *Archives from Elephantine*, op. cit., p. 110.

5 1 Kings 6:2: 'the length thereof was threescore cubits, and the breadth thereof twenty cubits.'

6 Emil G. Kraeling (ed.), *The Brooklyn Museum Aramaic Papyri: New Documents of the fifth century BC from the Jewish Colony at Elephantine*, Published for the Brooklyn Museum by the Yale University Press, New Haven and London, 1953, p. 101.

7 1 Kings 6:9.

8 Bezalel Porten, *Archives from Elephantine*, op. cit., p. 133; Emil G. Kraeling, *The Brooklyn Museum Aramaic Papyri*, op. cit., p. 100.

9 Bezaleel Porten, *Archives from Elephantine*, op. cit., pp. 13 and 133.

10 Ibid., pp. 109, 152. See also Emil G. Kraeling, *The Brooklyn Museum Aramaic Papyri*, op. cit., p. 85.

11 E.g. Numbers 10:33; 35–6.

12 I.e. after the promulgation of the Deuteronomistic code during the reign of Josiah – see Emil G. Kraeling, *The Brooklyn Aramaic Papyri*, op. cit., p. 85.

13 Ibid., p. 85.

14 Ibid., p. 85.

15 1 Samuel 4:4.

16 Bezalel Porten, *Archives from Elephantine*, op. cit., p. 299.

17 See Chapter 15 above.

18 Bezalel Porten, *Archives from Elephantine*, op. cit., pp. 121–2.

19 Ibid., p. 115.

20 Ibid., pp. 115–16.

21 1 Chronicles 28:2.

22 Emil G. Kraeling, *The Brooklyn Museum Aramaic Papyri*, op. cit., p. 24.

23 See Chapter 14 above.

24 In 609 BC. See 2 Kings 23:29–30. See also Bruce Metzger, David Goldstein, John Ferguson (eds), *Great Events of Bible Times*, Guild Publishing, London, 1989, p. 105. See also *Jerusalem Bible*, op. cit., Chronological Table, p. 345.

25 'The occasionally canvassed origin of the Falashas from the Jewish garrison of Elephantine or the conjecture that Jewish influences in Abyssinia had penetrated by way of Egypt are devoid of any reliable historical basis', Edward Ullendorff, *Ethiopia and the Bible*, published for the British Academy by the Oxford University Press, 1988, p. 117.

26 In the 1930s, for example, Ignazio Guidi, an Italian scholar, had canvassed exactly this possibility in his *Storia della letteratura etiopica* (Rome, 1932, p. 95). And later, in 1960, a former President of Israel had argued that the solution to the puzzle of Falasha origins must lie in Elephantine (Y. Ben-Zvi, *Erets Israel*,

Jerusalem, 1960, vol. VI, p. 146). The strongest and most persuasive case, however, had been put forward much more recently by David Kessler, Chairman of the Falasha Welfare Association of London and the author of an excellent book entitled *The Falashas: the Forgotten Jews of Ethiopia* (Schocken, New York, 1985). See in particular pp. 41–7.

27 This point is particularly cogently argued by David Kessler in *The Falashas*, op. cit.

28 See Chapter 6 above.

29 Bezalel Porten, *Archives from Elephantine*, op. cit., p. 201.

30 See Chapter 6 above.

31 Bezalel Porten, *Archives from Elephantine*, op. cit., pp. 109 and 154–5. Emil G. Kraeling (ed.), *The Brooklyn Museum Aramaic Papyri*, op. cit., p. 91.

32 Bezalel Porten, *Archives from Elephantine*, op. cit., p. 155.

33 See Chapter 6 above.

34 1 Kings 8:54.

35 Bezalel Porten, *Archives from Elephantine*, op. cit., p. 19.

36 Ibid., p. 20.

37 Emil G. Kraeling (ed.), *The Brooklyn Museum Aramiac Papyri*, op. cit., p. 102–3.

38 See Chapter 9 above.

39 James Bruce reports his discovery of Meroe in his *Travels to Discover the Source of the Nile in the Years 1768, 1769, 1770, 1771, 1772 and 1773*, Edinburgh, 1790, vol. IV, pp. 538–9. For independent confirmation that the Scottish explorer was indeed the discoverer of Meroe see William Y. Adams, *Nubia: Corridor to Africa*, Allen Lane, Princeton University Press, 1984, p. 295.

40 Bezalel Porten, *Archives from Elephantine*, op. cit., p. 45.

41 See Professor Edward Ullendorff, *The Ethiopians: An Introduction to Country and People*, Oxford University Press, 1973, pp. 1–2.

42 For example in 529 BC. See Bezalel Porten, *Archives from Elephantine*, op. cit., p. 15.

43 Herodotus, *The History*, translated by David Green, the University of Chicago Press, Chicago and London, 1988, pp. 142–3; emphasis added.

44 Herodotus was referring to Psammetichus II. Dates from John Baines and Jaromir Malek, *Atlas of Ancient Egypt*, Equinox Books, Oxford, 1990, p. 37.

45 Bezalel Porten, *Archives from Elephantine*, op. cit., p. 8, citing 'the letter of Aristeas'.

46 That tireless and prolific scholar of ancient Egypt and Ethiopia, Sir E. A. Wallis Budge, made his own analysis of the report of Herodotus and likewise concluded that the 'land of the Deserters'

'must have been situated in some part of western Abyssinia'. See
Sir E. A. Wallis Budge, *A History of Ethiopia, Nubia and Abyssinia*,
London, 1928, p. 62.

47 Edward Ullendorff, *Ethiopia and the Bible*, op. cit., p. 5.

48 Numbers 12:1 (King James Authorized Version translation). The
Jerusalem Bible refers to Moses's Ethiopian wife as a 'Cushite
woman'. So, too, does the New English Bible.

49 See, for example, Josephus, *Jewish Antiquities* (translated by H. St
J. Thackeray), Loeb Classical Library (Heinemann), London,
1978, vol. IV (books I-IV), pp. 269–75. See also Louis Ginzberg,
Legends of the Jews, Jewish Publication Society of America,
Philadelphia, 1909, vol. II, pp. 286–9, vol. V, pp. 407–10. For a
discussion see also Tessa Rajak. 'Moses in Ethiopia: Legend and
Literature', *Journal of Jewish Studies*, Oxford Centre for
Postgraduate Hebrew Studies, vol. 29, no.2, Autumn 1978.

50 Genesis 2:13 (King James Authorized Version translation).

51 See Part III above.

52 See Major R. E. Cheesman, *Lake Tana and the Blue Nile: An
Abyssinian Quest*, Cass, London, 1936, pp. 71 and 75. For a
discussion see also Professor Edward Ullendorff, *Ethiopia and the
Bible*, op. cit., p. 2. Ullendorff states of the Ethiopian traditions
regarding the Blue Nile/ Gihon: 'There is no valid reason to
doubt the essential accuracy of this identification.'

53 Jon D. Levenson, *Sinai and Zion: An Entry into the Jewish Bible*,
Harper & Row, San Francisco, 1987, p. 19.

54 Psalm 68:1: 'Let God arise, let his enemies be scattered: let them
also that hate him flee before him.' This is a virtual mirror-image
of the ancient passage in Numbers 10:35 which states: 'And it
came to pass, when the Ark set forward, that Moses said, Rise up
Lord, and let thine enemies be scattered; and let them that hate
thee flee before thee.'

55 Psalm 68:31.

56 See *Jerusalem Bible*, op. cit., 'Introduction to the Minor Prophets',
p. 1256.

57 Ibid.

58 Isaiah 18:1–2.

59 See Geoffrey Wigoder (ed.), *The Encyclopedia of Judaism*,
Jerusalem Publishing House, Jerusalem, 1989: 'modern scholars
maintain that the Book of Isaiah is a composite work written by
more than one prophet, and that only chapters 1–39 are the words
of Isaiah.' The verses quoted, from chapter 18 of Isaiah, fall
comfortably within this range.

60 See Chapter 15 above.

61 *Jerusalem Bible*, op. cit., Chronological Table, p. 345, for kings'

dates. For the dating of Isaiah's lifetime see F. L. Cross and E. A. Livingstone (eds), *The Oxford Dictionary of the Christian Church*, Oxford University Press, 1988, p. 715.

62 F. L. Cross and E. A. Livingstone (eds), *The Oxford Dictionary of the Christian Church*, op. cit., p. 715. See also Louis Ginzberg, *Legends of the Jews*, op. cit., vol. IV, pp. 278–9 and vol. VI, pp. 371 and 396.

63 See Chapter 9 above.

64 Genesis 21:33.

65 See Frederick C. Gamst, *The Qemant: A Pagan Hebraic Peasantry of Ethiopia*, Holt, Reinhart & Winston, New York, 1969, pp. 5–6.

66 See, for example, A. H. M. Jones and Elizabeth Monroe, *A History of Ethiopia*, Clarendon Press, Oxford, 1966, pp. 7–8.

67 See Donald N. Levine, *Greater Ethiopia: The Evolution of a Multi-ethnic Society*, University of Chicago Press, Chicago and London, 1974, pp. 34 and 37. The Agaw, Falasha and Qemant all belong to the 'Central Cushitic' language family and ethnic group. See also Frederick C. Gamst, *The Qemant*, op. cit., p. 1: 'The Qemant, an ethnic group with an estimated population of 20,000 to 25,000, are a remnant of the Cushitic-speaking Agaw peoples, the original inhabitants of northern and central Ethiopia.' The Agaw language has today all but died out amongst the Falashas, although some elders in remote communities still speak it. See Wolf Leslau, *Falasha Anthology*, Yale University Press, New Haven and London, 1979, pp. xx–xxi. In general see also Edward Ullendorff, *The Ethiopians*, op. cit., pp 37–8.

68 Balthazar Tellez, *The Travels of the Jesuits in Ethiopia*, quoted in Sydney Mendelssohn, *The Jews of Africa*, London, 1920, p. 5.

69 Jacqueline Pirenne, 'Des Grecs à l'aurore de la culture monumentale Sabéenne', in T. Fahd (ed.), *L'arabe préislamique et son environment historique et culturel* (Actes de colloque de Strasbourg, 24–27 juin 1987), published by the Université des sciences humaines de Strasbourg, 1989.

70 Ibid., p. 262.

71 R. Schneider, 'Documents épigraphiques de l'Ethiopie', *Annales d'Ethiopie*, vol. X, 1976, pp. 88–9.

72 Ibid., pp. 88–9.

73 Jacqueline Pirenne, 'Des Grecs à l'aurore de la culture monumentale Sabéenne', op. cit., pp. 264–5.

74 *Sir Gawain and the Green Knight*, translated with an introduction by Brian Stone, Penguin Classics, London, 1974, p. 100.

75 Ibid., p. 100.

76 Ibid., p. 103.

Chapter 17 **Supping with Devils**

1 Graham Hancock, Richard Pankhurst, Duncan Willetts, *Under Ethiopian Skies*, Editions HL, London and Nairobi, 1983 (reprinted 1987 and 1989).
2 Graham Hancock, *Ethiopia: the Challenge of Hunger*, Gollancz, London, 1985, p. 110.

Chapter 18 **A Treasure Hard to Attain**

1 J. Theodore Bent, *The Sacred City of the Ethiopians: Travel and Research in Abyssinia in 1893*, Longmans, Green, London, New York and Bombay, 1896, p. 196.
2 See Chapter 1 above.
3 See Chapter 5 above.
4 See Chapter 5 above. See also B. T. Evetts (trans. and ed.), Abu Salih, *Churches and Monasteries of Egypt and some Neighbouring Countries*, Oxford, 1895, p. 288.
5 See Chapter 5 above.
6 Wolfram von Eschenbach, *Parzival*, Penguin Classics, London, 1980. See for example pp. 393 and 397.
7 Wolfram von Eschenbach, *Parzival*, op. cit., p. 232.

Index